HUMAN KINETICS WEB STUDY GUIDE

How to access the supplemental web study guide

We are pleased to provide access to a web study guide that supplements your textbook, *Life Span Motor Development, Seventh Edition.* This resource offers learning exercises and lab activities, record sheets, and questions. The lab activities include video clips with footage of infants and toddlers; additional footage of people performing the fundamental motor skills; and context-specific, constraint-rich video for all chapters.

D0139196

Accessing the web study guide is easy! Follow these steps if you purchased a new book:

1. Visit **www.HumanKinetics.com/LifeSpanMotorDevelopment.**
2. Click the seventh edition link next to the corresponding seventh edition book cover.
3. Click the Sign In link on the left or top of the page. If you do not have an account with Human Kinetics, you will be prompted to create one.
4. If the online product you purchased does not appear in the Ancillary Items box on the left of the page, click the Enter Key Code option in that box. Enter the key code that is printed at the right, including all hyphens. Click the Submit button to unlock your online product.
5. After you have entered your key code the first time, you will never have to enter it again to access this product. Once unlocked, a link to your product will permanently appear in the menu on the left. For future visits, all you need to do is sign in to the textbook's website and follow the link that appears in the left menu!

→ Click the Need Help? button on the textbook's website if you need assistance along the way.

How to access the web study guide if you purchased a used book:

You may purchase access to the web study guide by visiting the text's website, **www.HumanKinetics.com/LifeSpanMotorDevelopment**, or by calling the following:

800-747-4457 . . . . . U.S. customers
800-465-7301 . . . . . Canadian customers
+44 (0) 113 255 5665 . . . . . European customers
217-351-5076 . . . . . International customers

For technical support, send an email to:
support@hkusa.com . . . . . U.S. and international customers
info@hkcanada.com . . . . . Canadian customers
academic@hkeurope.com . . . . . European customers

HUMAN KINETICS

4-2019

Product: Life Span Moto
web study guid
, Seventh Edition,

Key code: HAYWOOD-FTAZLX-OSG

This unique code allows you access to the web study guide.

Access is provided if you have purchased a new book.
Once submitted, the code may not be entered for any other user.

Seventh Edition

LIFE SPAN MOTOR DEVELOPMENT

Kathleen M. Haywood, PhD
University of Missouri-St. Louis

Nancy Getchell, PhD
University of Delaware

HUMAN KINETICS

Library of Congress Cataloging-in-Publication Data

Names: Haywood, Kathleen, author. | Getchell, Nancy, 1963- author.
Title: Life span motor development / Kathleen M. Haywood, Nancy Getchell.
Description: Seventh edition. | Champaign, IL : Human Kinetics, [2020] |
Includes bibliographical references and index.
Identifiers: LCCN 2019010429 (print) | LCCN 2019011146 (ebook) | ISBN
9781492587255 (epub) | ISBN 9781492566915 (PDF) | ISBN 9781492566908
(print) | ISBN 9781492587248 (loose leaf)
Subjects: | MESH: Motor Skills | Human Development
Classification: LCC RJ133 (ebook) | LCC RJ133 (print) | NLM WE 103 | DDC
612.7/6--dc23
LC record available at https://lccn.loc.gov/2019010429

ISBN: 978-1-4925-6690-8 (paperback)
ISBN: 978-1-4925-8724-8 (loose-leaf)

Copyright © 2020, 2014, 2009, 2005, 2001 by Kathleen M. Haywood and Nancy Getchell
Copyright © 1993, 1986 by Kathleen M. Haywood

All rights reserved. Except for use in a review, the reproduction or utilization of this work in any form or by any electronic, mechanical, or other means, now known or hereafter invented, including xerography, photocopying, and recording, and in any information storage and retrieval system, is forbidden without the written permission of the publisher.

Permission notices for material reprinted in this book from other sources can be found on page(s) xix-xxiv.

The web addresses cited in this text were current as of December 2018, unless otherwise noted.

Acquisitions Editor: Andrew L. Tyler; **Senior Developmental Editor:** Christine M. Drews; **Managing Editor:** Anne E. Mrozek; **Copyeditor:** Patricia L. MacDonald; **Indexer:** Nancy Ball; **Permissions Manager:** Dalene Reeder; **Graphic Designer:** Sean Roosevelt; **Cover Designer:** Keri Evans; **Cover Design Associate:** Susan Rothermel Allen; **Photograph (cover):** Zing Images/Digital Vision/Getty Images; **Photographs (interior):** © Human Kinetics, unless otherwise noted; **Photo Asset Manager:** Laura Fitch; **Photo Production Manager:** Jason Allen; **Senior Art Manager:** Kelly Hendren; **Illustrations:** © Human Kinetics, unless otherwise noted; **Printer:** Walsworth

The video contents of this product are licensed for educational public performance for viewing by a traditional (live) audience, via closed circuit television, or via computerized local area networks within a single building or geographically unified campus. To request a license to broadcast these contents to a wider audience—for example, throughout a school district or state, or on a television station—please contact your sales representative **(www.HumanKinetics.com/SalesRepresentatives)**.

Printed in the United States of America 10 9 8 7 6 5 4 3 2 1

The paper in this book was manufactured using responsible forestry methods.

Human Kinetics
P.O. Box 5076
Champaign, IL 61825-5076
Website: www.HumanKinetics.com

In the United States, email info@hkusa.com or call 800-747-4457.
In Canada, email info@hkcanada.com.
In the United Kingdom/Europe, email hk@hkeurope.com.

For information about Human Kinetics' coverage in other areas of the world, please visit our website:
www.HumanKinetics.com

E7301 (paperback) / E7510 (loose-leaf)

Tell us what you think!
Human Kinetics would love to hear what we can do to improve the customer experience. Use this QR code to take our brief survey.

To the many motor development researchers (past, present, and future)
who continue to push our field forward. Your work inspires ours.

CONTENTS

Preface ix
About the Web Study Guide xv
Acknowledgments xvii
Credits xix

Part I Introduction to Motor Development

1 Fundamental Concepts 3

Defining Motor Development 4
Constraints: A Model for Studying Motor Development 6
How Do We Know It Is Change? 9
A Developmental Paradox: Universality Versus Variability 14
Summary and Synthesis 14

2 Theoretical Perspectives in Motor Development 17

Maturational Perspective 18
Information Processing Perspective 21
Ecological Perspective 22
Current Interests 26
Summary and Synthesis 27

3 Principles of Motion and Stability 29

Understanding the Principles of Motion and Stability 31
Using the Principles of Motion and Stability to Detect and Correct Errors 40
Summary and Synthesis 41

Part II Development of Motor Skills Across the Life Span

4 Early Motor Development 45

How Do Infants Move? 47
Why Do Infants Move? The Purpose of Reflexes 53
Motor Milestones: The Pathway to Voluntary Movements 54
Development of Postural Control and Balance in Infancy 60
Summary and Synthesis 62

5 Development of Human Locomotion 65

The First Voluntary Locomotor Efforts: Creeping and Crawling 67
Walking Across the Life Span 68
Running Across the Life Span 73
Other Locomotor Skills 77
Summary and Synthesis 96

6 Development of Ballistic Skills 99

Overarm Throwing 100
Kicking 112
Punting 114
Sidearm Striking 116
Overarm Striking 121
Interventions 125
Summary and Synthesis 125

7 Development of Manipulative Skills 127

Grasping and Reaching 128
Catching 136
Anticipation 139
Summary and Synthesis 145

Part III Physical Growth and Aging

8 Physical Growth, Maturation, and Aging 151

Prenatal Development 153
Postnatal Development 158
Summary and Synthesis 174

9 Development and Aging of Body Systems 177

Systems Development During the Prenatal Period 179
Systems Development During Childhood and Adolescence 183
Systems Development During Adulthood and Older Adulthood 192
Summary and Synthesis 196

Part IV Development of Physical Fitness

10 Development of Cardiorespiratory Endurance 201

Physiological Responses to Short-Term Exercise 202
Physiological Responses to Prolonged Exercise 205
Summary and Synthesis 216

11 Development of Strength and Flexibility 219

Muscle Mass and Strength 220
Development of Strength 221
Development of Flexibility 231
Summary and Synthesis 237

12 Weight Status, Fitness, and Motor Competence 239

A Model of Interrelationships 240
Body Composition 241
Obesity 248
Motor Competence, Activity, Fitness, and Body Composition 252
Summary and Synthesis 255

Part V Perceptual-Motor Development

13 Sensory-Perceptual Development 259

Visual Development 261
Kinesthetic Development 268
Auditory Development 274
Intermodal Perception 278
Summary and Synthesis 282

14 Perception and Action in Development 285

The Role of Action in Perception 286
Postural Control and Balance 295
Summary and Synthesis 299

Part VI Functional Constraints in Motor Development

15 Social and Cultural Constraints in Motor Development 303

Social and Cultural Influences as Environmental Constraints 305
Other Sociocultural Constraints: Race, Ethnicity, and Socioeconomic Status 318
Summary and Synthesis 319

16 Psychosocial Constraints in Motor Development 321

Self-Esteem 323
The Link Between Perceived and Actual Motor Competence 328
Motivation 329
Summary and Synthesis 334

17 Developmental Motor Learning 337

Unpacking the Definition of Motor Learning 338
Stages of Learning and the Development of Expertise 340
Practice and Motor Learning 344
Augmented Feedback and Motor Learning 347
Other Factors That Influence Motor Learning 349
Summary and Synthesis 353

18 Conclusion: Interactions Among Constraints 355

Using Constraints to Enhance Learning in Physical Activity Settings 357
Interacting Constraints: Case Studies 366
Summary and Synthesis 368

Appendix: Skinfold, Body Mass Index, and Head Circumference Charts 369
References 375
Index 411
About the Authors 423

PREFACE

Few of us go very long in life without watching people change. Our younger siblings or infant sons, daughters, nieces, or nephews grow into toddlers and then preschoolers, acquiring countless new skills, great knowledge, and communication tools. Middle schoolers, before we know it, are in high school, begin driving a car, and may be becoming accomplished musicians or talented athletes. We also see parents or grandparents changing, perhaps becoming less able to do the things they once enjoyed, perhaps adapting so they can continue to do things they enjoy. So you are a developmentalist. This text focuses on the study of motor development, observing changes in movement across the life span and attempting to sort out why and how these changes occur. You have a head start. Whether you have thought about it or not, you have watched individuals across the life span change in how they perform motor skills. Now, as you become a professional in your chosen field, or even a parent, you have the opportunity to learn more and reflect on these life span changes.

In this text we focus on an interactive model of constraints to serve as a guide for better understanding these changes in movement. The model of constraints uses the individual (or mover), the environment in which the mover acts, and the task the mover is performing. Moreover, it stresses the interaction of the three that gives rise to movement. We know that individuals are on a continual path of physical change—growing and maturing and then aging. The value of the model of constraints for a motor developmentalist is that it guides our observations of the movement outcome as the individual changes and, therefore, the interaction of the individual, environment, and task changes. The model allows us to anticipate how we might change movements by altering the environment, the task, or both (something that future physical educators, physical and occupational therapists, and other practitioners will find quite useful). Using the model of constraints will help you gain a more complete view of motor development across the life span and a means for solving motor development problems long after you finish your course. In fact, understanding life span motor development will assist your progress in all movement-related fields. You will learn what motor development is as well as the theoretical and historical roots of the field. You will also observe many factors related to development of movement skills, such as growth, aging, and perception. In addition, you will discover how constraints and other factors can encourage or discourage various movements—perhaps in ways you hadn't thought about yet!

Who can benefit from reading this text? Many people interested in movement can benefit. Educators at all levels—from early childhood educators to gerontologists—can enhance their teaching by becoming aware of various systems of the body and how they change over time. Those in the health sciences, such as physical and occupational therapists, will find tools that assist them in observing patterns of movement. Readers in exercise science will receive guidance from the descriptions and explanations of developmental physical fitness and of processes underlying change. However, you don't need extensive experience in movement studies to profit from this text. Because all people go through these developmental changes during their lives, all people can benefit from understanding more about motor development. In fact, parents and future parents will gain understanding of the motor development of their children and how to foster healthful motor development. Thus, many readers of this text will be able to use the information personally no matter how extensively they use it in their professional roles.

What's New in the Seventh Edition

The seventh edition of *Life Span Motor Development* continues our tradition of making your experience with motor development an interactive one. At the beginning of every chapter we try to place an aspect of motor development into the real world so you can see its real relevance to people of various ages. Application questions throughout the chapters engage readers in considering how parents or professionals in various roles might use the material discussed. The number and variety of lab activities, delivered on the website, have been increased. Videos are included to provide more opportunities for student-centered learning and, in some cases, for you to choose projects related to your career goals.

The content in the seventh edition has been updated to reflect new research in the field. We have also changed the presentation of material to move through the life span, with every aspect of importance to a portion of the life span presented together. New material in chapter 12 reflects current research frontiers on the role of motor skill competence in good health, including higher levels of fitness and ideal weight status. A new chapter, chapter 17, demonstrates the overlap between the study of motor development and the study of motor learning, a value to those who anticipate becoming teachers, instructors, or coaches. We have also reorganized the presentation of material in the text so that the core section on the development of motor skills is presented early. The section on physical growth and aging now leads directly into the section on fitness development.

Features of the Book

The seventh edition of *Life Span Motor Development* continues several important features of previous editions.

- **Chapter objectives.** The chapter objectives list the most important concepts you should learn and understand in each chapter.
- **Motor development in the real world.** To remind you that motor development is a common part of our human experience, we begin each chapter with a real-life experience—something that is a common experience for many of us or something we see reported frequently in the media.
- **Running glossary.** A running glossary appears in the margins throughout each chapter. The **running glossary words** are highlighted in the text with color so that you know to check the margin definition. Some terms don't require a margin definition because they are defined sufficiently in the text. Those words are boldfaced to help you locate them.
- **Application questions.** We distribute application questions as shown here, throughout the chapters. These questions challenge you to consider how parents or professionals could use the material under discussion in a real-world situation.

This is an example of a **running glossary word**; it is highlighted in color in the text and is defined in the margin.

Who can benefit from learning about motor development?

- **Key points.** Key points appear periodically throughout the chapter to point out the theme of a discussion or a broad conclusion amid chapter details. These key points are identified by the key point icon.

▶ **KEY POINTS** look like this and can be important for studying the material.

- **Web study guide cues.** Each chapter includes cues, such as the example that follows, that point to the lab activities in the web study guide. If you purchased a print book, you received access to the web study guide via a key code. If you purchased a used print book or an ebook that does not provide access to the web study guide, you will have to purchase the web study guide for access to the lab activities and videos. To access the web study guide, go to www.HumanKinetics.com/LifeSpanMotorDevelopment.

Web Study Guide Gain experience in observing movement by doing Lab Activity 1.1, Observation as a Tool of Inquiry, in the web study guide.

- **Assessment elements.** Most chapters contain an assessment element that will aid you in observing and assessing some aspect of motor development. These elements also help you understand how researchers and other professionals measure certain aspects of motor development.
- **Summary.** This section appears toward the end of a chapter and offers a concise wrap-up of the material presented in the chapter.
- **Reinforcement of chapter content.** To help you integrate the concepts you've learned throughout the chapter into a constraints perspective, each chapter ends with a section titled Reinforcing What You Have Learned About Constraints. Here you'll find subsections that encourage you to
  - take a second look at the real-life experience that opened the chapter,
  - test your knowledge by answering questions about the material, and
  - complete learning exercises that provide hands-on ways to apply what you have learned.
- **Assistance in meeting national standards.** The seventh edition continues to assist students in meeting national standards. The text and the approach are consistent with the revised guidelines for minimum competencies drafted by the Motor Development Academy of the National Association for Sport and Physical Education, which is part of SHAPE America (formerly the American Alliance for Health, Physical Education, Recreation and Dance). For those preparing to teach, the seventh edition provides guidelines for constructing developmentally appropriate activities and designing learning activities to help your students meet grade-level expectations.

Organization

Part I contains three chapters of fundamental concepts. Key to part I is the introduction of Newell's constraints model, around which the entire text is organized. Chapter 1 defines terms and methods of study in motor development. Chapter 2 offers a historical and theoretical overview of the field. Chapter 3 introduces the principles of motion and stability that underlie all movements and guide motor development.

Part II describes changing motor patterns over the life span. Chapter 4 explores motor development during infancy. Chapter 5 examines the development of locomotor skills, chapter 6 the development of ballistic skills, and chapter 7 the development of manipulative skills. These chapters provide much detail related to the specific sequence of changes one sees through development.

Part III examines physical growth and aging—how these individual constraints affect the body as a whole and specific body systems as well as how they change over the life span. This leads directly to part IV, which looks at the four important components of physical fitness and how they interact with the development of motor skills. Many professionals apply adult training principles to children, youths, and older adults without appreciating their unique constraints. These chapters present developmentally appropriate guidelines. For those concerned about the obesity epidemic among children and youths, part IV contains useful information.

The remaining parts focus on additional constraints that influence the movement arising from the interaction of these constraints, emphasizing those that change over the life span. Part V focuses on the role of sensory-perceptual development as it interacts with movement actions. Part VI begins with the social, cultural, and psychosocial influences on movement, followed by the new chapter on developmental motor learning. The concluding chapter encourages readers to apply what they have learned about changing constraints and their interactions to actual people and situations. Enhanced opportunities are provided so readers can reflect on all they have learned about motor development over the life span and use that knowledge in specific cases.

Ancillaries

The seventh edition of *Life Span Motor Development* includes a web study guide for students as well as video clips, an instructor guide, a presentation package plus image bank, a test package, and chapter quizzes for instructors.

The *web study guide* contains learning exercises and lab activities for every chapter. These exercises and activities might be done during class, in the laboratory, or as homework assignments. Lab activity record sheets and questions are available as fillable documents so that students can complete and submit them electronically, resulting in increased efficiency and reduced paperwork for instructors. The lab activities include video clips so that instructors whose classes cannot perform live observations will still be able to use all the labs. Clips include footage of infants and toddlers; additional footage of people performing the fundamental motor skills; and context-specific, constraint-rich video for chapters 1 through 18.

New to this edition are downloadable video clips that instructors can upload and access directly through learning management systems and use in a variety of ways, including through PowerPoint slides. In this way, instructors will be able to advance the videos frame by frame, fast forward, rewind, loop the videos, and so forth, depending on the media player used.

The *instructor guide* includes an overview, list of major concepts, suggested class activities, and suggested readings for each chapter. In addition, we have added suggested answers for all end-of-chapter Test Your Knowledge questions and the lab questions that students will complete in the web study guide.

The *test package*, created with Respondus 4.0, includes a bank of more than 540 questions updated especially for this edition of *Life Span Motor Development*. Question types include true or false, fill in the blank, short answer, essay, and multiple choice.

Answers are provided for some of the short-answer and essay questions, although you will likely want your students' answers to these questions to reflect the particular discussions held by your class. With Respondus LE, a free version of the Respondus software, instructors can create print versions of their own tests by selecting from the question pool; create, store, and retrieve their own questions; select their own test forms and save them for later editing or printing; and export the test forms into a word-processing program.

Ready-made chapter quizzes will help instructors assess students' comprehension of the most important concepts in each chapter. Each quiz contains 10 questions.

The *presentation package* includes a comprehensive series of PowerPoint slides for each chapter. The slides highlight the most important concepts from the book and include selected video clips from the lab activities. We have tried to include something from every section of each chapter. Depending on the particular emphasis an instructor wants to give the chapter—or on the background and expertise of the students—instructors may want to delete some slides or embellish others.

The *image bank* includes most of the art, photos, and tables from the book. A blank PowerPoint template is also provided so that instructors can customize or create a PowerPoint presentation if they so choose. Easy-to-follow instructions are included.

The web study guide, video clips, instructor guide, test package, chapter quizzes, and presentation package plus image bank are all accessible at www.HumanKinetics.com/LifeSpanMotorDevelopment.

ABOUT THE WEB STUDY GUIDE

The *web study guide* contains learning exercises and lab activities for every chapter. These exercises and activities might be done during class, in the laboratory, or as homework assignments.

Each lab comes with a clear introduction, a purpose statement, and instructions.

Lab Activity 5.1

LAB ACTIVITY 5.1

Assessing the Developmental Levels of Runners

Purpose: To gain experience in assessing the developmental levels of runners.

Developmental changes in running—from the time at which toddlers start to run to the time at which adolescents become proficient in running—were identified long ago. It has been proposed that these developmental trends form a series of step-by-step changes, but no one has validated these steps as developmental stages; as a result, you will use a hypothesized developmental sequence as an assessment tool in this lab activity. The sequence for the leg action in running has three steps, and the sequence for arm action in running has four steps. You will be required to identify where each runner falls in the developmental sequences for the arms and legs. You can read more about the developmental sequences in chapter 5 of the textbook.

Instructions

1. Start with the two runners featured in the guided assessment videos, which will help you learn the process of identifying developmental levels. The questions in the guided video are the same questions in the observation and will prompt you to watch for the critical elements. Follow the observation plan to determine the runner's level—first for leg action, then for arm action.
2. Categorize runners' developmental levels on your own using the nonguided assessment videos. Follow the observation plan to determine the level of each runner—again, first for leg action, then for arm action. Open the Record Sheet for this lab, which includes the first two columns dedicated to video assessments. Each column is used for one runner. Once you determine the level of the leg or arm action, place an X in the appropriate box in the runner's column. You should have just one X per action.

Lab activity record sheets and questions are available as fillable documents so students can complete and submit them electronically.

Lab Activity 5.1

Record Sheet for Lab Activity 5.1

Assessing the Developmental Levels of Runners

Observation Checklist: Running

OBSERVATION NUMBER	1	2	3	4	5	6	7
Runner's name or video number							
Runner's age, if known							
Date							
Observation type	Video	Video					

The lab activities include video clips so classes that cannot perform live observations will still be able to use all the labs.

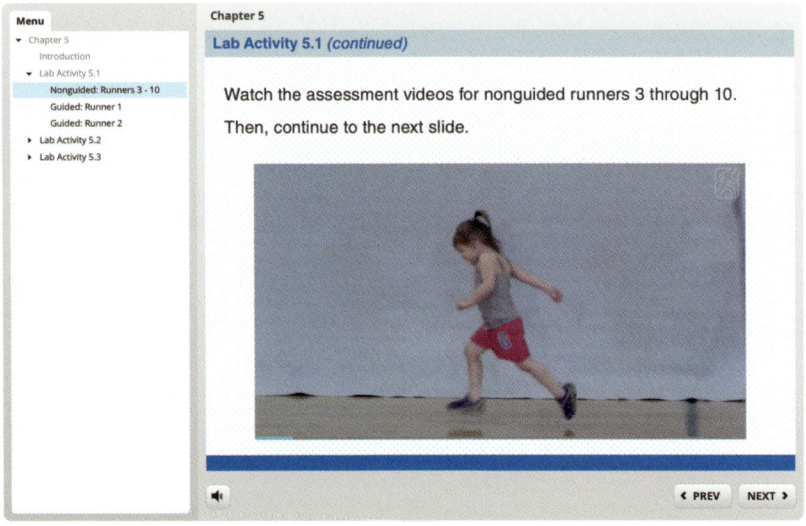

Clips include footage of infants and toddlers; additional footage of people performing the fundamental motor skills; and context-specific, constraint-rich video for chapters 1 through 18. Unique to this web study guide is video of the same infant at 1 month, 4 months, and 6.5 months.

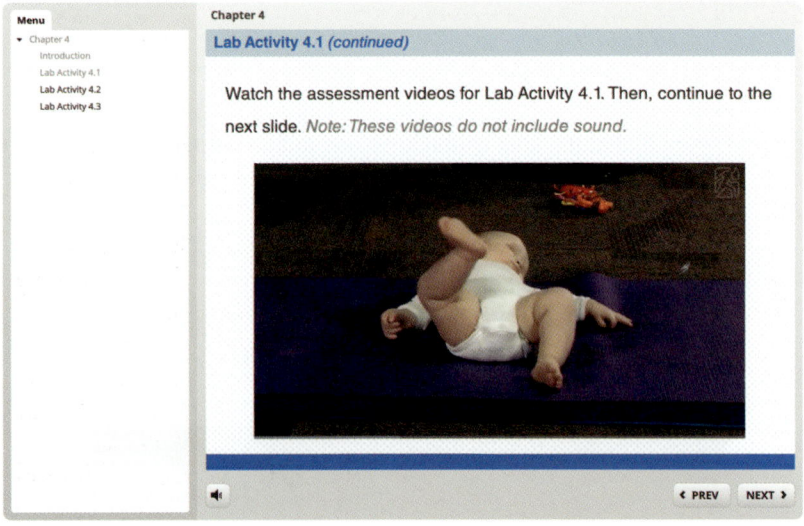

New to this edition are downloadable video clips that instructors can upload and access directly through learning management systems and use in a variety of ways, including through PowerPoint slides. In this way, instructors will be able to advance the videos frame by frame, fast forward, rewind, loop the videos, and so forth, depending on the media player used.

ACKNOWLEDGMENTS

The *Life Span Motor Development* project began in 1983. Each edition and each addition to what has now become a comprehensive instructional package reflects the contributions of many. We acknowledge some of those contributions here. Any undertaking this ambitious could be completed only with the help and support of those contributing their unique expertise and talents. This seventh edition continues to expand on the previous editions, and contributions anywhere along the way have made this work what it is today. We can only hope that everyone who has contributed in any way knows how much we appreciate their help.

First, we extend our appreciation to those who have appeared in photographs or video clips over the years: Jennifer, Douglas, and Michael Imergoot; Laura, Christina, and Matthew Haywood; Anna Tramelli; Cathy Lewis; Jules Mommaerts; Connor Miller; Franklin McFarland; Rachel Harmon; Jessica Galli; Charmin Olion; Chad Hoffman; Stephanie Kozlowski; Julia and Madeleine Blakely; Valeria Rohde; Ian Stahl; Amelia Isaacs; Reese and Nicholas Rapson; Janiyah Bell; Parker Lehn; Logan Allen; Jane Laskowski; Rachel and Jessica Wiley; Diane Waltermire; Jase Elliott; Susan Allen; Susan and Lisa Miller; Emily and Jeremy Falkenham, Sarah Poe; Alex Mitsdarfer; Lyna Buzzard; Blair Mathis; Parker, Addison, Zander, and Willow Burk; Robert, James, and Lillian Hall; Susan Outlaw; Julie and Johnathan Lyons; Grace and Dylan Taylor; Emily and Abram George; Reid and Madi Henness; Kaleb Curry; Kelly Taylor; Luci and Lynette Morris; Tony and Mary Graham; William Gingold; Anna Clark; Sarah, Mary, and Grace White; Neil Hollwedel; Daniel Fishel; Cole and Logan Hasty; Marcia Siebert; and Joshua, Shagra, and Holden Stone; among others.

Next, we acknowledge friends who took or donated some of the photographs, in this or previous editions: Brian Speicher, William Long, Rosa Angulo-Barroso, Susan Miller, Dale Ulrich, Mary Ann Roberton, Ann VanSant, John Haubenstricker, B.D. Ulrich, and Jill Whitall, contributed film tracings from which some of the art was drawn. Additional thanks to Mary Ann Roberton for supplying a great picture of Hal in action.

The content of *Life Span Motor Development* touches many subdisciplines and specialty areas of study. We extend our thanks to John Strupel, the late Elizabeth Sweeney, Bruce Clark, Jane Clark, Maureen Weiss, Kathleen Williams, Ann VanSant, and Mary Ann Roberton, who were all kind enough to read sections of the text or contribute information. Thanks to Paul M. Spezia, DO, of Advanced Bone and Joint, who provided wrist X rays for the laboratory exercise on skeletal age.

Ann Wagner and Cynthia Haywood Kerkemeyer helped by keyboarding and checking parts of the earlier editions, and the late Lynn Imergoot, Linda Gagen, Patricia Hanna, and Cathy Lewis were kind enough to help with the index of an earlier edition.

We especially thank our many colleagues in motor development who have made suggestions along the way. Their dedication to helping students of motor development appreciate this area of study is always an inspiration. Lisa Barnett, Dale Ulrich, and Kip Webster all helped with new material for the seventh edition. Last but not least, we appreciate the patience and dedication of our team at Human Kinetics for keeping us on track through the many facets of the seventh edition in the face of a very tight schedule.

We also acknowledge our families and friends, who have prevailed through many revisions of this textbook. Their continued support over the years makes our work possible.

CREDITS

Figure 2.3 Adapted by permission from E. Thelen, B.D. Ulrich, and J. L. Jensen, The Developmental Origins of Locomotion, in *Development of Posture and Gait Across the Life Span,* edited by M.H. Woolacott and A. Shumway-Cook (Columbia, SC: University of South Carolina Press, 1989), 28.

Figure 3.2 Reprinted from J.E. Donnelly, *Living Anatomy,* 2nd ed. (Champaign, IL: Human Kinetics, 1990), 32. Permission by J.E. Donnelly.

Figure 4.7 Reprinted by permission from B.I. Bertenthal, J.L. Rose, and D.L. Bai, 1997, "Perception-Action Coupling in the Development of Visual Control of Posture," *Journal of Experimental Psychology: Human Perception and Performance* 23: 1631-1634, fig. 1. Copyright © by the American Psychological Association.

Figure 5.2 Parts a and c are drawn from film tracings taken in the Motor Development and Child Study Laboratory, University of Wisconsin-Madison and now available from the Motor Development Film Collection, Kinesiology Division, Bowling Green State University. © Mary Ann Roberton. Part b is adapted from R.L. Wickstrom, *Fundamental Motor Patterns,* 3rd ed. (Philadelphia: Lea & Febiger, 1983), 29. © Mary Ann Roberton and Kate R. Barrett.

Figure 5.4 Part a is drawn from film tracings taken in the Motor Development and Child Study Laboratory, University of Wisconsin-Madison and now available from the Motor Development Film Collection, Kinesiology Division, Bowling Green State University. © Mary Ann Roberton. Part b is redrawn from R.L. Wickstrom, *Fundamental Motor Patterns,* 3rd ed. (Philadelphia: Lea & Febiger, 1983). © Mary Ann Roberton and Kate R. Barrett.

Figure 5.5 Adapted by permission from R.L. Wickstrom, *Fundamental Motor Patterns,* 3rd ed. (Philadelphia: Lea & Febiger, 1983), 29. © Mary Ann Roberton and Kate R. Barrett.

Table 5.2 Reprinted by permission from R.L. Wickstrom, *Fundamental Motor Patterns,* 3rd ed. (Philadelphia: Lea & Febiger, 1983), 68. © Mary Ann Roberton and Kate R. Barrett.

Table 5.3 Reprinted by permission from R.L. Wickstrom, *Fundamental Motor Patterns,* 3rd ed. (Philadelphia: Lea & Febiger, 1983), 68. © Mary Ann Roberton and Kate R. Barrett.

Table 5.4 Adapted by permission from V. Seefeldt, S. Reuschlein, and P. Vogel, *Sequencing Motor Skills Within the Physical Education Curriculum.* Paper presented to the annual conference of the American Association for Health, Physical Education and Recreation, 1972. © Vern D. Seedfeldt.

Table 5.5 Adapted by permission from J.E. Clark and S.J. Phillips, A Developmental Sequence of the Standing Long Jump, in *Motor Development: Current Selected Research,* Vol. 1, edited by J.E. Clark and J.H. Humphrey (Princeton Book, 1985), 76-77. Copyright 1985 by Princeton Book Company, Publishers.

Figure 5.7 Adapted by permission from R.L. Wickstrom, *Fundamental Motor Patterns,* 3rd ed. (Philadelphia: Lea & Febiger, 1983), 74. © Mary Ann Roberton and Kate R. Barrett.

Figure 5.8 Drawn from film tracings taken in the Motor Development and Child Study Laboratory, University of Wisconsin-Madison and now available from the Motor Development Film Collection, Kinesiology Division, Bowling Green State University. © Mary Ann Roberton.

Table 5.6 Reprinted by permission from A.P Lane et al., "Developmental Sequences for the Standing Long Jump Landing: A Pre-Longitudinal Screening," *Journal of Motor Learning and Development* 6 (2018): 114-120.

Figure 5.10 Adapted from by permission R.L. Wickstrom, *Fundamental Motor Patterns,* 3rd ed. (Philadelphia: Lea & Febiger, 1983), 77. © Mary Ann Roberton and Kate R. Barrett.

Figure 5.13 Drawn from film tracings taken in the Motor Development and Child Study Laboratory, University of Wisconsin–Madison and now available from the Motor Development Film Collection, Kinesiology Division, Bowling Green State University. © Mary Ann Roberton.

Figure 5.14 Drawn from film tracings taken in the Motor Development and Child Study Laboratory, University of Wisconsin–Madison and now available from the Motor Development Film Collection, Kinesiology Division, Bowling Green State University. © Mary Ann Roberton.

Table 5.7 Reprinted from M.A. Roberton and L.E. Halverson, *Developing Children: Their Changing Movement* (Philadelphia: Lea & Febiger, 1984), 56-63. © Mary Ann Roberton.

Figure 5.15 Drawn from film tracings taken in the Motor Development and Child Study Laboratory, University of Wisconsin–Madison and now available from the Motor Development Film Collection, Kinesiology Division, Bowling Green State University. © Mary Ann Roberton.

Figure 5.16 Drawn from film tracings taken in the Motor Development and Child Study Laboratory, University of Wisconsin–Madison and now available from the Motor Development Film Collection, Kinesiology Division, Bowling Green State University. © Mary Ann Roberton.

Figure 5.17 Reprinted from L. Halverson and K Williams, "Development Sequences for Hopping over Distance: A Prelongitudinal Screening," *Research Quarterly for Exercise and Sport,* 56 (1985): 38. By permission of SHAPE America.

Figure 5.19 a and b Adapted by permission from J.E. Clark and J. Whitall, Changing Patterns of Locomotion: From Walking to Skipping, in *Development of Posture and Gait Across the Life Span,* edited by M.H. Woollacott and A. Shumway-Cook (Columbia, SC: University of South Carolina Press, 1989), 132.

Figure 5.20 Adapted by permission from J.E. Clark and J. Whitall, Changing Patterns of Locomotion: From Walking to Skipping, in *Development of Posture and Gait Across the Life Span,* edited by M.H. Woollacott and A. Shumway-Cook (Columbia, SC: University of South Carolina Press, 1989), 132.

Table 5.8 Adapted by permission from D.A. Ulrich, "The Test of Gross Motor Development-3 (TGMD-3): Administration, Scoring, and International Norms," *Hacettepe Journal of Sport Sciences* 24, no. 2 (2013): 27-33.

Figure 6.1 Drawn from film tracings taken in the Motor Development and Child Study Laboratory, University of Wisconsin–Madison and now available from the Motor Development Film Collection, Kinesiology Division, Bowling Green State University. © Mary Ann Roberton.

Figure 6.2 Drawn from film tracings taken in the Motor Development and Child Study Laboratory, University of Wisconsin-Madison and now available from the Motor Development Film Collection, Kinesiology Division, Bowling Green State University. © Mary Ann Roberton and Kate R. Barrett.

Figure 6.3 Drawn from film tracings taken in the Motor Development and Child Study Laboratory, University of Wisconsin–Madison and now available from the Motor Development Film Collection, Kinesiology Division, Bowling Green State University. © Mary Ann Roberton.

Table 6.1 Reprinted from M.A. Roberton and L.E. Halverson, *Developing Children: Their Changing Movement* (Philadelphia: Lea & Febiger, 1984), 103, 106–107, 118, 123. © Mary Ann Roberton.

Figure 6.4 Drawn from film tracings taken in the Motor Development and Child Study Laboratory, University of Wisconsin–Madison and now available from the Motor Development Film Collection, Kinesiology Division, Bowling Green State University. © Mary Ann Roberton.

Figure 6.5 Drawn from film tracings taken in the Motor Development and Child Study Laboratory, University of Wisconsin–Madison and now available from the Motor Development Film Collection, Kinesiology Division, Bowling Green State University. © Mary Ann Roberton.

Figure 6.6 Drawn from film tracings taken in the Motor Development and Child Study Laboratory, University of Wisconsin–Madison and now available from the Motor Development Film Collection, Kinesiology Division, Bowling Green State University. © Mary Ann Roberton.

Figure 6.7 The line drawings within this Observation Plan are: Drawn from film tracings taken in the Motor Development and Child Study Laboratory, University of Wisconsin–Madison and now available from the Motor Development Film Collection, Kinesiology Division, Bowling Green State University. © Mary Ann Roberton.

Figure 6.7b The line drawings within this Observation Plan are: Drawn from film tracings taken in the Motor Development and Child Study Laboratory, University of Wisconsin–Madison and now available from the Motor Development Film Collection, Kinesiology Division, Bowling Green State University. © Mary Ann Roberton.

Figure 6.8 Drawn from film tracings taken in the Motor Development and Child Study Laboratory, University of Wisconsin–Madison and now available from the Motor Development Film Collection, Kinesiology Division, Bowling Green State University. © Mary Ann Roberton.

Figure 6.9 Drawn from film tracings taken in the Motor Development and Child Study Laboratory, University of Wisconsin–Madison and now available from the Motor Development Film Collection, Kinesiology Division, Bowling Green State University. © Mary Ann Roberton.

Figure 6.10 Drawn from film tracings taken in the Motor Development and Child Study Laboratory, University of Wisconsin–Madison and now available from the Motor Development Film Collection, Kinesiology Division, Bowling Green State University. © Mary Ann Roberton.

Figure 6.11 Drawn from film tracings taken in the Motor Development and Child Study Laboratory, University of Wisconsin–Madison and now available from the Motor Development Film Collection, Kinesiology Division, Bowling Green State University. © Mary Ann Roberton.

Figure 6.12 Drawn from film tracings taken in the Motor Development and Child Study Laboratory, University of Wisconsin–Madison and now available from the Motor Development Film Collection, Kinesiology Division, Bowling Green State University. © Mary Ann Roberton.

Table 6.2 Reprinted from M.A. Roberton and L.E. Halverson, *Developing children: Their changing movement* (Philadelphia: Lea & Febiger, 1984), 103, 106–107, 118, 123. © Mary Ann Roberton.

Figure 6.14 Drawn from film tracings taken in the Motor Development and Child Study Laboratory, University of Wisconsin–Madison and now available from the Motor Development Film Collection, Kinesiology Division, Bowling Green State University. © Mary Ann Roberton.

Figure 6.16 Drawn from film tracings taken in the Motor Development and Child Study Laboratory, University of Wisconsin–Madison and now available from the Motor Development Film Collection, Kinesiology Division, Bowling Green State University. © Mary Ann Roberton.

Figure 6.17 Drawn from film tracings taken in the Motor Development and Child Study Laboratory, University of Wisconsin–Madison and now available from the Motor Development Film Collection, Kinesiology Division, Bowling Green State University. © Mary Ann Roberton.

Table 6.4 The preparatory trunk action and the parenthetical information in step 3 of racket action are reprinted, by permission, from J.A. Messick, "Prelongitudinal Screening of Hypothesized Developmental Sequences for the Overhead Tennis Serve in Experienced Tennis Players 9-19 Years of Age," *Research Quarterly for Exercise and Sport* 62 (1991): 249-256. The remaining components are reprinted by permission from S. Langendorfer, Prelongitudinal Screening of Overarm Striking Development Performed Under Two Environmental Conditions, in *Advances in Motor Development Research,* Vol. 1, edited by J.E. Clark and J.H. Humphrey (New York: AMS Press, 1987), 26.

Table 6.5 Reprinted by permission from D.A. Ulrich, "The Test of Gross Motor Development-3 (TGMD-3): Administration, Scoring, and International Norms," *Hacettepe Journal of Sport Sciences* 24, no. 2 (2013): 27-33.

Figure 7.3 Reprinted by permission from L. Hay, Developmental Changes in Eye-Hand Coordination Behaviors: Preprogramming Versus Feedback Control, in *Development of Eye-Hand Coordination Across the Life Span,* edited by C. Bard, M. Fleury, and L. Hay (Columbia, SC: University of South Carolina Press, 1990), 235.

Figure 7.5 Drawn from film tracings taken in the Motor Development and Child Study Laboratory, University of Wisconsin–Madison and now available from the Motor Development Film Collection, Kinesiology Division, Bowling Green State University. © Mary Ann Roberton.

Table 7.1 Reprinted from H.S. Strohmeyer, K. Williams, and D. Schaub-George, "Developmental Sequences for Catching a Small Ball: A Prelongitudinal Screening," *Research Quarterly for Exercise and Sport,* 62 (1991): 249-256. Reprinted by permission of SHAPE America.

Figure 7.7 Illustrations are drawn from film tracings taken in the Motor Development and Child Study Laboratory, University of Wisconsin–Madison and now available from the Motor Development Film Collection, Kinesiology Division, Bowling Green State University. © Mary Ann Roberton.

Figure 7.8 Adapted by permission from P. McLeod and Z. Dienes, "Do Fielders Know Where to Go to Catch the Ball or Only How to Get There?" *Journal of Experimental Psychology: Human Perception and Performance* 22 (1996): 541. Copyright © 1996 by the American Psychological Association.

Figure 7.9 Redrawn from M. Lenoir et al. "Intercepting Moving Objects During Self-Motion," *Journal of Motor Behavior* 31, no. 1 (1999): 55-67.

Table 8.1 Adapted by permission from P.S. Timiras, *Developmental Physiology and Aging* (New York; Macmillan, 1972), 63-64.

Figure 8.4 a and b Data from the National Center for Health Statistics in collaboration with the National Center for Chronic Disease Prevention and Health Promotion 2000. www.cdc.gov/nchs/about/major/nhanes/growthcharts.clinical_charts.htm.

Figure 8.5 a and b Data from the National Center for Health Statistics in collaboration with the National Center for Chronic Disease Prevention and Health Promotion 2000. www.cdc.gov/nchs/about/major/nhanes/growthcharts.clinical_charts.htm.

Table 8.2 Adapted by permission from M.L. Feldkamp, L.D. Botto, and J.C. Carey, "Reflections on the Etiology of Structural Birth Defects: Established Teratogens and Risk Factors," *Birth Defects Research Part A: Clinical and Molecular Teratology* 103, no. 8 (2015):

Figure 8.7 Adapted by permission from P.S. Timiras, *Developmental Physiology and Aging* (New York: Macmillan, 1972), 284.

Figure 8.8 a, b and c Biro, F.M., & Kiess, W. (2016). Contemporary trends in onset and completion of puberty, gain in height and adiposity. In J.-P. Bourguignon & A-.S. Parent (Eds), *Puberty from bench to clinic* (Vol. 29, pp. 122-133). Basel, Switzerland: Karger; Susman, E.J., Houts, R.M., Steinberg, L., Belsky, J., Cauffman, E., DeHart, G., et al. (2010). Longitudinal development of secondary sexual characteristics in girls and boys between ages 9½ and 15½ years. *Archives of pediatrics and adolescent medicine, 164*(2), 166-173; Fryar, C.D., Gu, Q., & Ogden, C.L. (2012). Anthropometric reference data for children and adults: United States, 2007–2010. National Center for Health Statistics. *Vital Health Stat* 11(252).

Figure 8.10 Fryar, C.D., Gu, Q., & Ogden, C.L. (2012). Anthropometric reference data for children and adults: United States, 2007-2010. National Center for Health Statistics. *Vital Health Stat* 11(252).

Figure 8.12 Fryar, C.D., Gu, Q., & Ogden, C.L. (2012). Anthropometric reference data for children and adults: United States, 2007-2010. National Center for Health Statistics. *Vital Health Stat* 11(252).

Figure 9.1 Printed in U.S.A. © Carolina Biological Supply Company. Reproduction of all or any part of this material without written permission from the copyright holder is unlawful.

Figure 9.7 a and b Reprinted, by permission, from S.I. Pyle, 1971, *A radiographic Standard of Reference for the Growing Hand and Wrist* (Chicago: Year Book Medical), 53, 73. Copyright Bolton-Brush Growth Study—B.H. Broadbent D.D.S.

Figure 9.9 Reprinted by permission from R.M. Malina and C. Bouchard, Subcutaneous Fat Distribution During Growth, in *Fat Distribution During Growth and Later Health Outcomes,* edited by C. Bouchard and F.E. Johnston (New York: Liss, 1988), 70. Copyright © 1988 by Alan R. Liss, Inc.

Figure 10.1 a and b Reprinted by permission from R.M. Malina, C. Bouchard, and O. Bar-Or, *Growth, Maturation, and Physical Activity,* 2nd ed. (Champaign, IL: Human Kinetics, 2004), 259.

Figure 10.2 a and b Reprinted from O. Bar-Or, *Pediatric Sports Medicine for the Practitioner* (New York: Springer, 1983), 4, 5. By permission of Marilyn Bar-Or.

Figure 10.3 a and b Shephard, R.J. (1982). *Physical activity and growth.* Chicago: Year Book Medical.

Figure 10.5 a and b Reprinted by permission from B.A. Stamford, Exercise and the Elderly, in *Exercise and Sport Sciences Reviews,* Vol. 16, edited by K.B. Pandolf (New York: Macmillan, 1986), 344. © The McGraw-Hill Companies.

Figure 10.6 Reprinted by permission from W.W. Spirduso, K. Francis, and P. MacRae, *Physical Dimensions of Aging,* 2nd ed. (Champaign, IL: Human Kinetics, 2005), 108.

Figure 11.1 Shephard, R.J. (1982). *Physical activity and growth.* Chicago: Year Book Medical.

Figure 11.2 Reprinted by permission from R.M. Malina, C. Bouchard, and O. Bar-Or, *Growth, Maturation, and Physical Activity,* 2nd ed. (Champaign, IL: Human Kinetics, 2004), 495.

Figure 11.3 Reprinted by permission from R.M. Malina, C. Bouchard, and O. Bar-Or, *Growth, Maturation, and Physical Activity,* 2nd ed. (Champaign, IL: Human Kinetics, 2004), 498.

Figure 11.5 Shephard, R.J. (1982). *Physical activity and growth.* Chicago: Year Book Medical

Table 11.1 Reprinted by permission from W.W. Spirduso, *Physical Dimensions of Aging* (Champaign, IL: Human Kinetics, 1995), 127.

Figure 11.6 Reprinted by permission from A. Aniansson, M. Hedberg, G.B. Henning, and G. Grimby, "Muscle morphology, enzymatic activity, and muscle strength in elderly men: A follow-up study," *Muscle & Nerve* 9 (1986): 588. Copyright © 1986 by John Wiley & Sons.

Figure 11.7 Reprinted by permission from W.W. Spirduso, K. Francis, and P. MacRae, *Physical Dimensions of Aging,* 2nd ed. (Champaign, IL: Human Kinetics, 2005), 112.

Figure 11.8 a, b, and c Soucie, J.M., Wang, C., Forsyth, A., Funk, S., Denny, M., Roach, K.E., Boone, D. and the Hemophilia Treatment Center Network. (2011). Range of motion measurements: Reference values and a database for comparison studies. *Haemophilia,* 17, 500–507. doi:10.1111/j.1365-2516.2010.02399.x

Figure 11.10 Reprinted by permission from W.K. Hoeger et al., "Comparing the Sit and Reach With the Modified Sit and Reach in Measuring Flexibility in Adolescents," *Pediatric Exercise Science* 2 (1990): 156-162.

Figure 11.11 Reprinted by permission from J. Simons et al., *Growth and Fitness of Flemish Girls* (Champaign, IL: Human Kinetics, 1990), 118.

Figure 12.2 a and b From J. Parizkova, *Body Fat and Physical Fitness* (The Hague, The Netherlands: Martinus Nijhoff B.V., 1977). By permission of J. Parizkova.

Figure 12.3 From J. Parizkova, *Body Fat and Physical Fitness* (The Hague, The Netherlands: Martinus Nijhoff B.V., 1977). By permission of J. Parizkova.

Figure 12.5 Data from the U.S. Department of Health and Human Services, Centers for Disease Control and Prevention, National Center for Health Statistics, 2016. https://www.cdc.gov/nchs/data/hus/hus16.pdf#listtables.

Figure 13.1 Reprinted from WikiCommons. https://commons.wikimedia.org/wiki/File:Facevase.png.

Figure 13.5 a and b Selected material from the *Sensory Integration and Praxis Tests- Figure-Ground Perception Test* © 1972 by Western Psychological Services. Reprinted by Human Kinetics Publishing Inc. by permission of WPS, 625 Alaska Avenue, Torrance, California, 90503, U.S.A., rights@wpspublishi.com. Not to be reprinted in whole or in part for any additional purposes without the expressed written permission of the publisher. All rights reserved.

Figure 13.10 Reprinted from T.G.R. Bower, *A Primer of Infant Development* (San Francisco: W.H. Freeman, 1977). Copyright 1977.

Figure 13.11 Morrongiello, B.A. (1988a). The development of auditory pattern perception skills. In C. Rovee-Collier & L.P. Lipsitt (Eds.), *Advances in infancy research* (Vol. 6, pp. 135–172). Norwood, NJ: Ablex.

Figure 14.1 Adapted by permission from R. Held and A. Hein, "Movement-Produced Stimulation in the Development of Visually Guided Behavior," *Journal of Comparative and Physiological Psychology* 56 (1963): 872-876, fig. 1. Copyright © 1963 by the American Psychological Association.

Chapter 15 opening text Reprinted by permission from T.B. Wiese, "Women's Lacrosse Players Must Adhere to Traditional Gender Roles," *The Beacon* April 13, 2016. www.theonlinebeacon.com/womens-lacrosse-players-must-adhere-to-traditional-gender-roles/

Figure 15.2 Kenyon, G.S., & McPherson, B.D. (1973). Becoming involved in physical activity and sport: A process of socialization. In G.L. Rarick (Ed.), *Physical activity: Human growth and development* (pp. 301–332). New York, NY: Academic Press.

Figure 16.1 Horn, T.S., & Hasbrook, C.A. (1987). Psychological characteristics and the criteria children use for self-evaluation. *Journal of Sport Psychology,* 9, 208-221.

Figure 16.6 Reprinted from J.L. Duda and M.K. Tappe, Personal Investment in Exercise Among Adults: The Examination of Age and Gender-Related Differences in Motivational Orientation, in *Aging and Motor Behavior,* edited by A.C. Ostrow (Dubuque, IA: Benchmark Press, 1989), 246, 248. By permission of J.L. Duda.

Figure 17.4 Colcombe, S.J., Erickson, K.I., Raz, N., Webb, A.G., Cohen, N.J., McAuley, E., et al. (2003). Aerobic fitness reduces brain tissue loss in aging humans. *Journal of Gerontology: Series A: Biological Sciences and Medical Science,* 55, 176-180.

Figure 18.7 Reprinted by permission from J. Herkowitz, Developmental Task Analysis: The Design of Movement Experiences and Evaluation of Motor Development Status, in *Motor Development,* edited by M.V. Ridenour (Princeton, NJ: Princeton Book, 1978), 141.

Figure 18.8 Reprinted by permission from J. Herkowitz, Developmental Task Analysis: The Design of Movement Experiences and Evaluation of Motor Development Status, in *Motor Development,* edited by M.V. Ridenour (Princeton, NJ: Princeton Book, 1978), 149.

I

Introduction to Motor Development

When you begin to learn any new area of study, you must start out by deciphering the lingo used by the field's professionals. In motor development, the professionals include physical educators, athletic trainers, coaches, physical and occupational therapists, and professors. This is quite a variety! It may not surprise you, then, that the first part of this text is dedicated to providing a sound base of information—terms, theories, concepts, and important historical notes—on which you can build your knowledge of motor development. You must learn basic terms so you can read about motor development and converse with others about this field of study. You must learn the scope of the field and how it goes about researching the developmental aspects of motor behavior. It benefits you to learn how information is pictured or presented within the field of study. All these topics are addressed in chapter 1.

You also need to know the various perspectives that professionals in the field of motor development have adopted to view motor behavior and interpret studies of that behavior. Often, what is known within a discipline of study is a function of the perspectives adopted by those studying in the field. Chapter 2 introduces you to these perspectives.

In chapter 3, you will learn about the principles of motion and stability that influence all your movements at all times. Understanding these principles will help you see patterns in the way motor skills change over time (addressed in the chapters that follow). The goal of chapter 3 is to help you understand in a general way how these principles work.

Most importantly, part I introduces you to a model that will guide your study of motor development: Newell's model of constraints (Newell, 1986). Chapter 1 describes the model's parts and what it depicts. Newell's model gives you a way of organizing new pieces of information. Right now, the most important notion you can gain from this model is that motor development does not focus only on the individual; it also examines the importance of the environment in which an individual moves and the task the individual is trying to accomplish. Moreover, the model gives you a way to analyze and think about issues and problems in motor development. Thus it will be useful not only in the short term of your study of motor development but also in the long term, as you move into a professional position or interact with family and friends regarding their motor skills.

Suggested Reading

Adolph, K.E. (2018). Motor development. In M. Bornstein & M. Arterberry (Eds.). *The SAGE encyclopedia of lifespan human development* (pp. 1450–1453). Thousand Oaks, CA: Sage.

Adolph, K.E., & Franchak, J.M. (2016). The development of motor behavior. *WIREs Cognitive Science,* 8, 1–18. DOI: 10.1002/wcs.1430

Clark, J.E. (2017). Pentimento: A 21st century view on the canvas of motor development. *Kinesiology Review,* 6, 232–239. DOI:10.1123/kr.2017-0020

Gagen, L., & Getchell, N. (2008). Applying Newton's apple to elementary physical education: An interdisciplinary approach. *Journal of Physical Education, Recreation, and Dance,* 79, 43–51.

Gagen, L., & Getchell, N. (2018). Using 'constraints' to design developmentally appropriate movement activities for early childhood education. In H. Brewer & M. Ranck Jalongo (Eds.), *Physical activity and health promotion in the early years: Effective strategies for early childhood educators* (pp. 57-74). Springer: Champ, Switzerland.

Jensen, J. (2005). The puzzles of motor development: How the study of developmental biomechanics contributes to the puzzle solutions. *Infant and Child Development, 14*(5), 501–511.

1

Fundamental Concepts

CHAPTER OBJECTIVES

This chapter

- defines motor development,
- distinguishes developmental issues from other concerns,
- describes some of the basic tools used by researchers in motor development,
- explains why development occurs over a life span, and
- introduces a model that guides our discussion of motor development.

Motor Development in the Real World

The *Up* Series

In 1964, director Paul Almond filmed a group of 14 British children, all 7 years old, from diverse socioeconomic backgrounds and created a documentary about their lives titled *7 Up!* In 1971, Michael Apted followed up with *7 Plus Seven*, and he brought out a new installment of the series every 7 years, following these same individuals through childhood and adolescence, into adulthood, and then into middle age. Apted hoped to explore the influence of the British class system over time and see if the Jesuit motto "Give me a child until he is seven and I will give you the man" held true. The latest installment, *56 Up*, premiered on British television on May 14, 2012, and was released in the United States in January 2013. In total, the *Up* series showed the lives of the participants over the course of 49 years, from childhood into middle adulthood, thus providing a window into the group and individual development.

If we developed a series of documentaries addressing motor development, who might watch? Many professionals might be interested. Educators, especially physical and early childhood educators, might be interested in which practices work best and whether they are developmentally appropriate. Therapists would want to know the factors that affect movement abilities. Engineers and designers might be interested in changes throughout adulthood in order to make appropriately sized and arranged living spaces, control panels, work equipment, sport gear, and vehicles. Health care providers might want to determine how movement and exercise early in life affect health status later on. Clearly, then, motor development interests many people for many reasons. Indeed, we can learn a great deal by examining change in movement patterns—and why it occurs—from birth until old age. Movement is an integral part of our lives, and its change is inevitable.

Defining Motor Development

Our imaginary documentary series might give you a rough idea of what motor development is. Let's now be more exact and give the field some boundaries, much as a producer would do in order to decide which segments are appropriate for the motor development film and which are not.

Development is defined by several characteristics. First, it is a continuous process of change in functional capacity. Think of functional capacity as the capability to exist—to live, move, and work—in the real world. This is a cumulative process. Living organisms are always developing, but the amount of change may be more noticeable, or less noticeable, at various points in the life span.

Second, development is related to (but not dependent on) age. As age advances, development proceeds. However, development can be faster or slower at different times, and rates of development can differ among individuals of the same age. Individuals do not necessarily advance in age and advance in development at the same rate. Further, development does not *stop* at a particular age but rather continues throughout life.

Third, development involves sequential change. One step leads to the next step in an orderly and irreversible fashion. This change results from interactions both within the individual and between the individual and the environment. All individuals of a species undergo predictable patterns of development, but the result of development is always a group of unique individuals.

Individuals function in a variety of arenas, including the physical, social, cognitive, and psychological. Hence, we use terms such as **cognitive development** or **social development** to address the process of change in particular arenas. Social scientists often specialize in the study of one aspect of development.

We use the term **motor development** to refer to the development of movement abilities. Those who study motor development explore developmental changes in movements as well as the factors underlying those changes. Such study addresses both the process of change and the resultant movement outcome. Not all change in movement constitutes development. For example, if a tennis teacher elicits a change in a student's forehand stroke by changing the student's grip on the racket, we do not view the change as motor development. Rather, we use the term **motor learning**, which refers to movement changes that are relatively permanent but related to *experience* or practice rather than age. We use the term **motor behavior** when we prefer not to distinguish between motor learning and motor development or when we want to include both.

Motor control refers to the nervous system's control of the muscles that permits skilled and coordinated movements. In recent years, researchers in motor development and in motor control have found much in common. Understanding how the nervous system and movement abilities change with age expands our knowledge of motor control, and we now see much overlap in motor development and control research.

Motor development refers to the continuous, age-related process of change in movement as well as the interacting constraints (or factors) in the individual, environment, and task that drive these changes.

Motor learning refers to the relatively permanent gains in motor skill capability associated with practice or experience (Schmidt & Lee, 2014).

Motor control is the study of the neural, physical, and behavioral aspects of movement (Schmidt & Lee, 2014).

Scan news websites such as MSNBC.com or CNN.com for stories related to motor development. What key words did you search for besides *motor* and *development* in order to focus in on this topic?

Undoubtedly, you have heard the term *development* paired with the term *growth*, as in "growth and development." **Physical growth** is a quantitative increase in size or magnitude. Living organisms experience a period of growth in physical size. For humans, this growth period starts with conception and ends in late adolescence or the early 20s. Changes in the size of tissues after the physical growth period (e.g., an increase in muscle mass with resistance training) are described with other terms. Thus, the phrase *growth and development* includes change in both size and functional capacity.

The term *maturation* is also paired with the term *growth*, but it is not the same as development. **Maturation** connotes progress toward physical maturity, the state of optimal functional integration of an individual's body systems and the ability to reproduce. Development continues long after physical maturity is reached.

Physiological change does not stop at the end of the physical growth period. Rather, it can occur throughout life. Physiological change tends to be slower after the growth period but nevertheless remains prominent. The term **aging** can be used in a broad sense to refer to the process of growing older regardless of chronological age; it can also refer specifically to changes that lead to a loss of adaptability or function and eventually to death (Spirduso, Francis, & MacRae, 2005).

The physiological processes of growth and aging fall on a continuum of life span development. For many years, researchers examined motor development almost exclusively from early childhood through puberty. However, the population across the globe has aged. In many countries—including the United States, China, Russia, Australia, Canada, and the majority of the European Union's nations—by 2030 at least 13% of the population will be aged 65 years or older (Kinsella & Velkoff, 2001). This change brings more urgency to the need for better understanding of motor development in the later years. Although some motor development students might be particularly interested in one portion of the continuum, motor development as a field still concerns change in movement across the life span. Understanding what drives change in one part of the life span often helps us understand change in another part. This process of examining change is part of adopting a developmental perspective.

Physical growth is an increase in size or body mass resulting from an increase in complete, already formed body parts (Timiras, 1972).

Physiological **maturation** is a qualitative advance in biological makeup and may refer to cell, organ, or system advancement in biochemical composition rather than to size alone (Teeple, 1978).

Aging is the process, occurring with the passage of time, that leads to loss of adaptability or full function and eventually to death (Spirduso, Francis, & MacRae, 2005).

Constraints: A Model for Studying Motor Development

It is useful to have a model or plan for studying the change in movement that occurs over the life span. A model helps us include all the relevant factors in our observation of motor behavior. This is particularly true as we think about the complexity of motor skills and how our skills change over the life span. For this textbook, we adopted a model associated with a contemporary theoretical approach known as the ecological perspective (see chapter 2). We find that this model helps us make sense of developmental changes by providing a framework for observing change. We believe this model—Newell's constraints model—will help you better understand motor development across the life span.

Newell's Model

Karl Newell (1986) suggested that movements arise from the interactions of the organism, the environment in which the movement occurs, and the task to be undertaken. If any of these three factors change, the resultant movement changes. We can picture the three factors as points on a triangle with a circle of arrows representing their interaction (figure 1.1). Because we are concerned only with human movement here, we use the term *individual* instead of *organism*. In short, to understand movement, we must consider the relationships between the characteristics of the individual mover, his surroundings, and his purpose or reasons for moving. From the interaction of all these characteristics, specific movements emerge. This model reminds us that we must consider all three corners of the triangle in order to understand motor development.

Picture the different ways in which individuals can walk—for example, a toddler taking her first steps, a child walking in deep sand, an adult moving across an icy patch, or an older adult trying to catch a bus. In each example, the individual must modify his or her walking pattern in some way. These examples illustrate that changing one of the factors often results in a change in the interaction with one or both of the other factors, and a different way of walking arises from the interaction. For example, whether you are barefoot or wearing rubber-soled shoes might not make a difference when you're walking across a dry tile floor, but your walk might change notably if the floor were wet and slippery. The *interaction* of individual, task, and environment changes the movement, and, over time, patterns of interactions lead to changes in motor development.

Why is Newell's model so helpful in studying motor development? It reflects the dynamic, constantly changing interactions in motor development. It allows us to look at the individual

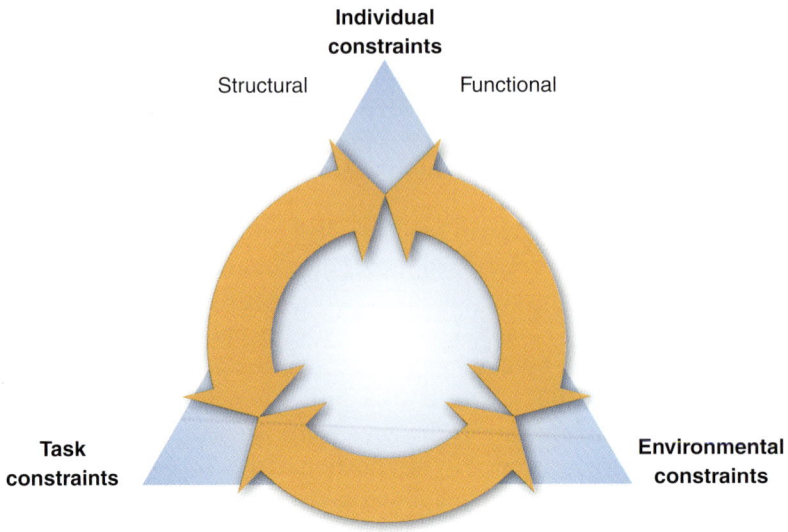

FIGURE 1.1 Newell's model of constraints.

and the many body systems that constantly undergo age-related changes. At the same time, the model emphasizes the influence of where the individual moves (environment) and what the individual does (task) on individual movements. Changes in the individual lead to changes in his or her interaction with the environment and task and subsequently change the way the individual moves. For example, a young child may enjoy tumbling on mats in his preschool. His parents may put him in a gymnastics class (change in environment); at that class, the instructors may focus on equipment rather than tumbling stunts (change in task). Over time and through his experience focusing on specific equipment in the gymnastics class, the boy may become proficient at the pommel horse. Another example is an older adult who, because of hip arthritis, chooses to walk only when absolutely necessary and stops attending her walking group. Changes in her social environment lead to disengagement in exercise, which in turn leads to loss of strength, flexibility, and mobility and, ultimately, to more hip pain. In both of these examples, the individual, environment, and task influence—and are influenced by—each other.

Newell calls the three factors we placed on the points of our triangle **constraints**. A constraint is somewhat like a restraint: It *limits* or *discourages* (in this case, movement), but at the same time it *permits* or *encourages* (in this case, other movements). It's important not to consider constraints as negative or bad. Constraints simply provide channels from which movements most easily emerge. A riverbed acts as a constraint: It restrains the river water from flowing anywhere and everywhere, but it also channels the water to follow a specific path. Movement constraints are characteristics that shape movement. They restrain and channel movement to a particular time and place in space; that is, they give movement a particular form.

A **constraint** is a characteristic of the individual, environment, or task that encourages some movements while discouraging others.

Individual constraints, the top point on our triangle, are a person's unique physical and mental characteristics. For example, height, limb length, strength, and motivation can all influence the way an individual moves. Consider the swimmer with a disability in figure 1.2. The disability constrains, but does not prevent, this individual's ability to swim; it simply modifies the way in which the swimmer performs his strokes. Individual constraints are either structural or functional.

Individual constraints are a person's or organism's unique physical and mental characteristics.

- **Structural constraints** relate to the individual's body structure. They change with growth and aging; however, they tend to change slowly over time. Examples include height, weight, muscle mass, and leg length. As we discuss these changes throughout the text, you will see how structural factors constrain movement.
- **Functional constraints** relate not to structure but to behavioral function. Examples include motivation, fear, experiences, and attentional focus. Such constraints can change over a much shorter period of time. For instance, you might be motivated to run several miles in cool weather but not in hot, humid weather. This functional constraint shapes your movement to running, walking, or even sitting.

Structural constraints are individual constraints related to the body's structure.

Functional constraints are individual constraints related to behavioral function.

For many professionals, it is important to know whether the student's or client's movement is being shaped by structural or functional constraints. Such information can help one understand how much a movement could change in a short time and whether a change in an environmental or task constraint would be necessary in order to modify the resultant movements. For example, knowing that young volleyball players cannot block a ball at the net because they are not yet at their adult height would lead a youth sports organizer to change the task by using a lower net height.

Environmental constraints exist outside the body, as a property of the world around us. They are global rather than task specific and can be physical or sociocultural. Physical environmental constraints are characteristics of the environment, such as temperature, amount of light, humidity, gravity, and the surfaces of floors and walls. The example of a runner not feeling motivated to run in humidity represents the functional constraint of motivation interacting with two environmental constraints—temperature and humidity—to constrain movement.

Environmental constraints are constraints related to the world around us.

One's sociocultural environment can also be a strong force in encouraging or discouraging behaviors, including movement behaviors. One example is how change in the sociocultural environment in Western society has changed the involvement of girls and women in sport over the past three decades. In the 1950s, society did not expect girls to participate in sport. As a

FIGURE 1.2 This swimmer's truncated limb is a structural constraint that gives rise to a swimming movement that is different from that of someone without a truncated limb.
Michael Svoboda/E+/Getty Images

result, girls were channeled away from sport.

Task constraints include the goals and rule structure of a particular movement or activity.

Task constraints are also external to the body. They include the goals of a movement or activity. These constraints differ from individual motivation or goals in that they are specific to the task. For example, in basketball the goal is to get the ball in the hoop—this is true for any individual playing the game. Second, task constraints include the rules that surround a movement or activity. If we think about basketball, players could get down the court much more quickly if they could simply run with the ball rather than dribble it. However, the rules dictate that players *must* dribble while running with the ball, meaning that the resultant movement is constrained to include bouncing the ball. Finally, the equipment we use is a task constraint. For example, using a strung racket rather than a wood paddle changes the game played on an enclosed (racquetball) court. Recall also the case of the youth sports organizer, who by lowering net height used the interaction of a structural individual constraint (body height) and a task constraint to allow a certain movement (blocking) to emerge in the game played by young volleyball players. You can probably imagine many of the task constraints in the depicted situation. The basketball player must pass the ball to a teammate while protecting the ball from a defender.

Throughout this discussion of motor development we demonstrate how changing individual, environmental, and task constraints shape the movement that arises from their interaction. Newell's model guides us in identifying the developmental factors affecting movements, helps us create developmentally appropriate tasks and environments, and helps us understand individual movers as different from group norms or averages.

Changing Views on the Role of Constraints

It is important to recognize that in the history of motor development research certain researchers and practitioners focused primarily on individual factors to the exclusion of others. For example, in the 1940s it was assumed that an individual constraint—specifically, the structural constraint of the nervous system alone—shaped movement in infants and children (see chapter

2 for a discussion of this concept). Later, in the 1960s, developmentalists commonly believed that environmental and task constraints, more than individual constraints, shaped movement. Only recently have motor developmentalists begun focusing on all three types of constraints simultaneously as well as carefully examining how constraints interact with and influence each other over time.

When one or two types of constraints are deemphasized, so is the rich effect of the three constraints interacting to shape movement. Thus, such an approach limits the resulting view of the emerging movement. In our survey of motor development we identify the effects of these various viewpoints on the importance of the three constraints. Sometimes what we know about an aspect of motor development is influenced by the perspective of the researcher who studied that behavior. It is much like seeing the color of a flower change as we try on sunglasses with lenses of different colors. We might "color" our conclusions about motor development as we emphasize one type of constraint and deemphasize other types.

Imagine you are a physical educator or a coach. Knowing how height and body size change with growth, how would you adapt the game of basketball (especially the task, through the equipment used) so that movements (shooting, dribbling, passing) remain nearly the same during the growth years?

Newell's model is more global than most models previously used in the study of motor development. We can better account for the complexity of age-related change in movement with this model through the interactions of individual, environment, and task. Keep the model in mind throughout our survey of motor development.

Constraints and Atypical Development

To understand the basics of constraints, we explain concepts using typical motor development. That is, we use examples that describe what we might expect in people with average individual constraints (strength, height, motivation), who move in typical environments (gymnasiums, playgrounds, grocery stores), and who perform normal tasks (sport, activities of daily living). Essentially, this is motor development "on average." People can develop in different ways and still be considered to be in an average range. However, individuals can deviate from the average developmental course in a variety of ways. In some instances, development is advanced (motor skills appear sooner than expected) or delayed (motor skills appear later than expected). In others, development is actually different (the person moves in unique ways). When we discuss constraints and atypical development, we focus on delayed and different development, particularly in individuals with disabilities. Interacting constraints lead to movement changes over individuals' lives. Therefore, we know that differences in structural and functional individual constraints can lead to atypical developmental trajectories. For example, a child with cerebral palsy may be delayed in the acquisition of fundamental motor skills because of muscle spasticity, or an adult with multiple sclerosis will see motor proficiency diminish as a function of deteriorating myelin sheaths in the brain and spinal cord. In certain conditions, people may exhibit motor coordination delays that can be overcome with enhanced practice or experience. In the language of constraints, enhanced practice represents a change in task constraints. Movement practitioners must keep in mind how movement can change as a result of changing constraints and thereby adjust environment and task constraints to accommodate differences in individual constraints. Throughout the text we provide examples of research related to atypical development.

How Do We Know It Is Change?

We've established that age-related change is fundamental in the study of motor development and the developmental perspective. Developmentalists are focused on change. How do we know, though, that a change is age related and not a fluctuation of behavior (a good or bad day on the court, for example) or a product of our measuring instrument (a radar gun versus video motion analysis)? One way to discern developmental change is to carefully observe individuals' movements and then describe differences between people of different age groups or instances of observation.

Web Study Guide **Gain experience in observing movement by doing Lab Activity 1.1, Observation as a Tool of Inquiry, in the web study guide.**

In addition, behavioral scientists use statistical techniques that can identify significant change. We sometimes discuss these techniques in the context of a research study. For now, let's focus on the straightforward technique of picturing change by graphing an aspect of development over time. We can then see whether a trend is emerging.

Picturing Change

When we picture age-related measurements by graphing, we traditionally put time or age on the horizontal axis. Time can be measured in days, weeks, months, years, or decades, depending on our frame of reference. A measurement of interest in infancy might be plotted in days or weeks, whereas a measurement of interest over the life span might be plotted in years or decades.

The measurement is plotted on the vertical axis. We usually arrange the measurements so that "more," "faster," or "more advanced" is higher on the scale. Figure 1.3 shows a typical graph of the measurement of growth in childhood. It is common to take a measurement periodically and plot its value at selected chronological ages. We assume that change has occurred consistently in the time between our measurements, so we often connect our data points to make a line. When we graph change using a developmental perspective, we should not make the assumption that more is always better. Individuals move in a variety of ways that are qualitatively different. Some ways of moving may result in longer throws or faster runs, but that does not imply that children who do not move this way are in error or are wrong. It simply means these children move at a different or lower developmental level.

A **developmental trajectory** is the course of a behavior over age or time (Nagin, 1999).

The curve plotted in describing developmental change can be called a **developmental trajectory**. This notion is useful in thinking about the early influences or constraints on some aspect of development and how they might influence development over the balance of the life span. A hypothetical behavior is plotted in figure 1.4 as a red line. Let us say that at age 3 years some constraint is imposed on the behavior. If that constraint restrains the behavior, the developmental trajectory for the behavior is changed, perhaps for the balance of the life span, as pictured by the blue line. If that constraint instead facilitates an advancement in the behavior, the developmental trajectory is also altered, but in a positive way, as pictured by the green line. Hence we can see that a small change in development can set an individual on very different development trajectories.

Arrested development is a failure to develop beyond a particular point of development.

Note that a severely negative influence or constraint could result in **arrested development**. This is pictured in figure 1.4 by the purple line. Truly arrested development is rare, but Seefeldt (1980) proposed the notion of a proficiency barrier in regard to the motor development of children. Seefeldt hypothesized that if an individual does not attain a certain level of motor skill proficiency in

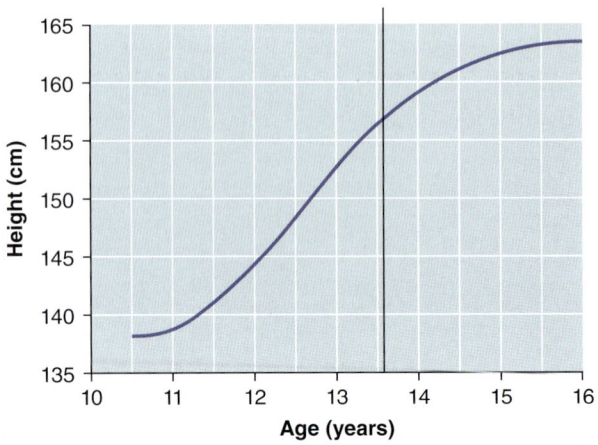

FIGURE 1.3 A typical graphical representation of growth in childhood.

middle childhood, that individual at older ages would find it difficult to become a proficient mover. If a proficiency barrier for the behavior in figure 1.4 existed at age 3, the purple line might show the developmental trajectory of an individual who was unable to cross the barrier.

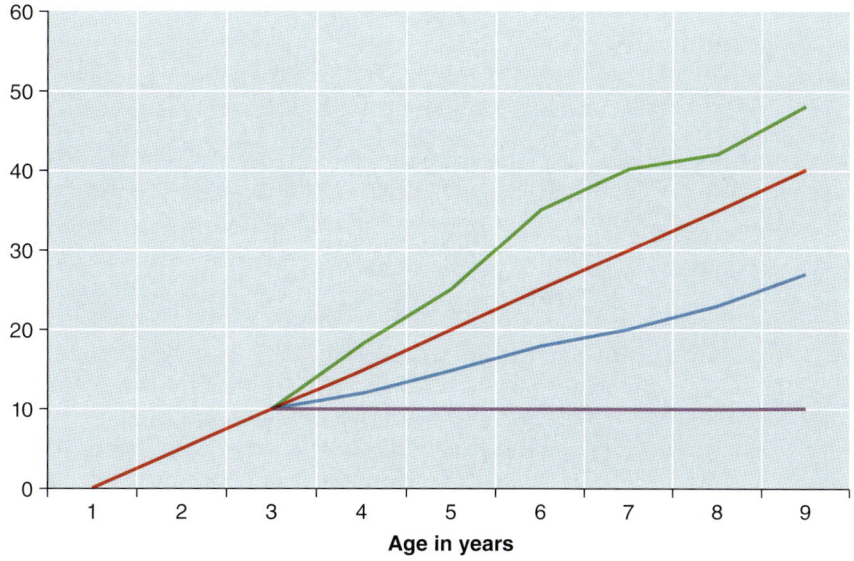

FIGURE 1.4 Developmental trajectories.

Web Study Guide Practice graphing to help picture change in Lab Activity 1.2, Graphing Developmental Data, in the web study guide.

Researching Developmental Change

In the study of development, we ideally watch an individual or group change with age for the entire length of the period we are interested in. This is termed a **longitudinal research study**. The difficulty here comes when our frame of reference is years or decades. For example, a teacher may be interested in the changes in locomotor skills across childhood. We can see that an individual researcher might be able to do only a few such studies in his or her lifetime. This approach would not inform us about motor development very quickly!

A **longitudinal research study** is one in which the same individual or group is observed performing the same tasks or behaviors on numerous occasions over a long time.

Researchers have several ways of learning more in a shorter time. One of these techniques is termed a **cross-sectional research study**. In a cross-sectional study, researchers select individuals or groups at chosen points in the age span of interest. For example, researchers interested in change during adolescence might measure a group of 13-year-olds, a group of 15-year-olds, a group of 17-year-olds, and so on. When the measurements of each group are plotted, we assume that any observed change reflects the same change we would observe in a single group over the whole time period. The advantage of this method is that researchers can study development in a short time. The disadvantage is that we never really observe change; we merely infer it from age group differences. If something else were responsible for the age group differences, we could be fooled into thinking the differences were caused by developmental change.

A **cross-sectional research study** is one in which developmental change is inferred by observing individuals or groups of varying ages at one point in time.

Consider the example of tricycles. At one time, all tricycles were metal and shaped so that the seat was relatively high off the ground. Children under 3 years of age had difficulty just getting on the tricycle. Then someone invented the Big Wheel tricycle, with the large front wheel and the seat only inches off the ground. Toddlers can easily sit on this vehicle.

Let's pretend that a researcher did a cross-sectional study on coordination of the cycling motion of the legs in toddlers at the ages of 1.5, 2.0, 2.5, and 3.0 years. The study was done just 1 year after the Big Wheel tricycle came on the market (note: as a piece of equipment, the Big Wheel is a task constraint). The researcher observed that toddlers 2.5 and 3.0 years of age

Can You Tell It's Developmental? A Litmus Test

Armed with definitions of motor development and motor learning, you still might find it difficult to distinguish whether a particular behavior is a matter of learning or development. Mary Ann Roberton (1988, p. 130) suggests that the answers to three questions help us distinguish developmental issues and topics:

1. Are we interested in what the behavior is like now and why the behavior is the way it is?
2. Are we interested in what the behavior was like before our present observation, and why?
3. Are we interested in how the present behavior is going to change in the future, and why?

Students of both motor learning and motor development answer yes to the first question, but only developmentalists answer yes to the second and third questions. Motor learning specialists are concerned with making changes that bring about a relatively permanent change in behavior within a short time. Motor developmentalists focus on a longer time during which a sequence of changes occurs. Developmentalists might introduce a change in task or environmental constraints to make either or both age appropriate while realizing that the task or environment will have to change again and again as individuals age and change.

could coordinate this movement and concluded that approximately 2.5 years was the age at which toddlers could coordinate the cycling movement of the legs. But what if the researcher had done the study a year earlier, before any of the children would have been on a Big Wheel? The researcher might have observed that *none* of the children could coordinate the cycling movement because none would have been able to ride the high-seat tricycle. The researcher would then have concluded that this coordination developed after the age of 3.0 years.

A **cohort** is a group whose members share a common characteristic, such as age or experience.

The invention of the Big Wheel gave a **cohort**, or mini-generation, of toddlers earlier practice in coordinating the cycling movement. Older cohorts could not practice the movement until they were big enough to get up on the higher tricycle. Thus, one cohort had an experience that another did not. Such a cohort difference can fool researchers in a cross-sectional study, leading them to associate performance differences between age groups with age alone and not factors such as exposure to new inventions. Researchers must be particularly aware of cohort differences when examining aging populations because of rapidly changing technologies. For example, many older adults may not own or frequently use computers. Let's say a researcher wants to examine differences in driving techniques among drivers of different age groups and uses a computer simulation in which the car is controlled by a joystick. Older adults may show differences in performance because they are unfamiliar with computer joysticks rather than because of true differences in driving technique. (In fact, children who are not yet eligible to drive may perform better because of their experiences with video games.) Researchers must take care to control for cohort differences.

Researchers have, however, devised a clever way to identify cohort influences while at the same time conducting developmental research in less time than required by a longitudinal study. They do it by combining longitudinal and cross-sectional studies. In effect, they conduct several small longitudinal studies with subjects of different ages of the period of interest. For example, in the first year they would measure three groups of children, one at 4 years of age, one at 6 years of age, and one at 8 years of age. Notice that if the researchers stopped here they would have a cross-sectional study. Instead, a year later they measure all the children again. This time the children are 5, 7, and 9 years of age. They do the same thing another year later, when the children are 6, 8, and 10. In the end they have done three small longitudinal studies: one cohort that was the original 4-year-olds at 4, 5, and 6; one cohort that was the original 6-year-olds at 6, 7, and 8; and one cohort that was the original 8-year-olds at 8, 9, and 10.

Thus, information is made available about ages 4 through 10, but only 2 years were needed to obtain it. What about the possibility of cohort differences? Note that the mini-longitudinal studies cover overlapping ages. Two groups were tested at age 6 and two groups were tested at age 8. If performance of the different cohorts is the same at a given age, then it is likely that cohort differences are not present. If the cohorts perform differently at the same age, cohort influences might well be present. This type of design is called a **mixed-longitudinal**, or **sequential, research study**.

In a **mixed-longitudinal**, or **sequential, research study**, several age groups are observed at one time or over a shorter time span, permitting observation of an age span that is longer than the observation period.

New students of motor development can tell whether a research study is developmental by considering the design of the study. The study is developmental if the design is longitudinal, cross-sectional, or sequential (figure 1.5). Research studies that focus on one age group at one point in time are not developmental.

Meta-Analyses and Reviews

Researchers make use of two analytical methods of studies that have been conducted and published. For researchers to generalize findings from studies of a limited number of participants to a larger group, it is important to replicate studies with different participants or perhaps in a different way. Meta-analysis is an analytical method that allows a researcher to pool many smaller studies. After setting criteria for the studies to be included, the researcher uses statistical techniques to integrate the effects observed in the individual studies into one, more generalizable estimate of an effect. This is a way that researchers can strengthen our knowledge of effects on development, even from individual cross-sectional studies.

Researchers use another technique, writing a review paper that selects many individual studies on a topic and then groups the studies, comparing and contrasting the participants, research methods, and outcomes. The researcher can point out factors that might explain conflicting results or highlight common findings across the studies. Sometimes researchers combine this

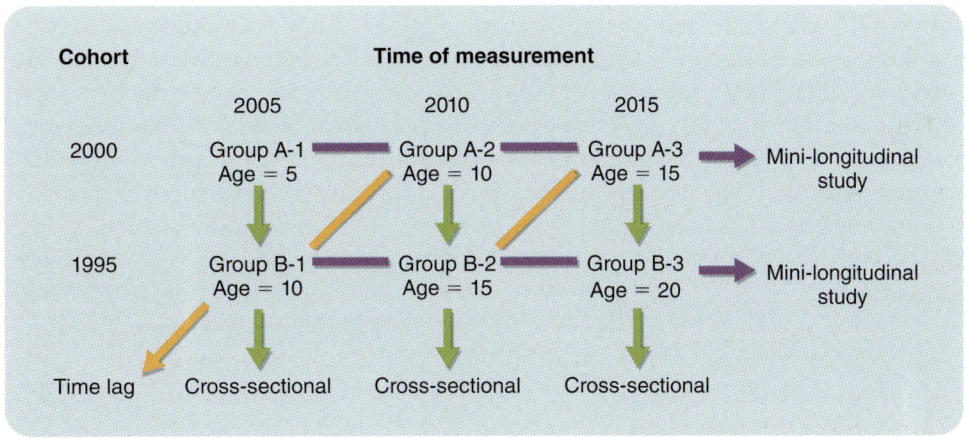

FIGURE 1.5 A model of a sequential research design. Note that each row is a short longitudinal study and that each column is a small cross-sectional study. The time-lag component of sequential research design, shown by the diagonal lines, allows comparison of groups from different cohorts but at the same chronological age, thus identifying any cohort differences. Ages 5 to 20 can be studied in 10 years—2005 to 2015.

type of review with a meta-analysis. Students of motor development value reviews and meta-analyses as information that might be better generalized to a larger group of students, clients, or patients than individual studies.

A Developmental Paradox: Universality Versus Variability

Picture yourself in a gymnasium filled with preschool students. Many children move similarly: They begin to display rudimentary catching and throwing; they walk and run with proficiency but have difficulty skipping. On average, the children perform many of the same motor skills. Yet if you look at an individual child, he or she may move in more or less advanced ways than a child standing a foot away. This difference highlights the paradox of universality of development as opposed to individual differences (Thelen & Ulrich, 1991). Individuals in a species show great similarity in their development in that they go through many of the same (stereotypical) changes. You have heard reference to "stages of development." Stages, of course, describe the emergence of universal behaviors. Those who anticipate working with individuals in a particular age range are often interested in the behaviors typical of those in that range.

However, individual differences in development do exist. Any individual we observe is more likely to be above or below average, or to achieve a milestone earlier or later than average, than he or she is to be exactly average. In addition, children can arrive at the same point in development by very different pathways (Siegler & Jenkins, 1989). All individuals, even identical twins, have different experiences, and people who work with any group of individuals supposedly at the same stage of development are usually amazed by the variability in the group.

Thus, developmentalists, educators, parents, and health professionals must consider an individual's behavior in the context of both universal behaviors and individual differences. It is also important to recognize when others are using a perspective that focuses on the universality of behavior and when they are focusing on variability in behavior. Systematic and controlled observation—that is, *research*—helps us distinguish between behaviors that tend to be universal and behaviors that reflect human variability. Research also helps us identify the role of constraints such as the environment and individual experiences in creating variability of behavior.

As much as possible, the ideas presented in this text are based on research studies; the information comes from an objective source. Keep in mind that this is not the same as saying that any one or two research studies provide us with all the answers we need. Individual research studies do not always rule out all the other possible explanations for the results—to do that, additional research might be required.

Deriving the principles and theories from research to guide educational and health care practice is a *process*. Although practitioners are sometimes frustrated to see that researchers are only in the middle of the process, it is better to recognize that this is the case than to take all research results as the final word. Our goal here is not only to use available research information to make insightful conclusions and decisions about the motor development of individuals but also to learn how to obtain and analyze further research information as it becomes available.

Think of generalizations we tend to make about people, such as "tall people are thin," and then think of at least one person you know who is an exception to this "rule." What is the consequence of expecting a student or patient to follow a generalization?

Summary and Synthesis

Now that we understand the developmental perspective, it is easy to see why a documentary series on motor development spanning several decades would be of interest to many viewers. At the present moment each of us is a product of "what we were like before," and each of us will change to become something different in the future. We are all developing, and our individual constraints constantly change! Add changing environmental and task constraints and you have a very interesting mix related to motor development.

Many professions involve relationships with people at critical points of the life span—points at which the change taking place influences life thereafter. This is especially true in regard to the physical being and physical skills. As a result, your knowledge of motor development and the constraints related to it will help you and those around you throughout life. If you choose a profession such as teacher, coach, or therapist, this knowledge will help you help others by providing developmentally appropriate activities.

Your study of motor development will be easier if you equip yourself with a few basic tools. Most important is a framework or model to which you can relate new information, and we use Newell's model of constraints throughout this text. Another important tool is knowledge of how research in motor development is designed, which helps you understand how researchers address developmental issues.

Yet another important tool, which we have yet to discuss, is knowledge of the various perspectives that developmentalists adopt as they approach their research. Because the same problem can be approached from many perspectives, it is valuable to know which approach is taken. The next chapter explores various approaches and discusses the theoretical roots of motor development.

Reinforcing What You Have Learned About Constraints

TAKE A SECOND LOOK

At the start of this chapter you learned about the *Up* series, which has been very successful in Great Britain and the United States. Viewers are interested in how the participants change over time as well as how they stay the same and in what factors (or constraints, as we now call them) influence their life trajectories. In other words, they want to see how the lives of these children (and later adults) develop. Just like viewers of these films, readers of this text will examine motor development interactively, considering the influences that individual, environmental, and task constraints have on an individual's movement skills over his or her entire life. It is important that the documentaries do not end (nor do they become less interesting) once childhood ends; rather, they continue because individuals continue to develop and change across the entire life span. For this reason, we adopt a life span perspective for motor development.

TEST YOUR KNOWLEDGE

1. How does the field of motor development differ from that of motor learning? What key perspective separates the two?
2. How do physical growth and physiological maturation differ?
3. Think of your favorite physical activity, exercise, or sport. Describe some of the individual (both structural and functional), environmental, and task constraints of this activity.
4. Why might a person planning a career in teaching children choose also to study older adults?
5. What are the differences between longitudinal research studies and cross-sectional research studies? What characteristics of each are used in sequential, or mixed-longitudinal, research studies?
6. What does it mean if a physical educator uses "developmentally appropriate" teaching practices? Provide some examples using constraints.

LEARNING EXERCISE 1.1

Searching the Internet for Information on Motor Development

The Internet can be a valuable resource for any practitioner. Many organizations and advertisers provide information that anyone with a computer can access. It is important, however, to keep in mind that there are few regulations on the Internet; anyone can make almost any claim (whether it is based on research, opinion, or something else). You, as an informed consumer, must examine websites carefully and determine the usefulness and accuracy of their information, just as you would with library research. In this learning activity you will determine the theoretical assumptions and underpinnings of various websites.

1. Enter the term *motor development* into the search engine of your choice (e.g., Google, Bing). How many hits are there using these two words? Do any of the websites surprise you? How so?
2. Find a website that sells motor development products. Pick a product. What is it, and what is its purpose? How is it developmental, according to the advertiser? Based on what you've learned, is it *really* developmental?
3. Repeat your Internet search, adding the term *infancy* to *motor development*. From the resulting list, examine at least three types of websites (e.g., academic, sales, medical). Identify some unusual or particularly interesting sites. If you were a parent searching for information, what could you learn from these websites?

2

Theoretical Perspectives in Motor Development

Changing Interpretations of Constraints

CHAPTER OBJECTIVES

This chapter

- describes the theories currently used to study motor development,
- illustrates how various theories explain changes in motor behavior, and
- describes the history of the field of motor development.

Motor Development in the Real World

The Birth of Your First Nephew

Imagine that you visit your older sister in a neighboring state just after she has had her first child. You see the infant as a newborn, just 1 week old. He does not really respond to you unless you place a bottle in his mouth or your finger in his hand. His movements include seemingly random flapping of the arms and legs—unless he is hungry, in which case he flails his limbs and cries! When you leave you think, "He seems pretty uncoordinated and weak." After 9 months, you visit your sister and nephew again. What a change! He sits up on his own, reaches for toys, and has started to crawl. He can even stand when you hold him. He begins to coordinate his actions so that he can move purposefully. Now, let's say you visit again, another 9 months later. Your nephew is no longer an infant but a full-fledged toddler. He can now walk—pretty quickly when he wants to—and has no problem with reaching and grasping. He is beginning to respond to language, particularly with the word *no*. He seems so very different from the newborn you met a mere 18 months before!

In this scenario it would be natural to wonder, *What happened during the past year and a half that resulted in these changes?* In other words, how can you (or anyone else) explain the changes seen across development? Given that there appear to be similarities in the development of different people (universality, described in chapter 1), how do we organize and understand these changes so we can explain them and predict future development? Certain facts exist. How can we make sense of them? We must look at the different theoretical perspectives on motor development. Theories provide a systematic way to look at and explain developmental change.

Theories of motor development have roots in other disciplines, such as experimental and developmental psychology, embryology, and biology. Contemporary research in motor development often uses what is called an ecological perspective to describe, explain, and predict change. To interpret developmental "facts," it is important to understand the different theoretical perspectives from which the supposed facts emerge. Knowing these theoretical perspectives will help us understand the explanations and form interpretations when several explanations conflict.

Maturational Perspective

In a nutshell, the maturational perspective explains developmental change as a function of maturational processes (in particular, through the central nervous system, or CNS) that control or dictate motor development. According to the assumptions of this theory, motor development is an internal or innate process driven by a biological or genetic time clock. The environment may speed or slow the process of change but it cannot change one's biologically determined course.

► **KEY POINT** Maturationists believe that genetics and heredity are primarily responsible for motor development and that the environment has little effect.

The maturational perspective became popular during the 1930s, led by Arnold Gesell (Gesell, 1928, 1954; Salkind, 1981). Gesell believed that the biological and evolutionary history of humans determined their orderly and invariable sequence of development (i.e., each stage of development corresponds with a stage of evolution). The rate at which people pass through that developmental sequence, however, can differ from one individual to another. Gesell explained maturation as a process controlled by internal (genetic) factors rather than external (environmental) factors. He believed that environmental factors would affect motor development only temporarily because hereditary factors were ultimately in control of development.

Using identical twins as subjects, Gesell and his associates introduced the co-twin control strategy to developmental research (figure 2.1). What better way to test the effects of environment and heredity than to look at twins? In this strategy, one twin receives a specific training (the experimental, environmental treatment) while the other receives no special training (the control treatment). Thus, the control develops naturally, as any child would without special training. In this manner, Gesell examined the effects of the environment on development.

After a certain period, the twins were measured and compared with previously determined developmental criteria to see whether the enhanced experience affected the experimental child in any way. Co-twin research provided significant contributions to the study of motor development. In particular, these studies allowed developmentalists to begin identifying the sequence of skill development and noting variations in the rate of skill onset. Gesell concluded from his research that children develop in an orderly fashion (i.e., developmental change came in a predictable, predetermined order over childhood).

Another prominent researcher at the time, Myrtle McGraw, used twins to examine the influence of enhanced experience on motor development (Bergenn, Dalton, & Lipsett, 1992; McGraw, 1935). In her classic study, *Growth: A Study of Johnny and Jimmy*, McGraw started observing the twins several months after their birth. She provided one twin (Johnny), at around 12 months of age, with challenging environments and unique tasks such as climbing a ramp at a progressively higher incline and roller skating. The tasks often required both motor and problem-solving skills. Johnny did excel in certain motor skills but not in others, which did little to resolve the nature-versus-nurture debate prominent in psychology at the time. McGraw's results were equivocal, which may have been due (at least in part) to the fact that the twins were fraternal rather than identical.

FIGURE 2.1 Using twins in studies allowed researchers such as Gesell and McGraw to "control" genetics while manipulating the environment.

Courtesy of the authors.

In addition to describing the course of motor development, many maturationists were interested in the processes underlying development. McGraw (1943), for example, associated changes in motor behavior with development of the nervous system. She considered maturation of the CNS to be the trigger for the appearance of new skills. McGraw was also interested in learning (and therefore was not strictly a maturationist), but those who followed in the study of development generally overlooked this aspect of her work (Clark & Whitall, 1989a).

Use of the maturational perspective as a research tool in motor development began to wane by the 1950s, but the theory's influence is still felt today. For example, the focus on maturation as the primary developmental process led researchers and laypersons alike to assume that basic motor skills will automatically materialize. Hence, even today, many researchers, teachers, and practitioners feel it is unnecessary to facilitate development of basic skills. In addition, the maturationists' emphasis on the nervous system as the *one* system triggering behavioral advancement evolved to almost single-minded emphasis on that system—to the point that no other system was believed to have much significance. The cardiovascular, skeletal, endocrine, and even muscular systems were not deemed of primary importance to motor development. By the mid-1940s, developmental psychologists began to change the focus of their research, and their interest in motor development waned. At that point, physical educators took up the study of motor development, influenced by the maturational perspective. From then until about 1970, people studied motor development by describing movement and identifying age group norms (Clark & Whitall, 1989a). During this period, motor developmentalists from the physical education discipline focused their attention on school-age children. Researchers still used the maturational perspective, and their task therefore was to identify the naturally occurring sequence of changes.

▶ **KEY POINT** People have interpreted the maturationist perspective to mean that motor skills will automatically emerge regardless of differing environments. This assumption has influenced many teaching, parenting, and research concepts during the 20th and 21st centuries.

Normative Descriptive Period

Anna Espenschade, Ruth Glassow, and G. Lawrence Rarick led a normative description movement during this era. In the 1950s, education became concerned with standardized tests and norms. Consistent with this concern, motor developmentalists began to describe children's average performance in terms of quantitative scores on motor performance tests. For example, they described the average running speed and jumping and throwing distances of children at specific ages. Although motor developmentalists were influenced by the maturational perspective, they focused on the *products* (scores, outcomes) of development rather than on the developmental *processes* that led to these quantitative scores.

Biomechanical Descriptive Period

Ruth Glassow also led another descriptive movement during this era. She made careful biomechanical descriptions of the movement patterns children used in performing fundamental skills such as jumping. Lolas Halverson (figure 2.2) and others continued these biomechanical descriptions with longitudinal observations of children. As a result, the developmentalists were able to identify the course of sequential improvement that children followed in attaining biomechanically efficient movement patterns. The knowledge obtained from the normative and biomechanical descriptive periods was valuable in that it provided educators with information on age-related changes in motor development. Because description prevailed as the primary tool of these researchers during this time, motor development was labeled as descriptive. Interest in the processes underlying age-related changes, which had been so meticulously recorded before this period of history, seemed to disappear.

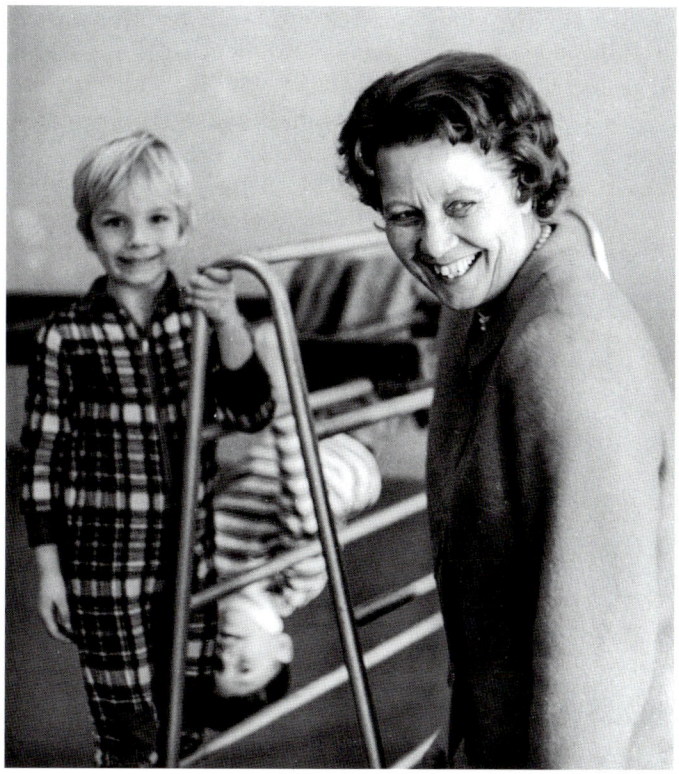

FIGURE 2.2 Lolas Halverson paved the way in the 1960s and 1970s for contemporary research in motor development.

Courtesy of the authors.

Information Processing Perspective

Another theoretical approach focuses on behavioral or environmental causes of development (e.g., Bandura's social learning [Bandura, 1986] and Skinner's behaviorism [Skinner, 1938], among others). The perspective most commonly associated from the 1960s to the 1980s with motor behavior and development is called **information processing**. According to this perspective, the brain acts like a computer, taking in information, processing it, and outputting movement. The process of motor learning and development, then, is described in terms of computer-like operations that occur as a result of some external or environmental input.

This theoretical perspective appeared around 1970 and became the dominant perspective among experimental psychologists, developmental psychologists, and motor learning scientists specializing in physical education during the 1970s and 1980s (Schmidt & Lee, 2014). This perspective emphasized concepts such as the formation of stimulus–response bonds, feedback, and knowledge of results (for more detailed information, see Pick, 1989). Although some motor developmentalists continued with the product-oriented work of the normative and biological descriptive era, many others adopted the information processing perspective. Researchers studied many aspects of performance, such as attention, memory, and effects of feedback, across age levels (French & Thomas, 1987; Thomas, 1984). Motor learning researchers and experimental psychologists tended to study the perceptual-cognitive mechanism in young adults first. Then, developmentalists studied children and older adults, comparing them with the young adults. In this way, they could identify the processes that control movement and change with development (Clark & Whitall, 1989a). Today, the information processing perspective is still a viable approach to the study of motor development.

Within the framework of information processing, some developmentalists continued to study perceptual-motor development in children. This work began in the 1960s with proposals that linked learning disabilities to children's delayed perceptual-motor development. Early research focused on this link; by the 1970s, researchers had turned their attention to the development of sensory and perceptual abilities, adopting information processing research strategies (Clark & Whitall, 1989a). Therefore, much of what we know about perceptual-motor development resulted from researchers working within an information processing and mechanistic theoretical framework.

Ecological Perspective

A new perspective on development appeared during the 1980s and has become increasingly dominant as the theoretical perspective used by motor development researchers today. This approach is broadly termed the **ecological perspective** because it stresses the interrelationships between the individual, the environment, and the task. Does this sound familiar? It should—it's the perspective adopted by this text! We adopted this perspective because we feel it best describes, explains, and predicts motor development. According to the ecological perspective, you must consider the interaction of all constraints—for example, body type, motivation, temperature, and ball size—in order to understand the emergence of a motor skill—such as kicking (Roberton, 1989). Although one constraint or system may be more important or may cast a larger influence at any given time, all systems play a role in the resultant movement. This point makes the ecological perspective very appealing: At any given moment, how you move is related not only to your body or your environment but also to the complex interplay of many internal and external constraints.

▶ **KEY POINT** The ecological perspective takes into account many constraints or systems that exist both in the body (e.g., cardiovascular, muscular) and outside the body (e.g., ecosystem related, social, cultural) when observing the development of motor skills across the life span.

The ecological perspective has two branches, one concerned with motor control and coordination (dynamical systems) and the other with perception (perception–action). The two branches are linked by several fundamental assumptions that differ notably from the maturational and information processing perspectives. In contrast to the maturational perspective, the ecological perspective considers motor development to be the development of multiple systems rather than only one (the CNS). In other words, many constraints change over time and influence motor development. Because these constraints or systems change throughout one's life, motor development is considered a life span process. This contrasts sharply with the view of maturationists, who felt that development ended with the end of puberty (or at adulthood). Another difference relates to the cause of change. In information processing theory, an executive function is thought to decide all action, based on calculations of perceptual information resulting in hundreds of commands to control the individual muscles. That is, the executive directs all movement and all change. The ecological perspective maintains that a central executive would be overwhelmed by the task of directing all movement and change. In addition, this is a very inefficient way to move. Rather, perception of the environment is direct, and muscles self-assemble into groups, reducing the number of decisions required of the higher brain centers (Konczak, 1990). Let's look more closely now at each branch of the ecological perspective.

Dynamical Systems Approach

One branch of the ecological systems perspective is called the **dynamical systems approach**. In the early 1980s, a group of scientists—working at Haskins Laboratory in New Haven, Connecticut, whose mission was and remains to research spoken and written language, and in the psychology department at the University of Connecticut—began to question the effectiveness of understanding motor control through the then-dominant information processing perspective.

Peter Kugler, Scott Kelso, and Michael Turvey (1980, 1982), along with others from UConn and Haskins Laboratory, introduced a new approach, called dynamical systems, as an alternative to existing motor control and coordination theories. Following the writings of Soviet physiologist Nikolai Bernstein, they suggested that the very organization of physical and chemical systems constrains behavior. Think about it: Your body can move in many different ways. However, because of the structure of your hip joints and legs (part of your skeletal system), you, as an adult, tend to walk (as opposed to crawl, scoot, or squirm) as a primary mode of transportation. Thus, the structural organization of your body encourages—constrains—you to walk. In other words, your body's structure removes some of the movement choices your CNS might have to make (i.e., among crawling, scooting, squirming, or walking). It's not that you cannot perform these movements; it's just that because of your body structure, you are more attracted to (or constrained to) walking. Walking provides speedy movement that can be sustained over time.

Imagine that a human infant is born in a space station on the moon. The pull of gravity is less than on earth. Predict the types of movements you would see during the first 2 years of life. In particular, how would you expect the infant to get around?

Unlike the maturational and information processing perspectives, the dynamical systems approach suggests that coordinated behavior is softly assembled rather than hardwired, meaning the interacting constraints in your body act together as a functional unit to enable you to walk when you need to. By *not* having a hardwired plan, you have greater flexibility in walking, which allows you to adapt your walk to many different situations. This process is called spontaneous self-organization of body systems. As we state in chapter 1, movement emerges from the interaction between constraints (individual, environmental, task). The resultant behavior emerges or self-organizes from these interrelationships. If you change any one of them, the emergent movement may change (Clark, 1995). This is the concept of constraints in the dynamical systems approach.

An important motor development concept produced by the dynamical systems approach is the notion of **rate limiters**, or **controllers**. The body's systems do not develop at the same rate; rather, some might mature quickly and others more slowly, and each system should be considered a constraint. Consider the hypothetical example graphed in figure 2.3. The development of four hypothetical systems is pictured in each of the small graphs numbered 1 to 4. As time passes, the development of system 1 remains at a constant value. System 2 plateaus, advances in a large step, then plateaus again. System 3 advances gradually and more continuously, whereas system 4 alternately advances and plateaus in a steplike fashion. The exhibited behavior, represented in the large graph, is affected by all the individual systems as they interact among themselves and with the task and environment.

A **rate limiter** is an individual constraint or system that holds back or slows the emergence of a motor skill because it develops more slowly than other systems. In the later portions of the life span an individual constraint or system can act as a **rate controller** by changing or aging more quickly than other systems.

An individual might begin to perform a new skill, such as walking, only when the slowest of the necessary systems for that skill reaches a certain point. Any such system or set of systems is known as a rate limiter for that skill because that system's development controls the individual's rate of development at that time. In other words, the system acts as a constraint that discourages the motor skill until the system reaches a specific, critical level. Suppose that system 4 in figure 2.3 is the muscular system. Perhaps an infant's muscular strength must reach a certain level before the legs are strong enough to support the infant's weight on one leg in order to walk. Hence, muscular strength would be a rate limiter, or controller, for walking. Until the infant reaches a critical level of leg strength (enough to support the body), strength discourages walking and encourages other forms of transportation, such as creeping, crawling, or rolling. The notion of rate limiters fits well in the model of constraints.

These tenets of the dynamical systems approach differ significantly from those of the maturational perspective. Maturationists tend to focus on the CNS as the only system relevant to development and the only rate limiter. The dynamical systems approach focuses on many systems and acknowledges that different systems might act as rate limiters or controllers for different skills and at different times (Thelen, 1998).

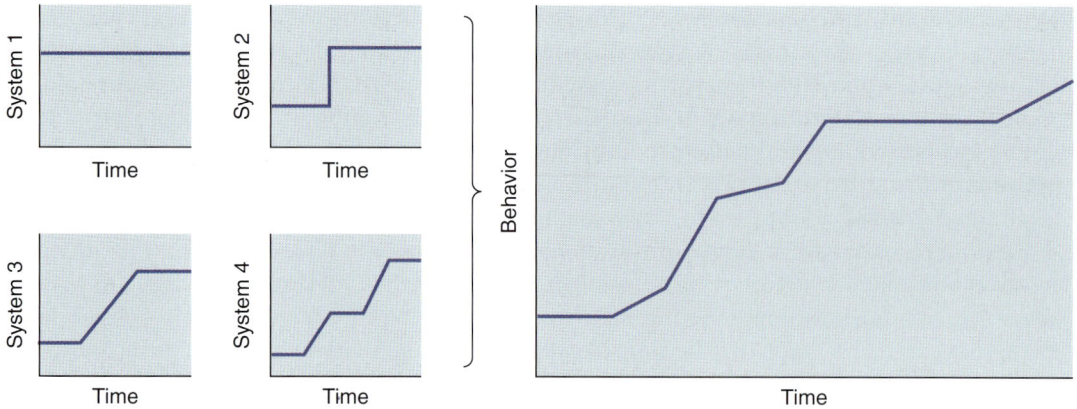

FIGURE 2.3 Four developing systems are depicted as contributing to behavior in an environmental context and for some particular task. The horizontal axis is time, and the vertical axis represents several parallel systems (which act as constraints) developing in different ways.

Adapted by permission from Thelen, Ulrich and Jensen (1989).

In your experience, what rate limiters have affected your motor behavior? How have these changed at different times in your life?

Another feature of the dynamical systems approach is that it allows for the study of development across the life span. The concept of a system acting as a rate limiter, or controller, for a movement behavior applies into older adulthood as well. The maturational perspective does not address aging because the predetermined endpoint of motor development is maturation, which occurs in the first several decades of life. In contrast, the dynamical systems approach accounts for changes in older adults as well as advancement in youths. When one or more of an individual's systems has declined to a critical point, a change in behavior might occur. This system is a rate controller; because it is the first to decline to some critical point, it triggers the reorganization of a movement to a less-efficient pattern. For example, if an individual's shoulder joint deteriorates as a result of arthritis and loses flexibility, at some point that individual might have to use a different overhand throwing motion or even throw underhand. The dynamical systems approach is appropriate for explaining developmental changes because changes do not necessarily occur in all systems over the entire span of older adulthood. Disease or injury may strike one system, and systems may be differentially affected by lifestyle. An active older adult who maintains a regular and balanced exercise program may experience fewer declines in many of the systems than a sedentary peer does.

Perception–Action Approach

When a person looks at an object, he or she directly perceives the function that the object will allow, based both on his or her body and on the object's size, shape, texture, and so forth. This function is called an **affordance**.

The second branch of the ecological perspective is the **perception–action approach**. J.J. Gibson proposed this model in his writings during the 1960s and 1970s (1966, 1979), but it took several decades before those who study movement adopted this approach. Gibson proposed that a close interrelationship exists between the perceptual system and the motor system and emphasized that these systems evolved together in animals and humans. In this approach, we cannot study perception independent of movement if our findings are to be *ecologically valid*—that is, applicable to real-world movement behavior. Likewise, the *development* of perception and the *development* of movement must be studied together.

In addition, we cannot study the individual while ignoring the surrounding environment. Gibson used the term **affordance** to describe the function an environmental object provides to an individual; this is related to the size and shape of the object and the individual in a particular setting. For example, a horizontal surface affords a human a place to sit, but a vertical surface does not. A squirrel can rest on a vertical tree trunk, so a vertical surface affords a squirrel a resting place. A heavy baseball bat affords an adult, but not an infant, the opportunity to swing. Hence, the relationship between individual and environment is so intertwined that one's characteristics define objects' meanings, which implies that people assess environmental properties in relation to themselves, not according to an objective standard (Konczak, 1990). For example, an individual perceiving whether he or she can walk up a flight of stairs with alternating footsteps considers not just the height of each stair alone but also the height of each stair in relation to the climber's body size. A comfortable step height for an adult is not the same as that for a toddler. The use of intrinsic (relative to body size) rather than extrinsic dimensions is termed **body scaling**.

Body scaling is the process of changing the dimensions of the environment or an environmental object in relation to the structural constraints of a performer.

Web Study Guide **Create body-scaled contexts for individuals with different disabilities by doing Lab Activity 2.1, Equipment That Affords Action, in the web study guide.**

The implications of these ideas for motor development are that affordances change as individuals change, resulting in new movement patterns. Growth in size, for example, or enhancement in movement capabilities, might allow actions not previously afforded. When an infant first faces stairs, her perception of their function is not likely to be one of "climbability" because of her small size and relative lack of strength. As a toddler, though, she grows to a size that makes climbing stairs with alternating footsteps easy. Scaling environmental objects to one's body size permits one to conceive of actions that otherwise seem impossible. Body scaling also applies to other age periods. For example, steps that are an appropriate height for most adults might be too high for an older adult with arthritis to climb comfortably with alternating footsteps. A wall-mounted light switch might be at a comfortable height for most adults yet rest a frustrating inch too high for someone sitting in a wheelchair. At any age, achievement of a movement goal relates to the individual, who is a certain shape and size, and to environmental objects, which afford certain movements to that individual.

▶ **KEY POINT** The concept of body scaling means that an object, though possessing an absolute size and shape, affords a function *relative* to the size and shape of the person using it. An activity may become easier or more difficult if the equipment size is changed relative to a person's body dimensions.

Viewed another way, body scaling represents an excellent example of the interaction or interface between individual and task constraints. When walking up stairs, individuals must relate the length of their legs, their strength, and their dynamical range of motion (individual constraints) to the height of the stairs they are about to step on (task constraint). Changes in constraints, such as an ankle sprain, high-heeled shoes, or an icy staircase, will result in changes in the way an individual steps on the stairs. In physical education settings, instructors often assist children in body scaling by providing them with smaller equipment that is more appropriate for their smaller body size. By doing so, instructors manipulate the interaction between individual and task constraints to encourage a more advanced movement pattern (Gagen & Getchell, 2004).

What activities would a 10-speed bicycle afford an infant, a typically able adult, an individual with paraplegia, or a chimpanzee? What individual constraints affect the activities afforded to each?

Gibson also rejected the notion of a CNS executive that performs almost limitless calculations on stimulus information to determine the speed and direction of both the person and the moving objects. The information processing perspective holds that such calculations are used to anticipate future positions so that we can, for example, reach up to catch a thrown ball. Instead, according to Gibson, individuals perceive their environments directly by constantly moving their eyes, heads, and bodies. This activity creates an optic flow field that provides both space and time information. For example, the image of a baseball approaching a batter not only indicates the ball's location but also expands on the eye's retina, and the batter uses the rate of image expansion to time his swing—that is, the rate of expansion gives the batter's CNS direct information about when the ball will be in range. Likewise, the expansion rate of the image of an oncoming car on a driver's retina yields the time to collision. From Gibson's perspective, an individual can perceive time to collision directly and does not need to perform a complicated calculation of speeds and distances to predict where and when collisions and interceptions will occur.

Once the ecological perspective took hold, developmentalists started asking different types of questions: How does an infant's immediate environment affect her motor behavior? What constraints act as rate limiters to children's throwing? How will changing specific individual constraints in a rehabilitation setting alter motor patterns? Concurrently, they have developed types of research studies to answer such questions, such as examining the relationship between infant reflexes and adult movements (Thelen & Ulrich, 1991). The ecological perspective encourages professionals to view developing individuals in a very different way than before. As a result, these perspectives will excite and challenge students in the field. In many sections of this text, we examine the maturation and dynamical systems approaches on a particular issue and highlight the differences between these perspectives.

Current Interests

Motor development research has not seen a paradigm shift since the ecological perspective emerged in the 1980s. Yet researchers often develop new interests within a theoretical perspective. A recent interest has been understanding the role of motor skill development in good health. The increasing numbers of overweight and obese individuals across the life span and around the world have led researchers to consider both the causes of and remediation for obesity rates. Overweight and obesity are associated with numerous health problems as well as quality and quantity of life. Much of the research leading into the 21st century focused on the relationship between obesity and physical activity; however, a growing number of researchers began to examine a broader range of determinants such as motor skill competency. They reasoned that while exercise can help individuals maintain ideal body weight since it burns calories, motor skill proficiency can influence both quantity and quality of physical activity. Proficient movers of any age can sustain exercise for a longer period than inefficient movers. Inefficient movers are also more likely to view exercise as difficult and burdensome because their inefficient movement patterns waste energy. Furthermore, because motor skills change developmentally, any relationships must be viewed with a developmental lens.

A group of motor development leaders (Stodden & Goodway, 2007; Stodden et al., 2008) proposed a model demonstrating the interrelationships among actual and perceived motor skill competence, activity levels, health-related fitness, and body composition or weight status over the course of childhood. The model illustrates how children lacking motor skills might not reach the level of exercise that would help them attain an adequate level of fitness and an optimal weight status as childhood progresses, leading to a negative spiral of engagement and greater risk of obesity. This model stimulated a great deal of research related to the associations among these interrelated factors and publication of numerous research studies (for reviews, see Figueroa & An, 2017; Logan, Webster, Getchell, Pfeiffer, & Robinson, 2015) as well as an initial validating of parts of the model (Robinson et al., 2015). The interest of motor development researchers in this topic relies on an ecological perspective that takes into account numerous factors that play a role in good health. We will examine this model more closely in chapter 12.

If you were a physical education teacher in an elementary school with students of varying motor skill competence in your class, how would the Stodden and Goodway approach influence your learning objectives for the class?

Summary and Synthesis

This chapter reviews the history and theoretical viewpoints specific to motor development—the maturational, information processing, and ecological perspectives. The maturational perspective emphasizes biological development, specifically maturation of the CNS. The information processing perspective sees the environment as the main force driving motor development. Unlike followers of the previous perspectives, ecological theorists stress interaction between all body systems (or, as Newell called them, constraints) as well as the inseparable factors of individual, environment, and task. In the ecological perspective, two related approaches to research exist: dynamical systems and perception–action approaches. This textbook adopts an ecological perspective and focuses on how individual, environmental, and task constraints interact to encourage or discourage movements. The concepts of rate limiters, or controllers, and body scaling exemplify how a motor developmentalist must consider the individual's performance of a particular task in a given environment in order to fully understand the individual's motor development over the course of a lifetime. Recent research uses an ecological perspective as it takes into account numerous factors that play a role in good health, including how perceived motor competence may affect a person's level of physical activity.

Diametrically opposed perspectives cannot be merged, but students of motor development are free to view behavior from different perspectives. It is important to remember that these theoretical viewpoints often focus only on specific aspects of development; that is, developmentalists with a particular perspective tend to study certain behaviors or age spans. Maturationists focus on infancy, whereas descriptive developmentalists focus on late childhood and adolescence. Information processing theorists search for age differences, whereas those studying from an ecological perspective observe transitions from one skill to another (e.g., from crawling to walking).

Reinforcing What You Have Learned About Constraints

TAKE A SECOND LOOK

Let's revisit the first 18 months of your hypothetical nephew's life from an ecological perspective. Thinking about his first week of life, what constraints most influence his motor behavior? That is, what rate limiters keep him moving the way he does? As we suggest in chapter 1, in order to understand developmental change, we should think about where he was, where he is, and where he will be. The first big change, therefore, would be moving from an aqueous environment (his mother's womb) to one where gravity's full force can be felt. Keeping this in mind, part of the reason your nephew may move his arms in a seemingly uncoordinated fashion may relate to his strength (or lack thereof). As his environment changes, a need is created for greater strength to move his arms (individual–environmental constraint interaction). Over time, he builds strength, which interacts with other developing systems. When you see him at 9 months, all the systems have converged to allow him to use his arms more effectively. In terms of the rate limiter of strength, he has reached a critical level that allows him to move more functionally. He has sufficient strength to sit up, move his arm toward a toy, grasp it, and bring it to his mouth. He even has enough strength to stand on both legs and support his weight (with a little help from you).

Consider his next objective: moving independently around his environment. He might eye a chair (which to you affords sitting), scale the height of the seat to the length of his trunk, and pull himself up to a standing position. Can he walk yet? Probably not, as another rate limiter—balance—prevents him from standing alone unsupported. We could go on and on, examining the different ways in which your nephew uses affordances and body scaling, and you can think of examples on your own. Hopefully the interactions between the various constraints become clearer and clearer to you, and by the end of the text you will naturally evaluate the influence of different constraints on motor development.

TEST YOUR KNOWLEDGE

1. List the key researchers in the field of motor development from the maturational, information processing, and ecological perspectives.
2. How can a physical educator or physical therapist use the concept of body scaling to help individuals develop motor skills?
3. Why should physical educators be interested in affordances?
4. Explain, based on the different theoretical perspectives, how an infant learns to walk. What are the most important influences on the infant, according to each perspective?
5. Why does the recent interest in the role of motor skill proficiency in good health fit into an ecological perspective?

LEARNING EXERCISE 2.1

Body Scaling to Design Sport Equipment

You have been hired by Haywood's Tennis Supplies to design a line of body-scaled tennis rackets. Because the company would like to distinguish its product line from others on the market, you must prepare an initial report addressing important aspects of the new rackets, available product lines from other companies, and how your rackets will be different. Develop this report; you can use the following questions as a guide.

1. What are the important individual constraints to consider when body-scaling tennis rackets?
2. Have other companies body-scaled their rackets and if so, how? On what individual constraint or constraints do they scale?
3. What are some novel ways to scale Haywood's new rackets? What have other companies overlooked?

LEARNING EXERCISE 2.2

Hunting for Rate Limiters in Everyday Situations

Physical educators, physical therapists, parents, and many others want to encourage proficient motor skills in those with whom they interact. One important consideration in working to improve motor skill performance is this: What is holding a person back, or limiting the rate at which he or she acquires a skill? In this exercise you will determine the key rate limiter for a particular skill, given the constraints described.

1. An 11-month-old infant can use furniture to pull himself upright, can cruise the length of the couch if he keeps one hand in contact, and can push a toy shopping cart down the hall. However, when placed standing in the center of the room, he does not walk but rather gets down on all fours and crawls. What is his primary rate limiter for walking?
2. A stroke patient has control over her limbs and has little difficulty walking. She can lift a pencil and write lists and letters. She can comb her hair and brush her teeth. She experiences problems, however, when she tries to lift cans and jars overhead onto shelves. What is her primary rate limiter for reaching?
3. A 5-year-old can easily walk, run, jump, and hop. She plays games with other children on the playground and is very attentive in physical education class. She has problems, however, with galloping and skipping; she cannot seem to master the asymmetrical rhythms of these skills. What is her primary rate limiter for galloping and skipping?

3

Principles of Motion and Stability

Mechanical Laws Guiding Constraint Interactions

CHAPTER OBJECTIVES

This chapter

- outlines the principles of motion and stability that lead to proficient motor performance,
- discusses the relationships between these principles and motor behaviors of individuals of various skill levels, and
- explains how skilled performers take advantage of specific principles.

Motor Development in the Real World

Running to the Best of Her Abilities

In 1975, Aimee Mullins was born with fibular hemimelia, a congenital condition that results in malformed or absent fibula bones. As a result, she had both her legs amputated below the knee by her first birthday, and doctors believed she would never be able to walk. To some, pursuing an athletic career with this condition may seem daunting or even impossible. Not to Aimee. Early in her childhood, she began walking with prosthetic limbs. By her high school years, she participated in a variety of sports, including softball, downhill skiing, and track. In fact, Aimee was so fast she competed against able-bodied athletes while attending NCAA Division I Georgetown University, becoming the first amputee ever to do so. Aimee also competed in the 1996 Atlanta Paralympics, setting three world records in track events. For Aimee, running to the best of her abilities means running very, very fast.

Aimee Mullins, a world-class athlete, model, and actor, has never let physical differences become obstacles to success. Rather, she challenged conventional wisdom by finding a way to excel in athletics against extreme odds. Both beautiful and eloquent, Aimee discussed the different designs of her prosthetics in the 2009 Technology, Entertainment, and Design (TED) talk titled "My 12 Pairs of Legs." Her use of a mechanically efficient design in the 1996 Paralympics helped revolutionize the use of "cheetah" polycarbon-fiber sprinting legs, which are more biomechanically efficient than other legs and are the gold standard for athletes today. Such a design takes advantage of certain principles of motion and stability in order to improve the energy efficiency of the runner.

As we note in chapter 1, many elements of motor development tend to occur similarly in different people. That is, humans change patterns of motor behavior in a somewhat predictable fashion. This similarity is not surprising when you consider that most humans share similar individual constraints (two arms, two legs, and upright posture). Similarities also occur because humans operate under a system of rules or principles that dictate how constraints interact in the context of life on this planet. Humans on Earth live in a context that features certain predictable characteristics, such as gravity. Part of the process of developing motor skills involves learning how the human body works within the boundaries of these physical laws. During early life this is not a simple task because individuals must learn to refine their movements while experiencing changes in physical parameters. Furthermore, they must learn to calibrate their movements to the environment while performing specific tasks based on these principles. (Think, for example, of picking up an empty box you thought was full. You must quickly recalibrate your movements in order to maintain your posture or you will fall over.) The process of calibrating movements to task and environment in accordance with mechanical principles can also be difficult for individuals who develop atypically or who must relearn skills after an injury. This chapter considers the physical and mechanical principles under which humans move. In the context of motor development, these are known as the principles of motion and stability.

How would you describe the movements of early, inexperienced movers? Often, their initial attempts at performing skills seem to be inefficient and jerky. They may move the body in separate, discrete steps rather than in a whole movement. They often try to optimize one aspect of the movement (e.g., balance) at the expense of another (e.g., speed) to increase the likelihood of success. As individuals become more proficient at skills, their movements become smoother and more efficient; indeed, their movement patterns often change entirely. Many of children's improvements are due to increases in body size and strength and therefore in their ability to produce force. Yet size and strength alone do not account for how children progress from unskilled to skilled performance. Another part of the process of change involves mastering and exploiting the principles of motion and stability. In fact, all individuals can use these principles to their advantage, in athletic performances as well as in activities of daily living.

Understanding the Principles of Motion and Stability

Movements occur in a context that is governed by certain principles of motion and stability; that is, certain physical laws of motion limit your movements. Consider gravity as an example of a rule that dictates how constraints interact and objects move. The simplest way to think about gravity is that all objects are attracted to each other and that the amount of attraction depends on the objects' masses. Because the mass of the earth is so large, objects on its surface are drawn toward its center. If you jump up, you don't continue to rise. Instead, you come back toward the earth as a result of gravity. What goes up must come down (figure 3.1). The force of gravity exists all around us, dictating that each of us must eventually return to Earth after jumping. Now, let's look at this rule as it applies to constraints. Given that all objects eventually return to Earth, people must calibrate their movements based on their individual constraints (e.g., overall body mass and strength), acting in an environment governed by specific task rules. The interaction of constraints in this context encourages certain motor patterns while eliminating others. What are some of the behaviors encouraged by gravity? An individual must activate certain postural muscles to assume and maintain a position, even while executing a skilled movement. Furthermore, she must work against gravity to become airborne. If a person projects herself or an object at an angle (as opposed to straight up and down), then the force of gravity will ensure that the flight path is parabolic. As you can see, then, principles of motion influence the interaction of constraints.

FIGURE 3.1 Because gravity acts on the long jumper equally and at all times, his flight path resembles a parabola, or semicircle.

► **KEY POINT** Principles of motion and stability act on all movements and movers. As movers become more proficient at skills, they often use these principles to their advantage.

At the same time, the individual constraints or characteristics of the performer influence the movement pattern undertaken. People throw using a movement pattern that is dictated by the shape and structure of the human body and limbs. Consider the shape and structure of the bones in the shoulder (figure 3.2). Muscles also have particular functional shapes and sizes, and they connect bones to each other. In addition, the nervous system coordinates muscular contractions. Furthermore, individuals use their bodies to move with a particular task goal in mind, which also acts to constrain movements. Here lies the interconnectedness of constraints: The individual, with a task goal in mind, acts in the environment to perform a skill. Thus, individual, environment, and task interact to shape or constrain a movement pattern.

▶ **KEY POINT** Children may execute the most efficient movement pattern for themselves given their body size, strength, posture, and experience, but this pattern can change if any one of the constraints changes.

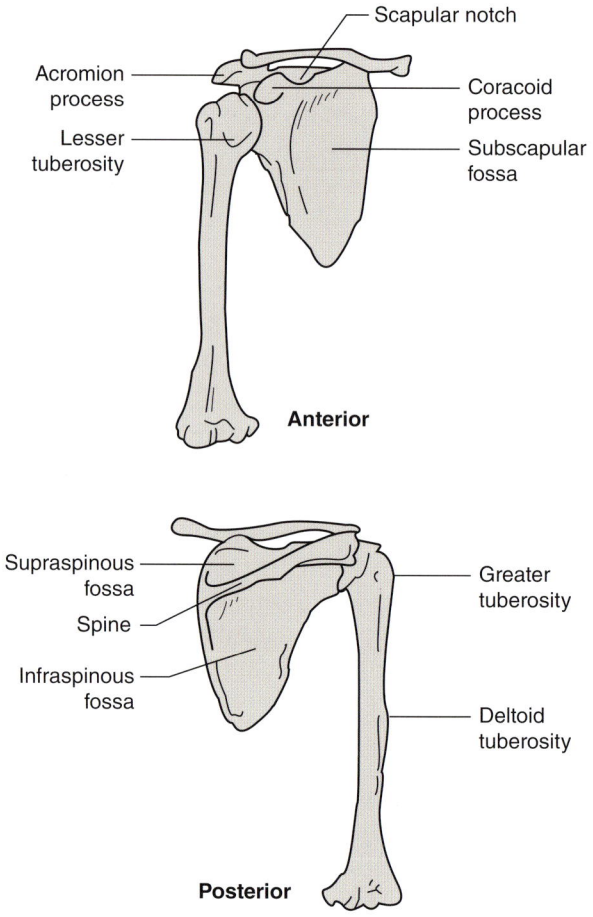

FIGURE 3.2 The structure of the articulating bones in the shoulder joint encourages movement in some directions while preventing it in others. For example, the acromion process prevents movement of the upper arm past 90° without movement of the scapula.

Reprinted by permission from Donnelly (1990).

Clearly, some movement patterns optimize the product of skill performance whereas others do not. Given the task of throwing a rock as far as possible, an individual can produce a variety of motor patterns that will move the rock, but only one will move the rock as far as possible. To develop their skills, children and adults must learn to use movement patterns that optimize performance. The changes taking place in children's bodies complicate this process because growth alters an individual's overall size and proportions.

As children grow and mature, their skeletal, muscular, and nervous systems allow them to produce greater force. Changing bodies mean changing individual constraints, and the individual must recalibrate the interactions between individual and environmental constraints. By taking advantage of the principles of motion and stability, children discover qualitatively different movement patterns that improve the outcome of their skill performance (Jensen, 2005; Jensen & Korff, 2005). Thus, young children, given their body size, shape, and strength, might execute what is for them the most successful or efficient movement pattern possible. However, as they grow, mature physiologically, and gain experience, other movement patterns become possible that allow them to execute skills with greater proficiency (Gagen & Getchell, 2008, 2018).

Injury or disability status can change individual constraints for either short or long periods (e.g., Pope, Lui, Breslin & Getchell, 2012). Affected individuals must relearn how to use mechanics of movement given their unique body structure and function. Adults can also take advantage of these principles of motion and stability. Just as with children, an adult might execute the movement pattern that affords the greatest success, but with time and experience (and, in some cases, with technologically advanced equipment) new patterns may emerge that provide for more adept performance (Getchell & Gagen, 2006).

▶ **KEY POINT** Observations of developmental change in basic skill performance benefit from application of the principles of motion and stability.

Understanding the principles of motion and stability is critical in observing motor performance. These principles help us determine which movement patterns are likely to produce optimal results. Knowledge of the principles also helps us focus on critical aspects of movement that often distinguish skilled movement patterns from unskilled ones. Thus, taking advantage of these principles can help us get much more out of our movements. For these reasons, this chapter reviews and evaluates the principles of motion and stability—the physics of movement—as they apply to basic skill performance. Only some of the more salient principles are discussed here; a more complete analysis of the physics of movement falls in the domain of biomechanics—the mechanics of muscular activity—which is an area of study in itself that lies beyond the scope of this text. A more detailed explanation of these principles can be found in any biomechanics text (Hall, 2019; Knudson, 2013; McGinnis, 2013).

Moving Against Gravity: The Application of Force

To move either themselves or objects, individuals must produce force; a stationary object or individual will not move until some force is applied to it (McGinnis, 2013). You may recognize this as **Newton's first law of motion**: An object at rest stays at rest, or an object in motion stays in motion, until acted on by a force (McGinnis, 2013). You probably understand Newton's first law without ever thinking about it. Or perhaps if you were a messy teen, your parents told you, "If you leave your socks on the floor, they will be there when you get back!" This is an excellent example of Newton's first law. Simply put, to move something, you must apply force to it.

Newton's first law of motion states that an object at rest stays at rest and an object in motion stays in motion with the same speed and in the same direction until acted upon by an external force.

Lie on the floor on your back and then stand up. What are some of the different ways you can achieve this task goal? Do some movements seem more comfortable or efficient than others? Why?

According to Newton's first law of motion, you must apply force to a stationary object to move it and apply force to a moving object to change its movement. Newton's first law is relatively simple and straightforward: It takes force to move something standing still and force to change the direction of something moving. **Newton's second law of motion** is related to force production, acceleration, and mass. If you exert force on an object, the object will accelerate in the direction of the force. Further, the amount of acceleration an object has when you apply force to it is proportional to the force and inversely proportional to its mass. This relationship is easier to understand when described with examples. It takes more force to "put" or throw a shot (which has more mass) than to throw a baseball (which has less mass) at the same speed. Also, if you kick a soccer ball harder (more forcefully), it will accelerate faster and thus go farther. Understanding Newton's second law is important when attempting to move proficiently.

Newton's second law of motion states that the acceleration of a person or object is proportional to the force applied to it and inversely proportional to its mass.

You can use these laws with other principles related to force to understand how to maximize performance (Gagen & Getchell, 2008). First, a relationship exists between force applied and the distance over which you apply it. You can improve your performance by applying force over a greater distance. For example, a young child throwing a ball may throw the ball without moving her legs. By keeping her feet in place, she can reduce compromises to her balance; however, the ball will not travel as far. An experienced thrower will take a step forward with her opposite leg, thus increasing the linear (straight-line) distance over which the force is applied. Try throwing a ball with and without a step and you will discover how much increasing your linear distance with a step aids your performance.

We can also consider rotary or angular distance in addition to linear distance. When you throw a ball, your arm rotates around a joint; hence, it moves a certain number of degrees, or a certain angular distance. By increasing their range of body motion, individuals can increase the rotary distance over which force is applied and therefore maximize their performance. Using a preparatory windup puts the performer in a position to maximize the linear and rotary distances of force application. The preparatory positioning also stretches the muscles the performer will use, thus readying them for maximal contraction. These actions permit the person to project the object at a greater velocity than could be accomplished without a windup and a full range of motion.

Imagine you are a physical educator. Throw a ball with and without using a contralateral (opposite side) step. What differences do you find in several quantitative measures (e.g., distance, accuracy)? What differences do you find in movement form? What might be the reason for these changes?

It is important to note that in most movement skills an optimal relationship exists between force and distance. That is, simply increasing linear or angular distance for a given force will not automatically result in an improved performance. The performer must first recognize what is a complete or full range of motion for a given skill. By observing children during movement, you will see them begin to explore relationships between force and distance (Gagen & Getchell, 2008). The changes in movement patterns related to the application of force often allow for a greater velocity and may come at the expense of stability. You can imagine that although a soccer player generates a lot of force in her leg and therefore in a kick, it would not take much effort for another person to move her from her spot on the field (figure 3.3).

▶ **KEY POINT** To improve movement performance, individuals must find the optimal relationship between force and distance in a given movement. Two important phases in this process are preparation (preparatory movement) and the application of force through a full range of motion.

Imagine you are the coach of a wheelchair basketball team. How could a wheelchair basketball player take advantage of Newton's first and second laws and the related principles of motion?

FIGURE 3.3 When trying to optimize performance of a skill, athletes must learn the proper relationship between force and distance. This soccer player takes a step to increase distance; any longer step would lead to instability.

Hero Images/Getty Images

Moving Against Gravity: Action and Reaction

When observing changes in motor behavior across the life span, we also notice that performers take advantage of **Newton's third law of motion**: To every action there is an equal and opposite reaction. This means that if you exert a force on an object, it exerts a force (equal and opposite) back on you. This may seem confusing at first, but an example may make it clearer. As you walk, you push down on the floor or surface you walk on. What would happen if the floor did not "push" back up on you? If you guessed that your foot would go through the floor, you are right. Perhaps you have experienced this situation when walking on thin ice or unstable floorboards.

Newton's third law of motion, the law of action–reaction, states that for every force you exert on an object, the object exerts an equal force back on you in the opposite direction.

How does the law of action–reaction affect movement patterns? To move forward while walking, an individual must push down and back so that the surface can push up and forward. Watch the movement pattern of newly walking toddlers. Much of their force is directed downward, not backward. This allows them to move without compromising their balance; however, forward progression is slow. With more walking experience, individuals begin to exert more force backward and therefore move forward faster.

Consider the implications of Newton's third law: If every action that a performer makes results in an equal and opposite reaction, then any forces that are applied outside of the plane of motion will lead to undesired reaction forces. These forces will in turn detract from the performance (Gagen & Getchell, 2008). For example, if you want to move forward, then any force exerted in other directions will make your walk less efficient. Athletes attempting maximal performance, such as kicking for the maximal force possible, want to exert as much force as possible in one plane of motion. In a skill such as kicking, maximal effort is characterized by full extension (straightening) of the striking limb.

We can also see the law of action–reaction applied among parts of the body. For example, in locomotor skills such as running, the lower body twists one way and the upper body twists the opposite way. One leg swings forward and the arm on that side of the body swings backward in reaction; thus, the leg on one side of the body and the arm on the opposite side swing forward and back in unison. This familiar pattern is termed **oppositional arm and leg movement** and is a characteristic of skilled locomotor movements.

Imagine the result of several everyday movements if the law of action–reaction did not exist. Have you ever experienced a situation in which you expected a reaction force and it did not occur? What happened?

Relationship Between Rotating Limbs and Projected Objects

As we discussed previously, individuals move when their limbs rotate around one or several joints. This is called rotational movement. In essence, when projecting an object (e.g., throwing or kicking), an individual's limb traces part of a circle—the arm travels in an arc in throwing, and the leg does so in kicking. Releasing or striking an object causes it to fly away from this curved path in a straight line from the release or impact point. A relationship exists between the velocity of the rotating arm and the velocity of the projected object. For example, if a baseball player throws a ball from the outfield, the velocity of the ball as it leaves the player's hand is dependent on how fast the player's arm moves and on the length of his arm at the release point. In more scientific terms, an object's linear velocity is the product of its rotational velocity and its radius of rotation.

What does this mean in terms of optimizing performance? First of all, as children grow, their limb length increases, which should lead to changes in projectile velocity (and consequently distance) that may appear even without changes in movement form (Gagen & Getchell, 2008). Increases in rotational velocity also cause these changes. However, at any given time, people cannot increase their absolute limb length or rotational velocity. What if an athlete already rotates his limb as fast as possible? There is one other way to increase a projected object's velocity. The athlete must extend his limb—and thus increase the radius of rotation—by straightening it out just before the point of release or contact. Consider a tennis server trying to get the most velocity possible on his first serve (figure 3.4). At the point of contact, the player's arm is extended as far as it can be, which will increase the ball's release velocity.

▶ **KEY POINT** Individuals can increase the velocity of an object they project (throw, kick, hit) by extending the rotating limb as much as possible at the point of release.

Imagine you are a physical educator. In which sports and physical activities, besides tennis, do athletes extend their limbs to increase the velocity of a projected object? Try to think of three obvious examples and three not-so-obvious examples.

FIGURE 3.4 To increase the velocity of a tennis ball, a tennis player extends her arm (thereby increasing her radius of rotation) as much as possible at the moment of contact.

At this point, you may wonder why skilled athletes do not keep their limbs extended as far as possible during the entire movement. If an extended limb leads to greater velocity, why do athletes often begin their movements in a bent or cocked position and not straighten the limb throughout? The answer lies in another law of motion: that of inertia. You have probably heard the term *inertia*; it refers to an object's resistance to motion, and it is related to the mass of the object. When dealing with rotating objects (e.g., arms and legs) in sports and physical activities, resistance to motion depends not only on mass but also on limb length. As the limb length increases for a given mass, so does the resistance to motion. As the resistance to motion increases, so does the amount of energy required to move the object. In short, bending the limb decreases the energy necessary to move the limb.

Let's consider several skills in which athletes take advantage of these two principles to maximize performance. First, consider sprinters (figure 3.5). Just before contact with the ground, the sprinters fully extend their legs to maximize their projected velocity. However, the sprinters bend these limbs as they recover and swing forward. This conserves energy and effort in that limb. Another example is that of batters swinging at pitched balls. The batters conserve effort at the beginning of the swing by keeping their elbows bent. Just before the point of contact, the batters extend their arms as fully as possible.

Open Kinetic Chain

Open kinetic chain refers to the correctly timed sequence of movements an individual uses to successfully perform a skill.

A person can toss or kick an object a short distance with a flick of the wrist or a tap of the toe. But a maximal ballistic effort must involve not only more body parts but also sequential movement of those parts. The sequence must be timed so that the performer applies the force of each succeeding movement just after the previous movement to accelerate the object. For example, recall that an effective thrower steps forward and rotates the pelvis, then rotates the upper trunk as the throwing arm comes forward, extends, and rotates inward. We term a movement sequence such as this an **open kinetic chain** of movements (Jensen, 2005).

▶ **KEY POINT** One of the most significant changes we see in the skill development of children and beginners is the transition from using a single action to executing skills in a pattern of efficient, properly timed sequential movements.

FIGURE 3.5 A sprinter changes relative leg length during the course of a stride. The leg is bent to decrease momentum and energy requirements; it is then extended to increase force production.
Nick Wilson/Allsport Concepts/Getty Images

Imagine you are a physical therapist. How important are sequencing and timing to activities of daily living? What results from changing either sequence or timing in a given movement?

Two elements are essential to the open kinetic chain of movements. First, an optimal sequence of movements exists. Equally important is the timing of events in this sequence. For example, we have discussed how taking a step before a throw increases the amount of work done; however, the step must occur immediately before the throw in order to provide benefit. You may have observed individuals—particularly children—learning to throw who take a step but do not time the step and throw together. In fact, beginners often use single actions or movements when executing motor skills. As they continue to perform these skills, they begin to link together and time these single movements; as a result, they become more proficient movers.

Force Absorption

Have you ever landed from a jump without bending your knees? If so, you understand the concept of action–reaction firsthand: The earth immediately returned the force of your landing body back to you. Obviously, you do not want to land this way every time you jump because injury will surely ensue. To decrease the impact of the landing, you simply bend your knees. Bending your knees during landing increases the time and distance of the landing. This brings us to our next principle of motion, related to force absorption. Simply put, to decrease the impact of a reaction force, you must either increase the amount of time in which the impact occurs or increase the area over which the impact occurs (Carr, 1997).

You can observe individuals using this principle to decrease impact force in a wide variety of motor activities. When catching a ball, a softball player extends the arms in front of the body, then brings the glove, hand, and arm into the body; this sequence helps absorb the force of a hard-driven ball. Gymnasts are experts at landings, bending their hips, knees, and ankles as fully as possible. Individuals practicing judo increase the time and area of their falls, rolling from the arms to the back (Gagen & Getchell, 2008). Using this principle of motion is important for preventing injury when attempting a maximal performance.

▶ **KEY POINT** To absorb forces transmitted to their bodies, individuals must increase the amount of time of the impact (by allowing the limbs to flex) or increase the area over which the force is absorbed.

Stability and Balance

We have discussed principles of motion, but principles of stability are equally important. Most people would have difficulty optimizing their movements from an unstable position. That is, stability and balance are essential elements of many sports and other physical activities. Some activities, such as powerlifting and golf, require maximum stability. In others, such as judo and wrestling, athletes try to maintain their stability while disturbing that of their opponents. Still other activities, such as gymnastics and ice skating, require athletes to maintain balance in relatively unstable positions.

Balance relates to the ability of an object or person to maintain equilibrium.

Center of gravity is the concentration point of the earth's gravitational pull on an individual.

From the previous examples, you can see that **stability** and **balance** do not refer to exactly the same concept. A stable object or person is one that resists movement. You would have a difficult time tipping over a large, wide, heavy box—it is very stable. Balance, on the other hand, relates to the ability of an object or person to maintain equilibrium. If you can stand on one foot while closing your eyes, you exhibit great balance in an unstable condition.

In most cases, increasing stability ensures balance; however, maintaining balance does not guarantee stability. In fact, a person may not want stability because it will inhibit mobility. People can readily become more stable by increasing the size of their base of support—for example, by spreading their legs when standing or by spreading their hands when doing a handstand. Individuals can add to their stability by keeping their **center of gravity** low and inside their base of support. In the example of a handstand, individuals must keep the legs directly above the trunk to maintain optimum stability; otherwise, they will either move or fall.

▶ **KEY POINT** An individual's stability is related to the ability to resist movement or disruption. You can increase your stability by increasing your base of support, lowering your center of gravity, and keeping your center of gravity within your base of support.

In many activities, maximal performance of the skill requires performers to minimize stability in order to increase mobility. In locomotor skills, a person momentarily sacrifices stability (two-foot support base) in order to move by alternately losing and gaining balance (one-foot support base). The body's weight is pushed forward, ahead of the base of support, and the person moves the leg forward to regain balance.

▶ **KEY POINT** Although increasing stability leads to improved balance, it also leads to decreased mobility. Therefore, a skilled performer uses a base of support just wide enough to provide sufficient stability for his or her activity.

Figure 3.6 shows individuals with varying degrees of stability and balance. In figure 3.6*a*, the individual is very stable and has a wide base of support and a low center of gravity. It would be difficult to move him. The person in figure 3.6*b* is less stable but more mobile. Figure 3.6*c* shows an athlete with great balance in a highly unstable position.

Young children, people with certain disabilities, older adults, and people learning new skills often attempt to improve balance by increasing their stability. In locomotor tasks, they will increase their base of support by planting their feet wide or out-toeing (what would be considered "duck-footing") their feet. They keep their center of gravity well within their base of support by avoiding excessive trunk rotation or limb movement. In reception skills such as catching, they also increase the base of support and lower their center of gravity. In many cases, if such

FIGURE 3.6 Different degrees of stability: *(a)* highly stable, *(b)* moderately stable, and *(c)* not very stable.
(a) Sanda Stanca/EyeEm/Getty Images, *(b)* Westend61/Getty Images, *(c)* Fuse/Corbis/Getty Images

people gain greater muscle control, more experience, proper training, or confidence, they will narrow the base of support and therefore increase their mobility and ability to move quickly.

Imagine you are a physical therapist. Think of four activities of daily living that range from requiring maximum stability to requiring maximum mobility. What are the consequences of losing balance in each activity?

Web Study Guide **Compare and contrast motion principles in different movements in Lab Activity 3.1, Searching for Movement Similarities and Differences, in the web study guide.**

Stability–Mobility Trade-Off in Motor Development

The ability to maintain balance (e.g., postural support) is essential for becoming proficient in many skills. For example, if movers cannot maintain an upright posture while shifting their center of gravity over their base of support (either one or both feet) to respond to reactive forces generated by their own movements, they cannot walk. In fact, the strategies taken in order to successfully move from one place to another have common developmental elements regardless of whether the mover walks, runs, hops, skips, or gallops. New movers adopt stability movement strategies that maximize stability *and* balance, but at the expense of the ability to move quickly. As they improve their ability to maintain an upright posture during movement, they shift to mobility movement strategies that allow for faster movements at the expense of stability. These mobility strategies provide a gateway to more proficient movement solutions (Brian, Taunton, Liebermain, Haibach-Beach, Forley, & Santarossa, 2018).

Let's look at walking as an example. A new walker's greatest challenge is to maintain an upright posture while projecting the body forward. Walking requires the ability to balance on one foot while moving the entire body forward to transfer weight to the other foot. Early walkers accomplish this by maximizing their overall stability (see chapter 5 for a complete description of early walking), which in turn minimizes their odds of falling. Before walking independently, infants will use furniture or other objects to support themselves in order to repetitively step. Biomechanically, the first few independent steps optimize stability: Feet are placed wide, which increases base of support, and trunk rotation and leg range of motion are minimized, decreasing reactive forces created during movement. Also, the arms are raised high in a guarded position to assist with balance. This configuration of limbs and trunk allows the new walker to move . . . slowly. Using a stability strategy as a means for locomotion ensures that the walker can maintain an upright posture while moving but also limits the speed at which that locomotion can occur.

Soon, however, toddlers begin to adapt to their environments. With practice, two things happen. The toddlers' experiences (1) allow them to implicitly learn important relationships within and among limbs and (2) lead to physiological changes such as increases in strength. These changes, plus the improved balance gained by the stability strategy in the early weeks of walking, begin to offer toddlers alternatives. Within several months of independent walking, young children explore ways they can move faster. In other words, with their new body configurations, they trade stability for mobility: They begin to use repetitive, alternating step patterns; rotate the trunk; and pump the arms.

Using the Principles of Motion and Stability to Detect and Correct Errors

Once you understand the principles that underlie human movement, you can use them to recognize and fix mechanical errors in a person's technique. At first, the amount of information may seem overwhelming. However, Carr (1997) has provided a simple five-step process for systematically observing and analyzing skill performance. This process provides you with a straightforward method for noticing and assisting with a person's mechanics.

- **Step 1: Observe the complete skill.** Although this seems self-evident, it is surprising how often novice teachers and coaches put themselves in a position where they cannot see a person's complete movement. Planning before performance of the skill is key, and you should keep several concerns in mind. If you can watch the performance only once or twice, focus on only a few elements. Videotape the performance for future analysis. Make sure the person warms up before the movement and performs in a natural environment, and always ensure the safety of the person and others who may be nearby.

- **Step 2: Analyze each phase and its key elements.** Home in on specific phases of the skill and their key elements. Break the skill into phases; for example, an overarm throw could be divided into preparatory backswing, force production, and follow-through. Next, look at a person's performance of the skill in these phases. Carr suggests two ways to do this. One is to start with the result and work backward. If a person is trying to serve a tennis ball over a net but continues to hit the net, you concentrate on the action of the racket when it contacts the ball and then work back from that point to identify which part of the performance may be leading to this result. Alternatively, you can watch the movement from start to finish. Watch the person's preparatory stance, balance, and weight shift before movement; then focus on each phase of the skill.

- **Step 3: Use your knowledge of mechanics in your analysis.** You have learned a good deal about mechanics, and now is the time to use it. Observers must focus on how the mover applies muscular force to generate movements. Carr suggests a series of questions to guide your analysis.

  - Does the mover have optimal stability when applying or receiving force?
  - Is the mover using all the muscles that can make a contribution to the skill?
  - Is the mover applying force with the muscles in the correct sequence?
  - Is the mover applying the right amount of force over the appropriate time frame?
  - Is the mover applying the force in the correct direction?
  - Is the mover correctly applying torque and momentum transfer?
  - Is the mover manipulating any linear or rotary inertia properly?

Use these questions to evaluate skill performance. Remember, you are not determining a right and wrong way to perform a skill; rather, you are looking for elements of the movement that can be modified to make the skill performance more proficient.

- **Step 4: Select errors to be corrected.** Many novice performers do not move in a mechanically efficient manner. This is not necessarily good or bad—it is simply how that person performs a skill. You, as a teacher or coach, can pick out certain aspects of movement that the person can improve to become more proficient at a skill. Keep in mind that there are many different ways that people can successfully perform a skill. However, improving the mechanics in several phases of a skill allows for improved performance. Focus on major errors—a performance that lacks in the areas listed in step 3—and ignore minor problems. Work on one aspect of performance at a time. In many cases, improvement in one area will lead to improvement in several other areas.
- **Step 5: Decide on appropriate methods for the correction of errors.** Educators can have different ideas about how to teach or coach motor skills. It's best to take a class or attend a coaching clinic to learn a variety of activity-specific teaching methods. Regardless of which methods you use, here are some keys to remember. First and foremost, keep safety in mind when attempting to correct errors. Highly complex skills and skills that involve flight can become dangerous if the mover diverts attention from the skill to try to correct errors. Next, communicate with your students in understandable language rather than mechanical terms. Consider also how much time you have with the students to correct errors; this will dictate the number of errors you attempt to correct. Finally, use outside resources, such as textbooks or the Internet, to help you find new and innovative ways to teach movement skills.

Web Study Guide **Uncover motion principles underlying developmental change in three skills (Lab Activity 3.2, Developmentally Sequencing Locomotor Movement Based on the Principles of Motion and Stability; Lab Activity 3.3, Developmentally Sequencing Ballistic Skills Based on the Principles of Motion and Stability; and Lab Activity 3.4, Developmentally Sequencing Manipulative Skills Based on the Principles of Motion and Stability) in the web study guide.**

Summary and Synthesis

Mechanical principles govern all our movements. The principles themselves act as constraints in that they dictate how an individual interacts with the environment when performing a task. For example, the force of gravity is an environmental constraint that influences how we move on Earth. These principles include Newton's laws of inertia, acceleration, and action–reaction as well as relationships based on these laws dealing with force production and absorption, open kinetic chain, and stability and balance. These principles define relationships that dictate how we move.

Over time, individuals gain understanding of these principles (either explicitly or implicitly) and can learn to control certain factors that allow them to perform skills more proficiently. The qualitative changes in motor performance that occur during childhood reflect changes in the interaction between the environment and the changing individual constraints in the growing child. The progress of children, beginners, and relearners is characterized by their selection of movement patterns that increasingly optimize the movement product in a manner consistent with the principles of motion and stability. The major mechanical principles involved in efficient, skilled movement include the application and absorption of force as well as action and reaction, linear and rotational velocity, sequentially timed movements, and stability and balance. Knowledge of these principles allows us to generalize across various basic skills. We need not approach developmental changes in each of the basic skills as a completely new study because some aspects of change in skills overlap, especially in the categories of locomotion, ballistics, reception, and skills requiring balance.

Reinforcing What You Have Learned About Constraints

TAKE A SECOND LOOK

Aimee Mullins has challenged preconceived notions of ability and disability her entire life. While in college, she successfully competed against able-bodied athletes in track and field. In recent years, some have argued that "cheetah" legs provide an unfair advantage for the individual using them. Both during and after her athletic career, Mullins argued that track athletes with and without prosthetics should compete against each other on national and international stages. Focusing on only the idea that "cheetah" legs are mechanically efficient overlooks the fact that the resultant movement comes from an interaction of many constraints. In other words, each athlete must master the different principles of motion and stability with respect to their own individual constraints.

TEST YOUR KNOWLEDGE

1. Describe some characteristics of two different motor skills that indicate the individual is optimizing stability instead of mobility.
2. List Newton's three laws and explain their relationship to movements.
3. What are some of the ways a baseball player can increase the force of a throw?
4. How can a child's growth contribute to greater proficiency at certain motor skills?

LEARNING EXERCISE 3.1

Understanding the Relationship Between Forces and Balance

What are the influences on balance when you stand on one leg? Start by standing and balancing on one leg. Now, move your support foot. How does this affect balance, and what is the ideal position? Next, move your free leg to different positions. How does this affect balance, and what is the ideal position? Repeat this process with your arms and head until you find your own ideal balance position. After you finish, compare your ideal position with that (or those) of a partner (or group).

LEARNING EXERCISE 3.2

Examining Principles of Motion and Stability in Specific Sports Skills

In this exercise you will examine the interplay between force and balance in certain sports skills. Start with the overarm throw. Throw a ball as hard as you can.

1. Where does your balance come from? Examine the specific movements that lead to greater balance.
2. Where does your force come from? Examine the specific movements that lead to greater force production.
3. Now, consider the relationship between force and balance. Describe how you would have to change your movements to create *more* force. What would have to change so that you could maintain balance when doing the movement as revised for more force?
4. Try to make these changes in your movements. What happens?

Try this experiment for different sports skills, such as a volleyball spike, a football punt, or a soccer kick.

II

Development of Motor Skills Across the Life Span

In part II, the pieces of the motor development puzzle begin to come together as we examine motor development over the life span, with consideration of the associated constraints influencing the course development takes. That is, this part of the book discusses the changes in skill performance observed from birth to older adulthood; it also identifies the individual, environmental, and task constraints that may bring about these changes.

Chapter 4 discusses early motor development. During the first year of life, infants and toddlers rapidly acquire new motor skills, progressing toward the ability to move adaptively in their environments. Because of the scope and speed of change in young children, the entire chapter is devoted to the period between birth and the onset of walking (at approximately 11 to 15 months of age). This is a critical time in atypical development as well, since small differences in individual constraints early on can evolve into large differences later in life.

Chapter 5 discusses changes in locomotor skills from approximately 1 year of age through the life span. These skills include the most commonly used locomotor patterns—walking and running—as well as skills used in play and sport contexts, such as jumping, hopping, and galloping. You should begin to see similarities in developmental trajectories, known as developmental sequences, given the similarity in individual constraints and the guiding principles of motion and stability. You will also see how the development of specific individual constraints influences developmental sequences.

Chapter 6 addresses ballistic skills, such as throwing, striking, and kicking. Again, you will see many similarities in the developmental sequences for various ballistic tasks. Finally, chapter 7 covers manipulative skills—both fine motor skills, such as reaching and grasping, and gross motor skills, such as catching.

Suggested Reading

Adolph, K.E., Rachwani, J., & Hoch, J.E. (2018). Motor and physical development: Locomotion. In *Neuroscience and biobehavioral psychology*. Elsevier (pgs 1–17). Retrieved from https://www.elsevier.com/solutions/sciencedirect/content/reference-modules/neuroscience-and-biobehavioral-psychology-module

Corbetta, D., DiMercurio, A., Weiner, R.F., Connell, J.P., & Clark, M. (2018). How perception and action fosters exploration and selection in infant skill acquisition. *Advances in Child Development and Behavior, 55*, 1–29.

Gagen, L.M., Haywood, K.M., & Spaner, S.D. (2005). Predicting the scale of tennis rackets for optimal striking from body dimensions. *Pediatric Exercise Science, 17*, 190–200.

Hall, M.L, & Lobo, M.A. (2017). Design and development of the first exoskeletal garment to enhance arm mobility for children with movement impairments. *Assistive Technology, 30*(5), 251–258. DOI: 10.1080/10400435.2017.1320690

Lane, A.P., Molina, S.L., Tolleson, D.A., Langendorfer, S.J., Goodway, J.D., & Stodden, D.F. (2018). Developmental sequences for the standing long jump landing: A pre-longitudinal screening. *Journal of Motor Learning and Development, 6*, 114–129.

Lobo, M.A., Kokkoni, E., de Campos, A.C., & Galloway, J.C. (2014). Not just playing around: Infants' object behaviors reflect ability, constraints, and object properties. *Infant Behavior and Development, 37*(3), 334–351. DOI: 10.1016/j.infbeh.2014.05.003

Logan, S.W., Barnett, L.M., Goodway, J.D., & Stodden, D.F. (2017). Comparison of performance on process- and product-oriented assessments of fundamental motor skills across childhood. *Journal of Sports Sciences, 35*(7), 634–641. DOI: 10.1080/02640414.2016.1183803

4

Early Motor Development

Fundamental Individual Constraints

CHAPTER OBJECTIVES

This chapter

- describes types of movement that occur in infancy,
- lists infantile reflexes and postural reactions,
- explains the relationship between infants' earlier and later movements,
- describes motor milestones,
- explains how early movements are shaped by a variety of constraints, and
- examines postural development and balance in infancy.

Motor Development in the Real World

Why Do Infants Quit Crawling After They Become So Good at It?

During the last few months of their first year, infants become proficient crawlers, skillfully zipping from one place to the next almost faster than their parents can catch them. Given the efficiency with which they can locomote on their hands and feet, it is a wonder why they ever change to upright walking: New walkers are slow, unstable, and liable to fall after a step or two. What motivates infants to change their entire mode of transportation, and how do they learn to do it?

Karen Adolph from New York University and her colleagues (Adolph et al., 2012) aimed to answer this question by examining infants in their natural environments (in contrast to most infant research of this kind, which occurs in a controlled laboratory setting). The researchers examined over 150 infants and toddlers (both crawlers and walkers) between the ages of 11 and 19 months for a 1-hour period while they interacted with a parent or caregiver. Through video analysis, they determined how frequently the infants fell and how they coordinated their limbs as they moved. Infants moved in short, frequent bursts for an average of about 20 minutes out of the 60-minute period. During this time, participants moved about 2,300 feet (700 m) on average (both walking and crawling), stepping almost 2,400 steps while at the same time falling an average of 17 times. Using these metrics, a typical toddler would take approximately 14,000 steps and fall 100 times over the course of 6 hours! This includes the group as a whole, but what happens when you compare experienced crawlers with beginning walkers? As noted before, new walkers often appear to be more unstable. The key is "appear." In fact, new walkers did not fall more frequently than the expert crawlers; the relative rate of falling was approximately the same. This suggests that the rewards of learning to walk—eventually moving a greater distance in a shorter time—come without additional risk of falling. This helps explain the mystery of why expert crawlers would give up a proven method of locomotion. According to the researchers, part of the answer to "why walk?" is "why not?"

In the past few years, researchers have taken a careful look at the relationship between movements that infants make and their developing minds. It appears as though this link is much stronger than originally believed. In other words, it is becoming clear that in order to understand cognitive development in infancy, we need to understand motor development and, eventually, determine the interactions and transactions between them. Such an approach fits with the ecological perspective as well as the constraints model. This chapter provides you with information about the motor behaviors exhibited by infants, which is the first step toward understanding how motor development is related to cognitive and perceptual development during infancy. There are also important practical reasons for knowing about infant motor development. In typically developing infants, many movements occur in fairly predictable order and timing. It is essential to learn about and understand typical development in order to be able to recognize deviance—either progression or regression—from the typical pattern.

In terms of motor development, most newborn infants exhibit spontaneous and reflexive movements. As infants move toward becoming toddlers, they begin to attain motor milestones. These gross movements slowly become more refined throughout infancy and early childhood.

In addition, infants gain the ability to lift their heads, sit up, and eventually stand with minimal support. In the past, parents and educators alike have thought of this process as maturation. In other words, maturation of the central nervous system was the sole individual constraint guiding early motor behavior. This notion, discussed in chapter 2, comes out of the maturational perspective. However, current research from an ecological perspective suggests that the interplay of many systems (cognitive, perceptual, motor) leads to the movement adaptations seen in infancy. Therefore, this chapter presents the concept that many constraints in addition to maturation encourage or discourage early motor behavior.

How Do Infants Move?

If you watch newborns, you will notice that some of their movements seem to be undirected and without purpose. For example, infants often kick their legs while lying on their backs. These spontaneous movements appear without any obvious stimulation. At other times, infants will move in a specific way every time they are touched in a certain place. Who can resist an infant "holding your hand"—that is, grabbing your finger when you touch her palm? An infant is born with a variety of reflexes that seem to disappear slowly as she ages, and she appears to move with discrete, purposeless actions that have little to do with future voluntary movements. However, there is more to infant motor behavior than meets the eye. Those seemingly random infant movements have an important relationship with intentional movements that occur later in life. After the first few months of life the infant will begin to attain motor milestones, which are particular movement skills that eventually lead to locomotion, reaching, and upright posture.

Newborn movements, then, have been classified into two general categories: (1) random or spontaneous movements and (2) infantile reflexes (Clark, 1995). These two types of movement are very different from each other.

Spontaneous Movements

People give much attention to the study of infantile reflexes; however, reflexes represent only a small portion of early motor behavior. Besides reflexes, how do newborns move? If not eating or sleeping, newborns might squirm, thrust their legs or arms, stretch or clench their fingers and toes, or make other **spontaneous movements**. These spontaneous movements seem very different from walking or reaching, and in the past, pediatricians, parents, and others believed that they had no particular purpose or relationship to the future movements the child would someday choose to make. However, this may not be the case.

Spontaneous movements are infants' movements that occur without any apparent stimulation.

Supine Kicking and Walking

If a baby is laid on his back (the supine position), he will likely spontaneously thrust his legs. This is called supine kicking. Thelen and her colleagues (Thelen, 1985, 1995; Thelen & Fisher, 1983; Thelen, Ridley-Johnson, & Fisher, 1983) studied the nature of supine kicking in infancy. In analyzing the position and timing of leg segments in these kicks as well as muscular activity in the leg muscles, they discovered some surprising results. The supine kicking was not random but rhythmical, and the kicks had a coordinated pattern. The ankle, knee, and hip joints moved cooperatively with each other, not independently from one another. It seems amazing that these supine kicks during infancy have a coordinated pattern. What is more remarkable is that the coordination of these kicks resembles the positioning and timing of an adult walking step (figure 4.1). The pattern of muscle use in infant supine kicking is also coordinated. Sometimes an infant kicks only one leg, but at other times an infant will kick both legs alternately, just as an adult alternates legs in walking. Even premature infants perform coordinated supine kicks (Geerdink, Hopkins, Beek, & Heriza, 1996; Heriza, 1986; Piek & Gasson, 1999).

What might account for some of the differences in infant kicking and adult walking? Think in terms of individual, environmental, and task constraints.

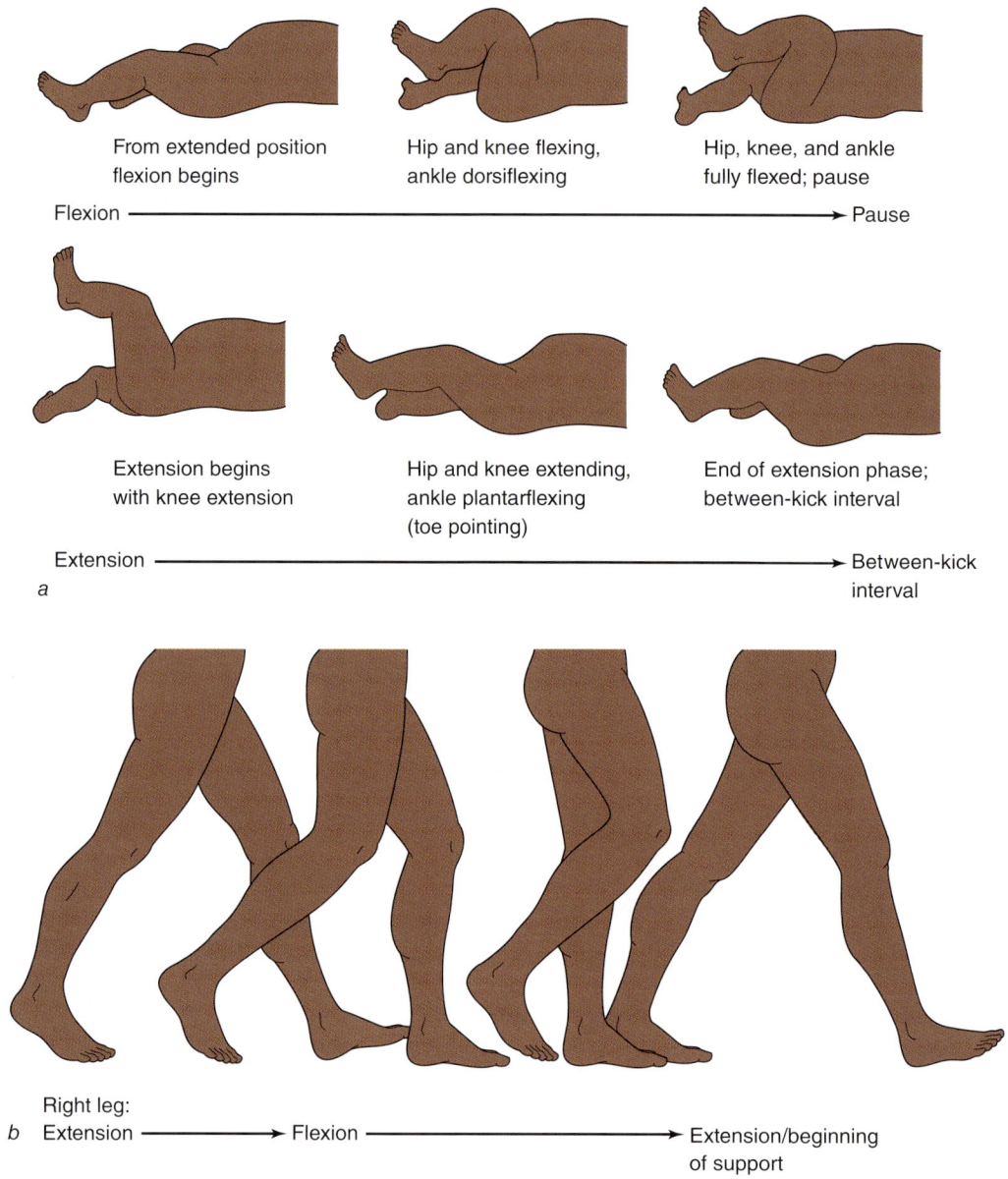

FIGURE 4.1 Kicking. *(a)* Infant kick. *(b)* Adult step.

Though an infant's supine kicks are similar to an adult's walking steps, they are not identical. Infants' timing is more variable from kick to kick, and they tend to move the joints in unison rather than in sequence. Infants also tend to activate both the muscles for flexing the limb (flexors) and the muscles for extending the limb (extensors). This is called cocontraction. In contrast, adults move by alternating flexor and extensor muscles. However, by the end of their first year, infants begin to move the hip, knee, and ankle sequentially rather than in tight unison. Both alternating and synchronous (i.e., with both legs in unison) kicks are evident after 6 months, indicating that infants are developing more ways to coordinate the two limbs (Thelen, 1985, 1995; Thelen & Fisher, 1983; Thelen et al., 1983).

Web Study Guide **Observe an infant throughout the first year of his life in Lab Activity 4.1, Identifying Rate Limiters During the First 6.5 Months, in the web study guide.**

Spontaneous Arm Movements

Infants also move their arms, and newborns' spontaneous arm movements show well-coordinated extension of the elbow, wrist, and finger joints. In other words, the fingers do not extend independently, or one at a time, but rather in unison with the hand, wrist, and elbow (just as with the kick). Arm movements are not as rhythmical and repetitious as leg kicks though (Thelen, 1981; Thelen, Kelso, & Fogel, 1987). As with the kick, early arm thrusts are not identical to adult reaching movements. It takes infants several months to begin opening their fingers independently of the other joints in anticipation of grasping objects as adults do (Trevarthen, 1984; von Hofsten, 1982, 1984). In addition, these spontaneous movements appear to be influenced by environmental constraints, as Kawai, Savelsbergh, and Wimmers (1999) found when they placed newborn infants in four environmental conditions and discovered differences in frequency and activity of spontaneous arm movements.

► **KEY POINT** Infants' movements, though not always goal directed or goal achieving, can be coordinated, and the coordination patterns may resemble patterns seen in adults.

Rhythmic flapping of arms and kicking of legs have been termed *stereotypies* because of the underlying, stereotypical temporal structure of the movements (Thelen, 1979, 1981). Other stereotypies exist, which Thelen identified according to specific regions of the body, such as legs and feet (e.g., alternating leg movements), head and face (e.g., head banging), and fingers (e.g., flexing fingers). What does the existence of stereotypies suggest? First, newborns may be weak and unable to produce intentional, precise, goal-directed movements, but even at a young age they exhibit underlying rhythmic coordination within limbs or pairs of limbs (Piek, Gasson, Barrett, & Case, 2002). Second, these coordination patterns resemble the coordination patterns we see in later voluntary movement, which suggests some relationship between random and voluntary movement. Perhaps spontaneous movements are part of the fundamental building blocks of voluntary, functional movement (Jensen, Thelen, Ulrich, Schneider, & Zernicke, 1995).

Infantile Reflexes

Reflexive movements are often visible in young infants. Unlike random movements, reflexes are involuntary movements that an individual makes in response to specific stimuli. Sometimes these responses occur only when the body is in a specific position. An infant does not have to think about making reflexive movements; they occur automatically. Some reflexes, such as eye blinking, occur throughout the life span, but others are present only during infancy (**infantile reflexes**). We can categorize those seen during infancy into three types of movements: primitive reflexes, postural reactions, and locomotor reflexes (table 4.1). Let's define each of these categories and discuss their purposes.

An **infantile reflex** is an involuntary, stereotypical movement response to a specific stimulus; the term refers specifically to such responses seen only during infancy. There are three types of infantile reflexes: the primitive and locomotor reflexes and the postural reactions.

Primitive Reflexes: Around From the Beginning

When a newborn infant grasps an object placed in her hand, she does so automatically and without conscious thought. This is an example of a primitive reflex, an involuntary response to specific stimulation that is often mediated by lower brain centers (Peiper, 1963). Generally, newborns exhibit strong reflexes at birth; these reflexes tend to lose their strength over time until they disappear around the fourth month. How can we tell primitive reflexes from spontaneous movements?

- Reflexes are responses to specific external stimuli, whereas spontaneous movements do not result from any apparent external stimuli.
- Reflexive movements are specific and often localized, whereas spontaneous movements tend to be nonspecific and generalized.
- The same stimulus will elicit a specific reflex over and over again (McGraw, 1943).

The palmar grasp and the asymmetric tonic neck reflex are shown in figure 4.2. The labyrinthine righting reflex and the stepping reflex are shown in figure 4.3.

TABLE 4.1 Infantile Reflexes

REFLEX OR REACTION	STARTING POSITION (IF IMPORTANT)	STIMULUS	RESPONSE	TIME	WARNING SIGNS
PRIMITIVE REFLEXES					
Asymmetrical tonic neck	Supine	Turn head to one side	Same-side arm and leg extend	Prenatal to 4 mo	Persistence after 6 mo
Symmetrical tonic neck	Supported sitting	Extend head and neck; flex head and neck	Arms extend, legs flex; arms flex, legs extend	6 mo to 7 mo	
Doll-eye		Flex head	Eyes look up	Prenatal to 2 wk	Persistence after first days of life
Palmar grasping		Touch palm with finger or object	Hand closes tightly around object	Prenatal to 4 mo	Persistence after 1 yr; asymmetrical reflex
Moro	Supine	Shake head, as by tapping pillow	Arms and legs extend, fingers spread; then arms and legs flex	Prenatal to 3 mo	Presence after 6 mo; asymmetrical reflex
Sucking		Touch face above or below lips	Sucking motion begins	Birth to 3 mo	
Babinski		Stroke sole of foot from heel to toes	Toes extend	Birth to 4 mo	Persistence after 6 mo
Searching or rooting		Touch cheek with smooth object	Head turns to side stimulated	Birth to 1 yr	Absence of reflex; persistence after 1 yr
Palmar-mandibular (Babkin)		Apply pressure to both palms	Mouth opens; eyes close; head flexes	1 to 3 mo	
Plantar grasping		Stroke ball of foot	Toes contract around object stroking foot	Birth to 12 mo	
Startle	Supine	Tap abdomen or startle infant	Arms and legs flex	7 to 12 mo	
POSTURAL REACTIONS					
Derotative righting	Supine	Turn legs and pelvis to other side	Trunk and head follow rotation	From 4 mo	
	Supine	Turn head sideways	Body follows head in rotation	From 4 mo	
Labyrinthine righting	Supported upright	Tilt infant	Head moves to stay upright	2 to 12 mo	
Pull-up	Sitting upright, held by 1 or 2 hands	Tip infant backward or forward	Arms flex	3 to 12 mo	
Parachute	Held upright	Lower infant toward ground rapidly	Legs extend	From 4 mo	
	Held upright	Tilt forward	Arms extend	From 7 mo	
	Held upright	Tilt sideways	Arms extend	From 6 mo	
	Held upright	Tilt backward	Arms extend	From 9 mo	
LOCOMOTOR REFLEXES					
Crawling	Prone	Apply pressure to sole of one foot or both feet alternately	Crawling pattern in arms and legs	Birth to 4 mo	
Stepping	Held upright	Place infant on flat surface	Walking pattern in legs	Birth to 5 mo	
Swimming	Prone	Place infant in or over water	Swimming movement of arms and legs	11 days to 5 mo	

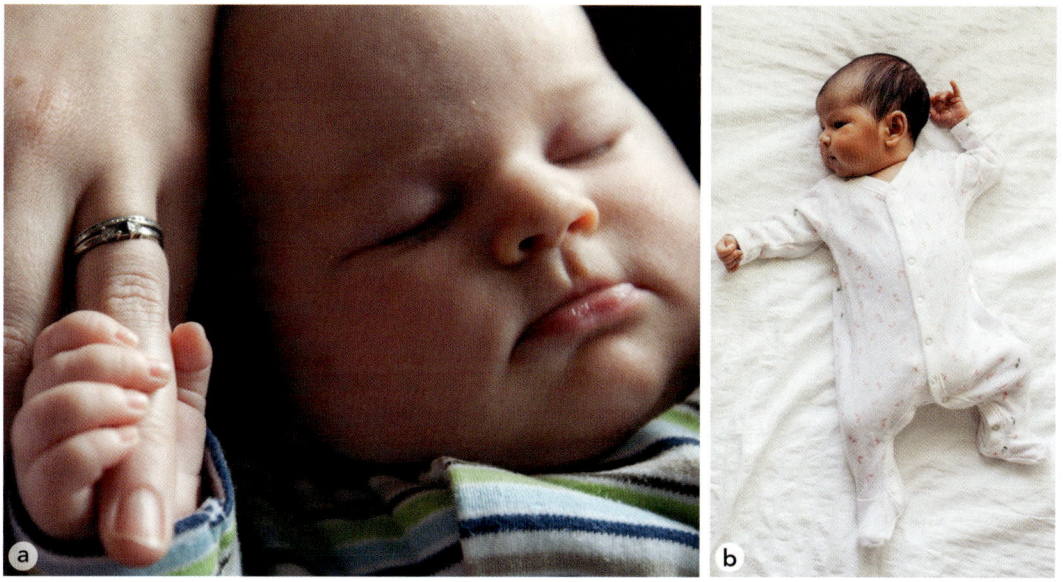

FIGURE 4.2 *(a)* Palmar grasp. The reflex is stimulated by touching or stroking the palm of the hand. *(b)* Asymmetrical tonic neck reflex. Note the "fencer's" position, which is one way to identify and describe this reflex.
(a) Geoff Kirby/PA Images; *(b)* Tuan Tran/Moment/Getty Images

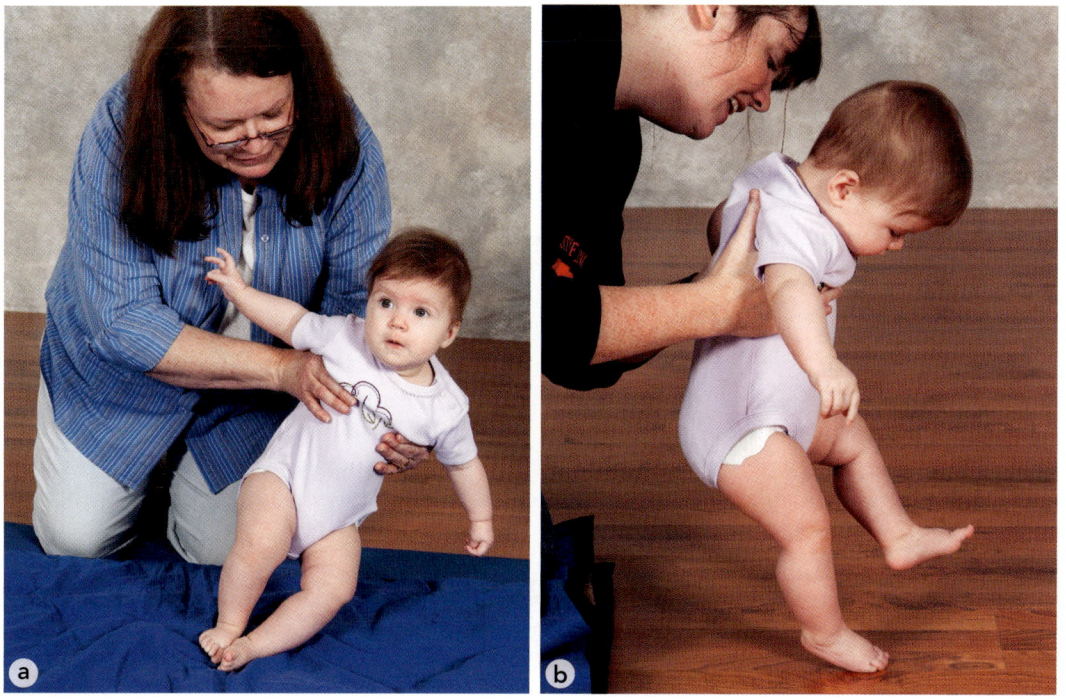

FIGURE 4.3 *(a)* Labyrinthine righting reflex. The infant rights the head when tipped backward. *(b)* Stepping reflex.

Postural Reactions: Moving Upright in the World

As their name implies, postural reactions, or gravity reflexes, help the infant automatically maintain posture in a changing environment (Peiper, 1963). Some of these responses keep the head upright, thereby keeping the breathing passages open. Others help the infant roll over and eventually attain a vertical position. Postural reactions generally appear after the infant is

2 months old. For example, an infant can roll over only after derotative righting appears after 4 months of age. By late in the first year or early in the second year of life, these isolated reactions requiring specific postures and stimuli drop out of the infant's repertoire of movements. However, these reflexes don't literally disappear. Children and adults react to being thrown off balance with specific muscle responses intended to bring the body back to balance. If you have recently tried in-line skating or snowboarding for the first time, you probably know this all too well! As you start to fall, you automatically extend your arms, and this automatic response results in many broken wrists—and unbroken skulls.

Locomotor Reflexes: Moving in Place

In the late 20th century, infant swim classes were all the rage. In these classes, parents placed their newborns in the water and the infants could actually swim! Precocious newborns? Perhaps, but more likely the infants were exhibiting the swim reflex, which, like other locomotor reflexes, gets its name because it appears similar and related to a voluntary movement (in this case, swimming). The locomotor reflexes appear much earlier than the corresponding voluntary behaviors and typically disappear months before the infant attempts the voluntary locomotor skill. There are three such locomotor reflexes: stepping, swimming, and crawling.

Appearance and Disappearance of Reflexes

In typically developing infants, infantile reflexes gradually show a less specific response with time; eventually, you can no longer stimulate these reflexes. In fact, the primitive reflexes start to weaken or become modified after about 2 weeks (Clark, 1995). Infants learn to adapt their reflexes after 2 weeks in order to modify the movement outcome (e.g., faster sucking leads to a faster supply of milk). Those who work with infants sometimes use the pattern of reflex appearance and disappearance to assess an individual infant's development. If the reflexes appear and disappear at an age close to the average, they consider the infant's development typical, whereas deviation from the typical pattern and typical execution of the response may signal a problem. An individual may deviate from typical in two ways:

1. Exhibiting a reflex when the individual should not
2. Not exhibiting a reflex when the individual should

A reflex that persists well after the average age of disappearance may indicate a pathological cerebral condition (Gieysztor, Choińska, & Paprocka-Borowicz, 2018; Peiper, 1963). A nonexistent or very weak response on one side of the body compared with the other also could reflect a pathological condition.

In the popular program *Grey's Anatomy*, emergency room doctors often check patients with suspected traumatic brain injury by running a probe along the bottom of the foot. This is a real technique, called the Babinski sign or test (see table 4.1 for a description of the Babinski reflex). This test is used to check for neurological problems in patients with head injuries. A positive Babinski sign indicates that the Babinski reflex as seen in infancy has returned—and that the patient most likely has an injury to the central nervous system.

Be careful when attempting to assess the neurological status of an infant (Bartlett, 1997). Remember that each individual develops as a result of interacting individual, environmental, and task constraints. This means that one infant may continue exhibiting reflexes after another of the same age has stopped without any pathological condition being involved. Most infants are ahead of or behind the average ages represented in normative data or scales. In addition, it is difficult to establish the exact time a reflex disappears. Only when the reflex persists for several months past the average might it constitute a warning sign of a pathological condition (Gieysztor et al., 2018). You should also be aware that reflexive responses are very sensitive to body position and environmental conditions (Adolph & Hoch, 2019). If you change an infant's body position or provide him with a stimulus that is different from those in table 4.1, you may not get the stereotypical response. It is easy for an untrained person to overlook some aspect of the environment and thus fail to elicit the anticipated response; as a result, he or she may incorrectly conclude that a pathological condition exists. Therefore, trained professionals should be consulted for such assessments.

▶ **KEY POINT** Parents, teachers, and others outside of the medical profession should bring infants in question to trained personnel for assessment.

Why Do Infants Move? The Purpose of Reflexes

Ask any mother and she will tell you that infant movements start well before birth! In fact, several reflexes appear as soon as 2 to 3 months in utero. But why are infants born with reflexes? Some, like the rooting reflex, seem to have an obvious purpose: to help an infant survive. Others, such as the asymmetrical tonic neck reflex or swimming reflex, seem to have no clear relevance to the infant at birth. Perhaps some reflexes are important before birth.

Researchers have explained the role of reflexes in three general ways: structural, functional, and applied. The structural explanation views reflexes as a byproduct of the human neurological system. That is, some theorists believe that reflexes merely reflect the structure of the nervous system—in other words, the way humans are wired. The functional explanation suggests that reflexes exist to help the infant survive—to eat, breathe, and grasp (Clark, 1995). Milani-Comparetti (1981; Milani-Comparetti & Gidoni, 1967) suggests that the fetus uses reflexes to position itself for birth, then to assist in the birthing process. Both the structural and functional explanations consider reflexes at birth but do not suggest anything about their purpose past birth. Applied theories, in contrast, examine the role of reflexes in future volitional movements. (Once again, we see some very different ideas depending on the theoretical viewpoints of the researchers.) Others take the view that reflexive movements lead to coordinated limb movements (Peiper, 1963), thus giving the infant the opportunity to practice coordinated movements before the higher brain centers are ready to mediate such actions.

Look at table 4.1 again. How do you see each reflex fitting into a role for future movements?

Relationship of Reflexes to Voluntary Movement

Ideas about the relationship between reflexes and later movement have changed dramatically over the past 50 years as a result of some unique experiments. Early researchers such as McGraw (1943) believed that infants could not move voluntarily until reflexes had been inhibited by the central nervous system—a theory termed *motor interference*. As time went on, researchers began to question this view. A relatively simple experiment by Zelazo, Zelazo, and Kolb (1972a, 1972b) challenged the notion that reflexes and voluntary movements are not related. The researchers elicited the stepping reflex daily in a small number of infants during their first 8 weeks. This daily practice not only increased the stepping reflex in these infants but also resulted in the earlier onset of voluntary walking in the trained infants compared with infants who did not practice the reflex. The investigators concluded that the involuntary walking reflex could be transformed into voluntary walking (see also Zelazo, 1983). They proposed that the disappearance of the reflex was due to disuse, that the period of reflex inhibition before onset of the voluntary skill was unnecessary, and that the systematic stimulation of a locomotor reflex could enhance infants' acquisition of voluntary locomotion.

Esther Thelen (1983, 1995; Thelen & Ulrich, 1991) also questioned whether reflexes had to be inhibited before voluntary movement could occur. With her colleagues, she proposed that other constraints, rather than strictly maturation, may be related to the disappearance of the stepping reflex. Thelen examined the changing individual constraints during early childhood and noticed that infants have a dramatic increase in leg weight, primarily from fat, during the first 2 months of life. She reasoned that this great increase in leg weight, along with the absence of a corresponding increase in muscle strength, may cause the stepping reflex to disappear because the infant has insufficient strength to lift the now-heavier legs. In other words, strength may be a rate limiter for stepping after 2 months or so of infancy.

To test this idea, Thelen and her associates took a group of 4- to 6-week-old infants who were still reflex-kicking and added small weights, equal to the amount of weight gain the infants were to experience, to their ankles. The amount of reflex stepping decreased, suggesting that the weight gain might be a viable explanation for the disappearing reflex. However, studies of these very young infants showed only half the picture. Thelen had to demonstrate that reflex stepping still existed in older infants if she accounted for the constraint of strength. To do so, she took older infants (who no longer reflex-stepped) and submerged them to their chests in a small tank of water. The water had the effect of buoying the legs (simulating an increase in strength), and these infants began to step with greater frequency. This result is similar to that of Zelazo's, whose training may have made the infants' legs strong enough to step despite weight gain. Finally, Thelen (1985; Thelen & Ulrich, 1991; Vereijken & Thelen, 1997) found that infants who did not reflexively step at 7 months *did* step when held over the moving belt of a motorized treadmill. The sum of these studies suggests that several individual constraints (rather than simply maturation) play a strong role as rate limiters on movement patterns during infancy. These studies have inspired several other infant research studies that utilized treadmills. Figure 4.4 illustrates the ongoing research that uses treadmills to elicit stepping in infants with Down syndrome.

FIGURE 4.4 To improve the onset and quality of independent walking, an infant with Down syndrome is trained on a motorized treadmill.
Photo courtesy of Dale Ulrich.

▶ **KEY POINT** The increase and decrease of stepping with changes in environmental and task constraints (e.g., addition of a moving treadmill belt, manipulation of leg weight) indicate that systems other than the nervous system must be involved in this aspect of motor development.

Motor Milestones: The Pathway to Voluntary Movements

A **motor milestone** is a fundamental motor skill, the attainment of which is associated with the acquisition of later voluntary movements. The order in which an infant attains these milestones is relatively consistent, although the timing differs among individuals.

Compare the movements of a newborn with those of the same child 12 months later. Somehow, those spontaneous and reflexive movements give way to complex, coordinated, purposeful activities such as walking, reaching, and grasping. What happens to the infant in the intervening months? Clearly, the infant does not suddenly acquire a complex skill; rather, he must learn how to coordinate and control the many interacting parts of his body. He must attain certain fundamental skills that lead to skilled performance. We call these fundamental skills **motor milestones** (figure 4.5), and each one is a landmark or turning point in an individual's motor development. Think of them this way: To walk, you must be able to stand; to stand, you must be able to hold your trunk upright; and to hold your trunk upright, you must be able to hold your head erect. Each skill is associated with a preceding milestone. Individual infants vary in the time at which they reach a motor milestone, but they acquire these rudimentary skills in a relatively consistent sequence. Table 4.2 gives the timing and sequence of selected motor milestones.

Bayley (1936, 1969), Shirley (1931, 1963), and other researchers observed infants and determined a sequence of motor milestones as well as the average ages at which the infants

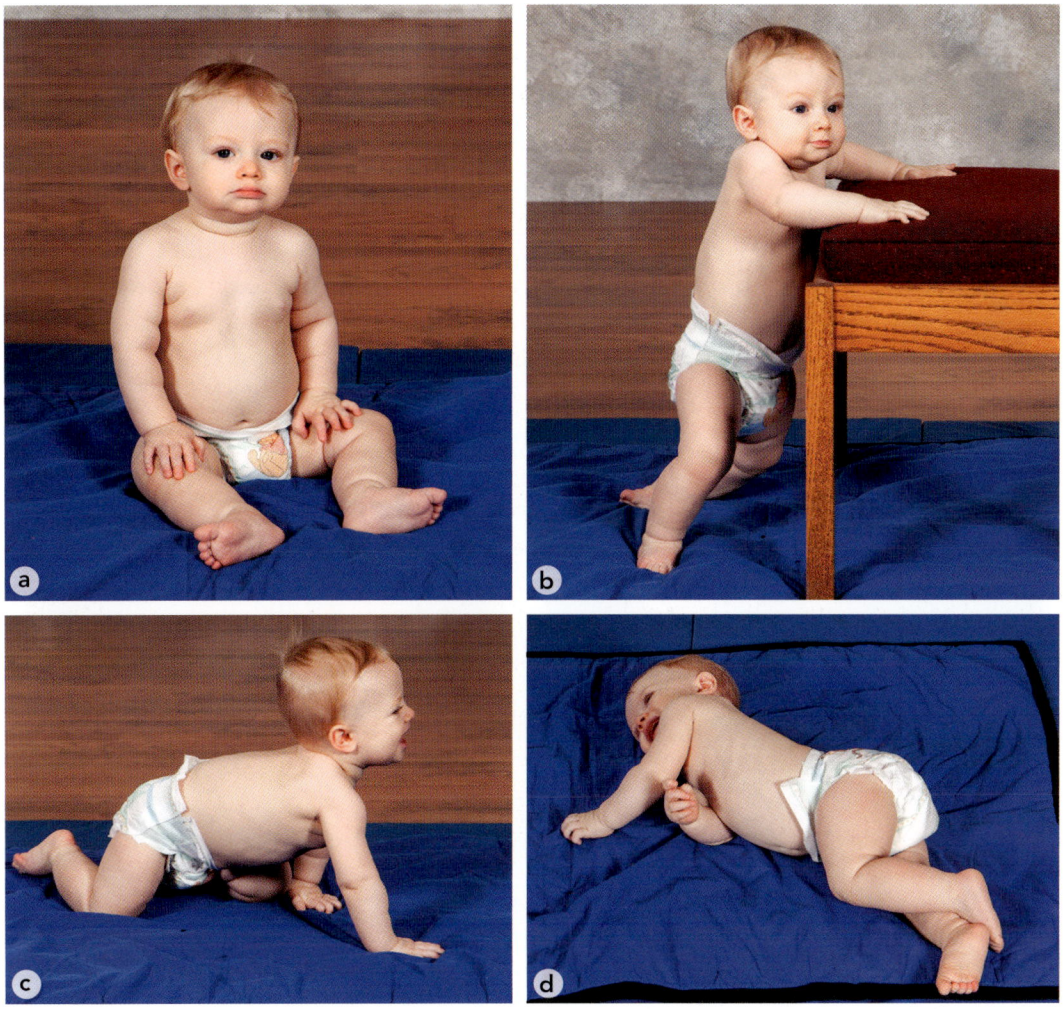

FIGURE 4.5 Some of the motor milestone skills: *(a)* sitting alone steadily, *(b)* standing up by furniture, *(c)* creeping, *(d)* rolling from back to front.

achieved them. This progressive pattern of skill acquisition can be related to predictable changes in individual constraints that occur in typically developing infants. These include

- maturation of the central nervous system,
- development of muscular strength and endurance,
- development of posture and balance, and
- improvement of sensory processing.

After reading this chapter, students may wonder whether the motor milestone research from Bayley and Shirley is still relevant. Haven't improvements in nutrition and child-rearing practices—as well as innovations in infant toys and equipment—led to quicker attainment of motor milestones? Or perhaps improvements in experimental methods and observation have resulted in more precise age-range windows? The World Health Organization (WHO) set out to answer these questions with its Multicentre Growth Reference Study (MGRS; de Onis et al., 2004, 2007; Wijnhoven et al., 2006; WHO Multicentre Growth Reference Study Group, 2006). The entire study involved six nations and thousands of children; for assessment of gross motor development, the group observed a total of 816 children from five countries (Ghana, India, Norway, Oman, and the United States). The groups focused on six motor milestones:

TABLE 4.2 Selected Motor Milestones

AVERAGE AGE (MO)	AGE RANGE (MO)	MILESTONE (BAYLEY SCALES OF INFANT DEVELOPMENT)	MILESTONE (SHIRLEY SEQUENCE)
0.1		Lifts head when held at shoulder	
0.1		Lateral head movements	
0.8	0.3–2.0	Arm thrusts in play	
0.8	0.3–2.0	Leg thrusts in play	Chin up (lifts head in prone)
0.8	0.3–3.0	Retains (i.e., grasps) red ring	
1.6	0.7–4.0	Head erect and steady	
1.8	0.7–5.0	Turns from side to back	
2.0			Chest up (lifts head and chest in prone position)
2.3	1.0–5.0	Sits with slight support	
4.0			Sits with support
4.4	2.0–7.0	Turns from back to side	
4.9	4.0–8.0	Partial thumb opposition	
5.0			Sits on lap; grasps object
5.3	4.0–8.0	Sits alone momentarily	
5.4	4.0–8.0	Unilateral reaching	
5.7	4.0–8.0	Rotates wrist	
6.0			Sits in chair; grasps dangling object
6.4	4.0–10.0	Rolls from back to front	
6.6	5.0–9.0	Sits alone steadily	
6.9	5.0–9.0	Complete thumb opposition	
7.0			Sits alone
7.1	5.0–11.0	Prewalking progression	
7.4	6.0–10.0	Partial finger prehension	
8.0			Stands with help
8.1	5.0–12.0	Pulls to standing	
8.6	6.0–12.0	Stands up by furniture	
8.8	6.0–12.0	Stepping movements	
9.0			Stands holding furniture
9.6	7.0–12.0	Walks with help	
10.0			Creeps
11.0	9.0–16.0	Stands alone	Walks when led
11.7	9.0–17.0	Walks alone	
12.0			Pulls to stand
14.0			Stands alone
14.6	11.0–20.0	Walks backward	
15.0			Walks alone
16.1	12.0–23.0	Walks up stairs with help	
16.4	13.0–23.0	Walks down stairs with help	
23.4	17.0–30.0+	Jumps off floor, both feet	
24.8	19.0–30.0+	Jumps from bottom step	

sitting without support, creeping, standing with assistance, walking with assistance, standing alone, and walking alone. Children were observed longitudinally from the age of 4 months until they could walk on their own. The fieldworkers making observations were highly trained, and high levels of interobserver reliability were set to ensure that all fieldworkers identified the milestones correctly and similarly.

What did the WHO Multicentre Growth Reference Study find in terms of age of attainment for the motor skills? The results for the 50th percentile ranking for the MGRS were remarkably similar to those found by Bayley in 1936 and within the ranges found by Shirley in 1963. The greatest discrepancies occurred in the earliest motor milestones; however, Bayley's average ages never differed from the ages found in the MGRS by more than 3 weeks. For example, the MGRS reported that the 50th percentile of infants sat without support at 5.9 months, whereas Bayley reported an average of 6.6 months and Shirley reported 7.0 months. Similarly, the MGRS reported that 50% of the infants attained the skill of standing with assistance at 7.4 months, whereas Shirley reported 8.0 months and Bayley reported 8.1 months. From this point on, however, the data from the MGRS and Bayley match closely. Shirley's average ages vary more and are always later than MGRS ages; however, her age ranges are still within the contemporary ranges found by the MGRS. Similar results were obtained by Darrah et al. (2014), using the Alberta Infant Motor Scale (AIMS), a Canadian norm-referenced instrument used to assess gross motor abilities (58 items) of infants (Piper & Darrah, 1994). Using the AIMS, they assessed 650 infants within the original age ranges to determine if the sequence of and age at emergence had changed over the course of 20 years. They found that the original percentile ranks remained the same for the new group, concluding that the normative values from 1994 were still valid.

What can we conclude from all this? First, based on the MGRS and AIMS studies, it appears that a secular trend in milestones does not exist. That is, infants are currently attaining motor milestones at about the same age as infants did more than 80 years ago. Second, the observation techniques that Bayley and Shirley used were both valid and reliable. Finally, we can still use the Bayley and Shirley scales with confidence that the age ranges represented indicate where typically developing infants should, on average, be.

Web Study Guide **Observe babies move in Lab Activity 4.2, Assessing Motor Milestones, in the web study guide.**

Constraints and the Attainment of Motor Milestones

Remember that individual constraints can act as rate limiters, or controllers. That is, for an infant to exhibit a certain skill, she needs to develop a certain system to a particular level. For example, in order to lift her head while lying on her belly, an infant must have sufficient strength in her neck and shoulders (figure 4.6). Because different systems advance earlier in some infants than in others, the rate of achievement of motor milestones varies. Experience and environmental constraints also play a role in individual variability (Adolph & Hoch, 2019; Adolph, Cole, & Vereijken, 2015). Infant development is also enculturated; that is, cultural norms shape social interactions between infants and others and guide parental child-rearing practices (Adolph & Hoch, 2019). In fact, culturally defined parental handling practices can alter the rate at which an infant attains motor milestones (Clark, 1995). For example, in an effort to reduce sudden infant death syndrome (SIDS), in 1992, the American Academy of Pediatrics recommended that infants be positioned on their sides or backs (called the Back for Sleep campaign). Although the campaign did reduce the incidence of SIDS, an unanticipated consequence was an increase in motor milestone delays (Jantz, Blosser, & Fruechting 1997; Davis, Moon, Sachs, & Ottolini, 1998; Pin, Eldridge, & Galea, 2007). In this case, the delays were not caused by disease or injury; rather, they emerged from a change in cultural practices for infant sleep position. Research has shown that these delays can be prevented by placing infants on their abdomens during waking hours, termed *tummy time*. The Eunice Kennedy Shriver National Institute of

Child Health and Human Development, as part of its Safe to Sleep campaign, recommends two or three short (3 to 5 minutes) daily sessions of tummy time for healthy infants. Tummy time works; infants who spend some of their waking time in prone positions acquire prone-specific milestones earlier than infants who do not (Kuo et al., 2008).

Recent research suggests that the attainment of certain milestones themselves can act as rate limiters for other skills. Corbetta and Bojczyk (2002) looked at the reaching and nonreaching movements and hand preferences of nine infants from the age of 3 weeks until the time they could walk independently. The most striking finding was that when the infants attained certain motor milestones—such as sitting, crawling, or walking—they changed their hand preference and even reverted back to an earlier form of reaching (with two hands). In the attainment of walking, the change back to two-hand reaching is likely the result of the infants' balance acting as a rate limiter; this type of reach is less likely to compromise the infants' newfound ability to walk. The fluctuation in hand preference provides more evidence to suggest that many interacting constraints influence the development of motor skills.

FIGURE 4.6 In order to crawl, an infant must first be able to lift her head and shoulders in a prone position, which requires neck and shoulder strength. Tummy time helps this milestone emerge.

Motor Milestones and Atypical Development

Because of their sequential nature, motor milestones may provide clues for trained professionals, such as doctors and physical therapists, about an infant's neurological health or potential for future diseases or disorders such as autism spectrum disorder (Hatakenaka, Ninomiya, Billstedt, Fernell, & Gillberg, 2016). For example, in a study of 173 high-risk preterm infants, Allen and Alexander (1994) evaluated six motor milestones on sequential visits to screen for cerebral palsy. They found they could predict cerebral palsy accurately when looking for a 37.5% delay on each of the six motor milestones on subsequent evaluations. This finding underscores two important points. First, the milestone sequence is fairly predictable in typically developing infants. Second, although variability exists in the acquisition of milestones, substantial delay in several milestones may indicate a developmental problem. The types of problems are

Norm-Referenced Versus Criterion-Referenced Scales

It is clearly necessary and beneficial to assess individual children and groups of children. Assessment can, for example, help professionals identify children who need special attention, chart individual and group progress, and choose appropriate educational tasks. Professionals must recognize, though, that testing instruments have specific purposes and are best used when the purpose matches a particular need. For instance, we can broadly classify testing instruments as either norm referenced or criterion referenced.

The purpose of norm-referenced scales is to compare an individual or group with previously established norms. Such a comparison indicates where a person falls in a group of like individuals matched on relevant factors, such as age, sex, and race. The value of norm-referenced scales in identifying slowly developing children is obvious; at the same time, such scales give professionals no information about the nature or cause of a delay or about what educational experiences to prescribe to facilitate future development.

Criterion-referenced scales indicate where a child falls on a continuum of skills that we know are acquired in sequence. The developmentalist administers the criterion-referenced scale periodically and compares individuals with their own previous performances rather than with a population norm. Often, criterion-referenced scales indicate what skills the individual has mastered and what skills are just emerging. Educators can prescribe education and practice activities based on those emerging skills, thus guaranteeing that the educational task is developmentally appropriate for the individual.

Most of the scales developed for infants are of the norm-referenced type. (Typically, more expertise is needed to administer a criterion-referenced scale than a norm-referenced scale.) The Bayley Scales of Infant Development, discussed in this chapter, are norm referenced (Bayley, 1969). The complete Bayley Scales consist of a mental scale (163 items), a motor scale (81 items), and a behavior record for social and attentional behaviors. Users of these scales can compare infants and toddlers from 2 months to 2.5 years with mental and motor norms.

Another well-known norm-referenced scale is the Denver Developmental Screening Test (Frankenburg & Dodds, 1967). This test can be used from birth to 6 years of age to assess four areas:

1. Gross motor performance (31 items)
2. Fine motor performance (30 items)
3. Language development (21 items)
4. Personal–social skills (representing age-appropriate social skills; 22 items)

A third well-known norm-referenced scale is the Gesell Developmental Schedules (Gesell & Amatruda, 1949). All these instruments are well standardized, but their motor scales are less reliable and valid than is desirable. In this sense they are useful but limited in the information they provide about motor development.

not necessarily limited to the motor domain. In their systematic review of research related to motor milestones and the risk of adult schizophrenia, Filatova et al. (2018), found that delays in walking unsupported, standing unsupported, and sitting unsupported were all significantly associated with adult schizophrenia risk.

Other conditions can lead to differences in the onset of motor milestones. For example, early in development, infants with Down syndrome often experience hypotonia, which is best described as a lack of muscle tone. In fact, infants with Down syndrome have been characterized as "floppy." Hypotonia often improves later in development. However, this lack of muscle tone usually results in delayed acquisition of motor milestones, such as grasping, sitting, rolling, and pulling to stand, throughout infancy (Jobling & Virji-Babul, 2004). Because these milestones require a certain degree of strength, hypotonia can be considered a rate-limiting factor in their acquisition. Furthermore, infants acquire many of these milestones in a sequence that leads to the ability to maintain an upright posture. Therefore, delays in milestones lead to delays in the attainment of fundamental motor skills, such as walking, and activities of daily living, such as eating (Reid & Block, 1996; Ulrich, Ulrich, & Collier, 1992).

Because infant mobility appears to be important to early development, any condition that delays or impedes infant mobility may negatively affect cognitive and perceptual development (Galloway, Rhu, & Agrawal, 2008). Motor development and early movement influence social, perceptual, and cognitive development (Babik, Galloway, & Lobo, 2017). For example, an infant begins to explore his environment by reaching and grasping objects; this allows for a human–object interface that involves multiple sensory systems (e.g., vision, tactile, and, if the object is placed in the infant's mouth, taste; Lobo, Kokkoni, De Campos, & Galloway, 2015). Such movements help create neural pathways in the brain, which are critical in the first 3 years of life (Kail & Cavanaugh, 2017; Ulrich et al., 1992). If infants are significantly delayed in these experiences, they will miss out on some or all of these opportunities to learn to integrate sensory information (Babik et al., 2017; Ulrich, Lloyd, Tiernan, Looper, & Angulo-Barroso, 2008). Part of this learning is discovering cause–effect relationships in their surroundings. Further, independent locomotion provides infants and toddlers with a way to control and explore their environments as well as an opportunity to interact socially (Adolph, Rachwani, & Hoch, 2018; Adolph & Robinson, 2015; Lynch, Rhu, Agrawal, & Galloway, 2009). Therefore, delayed acquisition of motor skills can have a far more profound effect than simply the inability to move; it can influence the entire developmental process, leading to greater cognitive disabilities than would exist if the same child had had movement opportunities (Ulrich et al., 2008).

If you were a physical therapist, what types of delays would you expect to see if you were working with infants who had low muscle tone or muscle spasticity? Consider how the delay in one milestone would affect later milestones.

Web Study Guide **Use a criterion-referenced scale to assess toddlers in Lab Activity 4.3, Assessing Toddler Motor Behavior, in the web study guide.**

Development of Postural Control and Balance in Infancy

Many of the motor milestones of the first year of life involve the attainment of certain postures, of which sitting and standing are the most obvious examples. Once infants can maintain a posture, they are balancing. As a result, developmentalists have been interested in whether postural control and balance make up the rate-limiting system in the onset of certain milestone skills. They have also been interested in whether infants rely on the same cues for balance that adults do.

Some evidence shows that newborns make postural adjustments of the head in response to a visual display of optical flow, or the change in optic patterns that occurs while one moves (Jouen, 1990; Jouen, Lepecq, Gapenne, & Bertenthal, 2000). This finding might indicate that the rate-controlling factor is not the perception of optical flow but rather the making of appropriate postural responses. Researchers have studied this question using the moving-room technique (figure 4.7). Pope (1984) held infants in a seated position on a stationary platform and observed their muscular responses through electromyograph recordings when the walls and ceiling of the small room surrounding them were moved. The effect was to provide visual information that made it seem as if the body, not the room, were moving, while kinesthetic information from the vestibular and somatosensory receptors indicated that the body was not moving. Thus, the visual information and the kinesthetic information were in conflict. The 2-month-olds reacted to the visual information rather than the kinesthetic information. That is, they responded as if their bodies were swaying and activated muscle to regain their starting posture.

Bertenthal, Rose, and Bai (1997) observed 5-, 7-, 9-, and 13-month-olds sitting in a moving room when the room moved at two different speeds. This age span included some infants who could sit alone and some who could not. The investigators found that all the infants, even those not yet capable of sitting alone, responded to room movement (they believed the visual information more than the kinesthetic information), and their action was linked to the movement speed. Investigators also observed that infants' responses improved with sitting experience; those with experience made postural responses sooner, more accurately, and more consistently.

When infants who have just begun standing are placed in a moving room, they often sway, stagger, or fall—unlike adults, who can keep their balance (Bertenthal & Bai, 1989; Butterworth & Hicks, 1977; Lee & Aronson, 1974; Woollacott & Sveistrup, 1994). Newly standing children take longer than adults to use their postural muscles when thrown off balance and sway more before attaining stability (Forssberg & Nashner, 1982). The moving-room effect diminishes in children after their first year of standing.

More recently, Chen, Jeka, and Clark (2016) used a virtual moving room to examine the dynamic relationship between vision and posture throughout infancy. They observed 20 infants who were divided into four groups based on their developmental status (sitting onset, standing alone, walking onset, and 1 year postwalking), placing them in a virtual moving-room environment where the room appeared to move at different frequencies and distances. Infants in the sitting-onset group—the least developmentally advanced—had difficulty controlling their postural sway in response to the changing visual stimuli. The remaining groups demonstrated the ability to match their posture to visual stimuli, suggesting that sensory reweighting occurs

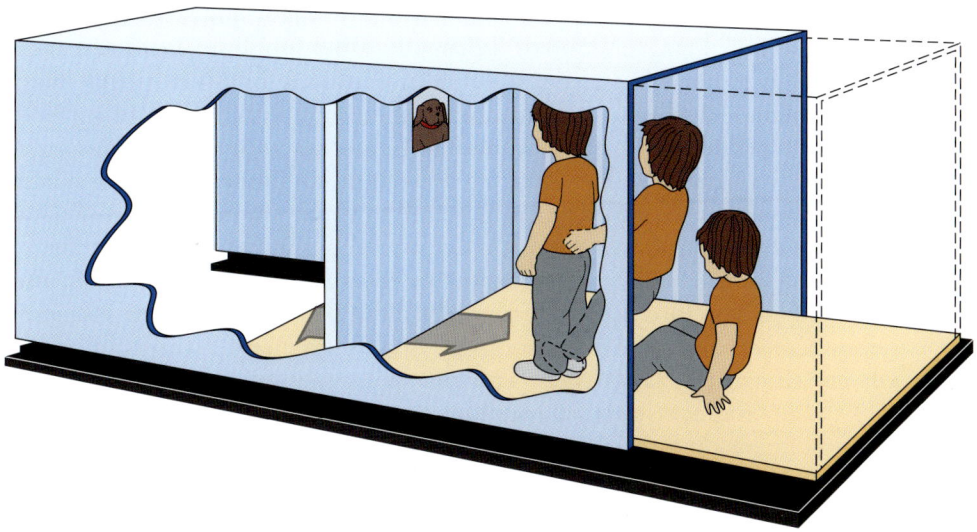

FIGURE 4.7 A moving room. In this drawing, the small "room" (made up of four walls and a ceiling) is moved toward the child, and the child falls backward. This response would occur if the child perceived the optical flow produced by the room movement as forward sway rather than as room movement.
Reprinted from Bertenthal, Rose, and Bai (1997).

soon after infants gain the ability to sit. It seems, then, that visual perception of self-motion is not the rate-controlling factor in infant posture and balance. Rather, the rate-controlling factor may be a *coupling* of the sensory information with the appropriate motor response. The refinement of this coupling occurs for every task, such as sitting and standing. This view is consistent with research on the neurological system, suggesting that vision must be linked to specific motor response loci (Goodale, 1988; Milner & Goodale, 1995). Once refined, these perception–action couplings provide very sensitive and rapid adjustments to the environment. As infants move, their environments change. As the environments change, infants must regulate and refine their movements based on continuous sensory information. In other words, infants must continuously calibrate their sensorimotor coupling (Chen, Metcalfe, Jeka, & Clark, 2007; Metcalfe et al., 2005). As systems develop and change, the sensorimotor coupling must change as well, requiring a recalibration to the environment.

Barela, Jeka, and Clark (1999) observed touch control in infants as they reached four important stages: pulling to stand, standing alone, beginning to walk, and reaching 1.5 months of walking experience. As the infants acquired standing experience, both their body sway and the force they applied to a nearby contact surface decreased. In the first three of these stages (pulling to stand, standing alone, and beginning to walk), the infants responded to body sway by applying force to the surface. After the infants gained walking experience, they used the touch information to control posture rather than simply react to sway. Somatosensory information certainly plays an important role in posture and balance. Infant research has established the important role of perceptual information from the various systems in actions that maintain our posture and balance, and more research is needed on how these various sources of information are integrated in the maintenance of posture and balance.

Summary and Synthesis

A newborn infant moves in a variety of ways. She may kick her legs and wave her arms in a seemingly random fashion; we call these spontaneous movements or stereotypies. She may also respond to a touch with a specific movement pattern; these responses are called infantile reflexes. During the first year she will begin to lift her head and sit alone. Such skills, which appear in a fairly well-defined sequence, are called motor milestones. She will sit, crawl, and stand, all of which demand postural control. In a typically developing infant, these motor behaviors come forward in a relatively predictable sequence and time frame, owing to rapidly changing individual constraints (both structural and functional). Infants do differ in the sequence and timing of these behaviors, however. The difference may simply indicate that for this particular infant, the interactions between individual, environmental, and task constraints encourage motor behaviors in a unique way. On the other hand, some infants may have some underlying condition, such as cerebral palsy or Down syndrome, that leads to a delay in the attainment of motor milestones.

What do the movements we see during infancy tell us about the infant himself? Developmentalists still debate the purpose of reflexes and spontaneous movements. However, several things are becoming clear. First, these movement patterns are not random; rather, they are coordinated (if not purposeful). Second, early movement patterns play some role in future movement, most likely creating the foundations of future movements. In any case, we cannot separate early movements from later skills. The infant's experiences—along with his physical characteristics, the environment, parental handling, and other constraints acting in the context of his infancy—all interact in the development of movement skills.

Reinforcing What You Have Learned About Constraints

TAKE A SECOND LOOK

Referring back to the anecdote about babies and walking at the start of the chapter, some people may ask, "Doesn't that just happen naturally?" Others may wonder why a person interested in teaching kindergarten through 12th grade or rehabilitating adults would study infancy at all. Two important reasons exist. First, infant motor behavior appears to form the basis of later voluntary behavior, as shown by a variety of researchers, such as Thelen and colleagues. Second, a positive relationship appears to exist between motor and cognitive behavior. As Cole Galloway, a researcher who studies infant mobility, explained about infancy, "As soon as you're reaching, as soon as you're walking, your cognition explodes." (Wolf, 2007) For infants and children who are developing atypically, observing developmental delays early on may allow for early intervention and a reduction in later deficits. Therefore, it is important to understand infant development because infancy provides an important piece of the motor development puzzle.

TEST YOUR KNOWLEDGE

1. For four of the infantile reflexes listed in table 4.1, describe either a survival function or a purpose later in life.
2. Consider the individual, environmental, and task constraints interacting during infancy, then give several reasons why an infant might be delayed in attaining a motor milestone.
3. Describe how both task and environmental constraints can have a profound effect on the emergence of motor skills.
4. On what perceptual system do young infants seem to rely for balance information?

LEARNING EXERCISE 4.1

Identifying Constraints During Infancy and Toddlerhood

The attainment of a milestone indicates a unique interaction of various constraints that allow the particular behavior to emerge. The rate at which motor milestones appear (and to a certain extent, the type of milestone) for one infant can differ from that for other infants. This suggests that particular constraints may act as rate limiters, or controllers, for a given infant and that when a critical value of that rate limiter is at last reached, the infant will achieve the motor milestone or skill.

One of the best ways to observe constraints in action is to watch a group of infants whose ages vary. Visit a local infant center and carefully observe the infants as their caretakers interact with them. Given your knowledge of infant development from this chapter, make a list of the constraints that affect the motor behavior of individual infants. Find individual, environmental, and task constraints in the context of the infant center. For individual constraints, explain which might act as rate limiters for motor milestones. For environmental and task constraints, explain how these either encourage or discourage different motor behaviors.

5

Development of Human Locomotion

CHAPTER OBJECTIVES

This chapter

- defines the concept of locomotion in humans,
- describes the types of locomotion,
- discusses the development of specific locomotor patterns, and
- explains the individual constraints that affect development of locomotor patterns.

Motor Development in the Real World

Senior Runners Say, "Catch Us If You Can!"

In early 2018, the USA Track and Field Masters Indoor Championships in Landover, Maryland, hosted a wide variety of athletes aged 30 years and older. Although any such event may provide record times, this meet had two world records set in the 60 m dash that were notable because the record holders' combined age was 202 years. In the women's 100-plus age group, Julia "Hurricane" Hawkins, at 102 years, set a new world record by finishing in a time of 24.79 seconds (Boren, 2018). She added this to her world record time in the 100-meter dash set at the same event in 2017 in her native Baton Rouge, Louisiana. This is quite an achievement for a runner who began her competitive career at age 100. Orville Rogers, who is relatively youthful at 100 years old, set a world record in the men's 100-plus 60-meter dash by finishing in 19.13 seconds (cruising ahead of the competition by several seconds). In addition to this record, Rogers also set a record in the 400-meter run with a time of 4:16.90. Compared with Hawkins, Rogers, who was a World War II bomber pilot, had a full 50 years of running experience, taking up the activity when he was 50 years old. Before turning 100, Rogers held seven world records in the 95- to 99-year-old bracket. Together these and other masters athletes demonstrate that getting older does not automatically mean slowing down, and for some athletes, it means being the fastest in the world!

People interested in motor development often focus on early acquisition of locomotor skills. Our introduction demonstrates, however, that locomotion is a lifelong movement activity. Changes do, of course, occur in walking, running, galloping, and other motor skills as individual, environmental, and task constraints change. This chapter examines various locomotor skills across the life span, how they change systematically, and how individual constraints act as rate controllers.

Locomotion is the act of moving from place to place.

Locomotion is the act of moving, or the capability to move, from place to place. Moving around, getting from here to there: Locomotion is something we do each day without much thought at all. However, this seemingly simple definition may hide the fact that moving from place to place is actually a complex activity that involves many interacting systems and constraints. The study of locomotion falls within many fields, from medicine to psychology, and includes many movements, from squirming to swimming. Across the life span, individuals use various methods of locomotion. Of course, the type of locomotion they use depends on interacting constraints. During the childhood years, height, weight, and lengths change dramatically and may act as rate controllers. During much of the life span, other types of constraints, such as motivation or even the perceived gender association of a skill (e.g., "skipping is for girls"), may encourage or discourage behavior. As one approaches old age, structural constraints such as physical characteristics may return as important rate controllers. However, functional constraints, such as fear of falling or loss of balance capability, may act just as strongly to discourage locomotion, as can environmental constraints, such as weather changes (e.g., snow and ice). As a result, we must examine many changing constraints to understand locomotion across the life span.

The First Voluntary Locomotor Efforts: Creeping and Crawling

What does it take for an infant to move from one place to another for the first time? Certain motor milestones must be achieved, such as lifting the head in the prone position. The infant must also have enough strength to support and move himself and must uncouple his limbs, which have primarily moved in unison and in the same direction. In addition to these individual constraints, the environment must allow for infant locomotion, and the infant must evaluate the environment to see how well it matches his or her individual constraints. Adolph (1997) suggests that the environment must afford the infant several things:

> The surface must provide a continuous path to support the body, must be large enough to allow passage as the body moves forward, must be sturdy enough to support body weight, and must be firm enough, flat enough, and have sufficient friction to maintain balance as weight shifts from limb to limb. (p. 6)

Certain systems act as rate limiters, or controllers, that hold an infant back from the initiation of locomotion. Once critical levels are reached in these systems, an infant can begin to move. The first types of locomotion that infants exhibit are usually **creeping** (moving on hands and knees) (figure 5.1) and **crawling** (moving on hands and stomach, in a "combat crawl"). The following progression of skills leads to creeping and crawling:

1. Crawling with the chest and stomach on the floor
2. Low creeping with the stomach off the floor but the legs working together (symmetrically)
3. Rocking back and forth in the high creep position
4. Creeping with the legs and arms working alternately

Creeping and **crawling** occur when all four limbs are in contact with the supporting surface. In crawling, the infant's chest and stomach also touch the surface. In creeping, only the hands and knees touch the surface.

Although not typically seen, another form of quadrupedal gait exists in infants: walking on hands and feet. Burton (1999) reviewed the work of Hrdlicka, who published a book in 1931 called *Children Who Run on All Fours*, and interpreted it using a dynamic systems approach. He concluded that the emergence of this gait pattern resulted from infrequently occurring interactions between constraints. First, environmental constraints related to crawling surface may make knee support uncomfortable (e.g., gravel, asphalt); thus, the infant changes to feet support. Next, the reinforcement or response of the parent or caregiver may encourage further use of this gait. Finally, average- or above-average strength and health of the infant must interact with these environmental factors to allow the hands-and-feet gait pattern to appear. Because these factors (and perhaps others that haven't been explored) often do not exist and interact to encourage the hands-and-feet gait pattern, we hardly ever see "running on all fours" in infants.

FIGURE 5.1 Infant creeping. Balance and strength must be sufficient for infants to support themselves, first on three limbs and eventually on one arm and the opposite leg.

Transitioning From Crawling to Walking

Toward the end of the first year, infants become expert crawlers with the ability to quickly and efficiently navigate their environments (Kretch & Adolph, 2013; Adolph & Tamis-LeMonda, 2014). Yet skilled crawlers transition from this well-learned mode of transportation to become novice walkers. Research has shown that the affordances infants had while crawling do not automatically transfer to walking. For example, in a laboratory setting, novice walkers placed themselves in harm's way, attempting to walk over cliffs, inclines, and drop-offs that they carefully avoided as crawlers (Adolph & Tamis-LeMonda, 2014). Still, they persist, as walking ultimately allows them to go, see, play, and interact more. This provides a rich array of physical, cognitive, and social experiences that further infants' overall development (Adolph & Robinson, 2013).

Walking Across the Life Span

Walking is defined by a 50% phasing relationship between the legs as well as a period of double support (when both feet are on the ground) followed by a period of single support.

Typically, a developing human can look forward to a long career as a walker. It's easy to assume that once people can walk, they won't change their walking technique much over the life span. As with other motor behaviors, however, people continually change the way they walk as constraints change. What remains the same across one's lifetime is the underlying timing of **walking**, which is 50% phasing between the legs (Clark, Whitall, & Phillips, 1988). In other words, individuals alternate their legs so that the left leg is halfway through its motion as the right leg begins its own. Also, there is a period of double support, when both feet contact the ground, followed by a period of single support. These are the relative timing relationships (coordination) that appear early in life, and they don't seem to change much (Clark, 1995). However, as an individual's body or the environment changes, the absolute timing (i.e., slower or faster) and placement (i.e., step height or length) can change substantially.

Imagine you are a parent. What sort of rate controllers might keep your crawling infant from creeping?

▶ **KEY POINT** After infancy, most humans move from place to place using upright bipedal locomotion. A particular pattern of locomotion is called a gait. Upright bipedal gait patterns include walking, running, galloping, skipping, and hopping.

First Steps: Characteristics of Early Walking

Most people—especially parents—know what a toddler's first solo steps look like. In fact, researchers have studied and described these first steps (Adolph, Vereijken, & Shrout, 2003; Burnett & Johnson, 1971; Clark et al., 1988; Sutherland, Olshen, Cooper, & Woo, 1980). At first, each step tends to be independent of the next. The toddler takes short steps with little leg and hip extension. She steps with flat feet and points her toes outward. The toddler spreads her feet wide apart when planted to improve her lateral balance. She doesn't use any trunk rotation. The toddler holds her arms up in high guard; that is, her hands and arms are carried high in a bent position (Adolph, Rachwani, & Hoch, 2018). All of the characteristics in early walking lead to improved balance for the new walker (figure 5.2, *a* and *b*). As the child continues to develop, her arms will drop to about waist level (middle guard) and later to an extended position at the sides (low guard; figure 5.2*c*), but they still will not swing. When children do begin to use the arm swing, it frequently is unequal and irregular; both hands might swing forward together (Roberton, 1978b, 1984).

▶ **KEY POINT** Rate limiters in early walking are muscular strength and balance.

Rate Limiters in Early Walking

Infants have the ability to move their legs in an alternating pattern from birth onward, yet they cannot walk for at least 7 months after birth. Clearly, several individual constraints must

FIGURE 5.2 *(a)* A beginning walker. Note the short stride and high-guard arm position. *(b)* To maintain balance, beginning walkers often plant their feet wide apart, with the toes out. *(c)* Rather than swing the arms in time with the legs, beginning walkers often hold their arms in high-, middle-, or low-guard position.

© Mary Ann Roberton and Kate R. Barrett.

develop to certain critical levels before the infant can support and move his own weight. His legs must be able to move alternately, and he must have enough strength to support himself on a single limb. He must also balance on one leg while transferring his weight to his other foot. These requirements suggest specific rate-controlling factors. Thelen, Ulrich, and Jensen (1989) suggest that infants must have muscle strength in the trunk and extensor muscles to allow them to maintain an upright posture on a small base of support. They must also develop balance, or an erect posture or body position, to the point where they can compensate for the shift of weight from one leg to the other (Adolph et al., 2018; Adolph et al., 2003; Clark & Phillips, 1993; Clark et al., 1988).

Addressing Atypical Walking Development in Down Syndrome

As we mention in chapter 4, children with Down syndrome often experience delays in motor milestones. The cascading effect of delayed early milestones leads to delayed onset of walking, sometimes significantly. As part of a series of studies investigating the use of a treadmill intervention to promote earlier onset of walking, Ulrich, Ulrich, Angulo-Kinzler, and Yun (2001) examined a group of infants with Down syndrome. On average, infants began the study at 10 months of age (±1.5 months) and began participating when they could sit independently for 30 seconds. All participants received physical therapy that infants with Down syndrome typically receive. In addition, the intervention infants received in-home practice stepping on a small motorized treadmill. During the intervention, the parents held the infants over the treadmill, which moved at 0.46 mile per hour. If the infants did not step, the parents repositioned them. This process was performed for 8 minutes a day (starting at 1 minute of intervention followed by 1 minute of rest) 5 days per week until the infant began walking independently. Further, the research team visited participants on a biweekly basis and carefully monitored motor development and growth.

The results indicated that the experimental protocol was successful. Before walking independently the intervention group could rise to a standing position as well as walk with assistance sooner than the control group could (the former not significant at $p = .09$ and the latter difference significant at $p = .03$). In addition, the group with treadmill training learned to walk with assistance sooner and to walk independently significantly sooner (at 19.9 months vs. at 23.9 months) than the control group. The researchers concluded that the treadmill intervention was successful in encouraging the emergence of independent walking in this sample of infants with Down syndrome.

Imagine you are a parent. What environmental or task constraints might limit the rate at which walking develops in your infant?

Observing Motor Skill Performance

An instructor of motor skills must be able to critically observe children's skill patterns. The instructor needs to give students feedback, provide further practice experiences, and formally assess their skills. The observation process requires a disciplined, systematic focus on the critical features of a skill pattern rather than on the outcome, or product, of a skill. The observer must learn observation techniques and practice them like any other skill in order to make them automatic.

Barrett (1979) provided a guide for improving the observation skills of instructors and coaches based on three principles:

1. Analysis
2. Planning
3. Positioning

To analyze developmental movement, the observer must first know the developmental sequences of the skill, including the critical features that characterize a given developmental step and the mechanical principles involved in proficient performance.

Observers must also organize and plan their observations in order to prevent their attention from wandering once activity begins. They may find it helpful to have written observation guidelines, many of which can be based on the developmental sequences suggested by researchers. One can, however, design suitable observation guidelines by simply listing the critical features of the skill to be watched. It might also be a good idea for observers to watch a given feature of a skill many times (two or three tries, or more).

The third principle is positioning. Many new observers rivet themselves to one location and attempt to watch everything from there. However, some critical features of motor skills can be seen only from the side; others are best seen from the front or back. It is important, then, for the observer to move about and to watch the performer from several angles.

The process of motor skill observation demands focused attention. New observers must plan ahead, know the critical features of the skill to be watched, position themselves properly, and practice observing.

You can see the key features that distinguish developmental levels by simply watching skill performance, but often there is a need to conduct a more formal assessment. Teachers, therapists, and researchers typically need to record an individual's development level in order to track progress, design activities, or make comparisons. Conducting a more formal assessment requires several tools:

- A description of the movements and positions that are characteristic of each step in a developmental sequence
- A plan for observing movement so that an individual can be quickly and accurately placed into a developmental step or level
- A recording sheet so that observations can be quickly recorded for future use

These tools are provided for many of the fundamental motor skills discussed in the next several chapters. A developmental sequence table lists the developmental steps as well as a description of the movements or positions characteristic of each step. They are organized by a body component, such as the legs or arms, or by a phase of the skill, such as the backswing. An observation plan follows. For each component, the observation plan directs you, by means of a question, to watch for one specific movement or position at a time. By indicating what you observe, you move through the observation plan until you arrive at the performer's developmental level. This information can be placed on a record sheet, much like the ones used in the lab activities for chapters 5 through 7.

Proficient Walking Patterns

Part of becoming a proficient walker involves taking advantage of the principles of motion and stability discussed in chapter 3. For example, new walkers optimize balance by widening their stance, which increases their base of support. However, stability is not always desirable, especially because it comes at the expense of mobility. Thus, once an infant's balance improves, she must decrease her base of support to become more mobile. Many of the characteristics of proficient walking relate to exploiting biomechanical principles as body dimensions change—in other words, recalibrating the body to the environment. Consider these developmental changes in walking that lead to a proficient level:

- Absolute stride length increases, reflecting greater application of force and greater leg extension at push-off. Also, as children grow, increased leg length contributes to a longer stride.
- Planting the foot flat on the ground changes to a heel-then-forefoot pattern, which results from an increased range of motion.
- The individual reduces out-toeing and narrows the base of support laterally to keep the forces exerted in the forward–backward plane.
- The skilled walker adopts the **double knee-lock** pattern to assist the full range of leg motion. In this pattern, the knee extends at heel strike, flexes slightly as the body weight moves forward over the supporting leg, and then extends once more at foot push-off. Because the knee extends twice in one step cycle, we call this pattern a double knee-lock.
- The pelvis rotates to allow the full range of leg motion and oppositional movement of the upper and lower body segments.
- Balance improves, and forward trunk inclination is reduced.
- The skilled walker coordinates oppositional arm swing (with the arms extending at the sides) with the movement of the legs. This pattern is consistent with the principle of action and reaction; that is, the opposite arm and leg move forward and back in unison. The arm swing must become relaxed and move from the shoulder, with a slight accompanying movement at the elbow.

Developmental Changes in Walking During Early Childhood

Children usually achieve developmental changes in walking by an early age; by age 4, most children have the essential ingredients of an advanced walk (Sutherland, 1997). Adolph and her colleagues provide an excellent overview of the development of infant walking in a 2003 paper, aptly titled "What Changes in Infant Walking and Why." Children exhibit pelvic rotation at an average age of 13.8 months, knee flexion at midsupport at 16.3 months, foot contact within a trunk-width base of support at 17.0 months, synchronous arm swing at 18.0 months, and heel-then-forefoot strike at 18.5 months (Burnett & Johnson, 1971). The length of time for which one foot supports body weight while the other swings forward increases, especially from 1.0 years to 2.5 years of age (Sutherland et al., 1980).

Stride length increases throughout midadolescence, partly because of the fuller range of motion at the hips, knees, and ankles and partly because of the increase in leg length resulting from growth. The velocity of the walk also increases, especially between 1.0 and 3.5 years of age (Sutherland et al., 1980). The rhythm and coordination of a child's walk improve observably until age 5 or so, but beyond this age, pattern improvements are subtle and probably not detectable by the novice observer.

Developmental Changes in Walking During Older Adulthood

We do not wish to imply that no development occurs between early childhood and older adulthood. However, the changes that do occur represent individual (rather than universal) differences, as discussed in chapter 1. Individuals may change their walking patterns over time because of weight gain or loss, changes in strength or balance, injury, or gait training. Any of these changes will change the constraint interactions during walking. Therefore, we cannot make generalizations about any specific developmental trends in walking in the late teens or early 20s. As for middle adulthood, we cannot predict developmental changes for these years as we can for early childhood because change is individualized and based on changing individual constraints. As individuals enter older age, they will again tend to change in a more predictable way as certain individual constraints tend to change more (figure 5.3). Again, the changes in walking patterns seen in older adults represent a recalibration to the environment and the task based on changes in individual constraints.

A number of research studies have focused on walking patterns in adults over 60 years old. Murray and coworkers (Murray, Drought, & Kory, 1964; Murray, Kory, Clarkson, & Sepic, 1966; Murray, Kory, & Sepic, 1970) conducted a series of studies on gait patterns in older men and women in which they measured the linear and rotary displacements and the velocity of the limbs during walking. They found that the older men walked in a pattern similar to that of younger men but with these differences:

- Step length of the older men was approximately 3 cm shorter.
- Older men toed out approximately 3° more than younger men.
- Older men had a reduced degree of ankle extension.
- Pelvic rotation was diminished in older men.

Similarly, older women showed greater out-toeing, shorter stride length, and less pelvic rotation than younger women. These results have been found in other, more recent research studies as well (Jerome et al., 2015; Ko, Ling, Winters, & Ferrucci, 2009; Ko, Stenholm, Metter, & Ferrucci, 2012).

Another common finding is that older adults walk more slowly than younger adults (Drillis, 1961; Gabel, Johnston, & Crowninshield, 1979; Jerome et al., 2015; Molen, 1973). Schwanda (1978) confirmed the finding of a shorter stride length among older men and further demon-

FIGURE 5.3 Walking patterns in adulthood tend to change as a result of changing individual constraints.
Maskot/Getty Images

strated that most other aspects of the walking pattern (stride rate, swing time of the recovering leg, time of support, and vertical displacement of center of gravity) remain similar to those of middle-aged men.

You may recall that new walkers also had greater out-toeing and a shorter stride length to assist in balance. Could balance be the reason older adults demonstrate similar movement characteristics? That possibility exists because balance can be affected by the aging process. On the other hand, researchers have associated some of these changes with differences in walking speed. When younger adults walk slowly, they too shorten their strides and decrease joint rotation (Craik, 1989; Winter, 1983). Gabell and Nayak (1984) observed walking in a group of 32 older adults, aged 66 to 84 years, who were selected from a group of 1,187. (The researchers repeatedly screened members of the large group for various types of pathology in order to select the small healthy group.) They found no significant differences between walking patterns of the 32 older adults and those of younger adults. Thus, some of the changes in older adults' movement patterns might relate to disease and injury in the various body tissues, especially those that result in loss of muscle strength. Even so, these and other studies (Adrian, 1982) indicate that the changes in older adults' walking patterns are minor.

▶ **KEY POINT** Rate controllers in walking during older adulthood may be caused by factors such as disuse and fear of falling and therefore may be altered and improved.

Rate Controllers in Later Walking

Any of the changes associated with the aging process can act as rate controllers in the task of walking. Structural constraints may result from osteoarthritis in the joints or from a decline in muscle mass. However, as noted previously, older adults do not necessarily change their gait in a drastic way. A disease state must progress to a critical level before it will discourage all walking. More often, older adults modify their gait to accommodate pain or changes in balance. Functional constraints, such as balance and fear, can also affect walking patterns. Often, two types of individual constraints will interact and their sum will act as a rate controller. If older adults fall, they may develop a fear of falling. That fear of falling results in a gait designed to assist with balance (wide base of support, short step length). If these factors are combined with pain from osteoarthritis, older adults may be less inclined to walk long distances. Unfortunately, a decrease in walking (and other physical activities) leads to a decrease in muscle mass and flexibility, which in turn affects walking patterns. What results is a sequence of events that eventually discourages walking—a sequence that can be altered if one or several individual constraints are actively manipulated.

Running Across the Life Span

Picture this scenario: You leave your house late and must rush to catch the bus to get to class. As you approach the bus stop, you notice the bus pulling away from the curb. What do you do? This is not a trick question; of course you run to catch the bus. Humans often run when they need to get from one place to another quickly. **Running** is a more advanced motor skill than walking, but the two motor patterns have many similar features. For example, in both patterns an individual's legs move symmetrically but in an alternating pattern with each other. Walking and running also have distinct differences. Walking has a period of double support when both feet are in contact with the ground. This never occurs in running; in fact, running has a flight phase, during which neither foot is on the ground.

Running, like walking, has a 50% phasing relationship between the legs. Unlike walking, running has a period of flight, during which neither foot is in contact with the ground.

Children typically start to run about 6 to 7 months after they begin to walk (Clark & Whitall, 1989b; Whitall & Getchell, 1995). Remember, for a gait to be considered a run it must include a flight phase. That means an infant's earliest attempts to run are actually fast walks. Infants running for the first time may exhibit some of the characteristics of an early walk, even though the infant no longer uses these characteristics in her walk (Burnett & Johnson, 1971). When first learning to run, the child may adopt a wide base of support, a flat-footed landing, leg extension at midsupport, and the high-guard arm position. This regression probably reflects an attempt by the child to simplify the task (e.g., by eliminating the arm swing) until she acquires more experience. As the child practices the running stride and gets used to its balance demands, she will put the swing back into the movement pattern.

Characteristics of Early Running

Imagine toddlers attempting to run for the first time. All prior attempts at upright locomotion involved at least one limb on the ground at all times. Now they must propel themselves into the air with one leg and then catch themselves with the other. For a toddler, this feat takes tremendous strength and balance.

Early characteristics of running reflect the changes in speed (task constraint) between walking and running (see table 5.1 for the developmental sequence). Some of these characteristics are pictured in figure 5.4*a*. Notice the leg action. You see a brief period of flight, but the legs still have a limited range of motion. The rear leg does not extend fully as the child pushes off the ground. As the swinging leg comes forward, the recovering thigh moves with enough acceleration that the knee bends but without too much acceleration, which would carry the thigh to a position parallel to the ground at the end of the leg swing. Therefore, the range of motion is limited and the stride length is short.

Next, examine the arm swing and note the opposition of the arms to the legs. The arms swing to accompany the trunk's rotation rather than drive forward and back as they would in a skilled sprinter's movement. The elbows extend when they swing back, which is unnecessary movement; the arms swing out slightly to the side, wasting energy. Beginning runners sometimes swing their arms horizontally, across the body, rather than forward and back, probably to aid their unsteady balance.

TABLE 5.1 Hypothesized Developmental Sequence for Running

SEQUENCE	ACTION
	LEG ACTION
Step 1	Minimal flight. The running step is short and flat-footed. On the recovery swing forward, the leg is rather stiff.
Step 2	Crossover swing. The stride is long, and the knee of the recovery leg flexes to at least a right angle. The leg action, though, has lateral movements wherein the legs swing out and in during the recovery.
Step 3	Direct projection. The stride is long, and the recovery leg tucks to swing forward. The legs project directly backward on takeoff and swing directly forward for the touchdown.
	ARM ACTION
Step 1	High or middle guard. Both of the arms are held up between waist and shoulder level and move very little as the legs stride forward and back.
Step 2	Bilateral arm swing. The arms swing but are coupled, moving forward and backward together.
Step 3	Opposition, oblique. The arms drive forward in the opposition pattern, each moving forward and backward with the opposite leg, so that one arm is moving forward while the other is moving backward. The arms, though, swing across the chest or out to the side in a plane oblique to the plane of movement.
Step 4	Opposition, sagittal. The arms swing forward and back in the opposition pattern and stay nearly in the sagittal (or forward–backward) plane of movement.

FIGURE 5.4 A beginning runner. *(a)* The legs have a limited range of motion. The arms extend at the elbows and swing slightly to the side rather than driving forward and back. *(b)* The thigh and arms swing out rather than forward and back.

© Mary Ann Roberton and Kate R. Barrett.

Figure 5.4*b* portrays some characteristics of early running that one can observe from the rear. As the child swings the recovering thigh forward, it inefficiently rotates to the side rather than moving straight forward. The arm swings to the side and away from the body, probably to assist with balance, but, again, this movement pattern wastes energy that could be directed toward running forward.

Rate Limiters in Early Running

To understand the rate limiters in early running, we must review similarities and differences between walking and running. First of all, the coordination patterns are quite similar; both have a 50% phasing relationship between the legs. Therefore, coordination is not likely to be a rate limiter for running. However, running requires a flight phase. To propel themselves into the air, toddlers must have sufficient strength in each leg to lift themselves off the ground. Clearly, then, strength is a very important rate limiter in running (Clark & Whitall, 1989b). Also, once in the air, infants must catch themselves on the other leg and then balance on that leg while shifting their weight forward. Thus, balance is another important rate limiter for running.

Proficient Running

Like walking, proficient running requires effective use of the biomechanical principles discussed in chapter 3. When running, you must optimize movement forms that allow you to move quickly, even at the expense of balance. Keeping this in mind, we can identify the developmental changes that beginning runners make to optimize their performance, as pictured in figure 5.5, as follows:

- Stride length increases, indicating that the runner is applying greater force. As greater force is used, several characteristics of mature running emerge: the rear leg is fully extended at push-off; the heel is tucked close to the buttocks and the thigh swings forward with greater acceleration; and the thigh comes parallel to the ground before foot strike. When the recovery leg is swung forward in a tuck position, the runner's effort is conserved.
- The runner eliminates lateral leg movements so that forces are kept in the forward–backward plane.
- For extended running, each foot strikes the ground with the heel first and then the forefoot or strikes the ground in an approximately flat pattern.
- The runner eliminates out-toeing and narrows the base of support.
- The runner's support leg flexes at the knee as the body's weight comes over the leg.
- Trunk rotation increases to allow for a longer stride and better arm–leg opposition. The trunk leans slightly forward.
- The arms swing forward and back, with the elbows approaching right angles, and move in opposition to the legs.

FIGURE 5.5 An advanced runner. Note the full range of leg motion.
© Mary Ann Roberton and Kate R. Barrett.

Imagine you are a spectator at an Olympic track meet. Most elite sprinters look very similar—their form is almost identical. However, the form of marathon runners differs greatly among individuals. What can you speculate about why sprinters have similar running forms but distance runners have different ones?

Developmental Changes in Early Running

As children grow, these qualitative changes in running pattern, together with increased body size and strength and improved coordination, typically result in improved quantitative measures of running speed and time in flight. Such changes have been well documented in several University of Wisconsin studies of children between ages 1.5 and 10 years (Beck, 1966; Clouse, 1959; Dittmer, 1962) and in other studies (Branta, Haubenstricker, & Seefeldt, 1984; Roberton, 1984). Therefore, we can expect improvement in the process and product of running performances as children grow, and improvements in the product—increased speed, for example—certainly may continue throughout adolescence. However, not every individual achieves all the improvements in running pattern during childhood. Most teenagers continue to refine their running form, and it is not uncommon to observe inefficient characteristics in adults' running, especially out-toeing, lateral leg movements, and limited stride. Perhaps these tendencies reflect skeletal and muscular imbalances in individual runners. Thus, age alone does not guarantee perfect running form; adolescents and adults may have inefficient running patterns.

Developmental Changes in Later Running

Some research exists on the developmental changes that occur as people age. Nelson (1981) studied the walking and running patterns of older women (aged 58 to 80). She asked the participants in her study to walk normally, walk as fast as possible, jog, and then run as fast as possible. Average speed, stride length, and stride frequency all tended to increase over this sequence, but individuals varied greatly in how they changed from walking to jogging. The older women generally increased their walking speed by lengthening their stride, but they increased their running speed by increasing stride frequency, as do young women. However, major differences were found between younger and older women in the pattern used for fast running:

- Older women did not tuck their recovering leg as completely.
- Older women had a shorter stride length.
- Older women took fewer strides than younger women.

The absolute speeds of jogging and running also differed between the age groups. Older women jogged more slowly (1.85 vs. 3.93 m/s) and ran more slowly (2.60 vs. 6.69 m/s) than a group of 20-year-old women (Nelson, 1981).

Rate Controllers in Later Running

Many of the rate controllers mentioned for later walking also affect running. However, because running requires greater generation of force and greater ability to balance, considerably smaller changes in these constraints may lead to the disappearance of this skill. Furthermore, one may have the ability to run but not the desire or the opportunity; in other words, an older adult may run only in an urgent situation, such as escaping a burning house. However, as more and more seniors discover that maintaining fitness levels can postpone undesired changes associated with aging, more and more opportunities for running exist. The Senior Games (formerly known as the Senior Olympics) have expanded greatly in the past decade; many states have statewide games, and the Huntsman World Senior Games are held in Utah each year. The running events range from the 100-meter dash to the half-marathon and even the triathlon. Age categories for runners range from 50 to 85- or 90-plus for men and women. Still, participants in the Senior Games represent a small portion of the population over 50. In fact, it is still noteworthy when an older adult participates in athletics.

Not all of the constraints that discourage running in older adults are structural. Imagine you are a physical therapist, and think of at least two other constraints in each of the constraint categories.

Assessment of Running: Observation Plan

Assessing motor skills using developmental sequences can seem like a daunting task to a novice observer. Fortunately, using an observation plan can make the task much simpler (see figure 5.6, Observation Plan for Running). In a nutshell, an observation plan allows you to make quick judgments about the developmental level of a particular runner by completing a flow chart of quick yes or no checkpoints. By observing a runner and making decisions about movements, you can establish developmental levels very efficiently and effectively.

Web Study Guide **Identify developmental differences among runners in Lab Activity 5.1, Assessing the Developmental Levels of Runners, in the web study guide.**

Other Locomotor Skills

Most other locomotor skills have not received the amount of empirical attention given to walking and running. However, many researchers, teachers, and therapists have observed these skills, and we can gain valuable insights from their observations. The skills we discuss here are jumping, hopping, galloping, sliding, and skipping, and like many of the observers, we focus primarily on the childhood years.

Jumping occurs when individuals propel themselves off the ground with one or both feet and then land on both feet.

Hopping occurs when individuals propel themselves with one foot and then land on the same foot.

Leaping occurs when individuals propel themselves with one foot and then land on the other foot.

Jumping

Typically, children attempt jumping tasks at a young age and often achieve the simplest forms before age 2. In **jumping**, individuals propel their bodies from a surface with either one or both feet and land with both feet. Children also acquire specialized forms of jumping during childhood, such as hopping and leaping. **Hopping** requires taking off and landing on the same leg, often repeatedly. **Leaping** involves a run with a projection forward from one foot to a landing on the other (increased flight time). Table 5.2 outlines several examples of jumping, hopping, and leaping. Let's first look at jumping.

Characteristics of Early Jumping

We can gauge developmental changes in jumping in various ways:

- The age at which a child can perform certain kinds of jumping (age norms)
- The distance or height of a jump
- The jumping form or pattern

Figure 5.6
OBSERVATION PLAN FOR RUNNING

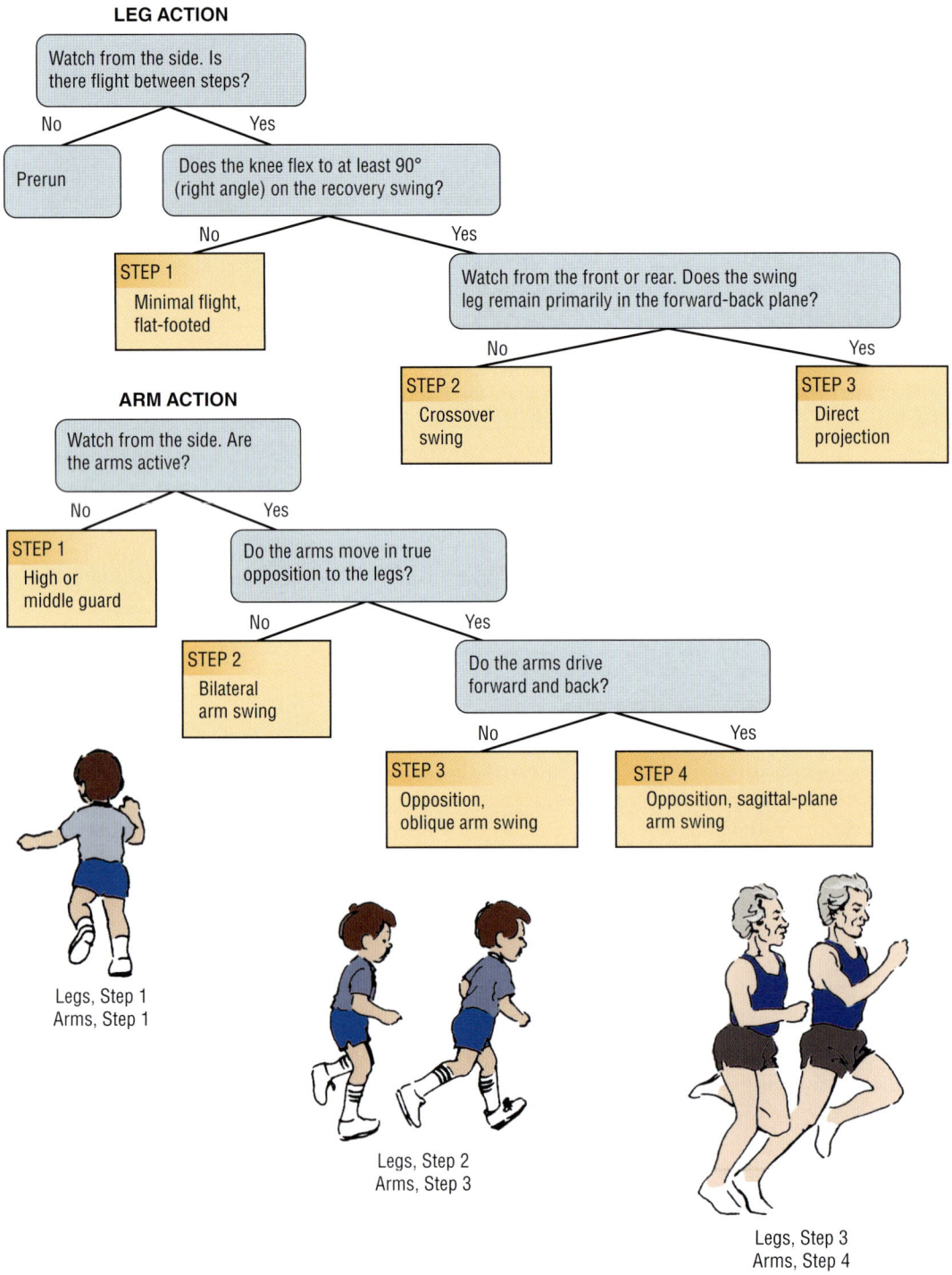

Early developmentalists determined age norms for jumping achievements in preschool children (Wickstrom, 1983). These norms appear in table 5.3, which indicates that children learn to step down off of a higher surface from one foot to the other before jumping off the floor with both feet. Children then learn to jump down from progressively greater heights onto both feet. Later, they master forward jumps, jumps over objects, and hopping a few times on one foot. By school age, children can usually perform all of these jumps.

Because of a secular trend, the exact ages at which children today can perform the various jumps might be younger than those in table 5.3, but the order in which they acquire those skills is the same. Developmentalists frequently use product assessments—that is, they measure the horizontal or vertical distance jumped—to assess jumping skill after children have refined the movement process. We focus here on the movement pattern because the measurement of distance jumped is rather self-explanatory and straightforward.

TABLE 5.2 Types of Jumps Arranged by Progressive Difficulty

LEVEL OF DIFFICULTY	TYPE OF JUMP
1	Jump down from one foot to the other foot.
2	Jump up from two feet to two feet.
3	Jump down from one foot to two feet.
4	Jump down from two feet to two feet.
5	Run and jump forward from one foot to the other.
6	Jump forward from two feet to two feet.
7	Run and jump forward from one foot to two feet.
8	Jump over object from two feet to two feet.
9	Jump from one foot to the same foot rhythmically.

© Mary Ann Roberton and Kate R. Barrett.

TABLE 5.3 Jumping Achievements of Young Children

ACHIEVEMENT	MOTOR AGE (MO)	SOURCE
Jump from 12 in. (30 cm) height; one foot	24	M & W
Jump off floor; both feet	28	B
Jump from 18 in. (46 cm) height; one foot	31	M & W
Jump from chair 10 in. (26 cm) high; both feet	32	B
Jump from 8 in. (20 cm) height; both feet	33	M & W
Jump from 12 in. (30 cm) height; both feet	34	M & W
Jump from 18 in. (46 cm) height; both feet	37	M & W
Jump from 12 in. (30 cm) height; both feet	37.1	B
Jump forward 4 to 14 in. (10–35 cm) from 12 in. (30 cm) height; both feet	37.3	B
Hop on two feet 1 to 3 times	38	M & W
Jump over rope 8 in. (20 cm) high; both feet	41.5	B
Hop on one foot 1 to 3 times	43	B

Note: Adapted from information in studies by Bayley (1936) (B) and McCaskill & Wellman (1938) (M&W).

© Mary Ann Roberton and Kate R. Barrett.

Basic skill development in children is a gradual process of refining skills. Oftentimes, this process includes a qualitative change in the skill, such as taking a step forward when throwing. Authors have described development of a particular skill through successive steps, or developmental sequences, based on qualitative changes in critical features of the skill. Two types of developmental sequences exist. The whole-body approach describes all characteristic positions of various body components in a step (table 5.4). The component approach follows each separate body component through whatever number of steps accounts for the qualitative changes observed over time (table 5.5).

Several published developmental sequences help us examine the developmental changes that occur in jumping movement patterns. Such sequences identify the steps that children achieve in making the transition from inefficient to proficient movement patterns. The advancements reflect the children's adoption of movements that take advantage of the principles of motion. We can see improvements in both the vertical jump and the horizontal (standing long) jump, but the developmental sequences that researchers have suggested thus far are based on the standing long jump (Clark & Phillips, 1985; Roberton, 1978b, 1984; tables 5.4 and 5.5).

We first identify some of the characteristics of beginning jumpers in both the vertical jump and the standing long jump. Most young jumpers begin by executing a vertical jump, even if they intend to jump horizontally. Look at the beginning jumpers in figures 5.7, 5.8, and 5.9. A vertical jump is shown in figure 5.7 and a horizontal jump in figures 5.8 and 5.9. Note that in all three jumps, the preparatory crouch is slight and the legs are not fully extended at liftoff. In fact, the vertical jumper in figure 5.7 tucks the legs to leave the ground rather than extend them at takeoff to project the body up. In this example, the head is no higher at the peak of the jump than at takeoff.

TABLE 5.4 Developmental Sequence of the Standing Long Jump for the Whole Body

SEQUENCE	ACTION
Step 1	Vertical component of force may be greater than horizontal; resulting jump is then upward rather than forward. Arms move backward, acting as brakes to stop the momentum of the trunk as the legs extend in front of the center of mass.
Step 2	The arms move in an anterior–posterior direction during the preparatory phase but move sideward (winging action) during the in-flight phase. The knees and hips flex and extend more fully than in step 1. The angle of takeoff is still markedly greater than 45°. The landing is made with the center of gravity above the base of support, with the thighs perpendicular to the surface rather than parallel as in the reaching position of step 4.
Step 3	The arms swing backward and then forward during the preparatory phase. The knees and hips flex fully before takeoff. On takeoff the arms extend and move forward but do not exceed the height of the head. The knee extension may be complete, but the takeoff angle is still greater than 45°. On landing, the thigh is still less than parallel to the surface, and the center of gravity is near the base of support when viewed from the frontal plane.
Step 4	The arms extend vigorously forward and upward on takeoff, reaching full extension above the head at liftoff. The hips and knees extend fully, and the takeoff angle is 45° or less. In preparation for landing, the arms are brought downward and the legs are thrust forward until the thighs are parallel to the surface. The center of gravity is far behind the base of support on foot contact, but at the moment of contact the knees are flexed and the arms are thrust forward to maintain the momentum to carry the center of gravity beyond the feet.

Note: Degrees are measured from horizontal.

© Vern D. Seedfeldt

TABLE 5.5 Developmental Sequence of the Standing Long Jump Takeoff for Body Components

SEQUENCE	ACTION
	LEG ACTION
Step 1	One-foot takeoff. From the beginning position, the jumper steps out with one foot. Usually there is little preparatory leg flexion.
Step 2	Knee extension first. The jumper begins to extend the knee joints before the heels come off the ground, resulting in a jump that is too vertical to achieve maximum horizontal distance.
Step 3	Simultaneous extension. The jumper extends the knees at the same time the heels come off the ground.
Step 4	Heels up first. The jump begins with the heels coming off the ground, then the knees extend; the jumper appears to start the takeoff by tipping forward.
	ARM ACTION
Step 1	No action. The arms are stationary. After takeoff, they may "wing" (shoulder girdle retracts).
Step 2	Arms swing forward. The arms swing forward at the shoulder from a starting position at the sides. The arms might also swing out to the side (abduct at the shoulder).
Step 3	Arms extend, then partially flex. The arms extend back together during leg flexion, then swing forward together at takeoff. Arm swing never reaches a position overhead.
Step 4	Arms extend, then fully flex. The arms extend back together during leg flexion, then swing forward to a position overhead.

Adapted by permission from Clark and Phillips (1985).

Another characteristic of beginning jumpers is that they do not use a two-foot (symmetrical) takeoff or landing, as shown in figure 5.7, even when they intend to do so. A one-foot takeoff, or step-out, is the lowest level of leg action in the developmental sequence of the standing long jump takeoff. The legs may also be asymmetrical during flight. To improve this leg action, the jumper needs to (1) make a symmetrical two-foot takeoff, flight, and landing and (2) fully extend the ankles, knees, and hips at takeoff after a deep preparatory crouch. The knees and hips flex together in the flight phase of the standing long jump after a full and forceful extension of the legs at takeoff.

To jump a long distance, the skilled performer leans the trunk forward at least 30° from the vertical. By age 3, children can change their trunk angle at takeoff

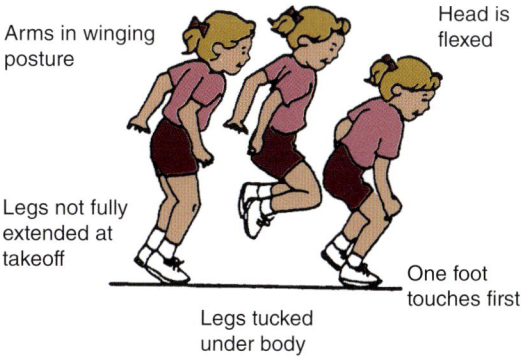

FIGURE 5.7 Sequential views of a vertical jump. The form here is inefficient. The legs are tucked up under the body rather than fully extended to project the body off the ground. Notice that one foot touches down first. The arms do not assist in the jump; the jumper holds them in the winging posture.

© Mary Ann Roberton and Kate R. Barrett.

to make either a vertical or a horizontal jump (Clark, Phillips, & Petersen, 1989). However, beginning jumpers often keep the trunk too erect during a horizontal jump. When a skilled jumper leans the trunk forward to facilitate jumping for distance, the heels usually come off the ground before the knees start to extend (Clark & Phillips, 1985). Skilled jumpers appear to tip forward at the start of the takeoff. The leg action in which "heels up" begins the takeoff is the most advanced step in the developmental sequence for the leg action of the horizontal jump.

Lack of coordinated arm action also characterizes beginning vertical and horizontal jumpers. Rather than use their arms to assist in the jumping action, they may use their arms asymmetrically, hold them stationary at the side, or keep them in a high-guard position as a precaution against falling. Arms may wing (extend backward) ineffectively during flight (figure 5.7) or parachute (extend down and out to the side) during landing (figure 5.8). To achieve a proficient jump, the jumper must use the arms symmetrically to lead the jump from a preparatory extended position to an overhead swing. The developmental sequence for the arm action of the standing long jump progresses from no arm action to limited arm swing; to extension, then partial flexion; and finally to extension, then complete arm swing overhead.

FIGURE 5.8 A beginning long jumper. As the jumper's weight shifts forward, the toes are pulled off the floor to "catch" the body at landing. The trunk lean at takeoff is less than 30° from the vertical. The arms are used at takeoff but are in an abducted position, laterally rotate in flight, and "parachute" for the landing.

© Mary Ann Roberton.

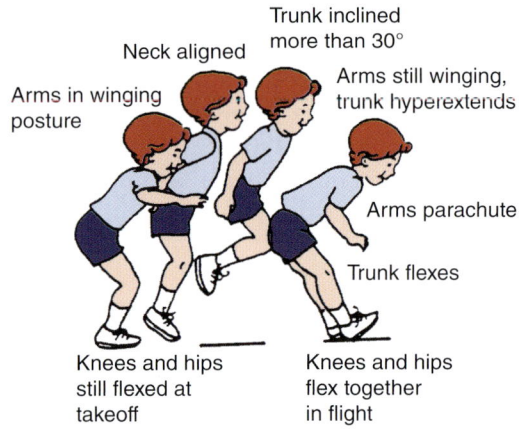

FIGURE 5.9 A beginning jumper. The leg action is in step 3 (table 5.5) at takeoff, as the knees extend at the same time the heels leave the ground. The knees and hips flex together during flight, and the knees then extend before landing. The trunk is somewhat erect at takeoff; it hyperextends in flight, then flexes for landing. The arms wing at takeoff (step 1) before parachuting for the landing.

Screening for a Standing Long Jump Developmental Sequence

Recently, Lane et al. (2017) used a technique called prelongitudinal screening to validate the developmental sequences associated with landing in the standing long jump. This process involves examining a cross section of individuals from a broad range of ages to screen for the hypothesized sequences (to be followed by a longitudinal study in the future). They examined 395 children between the ages of 4 and 12 years as well as 48 adults as they performed standing long jumps. Using video analysis to determine the shank, foot, and arm action at landing, the researchers found that each of the components demonstrated a developmental trend (see table 5.6). Because of the sufficiency of the developmental trends within the different limb actions, the authors believe the sequences received strong support and, in the future, can be studied longitudinally in order to be validated.

TABLE 5.6 Hypothesized Developmental Sequences for the Long Jump Landing

SEQUENCE	ACTION
	SHANK ACTION
Step 1	Acute or perpendicular. Anterior shank angle at contact is acute or approximately perpendicular to the ground.
Step 2	Obtuse. Anterior shank angle at contact is clearly obtuse relative to the ground.
	FOOT ACTION
Step 1	Asymmetrical contact. One foot clearly lands before the other; leg configuration during flight is often asymmetrical.
Step 2	Symmetrical neutral or plantar flexed. Two-foot landing; ankle is plantar flexed or neutral just before contact, resulting in a forefoot or flat-footed landing.
Step 3	Symmetrical dorsiflexed. Two-foot landing; ankle is actively dorsiflexed at contact, resulting in a distinct heel landing.
	ARM ACTION
Step 1	No reach. Arms wing during flight and act only to parachute (i.e., used for balance) during landing.
Step 2	Slight forward reach. Shoulders flex to bring arms in front of the body during flight, but the reach is abandoned as shoulders abduct to parachute; arms are often dropped straight in line with the trunk at contact.
Step 3	Full forward reach. Shoulder flexion of ≥ 90° relative to the trunk is observed at foot contact.
Step 4	Neutral or hyperextension. Arms are forcefully thrown down and back into full shoulder extension or hyperextension as hips simultaneously flex.

Reprinted by permission from Lane et al. (2018).

Proficient Jumping

Through these developmental changes, performers can develop a proficient jumping pattern, as shown in figures 5.10 and 5.11. To execute proficient jumps, they do the following:

- Get into a preparatory crouch that will stretch the muscles and allow the legs to apply maximal force as they fully extend at the moment of liftoff.
- Take off for a horizontal jump with the heels coming off the ground and with both feet leaving the ground at the same time.
- Extend the arms backward, then initiate the takeoff with a vigorous arm swing forward to a position overhead.

In jumping for height, proficient jumpers do the following:

- Direct force downward and extend the body throughout flight. If they are to strike an object or touch something overhead, the dominant arm reaches up and the opposite arm swings down. They gain height through a lateral tilt of the shoulders.
- Keep the trunk relatively upright throughout the jump.
- Flex the ankles, knees, and hips on touchdown to allow the force of landing to be absorbed.

In jumping for distance, proficient jumpers do the following:

- Direct force down and back by beginning the takeoff with the heels leaving the ground before the knees extend. The trunk appears to tip forward.

- Flex the knees during flight, then bring the thighs forward to a position parallel with the ground.
- Swing the lower legs forward for a two-foot landing.
- Let the trunk come forward in reaction to the thigh flexion, putting the body in a jackknife position.
- Flex the ankles and knees when the heels touch the ground to absorb the momentum of the body over distance as the body continues to move forward.

FIGURE 5.10 An advanced vertical jump for the purpose of reaching high. From a preparatory crouch, this basketball player swings his arms forward and up to lead the jump. The hips, knees, and ankles extend completely at takeoff. Near the peak of the jump, one hand continues up while the other comes down, tilting the shoulder girdle to assist in the high reach. Note that the trunk tends to remain upright throughout.

© Mary Ann Roberton and Kate R. Barrett.

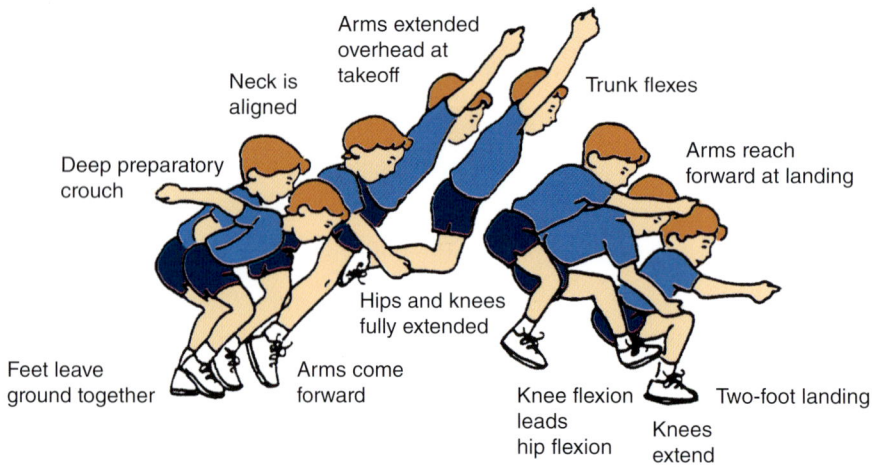

FIGURE 5.11 An advanced long jump. The feet leave the ground together and touch down together. The legs fully extend at takeoff, beginning with heels up. The knees then flex in flight, followed by hip flexion and finally knee extension to reach forward for landing. The trunk is inclined more than 30° at takeoff, and the jumper maintains this lean in flight until the trunk flexes for landing. The arms lead the jump and reach overhead at takeoff, then lower to reach forward at landing.

Web Study Guide Identify developmental differences among long jumpers in Lab Activity 5.2, Assessing the Developmental Levels of Long Jumpers, in the web study guide.

Developmental Changes in Jumping

With practice, then, children can eventually make refinements in their jumping pattern as described. Continuous growth in body size and strength also contributes to quantitative improvements in how far children can jump. During the elementary school years, children average increases of 3 to 5 inches (~8 to 13 cm) a year in the horizontal distance they can jump and approximately 2 inches (5 cm) a year in vertical distance (DeOreo & Keogh, 1980). Qualitative improvements in jumping vary among children. For example, Clark and Phillips (1985) observed that fewer than 30% of the 3- to 7-year-olds they filmed had the same level of leg and arm action. Most had more advanced leg action than arm action, but some had more advanced arm action than leg action. If one component was more advanced than the other, it was usually by only one step, but some children were two steps more advanced in one component than in the other. Thus, we see many movement patterns among developing children.

The differences between a vertical jump and a standing long jump involve position and movement speed. For example, in the standing long jump, the hips are more flexed than in the vertical jump as the jumper makes the transition from the preparatory crouch to the takeoff. The hips extend faster in the standing long jump, whereas the knees and ankles extend faster in the vertical jump. Other characteristics of jumping remain stable across developmental steps and type of jump. Clark et al. (1989) found that 3-, 5-, 7-, and 9-year-olds and adults all used the same pattern of leg coordination. In addition, all used that same pattern for both standing long jumps and vertical jumps. Specifically, the timing of hip, knee, and ankle joint extension at takeoff was similar in all groups. Perhaps this similarity reflects the mechanics involved in propelling the body's mass off the ground. The neuromuscular system must use a leg coordination pattern that gets the body off the ground, but limb positions and movement speeds change as the jumper is better able to optimize jumping distance or adapt the jump to a specific task, such as shooting a jump shot in basketball.

It is clear that not all persons master jumping in childhood or even in adolescence. Zimmerman (1956) found many inefficient jumping characteristics in college women, including limited arm swing and incomplete leg extension at takeoff. For children and teens to receive assistance from their instructors in perfecting an advanced jumping pattern, instructors must be able to critically observe and analyze jumping performance. Use figure 5.12, Observation Plan for the Standing Long Jump, to assess the developmental level of the standing long jump takeoff.

Rate Limiters in Jumping

For children to perform a two-foot jump, they must be able to develop enough force to bring their bodies into the air from a still position. Unlike in walking and running, they cannot take advantage of a "fall and catch" motion but rather must project their entire bodies into the air.

Hopping

Adults rarely use hopping to move around, yet to become a skillful mover, an individual should develop hopping skills during childhood. To hop, especially repeatedly, one must project and absorb body weight with just one limb and maintain balance on the small base of support that one foot provides. Complex sport and dance skills often incorporate these movement abilities.

Characteristics of Early Hopping

Children may move through the levels of arm action and leg action at different rates. Look at the two early hoppers shown in figures 5.13 and 5.14. The leg action of the hopper in figure 5.13 is ineffective as a force producer. The child momentarily lifts the support leg from the floor by flexing it rather than projecting the body up by leg extension; the swing leg is inactive. The arms are also inactive, and the child's leg and arm actions fall into the first developmental step (see table 5.7 for the developmental sequence). The hopper in figure 5.14 has achieved some leg extension; this child is in step 2 of leg action but still in step 1 of arm action.

Figure 5.12
OBSERVATION PLAN FOR THE STANDING LONG JUMP

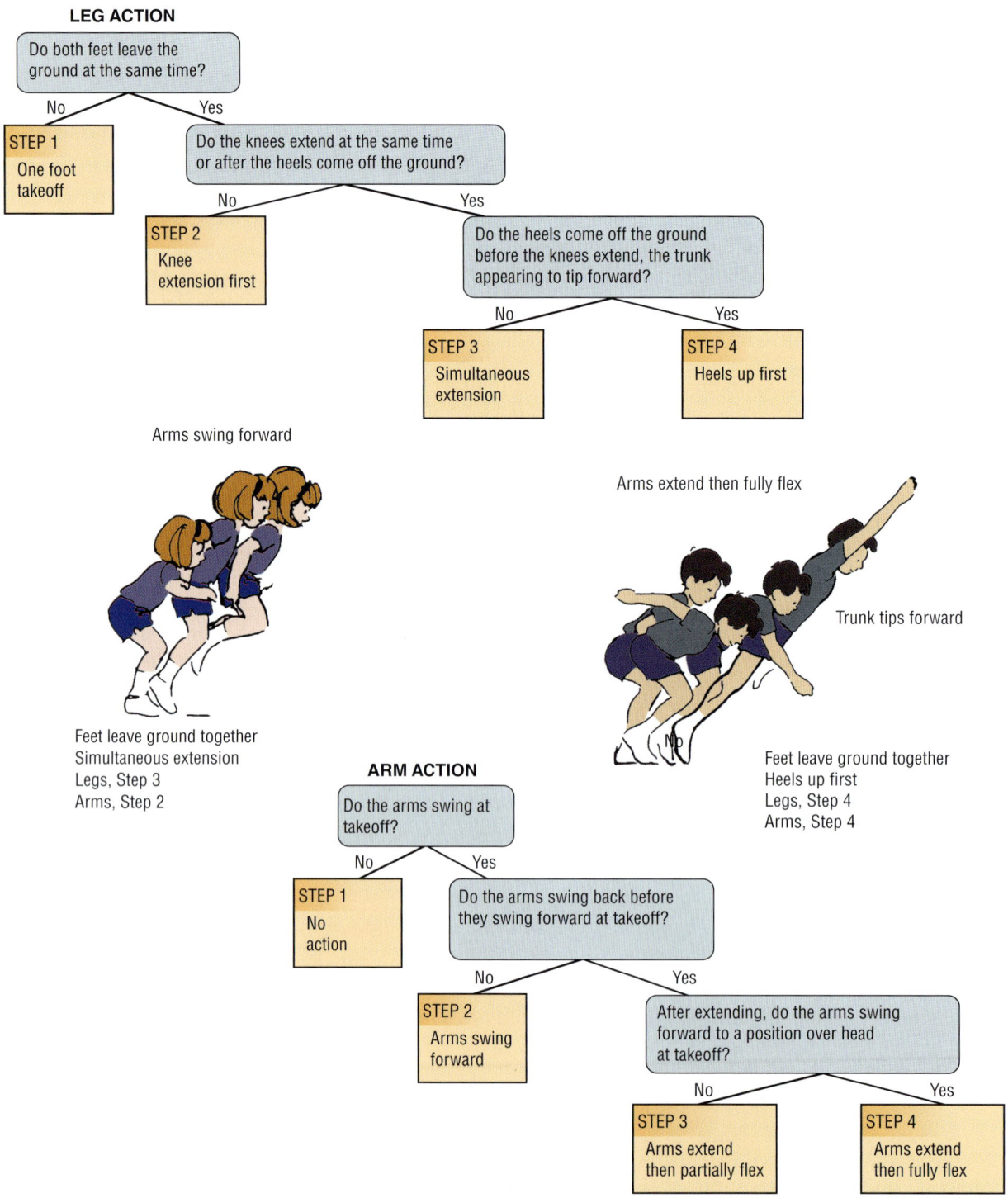

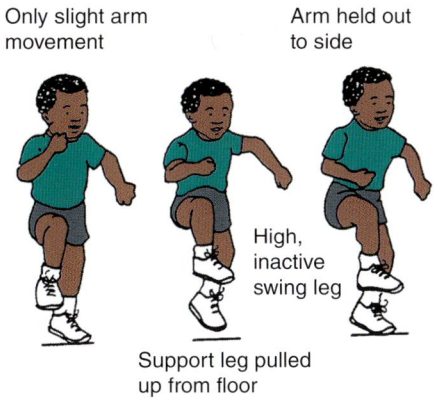

FIGURE 5.13 An early hopping attempt exhibiting step 1 leg action and step 1 arm action. The support leg is pulled off the floor to produce only momentary flight. The arms are high and are not working in opposition.
© Mary Ann Roberton.

TABLE 5.7 Developmental Sequence for Hopping

SEQUENCE	ACTION
	LEG ACTION
Step 1	Momentary flight. The support knee and hip quickly flex, pulling (instead of projecting) the foot from the floor. The flight is momentary. Only one or two hops can be achieved. The swing leg is lifted high and held in an inactive position to the side or in front of the body.
Step 2	Fall and catch; swing leg inactive. Forward body lean allows minimal knee and ankle extension to help the body "fall" forward of the support foot, then quickly catch itself again. The swing leg is inactive. Repeat hops are now possible.
Step 3	Projected takeoff; swing leg assists. Perceptible pretakeoff extension occurs in the hip, knee, and ankle in the support leg. There is little or no delay in changing from knee and ankle flexion on landing to extension before takeoff. The swing leg now pumps up and down to assist in projection. The range of the swing is insufficient to carry it behind the support leg when viewed from the side.
Step 4	Projection delay; swing leg leads. The weight of the child on landing is now smoothly transferred along the foot to the ball before the knee and ankle extend to takeoff. The support leg nearly reaches full extension on the takeoff. The swing leg now leads the upward-forward movement of the takeoff phase, while the support leg is still rotating over the ball of the foot. The range of the pumping action in the swing leg increases so that it passes behind the support leg when viewed from the side.
	ARM ACTION
Step 1	Bilateral inactive. The arms are held bilaterally, usually high and out to the side, although other positions behind or in front of the body may occur. Any arm action is usually slight and not consistent.
Step 2	Bilateral reactive. Arms swing upward briefly, then are medially rotated at the shoulder in a winging movement before takeoff. It appears that this movement is in reaction to loss of balance.
Step 3	Bilateral assist. The arms pump up and down together, usually in front of the line of the trunk. Any downward and backward motion of the arms occurs after takeoff. The arms may move parallel to each other or be held at different levels as they move up and down.
Step 4	Semi-opposition. The arm on the side opposite the swing leg swings forward with that leg and back as the leg moves down. The position of the other arm is variable, often staying in front of the body or to the side.
Step 5	Opposing assist. The arm opposite the swing leg moves forward and upward in synchrony with the forward and upward movement of that leg. The other arm moves in the direction opposite to the action of the swing leg. The range of movement in the arm action may be minimal unless the task requires speed or distance.

Note: This sequence has been partially validated by Halverson and Williams (1985).
© Mary Ann Roberton

Proficient Hopping

To become proficient hoppers, children need to make the following improvements:

- The swing leg must lead the hip.
- The support leg must extend fully.
- The arms must move in opposition to the legs.
- The support leg must flex at landing to absorb the force of the landing and to prepare for extension at the next takeoff.

The hopper in figure 5.15 has made one of these improvements by moving the arm opposite the swing leg in opposition, but the other arm does not move in a consistent way. The advanced hopper in figure 5.16 assists the hop by moving both arms in opposition to the legs. In terms of leg motion, the hopper in figure 5.15 extends the support leg at takeoff, reflecting good force application, and uses the swing leg, but not vigorously. The hopper in figure 5.16 has made this improvement—the swing leg leads the takeoff, allowing the momentum of several body parts to be chained together, and then swings back behind the support leg to lead the next takeoff.

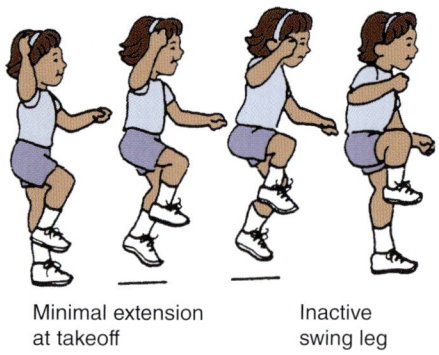

FIGURE 5.14 This girl uses some leg extension to leave the ground, but her swing leg is still inactive. She is in step 2 of the developmental levels for leg action.

© Mary Ann Roberton.

FIGURE 5.15 A more advanced hop: step 3 in the developmental sequence of leg action, step 4 in arm action. The swing leg leads the hop. Although the range of the swing leg is larger, it could increase even more.

© Mary Ann Roberton.

Developmental Changes in Hopping

Few children under age 3 can hop repeatedly (Bayley, 1969; McCaskill & Wellman, 1938). Developmentalists often cite the preschool years as the time when children become proficient hoppers (Gutteridge, 1939; Sinclair, 1973; Williams, 1983). Yet Halverson and Williams (1985) found that more than half of a group of 63 children (3-, 4-, and 5-year-olds) were at step 2 in the arm and leg action. They observed few attempts they could classify at the advanced levels, and hopping on the nonpreferred leg was developmentally behind hopping on the preferred leg. Figure 5.17 shows that many more children were at the lowest developmental step when hopping on their nonpreferred leg than when hopping on their preferred leg. Few children were

FIGURE 5.16 This boy demonstrates step 4 leg action in that the range of the swing is sufficient to carry the swing leg completely behind the support leg. Both arms move in opposition to the legs.

© Mary Ann Roberton.

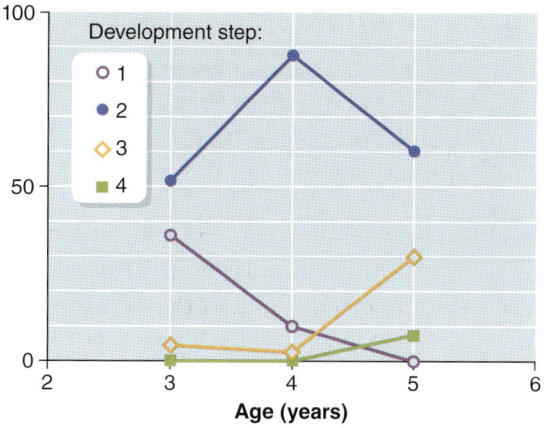

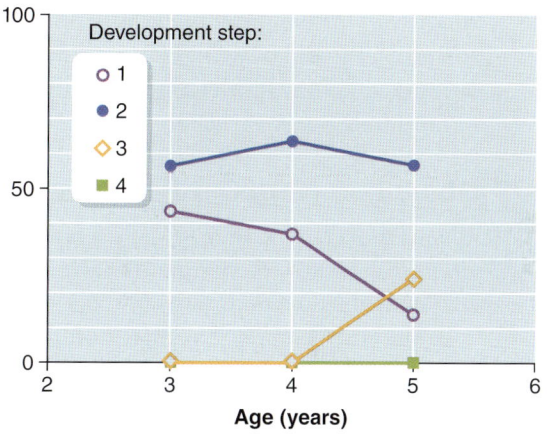

FIGURE 5.17 The developmental level of leg action in 3-, 4-, and 5-year-old hoppers on their preferred leg (top) and nonpreferred leg (bottom). Note that more children were at step 1 when hopping on their nonpreferred leg than when hopping on their preferred leg. Only at age 5 were any notable number of the children at step 3.

Reprinted by permission from Halverson and Williams (1985).

beyond step 2 when hopping on either leg. If the children in this study are representative of this age group, hopping continues to develop well past the age of 5.

Why do children advance from one developmental level of hopping to another? Several researchers attempted to answer this question by examining the force and stiffness of landing in hopping (Getchell & Roberton, 1989; Roberton & Halverson, 1988). Note that in step 2 the hopper lands flat-footed and holds the swing leg still. By step 3 the hopper uses a softer landing (more leg flexion to cushion the landing, followed by extension to the next takeoff) and swings the nonhopping leg. Researchers confirmed that the force of landing in a step 2 hop rises sharply on landing, whereas in a step 3 hop it rises gradually. To achieve a soft landing, the neuromuscular system probably prepares ahead of time (ahead of the landing) to moderate the force of landing by allowing the leg to "give" (flex). Perhaps, then, once children achieve a step 2 hop, their ability to project the body higher and travel faster—and perhaps their increasing body weight—increases the force of the landing. Once that force reaches a critical value that could cause a damaging, jarring landing, the neuromuscular system changes children's hopping movements to allow a softer, more cushioned landing. Hence, children advance to the next developmental level.

Web Study Guide **Identify developmental differences among hoppers in Lab Activity 5.3, Assessing the Developmental Levels of Hoppers, in the web study guide.**

Part of the rehabilitation process for some injuries to the lower limbs includes hopping on the injured leg (generally later in the rehabilitation process). Imagine you are a physical therapist and a patient has asked the following question: If adults do not hop regularly, why is hopping so important in rehabilitation? Consider your answer in terms of constraints.

An Integrated Approach to Understanding Hopping

If we dig deeper into understanding the change in developmental levels in the hop, we reveal the remarkable interaction of individual constraints in the body and within the framework of the principles of motion. Let's consider a child who hops with step 2 action. The swing leg is held in front; therefore, it simply reacts rather than contributes to the hop. For a lightweight child who needs to produce little force to move, a stationary swing leg does not prevent hopping. The child produces force, primarily downward, from the stance leg. As the child grows she adds body weight and size, which increase her inertia (which, in turn, increases the force required to overcome inertia). Projecting force downward from the stance leg no longer suffices for a hop; she adds swing leg movement to provide additional force, as the movement of the swing leg helps push the body down and back. The ground responds by pushing the body up and forward (Newton's third law), and the child hops into the air. What goes up, however, must come down—and the child returns to earth with a greater amount of force (because of her increased weight and the height of the hop) than in a step 2 hop. To break the fall, the child must "give" to land softly. This illustrates one way in which the body recalibrates and changes movement patterns to account for changing individual constraints. The changes in the swing leg in step 3 are complemented by changes in the stance leg, both of which lead to a higher, safer hop.

Observing Hopping Patterns

As with the other locomotor skills, a novice observer must practice hopping assessment. Halverson (1983; see also Roberton & Halverson, 1984) suggests a systematic pattern of observation that focuses on the body parts one at a time. As a novice observer, you should observe leg action from the side. Initially, pay attention to the swing leg. Is it active? If so, does it move up and down or swing past the support leg? Next, observe the support leg. Does it extend at takeoff? Does it flex on landing and extend during the next hop? Look at arm action from the side and the front. Watch first to see whether the arm movement is bilateral or opposing. If it is bilateral, you can then categorize arm movement as inactive, reactive, or backward in direction. If arm movement is opposing, note whether one or both arms move synchronously with the legs. Use figure 5.18, Observation Plan for Hopping, to assess the developmental levels of hoppers.

Rate Controllers in Hopping

Hopping likely depends on the postural system's ability to balance the body on one limb for a succession of hops. Also, to hop repeatedly, the individual must be able to generate enough force to lift the body with one limb, recover, and quickly generate enough force to hop again. Running also requires projection and acceptance of weight on one limb; however, in running, legs alternate and are able to regain energy as they swing in a flexed position. In the hop, the leg stays extended—thus, hopping requires more effort than running. Therefore, the ability to generate force can act as a rate controller.

Galloping, Sliding, and Skipping

Galloping, **sliding**, and **skipping** involve the fundamental movements of stepping, hopping, or leaping. Galloping and sliding, both asymmetric gaits, consist of a step on one foot, then a leap-step on the other foot (Roberton & Halverson, 1984; Whitall, 1988). The same leg always leads with the step. The difference between galloping and sliding is the direction of movement. In galloping, the individual moves forward; in sliding, the individual moves sideways. Skipping is a step and a hop on the same foot, with alternating feet: step-hop on the right foot, step-hop on the left foot, step-hop on the right foot, and so on. The movement is usually forward (figure 5.19, *a* and *b*).

Consider situations or contexts in which locomotor skills other than walking and running are socially acceptable. Do not limit yourself to sport and dance applications.

Characteristics of Early Skill Patterns

Children's early attempts at these skills are usually arrhythmic and stiff, as shown in figure 5.20. The arms are rarely involved in projecting the body off the floor. Children might hold their arms stiffly in the high-guard position or out to the side to aid their balance. Their stride or step length is short, and they land flat-footed. Little trunk rotation is used, and they exaggerate vertical lift. In early galloping attempts, a child's trailing leg may land ahead of the lead leg.

Proficient Skill Patterns

In contrast, children who are proficient at galloping, sliding, and skipping move in a manner that is rhythmical and relaxed, as seen in figure 5.21. Proficiency in these skills includes the following characteristics:

- The arms are no longer needed for balance.
- In skipping, the arms swing rhythmically in opposition to the legs and provide momentum.

Figure 5.18
OBSERVATION PLAN FOR HOPPING

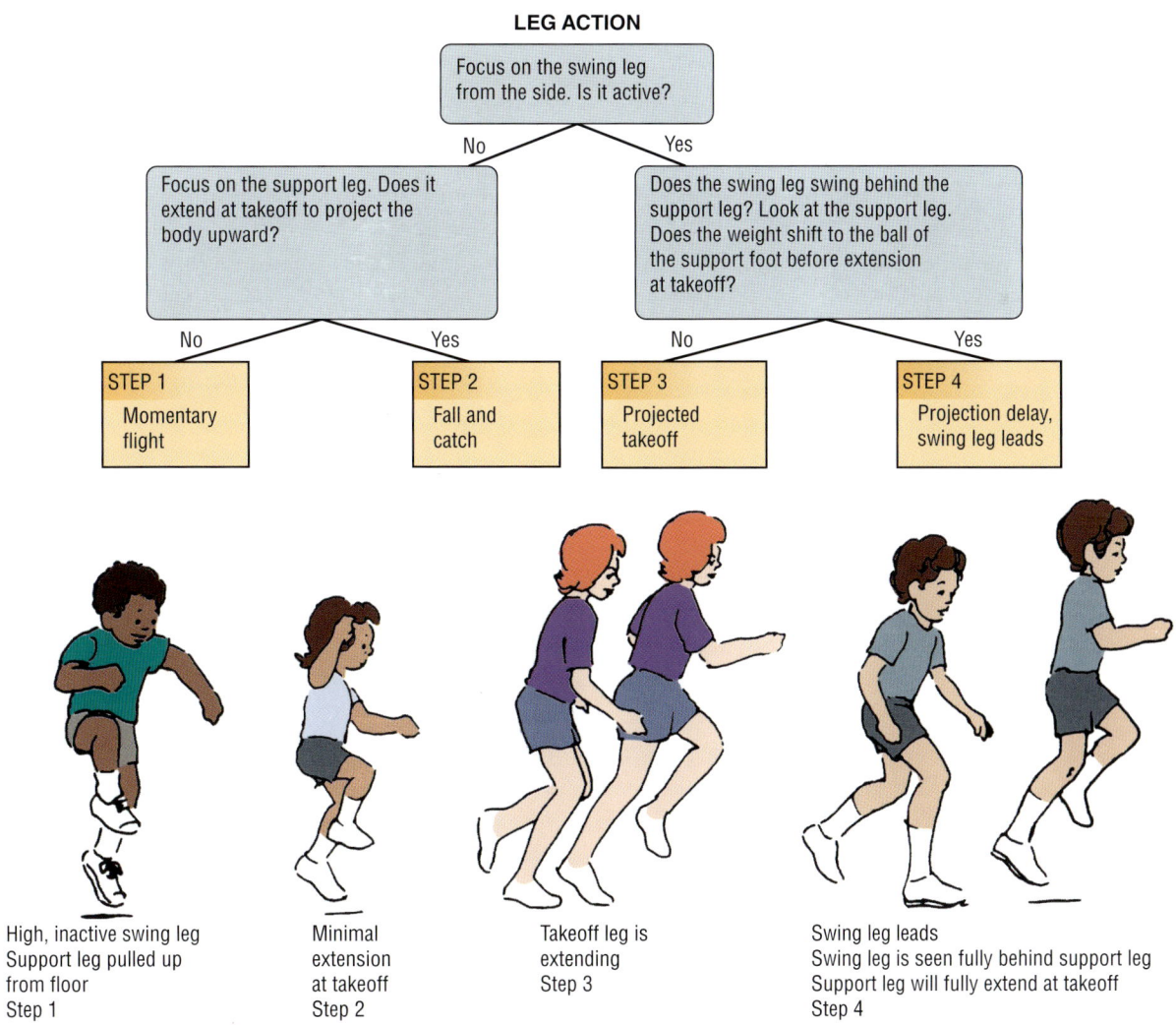

(continued)

Figure 5.18 continued

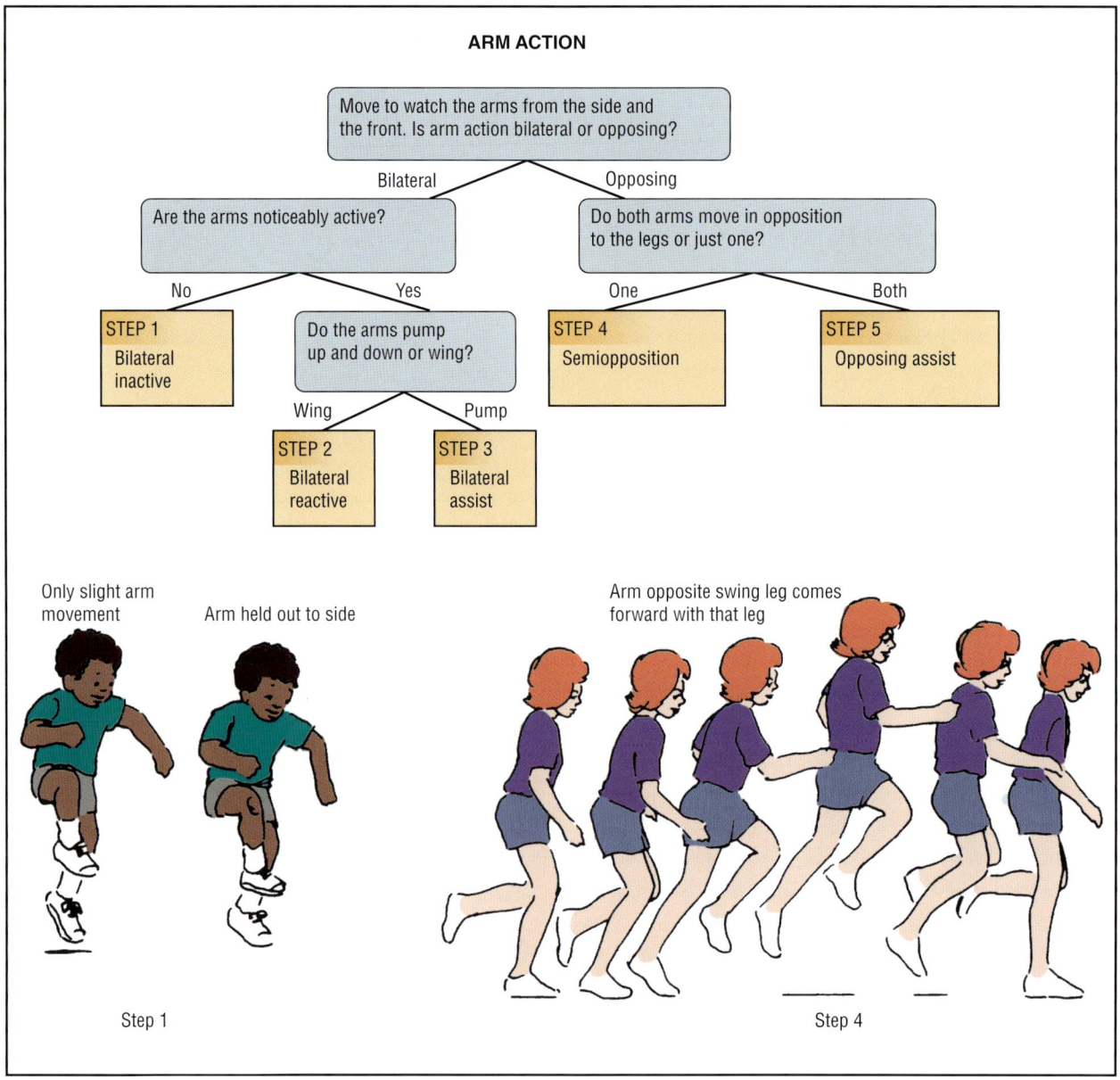

- The child can use the arms for another purpose during galloping and sliding, such as clapping.
- Forefoot or heel-to-forefoot landings prevail.
- The knees "give" on landing, remaining flexed while they support the body's weight, and then extend at takeoff, especially when the child is traveling quickly.

Developmental Changes

Galloping is the first of these three bipedal patterns to emerge. It develops sometime between 2 and 3 years of age, after the child has firmly established the running pattern (around age 2) and usually before hopping, which occurs at age 3 or 4. Galloping is the first asymmetrical locomotor pattern a child learns. As noted earlier, walking and running have 50% phasing—the legs make the same movement, but the cycle of one leg is halfway behind the cycle of the other. Galloping, in contrast, is uneven. The steps take longer than the leap-steps. Gallopers, regardless

FIGURE 5.19 *(a)* Galloping is a step on the lead leg and a leap-step on the trailing leg. *(b)* Skipping is a step and then a hop on the foot that just stepped followed by a step and a hop on the other foot, and so on, continuing alternatingly (e.g., step-hop left foot, step-hop right foot, and so on).

Adapted by permission from Clark and Whitall (1989).

FIGURE 5.20 A beginning galloper. The arms are held stiffly, the stride length is short, and vertical movement is exaggerated.

Adapted by permission from Clark and Whitall (1989).

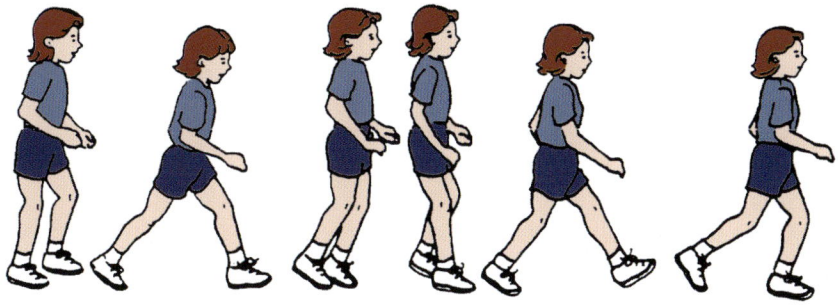

FIGURE 5.21 An advanced galloper. The arms move in opposition to the legs. Movements are rhythmic and landings are not flat-footed.

of age, tend to use one of two timing patterns: the step takes either approximately twice as long as the leap-step (a 66% to 33% phasing) or 3 times as long (a 75% to 25% phasing) (Clark & Whitall, 1989b; Whitall, 1988). Children master sliding next, and in both galloping and sliding they develop the ability to lead with the nondominant leg much later than the ability to lead with the dominant leg.

Skipping is usually the last of the locomotor patterns to emerge, usually between 4 and 7 years of age. A little more than half of 5-year-olds demonstrate skipping (Branta et al., 1984).

Assessing Locomotion Motor Skills: Test of Gross Motor Development

For any movement practitioner, the ability to assess motor proficiency and determine how it changes over time is essential. One assessment tool specifically designed to examine fundamental motor skills is the Test of Gross Motor Development (TGMD; Ulrich, 1985, 2000, 2013). The TGMD was originally developed by Dale Ulrich as part of his dissertation at Michigan State in 1981 and made available as an assessment tool in 1985 (Ulrich, 1985, 2017). Ulrich designed the TGMD to correspond to the typical elementary school curriculum, which focused on the acquisition of a variety of fundamental motor skills. The test provided a standardized criterion-referenced assessment based on skill-specific fundamental motor patterns observed in children; this could be used to establish children's levels of gross motor skill development at any one time and to chart developmental changes over time. Since developing the original assessment, Ulrich has revised two subsequent versions (TGMD-2: Ulrich, 2000; TGMD-3: Ulrich, 2013). The TGMD-3 is valid and reliable (Webster & Ulrich, 2017) and has been used with typically developing children as well as children with visual impairments (Brian et al., 2018), Down syndrome (Bouquet, 2016), and autism spectrum disorder (Allen, Bredero, Van Damme, Ulrich, & Simons, 2017), among other conditions and disabilities. Further, the TGMD-3 has been used in a wide variety of countries (e.g., Mohammadi, Bahram, Khalaji, & Ghadiri, 2017; Rintala, Saakslahti, & Iivonen; 2017) and has been translated into Portuguese (Valentini, Zanella, & Webster, 2017), Spanish (Estevan et al., 2017), and German (Wagner, Webster & Ulrich, 2017).

The TGMD-3 includes a total of 13 skills divided into two subscales: locomotor skills (6 skills) and ball skills (7 skills). This section reviews the locomotor portion of the assessment; chapter 6 covers assessment of ball skills using the TGMD-3. Within the locomotor subscale, the assessed skills include the run, gallop, one-leg hop, skip, jump, and slide. As Webster and Ulrich (2017) describe, a trained administrator demonstrates a particular skill to the child being tested and then allows for one practice trial. After this practice, the child performs two trials of the skill, which in turn are coded. Each skill has three to five performance criteria for each movement pattern. For example, for the run, gallop, hop, and horizontal jump, there are four performance criteria (see table 5.8).

Notice that the locomotor performance criteria align well with the locomotor developmental sequences provided in this chapter. As children become more developmentally advanced within a locomotor skill, they will exhibit higher developmental levels as well as score higher on the TGMD-3. If a child correctly demonstrates the locomotor skill performance criteria, he or she is awarded a score of 1 for the trial. On the other hand, if he or she

At first, a child might perform a unilateral step-hop—that is, a skip with the dominant leg and just a running step with the other leg. When the child begins to skip with both legs, occasional breaks, with a step or gallop interjected, are common (Gutteridge, 1939; Wickstrom, 1987).

Though no one has validated developmental steps for skipping, several changes are apparent. A beginning skipper uses a high hop and knee lift. The skip appears jerky, which perhaps reflects the need for much effort to project the body off the ground for the hop. Eventually, the child partially extends the leg on the hop and uses a lower but smoother knee lift, making the skip

does not demonstrate the appropriate criteria, a score of 0 is recorded. Total scores from the performance criteria over the two formal trials are summed to create a raw skill score; for the locomotor skills in table 5.8, this raw score can range from 0 (if no criteria are observed) to 8 (if all criteria are observed on both trials). Skill scores may be summed to provide a total raw score for the locomotor subtest, or they can be combined with the ball skills subscale to provide a total TGMD-3 raw score. The highest possible locomotor subscale raw score is 46 points. The higher the score, the better the performance on the assessment (for more information on the TGMD-3, see Ulrich, 2017, or Webster & Ulrich, 2017).

TABLE 5.8 Selected TGMD-3 Locomotor Skills Performance Criteria

SEQUENCE	LOCOMOTOR SKILL			
PERFORMANCE CRITERIA	RUN	GALLOP	HOP	HORIZONTAL JUMP
1	Arms move in opposition to legs, with elbow bending.	Arms are bent and lifted to about waist level at takeoff.	Nonhopping leg swings forward in a pendular fashion to produce force.	Before takeoff, both knees are flexed and arms are extended behind the back.
2	Both feet are off the surface for a brief period.	A step forward with the lead foot is followed by the trailing foot landing beside or a little behind the lead foot (not in front of the lead foot).	Foot on nonhopping leg remains behind hopping foot (does not cross in front of).	Arms extend forcefully forward and upward, reaching above the head.
3	Child exhibits narrow foot placement, landing on heels or toes (not flat-footed).	Both feet come off the surface for a brief period.	Arms flex and swing forward to produce force.	Both feet come off the floor together and land together.
4	Nonsupporting leg is bent about 90° so foot is close to buttocks.	Child maintains rhythmic pattern for 4 consecutive gallops.	Child hops 4 consecutive hops on the preferred leg before stopping.	Both arms are forced downward during landing.

Adapted by permission from Ulrich (2013).

smoother and more rhythmic. Perhaps greater leg strength allows the child to get the body off the ground with only partial leg extension.

Several changes occur in arm action. Beginners use the arms inconsistently, often swinging one or both arms up to the side. Skippers then begin to use the arms bilaterally, swinging them sometimes forward and back in circles, sometimes forward and down. Skilled skippers can use their arms in opposition to their legs (Wickstrom, 1987).

It is easy to speculate about why skipping is the last fundamental locomotor skill that children develop. The coordination between the legs is symmetrical, but in each leg the pattern of movement is asymmetrical. Girls typically perform these locomotor skills at an earlier age than do boys, perhaps reflecting their slight edge in biological maturity for chronological age, their imitation of other girls, or encouragement from family and friends.

Observing Galloping, Sliding, and Skipping Patterns

While observing galloping, first take a side view and note where the trailing foot lands in relation to the lead foot. The extent of vertical lift is also clearly visible from the side. Arms can be viewed from any angle. In proficient galloping the trailing foot lands alongside or behind the lead foot, the flight pattern is low, and the arms are free to swing rhythmically, clap, or engage in another activity. Note whether a child can lead with the dominant leg only or with either leg.

Sliding is best observed from the front. Focus on the knees to see if they are stiff, as in early sliding, or relaxed so that the child's steps have the spring characteristic of proficient sliding. Note whether the arms are in an inefficient guard position or are relaxed and free to be used for another task. As with galloping, you should see if a child can slide to the dominant side only or to both sides.

When watching skipping, observe whether the child skips with one leg and runs with the other or skips with both. If the child skips with both legs, look at the height of the hop and the knee lift from the side. Lower height and knee lifts characterize a more proficient, smoother skip. Finally, watch the arm pattern to see if it is bilateral or, in a more proficient skipper, in opposition to the leg movement.

Rate Limiters for Galloping, Sliding, and Skipping

Galloping generally follows running in the development of motor skills. What rate limiters exist for galloping? To gallop, individuals must uncouple their legs from the 50% phasing they use when walking and running. To do so requires rhythmic or coordination changes. At the same time, the two legs are performing different tasks (step vs. leap-step); therefore, they require different amounts of force, which requires changing force coordination (Clark & Whitall, 1989b). Thus, coordination appears to be a rate limiter for galloping. To slide, individuals must also turn to one side. The neuromuscular system may limit the rate at which these two skills required for galloping and sliding develop.

The emergence of skipping does not appear to be limited by generation of force for the hop because children hop before they skip. Nor is balance a probable rate limiter because it is more difficult to balance while hopping than while skipping. As mentioned earlier, skipping is the most complex fundamental locomotor pattern. Skipping might not appear until the individual's neuromuscular system can coordinate the two limbs as they alternately perform asymmetric tasks.

Summary and Synthesis

Transporting ourselves from here to there is an important part of human life. We consider locomotion to be one of the first signs of an infant's independence. Infants may creep, crawl, or move on hands and feet as their initial means of getting around. Not long after, they develop the ability to walk, which is the most basic form of upright bipedal locomotion. Walking involves alternating leg motion, with a period of single-foot support following a period of double-foot support. Next, toddlers run. Running is similar to walking, with alternating foot strikes, but has a period of flight rather than double support. Children then develop the ability to jump, gallop, hop, slide, and skip. All of these more complex locomotor patterns have different constraints that affect the timing and sequence in which they emerge. We can trace the changes in these motor skills throughout individual life spans as the forms of the movements change with the changing constraints of adolescence, adulthood, and older adulthood.

From crawling through skipping, children acquire fundamental locomotor skills as their bodies and the world around them change. Many individual constraints act as rate limiters to these emerging skills. After an individual acquires these skills, the form of the skills changes as the child becomes more proficient at them. If you look across locomotor skills, you can see similar patterns of change. For example, in all the locomotor skills, individuals narrow their base of support to increase mobility and widen it (as in infancy and older adulthood) to increase stability. The developmental changes described in this chapter can be used to generally estimate an individual's developmental status. Of course, the developmental sequences provide specific characteristics of these changes.

It is perhaps not surprising that researchers tend to focus on childhood when studying locomotor skills. Children not only acquire the skills rather quickly but also use the skills regularly, which is not the case for most adults. Try to remember the last time you galloped. If you can, you will probably remember that you galloped for some purpose, such as performing a dance. Adults generally do not use the entire range of fundamental locomotor patterns, at least not in the United States. What constrains these patterns from emerging? Farley (1997) describes the energetic inefficiency of human skipping; because skipping is "slow, jolting, and tiring," it makes an unlikely candidate for adult locomotion. In addition, sociocultural attitudes suggest that these motor skills are not appropriate for adults. The question remains: Do adults and older adults hop, gallop, jump, slide, and skip the same way children do?

Reinforcing What You Have Learned About Constraints

TAKE A SECOND LOOK

Julia "Hurricane" Hawkins, the world record holder for the 60-meter dash in the 100-plus division, only recently took up competitive running, but locomotion has been a part of her movement repertoire for a long time. Born in 1916 during World War I, Hawkins has 102 years of moving from place to place on her two feet. Hawkins and her fellow senior Olympians demonstrate that people can prevent or delay declines in individual constraints commonly associated with aging (e.g., strength, endurance) for a substantial period. Furthermore, adults can improve on their performance of locomotor skills long into adulthood.

TEST YOUR KNOWLEDGE

1. Describe the constraints that may act as rate controllers for specific locomotor activities.
2. How can a teacher or therapist manipulate task constraints to help a child acquire the skill of galloping?
3. What are some of the ways humans can move from place to place (without equipment)? Which ones are not currently observed in adults? Why are these locomotor forms rarely used?
4. What movement characteristics might you see in an older adult who is galloping? Why?

LEARNING EXERCISE 5.1

Comparing Preferred and Nonpreferred Hopping Legs

What individual constraints could be involved in determining the developmental level of hopping?

1. Observe three people (try to include at least one child). Ask each person to hop on his or her preferred leg (i.e., whichever foot he or she naturally chooses). Assess each hopper's developmental level using the observation plan provided in chapter 5.
2. Now, ask each person to hop on his or her opposite, or nonpreferred, leg. What happens to the person's developmental level?
3. A difference of one developmental level often exists between the preferred leg and the nonpreferred leg, particularly in children. Generate a list of possible reasons to account for the difference.

6

Development of Ballistic Skills

CHAPTER OBJECTIVES

This chapter

- identifies developmental changes in throwing, kicking, punting, and striking movements;
- compares the characteristics of early performers across the various ballistic skills; and
- notes similar characteristics of proficient performance of ballistic skills.

Motor Development in the Real World

Tennis' Grande Dame Was Still Winning at Age 97

Dorothy "Dodo" Cheney, daughter of women's tennis pioneer May Sutton and doubles champ Thomas Bundy, was a tennis star in her own right. In 1938 she won the Australian Open, but she didn't stop winning. In fact, she won more than 300 senior titles—a record in the United States Tennis Association—since the time she turned 40 years old in 1956. In 2004, she was inducted into the International Tennis Hall of Fame, and in 2010, she received a lifetime achievement award from the San Diego Hall of Champions. In 2011, she won her 381st national championship at age 95 and then won 13 more before her death at age 98. Dodo Cheney is proof that ballistic skills can be executed—and executed well—over the life span.

Ballistic skills are those in which a person applies force to an object in order to project it. The ballistic skills of throwing, kicking, and striking have similar developmental patterns because the mechanical principles involved in projecting objects are basically the same. The ballistic skill that researchers have studied most is the overhand throw for distance. Much of the discussion on overhand throwing also applies to other types of throwing and to kicking and striking, which we examine later in this chapter.

Overarm Throwing

Throwing takes many forms. The two-hand underhand throw (with windup between the legs) and the one-hand underhand throw are both common in young children. There is also a sidearm throw and a two-hand overarm throw. The type of throw a person uses, especially among children, often depends on task constraints, particularly rules and the size of the ball. Our focus, though, is on the one-hand overarm throw, which is the most common type of throw in sport games and has been studied more widely than other types. Many of the mechanical principles involved in the overarm throw apply to other types of throws as well.

Researchers often make product assessments to gauge throwing skill development; that is, they measure the end product, or result, of the throwing movement, such as the accuracy, distance, or ball velocity. However, product measures have several drawbacks. Researchers must often change an accuracy assessment task when working with children of different ages. Young children need a short distance over which to throw to reach the target, but a short distance makes the task too easy for older children, who might all achieve perfect scores. Thus, researchers must either increase the distance or decrease the target size for older groups. In addition, scores on throws for distance often reflect not just throwing skill but also factors such as body size and strength. Two children may have equal throwing skills but quite different distance scores because one child is bigger and stronger. Finally, measuring ball velocity at release requires specialized equipment that may not be readily available. Thus, we could argue that product scores are not as useful to teachers, parents, and coaches as knowing how a child throws. Let's now turn our attention to the quality of the throwing pattern.

Characteristics of Early Overarm Throwing

It is helpful to contrast children's early attempts to throw with an advanced overarm throw. Young children's throwing patterns, especially those of children under 3 years, tend to be restricted to arm action alone (Marques-Bruna & Grimshaw, 1997). The child depicted in figure 6.1 does not step into the throw or use much trunk action. This child merely positions the upper arm, often with the elbow up or forward, and executes the throw by elbow extension alone. Figure 6.2 shows more movement but little gain in mechanical efficiency. These children demonstrate minimal throwing skill.

FIGURE 6.1 A beginning thrower simply brings the hand back with the elbow up and throws by extending the elbow without taking a step.

© Mary Ann Roberton.

FIGURE 6.2 A beginning thrower. Note the trunk flexion, rather than rotation, with the throw.

© Mary Ann Roberton and Kate R. Barrett.

▶ **KEY POINT** In very young children, throwing consists of arm action alone.

Proficient Overarm Throwing

By studying the characteristics of a proficient throw, we can identify the limitations in early throwing attempts. An advanced, forceful throw for distance involves the following movement patterns:

- The weight shifts to the back foot; the trunk rotates back; and the arm makes a circular, downward **backswing** for a windup.
- The leg opposite the throwing arm steps forward to increase the distance over which the thrower applies force to the ball and to allow full trunk rotation.
- The trunk rotates forward to add force to the throw. To produce maximal force, trunk rotation is "differentiated," which means the lower torso leads the upper torso, resulting in a movement that looks like the body "opens up."
- The trunk bends laterally, away from the side of the throwing arm.
- The upper arm forms a right angle with the trunk and comes forward just as (or slightly after) the shoulders rotate to a front-facing position. This means that from the side, you can see the upper arm within the outline of the trunk.
- The thrower holds the elbow at a right angle during the forward swing, extending the arm when the shoulders reach the front-facing position. Extending the arm just before release lengthens the radius of the throwing arc.

The **backswing** is the backward, or takeaway, movement to put the arm, leg, or racket in a position to move ballistically forward to project an object.

- The forearm lags behind the trunk and upper arm during the forward swing. While the upper trunk is rotating forward, the forearm and hand appear to be stationary or to move down or back. The forearm lags until the upper trunk and shoulders actually rotate in the direction of the throw (the front-facing position).
- The follow-through dissipates the force of the throw over distance. The greater portion of wrist flexion comes during follow-through, after the thrower releases the ball.
- Dissipating force after release allows maximal speed of movement while the ball is in the hand.
- The thrower carries out the movements of the body segments sequentially, progressively adding the contributions of each part to the force of the throw. Generally, the sequence is as follows:

  1. Forward step and pelvic rotation
  2. Upper spine rotation and upper arm swing
  3. Upper arm inward rotation and elbow extension
  4. Release
  5. Follow-through

Developmental Changes in Overarm Throwing

Validated developmental sequences are sequences of advances in the performance of a skill that have been determined by longitudinal study and shown to fall in the same fixed order for all individuals.

Now that we have discussed the characteristics of an advanced, forceful throw, we can examine how an individual progresses through the developmental steps from initial throwing attempts to advanced throwing skill. Several developmental sequences of overarm throwing have been proposed, beginning with a sequence outlined by Wild in 1938 and including that of Seefeldt, Reuschlein, and Vogel in 1972. Later, Roberton proposed a developmental sequence for the overarm throw using the body component approach. Two of the component sequences, arm action and trunk action, are **validated developmental sequences** (Roberton, 1977, 1978a; Roberton & DiRocco, 1981; Roberton & Langendorfer, 1980). In fact, Roberton and Konczak (2001) determined that changes in developmental sequences (i.e., a change from level 2 to level 3) accounted for more than half the change in velocity in throwing among 39 children studied over 7 years. Carefully studying the developmental overarm throw sequence outlined in table 6.1 will help you compare these steps with the characteristics of early throwers depicted in figures 6.1 and 6.2 and those of the more advanced throwers shown in figures 6.3 through 6.6.

FIGURE 6.3 A thrower with stage 2 arm action. The forearm reaches its farthest point back before the shoulders rotate to front-facing, but the humerus then swings forward before the shoulders; the elbow is consequently visible outside the body outline. Note the right angle between the humerus and the trunk.

© Mary Ann Roberton.

If you were a physical education teacher, what factors would you expect to increase the likelihood that a developing child would reach the advanced steps in each component of throwing?

TABLE 6.1 Developmental Sequence for Throwing

SEQUENCE	ACTION
	TRUNK ACTION IN THROWING AND STRIKING FOR FORCE
Step 1	No trunk action or forward or backward movements. Only the arm is active in force production. Sometimes the forward thrust of the arm pulls the trunk into a passive left rotation (assuming a right-handed throw), but no twist-up precedes that action. If trunk action occurs, it accompanies the forward thrust of the arm by flexing forward at the hips. Preparatory extension sometimes precedes forward hip flexion.
Step 2	Upper trunk rotation or total trunk ("block") rotation. The spine and pelvis rotate away from the intended line of flight and then simultaneously begin forward rotation, acting as a unit, or block. Occasionally, only the upper spine twists away, then toward the direction of force. The pelvis, then, remains fixed, facing the line of flight, or joins the rotary movement after forward spinal rotation has begun.
Step 3	Differentiated rotation. The pelvis precedes the upper spine in initiating forward rotation. The child twists away from the intended line of ball flight and then begins forward rotation with the pelvis while the upper spine is still twisting away.
	BACKSWING, HUMERUS, AND FOREARM ACTION IN THE OVERARM THROW FOR FORCE PREPARATORY ARM BACKSWING COMPONENT
Step 1	No backswing. The ball in the hand moves directly forward to release from the arm's original position when the hand first grasped the ball.
Step 2	Elbow and humeral flexion. The ball moves away from the intended line of flight to a position behind or alongside the head by upward flexion of the humerus and concomitant elbow flexion.
Step 3	Circular, upward backswing. The ball moves away from the intended line of flight to a position behind the head via a circular overhead movement with elbow extended, or an oblique swing back, or a vertical lift from the hip.
Step 4	Circular, downward backswing. The ball moves away from the intended line of flight to a position behind the head via a circular down-and-back motion, which carries the hand below the waist.
	HUMERUS (UPPER ARM) ACTION COMPONENT DURING FORWARD SWING
Step 1	Humerus oblique. The upper arm moves forward to ball release in a plane that intersects the trunk obliquely above or below the horizontal line of the shoulders. Occasionally, during the backswing, the upper arm is placed at a right angle to the trunk, with the elbow pointing toward the target. It maintains this fixed position during the throw.
Step 2	Humerus aligned but independent. The upper arm moves forward to ball release in a plane horizontally aligned with the shoulder, forming a right angle between humerus and trunk. By the time the shoulders (upper spine) reach front-facing, the upper arm and elbow have moved independently ahead of the outline of the body (as seen from the side) via horizontal adduction at the shoulder.
Step 3	Humerus lags. The upper arm moves forward to ball release horizontally aligned, but at the moment the shoulders (upper spine) reach front-facing, the upper arm remains within the outline of the body (as seen from the side). No horizontal adduction of the upper arm occurs before front-facing.
	FOREARM ACTION COMPONENT DURING FORWARD SWING
Step 1	No forearm lag. The forearm and ball move steadily forward to ball release throughout the throwing action.
Step 2	Forearm lag. The forearm and ball appear to lag (i.e., to remain stationary behind the child or to move downward or backward in relation to the child). The lagging forearm reaches its farthest point back, deepest point down, or last stationary point before the shoulders (upper spine) reach front-facing.

(continued)

Table 6.1 continued

SEQUENCE	ACTION
Step 3	Delayed forearm lag. The lagging forearm delays reaching its final point of lag until the moment of front-facing.
FOOT ACTION COMPONENT IN FORCEFUL THROWING AND STRIKING	
Step 1	No step. The child throws from the initial foot position.
Step 2	Homolateral step. The child steps with the foot on the same side as the throwing hand.
Step 3	Short contralateral step. The child steps with the foot on the opposite side of the throwing hand.
Step 4	Long contralateral step. The child steps with the opposite foot over a distance of more than half the child's standing height.

Note: Validation studies support the trunk sequence (Langendorfer, 1982; Roberton, 1977, 1978a; Roberton & DiRocco, 1981; Roberton & Langendorfer, 1980). Validation studies also support the arm sequences for the overarm throw (Halverson, Roberton, & Langendorfer, 1982; Roberton, 1977, 1978a; Roberton & DiRocco, 1981; Roberton & Langendorfer, 1980), with the exception of the preparatory arm backswing sequence, which was hypothesized by Roberton (1984) from the work of Langendorfer (1980). Langendorfer (1982) believes the humerus and forearm components are appropriate for overarm striking. The foot action sequence was hypothesized by Roberton (1984) from the work of Leme and Shambes (1978); Seefeldt, Reuschlein, and Vogel (1972); and Wild (1937).

© Mary Ann Roberton

FIGURE 6.4 A relatively advanced thrower. Arm, leg, and preparatory action are characteristic of the most advanced step, but the trunk action is characteristic of stage 2, or block rotation, rather than differentiated rotation.

© Mary Ann Roberton.

FIGURE 6.5 From the rear you can see that this advanced thrower flexes the trunk laterally away from the ball at release.

© Mary Ann Roberton.

FIGURE 6.6 This still drawing of a baseball pitcher captures the forward movement of the hips while the upper trunk is still back. This is called differentiated trunk rotation because the hips and upper trunk rotate at different times.

© Mary Ann Roberton.

Just as with locomotor skills, you can more easily assess the developmental sequences of throwing using an observation plan (see figure 6.7, Observation Plan for Throwing).

Begin the comparison by focusing on the trunk action component. In the first step of the developmental sequence, you do not see trunk action or forward or backward movements before the thrower releases the ball (figures 6.1 and 6.2). In the second step, the thrower proceeds to a **block rotation** of the trunk. Block rotation occurs between the third and fourth positions in figure 6.4. Distance throwers typically flex the trunk laterally (figure 6.5). The most advanced trunk action—**differentiated trunk rotation**—is often observable in pictures of baseball pitchers. In figure 6.6, the pitcher has started to rotate the lower trunk toward the direction of the throw while the upper trunk is still twisting back in preparation to throw. Specific parts of the trunk start rotating forward at different times.

Block rotation of the trunk is forward rotation of the lower and upper trunk as a unit.

In **differentiated trunk rotation**, the lower trunk (hip section) rotates forward while the upper trunk (shoulder section) is rotating backward, still preparing to rotate forward.

To analyze the complexity of arm movements in throwing, first study the preparatory backswing, then the upper arm (humerus) motions, and finally the forearm motions. An unskilled thrower often does not use a backswing (figure 6.1). At the next step in the developmental sequence, a thrower flexes the shoulder and elbow in preparation for elbow extension, as in figure 6.2. A more advanced preparation involves using an upward backswing, but the most desirable backswing for a throw for distance is circular and downward. The thrower pictured in figure 6.4 is using this pattern.

As an unskilled thrower begins to swing the upper arm forward to throw, he or she often swings it at an angle oblique to the line of the shoulders—that is, with the elbow pointed up or down. A desirable advancement is to align the upper arm horizontally with the shoulders, forming a right angle with the trunk, as seen in figure 6.3. Even so, the upper arm may move ahead of the trunk's outline, which results in a loss of some of the momentum the thrower gains from moving the body parts sequentially for a forceful throw. In the most advanced pattern, the upper arm lags behind so that when the thrower reaches a front-facing position, you can see the elbow from the side within the outline of the trunk, as in figure 6.4.

It is also desirable for the forearm to lag behind. The thrower in figure 6.3 has some forearm lag, but the deepest lag comes before rather than at the front-facing position. The thrower in figure 6.4 demonstrates the advanced pattern of delayed forearm lag.

▶ **KEY POINT** Letting distal body sections lag behind more proximal ones allows momentum to be transferred and distal sections to increase speed, providing the movements are well timed.

Most unskilled throwers throw without taking a step, like the child in figure 6.1. When a child learns to take the step, he or she often does so with the homolateral leg—the leg on the same side of the body as the throwing arm—which reduces the extent of trunk rotation and the range of motion available for a forceful throw. When the child acquires the advanced pattern of a contralateral step, he or she may initially take a short step, as in figure 6.2. A long step (more than half of the thrower's height) is desirable.

The body component analysis of overarm throwing demonstrates that individuals do not achieve the same developmental step for all body components at the same time. For example, the thrower in figure 6.2 is in step 1 of trunk, humerus, and forearm action but in step 3 of foot action. The thrower in figure 6.4 is in step 3 of humerus, forearm, and foot action but in step 2 of trunk action. Children who are the same age may be moving at various levels of the body component sequences, so they look different from one another as they advance through the developmental sequence.

However, not every possible combination of steps within the components is observed. In considering the trunk, humerus, and forearm components, Langendorfer and Roberton (2002a) observed just 14 of the possible 27 combinations of developmental steps for these three components. It is likely that structural constraints limit the movements that some body sections can make while other body sections are moving in a particular way. When you observe throwing, then, you will tend to see certain common combinations and you probably will not see others at all. Langendorfer and Roberton (2002a) also studied the common combinations of steps within components as children develop. They found a tendency for children to change from no trunk rotation to trunk rotation before the upper arm and forearm advanced to intermediate levels. The shift of the humerus to an advanced level occurred after both the upper arm and forearm

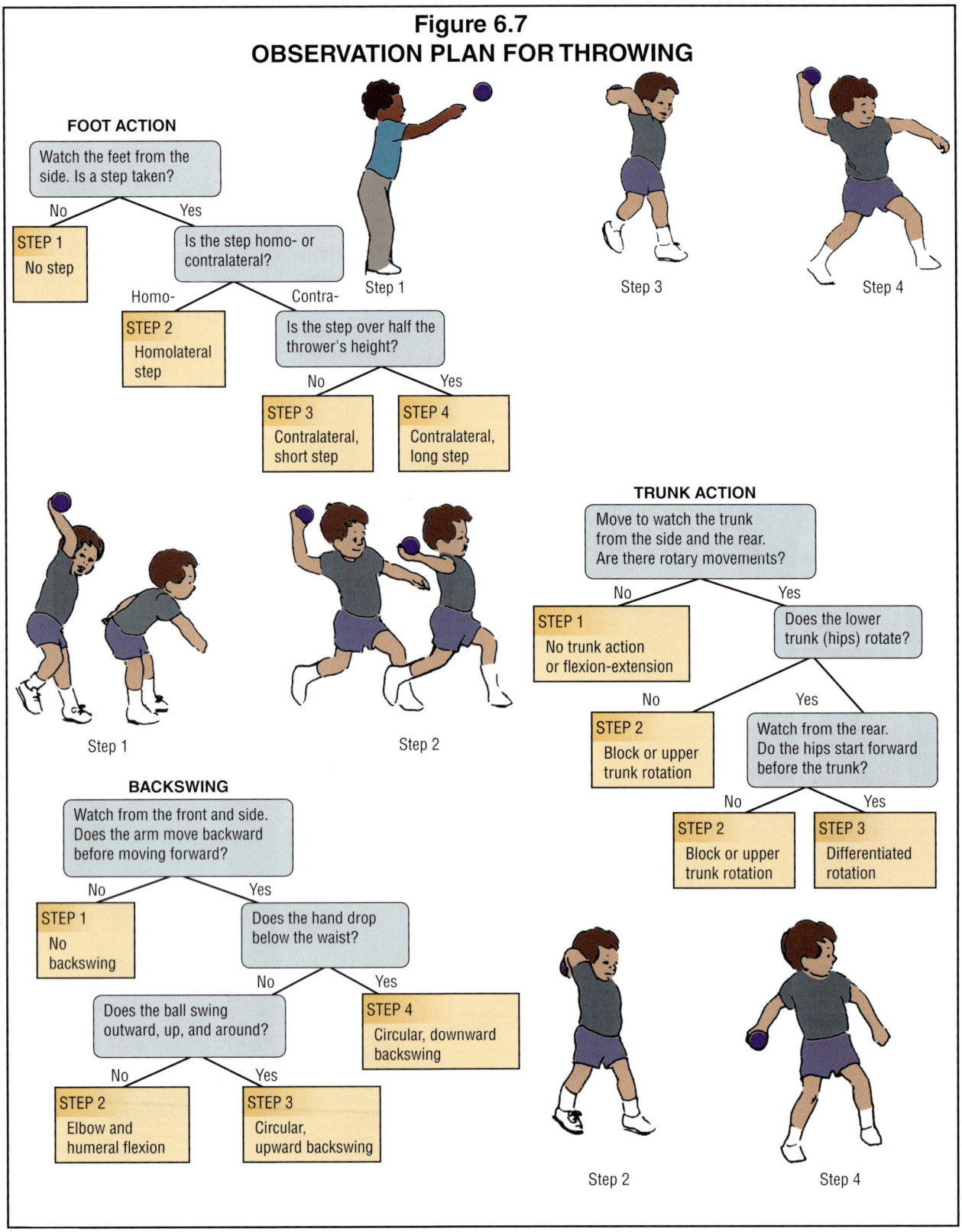

Figure 6.7
OBSERVATION PLAN FOR THROWING

© Mary Ann Roberton.

advanced to the intermediate level. It is likely that mechanical constraints and neurological development are responsible for these trends; that is, they are likely to be rate controllers in the development of throwing.

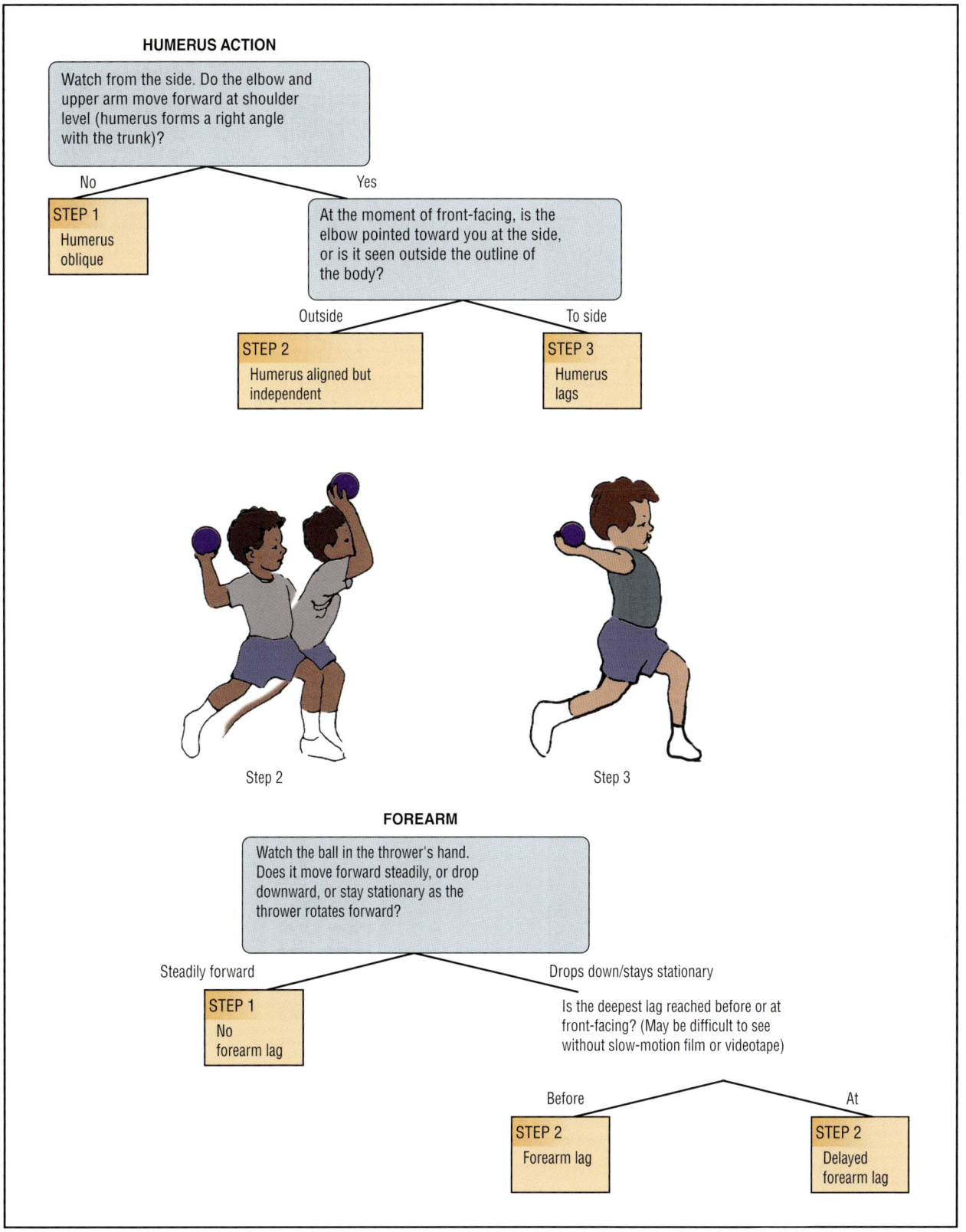

© Mary Ann Roberton.

It is desirable for all individuals to move through the various developmental steps during childhood in order to achieve an advanced throwing pattern they can use in a number of physical activities, from softball to football to team handball. Yet forceful overarm throwing is a complex skill. Yan, Payne, and Thomas (2000) recorded 51 girls approximately 3, 4, and 6 years of age. They then determined each child's developmental level for the foot, trunk, humerus, and forearm components. All but one of the 13 3-year-olds were in step 1 in each component. Thirteen of 17 4-year-olds were in step 1, and the remaining 4 were in step 2 across all body components. Eighteen of 20 6-year-olds were in step 2, using block rotation of the trunk and an aligned but independent humerus. Still, most did not take a step with their throw. Six-year-olds better coordinated their joint actions, using the open kinetic chain, than did younger girls.

Earlier, Halverson, Roberton, and Langendorfer (1982) had filmed a group of 39 children in kindergarten and first, second, and seventh grades and classified them according to Roberton's developmental sequence. Their analysis of upper arm action demonstrated that most of the younger boys were already at step 2 of humerus action, and by the seventh grade, more than 80% of boys had achieved the most advanced level (step 3). In contrast, approximately 70% of the girls were still in step 1 of humerus action when initially filmed. By the seventh grade, only 29% of the girls had reached step 3.

This trend was also apparent for forearm action. Almost 70% of the boys demonstrated step 2 forearm action when initially filmed. Some were still at this level by the seventh grade, but considerably more—a total of 41% of the boys—had reached step 3. More than 70% of the girls began in step 1, and the majority—71% of all the girls—were at only the second level in the seventh grade. Sex differences in developmental throwing progress were even more apparent for trunk action. Almost all the boys started in step 2, and 46% advanced to step 3 by the seventh grade. Similarly, almost 90% of the girls were in step 2 in kindergarten, but by the seventh grade all the girls remained in step 2; none had advanced to step 3. Additional research published in the early 2000s established that not every individual attains the advanced steps of overarm throwing (Langendorfer & Roberton, 2002a, 2002b), and no change in the gender difference favoring boys had been observed in the previous 20 years (Pulito Runion, Roberton, & Langendorfer, 2003).

These studies demonstrate developmental trends in overarm throwing, but the Halverson et al. (1982) study documented significant gender differences. Perhaps this study reflected a culture of discouraging girls to practice overarm throwing, which existed up to the 1980s in the United States. In 2008, Lorson and Goodway recorded 6- to 8-year-olds using overarm throwing in a ball game. Students were recorded before, after, and 10 days following four instruction and practice classes. Using modified developmental-level categories, the researchers found that boys were more likely than girls to take a contralateral step and more likely than girls to use trunk rotation. Forearm lag was more likely to be seen in boys than in girls and seen after the instructional classes. Although the boys tended to use more advanced throwing patterns than girls did as a group at all time points, the girls showed more advanced patterns after the instructional classes. While this more recent study still found gender differences, there are indications that instruction and practice may particularly help girls in their skill development and narrow the gender gap.

Gender differences in overarm throwing were recently studied in adolescents and adults (Lorson, Stodden, Langendorfer, & Goodway, 2013). The adolescent throwers were 14 to 17 years old, the young adults 18 to 25 years, and the midadults 35 to 55 years. Considering the three age groups and males and females together, most throwers were in either step 3 or 4 in foot action (contralateral step), step 2 of trunk action (block rotation), step 2 of humerus action (aligned but independent), and step 2 of forearm action (forearm lags). Adolescent boys were significantly more advanced than adolescent girls in foot, trunk, and forearm action. Young adult men had significantly higher developmental levels than young adult women in foot, trunk, humerus, and forearm action. Midadult men were better than only midadult women in humerus action. Although these findings agree with earlier studies documenting gender differences in component levels, this is the first study to observe a narrowing of the gender differences in the 35- to 55-year-old group. Also, there was a regression of the developmental levels in component body areas between young adulthood and middle adulthood. Future research is needed to determine the constraints responsible for the regression.

The persistence of gender differences in forceful overarm throwing has prompted much discussion among motor developmentalists, particularly on the topic of why there has not been a significant narrowing of the gender differences as girls are given more opportunities to participate in ball sports, more coaching, and more motivation to succeed in sport (e.g., college scholarships, professional careers). We will discuss sociocultural constraints on development more completely in a later chapter. For now, we can acknowledge that researchers have debated this question regarding overarm throwing.

First, researchers have examined whether biological factors (Nelson, Thomas, & Nelson, 1991) or environmental (sociocultural) factors (Williams, Haywood, & Painter, 1996) are responsible. Second, researchers have examined gender differences in other cultures. Ehl, Roberton, and Langendorfer (2005) found that German girls were behind German boys in backswing, humerus, and forearm action, but girls also reported engaging in less throwing practice than boys. Sakurai, Chentanez, and Elliott (1998) found gender differences in throwing distance in Australia, Japan, and Thailand. Thomas, Alderson, Thomas, Campbell, and Elliott (2010) researched 6-, 8-, and 10-year-old Aboriginal Australian children because of their history as hunters who relied on throwing weapons. The researchers did not assess developmental level but measured ball velocity and several kinematic variables. There were still gender differences between Aboriginal boys and girls, but the differences were much smaller than in children from the United States. The Aboriginal girls were much better throwers than were American girls. Most of the research on gender differences in overarm throwing included throwing velocity as well as developmental level, but the results for velocity have paralleled those for developmental level.

Likely, gender differences in overarm throwing are a mix of biological and sociocultural factors. The persistence of gender differences over a long arc of research history serves as a reminder that increased opportunity for participation alone is not sufficient to promote girls' throwing development. Practice is important for girls (Petranek & Barton, 2011), but more research on setting task goals to elicit maximal effort for girls is needed.

▶ **KEY POINT** Not every individual reaches the highest developmental levels of forceful overarm throwing. Gender differences in throwing likely reflect a large number of individual and environmental constraints.

Observing Overarm Throwing Patterns

Overarm throwing is complex and difficult to observe in detail. The best procedure is to focus on a small number of components, or even a single component, at any one time. Some characteristics are best observed from the front or back:

- Trunk-to-upper-arm angle
- Elbow angle
- Lateral trunk bend

Others are best observed from the throwing side:

- The step
- Trunk rotation
- Upper arm and forearm lag

Videotaping is particularly valuable in helping you observe the overarm throw. By videotaping, one can go back and review the different arm actions separately and in slow motion.

Web Study Guide **Identify developmental differences among throwers in Lab Activity 6.1, Assessing the Developmental Levels of Overarm Throwing, in the web study guide.**

Throwing in Adulthood

As we have seen, throwing is a complex skill that requires the coordination of many body segments. To execute a maximum throw, the thrower must move many joints through a full range of motion with precise timing. This makes throwing an interesting skill to study in older adults. For example, we can ask whether older adults coordinate their movements for throwing just as young adults do or use different movement patterns. If they use the same patterns, we can ask whether older adults control those movements as young adults do or vary the extent or speed of movements in ways different from the movements of young adults.

Let's begin with observations that tell us what movement patterns older adults use. Williams, Haywood, and VanSant (1990, 1991) used the developmental steps in table 6.1 to categorize active older adult men and women between the ages of 63 and 78. Although the developmental steps were identified to monitor change in children and youths, they can be used to describe the movement patterns of throwers at any age.

▶ **KEY POINT** In comparing younger and older adult throwers, we can observe both the movement patterns used and how the movements are controlled.

The older adults were active in a university-sponsored physical activity program but did not practice throwing or participate in activities with overarm movement patterns. The investigators found their throwing movements to be only moderately advanced on the developmental sequences. Most older throwers took a short contralateral step (step 3) and were categorized at step 1 or 2 of humerus action and step 1 or 2 of forearm action. Almost all used block rotation of the trunk (step 2). Sex differences similar to those in children existed; that is, men generally had better form. However, qualitative throwing status also related to childhood and young adult experiences. Those who had participated in sports with overarm movement patterns at younger ages had better throwing form.

The ball velocities generated by the older adults were moderate (similar to velocities generated by 8- to 9-year-olds). The men averaged 54.4 ft/s (16.6 m/s), and the women averaged 39.1 ft/s (11.9 m/s). Hence, the older adults also confirmed the sex differences in velocity noted in youths.

Because actions during the backswing in ballistic skills generally are related to ball velocity, Haywood, Williams, and VanSant (1991) closely examined the backswing used by older adults. Those who used a circular, downward backswing threw faster than those using an upward (therefore shorter) backswing. Many older adults used backswing movement patterns that seemed different from those that children use. For example, many started the circular, downward backswing (step 4) but did not continue the circle. Instead, they bent the elbow to bring the ball up behind the head. A possible reason for this could be a change in the musculoskeletal system, such as decreased shoulder flexibility or a loss of fast-twitch muscle fibers. Possibly the throwers could not continue arm movement at the shoulder joint, or would experience pain in doing so, and thus they reorganized the movement.

The older adults in these studies were not observed when they were young adults, so we do not know whether any or all of them reached the highest developmental level in all the body components when they were younger. We can only hypothesize that their moderate status as older adults reflects at least some change from the movement patterns of their youth.

A commonly held notion of skill performance in older adulthood is one of consistent decline with advancing age. To observe throwing with advancing age, Williams, Haywood, and VanSant (1998) observed eight older adults over a period of 7 years. One individual was in her 60s, but most were in their late 70s. In contrast to what many would predict, throwing movements were relatively consistent over the years. Participants were placed in the same sequential step in 80% of the possible observations of body components over all the years. In cases where individuals changed, the change often (though not always) involved a decline. Increased variability was associated with change; that is, if participants changed their developmental level from a previous session, they would often be inconsistent over the five trials, showing a variety of developmental levels. Williams and colleagues also observed small changes over the years that did not necessarily result in a change in developmental step. These small changes included decreased range of motion and slower movement speeds. This longitudinal observation shows that throwing performance in older adulthood is relatively stable. Small changes are more typical of performance than are large declines. Moreover, short-term training improved the anticipatory postural adjustments of older adults throwing a medicine ball (Aruin, Kanekar, Lee, & Ganesan, 2015). It might be possible to reverse some of these small changes with training.

▶ **KEY POINT** Throwing movements of older adults are characterized more by stability in the developmental steps than by rapid decline. Change is more often typified by increased variability from throw to throw, a slight slowing of movement, or a more limited range of movement.

It's clear that older adults coordinate their throwing movements in the same way as young adults of moderate throwing skill. Few older adults are observed to use the same movement patterns as the most advanced young adults, but this could reflect the limited number of observations of older adults as well as the constraints imposed by rate-controlling systems. The change observed over time in older adulthood is most likely to be change in the control of movements, especially a slowing of speed or a decrease in range of motion.

Though we need more research and more longitudinal observation of older adults, the model of constraints can guide our study of older adult performance. One or more body systems might regress, causing a slowing or limitation of movement, then reach a critical point at which the movement pattern must change. For example, advancing arthritis in the shoulder joint could cause the musculoskeletal system to act as a rate controller for throwing movements. Some movement patterns might be unique to older adulthood because declines in the various body systems that occur with aging might not be exactly the opposite of the advances that occur with physical growth. Others might well be the same movement patterns seen in children and youths as they advance through the developmental sequence.

Throwing for Accuracy

The developmental sequences constructed for overarm throwing specifically address a throw for distance rather than for accuracy. The model of constraints would lead us to predict that changing the task from throwing for distance to throwing for accuracy results in a change in the movement pattern, and Langendorfer (1990) demonstrated this to be the case. He had young adults and 9- to 10-year-olds throw for distance and accuracy. The accuracy task was to hit an 8 foot (2.4 m) circular target at a distance of 11 yards (10 m) for adults and 6.6 yards (6 m) for children. Male throwers were categorized at significantly lower developmental steps when throwing for accuracy than for distance. Female throwers tended toward lower steps but were not significantly different in the two task conditions. Langendorfer believed the distance for the accuracy throw for females resulted in a forceful task condition, which suggests that under true accuracy conditions throwers use movement patterns that are different from those for distance conditions.

▶ **KEY POINT** If the developmental sequences for forceful throwing are used to describe a short throw for accuracy, even the most proficient throwers might not use the most advanced movement patterns.

Think of throwing as it is required in three or four sports or games. Do these activities emphasize distance, accuracy, or a combination of both? In which of these conditions would it be appropriate to use the developmental sequences with the perspective that the most proficient throwers would place in the upper steps?

Williams, Haywood, and VanSant (1993, 1996) replicated Langendorfer's study with older adults, asking them to throw for distance and for accuracy to a target 11 yards (10 m) away. Throwing velocity was measured for both task conditions, and the observers found that throwers used a slower velocity in the accuracy condition. As a group, the older adults changed little from one condition to the other, but most individuals adapted their movements in at least one body component. As with Langendorfer's female throwers, the older adults likely found the 11 yards distance of the accuracy throws to require relatively more force than young men would perceive was necessary. An accuracy condition at a shorter distance might have elicited more differences in the movements used.

Of course, in sports and games, throws are rarely made for distance without some accuracy constraint, or for accuracy without the need for force. What this research demonstrates is that different movement patterns arise for different task constraints, even for the same person in the same environment. When we compare movement patterns, then, by using either developmental categories or some other description of a movement pattern, we must recognize that the comparisons are valid only when the task constraints are identical. Even then, the person–task interaction influences the movement. For example, a strong individual could throw a given distance without the need for a step of the contralateral foot, whereas a weaker individual needs a step to reach that same distance. Parents, coaches, teachers, and recreational leaders must keep such factors in mind when comparing throwers.

Web Study Guide **Compare throwing for force versus for accuracy by doing Lab Activity 6.2, Comparing Throws for Force With Throws for Accuracy, in the web study guide.**

Kicking

A **kick** is a ballistic strike of an object from the foot.

Like throwing, kicking projects an object; unlike throwing, however, the kicker strikes the object. Thus, children must have sufficient perceptual abilities and eye–foot coordination in order to execute a **kick** and consistently make contact with the ball. Teachers and parents can simplify the task for young children by challenging them to kick a stationary ball.

Characteristics of Early Kicking

As with throwing, unskilled kickers tend to use a single action rather than a sequence of actions. As you can see in figure 6.8, there is no step forward with the nonkicking leg, and the kicking leg merely pushes forward at the ball. The knee of the kicking leg may be bent at contact, and an unskilled kicker may even retract the leg immediately after contacting the ball. The trunk does not rotate, and the child holds the arms stationary at the sides. The child in figure 6.9 demonstrates more advanced kicking skill by stepping forward with the nonkicking foot, thus putting the kicking leg in a cocked or wind-up position.

FIGURE 6.8 A beginning kicker simply pushes the leg forward.
© Mary Ann Roberton.

▶ **KEY POINT** Just as young children throw with arm action alone, young kickers use only leg action.

FIGURE 6.9 This kicker has made some improvements compared with the beginning kicker. He steps forward, putting the leg in a cocked position, but the leg swing is still minimal. The knee is bent at contact, and some of the momentum of the kick is lost.

© Mary Ann Roberton.

Proficient Kicking

Compare the characteristics of early kicking with the critical features of advanced kicking shown in figure 6.10. The advanced kicker does the following:

- Starts with a preparatory windup. The kicker achieves this position, with the trunk rotated back and the kicking leg cocked, by leaping or running up to the ball. As a natural consequence of the running stride, the trunk is rotated back and the knee of the kicking leg is flexed just after the push-off of the rear leg. Hence, the kicker is able to apply maximal force over the greatest distance. Running up to the ball also contributes momentum to the kick.
- Uses sequential movements of the kicking leg. The thigh rotates forward, then the lower leg extends (knee straightens) just before contact with the ball to increase the radius of the arc through which the kicking leg travels. The straightened leg continues forward after contact to dissipate the force of the kick in the follow-through.
- Swings the kicking leg through a full range of motion at the hip.
- Uses trunk rotation to maximize the range of motion. To compensate for the complete leg swing, the kicker leans back at contact.
- Uses the arms in opposition to the legs as a reaction to trunk and leg motion.

FIGURE 6.10 An advanced kicker. Note the full range of leg motion, trunk rotation, and arm opposition.

© Mary Ann Roberton.

Developmental Changes in Kicking

The study of kicking development in children has not been as extensive as educators would like. Although we know the overall changes children must undergo to perform an advanced kick, the qualitative changes that each body part makes are not well documented. Haubenstricker, Seefeldt, and Branta (1983) found that only 10% of the 7.5- to 9.0-year-old children they studied exhibited advanced kicking form. So we have reason to speculate that, as with throwing, children do not automatically achieve proficient kicking.

What other factors can modify the movement pattern used in kicking? Mally, Battista, and Roberton (2011) investigated the effect of distance on kicking form. Using a dynamical systems perspective (see chapter 2), they postulated that distance acts as a control parameter for kicking, much as the way speed, when scaled up or down, changes a walk to a run or vice versa. Following this logic, individuals will change their kicking pattern once a critical kicking distance is reached. Mally and colleagues tested 19 children at an average age of 8.1 years. The children kicked at five randomly ordered distances (approximately 1.5, 3, 6, 9, and 12 m). They kicked three times each while being videotaped. The authors analyzed the kicks based on key features of kicking, such as the final foot position in the approach, arm position on the final step, and leg and arm action during the forward swing of the leg. Of these features, four changed significantly as a function of distance (number and type of forward steps in the approach, position of the shank in the forward leg swing, leg action in the follow-through). The fact that significant differences existed suggests that distance may act as a control parameter for kicking. This also offers clues into the basis of developmental change in the kick, in that the pattern of changes resembles that seen in prelongitudinal screening of other skills. In other words, children changed movement form when asked to kick longer distances much in the way children improve proficiency over their childhood. This suggests that the ability to generate force may be a key component driving developmental change in kicking.

Observing Kicking Patterns

To give children adequate instruction in kicking, it is especially important to observe individual children. From the side, a teacher or coach can look for

- placement of the support foot,
- range of motion and precontact extension in the kicking leg,
- range of trunk motion, and
- arm opposition.

Let's now turn to the development of punting—a special form of kicking for which researchers have hypothesized a developmental sequence.

Punting

A **punt** is a form of kicking where an object is dropped from the individual's hands before impact with the foot.

The ballistic skill of punting is mechanically similar to kicking, yet punting tends to be more difficult for children to learn. To **punt**, a child drops the ball from the hands and must time the leg swing to the dropping ball.

Characteristics of Early Punting

A beginning punter tends to toss the ball up rather than drop it and will often release the ball after the support leg contacts the ground, if the child even takes a step at all. The arms drop to the sides. The child might rigidly extend the kicking-leg knee or bend it at a right angle, as in figure 6.11. The child typically holds the foot at a right angle to the leg so that the ball contacts the toes rather than the instep, resulting in an errant punt.

Proficient Punting

To execute a sound punt, as shown in figure 6.12, a child must

- extend the arms forward with the ball in hand before dropping it as the final leg stride is taken;
- move the arms to the side after releasing the ball, then move into an arm opposition pattern;
- leap onto the supporting leg and swing the punting leg vigorously up to contact the ball, such that the body leaves the ground with a hop of the supporting leg; and
- keep the kicking-leg knee nearly straight and the toes pointed at time of contact.

FIGURE 6.11 A beginning punter takes only a short step and flexes the kicking-leg knee 90° at contact (step 1). The ball is dropped from waist height (step 3), but the arms drop to the sides at contact (step 1).

© Mary Ann Roberton.

FIGURE 6.12 An advanced punter. The last step is a leap, the ankle is extended (plantar flexed) at ball contact, and the punt is completed with a hop on the support leg (step 3). The ball is dropped early from chest height (step 4), and the arms abduct and move in opposition to the legs (step 3).

© Mary Ann Roberton.

Developmental Changes in Punting

Roberton (1978b, 1984) hypothesized a developmental sequence for punting (table 6.2). Arm action is divided into two sequences, one for the ball-release phase and one for the ball-contact phase. The ball-release sequence outlines progress that moves from tossing the ball up to begin the punt, to dropping the ball late, and finally to timing the drop appropriately. The ball-contact sequence shows that the arms make a transition from nonuse to bilateral movement, then to the arm opposition pattern that characteristically accompanies forceful lower trunk rotation.

The leg action sequence reflects a developmental transition from a short step of the nonkicking leg to a long step and finally to a leap. At contact, the ankle of the kicking leg changes from a flexed to an extended position.

TABLE 6.2 Developmental Sequence for Punting

SEQUENCE	ACTION
	ARM ACTION: BALL-RELEASE PHASE
Step 1	Upward toss. Hands are on the sides of the ball. The ball is tossed upward from both hands after the support foot has landed (if a step was taken).
Step 2	Late drop from chest height. Hands are on the sides of the ball. The ball is dropped from chest height after the support foot has landed (if a step was taken).
Step 3	Late drop from waist height. Hands are on the sides of the ball. The ball is lifted upward and forward from waist level. It is released at the same time as or just prior to the landing of the support foot.
Step 4	Early drop from chest height. One hand is rotated to the side and under the ball. The other hand is rotated to the side and top of the ball. The hands carry the ball on a forward and upward path during the approach. It is released at chest level as the final approach stride begins.
	ARM ACTION: BALL-CONTACT PHASE
Step 1	Arms drop. Arms drop bilaterally from ball release to a position on each side of the hips at ball contact.
Step 2	Arms abduct. Arms bilaterally abduct after ball release. The arm on the side of the kicking leg may pull back as that leg swings forward.
Step 3	Arm opposition. After ball release, the arms bilaterally abduct during flight. At contact, the arm opposite the kicking leg has swung forward with that leg. The arm on the side of the kicking leg remains abducted and to the rear.
	LEG ACTION: BALL-CONTACT PHASE
Step 1	No step or short step; ankle flexed. The kicking leg swings forward from a position parallel to or slightly behind the support foot. The knee may be totally extended by contact or, more frequently, still flexed 90°, with contact above or below the knee joint. The thigh is still moving upward at contact. The ankle tends to be dorsiflexed.
Step 2	Long step; ankle extension. Several steps may be taken. The last step onto the support leg is a long stride. The thigh of the kicking leg has slowed or stopped forward motion at contact. The ankle is extended (plantar flexed). The knee has 20° to 30° of extension still possible by contact.
Step 3	Leap and hop. The child may take several steps, but the last is a leap onto the support foot. After contact, the momentum of the kicking leg pulls the child off the ground in a hop.

Note: This sequence was hypothesized by Roberton (1984) and has not been validated.

© Mary Ann Roberton

Observing Punting Patterns

Observing a punter from the side offers you a view of the ball drop, the arm position, and the foot position (see figure 6.13, Observation Plan for Punting). You can clearly see the degree of foot extension at ball contact from this position.

Sidearm Striking

Although many sports and physical activities incorporate striking, research data on the development of striking is sparse. Striking encompasses numerous skills. It can be done with various body parts, such as the hands or feet. People can also use a variety of implements in various orientations, such as swinging a bat sidearm, a racket overhand, or a golf club underhand. In our discussion, we focus on one-hand **sidearm striking** with an implement and one-hand overarm striking with an implement.

Figure 6.13
OBSERVATION PLAN FOR PUNTING

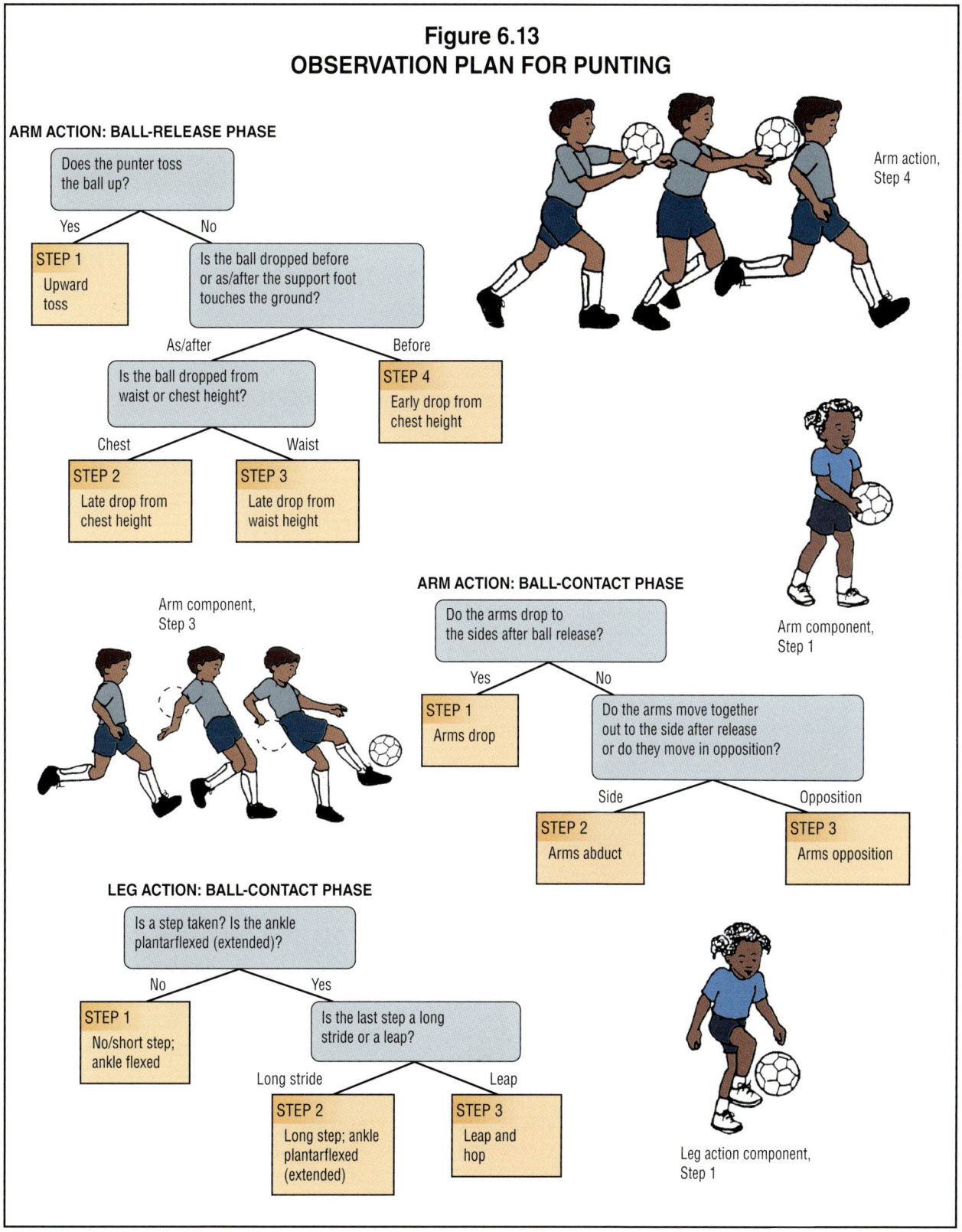

Sidearm striking is a form of striking where the arm remains at or below shoulder level. One example of sidearm striking is a person swinging a baseball bat.

Of the basic skills we've discussed so far, striking involves the most difficult perceptual judgment. Success in meeting a moving object is limited in early childhood; therefore, it is difficult to assess striking of a moving object by young children. For this reason, teachers often adapt striking tasks for young children by making the ball stationary. Researchers often base the developmental sequences on striking a stationary ball so they can describe the changes in young children's movement patterns.

We can apply the mechanical principles and developmental aspects of one-hand striking of a stationary object to other types of striking tasks. Keep this in mind as we examine the development of the striking pattern. Table 6.3 shows the developmental sequence of the sidearm strike.

TABLE 6.3 Developmental Sequence for Sidearm Striking

SEQUENCE	ACTION
RACKET ACTION COMPONENT	
Step 1	Chop. The racket is swung in the vertical plane.
Step 2	Arm swing only. The racket swings ahead of the trunk.
Step 3	Racket lag. The racket lags behind trunk rotation but goes ahead of the trunk at front-facing.
Step 4	Delayed racket lag. The racket is still lagging behind the trunk at front-facing.
FOOT, TRUNK, AND UPPER ARM ACTION COMPONENT	
See the foot, trunk, and upper arm sections in table 6.1.	

Characteristics of Early Sidearm Striking

A child's first attempts to strike sidearm often look like unskilled attempts to throw overhand. The child chops at the oncoming ball by extending at the elbow, using little leg and trunk action. As in figure 6.14, the child often faces the oncoming ball.

Proficient Sidearm Striking

An advanced sidearm strike incorporates many of the characteristics of an advanced overarm throw. Such characteristics include the following:

- Stepping into the hit, thus applying linear force to the strike. The step should cover a distance more than half the individual's standing height (Roberton, 1978b, 1984). The preparatory stance should be sideways to allow for this step and the sidearm swing.
- Using differentiated trunk rotation to permit a larger swing and to contribute more force through rotary movement.
- Swinging through a full range of motion to apply the greatest force possible.
- Swinging in a roughly horizontal plane and extending the arms just before contact.
- Linking or chaining the movements together to produce the greatest force possible. The sequence is as follows: backswing and forward step, pelvic rotation, spinal rotation and swing, arm extension, contact, and follow-through.

FIGURE 6.14 This young girl executes a striking task with arm action only. She faces the ball and swings down rather than sideways.

© Mary Ann Roberton.

Developmental Changes in Sidearm Striking

Researchers have not validated a completed developmental sequence for sidearm striking, but we can apply the sequences for foot and trunk action in the overarm throw to striking (see figure 6.15, Observation Plan for Sidearm Striking). In addition, we know some of the qualitative changes individuals make in the arm action for sidearm striking. The arm action for sidearm striking is distinct from that for overarm and underarm (as in the golf swing) striking, but all three forms share many of the same mechanical principles. We discuss sidearm striking first, but keep in mind that many of the qualitative changes in the arm action for sidearm striking, as well as the mechanical principles involved, apply to overarm striking as well.

The first obvious change in sidearm striking from the technique shown in figure 6.14 occurs when a striker stands sideways to the path of the incoming ball. By transferring the weight to the rear foot, taking a step forward, and transferring the weight forward at contact, a striker is able to improve striking skills. The child pictured in figure 6.16 turns sideways but has not yet learned to step into the strike.

Figure 6.15
OBSERVATION PLAN FOR SIDEARM STRIKING
(for foot, trunk, and humerus components, use the throwing observation)

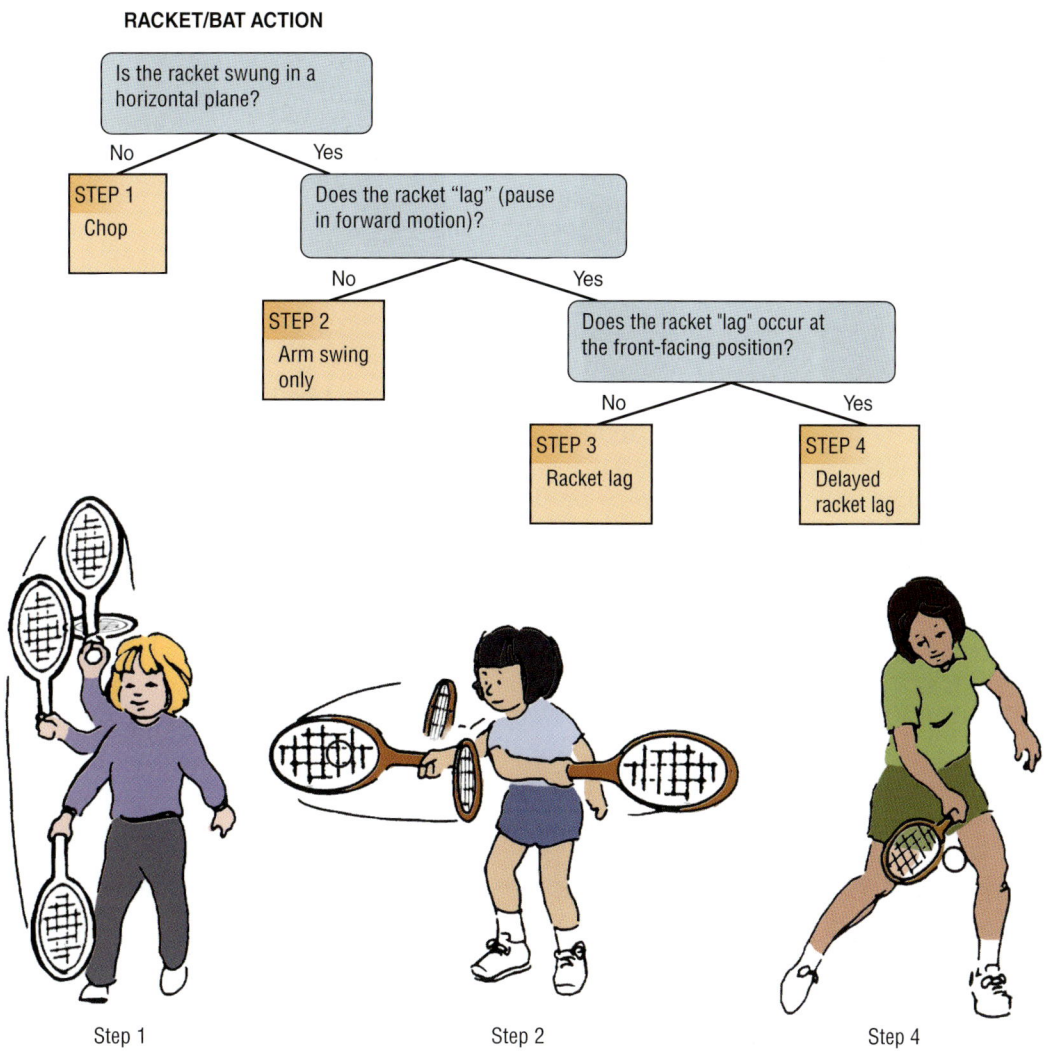

A second beneficial change is the use of trunk rotation. In a developmental sequence similar to that for throwing, individuals first use block rotation before advancing to differentiated (hip, then shoulder) rotation. A skilled striker who uses differentiated rotation appears in figure 6.17.

Strikers also progressively change the plane of their swing from the vertical chop seen in figure 6.14 to an oblique plane and finally to a horizontal plane, as seen in figure 6.16. Eventually, they obtain a longer swing by holding their elbows away from their sides and extending their arms just before contact. A beginning striker frequently holds a racket or paddle with a power grip,

FIGURE 6.16 This girl has made improvements as compared with the beginning striker in that she stands sideways and executes a sidearm strike. However, she does not yet involve the lower body.

© Mary Ann Roberton.

FIGURE 6.17 An advanced striker. The swing arm moves through a full range of motion. The striker steps into the swing and uses differentiated trunk rotation.

© Mary Ann Roberton.

where the handle is held in the palm like a club (figure 6.18, *a* and *b*). With this grip the striker tends to keep the elbow flexed during the swing and to supinate the forearm, thus undercutting the ball. Although children tend to use the power grip with any striking implement, they most often adopt it when given implements that are too big and heavy for them. Educators can promote use of the proper "shake-hands" grip by giving children striking implements that are an appropriate size and weight (Roberton & Halverson, 1984)—that is, by scaling the size and weight of the implement to the size and strength of the child.

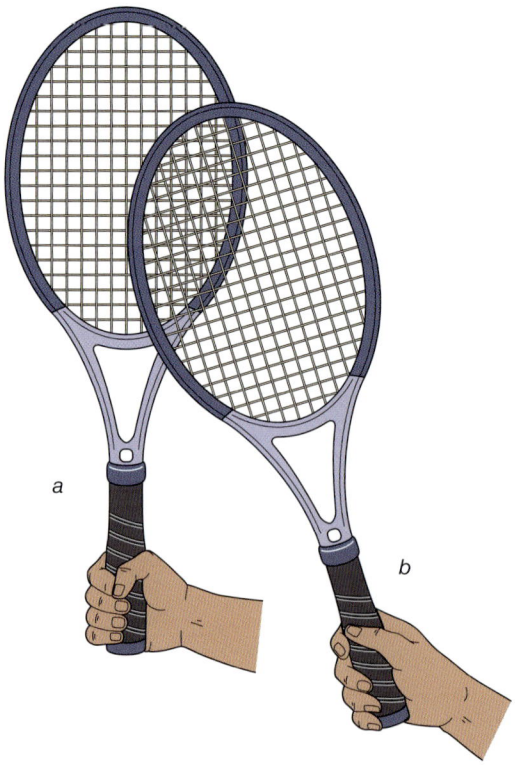

FIGURE 6.18 *(a)* Beginners often use a power grip, causing them to undercut the ball. *(b)* A "shake-hands" grip is desirable for sidearm striking.

Observing Sidearm Striking Patterns

As with many of the skills we've looked at thus far, studying a child's swing from more than one location yields the most information. From the "pitching" position (i.e., directly in front of the child, at a safe distance away and in a location where you can administer a pitch) you can observe the direction of the step, the plane of the swing, and arm extension. From the side you can check the step, the trunk rotation, and the extent of the swing.

Overarm Striking

One can execute **overarm striking** without an implement, as in the overarm volleyball serve, or with an implement, such as in the tennis serve. We focus on overarm striking with an implement.

Overarm striking is a form of striking where the arm travels above the shoulder level. One example of overarm striking is a person swinging a racket in a tennis serve.

Characteristics of Early Overarm Striking

A beginning striker demonstrates limited pelvic and spinal movement, swings with a collapsed elbow, and swings the arm and racket forward in unison, as in figure 6.19. If the striker is receiving a pitched ball, the collapsed elbow leads to a low point of contact between the racket and the ball. The movement pattern of early overarm striking, then, is similar to that of early overarm throwing and early sidearm striking.

Proficient Overarm Striking

A person who is skilled at overarm striking, as depicted in figure 6.20, does the following:

- Rotates both the pelvis and the spine more than 90°.
- Holds the elbow at an angle between 90° and 119° at the start of forward movement.
- Lets the racket lag behind the arm during the forward swing.

FIGURE 6.19 Beginning overarm striking. Trunk movement is minimal. The elbow is collapsed, and the arm and racket move together.

FIGURE 6.20 Proficient overarm striking. Trunk rotation is obvious. The racket lags behind the arm during the swing.

Racket lag is consistent with the open kinetic chain principle, where force is generated by a correctly timed sequence of movements. The humerus and forearm lag is an example of an open kinetic chain: The humerus lags behind trunk rotation, the forearm lags behind the humerus, and the racket lags behind the forearm to create the chain of sequential movements.

Developmental Changes in Overarm Striking

Langendorfer (1987) and Messick (1991) proposed developmental sequences for overarm striking. Both sequences are based on cross-sectional studies; neither has been validated with longitudinal research.

Overarm striking is similar to overarm throwing and sidearm striking, but it also has unique features. Langendorfer identified eight component sequences from a study of children 1 to 10 years old. The trunk, humerus, forearm, and leg sequences are similar to those for overarm throwing (table 6.1). Sequences unique to overarm striking include pelvic range of motion, spinal range of motion, elbow angle, and racket action (table 6.4). Messick observed 9- to 19-year-olds executing tennis serves. She identified elbow angle and racket sequences similar to those that Langendorfer identified, except that extending the forearm and racket up to contact the ball was characteristic of the tennis serves. She also noted a developmental sequence of preparatory trunk action in tennis overarm striking. This appears in table 6.4.

Neither Langendorfer nor Messick found the developmental sequences for foot action in throwing to apply to overarm striking, although they observed age differences in weight shift-

TABLE 6.4 Developmental Sequence for Overarm Striking

SEQUENCE	ACTION
PREPARATORY PHASE: TRUNK ACTION	
Step 1	No trunk action or flexion and extension of the trunk
Step 2	Minimal trunk rotation (<180°)
Step 3	Total trunk rotation (>180°)
BALL-CONTACT PHASE: ELBOW ACTION	
Step 1	Angle is 20°or less, or greater than 120°
Step 2	Angle is 21° to 89°
Step 3	Angle is 90° to 119°
BALL-CONTACT PHASE: SPINAL RANGE OF MOTION	
Step 1	Spine (at shoulders) rotates through less than 45°
Step 2	Spine rotates between 45° and 89°
Step 3	Spine rotates more than 90°
BALL-CONTACT PHASE: PELVIC RANGE OF MOTION	
Step 1	Pelvis (below the waist) rotates through less than 45°
Step 2	Pelvis rotates between 45° and 89°
Step 3	Pelvis rotates more than 90°
BALL-CONTACT PHASE: RACKET ACTION	
Step 1	No racket lag
Step 2	Racket lag
Step 3	Delayed racket lag (and upward extension)

The preparatory trunk action and the parenthetical information in step 3 of racket action are reprinted by permission from Messick (1991); Remaining components are reprinted by permission from Langendorfer (1987).

ing—older performers shifted their weight more than younger ones. Perhaps overarm striking requires a different sequence that has not yet been identified. This may be especially true in the context of tennis, where the rules specify that the server must not step on or over the baseline before striking the ball.

Observing Overarm Striking Patterns

Observation of overarm striking is similar to that of sidearm striking. You might prefer, though, to watch from behind rather than from the "pitching" position, in addition to watching from the side.

Web Study Guide **Identify developmental differences among strikers in Lab Activity 6.3, Assessing the Developmental Levels of Striking, in the web study guide.**

Older Adult Striking

As active middle-aged and older adults such as Dodo Cheney make sports news, we know that ballistic skills can be lifetime skills. The research on active adults performing ballistic skills is limited but likely to increase as larger numbers of seniors maintain an active lifestyle involving sports that require ballistic skills. It is not surprising that tennis and golf are two of the contexts for older adult research because both have a large senior following and established senior programs.

The tempo and rhythm of a short iron shot in golf have been compared in younger (19- to 25-year-old) and older (60- to 69-year-old) males who are experienced golfers (Jagacinski, Greenberg, & Liao, 1997). This task, of course, emphasizes accuracy more than distance. As a group, the older golfers had a slightly faster tempo, or overall speed of the shot. Differences in rhythm also existed. Older golfers reached peak force earlier in the swing, whereas younger players reached it just before impact. Older golfers also had larger force changes in later phases of the swing. This might indicate that the older golfers exert relatively more force to execute this short iron shot than younger golfers. In terms of accuracy, 3 of 12 older golfers made less than 10% of their shots, but the remainder were as accurate as the younger golfers. Increased variability in accuracy among members of the older group was found, then, and many older golfers showed no decrement. We should keep in mind that the strength and flexibility demands of this task were relatively low; thus, losses of strength and flexibility with advancing age would not have constrained the older golfers compared with younger ones.

What might be the rate controllers causing older adults to reorganize their movement patterns for striking? Would these controllers differ for those who remain active in a "striking" sport, as compared with those who are sedentary?

Haywood and Williams (1995) observed older adult tennis players as they executed an overarm serve. These older adults played tennis an average of 2.7 times per week. They were divided into a younger group (from 62 up to 68 years old) and an older group (69 up to 81 years old). The developmental steps described earlier for preparatory trunk action, elbow action, and forearm and racket action were used to categorize the servers by movement pattern. Ball impact velocity was also measured. The younger and older servers did not differ in any of these measures, nor did male and female servers differ. Most of the servers used moderate-level trunk, forearm, and racket movements, but the older group was somewhat more advanced in elbow action. So the investigators found little evidence of significant decline for a population continuing to use a striking skill.

▶ **KEY POINT** Many older performers can be as accurate as younger performers when strength and flexibility demands are not high, but it is likely that some performers in a group of elders will not be as accurate as the young.

▶ **KEY POINT** Well-practiced movement patterns might be well maintained over the life span.

Assessing Ballistic Skills: Test of Gross Motor Development

The developmental sequences for throwing, kicking, punting, sidearm striking, and overarm striking can be used to assess a performer's developmental progress, but assessment tools can be used as well. The previous chapter outlines the Test of Gross Motor Development (TGMD) and its evolution and describes the locomotor portion of the assessment. Here, the ball skills subscale of the TGMD-3 is presented. The skills assessed in the subscale are as follows: two-hand striking of a stationary ball, forehand striking of a self-bounced ball, one-hand stationary dribbling, two-hand catching, kicking a stationary ball, overhand throwing, and underhand throwing. The TGMD-3 provides exact specifications for materials and the directions to be given to the performer (Ulrich, 2013). The procedure for administering each item is the same as for locomotor skills: A trained administrator demonstrates the skill, one practice trial is permitted, and then two trials of the skill are performed for coding (Webster & Ulrich, 2017). The scoring procedure also is the same. Just as with the locomotor skills, there are four performance criteria for each skill. The criteria for three of the seven ball skills are presented in table 6.5. The two-hand catch is presented in the next chapter. Notice that many of the performance criteria are similar to the developmental steps described in this chapter for each of the skills.

TABLE 6.5 Selected TGMD-3 Ball Skills Performance Criteria

SEQUENCE PERFORMANCE CRITERIA	BALL SKILL		
	FOREARM STRIKE	KICK	OVERHAND THROW
1	Child takes a backswing with the paddle when ball is bounced.	Approach to the ball is rapid and continuous.	Windup is initiated with a downward movement of hand and arm.
2	Child steps toward the ball with nonpreferred foot.	Child takes an elongated stride or leap just before ball contact.	Hip and shoulder rotate to a point where the non-throwing side faces the wall.
3	Child strikes ball forward toward the wall.	Nonkicking foot is placed close to the ball.	The foot opposite the throwing hand steps toward the wall.
4	Paddle follows through toward nonpreferred shoulder.	Child kicks ball with instep of preferred foot (not the toes).	Throwing hand follows through after ball release across the body toward the hip on the nonthrowing side.

Reprinted by permission from Ulrich (2013).

The investigators measured static shoulder flexibility in the senior tennis players to determine whether a decline of flexibility might act as a rate controller for overarm striking movements. However, there was no difference in flexibility between the two age groups. Of course, as with the older throwers described earlier, these tennis players were not observed longitudinally, and we do not know whether they ever used more advanced movement patterns. Two of the servers, one man and one woman, were placed into the highest developmental category of each body component observed; both servers were former tennis teaching professionals. This investigation therefore suggests that well-practiced movement patterns tend to be maintained over the older adult years and perhaps even from younger years.

Interventions

There has been recent interest in interventions that promote development of the fundamental motor skills in preschool and early elementary school children. Much of this interest derives from the proficiency barrier hypothesis discussed in chapter 1. Children must cross the barrier to ever achieve advanced and sport-related skills. As we will discuss later in chapter 12, motor skill competency is important for achieving lifelong health and wellness. Recent research shows the benefits and characteristics of successful intervention programs.

Two systematic reviews and meta-analyses have examined multiple studies of interventions. Van Capelle, Broderick, van Doorn, Ward, and Parmenter (2017) focused on studies of 3- to 5-year-olds. They analyzed 20 studies, 13 of a teacher-led intervention, six of a child-centered intervention, and one of a parent-led intervention. Specialists trained the intervention leaders. The intervention time varied widely across the studies, but the average was 21 weeks in length, three times per week, for 35 minutes. The meta-analysis yielded evidence that teacher-led interventions significantly improved overall fundamental motor skills, as well as object control (ballistic and manipulative skills) and locomotor skills specifically, in children participating in the intervention compared with children who did not.

Wick et al. (2017) analyzed studies of interventions with children in a wider age range, 2 to 6 years old. Their meta-analysis on 26 studies led to the conclusion that fundamental motor skill interventions were beneficial to overall skill, object control, and locomotor skill proficiency. Interventions involving experts on motor skill development tended to have a larger effect than those programs that did not involve experts. The researchers pointed to the need for higher-quality research studies with better randomization of the study participants and research on whether the skill advantage young children attain in an intervention is maintained throughout childhood and adolescence.

Also, a study of children 3 to 8 years of age demonstrated a higher improvement in both locomotor and object control skills for children in an intervention program supplementing regular physical education compared with those not in the supplemental intervention (Bardid et al., 2017). This widens the age period over which interventions have been found to be beneficial.

Earlier it was noted that not as many girls as boys seem to reach the more advanced levels of throwing at the same age. Veldman, Palmer, Okley, and Robinson (2017) implemented a mastery-based, high-autonomy 9-week intervention that focused on ball skills in preschool-aged girls. They demonstrated both short- and long-term improvements in the girls' ball skills after the intervention program. Such intervention programs might be particularly important for increasing the opportunities for girls and women to advance in ball skills performance.

Although further research on this topic is needed, evidence supports the notion that children benefit from instruction and practice of the fundamental motor skills, that these skills do not develop automatically, and that childhood is an important period for developing skill proficiency that might provide a lifetime benefit. Again, we will look further into this possibility in chapter 12.

Summary and Synthesis

Proficient performance of ballistic skills requires movements that obey mechanical principles for maximizing force and speed (as discussed in chapter 3). As children and youths improve their ballistic skills, we see changes that make their movements more and more consistent with those mechanical principles. Examples include a forward step that transfers momentum into the direction of the throw or strike; rotary motions of the trunk, usually sequenced as lower trunk followed by upper trunk for arm throws and strikes; and sequential movement of the projecting limb to allow distal body components and striking implements to lag behind larger and more proximal body components so that momentum is transferred and speed is increased. We know that transition to the most efficient movement patterns is not automatic. Some adults continue to use movement patterns that produce moderate results when maximal ones are desired. Because little observation of life span striking performance is available, it is difficult to know the amount of decline in the throwing and striking performance of older adults. Active older adults, however, appear to maintain movement patterns fairly well, especially when the patterns are well practiced.

Task conditions and the interaction between the person and the task are important for determining what movement patterns emerge in performance. In assessing how youths are progressing or whether seniors are declining, we must not only consider the rate controllers possibly influencing those changes but also acknowledge the particular task conditions for the movement observed. An individual throwing a short distance for accuracy would not necessarily need to use the movements characteristic of the most advanced level in each body component.

Reinforcing What You Have Learned About Constraints

TAKE A SECOND LOOK

Dorothy "Dodo" Cheney integrated changing constraints in order to remain successful at tennis over eight decades. She adapted to changes in her own body, winning matches in every age group in which she played. She also won on every playing surface on which she competed (environmental constraints) and in singles, doubles, and mixed doubles (task constraints)!

TEST YOUR KNOWLEDGE

1. What distinguishes kicking from punting?
2. Identify four of the major qualitative changes in the development of each of the following ballistic skills: throwing, punting, and overarm striking.
3. What qualitative developmental changes are shared by throwing and overarm striking? Why might both skills change in these ways?
4. What characteristics of intervention programs result in the improved performance of young children?

LEARNING EXERCISE 6.1

Overarm Throwing: Changes in Form Related to Changes in the Throwing Arm

What individual constraints could be involved in determining the developmental level of overarm throwing for force?

1. Observe three people (try to include at least one child). Ask each person to throw with his or her preferred arm (i.e., the arm he or she naturally chooses). Assess each thrower's developmental level using the observation plan provided in chapter 6.
2. Now, ask each person to throw with the opposite, or nonpreferred, arm. What happens to the developmental level?
3. There will often be a difference of at least one developmental level between the preferred and nonpreferred throwing arms. Generate a list of possible reasons to account for the difference.

7

Development of Manipulative Skills

CHAPTER OBJECTIVES

This chapter

- documents a transition in infancy from the use of power grips to pick up objects to the use of precision grips;
- demonstrates how the size of an object, relative to the size of the hand, can influence the grip used to pick up the object;
- examines the role of vision in learning to reach for objects;
- identifies developmental changes in catching; and
- considers how catchers are able to intercept objects.

Motor Development in the Real World

Helping Hands

In January of 2018, Matthew Scott celebrated the 19th anniversary of his hand transplant, which was the first in the United States. Scott, who is left handed, lost his left hand in a firecracker accident in 1985. He received the transplant from a cadaver in a 15-hour operation (Composite Tissue Allotransplantation, 2012). A year and a half later, Scott was able to sense temperature, pressure, and pain in his new hand as well as turn pages, tie shoelaces, and throw a baseball. By his 8-year checkup he could hold a 15-pound weight with his transplanted hand and pick up small objects.

Those of us who have had an arm or wrist in a cast can probably begin to imagine what it would be like to attempt certain tasks or sports with one hand or without hands. Our hands allow us to perform a wide range of skills, from handling small, delicate objects to steering large ships. Today the use of cell phones to send text messages is commonplace, and most teens probably consider typing text messages to be a fundamental skill!

As with any other movement, we expect limb movements to arise from the interaction of individual, task, and environmental constraints. Consider the task of lifting a heavy crystal bowl from a table, as well as the question of whether an individual should pick it up with one hand or two. The environment plays a role because gravity acts on the object. Crystal is heavier than plain glass. The task is a factor in several ways. Consider the shape of the bowl. Does the shape and the weight—that is, the interaction of environment and task—afford lifting the bowl with one hand, or does it require two? Now consider the person's strength. Does this individual structural constraint interact with task and environment to afford lifting with one hand or two?

With growth and aging, many individual structural constraints change. The length and size of the limbs change with growth, as does strength. On the other hand, when we age, conditions such as arthritis can make manipulative skills difficult or even painful. Thus, just as with other types of skills, the performance of manipulative skills changes with growth and aging.

Grasping and Reaching

Prehension is the grasping of an object, usually with the hand or hands.

When a skilled adult wants to obtain a small object, the arm reaches forward and then the hand grasps the object. The reach and grasp form a smooth movement unit. To simplify our study of the development of reaching and grasping in infancy, however, we'll consider grasping, or **prehension**, first.

Grasping

In 1931, H.M. Halverson published a classic description of grasping development, the 10 phases of which are summarized in figure 7.1. Halverson filmed infants between 16 and 52 weeks of age grasping a 1-inch (2.5 cm) cube. In early grasping, the infant squeezes an object against the palm without the thumb providing opposition. Eventually, the infant uses the thumb in opposition but still holds the object against the palm. Such grips are collectively called power grips. Halverson observed that after about 9 months of age, infants began to hold objects

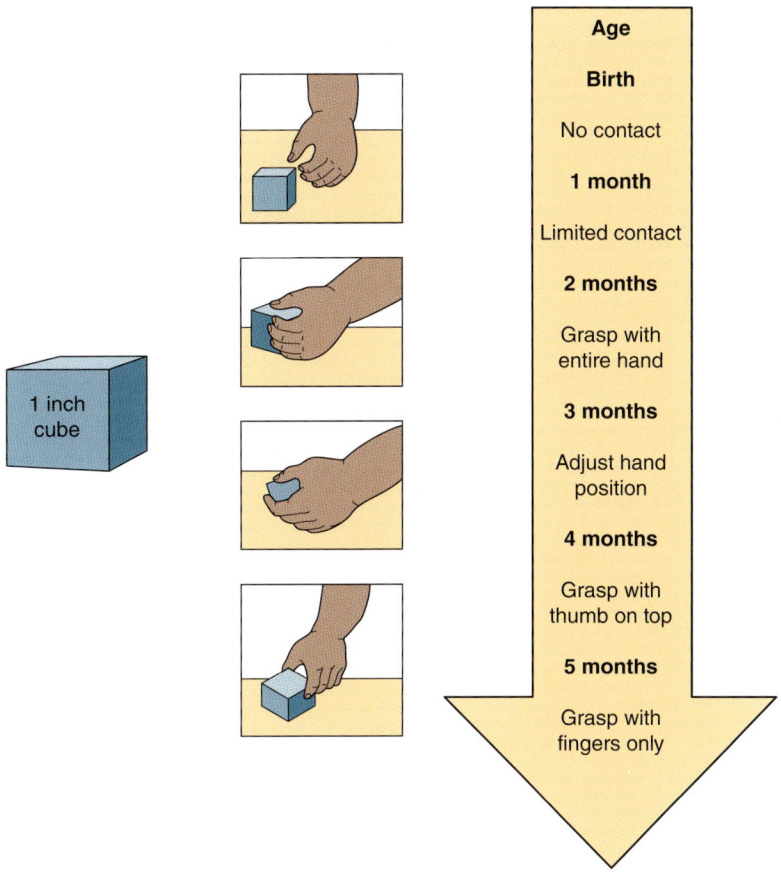

FIGURE 7.1 A developmental progression of grasping.
Illustration by Nancy Getchell.

between the thumb and one or more fingers; these are called precision grips. Thus, the first year is characterized by a transition from power grips to precision grips.

Hohlstein (1982) later replicated Halverson's study, but in addition to the 1-inch cube used in the original study, she provided objects of different sizes and shapes. The transition from power to precision grips was still evident, but shape and size of the object influenced the specific type of grasp used. In fact, by 9 months of age infants reliably shape their hand in anticipation of an object's shape as they go to grasp it (Lockman, Ashmead, & Bushnell, 1984; Piéraut-Le Bonniec, 1985).

▶ **KEY POINT** The first year sees a transition from power grips to precision grips, but the particular grip used is influenced by the shape and size of the object grasped.

Through Halverson's early work, developmentalists viewed prehension as a behavior acquired in steps. Maturationists of Halverson's era viewed these age-related changes in the same vein as motor milestones. They linked each progression to a new stage with neuromotor maturation, especially maturation of the motor cortex. However, the finding that shape and size of the object to be grasped influence the grip used suggests that the individual, the environment, and the task interact in prehension movements. Halverson studied only one set of environment and task characteristics. More variety of movement grips is observed with changing environment and task characteristics in the early months of life.

For example, Newell, Scully, McDonald, and Baillargeon (1989) watched 4- to 8-month-old infants grasp a cube and three cups of different diameters. They found that infants used five types of grip 95% of the time. The specific grip seemed to depend on the size and shape of the object. The investigators even observed precision grips with the smallest cup at a younger age than Halverson observed. Because we can observe this precision grip at such a young age, it's clear that the neuromotor system must be mature enough at this young age to control the precision grip. Lee, Liu, and Newell (2006), who observed prehension longitudinally from age 9 to 37 weeks, also found that the grasp used by infants depended on the properties of the object. Clearly, then, neuromotor maturation is not the only structural constraint involved in grasping.

▶ **KEY POINT** After infancy, visual information and body size appear to constrain the shape of the hands in grasping and the number of hands used to grasp a particular object.

Body scaling is adapting characteristics of the task or environment to the overall body size or to the size of a body component such that the same movement or action can be carried out by individuals of different sizes because the ratio of body size to object or dimension is the same—that is, a body-scaled ratio is relatively constant.

Newell, Scully, Tenenbaum, and Hardiman (1989) suggested, based on observations of older children, that the grip used to obtain any particular object depends on the relationship between hand size and object size. That is, the movement selected by individuals is related to their hand size compared with an object's size, or movements reflect **body scaling**. Butterworth, Verweij, and Hopkins (1997) tested this idea by having infants between 6 and 20 months of age pick up cubes and spheres of different sizes. They confirmed Halverson's general trend from power to precision grips. By early in the second year, precision grips predominated. Younger infants tended to use more fingers to grasp the objects than older infants did. Object *size* greatly influenced the grip selected, and *shape* had somewhat less influence on the grip. Butterworth and colleagues observed all but Halverson's inferior-forefinger grasp in the youngest infants, 6 to 8 months of age, so infants use a greater variety of grips than we would assume from Halverson's work. Thus, neuromotor development for grasping movements must be more advanced than those in Halverson's day thought. Task and environmental constraints clearly play an important role in infants' adaptations of their movements.

Think about making and eating your breakfast in the morning. How many objects do you grip, and how does the configuration of your hand change for each one? Have you ever broken your wrist and found it was difficult to do such tasks?

It so happened that the infant boys in Butterworth and colleagues' study had longer hands than the girls had. The hypothesis of Newell, Scully, Tenenbaum, and Hardiman predicted that these boys and girls would use different grips, but this was not the case. Thus, the influence of object size on grip used supports the idea that the ratio between hand size and object size is important, but the lack of a difference between the boys and girls does not. Therefore, more research is needed before we know whether infants do in fact use body scaling in selecting a grip. Still, this work affirms that interactions between the infant, the environment, and the task are important even in early grasping and that changes in movement patterns related to changing structural constraints occur even in infancy.

Is body scaling used at older ages? Do older children and adults use the ratio of hand size to object size in selecting a grip? Newell, Scully, Tenenbaum, and Hardiman (1989) observed 3- to 5-year-olds and adults. They found that a relatively constant ratio of hand size to object size determined when individuals chose to use two hands to pick up an object instead of one, no matter what their age. Thus, the ratio was consistent even though the adults had larger hands. The same has been found to be true in children 5, 7, and 9 years of age (van der Kamp, Savelsbergh, & Davis, 1998). The interaction of the individual's structural constraints with environmental and task constraints, then, gives rise to either a one-hand or a two-hand grasp.

Vision also plays a role in this type of task. From a young age, we select the grip appropriate for the size, weight, and shape of the object to be obtained (figure 7.2). Butterworth and colleagues (1997) observed that infants often knocked an object before actually grasping it. In contrast, adults configure, or shape, their hands for a particular object *before* making contact with it. Adults also make a decision about whether to reach for an object with one hand or two *before* making contact with it. That is, visual information is used in preparation for the grasp. During childhood, individuals acquire the experience with objects needed to precisely configure the hand. Kuhtz-Buschbeck et al. (1998) noted that 6- and 7-year-olds were more dependent than adults on visual feedback during the reach to shape their hand for the grasp. Similarly, Pryde, Roy, and Campbell (1998) observed 9- and 10-year-olds slowing down more than adults at the end of a reach, presumably taking more time to use visual information for grasping the object. Older children, in the 5- to 10-year-old range, and adults appear to use visual information to anticipate the grasp and optimize accuracy (Smyth, Katamba, & Peacock, 2004; Smyth, Peacock, & Katamba, 2004).

If indeed body scaling determines grip selection starting in childhood, grasping quickly becomes a well-practiced skill, with growing hand size and arm length taken into account in the body-scaled ratio. Grasping doesn't need to be relearned with increases in growth. Thus, we might expect it to be a very stable skill over the life span. Only conditions such as arthritis or a loss of strength in old age would influence hand configuration. Indeed Carnahan, Vandervoort, and Swanson (1998) found that young adults (average age 26 years) and older adults (average age 70 years) accurately adapted the opening of the hand to grasp moving objects of different sizes. Of course, most manipulative tasks are not just a matter of grasping an object but rather of bringing the hand to an object so that it can be grasped. We now examine the development of reaching over the life span.

Think about your experience in grasping objects. Have you ever said, "This is heavier than it looks"? Or "This is lighter than it looks"? What does this tell you about the role of vision in grasping?

Web Study Guide **Identify different grasping techniques during infancy in Lab Activity 7.1, Observing Grasping Development, in the web study guide.**

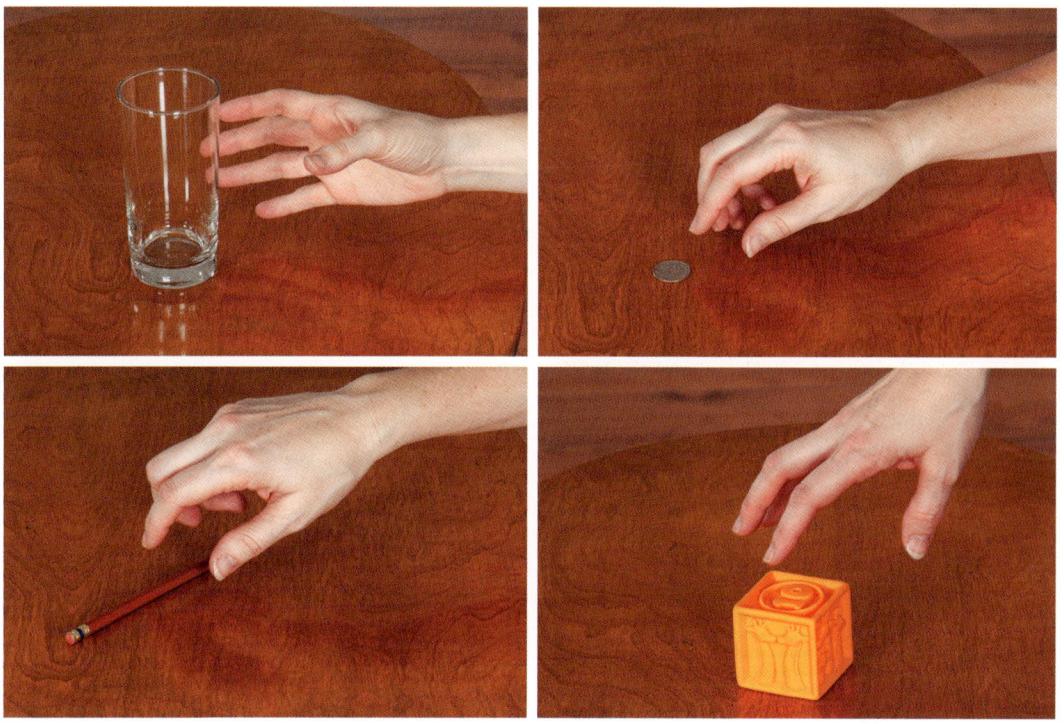

FIGURE 7.2 The type of grip one uses to pick up an object depends in part on the size and shape of the object. An adult configures, or shapes, the hand for the object to be grasped before making contact.

Reaching

Infants make a transition during their first year from random arm movements to reaches that allow them to grasp objects. The questions we ask about the developmental processes that bring about this change in reaching are similar to those asked about early leg movements in chapter 6. In the case of reaching, what is it that drives the change from random and reflexive arm movements (prereaching) in the first few months after birth to eventual successful reaching of objects? Beginning with Piaget (1952), many developmentalists proposed that reaching and grasping required seeing both the object and the hand in the visual field so that vision and proprioception could be matched. Bruner (1973; Bruner & Koslowski, 1972) further suggested that infants build a system of visually guided arm movements from initial, poorly coordinated movements. Others considered reaching development to be a process of fine-tuning abilities that are already in place (Bower, Broughton, & Moore, 1970; Trevarthen, 1974, 1984; von Hofsten, 1982).

It now seems, though, that there is not a continuous change from prereaching to reaching—that is, it seems that infants are *not* learning to match vision of the hand and arm with proprioception of the movement (von Hofsten, 1984). Infants are very good from the start at reaching in the dark when they cannot see their hands (Clifton, Muir, Ashmead, & Clarkson, 1993; McCarty & Ashmead, 1999). This is not to say that vision is not important to the task. Infants later rely on vision to refine the path of the reach and, as we said earlier, configure the hand to the object (figure 7.3). Rather, it might be the case that learning to reach is, more than anything else, a problem of learning to control the arm.

Thelen et al. (1993) examined this issue by recording the arm movements of four infants longitudinally from 3 weeks to 1 year of age. The investigators observed that infants made the transition from prereaching to reaching at 3 to 4 months of age. The infants began with ballpark reaches—movements of exploration and discovery—but each infant found his or her own means of controlling reaches based on the movements he or she already used. Two of the infants preferred fast, oscillating movements that they had to dampen when they reached to get near a toy. The other two infants had to apply muscle force to their preferred slow movements to reach a toy. After several months of practice, the infants became quite good at reaching for a toy, but each had generated a different solution to make the transition from crude initial reaching attempts to consistently successful reaches. The period of improvement was characterized by times when reaches improved and then regressed before improving again.

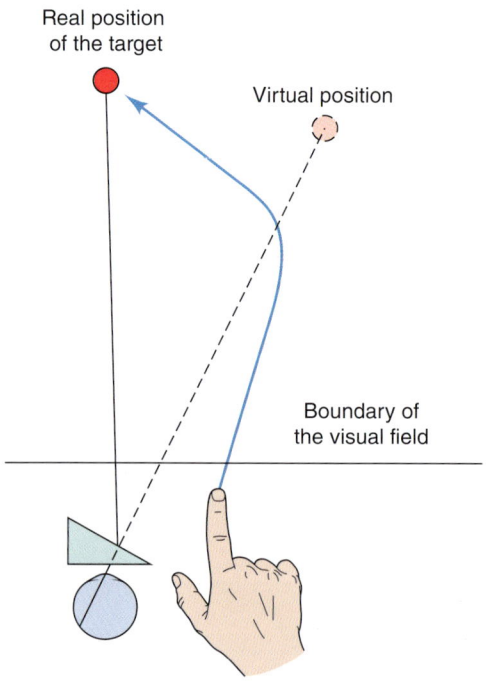

FIGURE 7.3 Displaced vision tasks demonstrate the role of vision in reaching. Prisms placed in front of the eyes shift the apparent location of an object from its real position. Individuals reach but grasp nothing because they reach directly for the location they identified by vision. They do not wait to see their hand in the visual field and then guide it to the location.

Reprinted by permission from Hay (1990).

▶ **KEY POINT** To reach objects, infants learn to control their arms; they learn by doing.

Thelen et al. believed their longitudinal study of infant reaching demonstrated that infants learn by doing. Rather than infants' central nervous systems planning a trajectory of arm movement, one that would carry the hand to a toy, infants adjust the tension in the arms and apply muscle energy to get the hand close to the toy. By repeating the reaching, infants found increasingly efficient and consistent reaching patterns, yet they found these movement solutions individually, adapting their actions based on perceptions of their self-generated movements.

Corbetta and colleagues (Corbetta, Thurman, Wiener, Guan, & Williams, 2014) further explored this embodied explanation by asking whether infants map vision onto their movement or map movements onto what they see as they learn to reach. By tracking the eye movements of infants in a weekly session during the reach learning process, they saw that infants learned to align their gaze to where they reached. So infants' self-generated movement provided proprioceptive and touch feedback to learn how to direct the reach. In doing so, infants learned to map vision onto these movements. This early visual-motor mapping is an important step toward movement control.

Although much of the research on infant reaching has used stationary objects, studies done with moving objects show that infants begin reaching for stationary objects and moving objects (in the horizontal plane) at about the same age and have similar success in reaching (von Hofsten & Lindhagen, 1979; von Hofsten, 1980). From 6 to 10 months of age, infants diversify their strategies in reaching for and grasping moving objects. They use reaches that are bimanual and reaches made with the arm on the same side as the object (Fagard, Spelke, & von Hofsten, 2009).

Hand–Mouth Movements

Another type of arm movement brings the hand, with or without an object, to the mouth. Between 3 and 4 months, infants become more consistent at bringing the hand to the mouth rather than to other parts of the face. At 5 months, they begin to open the mouth in anticipation of the hand's arrival (Lew & Butterworth, 1997). The role of vision in these movements has not yet been studied, nor has the relationship between hand–mouth movements and reaches for objects in the same infants.

▶ **KEY POINT** Infants exhibit bimanual reaching during the first year but cannot perform complementary activities with two hands until the second year.

Bimanual Reaching and Manipulation

The reaches we've discussed thus far are unimanual, or one-arm, reaches, but infants also acquire bimanual reaching and grasping (Corbetta & Mounoud, 1990; Fagard, 1990). Skilled performers know to use two hands when grasping objects that are too large for one hand, and they can use one hand to complement the other. For example, they might use one hand to hold a container and the other to open the lid.

▶ **KEY POINT** Infants in their first year alternate between periods when unimanual reaches predominate and periods when bimanual reaches predominate.

Newborns' random arm movements are asymmetrical (Cobb, Goodwin, & Saelens, 1966). The first bilateral movements—extending and raising the arms—are observed at approximately 2 months of age (White, Castle, & Held, 1964). Within a few months, infants can clasp their hands at the body midline. At approximately 4.5 months, infants often reach for objects with both arms (Fagard, 1990), but reaches begun with two hands usually result in one hand reaching and grasping the object first. Corbetta and Thelen (1996) studied the bimanual reaches of the infants described earlier (Thelen et al., 1993). During the first year, reaching fluctuated between periods of unimanual reaching and periods of bimanual reaching (figure 7.4). Infants tended to make synchronized nonreaching arm movements during periods of bimanual reaching but exhibited no pattern during periods of unimanual reaching. The four infants did not necessarily experience shifts from one kind of reaching to the other at the same ages. Manual activities might be influenced by postural control, yet it might also be the case that no single factor influences the predominance of unimanual or bimanual reaching. Rather, changing constraints can push infants to particular movement patterns.

After 8 months, infants start to dissociate simultaneous arm activity so they can manipulate an object cooperatively with both hands (Goldfield & Michel, 1986; Ruff, 1984). Late in the first year, infants learn to hold two objects, one in each hand, and often bang them together (Ramsay, 1985). By 12 months, they can pull things apart and insert one object into another. Soon infants can reach for two objects with different arms simultaneously. Not until the end of the second year, however, can infants perform complementary activities with the hands, such as holding a lid open with one hand while withdrawing an object with the other (Bruner, 1970).

Infants early in their second year can use objects as tools. Barrett, Davis, and Needham (2007) noted that infants with prior experience with a tool, such as a spoon, persisted in holding the handle of the spoon even when a task was better accomplished by holding the bowl. Infants could use a novel tool flexibly, though, and could be trained on what end of a tool to hold.

FIGURE 7.4 Obtaining large objects necessitates bimanual reaching. In young infants, one hand might reach the object before the other. Infants older than 7 months reach either unimanually or bimanually, depending on the object's characteristics.

▶ **KEY POINT** Early in the second year, infants can use tools flexibly.

The Role of Posture

Postural control is important in reaching. Consider that as adults we often lean forward or twist as we reach for an object. Infants typically sit independently by around 6 to 7 months. Before this, their trunks must be supported for them to achieve a successful reach. Reaching improves when infants are able to maintain postural control (Bertenthal & von Hofsten, 1998). Even at 4 months of age, infants adjust their posture as they reach, and improvements in these adjustments during the first year continue to facilitate reaching (Van der Fits & Hadders-Algra, 1998). The shift to bimanual reaching at the end of the first year has been associated with the onset of walking with support through longitudinal observation of infants starting at 7 months (Atun-Einy, Berger, Ducz, & Sher, 2014).

Learning exercise 7.1 at the end of this chapter provides an opportunity for you to observe the type of grasp that a particular infant uses to pick up various objects.

Manual Performance in Adulthood

The ability to reach and grasp remains an important motor skill throughout the life span. Many careers involve manipulation, and in older adults the ability to perform some activities of daily living—such as bathing and dressing, preparing meals, and making phone calls—can dictate whether the individual is able to live independently. We discussed earlier some of the changes in individual constraints that accompany aging. It is easy to see that some of these might be a significant factor in the performance of large motor activities, but would they also affect manipulative skills? Would fine motor skills be better maintained over the life span than large motor skills? Let's consider some of the research on manipulation in adulthood.

Kauranen and Vanharanta (1996) conducted a cross-sectional study of men and women between 21 and 70 years of age. A test battery was administered that included reaction time, movement speed, tapping speed, and coordination of the hands and feet. Scores declined on all of the hand measures after age 50; the reaction, movement, and tapping times slowed, and coordination scores declined.

What about manual performance at older ages? Hughes et al. (1997) observed older adults with an average age of 78 over a 6-year time span. Every 2 years, these adults completed the Timed Manual Performance Test and a grip strength measure. The Timed Manual Performance Test consists of 22 manipulative tests, 17 from the Williams board tests of manual ability and 5 from Jebsen's test of hand skills. Each subject's score consisted of the total time in seconds needed to complete the test. Generally, more individuals at older ages went over the time threshold on the performance test, and grip strength declined with advancing age. Declining manual performance was associated with loss of strength and upper joint impairment resulting from musculoskeletal disease. Also, in reaching for objects, older adults slow down more than young adults at the end of the reach, presumably to make more corrections in their trajectory (Roy, Winchester, Weir, & Black, 1993).

Contreras-Vidal, Teulings, and Stelmach (1998) observed younger (20s) and older (60s and 70s) adults making handwriting movements. These movements, of course, do not demand speed, nor do they require great precision. Compared with the younger adults, the older adults could control force well but did not coordinate their finger and wrist movements as well.

Loss of speed in movement with aging is a common finding for large and fine motor movements. Additionally, the research studies reviewed here indicate that movements might not be as finely coordinated with advancing age. We can see, however, that disuse and disease are every bit as important in the loss of manipulative skills as in the loss of locomotor or ballistic skills. Greater loss can be expected among those who curtail manipulative activities as they age, contributing in turn to a loss of strength, which may further hurt performance. Kornatz, Christou, and Enoka (2005) provided a 6-week manual steadiness training program for the nondominant hand to 10 older adults. The result was improved strength and manual dexterity on a functional assessment of hand control, the Purdue Pegboard Test. Continued use or practice of manipulative skills throughout the life span, then, might temper a loss of manipulative skills.

It is clear that the interaction of individual, task, and environmental constraints is as important in fine, manipulative motor skills as it is in large motor skills. Over the age span, changing individual constraints bring changes in the interaction with environmental and task constraints, thus causing changes in movement.

▶ **KEY POINT** Some aspects of older adults' reaches slow down, putting them at a disadvantage in making sequential movements, but accuracy of manipulation is stable, especially on well-known tasks.

Think about the increased use of e-mail, which involves typing on a standard-size keyboard, and of text messaging, which involves typing on a very small keyboard. Do certain age groups prefer one or the other? Why? Is preference related to experience or something else?

Rapid Aiming Movements

In some complex motor skills, participants make rapid aiming movements. Such arm movements involve an initiation and acceleration phase from the start of the movement to the point when peak velocity of the arm movement is reached, then a deceleration and termination phase from peak velocity to the end of the movement.

Young adults tend to make this movement symmetrically; that is, the acceleration and deceleration phases are equal. In contrast, older adults do not begin the movement as forcefully or travel as far in the acceleration phase. They tend to have a longer deceleration phase to compensate because they need more adjustments in the final phase, especially when the aiming movement needs to be very accurate (Vercruyssen, 1997).

Rapid aiming movements are involved in tasks requiring monitoring and manipulation of complex displays such as cockpits. In critical tasks, many such movements can be required in sequence, and any slowing effects can accumulate. Age differences, then, might not be important in single, simple, or self-paced arm movements but may be critical when many sequential movements are needed in a short time. The interaction of individual and task constraints is evident in this type of skill. Practice is important to older adults. They can compensate for some slowing when they know the location of buttons or levers very well.

Catching

Several manipulative skills are basic to sport performance. In these skills, a performer must gain possession or control of an object by reaching to intercept a moving object or stopping it with an implement. The most common manipulative skill is catching. Fielding in hockey also allows a player to control the ball or puck, such that it remains in the player's control rather than bouncing or rolling away. Of these reception skills, we know the most about the development of catching.

Baseball trivia buffs never tire of recounting great outfield catches. Perhaps the greatest was Willie Mays' over-the-shoulder catch in the 1954 World Series. The score was tied 2-2, with two runners on base and no outs. Vic Wertz hit a long drive to right center field. Mays turned and ran full speed, his back to home plate. Just a few feet from the wall (which was particularly deep at New York's Polo Grounds), he was able to stretch his arms and catch the ball, then make a tremendous throw back to the infield. The Cleveland Indians weren't able to score that inning, and the New York Giants went on to win the game and sweep the series.

Catching is relatively difficult as a developmental task. During early childhood we see children throw and kick, even if their movement patterns are not yet proficient. But if young children catch a ball, it often reflects the skill of the thrower in getting the ball to arrive in outstretched arms. It is the interception aspect of catching that makes it difficult. With this in mind, let's consider how catching develops and then examine interception in catching.

The goal of catching is to retain possession of the object you catch. It is better to catch an object in the hands than to trap it against the body or opposite arm because if the object is caught in the hands, the catcher can quickly manipulate it—usually by throwing it. A child's initial catching attempts involve little force absorption. The young child pictured in figure 7.5 has positioned his hands and arms rigidly. Instead of catching the ball in his hands, he traps it against his chest. It is common to see children turn away and close their eyes in anticipation of the ball's arrival. The next section discusses characteristics of proficient catching and then examines how children typically develop proficient catching.

FIGURE 7.5 Beginning catching. This young boy holds his arms and hands rigidly rather than giving with the arrival of the ball to absorb its force gradually.
© Mary Ann Roberton.

Proficient Catching

In moving from novice to proficient catching skills, as shown in figure 7.6, a child must

- learn to catch with the hands and give with the ball, thus gradually absorbing the ball's force;

- master the ability to move to the left or the right, or forward or back, to intercept the ball; and
- point the fingers up when catching a high ball and down when catching a low one.

FIGURE 7.6 Proficient catching. The ball is caught with the hands, and the hands and arms give with the ball.

Developmental Changes in Catching

It is more difficult to identify developmental sequences for catching skills than for most locomotor or ballistic skills because the sequence is specific to the conditions under which the individual performs the skill. Many factors are variable in catching—for example, the ball's size, shape (e.g., a round basketball vs. a football), speed, trajectory, and arrival point. Haubenstricker, Branta, and Seefeldt (1983) conducted a preliminary validation of a developmental sequence for arm action in two-hand catching. They used progressively smaller balls as children demonstrated better skill. Table 7.1 summarizes the sequence, which was originally outlined by Seefeldt, Reuschlein, and Vogel (1972). At 8 years of age, most of the boys and almost half of the girls tested were at the highest level of arm action. Virtually all the children had passed through steps 1 and 2 by this time. Slightly higher percentages of boys than girls performed at higher levels at any given age, but overall this group demonstrated well-developed arm action by age 8. The gender differences might reflect patterns of participation in ball games that were different for boys and girls when this study was done. Table 7.1 also suggests the key observation points that can help you place performers at a developmental level.

TABLE 7.1 Developmental Sequence for Two-Hand Catching

SEQUENCE	ACTION
	ARM ACTION
Step 1	Little response. Arms extend forward, but there is little movement to adapt to ball flight; ball is usually trapped against chest.
Step 2	Hugging. Arms are extended sideways to encircle (hug) the ball; ball is trapped against chest.
Step 3	Scooping. Arms are extended forward but move under (scoop) the object; ball is trapped against chest.
Step 4	Arms give. Arms extend to meet object with the hands; arms and body give; ball is caught in hands.
	HAND ACTION
Step 1	Palms up. The palms of the hands face up. (Rolling balls elicit a palms-down trapping action.)
Step 2	Palms in. The palms of the hands face each other.
Step 3	Palms adjusted. The palms of the hands are adjusted to the flight and size of the oncoming object. Thumbs or little fingers are placed close together, depending on the height of the flight path.
	BODY ACTION
Step 1	No adjustment. No adjustment of the body occurs in response to the ball's flight path.
Step 2	Awkward adjustment. The arms and trunk begin to move in relation to the ball's flight path, but the head remains erect, creating an awkward movement to the ball. The catcher seems to be fighting to remain balanced.
Step 3	Proper adjustment. The feet, trunk, and arms all move to adjust to the path of the oncoming ball.

Reprinted by permission from Wtrohmeyer, Williams, and Schaub-George (1991).

▶ **KEY POINT** Catching is specific to environmental and task constraints.

Strohmeyer, Williams, and Schaub-George (1991) proposed developmental sequences for the hands and body in catching a small ball (table 7.1). A unique feature of this work is that it is based on catching balls thrown directly to the catcher as well as balls thrown high or to the side of the catcher. These sequences suggest that as catchers improve, they

- are better able to move their bodies in response to the oncoming ball,
- adjust their hands to the anticipated location of the catch, and
- catch the ball in their hands.

The investigators tested their sequences on a cross section of children between 5 and 12 years old. All the children over 8 years made some adjustment in body position in response to the oncoming ball, and 11- to 12-year-olds successfully adjusted their body positions about 80% of the time. In contrast, this older group could properly adjust their hand positions in response to the ball only 40% of the time if the ball was thrown directly to them and less than 10% of the time if it was thrown to various positions around them.

A **developmental profile** is a combination of the developmental steps shown by a performer over all body components. For example, a developmental profile for catching could be arm 2, hand 3, body 2.

Utley and Astill (2007) conducted a prelongitudinal screening of the developmental sequences in table 7.1 and then evaluated 10 children 7 to 8 years of age. All the children were in steps 2, 3, or 4 of arm action, steps 2 or 3 of hand action, and steps 2 or 3 of body action. The modal profile of the group was arm action level 3, hand action level 3, and body action level 3, and this profile was observed on 63.3% of the 300 trials observed. Utley and Astill also observed 10 children with developmental coordination disorder and found they displayed less advanced **developmental profiles** that were also less stable since far more different profiles were observed. Typically developing children seem to reach the moderate steps of catching by midchildhood.

Think of your own skill level in catching. What kinds of catching tasks do you find easy? Is there a catching task you find difficult?

Catching, like striking, involves anticipating where a ball can be intercepted as well as the ability to complete the movements that position the hands at that location. As we would expect, children better predict the ball flight as they get older, especially when the viewing time (path of the ball) is short (Lefebvre & Reid, 1998). The anticipatory aspects of manipulative skills are discussed in more detail elsewhere in this chapter.

Observing Catching Patterns

Catching can be observed from the front, allowing you to toss the ball, or from the side. It is easy to assess the product in catching tasks. One can simply record a percentage of balls successfully caught, noting the task constraints, including the size and type of ball used, the throwing distance, and the trajectory of the ball.

▶ **KEY POINT** To assess catching skill, environmental and task constraints such as ball size and ball trajectory must be tracked and replicated.

Parents, teachers, and coaches often want to know about the movement process used in catching. Figure 7.7, Observation Plan for Catching, provides a suggested developmental sequence that indicates which step the catcher demonstrates for each body component. For example, if you observe a child who extends her arms, palms up, and scoops a large ball thrown to her, trapping it against her chest, all without moving her feet, the developmental levels would be step 3 for arm action, step 1 for hand action, and step 1 for body action.

Web Study Guide **Identify developmental differences among catchers in Lab Activity 7.2, Assessing the Developmental Levels of Catchers, in the web study guide.**

Figure 7.7
OBSERVATION PLAN FOR CATCHING

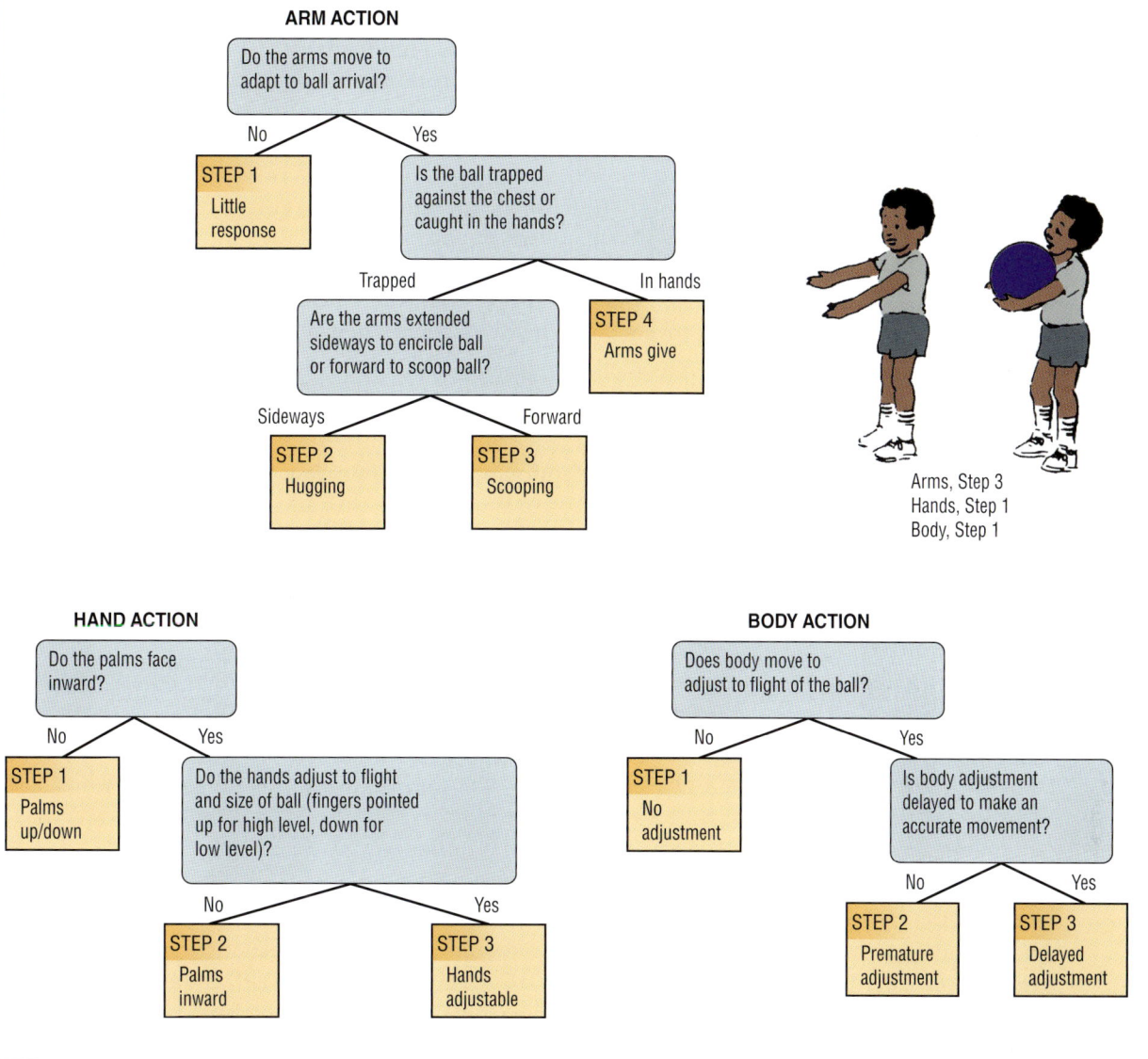

© Mary Ann Roberton.

Anticipation

It is clear that many manipulative tasks and interception skills involve anticipation. The ball or other moving object can approach at different speeds, from different directions, and along different trajectories and may be of varying size and shape. To be successful, performers must initiate movements well ahead of interception so that the body and hands (or implement, such as a hockey stick) can be in the proper position when the object arrives. In fact, the manipulative component of reception skills (e.g., positioning and closing the hands on the ball) is often perfected before an individual develops the ability to be in the right place at the right time.

Some developmentalists have researched this aspect of reception skills through the use of **coincidence-anticipation** tasks. With this approach, it is easy to vary task characteristics and

Coincidence-anticipation tasks are motor skills in which one anticipates the completion of a movement to coincide with the arrival of a moving object.

observe the effect on performance. Variations in task characteristics influence not only the product of performance—a hit or catch versus a miss—but also the process, or movement pattern, used in the task. For example, children who are capable of catching *small* balls in their hands may choose to scoop very *large* balls with their arms, perhaps as a surer means of retaining them. Thus, a task can be defined as requiring a simpler or more complex movement response, and the characteristics of the ball can be varied to further constrain the movement. Yet many research studies on coincidence-anticipation are conducted in a laboratory setting with an apparatus that allows factors such as ball speed, trajectory, and direction to be varied and are not very similar to the real-world task of catching a ball. Therefore, it is important to recognize that these studies might tell us more about the perceptual limits of performers for a specified interception task than for real-world catching.

Let's consider some of the task constraints in coincidence-anticipation tasks. Several researchers have found that coincidence-anticipation performance improves throughout childhood and adolescence (Bard, Fleury, Carriere, & Bellec, 1981; Dorfman, 1977; Dunham, 1977; Haywood, 1977, 1980; Lefebvre & Reid, 1998; Stadulis, 1971; Thomas, Gallagher, & Purvis, 1981). However, the exact pattern of improvement with advancing age depends on task constraints:

- Young children are less accurate as the movement required of them gets more complex (Bard et al., 1981; Haywood, 1977). So, response complexity is one task characteristic that influences how well children perform on interception tasks.
- Children's accuracy decreases if the interception point is farther away. For example, McConnell and Wade (1990) found that the number of successful catches and the efficiency of the movement pattern used decreased if children 6 to 11 years old had to move 2 feet instead of 1 foot, left or right, to make a catch.
- Young children are more successful at intercepting large balls than small balls (Isaacs, 1980; McCaskill & Wellman, 1938; Payne, 1982; Payne & Koslow, 1981).
- A high trajectory also makes interception more difficult for young children because the ball changes location in both horizontal and vertical directions (DuRandt, 1985).
- Some ball color and background combinations influence young children's performance. Morris (1976) determined that 7-year-olds could better catch blue balls moving against a white background than white balls against a white background. The effect of color diminished with advancing age.
- The speed of the moving object affects coincidence-anticipation accuracy but not in a clear pattern. A faster speed makes interception more difficult, especially when the object's flight is short. But researchers often note that children are inaccurate with slow velocities because they respond too early (Bard et al., 1981; Haywood, 1977; Haywood, Greenwald, & Lewis, 1981; Isaacs, 1983; Wade, 1980). Perhaps children prepare for the fastest speed an object might travel and then have difficulty delaying their responses if the speed is slow (Bard, Fleury, & Gagnon, 1990). Also, the preceding speeds might influence young children more than they do older performers. If the previous moving object came quickly, young children judge the next object to be moving faster than it really is (Haywood et al., 1981), just like baseball batters are fooled by a pitcher's changeup, or slow pitch. Educators should be aware, then, that children can have difficulty adjusting their responses when the speed of an object in an interception task varies greatly from one repetition to the next. This is particularly true if the object's flight is short or the response required is complex.

Kim, Nauhaus, Glazek, Young, and Lin (2013) observed young males from 11 to 18 years of age on a coincidence-anticipation task with fast stimulus speeds. There were no differences in performance across age, the subjects showing similar times to initiate movement and similar movement durations. All the performers were able to accommodate varying target locations and speeds. Altogether, this suggests coincidence-anticipation performance is well developed by the teens. The challenge for young adult and adult performers in sports situations likely centers around running to far interception points, discussed later in this chapter.

Imagine you're an elementary school physical education instructor. Recall the sports that involve moving objects, then identify the many ways in which pitchers and servers in various sports change the pitch or serve to make interception of the ball more difficult. In contrast, how would you throw a ball to small children to increase the likelihood that they will catch it?

▶ **KEY POINT** Interception success is often related to ball size, speed, trajectory, and other task and environmental constraints.

What underlies these age-related trends in coincidence anticipation? Early studies of these skills took an information processing perspective. That is, performers were thought to receive visual and kinesthetic information and perform calculations on that data, much like a computer, to project the future location of the moving object in order to intercept it.

The perception–action perspective, in contrast, holds that all the needed information is in the environment and that no calculations are necessary. Meaningful information in the environment specifies the action or movement possibilities of that environment and for specific events. This relationship is called an **affordance**. For catching, two important characteristics of the person–environment system are constant patterns of change, called **invariants**, and the expanding **optic array**. The optic array refers to the visual picture falling on our retinas as we approach an object or as a moving object approaches us. That picture expands in size on the retinas with approach and constricts with retreat.

An **affordance** is an action or behavior provided or permitted for an actor by the places, objects, and events in an environment; it is often related to the relative sizes of the actor and the objects.

Invariance is stability in the kinematic values of a set of movements (i.e., keeping patterns in the environment constant).

An **optic array** consists of the light waves reverberating from surfaces in the environment—in other words, the stimulus for visual perception. When movement of environmental objects or of the viewer in the environment occurs, the optic array expands when the movement is "toward" and constricts when the movement is "away."

From the perception–action perspective, it is possible that we use the rate of expansion of this image on our retinas to know when arrival or collision will occur (Lyons, Fontaine, & Elliott, 1997). Insects that intercept prey and birds that fold their wings back before diving into water both demonstrate perfect timing in these interceptions, and, given their small brains, it is more likely that they perceive aspects of the environment directly than that they perform complex calculations to predict arrival times. Van Hof, van der Kamp, and Savelsbergh (2008) investigated whether infants between 3 and 9 months could act on an approaching ball. They placed a ball on a mechanical apparatus so that the ball came directly over the right shoulder of a seated infant at various speeds. Infants aged 3 to 5 months often did not even reach for the balls and were not very accurate when they did. Individual differences occurred in age of improvement, but by 8 to 9 months the infants were relatively accurate. They also were more likely not to attempt to catch fast-moving balls they were unlikely to intercept.

▶ **KEY POINT** To reach objects, the expansion rate of the image of a directly approaching ball on the retina could be used to time an interception.

Several research teams have recently used the perception–action perspective to study the "real world" task of catching a ball projected in a high trajectory, much like the task faced by an outfielder in baseball. Such researchers are now able to track the position of both the ball and the catcher by using video technology. McLeod and Dienes (1993, 1996) demonstrated that catchers could intercept a directly approaching high-trajectory ball by keeping a ratio, based on the angle of gaze, at or near zero. (For those with a mathematical background, the ratio is the second derivative of the tangent of the angle of gaze.) If the ratio's value is positive, the ball will land behind the catcher; if it is negative, the ball will land in front. By keeping the ratio near zero, the catcher knows whether to move forward or backward and how quickly to move (figure 7.8).

Oudejans and colleagues (Michaels & Oudejans, 1992; Oudejans, Michaels, Bakker, & Dolne, 1996) similarly demonstrated that catchers could keep the vertical optical acceleration of the ball close to zero. This is called the optical acceleration cancellation (OAC) strategy. Unlike McLeod and Dienes' notion that the catcher focuses on angle of gaze, in this approach the catcher focuses on the ball's acceleration in the vertical plane as the catcher views the ball. Both approaches tell a catcher whether to move forward or backward.

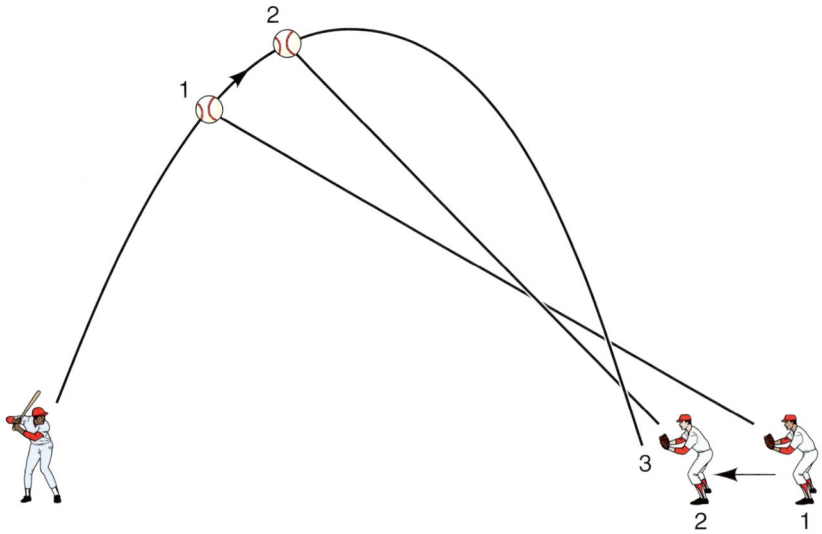

FIGURE 7.8 The catcher might intercept the approaching ball by keeping a ratio, based on the angle of gaze, at or near zero. When the ball and catcher are in position 1, this ratio is a negative number. The catcher must move forward to bring the ratio closer to zero. At position 2 the ratio is closer to zero but still not zero. The catcher continues to move until the ratio is zero, and both the catcher and the ball arrive at position 3.

Adapted by permission from McLeod and Dienes (1996, pg. 541).

Of course, many catches require sideways movement. A strategy proposed for this situation is keeping the lateral position of the ball constant with respect to the catcher. This is called the constant bearing angle strategy (figure 7.9) (Lenoir, Musch, Janssens, Thiery, & Uyttenhove, 1999). For example, a soccer goalie could keep this angle constant by moving sideways to intercept a ball. Researchers (McBeath, Shaffer, & Kaiser, 1995; Shaffer, 1999; Shaffer & McBeath, 2002) identified a relationship that incorporates both elevation of gaze and horizontal angle of gaze, as would be important for catching a high-trajectory ball projected to the side of a catcher. If this relationship is kept constant, a catcher can arrive at the correct place to catch the ball. The specific mathematics of the relationship are not important here; what matters for us is that we can see that invariant relationships are available to catchers in the environment and that it is possible to arrive at the correct place without our brains calculating a landing point based on the early part of the trajectory. Practically, a fielder (as long as he or she can move fast enough) can adopt the unconscious strategy of continuously moving to stay under the ball's trajectory as viewed. If the ball's path appears to arc up and past the catcher, the ball will land behind the catcher. If the ball's path appears to arc down, the ball will land in front. So, the catcher can adjust to maintain the proper visual appearance and adapt to changes in the path due to ball spin, air resistance, or wind in order to arrive at the right place.

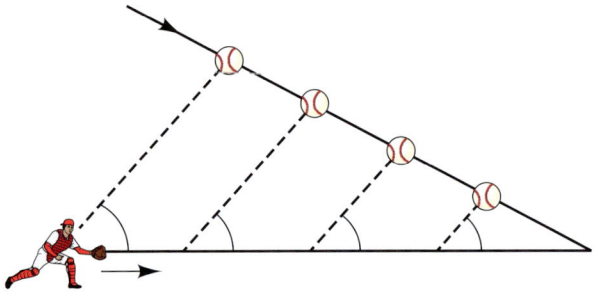

FIGURE 7.9 A catcher moves to the side to intercept a ball by keeping the bearing angle formed by the dashed line constant.

Redrawn from Lenoir et al. (1999).

Advancements in technology have allowed researchers to test the proposed strategies for catching fly balls. Using virtual reality to perturb the ball in midflight, investigators observed the catcher's response to determine which strategy accounted for that response. They found support for the OAC strategy (Fink, Foo, & Warrant, 2009; Khomut & Warren, 2007). On the other hand, Postma, Smith, Pepping, van Andel, and Zaal (2017) found that the OAC strategy could not account for predictions of the landing point when fly balls were out of reach. The perception of catchability certainly needs more investigation.

▶ **KEY POINT** Catchers are able to intercept balls by keeping certain relationships between themselves and the ball constant.

Imagine you are a baseball or softball coach. Keeping in mind the perception–action approach, how might you help a young fielder who is having trouble catching fly balls?

How Do Children Learn to Arrive at the Right Place?

From an information processing viewpoint, children must learn to make more precise calculations to become proficient catchers. Errors made in early attempts serve as informative feedback that can be used to refine the calculation process. From a perception–action viewpoint, however, what children need is to subconsciously discover an invariant. When children begin catching by standing still, for example, McLeod and Dienes' ratio is zero for balls that land in their arms and something else for balls that do not land in their arms. With sufficient exposure, children discover the relationship between the ratio and the catchability of a ball and eventually use the relationship when they begin moving for a ball.

▶ **KEY POINT** Children learn to catch fly balls from their experiences with catching. Both successful and unsuccessful catches contribute to learning a relationship between the visual display and the position of the body.

From the perception–action perspective, then, one role of parents, teachers, and coaches is to help children discover the various sources of perceptual information that constrain movement in interception tasks. They can do so by manipulating informational constraints during the exploratory process of practice. Bennett, Button, Kingsbury, and Davids (1999) recently demonstrated that 9- and 10-year-olds who were asked to practice one-hand catching with a restricted view of the ball later benefited when learning a catching task under new conditions. Thus, highlighting the useful sources of information by varying task constraints during practice can be helpful.

Some attempts to improve anticipatory sports skills with training in novice adults have been ineffective (Wood & Abernethy, 1997). Abernethy, Wood, and Parks (1999) suggest that training must be sport specific (environment and task specific) and must focus on the factors known to limit novice performance. They demonstrated that novice adults can benefit from such training; the novice adults performed a laboratory task similarly to experts after training. It is important to identify the perceptual information that constrains movement. This research suggests that whether the individual is a child or a novice adult, manipulating constraints to help the performer identify the important information in the environment subconsciously facilitates the movements that result in success. More information, however, is needed about the relative merits of simple exploratory practice and instruction.

Imagine you are a teacher and design an activity that helps children learn to catch fly balls.

Catching in Older Adulthood

Little research-based information is available about catching by older adults. We might suspect that experienced older adults know the invariant patterns that provide information about intercepting balls. Factors that might change, however, could include the quickness with which movement is initiated, the maximum speed that could be achieved in moving to the ball, and the extent of reach if the catchability of a given ball were at the limit for an individual's speed in moving. All these factors might contribute to an older adult's being unable to catch as many balls as a younger adult could.

Coincidence-anticipation research provides some information about the anticipatory aspects of skills such as catching. Older adults are somewhat less accurate and more variable in their performance than younger performers, and the differences are greater when the moving object moves faster and when the older adults are sedentary rather than active (Haywood, 1980, 1982; Wiegand & Ramella, 1983). Wiegand and Ramella (1983) observed that older adults improved with practice at the same rate as younger adults. Over a 7-year period, from an average age of 66.9 years to an average age of 73.5 years, active adults demonstrated improvement in performance on a coincidence-anticipation task (Haywood, 1989). Thus, repetition of such skills probably is important for maintaining skill. The task constraints on the movement response in the coincidence-anticipation tasks, however, were minimal. When task constraints are such that larger, more complex movements or movements over distance in a short time are required, a higher number of older adults might be less successful at these tasks given their individual constraints. Cesqui, Russo, Lacquaniti, and d'Avella (2016) determined that velocity of wrist movement and speed of hand closure are related to catching performance, so maintaining the speed of even fine movements could be related to older adults' catching performance.

Driving and Piloting

Although only a portion of older adults participate in sports involving interception, a large number drive automobiles. In fact, the issue of whether an older adult should continue driving is often an emotional one because driving often represents a considerable degree of independence and freedom. Driving is a complex perceptual-motor skill involving manipulation. Skillful driving depends on vision (and sometimes audition, or hearing), attentional focus, experience, speed, and coordination, all under occasionally stressful conditions.

Older adults have more difficulty than younger adults in dividing their attention and performing two tasks at once in driving situations (Brouwer, Waterink, Van Wolffelaar, & Rothengartter, 1991; Ponds, Brouwer, & Van Wolffelaar, 1988). Older adults also take longer to plan movements and are slower in executing movements, especially when speedy movement is needed (Goggin & Stelmach, 1990; Olson & Sivak, 1986). Goggin and Keller (1996) examined whether aging differentially affects the sensory-cognitive or motor functions in driving. They had older adult drivers take a written test about a videotape of 15 driving situations. The older drivers also made driving responses to the same videotaped situations on a driving simulator. Goggin and Keller reasoned that if older adults had difficulty only on the written test, aging likely affected sensory-cognitive functions, but if they had difficulty only with the simulator responses, aging likely affected motor functions. The adults performed less well on the written test and better on the simulator. Thus, sensory-cognitive factors such as attention and decision making might be more significant factors in poor performance of driving-related motor skills.

Think about the older adults in your family. How are their driving skills? Do any of them compensate for a loss of driving skill? How?

The effects of aging on airplane piloting performance have also been studied (see Morrow & Leirer, 1997, for a review). Mandatory retirement ages for commercial pilots are also an emotional issue for those involved. Like driving, piloting is affected more as task complexity increases. Perceptual aspects of piloting, attention, and working memory are particularly affected by aging. Expertise on familiar tasks, however, offsets the effects of aging, and highly practiced skills are well maintained.

Assessing Catching: Test of Gross Motor Development

In the previous two chapters, we describe the TGMD-3 as an assessment tool of fundamental motor skills. Within the ball skills subscale is a two-hand catching assessment. The two-hand catching item has three performance criteria: Child's hands are positioned in front of the body with elbows flexed; arms extend, reaching for the ball as it arrives; and ball is caught by hands only. Note that these criteria are similar to some of the steps in table 7.1 for the arm and hand components. The youngest group assessed on the TGMD-3 is 3 years of age. The lowest developmental steps in table 7.1 are likely seen in children younger than this; hence the TGMD performance criteria overlap more advanced developmental steps. Also, the TGMD test item requires the test administrator to toss underhand to the child's chest area, so no body adjustment is required.

Applying the model of constraints, we can see that an increased number of constraints on a task adds to its complexity, and when individual constraints change with aging, the interaction of constraints can quickly cause the difficulty of driving and piloting tasks to reach a critical point. As mentioned earlier in regard to rapid aiming tasks, experience with a set of environmental and task constraints allows older adults to compensate for slowing of manipulative movements. Thus, continued practice with tasks, whether sport or driving tasks, is important for maintaining skill. Eventually, however, decrements in sensory-cognitive systems, as well as in speed of movement, lead to a loss of skill.

Summary and Synthesis

Manipulative skills set humans apart from other species. Whether executing sports skills or tasks of everyday living, people need to reach, grasp, and maneuver objects. Infants become skilled at reaching and grasping stationary and moving objects early in life, during the first year, although using the two hands in complementary ways comes a little later.

Children can become accomplished catchers by 11 or 12 years of age, but in all catching tasks at any age, the farther the catcher must travel, the more difficult the catch. Aging probably affects a catcher's ability to get to a ball more than the ability to know where to be in order to catch the ball. Changing structural constraints influence the speed with which manipulative and locomotor movements can be initiated and completed. When tasks demand great speed, older adults are disadvantaged compared with younger adults.

Children need practice in order to learn, even if subconsciously, the information available in the environment that is important for catching success. Adults need practice in order to maintain their skills, especially in demanding conditions. Thus, at any age, a person's skill in completing challenging manipulative tasks often reflects experience and practice in dealing with the individual, task, and environmental constraints involved.

Reinforcing What You Have Learned About Constraints

TAKE A SECOND LOOK

As the case of Matthew Scott teaches us, being able to manipulate objects with two hands is important in activities of daily living and many activities that are uniquely human and enjoyable for us. When faced with the loss of manipulative skills, it is worth extraordinary effort to restore the ability to perform those skills. The development of manipulative skills certainly emphasizes the importance of task and environmental constraints in performance. As Matthew Scott undertook the journey to use his transplanted hand, he was challenged by environmental and task constraints that many of us take for granted. With continued therapy, he has been able to use his new hand while dealing with an increasing range of environmental and task constraints.

Manipulative skills are among the fundamental motor skills. The perception–action perspective in particular holds that the environment provides individuals with much of the information they need in order to intercept objects. Thus, manipulative skills such as catching do not improve just because individual constraints change. The changing interaction of individual constraints with task and environmental constraints is an important aspect of the development of manipulative skills. This interaction is equally important in the maintenance of manipulative skills in older adulthood. Experience with numerous interactions of our existing individual constraints and environmental and task constraints gives us the ability, eventually, to successfully manipulate objects even when we have not previously seen a particular ball trajectory and speed—or used a particular keyboard.

TEST YOUR KNOWLEDGE

1. How does the size of an object affect the grip that an infant uses? How might this factor influence where an infant falls on Halverson's prehension sequence? How does the shape of an object affect the grip used?
2. Do infants learn to reach for objects by better matching their hand position and the seen location of the object, or do they first learn to control the arm? Explain why you chose your answer.
3. How does reaching for stationary and moving objects compare in infants?
4. How does manipulative skill change in older adulthood, and how can older adults adapt to these changes?
5. What are the major developmental trends we see in children as they become increasingly proficient in catching?
6. When balls do not come directly to the catcher, what situations (environmental and task constraints) make catching success difficult for children? For adults?
7. Explain, from the information processing perspective and the perception–action perspective, how children learn to go to the proper place to catch a ball not traveling directly toward them.
8. What changing individual structural constraints might affect an older adult's skill in driving or piloting?
9. Think about the term *coincidence anticipation*. Explain why someone who prefers the perception–action approach might consider this to be a misnomer for interception skills.

LEARNING EXERCISE 7.1

Investigating Infant Reaching

Place an infant between 6 and 12 months of age in an upright sitting position in front of a table or tray. One at a time, place six small objects in front of the infant; the objects should vary in size, weight, and shape (all should be small enough for an infant to pick up with one hand but not so small that they could be swallowed). Consult figure 7.1 and note the type of grip the infant uses for each object. Be careful not to let the infant put small objects in his or her mouth because they can pose a choking hazard. Next, repeat the process to see whether the infant uses the same grip on each object as in the first round. Finally, prepare a report on the different grips you observed for the various objects; be sure to distinguish between power grips and precision grips. Discuss whether or how the grips changed as the weight or shape of the object changed. If the infant's parents approve, you could video record the grasps to better study and assess them.

III

Physical Growth and Aging

One reason the model of constraints is so useful to those studying motor development is that it shows how physical growth and aging, as changing individual structural constraints, in turn change individuals' interactions with the environment and with the task—and therefore change movement. The change in individual structural constraints through growth is particularly dramatic, as evident on a whole-body level and a system level. That is, there are changes not only in the size and proportion of the whole body but also in the body's systems (e.g., skeletal, muscular, endocrine). Changes are more subtle but still present in aging.

Chapter 8 considers the typical pattern of growth and aging of the body as a whole. It emphasizes body size and proportion as well as maturity. Chapter 9 examines five body systems and how they change prenatally as well as during childhood, adolescence, and adulthood into older adulthood. These are the five systems most related to the performance of motor skills. Taken together, these whole-body and system-specific changes play such a large role in a person's age-related change in skill performance that students must possess a thorough knowledge of physical growth and aging in order to effectively study the course of motor development. As we will see later, movement is influenced by size, mass, and leverage.

Suggested Reading

Coupé, P., Catheline, G., Lanuza, E., & Manjón, J.V., for the Alzheimer's Disease Neuroimaging Initiative. (2017). Towards a unified analysis of brain maturation and aging across the entire lifespan: A MRI analysis. *Human Brain Mapping, 38*, 5501–5518. DOI:10.1002/hbm.23743

Freitas, D.L., Lausen, B., Maia, J.A., Gouveia, E.R., Antunes, A.M., Thomis, M., et al. (2018). Skeletal maturation, fundamental motor skills, and motor performance in preschool children. *Scandinavian Journal of Medicine and Science in Sports, 28*(11), 2358–2368. DOI: 10.1111/sms.13233

Freitas, D.L., Lausen, B., Maia, J.A., Lefevre, J., Gouveia, E.R., Thomis, M., et al. (2015). Skeletal maturation, fundamental motor skills and motor coordination in children 7–10 years. *Journal of Sports Sciences, 33*(9), 924–934. DOI: 10.1080/02640414.2014.977935

Malina, R.M., Bouchard, C., & Bar-Or, O. (2004). *Growth, maturation, and physical activity* (2nd ed.). Champaign, IL: Human Kinetics.

Malina, R.M., Rogol, A.D., Cumming, S.P., Coelho e Silva, M.J., & Figueiredo, A.J. (2015). Biological maturation of youth athletes: Assessment and implications. *British Journal of Sports Medicine, 49*, 852–859.

Naaktgeboren, K., Dorgo, S., & Boyle, J.B. (2017). Growth plate injuries in children in sports. *Strength and Conditioning Journal, 39*(2), 59–68. DOI: 10.1519/SSC.0000000000000295

8

Physical Growth, Maturation, and Aging

Changing Individual Constraints Across the Life Span

CHAPTER OBJECTIVES

This chapter

- describes the course of body growth and aging over the life span,
- reviews the role of genes in the course of early physical growth and development,
- reviews the influence of extrinsic factors on growth and development and the increasing role of extrinsic factors as individuals proceed through the life span,
- identifies typical patterns of growth while recognizing individual differences in the timing of growth, and
- distinguishes between growth and maturation.

Do Growth Spurts Affect Motor Skills?

Likely you have heard jokes about teenage boys tripping over their own feet during their growing years. Is this temporary clumsiness a myth or does it have a basis in science? Maria Cristina Bisi and Rita Stagni of the University of Bologna in Italy decided to find out. They selected 15-year-old boys in a growth spurt (i.e., a gain in height of at least 3 cm in 3 months) to compare to boys in a steady growth period (i.e., a gain in height of less than 1 cm in 3 months). Various characteristics of walking gait were measured in both groups while simply walking and when doing the cognitive task of counting backwards while walking. When asked to do a cognitive task while they walked, the boys in their growth spurt were more affected in the variability, smoothness, and regularity in their gait than were the slower-growing boys. On the other hand, stability of their walk was not affected. The rapid change in trunk and limb length during the growth spurt obviously presents an additional challenge to the control of walking and this can be seen in subtle characteristics of walking. Yet, the system is able to handle these changes well enough to preserve the stability of walking in rapidly growing teenagers (Bisi & Stagni, 2016).

Physical growth and aging are fascinating. Humans, as members of a single species, experience many common steps and processes in growth and aging. One example is the adolescent growth spurt. Genetic factors drive a very orderly and sequenced pattern of growth and aging, so in many respects we know what to expect (Bisi & Stagni, 2016). On the other hand, individuals each have unique potential and their own timing. When we observe a group of preadolescents of the same chronological age, we find a huge range of sizes. Growth and aging are also affected by a variety of extrinsic factors, such as nutrition and disease.

Genetic and extrinsic factors combine to influence the physical growth and aging of humans. We can identify patterns and relationships (universality), but we are reminded over and over again of the individual differences (variability). It is important for us to know both the expected pattern and the range of variation.

You might wonder why motor developmentalists have any interest at all in physical growth and aging. Recall our triangular model, which pictures the interaction of individual, environmental, and task constraints, and think back to one of the reasons we gave for the usefulness of this model to developmentalists. As individuals grow and age (in other words, as the individual constraints related to the body's structure change), the interactions between the three types of constraints must change, giving rise to different movements. If our goal is to make the same movements possible over a long range of the life span, then we need to constantly change the environment or the task to accommodate the changing physical constraints. For example, if we want players of a variety of ages to be able to dunk a basketball, we have to adjust the task by changing the basket height as the height of the players or their jumping ability changes. We need to be constantly alert to changing the environment and task in order to help each individual achieve a desired movement.

Imagine for a moment that you are the youth sports coach of a sixth-grade basketball team. How much variation would you expect in the height and weight of your players? Would you assign each player a position (forward, center, or guard) based on size? As your players return for future seasons, would these assignments change? Why or why not?

Understanding the patterns and variations of growth and aging is fundamental to helping individuals develop their motor skills. One goal of educators and health care providers is to make motor tasks developmentally appropriate—that is, achievable by those at any age and with any set of abilities or disabilities. This would be impossible without knowledge of physical growth and aging.

Even for students who anticipate working with people past infancy, a good understanding of growth and aging begins with the study of prenatal growth and development. The talents and limitations that each individual brings to a task are often influenced by the course of prenatal growth and development. So, we begin a review of the growing and aging processes with prenatal development. This brief discussion highlights how sensitive individuals are to extrinsic influences, even in the relatively protective womb.

Prenatal Development

The growth process begins the instant an ovum (egg) and spermatozoon fuse in fertilization. Carried out under the control of genes, early development is astonishingly precise. Genes, then, determine the normal aspects of development and inherited abnormal development. At the same time, the growing embryo (and, later, the fetus) is very sensitive to extrinsic factors, which include the environment in which the fetus is growing—the amniotic sac in the uterus—and the nutrients delivered to the fetus via the mother's circulation and the placenta. Even in the womb, individual genetic factors and extrinsic factors interact in the fetus' development. Some extrinsic factors, such as abnormal external pressure applied to the mother's abdomen or the presence of certain viruses and drugs in the mother's bloodstream, are detrimental to the fetus. Other factors, such as delivery of all the proper nutrients, enhance the fetus' growth.

▶ **KEY POINT** Both genetic and extrinsic factors influence normal and abnormal embryonic and fetal growth.

Prenatal growth is divided into two phases: embryonic growth, from conception to 8 weeks, and fetal growth, from 8 weeks to birth. Let's consider the key features of each phase.

Embryonic Development

Development begins with the fusion of two sex cells: an ovum from the female and a spermatozoon from the male (see figure 8.1). The genes direct the continuous development of the embryo in a precise and predictable pattern.

The number of cells increases, and the cells **differentiate** to form specific tissues and organs. This process occurs in a predictable time line, summarized in table 8.1. At 4 weeks, the limbs are roughly formed and the heartbeat begins. By approximately 8 weeks, the eyes, ears, nose, mouth, fingers, and toes are formed. By this time, the human form has taken shape.

Differentiation is the process wherein cells become specialized, forming specific tissues and organs.

Hyperplasia is an increase in the absolute number of cells.

Hypertrophy is an increase in the relative size of an individual cell.

Fetal Development

The fetal stage, from 8 weeks to birth, is characterized by further growth and cell differentiation of the fetus, leading to functional capacity. This continued growth of the organs and tissues occurs in two ways: by **hyperplasia** and by **hypertrophy**. If you examine the landmarks of growth carefully, you will also see that growth tends to proceed in two directions. One direc-

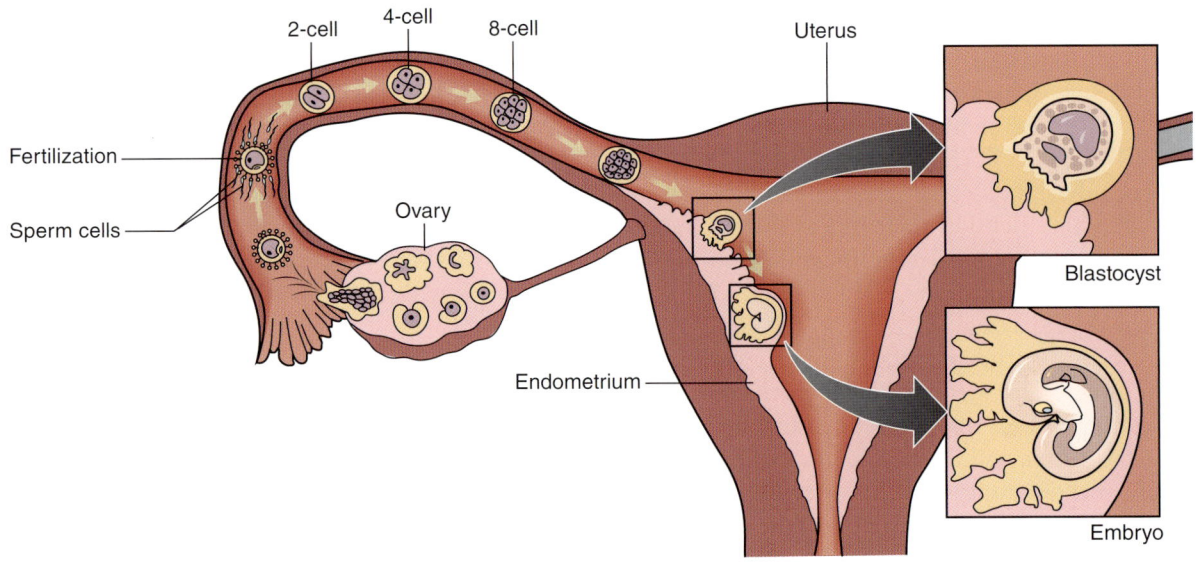

FIGURE 8.1 As the embryo moves through the oviduct, its cells divide and multiply. By the time it implants on the lining of the uterus, it is several hundred cells in size. It is embedded in nutrient cells that nourish it. Implantation in the uterus is facilitated by protuberances of sugar molecules on the surface of the blastocyst.

TABLE 8.1 Landmarks in Embryonic and Fetal Growth

AGE (WK)	LENGTH	WEIGHT	APPEARANCE	INTERNAL DEVELOPMENT
3	3 mm		Head, tail folds formed	Optic vesicles, head recognizable
4	4 mm	0.4 g	Limb rudiments formed	Heartbeat begins; organs recognizable
8	3.5 cm	2 g	Eyes, ears, nose, mouth, digits formed	Sensory organs developing; some bone ossification beginning
12	11.5 cm	19 g	Sex externally recognizable; head very large for body	Brain configuration nearly complete; blood forming in bone marrow
16	19 cm	100 g	Motor activity; scalp hair present; trunk size gaining on head size	Heart muscle developed; sense organs formed
20	22 cm	300 g	Legs have grown appreciably	Myelination of spinal cord begins
24	32 cm	600 g	Respiratory-like movements begin	Cerebral cortex layers formed
28	36 cm	1.1 kg	Increasing development of fat tissue	Retina layered and light-receptive
32	41 cm	1.8 kg	Weight increasing more than length	Taste sense operative
36	46 cm	2.2 kg	Body more rounded	Ossification begins in distal femur
40	52 cm	3.2 kg	Skin smooth with a pinkish tone; at least moderate hair on head	Proximal tibia begins ossification; myelination of brain begins; pulmonary branching two-thirds complete

Adapted by permission from Timiras (1972).

tion is **cephalocaudal**, meaning the head and facial structures grow fastest, followed by the upper body and then by the relatively slow-growing lower body. At the same time, growth is **proximodistal** in direction, meaning the trunk tends to advance, then the nearest parts of the limbs, and finally the distal parts of the limbs (figure 8.2). Body weight increases and the body tissues grow steadily, with the rate of growth increasing at about 5 months and continuing at that rapid rate until birth.

Although cells differentiate during growth to perform a specialized function, some cells have an amazing quality termed **plasticity**, which is the capability to take on a new function. If some of the cells in a system are injured, for example, the remaining cells might be stimulated to perform the role the damaged cells would ordinarily carry out. The cells of the central nervous system have a high degree of plasticity, and their structure, chemistry, and function can be modified both prenatally and postnatally (Ratey, 2001).

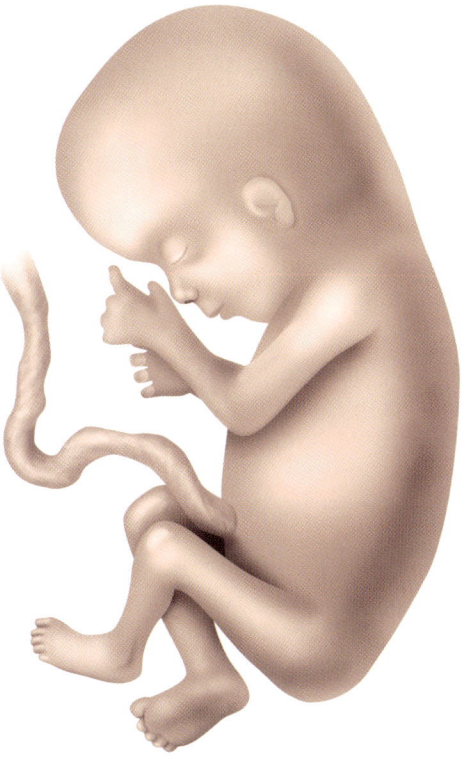

FIGURE 8.2 A fetus at 3 months.

Cephalocaudal is the direction of growth beginning at the head and extending toward the lower body.

Proximodistal is the direction of growth proceeding from the body toward the extremities.

Plasticity is modifiability or malleability; in regard to growth, it is the ability of tissues to subsume functions otherwise carried out by other tissues.

Fetal Nourishment

Many characteristics of the fetal environment have the potential to affect growth, either positively or negatively, and the nourishment system is the extrinsic factor that has the most influence on fetal development. The fetus is nourished by the diffusion of oxygen and nutrients between fetal blood and maternal blood in the placenta (figure 8.3). Carbon dioxide and excretory byproducts also are exchanged and carried away in the mother's blood.

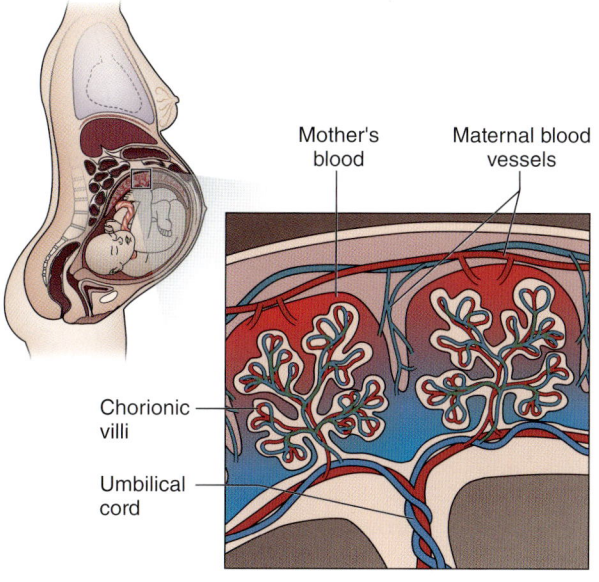

FIGURE 8.3 A diagram of the placenta showing the two circulations—that of mother and that of fetus—which come close enough to each other that substances diffuse from one to the other, though the bloodstreams never mingle.

The growing fetus needs energy, nutrients, and oxygen. If these are in short supply, mother and fetus compete for limited resources, possibly compromising the needs of the fetus. Obviously, then, maternal health status plays a role in prenatal development.

A woman who lives in better conditions (with an adequate, safe food supply and a protective, clean environment) and who receives early prenatal health care is more likely than a woman living in poorer conditions to meet the needs of the fetus. She is also more likely to be at lower risk for illnesses and infections that might compromise the health of the fetus and would result in low birth weight. Consequently, women at lower socioeconomic levels typically give birth to lighter infants than do women at higher socioeconomic levels. This is significant because low-birth-weight infants are at greater risk of disease, infection, and death in the weeks after birth than are normal-weight infants. Some of the differences in birth weight among ethnic groups can be attributed to parental height and are thus largely influenced by genetic factors (Troe et al., 2007). Further research is needed to distinguish the influences on birth weight that are primarily genetic from those that are environmental and thus might be modifiable to promote health in the early postnatal period.

If you were a doctor, would you have to travel to a poor country with primitive living conditions to treat pregnant women with poor health status? Or would you likely see some poor women in your practice in an affluent country? What groups of pregnant women in an affluent country might be at risk of poor health?

Abnormal Prenatal Development

Congenital defects are anomalies present at birth, regardless of whether their causes are genetic or extrinsic.

Abnormal growth may arise from either genetic or extrinsic factors. Genetic abnormalities are inherited and may be immediately apparent or may remain undetected until well into postnatal growth. A host of extrinsic factors can also negatively affect the fetus. Examples include drugs and chemicals in the mother's bloodstream, viruses in the mother's bloodstream, and excessive pressure applied to the mother's abdomen. Let's consider some examples of **congenital defects** in more detail.

Genetic Causes of Abnormal Prenatal Development

An individual may inherit genetic abnormalities as dominant or recessive (including sex-linked) disorders. Dominant disorders result when one parent passes on a defective gene. Recessive disorders occur in children who inherit a defective gene from each parent.

Genetic abnormalities can also result from a new mutation—that is, the alteration or deletion of a gene during formation of the egg or sperm cell. Researchers suspect irradiation and certain hazardous environmental chemicals of causing genetic mutations, and the potential for genetic damage to sex cells increases with advancing maternal age (Nyhan, 1990). Mutations can also occur spontaneously, without a known cause.

An example of a familiar genetic abnormality is trisomy 21, or Down syndrome. When an egg or sperm cell divides, its 46 chromosomes divide in half. When the sperm cell with 23 chromosomes fertilizes an egg with 23 chromosomes, an embryo ends up with a complete set of 46. Sometimes an egg or sperm cell keeps both chromosome 21s, and every cell in the resulting embryo's body will have an extra chromosome 21. A combination of birth defects can result, including mental retardation, distinctive facial features, visual and hearing impairments, and heart defects.

New mutations and inherited disorders can both result in single or multiple malformations of an organ, limb, or body region; deformations of a body part; or disruptions in development resulting from the breakdown of normal tissue. They can affect one or more of the body systems. Many of these abnormalities are obvious at birth, but some do not appear until later. Genetic abnormalities vary considerably in appearance and severity.

External Causes of Abnormal Prenatal Development

Our earlier discussion of fetal nourishment reveals how dependent the fetus is on the mother for the oxygen and nutrients it needs. Unfortunately, the fetal nourishment system can also deliver harmful substances to the fetus, and various other factors can potentially affect the fetus' physical environment and thereby its growth and development.

▶ **KEY POINT** Congenital disorders arising from extrinsic factors can affect the potential for postnatal growth and development. When medical professionals and parents are aware of negative influences, they can manage these influences to minimize the risk to the fetus.

Teratogens

In addition to oxygen and nutrients necessary for fetal life and growth, other substances—including viruses, drugs, and chemicals—can diffuse across the placenta and be harmful to the developing fetus. Sometimes even necessary vitamins, nutrients, and hormones can be harmful if their levels are too high or too low. In these cases substances can act as malformation-producing agents, or **teratogens**. The specific effect that a teratogen has on the fetus depends on when the fetus was exposed to the substance as well as the amount of the substance.

A **teratogen** is any drug or chemical agent that causes abnormal prenatal development upon exposure.

There are critical periods of particular vulnerability to change in the growth and development of tissues and organs. Exposure to a teratogen during a critical period has a more significant effect than exposure at another time. For example, the rubella virus is harmful if the embryo is exposed to it during the first 4 weeks of pregnancy. The earlier the infection, the more serious the resulting abnormalities. Very early exposure can result in miscarriage.

Some congenital defects result from the mere presence of a harmful substance in the maternal blood. Whether the fetus is exposed depends on the size of the substance. For example, small virus particles present in maternal blood can cross the placenta and harm the fetus. Drugs with molecular weights under 1,000 also cross the placenta easily, whereas those with molecular weights over 1,000 do not.

Parents can maximize fetal growth and development by avoiding substances that might be teratogenic. Mothers can maintain a diet that supplies adequate but not excessive nutrients; otherwise, the fetus might develop a specific malformation or be generally retarded in growth and small for age at birth. It is important to recognize that these conditions, including low birth weight, can affect postnatal growth and development. For example, a mother's alcohol consumption during pregnancy can result in a condition called fetal alcohol syndrome, which involves a cluster of birth defects that often include mental retardation; heart defects; facial, joint, and limb deformities; slowed growth and small brain size; short attention span; and hyperactivity. Although it is not clear when a small amount of alcohol consumption becomes an amount that affects a fetus, this birth defect is completely avoidable when a mother abstains from using alcohol.

Other Prenatal Extrinsic Factors

Malformation, retarded growth, and life-threatening conditions can also result from external risk factors affecting the fetus' environment. Examples include

- external or internal pressure on the infant, including pressure from another fetus in utero;
- extreme internal environmental temperature, as when the mother suffers from high fever or hypothermia;
- exposure to X rays or gamma rays;
- changes in atmospheric pressure, especially those leading to hypoxia (oxygen deficiency) in the fetus; and
- environmental pollutants.

The precise effects of these factors also depend on the fetus' stage of development. Like teratogens, external factors have the potential to affect present and future growth and development. Table 8.2 provides a list of external factors that are associated with an increased risk for abnormal prenatal development (Feldkamp, Botto, & Carey, 2015).

TABLE 8.2 Selected External Factors Associated With Increased Risk for Birth Defects

MEDICATIONS	ENVIRONMENT	CONDITIONS AND DISEASES
Asthma medications	Air pollution	Asthma
Hypertensive medications	Caffeine	Bacterial infections
Opioids	Maternal occupation	Maternal injuries
Statins	Phytoestrogens	Obesity
Weight-loss products	Secondhand smoke	Viral infections

Adapted by permission from Feldkamp, Botto, and Carey (2015).

Prenatal Development Summary

Prenatal development is influenced by genetic and extrinsic factors. The genes direct an orderly and precise course of development, but extrinsic factors can influence the process either positively or negatively. Many of these extrinsic factors exert their influence through the fetal nourishment system. A fetus that receives appropriate levels of oxygen and nutrients has the best chance of reaching its full genetic potential, including its potential for skill performance.

Prenatal abnormalities can arise from genetic or extrinsic influence. Some abnormal conditions are a product of *both* genetic inheritance and the environment; that is, a tendency for a disease might be inherited, and subsequently the disease will appear under certain environmental conditions (Timiras, 1972). We should view physical growth and development, then, as a continuous process that begins at conception. Individuals are, in part, products of the factors that affected their prenatal growth and development. Hence, the individual structural constraints that educators and therapists consider when planning activities for individuals reflect the course of prenatal development. The process of postnatal development is the continuation of prenatal development.

Postnatal Development

Is an 11-year-old capable of long-distance runs? How about a 60-year-old? We know that no single answer applies to all 11-year-olds or all 60-year-olds because we have acknowledged the coexistence of universality and specificity in development. Educators and therapists benefit from knowing the universal pattern of postnatal growth and physiological maturation as well as the typical pattern of aging in adults. Yet we work with individuals who have their own timing and potential for growth. Therefore, we must be able to evaluate an individual's status and potential in order to help him or her set reasonable personal goals. We must be able to compare an individual with the average and adjust expectations for performance accordingly.

Overall Growth

Overall body growth after birth is a continuation of prenatal growth. The growth pattern is predictable and consistent but not linear, no matter which measure of overall growth we choose to study. For example, look at the growth curves for height (figure 8.4, *a* and *b*) and weight (figure 8.5, *a* and *b*). They are characterized by rapid growth after birth, followed by gradual but steady growth during childhood, then by rapid growth during early adolescence, and finally by a leveling off. Thus, the curves are roughly S-shaped. We call this pattern of overall body growth a **sigmoid curve** after the Greek letter for S.

▶ **KEY POINT** Postnatal growth proceeds in a precise and orderly pattern, but individual variability, especially in the timing of landmark events, is increasingly obvious as individuals move through infancy, childhood, preadolescence, and adolescence.

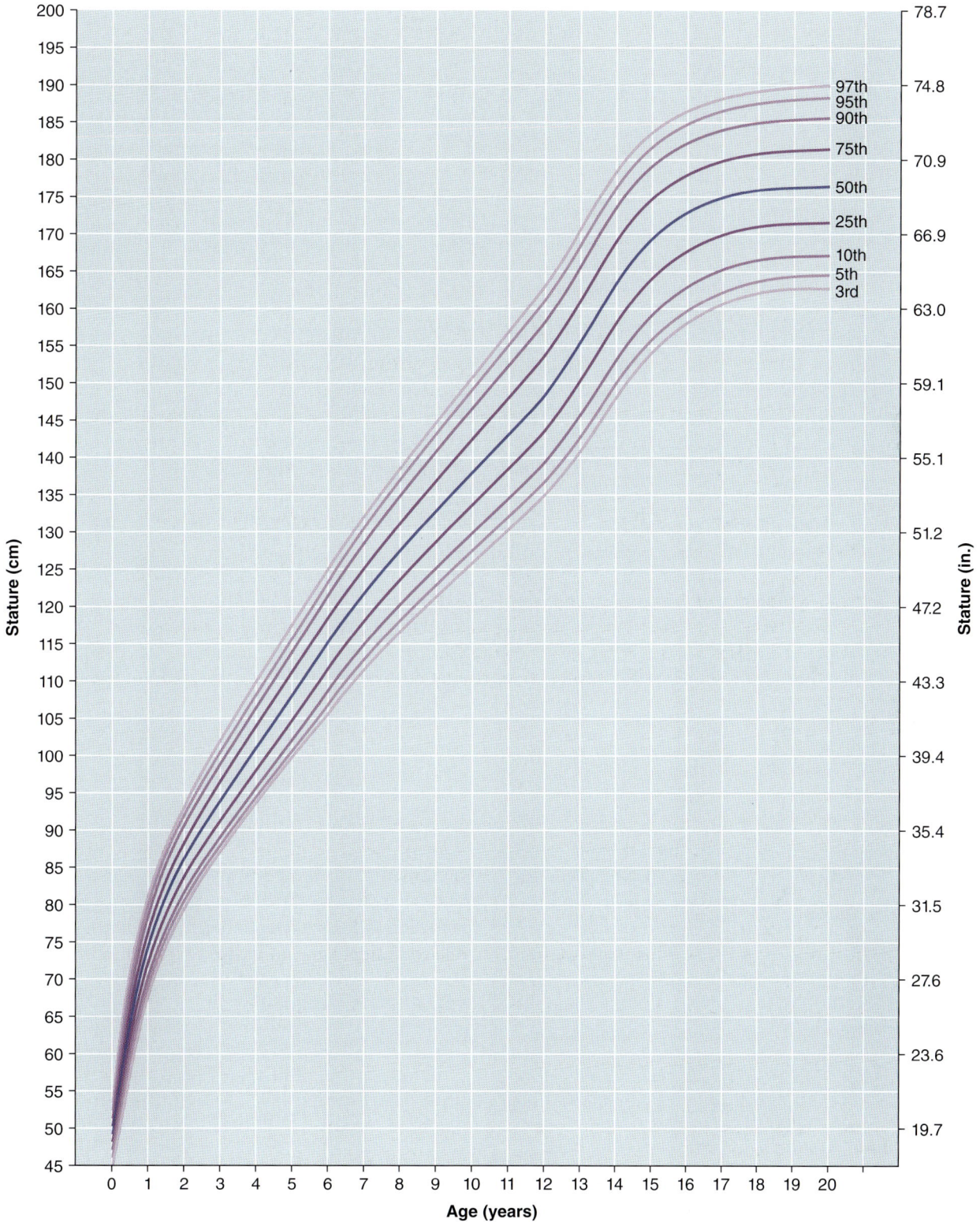

FIGURE 8.4*a* Stature (standing height) by age percentiles for boys. Note the sigmoid, or S-shaped, form of the curves.
Data from the National Center for Health Statistics (2000).

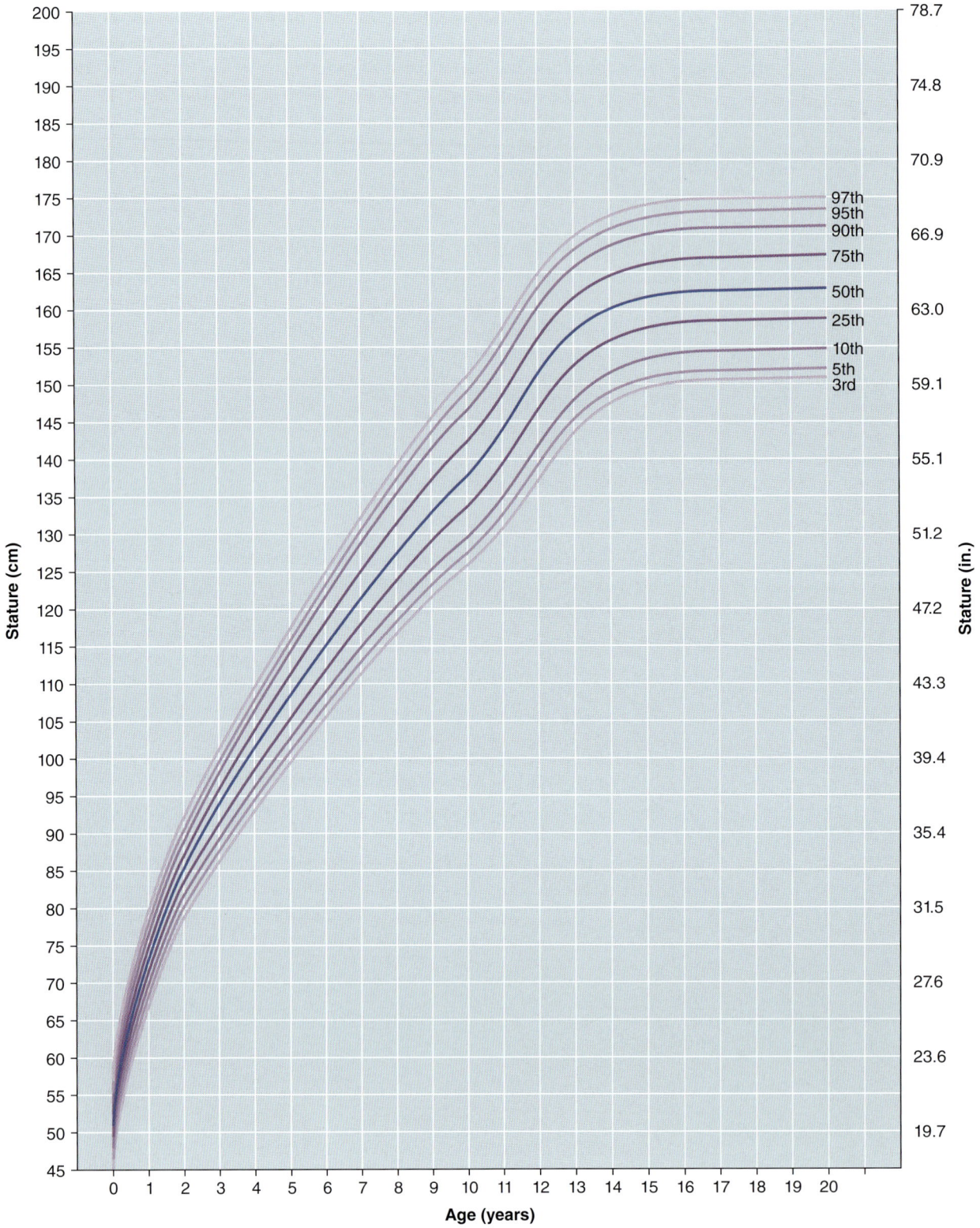

FIGURE 8.4*b* Stature by age percentiles for girls.

Data from the National Center for Health Statistics (2000).

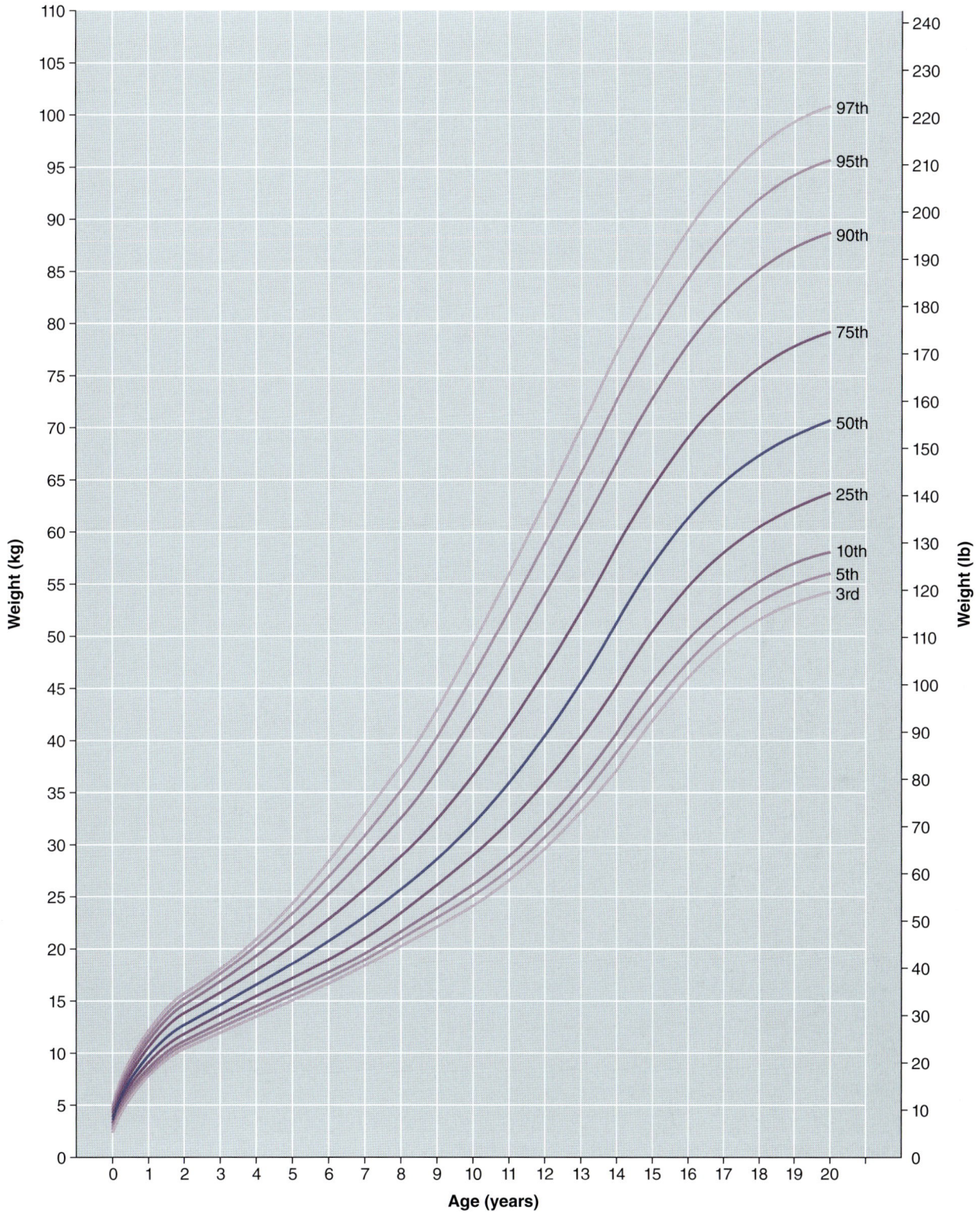

FIGURE 8.5*a* Weight by age percentiles for boys. Note that the curves are S-shaped, though flatter than the height curves.

Data from the National Center for Health Statistics (2000).

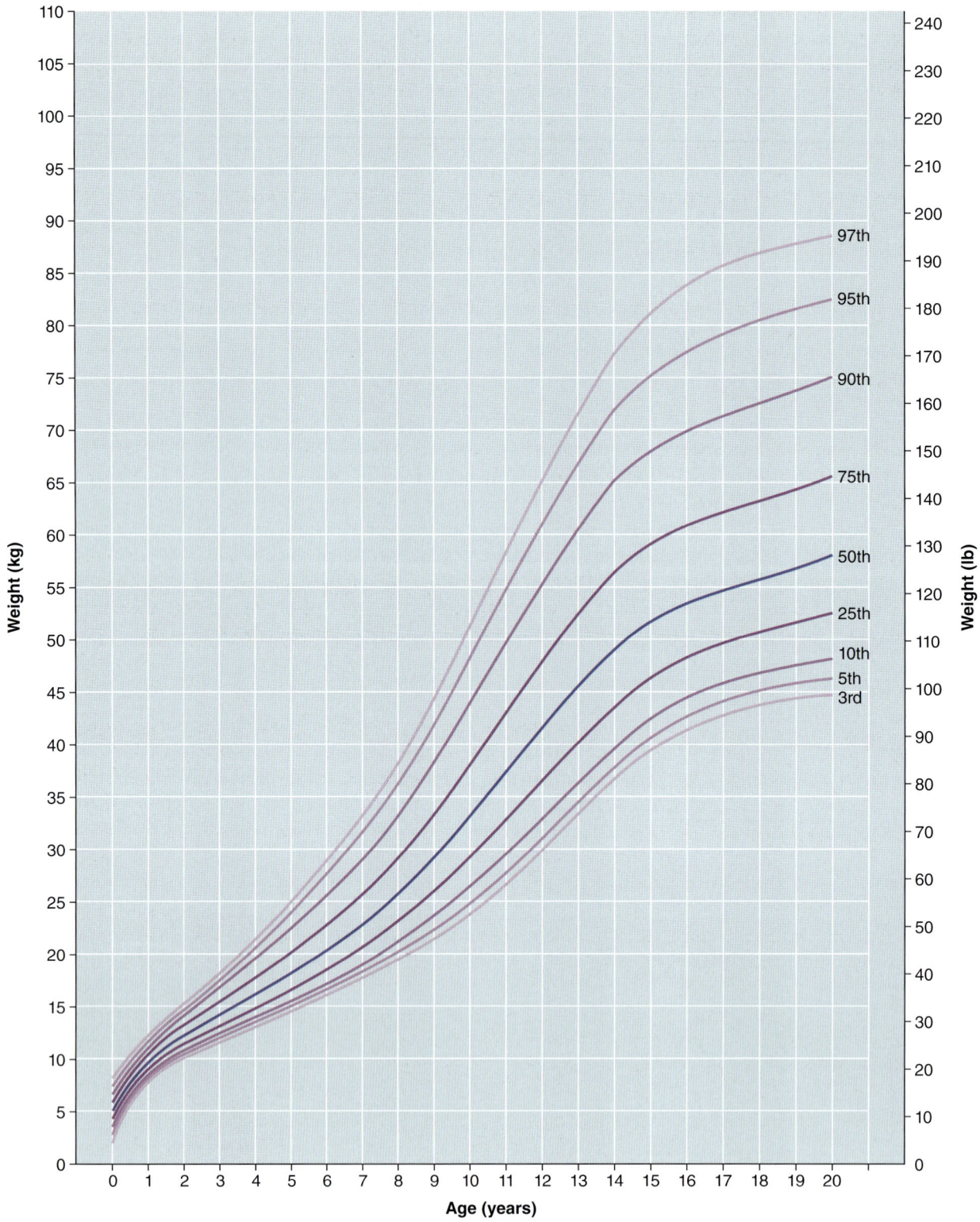

FIGURE 8.5*b* Weight by age percentiles for girls.

Data from the National Center for Health Statistics (2000).

Although a normal growth curve is always sigmoid, the timing of a particular individual's spurts and steady growth periods is likely to vary from the average. For example, one girl might begin her adolescent growth spurt at 8 years, whereas another might begin hers at 10. The slope of the curve can also vary from the average. One girl might grow more rapidly (i.e., have a steeper growth curve) than the other. Note that, on the growth charts, the range of variation—the gap between the 3rd and 97th percentiles—widens with age, especially for weight (Malina, Bouchard, & Bar Or, 2004). This is another example of universality and specificity in development. The sigmoid pattern of a graph of overall growth is universal, but the timing and steepness of segments of the curve are specific to the individual, and with advancing age the influence of environmental factors increases the variation among individuals.

Web Study Guide Learn to graph rate of change in height and weight in Lab Activity 8.1, Graphing a Velocity Curve, in the web study guide.

Sex

Sex is a major factor in the timing as well as the extent of growth. Sex differences are minimal in early childhood, with boys being very slightly taller and heavier. Throughout childhood, though, girls tend to mature faster than boys, so that at any given age girls as a group are biologically more mature than boys. Important sex differences in growth and development are especially pronounced at adolescence. Girls begin their adolescent growth spurt when they are about 9 years old (often termed the **age at takeoff** because the rate of growth begins to increase), whereas boys begin theirs at about age 11. Note that these ages are group averages. About two-thirds of all adolescents will initiate their growth spurt during the year before or the year after these averages, meaning that approximately one-third will initiate it even earlier or later.

Age at takeoff is the age at which the rate of growth begins to increase.

Height

Height follows the sigmoid pattern of growth: a rapid increase in infancy, tapering off to steady growth in childhood, followed by another rapid increase during the adolescent growth spurt, and finally a tapering off until the end of the growth period. An individual's height can be compared with group norms, and this comparison is often made using a family of height curves plotted against age. The individual curves represent various percentiles, usually the 3rd, 5th, 10th, 25th, 50th, 75th, 90th, 95th, and 97th (as in figures 8.4, *a* and *b*). This approach allows us to approximate an individual's percentile for height at a specific age or over time as well as whether he or she maintains position in the group or changes. For example, we might find one individual who remains in the 40th percentile for most of the growth period and another who begins the adolescent growth spurt early and goes from the 60th percentile at age 8 to the 90th percentile at age 10.

Children tend to maintain their relative percentile positions in comparison with group norms after they are 2 or 3 years old; that is, a 3-year-old child in the 75th percentile for height is most likely to be around the 75th percentile throughout childhood. A large fluctuation in relative position could indicate that some extrinsic factor is influencing growth (Martorell, Malina, Castillo, Mendoza, & Pawson, 1988) and that medical examination is warranted.

In addition to the extent of growth, it is interesting to examine the rate, or velocity, of growth (i.e., when individuals are growing rapidly or slowly). By plotting the rate of growth, we can find the age at which one is growing the fastest (**peak velocity**) or the age at which one changes from slow growth to rapid growth (age at takeoff) or vice versa (see the sidebar Assessing the Extent and Rate of Growth).

On average, girls reach peak height velocity during the adolescent growth spurt at 11.5 to 12.0 years of age (figure 8.6). Their growth in height then tapers off at approximately age 14, and notable increases in height end around age 16. Boys reach their peak height velocity at 13.5 to 14.0 years. This velocity is somewhat faster than that of girls—approximately 9 cm per year for boys compared with 8 cm per year for girls (Beunen & Malina, 1988; Brown, Patel,

Assessing the Extent and Rate of Growth

In chapter 1, we acknowledge that we often picture growth and development through graphs. This practice is common in describing physical growth. We often see measurements of height, weight, or length plotted against advancing age. These plots are called **distance curves** because they convey the extent of growth; figures 8.4 and 8.5 are examples. If we want to know the distance that growth has progressed at a certain age, we merely read the value opposite that age. For example, from a height curve we can determine how tall an individual was at any age (if using the plot of an individual person), or what the average height for a group was at any age (if using the plot of a group average).

If the line plotted is going up with age, we know that growth is taking place, provided that the axes of the graph are arranged from low (at the origin) to high. We expect growth measurements to increase with age during the growth period. In adulthood, measurements might go up or down as extrinsic factors influence the measurement. Body weight is a good example. If the slope of a distance curve is gradual, the change is moderate for that age period. If the slope is steep, the change is rapid for that age period. Thus, the slope of a distance curve can indicate changes in the *rate* of growth.

The rate of growth can be illustrated more dramatically on graphs of growth speed called **velocity curves**. These curves are plotted by first selecting small age spans, such as the time between the 8th and 9th birthdays, the 9th and 10th birthdays, and the 11th and 12th birthdays. Then, for each of these short spans, we find the change in growth as indicated by the distance curve. For example, we might check a distance curve for height and see that the increase in height between the 8th and 9th birthdays is 5 cm. We would then plot a point at 5 cm per year and at 8.5 years (representing the midpoint of the age span during which the growth was 5 cm). By doing this for a number of age spans and connecting our points with a smooth curve, we produce a velocity curve.

Velocity curves look very different from distance curves. They often have sections where the graphed line is decreasing, indicating that the rate of growth is slowing or decelerating. They also have peaks (i.e., points at which the rate of growth changes from faster to slower). Humans have a peak velocity in their overall growth measurements during early adolescence (termed peak height velocity, peak weight velocity, and so on). This is the age at which growth is the fastest for this portion of the life span. During the downslope of the peak, growth slows, although it may still be quite rapid. For example, a typical peak height velocity for girls is 8 cm per year (figure 8.6), and it typically occurs around 12 years of age. Immediately before this age, the velocity of growth in height increases from 5 to 6 to 7 to 8 cm per year. After this age, growth slows from 8 to 7 to 6 cm per year, and so on. Throughout the age span of 10.5 to 13 years, a fairly rapid increase in height (6–8 cm per year) occurs.

In reading a velocity curve, we must keep in mind that we are reading a rate of growth for a short age span, not the extent of growth. We can say how tall an individual girl is from her distance curve for height but not from her velocity curve. On the other hand, her velocity curve enables us to easily determine the age at which she was growing the fastest.

Readers who have studied calculus will recognize that a velocity curve is the first derivative of a distance curve. The second derivative would provide an acceleration curve, indicating the ages at which growth is accelerating or decelerating.

& Darmawan, 2017). Boys' growth tapers off at 17 years, and notable increases end by age 18. Note that males have about 2 more years of growth than females, amounting to 10 to 13 cm of height. This longer growth period accounts for much of the difference in average absolute height between adult men and women.

Weight

Growth in weight also follows the sigmoid pattern: a rapid increase in infancy, a moderate increase in childhood, a spurt in early adolescence, and a steady increase that tapers off at the end of the growth period. Weight, however, is very susceptible to extrinsic factors and can reflect variations in the amount of muscle with exercise as well as variations in the amount of fat tissue with diet and exercise. Disease can also influence body weight.

Peak weight velocity during the adolescent growth spurt follows peak height velocity in adolescents by 2.5 to 5.0 months in boys and 3.5 to 10.5 months in girls (Brown et al., 2017). The growth of various segment lengths and breadths can reach peak velocity before or after the individual reaches peak height velocity, but all reach their peak before or at peak weight velocity (Beunen, Malina, Renson, & Van Gerven, 1988). This is the factual basis for the commonly observed pattern of individuals first growing "up," then filling "out."

Relative Growth

Although the body as a whole consistently follows the sigmoid growth pattern, specific body parts, tissues, and organs have differential rates of growth. In other words, each part of the growing individual has its own precise and orderly growth rate. These differential growth rates can result in notable changes in the body's appearance as a whole. Observe how the proportions illustrated in figure 8.7 change dramatically throughout life. Body proportions at birth reflect the cephalocaudal (head to toe) and proximodistal (near to far) directions of prenatal growth. Therefore, a newborn's form is quite different from that of an adult. The head accounts for one-fourth of the total height at birth but only one-eighth of adult height. The legs make up about three-eighths of height at birth but almost half of adult height.

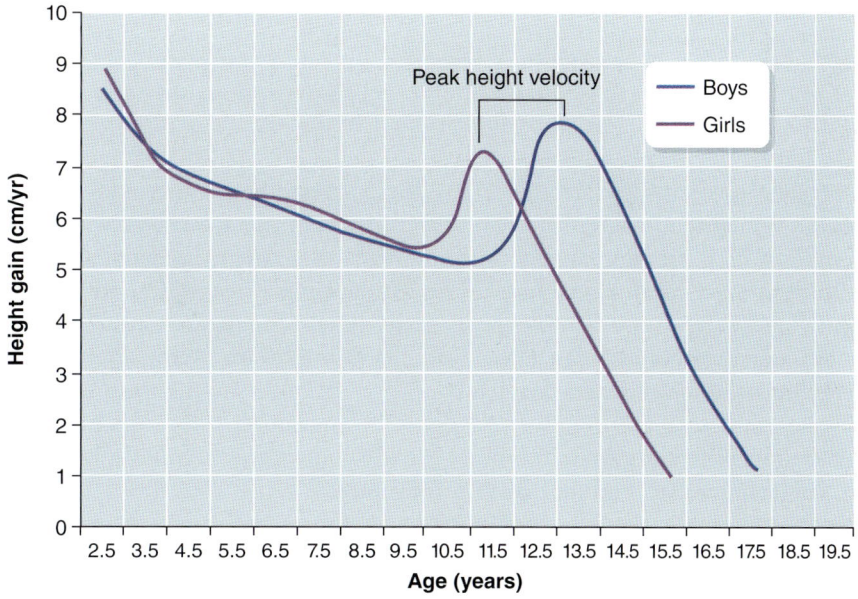

FIGURE 8.6 Velocity curves plotted from figure 8.4, *a* and *b*, ages 2 to 18 years. After age 2, the rate of growth slows until the adolescent growth spurt. Note the ages at peak height velocity for boys and girls.

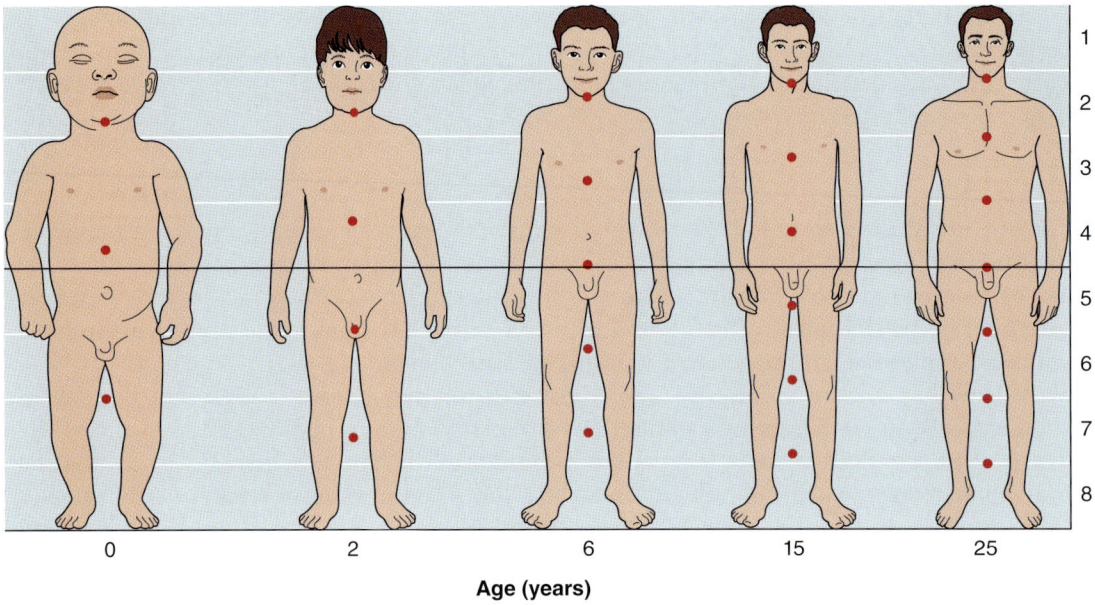

FIGURE 8.7 Postnatal changes in body proportion shown by placing individuals throughout the growth period on the same scale.

Adapted by permission from Timiras, (1972).

For a newborn to achieve adult proportions, some body parts must grow faster than others during postnatal growth. For example, the legs grow faster than the trunk and head in infancy and childhood, and they undergo a growth spurt early in adolescence. Growth in height results mostly from an increase in trunk length during late adolescence and early adulthood. Boys and girls have similar proportions in childhood, but by the time they are adults, relative growth of some body areas brings about noticeable differences between the sexes. In girls, shoulder and hip breadth increase at about the same rate, so their shoulder-to-hip ratio is fairly stable during growth. Boys undergo a substantial increase in shoulder breadth during their growth spurt, so their ratio changes as they move into adolescence and acquire the typical broad-shouldered shape of adult men.

▶ **KEY POINT** Although early maturing girls tend to be initially taller, girls who mature later have a longer growth period than the early maturers and consequently tend to be taller in adulthood. The results are not as clear-cut in boys, but the same trend seems to exist.

Teachers, personal trainers, physical therapists, doctors, researchers, and many other professionals take anthropometric measurements. These measurements must be taken with great precision if they are to be used for comparisons with norms or measurements taken at a later date.

Body form might have implications for skill performance in early childhood. For example, even if 5-month-old infants were neurologically ready to coordinate and control the walking pattern, it is unlikely they could balance their top-heavy bodies on such thin, short legs and small feet. Varying limb lengths and weights can affect balance, momentum, and potential speed in various movements. Recalling Newell's model from chapter 1, we realize that changing individual structural constraints related to body form and proportion could certainly interact with task and environment to produce different movements.

Specific tissues and organs also grow differentially. Although their prenatal growth tends to follow the increase in body weight, the postnatal growth of some tissues and systems follows unique patterns. The brain, for example, achieves more than 80% of its adult weight by the time the individual reaches age 4. Because various tissues of the body grow differentially after birth, our knowledge of individual structural constraints is made more complete by study of the individual body systems. Growth, development, and aging of each of the relevant body systems are discussed in chapter 9.

Physiological Maturation

Tissues of the growing body can advance without necessarily increasing in size. The biochemical composition of cells, organs, and systems can advance qualitatively in what is termed **physiological maturation**. Chronological age, growth in body size, and physiological maturation are related to one another in that as children and youths get older they tend to grow in size and to mature. These dimensions can, however, proceed with their own timing. For example, two children of the same age can be dramatically different in maturation status, with one being an early maturer and the other being a late maturer. Or, two children of the same size can be different ages, and they could be at similar levels of maturation or very different levels of maturation. Thus, it is difficult to infer maturity from age alone, from size alone, or even from age and size considered together. An individual child can appear to be small and slight of build but may actually be relatively mature for his or her chronological age.

Physiological maturation is the developmental process leading to a state of full function.

One indication of maturation status is the appearance of the **secondary sex characteristics** during the adolescent growth spurt. The secondary sex characteristics appear at a younger age in girls and boys who are early maturers and at an older age in those who are late maturers. As noted previously, girls as a group mature at a faster rate than boys; they enter their adolescent growth spurt sooner and their secondary sex characteristics appear sooner. Their breasts enlarge; pubic hair appears; and **menarche**, the first menstrual cycle, occurs. Regardless of the exact chronological age at which a girl begins her growth spurt, menarche typically follows the peak height velocity by 11 to 12 months. In the past several decades, the average age of menarche has decreased and has been reported to be between 12 and 12.5 years old (Biro et al., 2018). Figure 8.8 shows height attained as well as height velocity and acceleration curves, with the onset and completion of secondary sex characteristics and average age of menarche marked. In boys, the testes and scrotum grow in size and pubic hair appears. Boys have no landmark comparable with girls' menarche for puberty; the production of viable sperm is a gradual process.

Secondary sex characteristics are aspects of form or structure appropriate to males or females, often used to assess physiological maturity in adolescents.

Imagine you are a physical education teacher at an elementary school. What would be wrong with expecting all of the tall children in your class to be the most skilled because you assume they are the most mature? Would you be correct in assuming that the most coordinated children in your fifth-grade class are likely to be those you will see playing on their high school varsity team in 6 years?

Maturation status is relevant as a structural constraint influencing movement. Individuals who are more mature are likely to be stronger and more coordinated than those who are less mature, even at the same chronological age. Parents, educators, and therapists must consider maturation status when designing activities and therapies for youths and when setting performance goals. It is tempting to infer movement performance potential from size alone or age alone, but maturation status is a powerful predictor of performance potential. Motor performance during puberty can be significantly influenced by the process of growth and maturation. Periods of motor incoordination, or "adolescent awkwardness," may occur during the adolescent growth spurt (Brown et al., 2017). These are often temporary (lasting approximately 6 months) and not associated with any underlying dysfunction, but they may be associated with an increased risk of injury, although research is not conclusive (Quatman-Yates, Quatman, Meszaros, Paterno, & Hewett, 2012). Table 8.3 summarizes the developmental changes in growth and maturation during early childhood through adolescence.

▶ **KEY POINT** Postnatal growth patterns differ among body parts and body systems.

Extrinsic Influences on Postnatal Growth

As noted earlier, extrinsic factors can have a great influence on prenatal growth even in the relatively protective environment of the womb. It is no surprise, then, that extrinsic factors have an

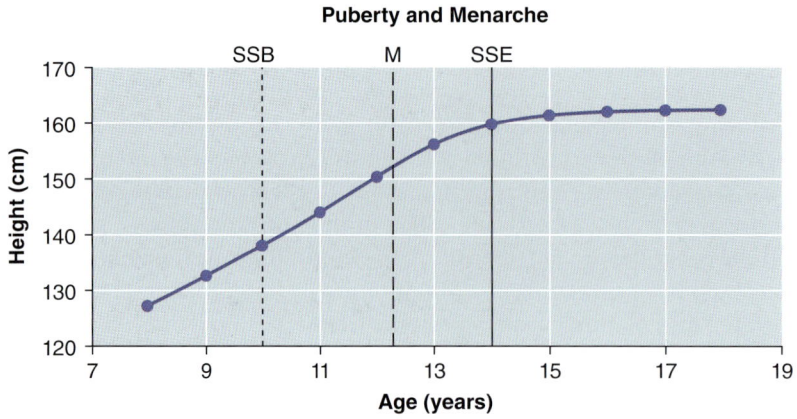

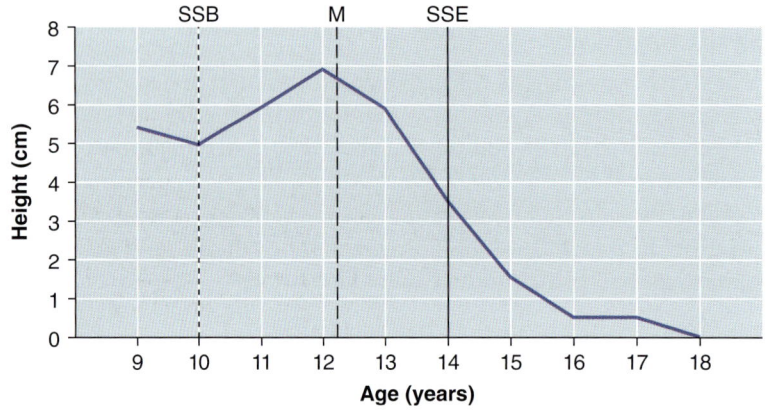

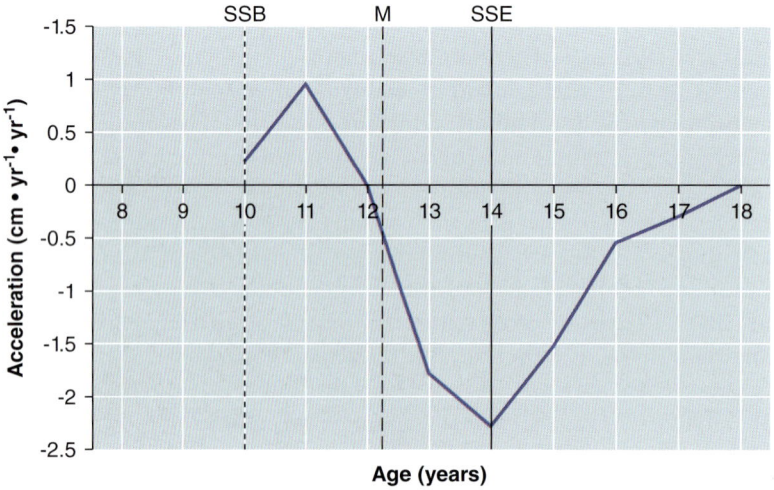

FIGURE 8.8 *(a)* Height attained (distance), *(b)* height velocity, and *(c)* height acceleration curves for a girl at adolescence. Note that menarche (M) comes after peak height velocity. Secondary sex characteristics begin to appear at approximately 10 years old (SSB) and reach adult form by approximately 14 years of age (SSE).

Data from Biro & Keiss (2016), Susman et al. (2010), and the National Health and Nutrition Examination Survey (NHANES): Fryar, Gu, and Ogden (2012).

TABLE 8.3 Summary of Developmental Changes in Growth and Maturation

AREA OF GROWTH	EARLY CHILDHOOD (0–5 YR)	LATE CHILDHOOD (6–9 YR)	EARLY ADOLESCENCE (10–14 YR)	LATE ADOLESCENCE (15–19 YR)
HEIGHT CHANGES	Rapid increases during first 2 yr	Steady	Rapid; peak velocity occurs between 11 and 14 yr, with girls reaching PHV earlier than boys	Slowing by 14 yr (girls) to 17 yr (boys)
WEIGHT CHANGES	Rapid increases during infancy	Steady	Rapid; peak velocity occurs 2 to 5 mo after height spurt	Extrinsic factors such as diet and exercise impact body weight
RELATIVE GROWTH	Head proportionally larger than body; legs grow faster than head and trunk	Legs continue to grow faster than trunk and head	Gender differences appear in shoulder to hip ratios	Adult proportions
MATURATION OF SEX CHARACTERISTICS	No signs of maturation present	Puberty-induced body changes may begin as early as 9 yr in females	Secondary sex characteristics appear	Physiological maturation complete

increased influence on growth and development after birth. Genetics control the timing and rate of an individual's growth and maturation, but extrinsic factors—especially those influencing body metabolism—can have a great effect. During periods of rapid growth, such as just after birth and in early adolescence, growth is particularly sensitive to alteration by environmental factors.

One way to study extrinsic influences on growth throughout the life span is to perform a large-scale prospective cohort study, such as the Generation R Study, which is being conducted in Rotterdam, Netherlands (Kooijman et al., 2016). Since 2002, researchers have followed a large cohort of newborns through childhood and adolescence, measuring exposures to different determinants (e.g., environmental, nutritional, lifestyle related) and the resulting health outcomes (e.g., body composition, cognition, infections, disease, immunity).

Early diet is a particularly important extrinsic influence. Duijts, Jaddoe, Hofman, and Moll (2010) observed that Generation R infants who were breastfed exclusively until 6 months of age had a lower risk of infection than those infants who were exclusively breastfed until 4 months of age and only partially thereafter.

▶ **KEY POINT** Extrinsic factors play a larger role as individuals proceed through adulthood, leading to great variability among individuals in older adulthood.

The phenomenon of **catch-up growth** illustrates the susceptibility of overall body growth to extrinsic influence. A child might experience catch-up growth after suffering a period of severe malnutrition or a bout with a severe disorder such as chronic renal failure (figure 8.9). During such a period, body growth is retarded. After the diet is improved or the child recovers from the disorder (i.e., after a positive environment for growth is restored), growth rate increases until the child approaches or catches up to what otherwise would have been the extent of growth during that period (Prader, Tanner, & von Harnack, 1963). Whether the child recovers some or all of the growth depends on the timing, duration, and severity of the negative environmental condition.

Catch-up growth is relatively rapid physical growth of the body to recover some or all potential growth lost during a period of negative extrinsic influence. It occurs once the negative influence is removed.

One of the Generation R studies (Ay et al., 2008) noted that children with slower prenatal growth in weight, especially during the third trimester, demonstrated catch-up growth in the early months after birth. Children who experienced this period of catch-up growth tended to have a higher percentage of fat weight at 6 months of age than did children who did not experience a period of catch-up growth. The Generation R project will continue to follow these children during adolescence to determine whether this early period of catch-up growth might predispose individuals to higher proportions of fat weight later in life.

Web Study Guide Collect anthropometric measures to assess children's growth in Lab Activity 8.2, Taking Growth Measures, in the web study guide. In this lab, you will use the figures found in this book's appendix.

Imagine you are a parent or, if you are in fact one, put on your "parenting cap." Early maturers are likely to demonstrate better athletic performance than their late-maturing counterparts. If you overlook this and expect your son or daughter who is an early maturer to maintain his or her performance edge over others into adulthood, what could be the repercussions when the late maturers catch up? If you have a late-maturing child, what could be the repercussions of an early assumption that the child has no future as an athlete?

Measuring Height, Lengths, and Breadths

Frequent measurement of children's growth and comparisons of the values with averages at a given age can help detect abnormal growth. Medical or environmental factors influencing abnormal growth can then be identified and moderated or corrected. Of course, such growth measurements reflect the individual's genetic potential for height and body build (which often correspond to the parents' height and build) as well as the individual's personal growth timing. Therefore, in screening growth measurements, children and teens who measure above the 90th or below the 10th percentile for their age—especially those whose parents are not exceptionally tall or short, respectively—should be referred to medical personnel for examination (Lowrey, 1986).

For growth screenings to be meaningful, measurements must be done accurately using the same measurement techniques used to establish group norms or averages. Descriptions of standard techniques are widely available. For example, the World Health Organization published a training course for assessing children's growth in 2008 (Onyango, De Onis, & WHO, 2008), and you should refer to these standards if you decide to conduct a screening program. A detailed description of standard techniques is beyond the scope of this text, but let's briefly consider the various measurements used to assess physical growth and body size.

Anthropometry is the science of the measurement of the human physical form.

The measurements used to assess growth and size are known as **anthropometric** measures, and they include height, weight, segment length, body breadth, and circumference. The measurements are sometimes used in ratios to illustrate a particular aspect of size. Standing height is the most common growth measure, but sitting height is an interesting measurement to observe during the growth period. Standing height minus sitting height yields a functional measure of leg length. Infants have relatively long trunks and short legs, so the proportion of standing height to leg length changes over the growth period to reach the typical adult proportion.

Various other segment lengths, such as those of the upper arm and the thigh, can also be measured, as can the breadth of the body at specified locations. Typically, length and breadth measurements are taken where skeletal landmarks can be located so that the measurement reflects skeletal structure and not soft tissues such as fat and muscle that

Adulthood and Aging

Growth ends for humans in the late teens or early 20s, but the status and size of the body attained during the growth years are not necessarily maintained in adulthood. Some measures of body size can change in adulthood. These changes reflect the aging of tissues and, probably to a greater extent, the influence of extrinsic factors. For example, a lack of weight-bearing exercise and calcium in the diet could contribute to osteoporosis and a resulting decrease in height. The extrinsic factors that might or might not influence an individual, as well as the timing of their influence, are extremely variable over the life span. Naturally, then, we expect to see more and more individual variability in changes of body size as we move through the life span.

Men and women grow slightly in height into their 20s. Trunk length may even increase very slightly into the mid-40s. Aside from these very small increases, height is stable through adulthood. It is common, however, for an individual's stature to decrease slightly over the adult years

can change with diet and exercise. The most common breadth measures are taken at the shoulders and hips, and shoulder width is often divided by hip width to form a ratio. This shoulder-to-hip ratio is also interesting to observe over the growth period because it undergoes dramatic change in boys during the adolescent growth spurt as they reach the typical male body build of broad shoulders and narrow hips.

Circumference measurements can be taken at numerous locations and often represent soft tissue—fat and muscle—as well as bone structure. We expect circumference measurements to increase with growth in size, but a circumference measurement by itself cannot provide information about the amount of fat tissue versus lean body tissue. Pediatricians closely monitor head circumference in infants and toddlers. An abnormally large measurement is associated with hydrocephalus (excess cerebrospinal fluid that could cause brain damage).

Body weight is another common measure of growth and body size. Growth in weight reflects the increase in lean body tissues, which is genetically driven, and the increase in adipose, or fat, tissues, which can be readily influenced by extrinsic factors such as exercise and nutrition. Body weight can be apportioned into lean body mass and fat tissue mass by one of several means described later in this text. The resulting measurement typically is expressed as "percent fat."

In another interesting ratio, body weight (in kilograms) is divided by the square of standing height (in meters). This ratio is called the body mass index (BMI), and it is useful for measuring obesity, especially in adults. The normal or healthy range for BMI is 18.5 to 24.9; obesity is defined as a BMI over 30.

Many methods exist for measuring physical growth and body size, and each measurement yields a specific type of information. Particularly in combination, these measurements can provide a great deal of information about the course of growth in size. This information can be used by medical professionals to screen for and possibly correct troubling conditions, thereby enabling individuals to reach their growth potential or to maintain good health after the growth period. Such information can also be used to help children and youths understand the changes their bodies undergo, especially during the adolescent growth spurt.

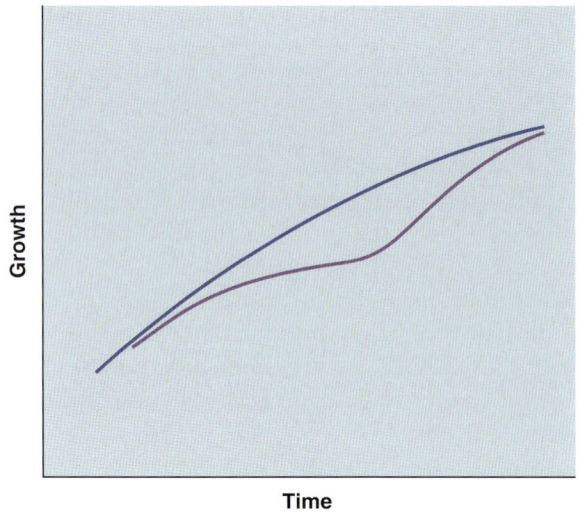

FIGURE 8.9 In this illustration of hypothetical catch-up growth, the blue line represents the course of normal growth as it might have been. The purple line represents actual growth as influenced by a negative extrinsic factor. As the factor exerts its influence, growth slows; however, with removal of the negative factor, growth speeds up in order to catch up to the level that otherwise would have been reached. How close actual growth comes to catching the line representing normal growth depends on the time of occurrence and the length of time the factor exerts its influence, as well as its severity.

Assessment of Physiological Maturation

Maturation can be assessed directly or indirectly. A direct measurement would be ideal, but direct measures of maturation are not always easy to obtain or applicable to the entire growth period. For example, dental eruption (the appearance of new teeth) indicates maturation status but is restricted to two age spans: between approximately 6 months and 3 years, when the deciduous (baby) teeth first appear, and between approximately 6 and 13 years, when the permanent teeth appear. The appearances of baby and permanent teeth follow a typical order. For early maturers, teeth appear at a younger age than for late maturers.

The appearance of the secondary sex characteristics can also be used to assess maturation. Tanner (Marshall & Tanner, 1969, 1970; Tanner, 1975) devised a system of assessment that separately places boys and girls into one of five stages based on breast, pubic hair, and genitalia development. Stage 1 is the immature, prepubertal state and stage 5 is the fully sexually mature state. The average individual moves through these stages in approximately 4 years, so even with several years of variation in the timing of maturation, this assessment can be used for only about 6 years of the growth period. In addition, there are many individual exceptions to the course of progression. Ratings for axillary hair, voice change, and facial hair are not precise enough for assessing maturation, although these are obvious characteristics of ongoing maturation.

(figure 8.10). Some of this decrease results from the compression and flattening of the body's connective tissues, especially the cartilage pads between the vertebrae in the spinal column. The result is a compression of the spinal column and a decrease in trunk length. The bones also lose density as a result of progressive modifications in the protein matrix of the skeleton (Timiras, 1972). This breakdown is more severe in persons with osteoporosis and can result in the collapse of one or more vertebrae; if this occurs, the loss of stature is pronounced (figure 8.11). Heightened awareness in recent years of the devastating effects of osteoporosis on well-being has

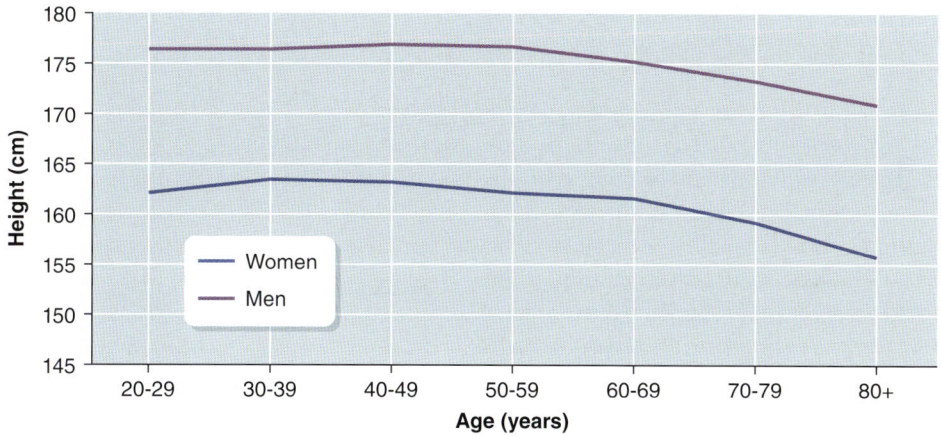

FIGURE 8.10 Body height in adulthood.

Data from the National Health and Nutrition Examination Survey (NHANES): Fryar, Gu, and Ogden (2012).

A relatively precise assessment of maturation can be obtained from skeletal maturation. By comparing an X ray of skeletal maturation with a set of standards, developmentalists can assign individuals a skeletal age. In early maturers skeletal age is older than chronological age, and in late maturers skeletal age is younger than chronological age. This maturation assessment is described in more detail in chapter 9.

Given the disadvantages of and difficulty obtaining direct assessments of maturation, many educators and therapists infer maturation status by comparing a set of growth measurements with group norms. That is, if a girl is in the 75th percentile for height, the 70th percentile for weight, the 80th percentile for shoulder breadth, and so on, we could infer that she is an early maturer. Of course, we could be fooled if her genetic potential is to be a large individual. She might be average in maturation status but larger than average for her age because she has inherited the genetic potential to be large. We must always keep in mind the limitations of inferring maturation from growth measurements, yet we still may find it useful to make an inference when considering the movement performance potential of an individual child or youth.

led to more interest in its prevention and treatment, which could at some point lead to less pronounced loss of height in older adulthood.

Imagine you are a doctor. As your patients enter their 50s, what might you do to decrease the likelihood that they will one day suffer a hip fracture due in part to bones that have lost density?

Adults typically start gaining excess fat weight in their early 20s (figure 8.12). This occurs in many individuals, even those who are initially at a normal or healthy body mass index (Stenholm et al., 2015). This increase may be related to changes in lifestyle. Young adults who begin careers and families commonly take less time to exercise and prepare healthy meals. In contrast, adults who exercise regularly and eat wisely often maintain their weight or even gain muscle and lose fat. Older adults sometimes lose weight, probably as a result of inactivity and a consequent loss of muscle tissue. Loss of appetite accompanying lifestyle changes can also be a factor. Again, active older adults are not as likely to lose muscle weight.

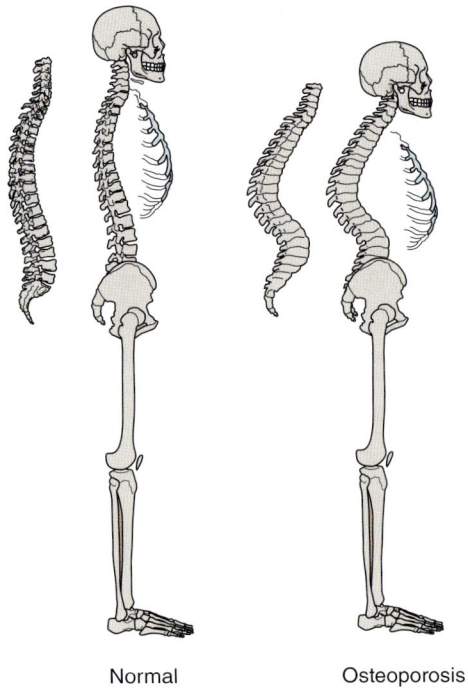

FIGURE 8.11 Loss of height in those with osteoporosis can be pronounced. Compression fractures of the vertebrae lead to kyphosis ("dowager's hump") and pressure on the viscera, causing abdominal distension.

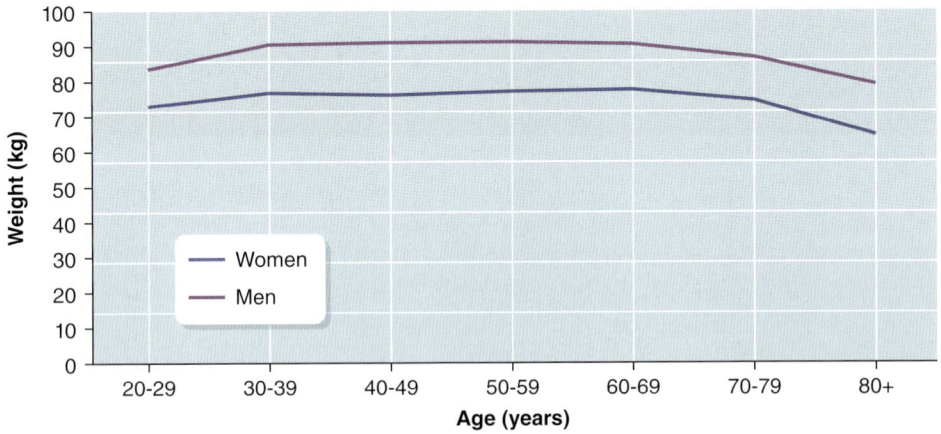

FIGURE 8.12 Body weight changes in adulthood.

Data from the National Health and Nutrition Examination Survey (NHANES): Fryar, Gu, and Ogden (2012).

Summary and Synthesis

Knowledge of the process of overall postnatal growth helps parents, educators, and therapists see how changing structural constraints affect the movement that arises from individual, task, and environmental constraints. Whole-body growth proceeds in a characteristic pattern known as the sigmoid pattern, but the rate of maturation varies between the sexes and among individuals.

Knowing the normal process and the normal variability among individuals helps professionals detect abnormal or retarded growth.

As individuals move through their growing years and then through their adult years, extrinsic factors contribute more and more to the individual variability we see. Because extrinsic factors can usually be manipulated (i.e., accentuated, minimized, or removed), everyone has an interest in knowing what factors have an effect and how they act on individuals.

The individual structural constraints that affect movement often do so at a system level rather than at a whole-body level. For example, muscle growth influences available strength for executing skills. Our understanding of the role of changing structural constraints requires a look at the development of those body systems involved in movement over the life span. This is our task in the next chapter.

Reinforcing What You Have Learned About Constraints

TAKE A SECOND LOOK

Think about the adolescents described at the beginning of the chapter. Imagine the frustration of mastering motor skill performance in childhood, only to become clumsy at the point of a growth spurt during puberty. The good news is that this clumsy period will soon pass. It is smart for teachers, coaches, and parents to patiently encourage all children to practice their skills and enjoy activities. It is very difficult to predict who might later pursue participation at an elite level or what activities individuals will later find fun and rewarding, especially based on size or maturity at a young age.

TEST YOUR KNOWLEDGE

1. Discuss the differences between measurements of growth and direct measurements of maturation. What does each measure? What are some examples of each?
2. What is the difference between a distance curve and a velocity curve? What does each type of curve tell you about growth? Why are peaks in velocity curves of interest?
3. What areas of a fetus' body advance first? In what directions does growth proceed?
4. Describe how teratogens reach a fetus. What are some factors that determine how a teratogen affects a fetus?
5. Describe sex differences in the course of overall growth from infancy to adulthood. Include the average ages for entering the adolescent growth spurt, peak height velocity, puberty, and the tapering off of growth in height.
6. What body measurements can change in older adulthood? How do they change?
7. What are some environmental factors that could affect middle-aged and older adults and reduce their health or wellness? How? Is it possible to alter these factors? Which ones?

LEARNING EXERCISE 8.1

Secular Trends

A secular trend is a change in a landmark of development over successive generations, usually due to the influence of extrinsic factors. Some researchers have hypothesized current secular trends toward earlier maturity, taller standing height, and greater body weight. Conduct an Internet search to locate information on these possible secular trends. Classify your information as (a) objective research conducted on a large number of participants, (b) anecdotal information about a single case, (c) an author's hypothesis, or (d) opinion. Considering the information altogether, do you find credible evidence that a secular trend exists for any of these three landmarks of development? Support your conclusion with examples.

9

Development and Aging of Body Systems

The Systems as Individual Constraints

CHAPTER OBJECTIVES

This chapter

- identifies developmental changes in the skeletal, muscular, adipose, endocrine, and nervous systems over the life span;
- notes the interaction of the systems during development and aging;
- discusses the periods when rapid change in the systems makes them particularly sensitive to external influences; and
- identifies a trend of increasing influence of external factors and decreasing influence of genetic factors as individuals proceed through the life span.

Motor Development in the Real World

Early Attention to Development of the Body's Systems

Nerlens Noel, born in 1994 in Malden, Massachusetts, was a successful high school basketball player with aspirations to play in the National Basketball Association (NBA). Despite having to sit out his sophomore year in high school with a fractured growth plate in his left knee, Noel excelled as a player throughout high school. By 2012, he ranked as the number one or two high school player in a variety of national polls. Recruited by many top-ranked programs, Noel ultimately decided to become a Wildcat and play for the University of Kentucky, a school that leads all others in NCAA tournament appearances and has eight national championships. During the first part of his freshman year, he wowed Kentucky fans with his blocking abilities, setting several school records for blocked shots in one game. That season came to a fast end when Noel tore his anterior cruciate ligament in mid-February while blocking a shot in a game against the University of Florida.

A torn ACL is not uncommon in basketball. However, after Noel's ACL tear, different medical professionals suggested this was not a random injury. Rather, they suggested that Noel's earlier fracture of his growth plate and rapid return to play in high school might have led to his later ACL tear in college due to a misalignment of his knee joint. Dr. Robin West, an orthopedic surgeon for the Pittsburgh Steelers, commented: "If the leg healed awkwardly and [Noel] had a malalignment in that knee, that could predispose him to future injuries in that leg" (Coleman, 2013). As many young players do, Noel was considering the NBA draft, and despite his injury, he declared his eligibility in 2013. But speculation about predisposition to knee injuries because of his fractured growth plate appears to have affected his place in the draft. Although he was projected to be one of the top overall picks, he ended up being selected sixth overall and then traded later in the evening to the Philadelphia 76ers. He has played professional basketball on several teams since that time.

Our discussion in chapter 8 of the physical growth, maturation, and aging of the body demonstrates that body size and maturity can be a structural constraint. Thinking about the model of constraints and height, for example, we can see that the movement of dunking a basketball is indeed the interaction of the task (dunking), the environment (the basket height as well as the size and weight of the ball), and the individual structural constraint of height. For individuals of differing heights, dunking success can vary. Yet as we think about this task, it quickly becomes clear that we must think beyond the body as a whole. We must also consider some of the body's specific systems. In considering how high one might jump, body height is a factor and a product of the body's skeletal system. We should also consider the muscular system, because someone with stronger muscles likely can jump higher than an individual with weaker muscles. The amount of adipose tissue influences body weight and thus how easily one can jump up. Finally, of course, the nervous system must coordinate the muscles to produce the jumping movement. So we often need to consider one or more body systems, or their interactions, as individual structural constraints to movement.

To understand the role of body systems as structural constraints to movement, we must know how the body systems normally develop, what can influence this development and when, and what effect all of this has on movement. Our discussion of these systems' effects on movement continues throughout this text as we consider how they act as constraints to various aspects of movement. We will discuss the development of the following systems that are related to movement, chronologically, starting with prenatal development and following through to old age:

- **The skeletal system.** The skeletal system defines an individual's structure. It is not, however, a hard and static structure; it is living tissue. It undergoes considerable change over the life span and reflects the influence of both genetic and external factors.
- **The muscular system.** Whereas the skeletal system provides the body's structure, the muscular system allows its movement. More than 200 muscles permit a vast number of movements and positions for the human body. Like the skeletal system, the muscular system changes over the life span under the influence of genetic and external factors.
- **The adipose system.** A common misconception about adipose (fat) tissue is that its presence in any amount is undesirable. In reality, adipose tissue plays a vital role in energy storage, insulation, and protection.
- **The endocrine system.** The endocrine system exerts its control over specific cellular functions through chemical substances called **hormones**. Those secreted by the hypothalamus in the brain regulate the pituitary gland, which, in turn, regulates the adrenal gland, the thyroid gland, and the release of sex hormones.
- **The nervous system.** No single system is as much the essence of an individual as the nervous system. We need only observe an individual with severe brain injury to know this. The nervous system controls movement and speech. It is the site of thinking, analysis, and memory, and its development is important for social, cognitive, and motor development.

Hormones are chemical substances secreted into body fluids by a gland. These substances have specific effects on the activities of target cells, tissues, or organs.

Systems Development During the Prenatal Period

In human development, the prenatal period exists from fertilization (when the ovum and spermatozoon fuse) through birth, which is approximately 40 weeks. In chapter 8, we described overall changes during the prenatal period. Now we will go through the changes within each system in greater detail.

The Skeletal System

Early in embryonic life, the skeletal system exists as a cartilage model of the bones. Sites gradually appear in the cartilage model where bone is deposited; these are called ossification centers. About 400 appear by birth and another 400 appear after birth. There are two types of ossification centers. **Primary ossification centers** appear in the midportions of the long bones, such as the humerus (upper arm) and femur (thigh), and begin to form bone cells starting at the fetal age of 2 months (figure 9.1). The bone shafts ossify outward in both directions from these primary centers until, by birth, the entire shafts are ossified.

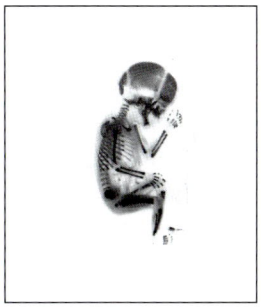

FIGURE 9.1 A human fetal skeleton at about 18 weeks. Dark areas indicate the ossified portions of the developing skeleton. Spaces between dark areas are occupied by cartilage models.

© Carolina Biological Supply Company

The **primary ossification centers** are areas in the midportion of the shafts of long bones where bone cells are formed so that the cartilage-model bones of the fetal skeleton begin ossifying, from the center outward, to form bone shafts.

The Muscular System

Muscle fibers (cells) grow during prenatal life by hyperplasia (an increase in the number of muscle cells) and hypertrophy (an increase in muscle cell size). At birth, muscle mass accounts for 23% to 25% of body weight. Hyperplasia continues for a short time after birth, but thereafter muscle growth occurs predominantly by hypertrophy (Malina, Bouchard, & Bar-Or, 2004). The sigmoid pattern of growth in weight reflects the growth of muscle tissue. (See chapter 8 for an explanation of the sigmoid pattern.)

Muscle cells grow in both diameter and length. The amount of increase in muscle fiber diameter is related to the intensity of muscle activity during growth. Naturally, muscles must also increase in length as the skeleton grows, and this increase is accomplished through the addition of sarcomeres (the contractile units of muscle cells; figure 9.2) at the muscle–tendon junction as well as through the lengthening of the sarcomeres (Malina et al., 2004).

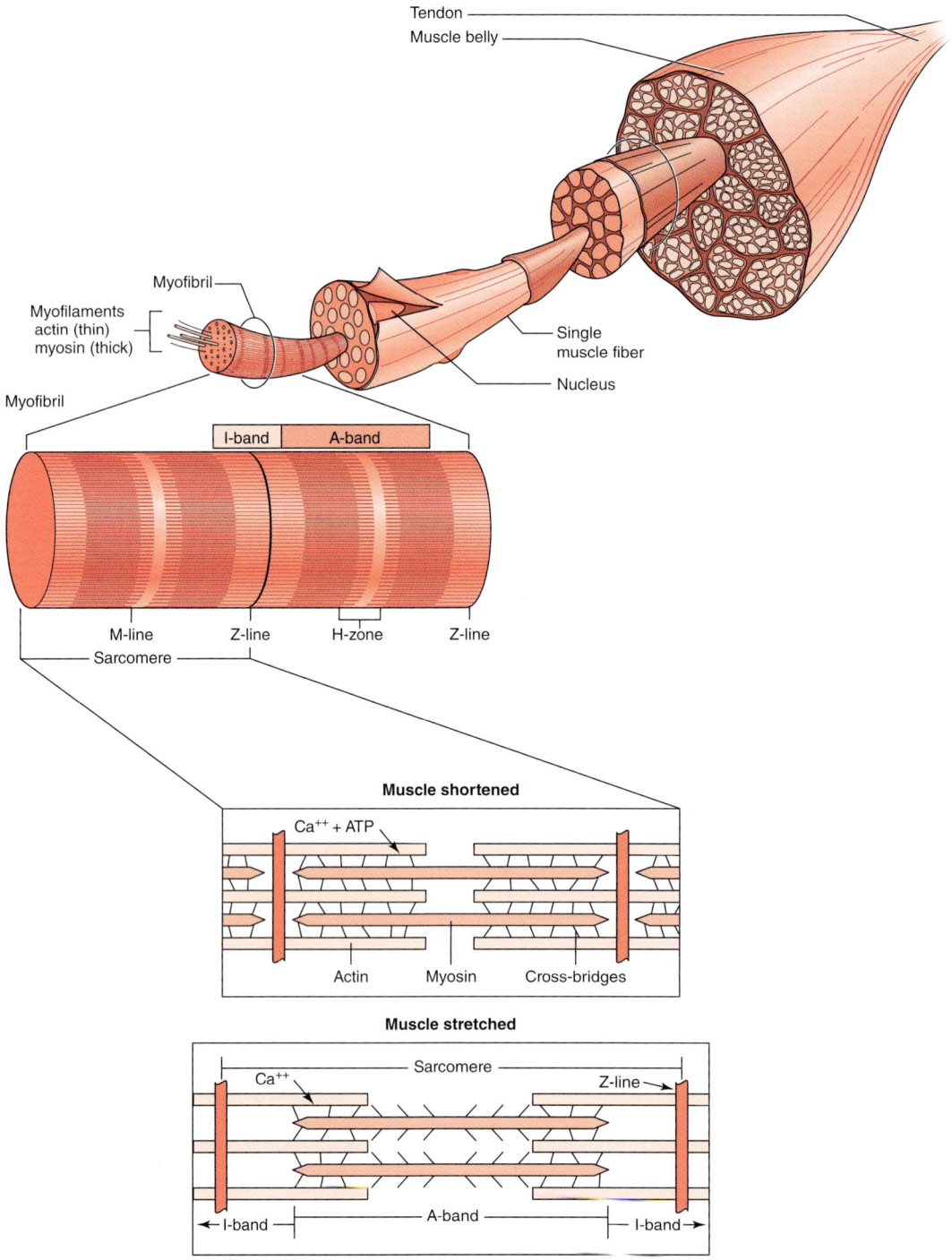

FIGURE 9.2 Muscle structure. The sarcomeres, or contractile units, compose muscle cells (myofibrils), which in turn make up a muscle fiber. Bundles of fibers compose the muscle.

Human muscle consists of two main types of fibers: **slow-twitch** (type I) fibers, which are suited to endurance activities, and **fast-twitch** (types IIa, IIx, and IIb) fibers, which are suited to intense short-duration activities (figure 9.3). At birth, approximately 15% of muscle fibers have yet to differentiate into slow- or fast-twitch fibers (Baldwin, 1984; Colling-Saltin, 1980), and 15% of type II fibers cannot be clearly categorized. These observations have led to speculation that an infant's early activities might influence the ultimate proportion of the different types of fibers, but the issue remains unresolved.

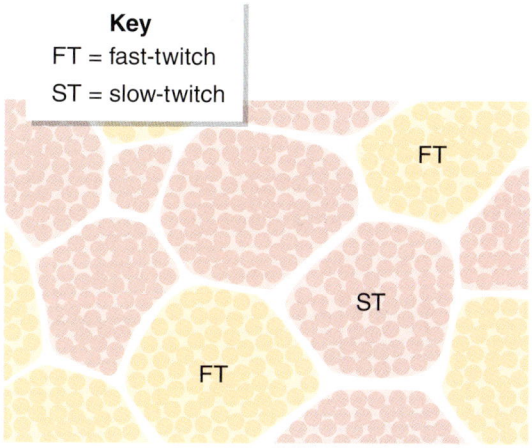

FIGURE 9.3 A cross section of muscle showing that fast-twitch (FT) and slow-twitch (ST) fibers are intermingled.

A **twitch** is a brief period of contraction of a muscle fiber (cell) followed by relaxation.

Muscles can be classified as **slow twitch** or **fast twitch**. Slow-twitch muscles have a slower contraction–relaxation cycle and greater endurance than do fast-twitch muscles.

The Adipose System

The amount of adipose tissue increases in early life. It first appears in the fetus at 3.5 months and increases rapidly during the last 2 prenatal months. Despite this late prenatal increase, adipose tissue accounts for only 0.5 kg (1.1 lb) of body weight at birth.

The Endocrine System

The endocrine system's regulation of growth is a complex and delicate interaction of hormones, genes, nutrients, and environmental factors that begin in utero. A large number of different hormones influence optimal prenatal development; a full discussion is beyond the scope of this textbook. The regulation of these hormones occurs through a convoluted collaboration among maternal, fetal, and placental endocrine systems. As surprising as it may seem, the placenta produces its own hormones and provides a barrier so that the mother's hormones do not flood the fetus' system.

The Nervous System

Much of neurological development occurs very early in the life span. The course of neurological development is a prime example of the interplay of genetic and extrinsic factors. Genes direct the development of the nervous system's structures and its main circuits. The trillions of finer connections between nervous system cells, however, are fine-tuned by extrinsic factors. Let's consider neurological development in more detail, including the role of extrinsic factors.

In general, the formation of immature **neurons**, their differentiation into a general type, and their migration to a final position in the nervous system occur prenatally. Neurons proliferate in the early prenatal period at an astonishing rate of 250,000 per minute. As many as 200 billion are formed. During the third and fourth prenatal months, almost all the neurons that the individual human brain will ever have are formed, although it seems that genes direct an overproduction of cells so that the system can later be pruned (Ratey, 2001). Neurons contain a cell body, which carries out functions to keep the cell alive; up to 100,000 dendrites, which receive impulses from other neurons; and an axon, which transmits impulses to another neuron, gland, organ, or muscle (figure 9.4).

Neurons are the cells of the nervous system that receive and transmit information.

The new neurons also travel to a final destination during the prenatal period. Some form the brain stem, which controls the heartbeat and breathing; some the cerebellum, which controls posture; and some the cerebral cortex, where perception and thought take place. Generally, neurons are in their final location by the sixth prenatal month. Neurons specialize. For example, visual neurons are specialized as a function of both their genes and the location to which they migrate, in this case a part of the brain where visual information arrives. The migration process is vital to normal brain development (Ratey, 2001).

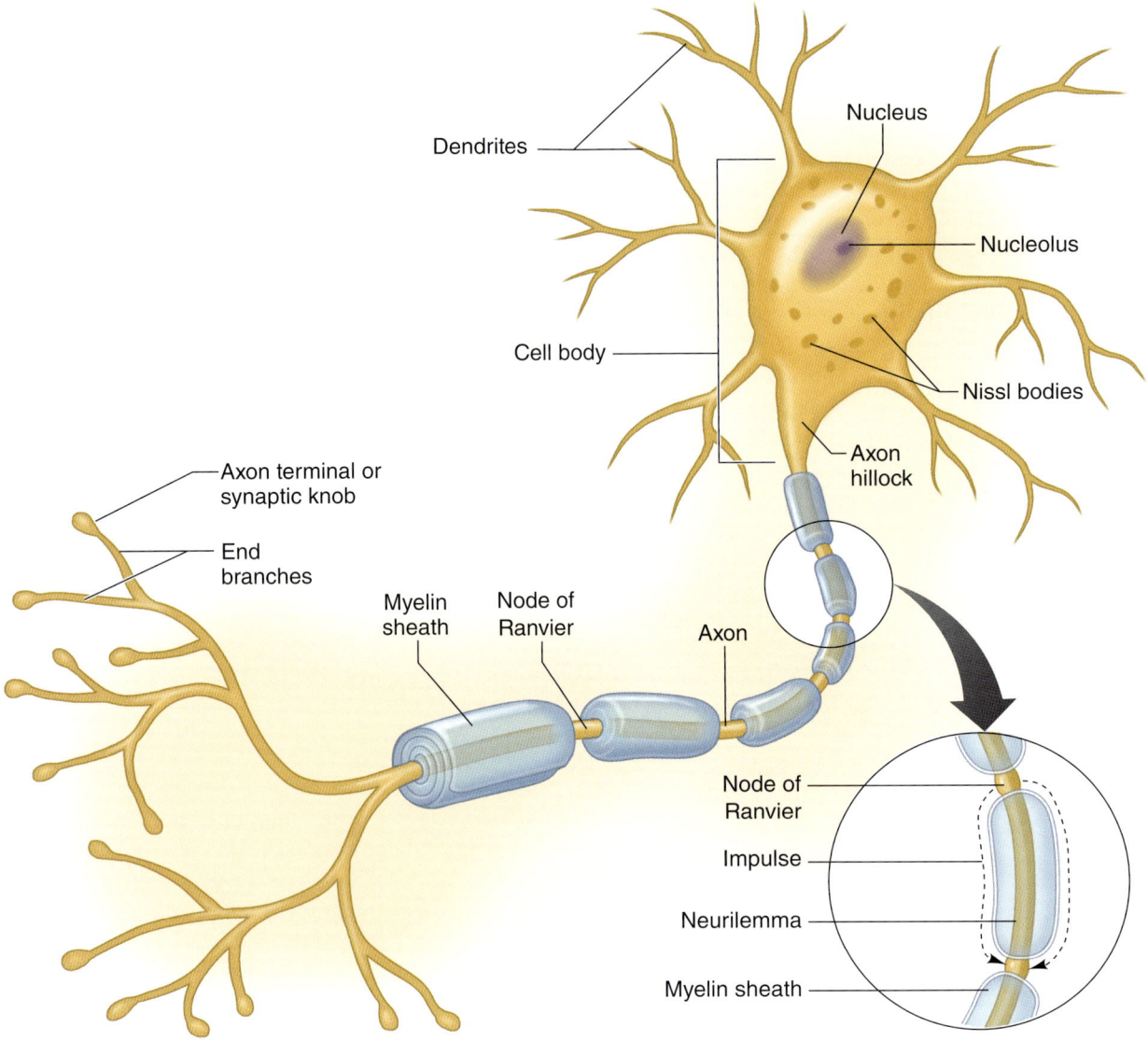

FIGURE 9.4 The structure of a nerve cell, or neuron. Note that there can be multiple dendrites to carry nerve impulses to the cell body, but only one axon emerges to carry an impulse to other neurons, glands, or muscles. The axon can, however, branch extensively.

A **synapse** is a connection between two neurons; it is made by the release of chemicals called neurotransmitters from an axon. These neurotransmitters cross a small gap between neurons, then permeate the cell wall at the dendrite, or cell body, of a receiving neuron to trigger an electrical impulse.

Once the neurons are in place, they grow an axon along a chemical trail to a general destination in order to connect to other neurons, forming the brain's circuitry of about 100 trillion connections, or **synapses**. Because of the overproduction of neurons, axons compete for the chemical trails. Some axons and their neurons die off. The neurons fire electrical impulses that strengthen some of the connections between neurons. The firing is somewhat random prenatally but more organized as the fetus, and later the infant, receives input from the environment (Ratey, 2001). Thus, a natural pruning occurs of both neurons (reducing the number to approximately 100 billion at birth) and their branches and connections. Weak or incorrect connections are sacrificed to make the neural network more efficient.

Assume you have just found out you will be a new mother. What substances would you avoid consuming until your baby is born? Why?

The migration of neurons and the branching of their processes are susceptible to the effects of environmental factors delivered via the fetal nourishment system described in chapter 8. Growing evidence shows that some disorders, such as epilepsy, autism, and dyslexia, are caused at least in part by faulty migration of neurons (Ratey, 2001). Nicotine that is introduced to a fetus by a mother's smoking might affect migration, branching, and pruning of the neurons, and we know that children of mothers who smoked while pregnant are at increased risk of mental retardation. Alcohol introduced by a mother's alcohol consumption can cause improper neuron migration, and babies with fetal alcohol syndrome are known to later exhibit lower IQs and more prevalent reading and mathematics disabilities than other children. There are many examples of fetal exposure to illicit drugs and toxins and of malnutrition influencing development of the nervous system. It is clear that the nervous system is one of the systems most susceptible to teratogenic exposure during the prenatal period.

Systems Development During Childhood and Adolescence

After birth, infants begin postnatal development. We divide this postnatal period, which lasts until approximately 20 years of life, into childhood and adolescence. The factors that drive system change during childhood change dramatically as individuals approach adolescence because of puberty and sexual maturity.

The Skeletal System

Postnatal bone growth in length occurs at **secondary ossification centers** at the end of the bone shaft. A secondary center can also be called the **epiphyseal plate**, growth plate, or **pressure epiphysis** (figure 9.5). The epiphyseal plate has many cellular layers (figure 9.6) where cartilage cells form, grow, align, and finally erode to leave new bone in place. Bone is thus laid down at the epiphyseal plates to increase the length of the bone. The process of laying down new bone depends on an adequate blood supply. Any injury that disturbs this blood supply threatens the bone's normal growth in length. In contrast to the long bones, small round bones such as those in the wrist and ankle simply ossify from the center outward.

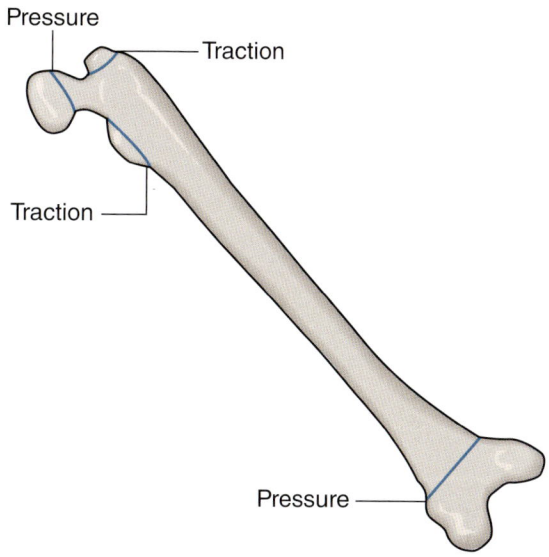

FIGURE 9.5 Pressure epiphyses are located at the ends of long bones, such as the femur (thigh bone) pictured here. Epiphyses also occur at muscle tendon attachment sites, called traction epiphyses.

The **secondary ossification centers**, or **epiphyseal plates**, are the areas near the ends of long bones where new bone cells are formed and deposited so that the bones grow in length. Active secondary ossification centers are indicated on X rays by a line (an area not opaque) that is a layer of cartilage cells. Such an area is also called a **pressure epiphysis**, especially if it is at the end of a weight-bearing bone.

Growth at the ossification centers ceases at different times in different bones. At the epiphyseal plates, the cartilage zone eventually disappears and the shaft, or diaphysis, of the bone fuses with the epiphysis. Once the epiphyseal plates of a long bone fuse, the length of the bone is fixed. Almost all epiphyseal plates are closed by age 18 or 19.

Recall that girls as a group mature faster than boys. It is no surprise, then, that the various ossification centers appear at younger chronological ages in girls than in boys. Likewise, the epiphyseal plates close at younger chronological ages in girls than in boys. For example, on average, the epiphysis at the head of the humerus closes in girls between 12 and 16 years but in boys between 14 and 19 years (Crowder & Austin, 2005; Hansman, 1962). Individuals, of course, have their own unique timing, and a group of children at the same chronological age could easily vary in skeletal age by 3 years or more, demonstrating how variable maturity is in comparison with chronological age during the growth period.

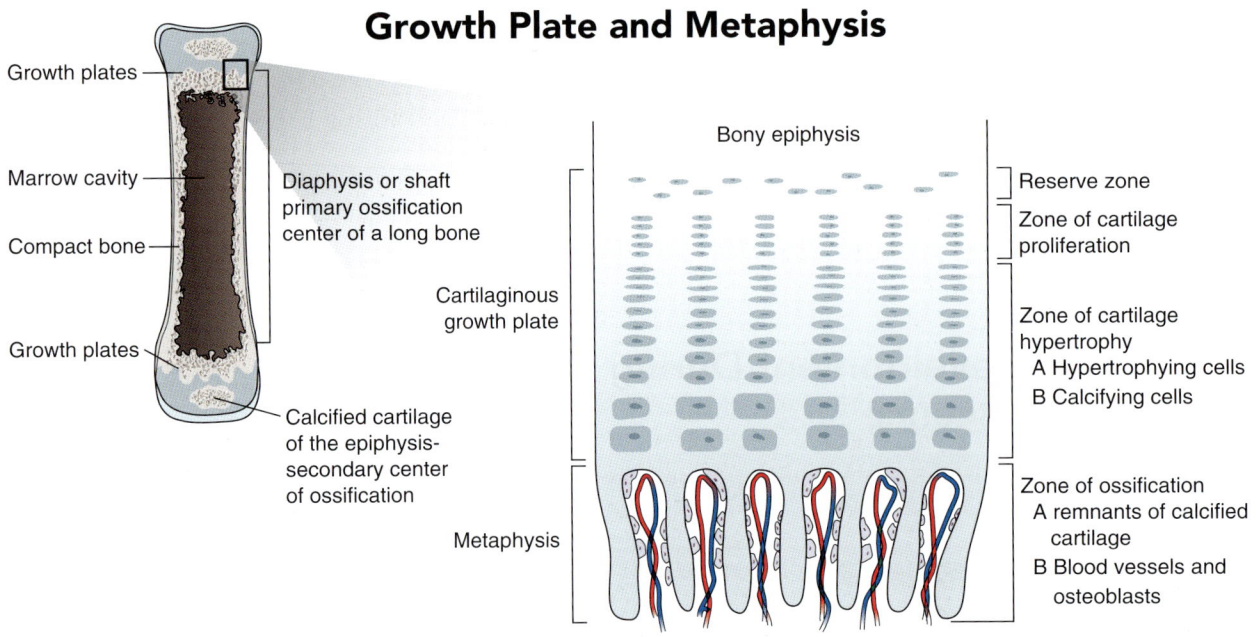

FIGURE 9.6 Development of a long bone in childhood. The epiphyseal growth plate, between the epiphysis and shaft, is enlarged on the right to show the zones in which new cells ossify.

Appositional bone growth involves the addition of new layers on previously formed layers so that a bone grows in girth.

While the long bones are growing in length they also increase in girth, a process called **appositional bone growth**. Girth is increased by the addition of new tissue layers under the periosteum, a very thin outer covering of the bone, much like a tree adds to its girth under its bark.

There are also epiphyses at the sites where the muscles' tendons attach to bones. They are called traction epiphyses. You might have heard of a familiar condition that occurs during the growth period in some youths—Osgood-Schlatter disease. This is an irritation of the traction epiphysis where the patellar tendon attaches to the shin bone below the knee. Pediatricians usually have youths with this condition refrain for a time from vigorous (in particular, weight-bearing and jumping) activities to prevent further irritation of the site. Overuse injuries to traction epiphyses during the growth period can threaten the pain-free movement at a joint in later life. For example, a traction epiphysis near the elbow can be injured by repeatedly and forcefully pronating the forearm, as in throwing.

Ay et al. (2011) found that infants in the Generation R Study with low birth weight as well as those in the lowest weight groups at age 6 months tended to have a low bone mineral density measure at age 6 months. A positive relationship existed between postnatal growth in weight and bone mineral density as well as bone mineral content. Even infants showing catch-up growth in weight during the first 6 weeks after birth were less likely to have low bone mineral density. As the Generation R Study continues, it will be interesting to observe the relationship between early levels of bone mineral density and content and later levels so that we might learn whether adults are at risk of bone fractures based on their early growth patterns.

Web Study Guide **Identify differences in skeletal development in Lab Activity 9.1, Estimating Skeletal Age, and learn about different types of children's skeletal injuries in Lab Activity 9.2, Exploring Skeletal Injuries in Youth Sports, in the web study guide.**

► **KEY POINT** Because linear growth of the body is almost completely the result of skeletal growth, measures of height reflect the increase of bone length.

Assessment of Skeletal Age

The growth status of the bones can be used to assess maturation by comparing an individual's state of development with those depicted in an atlas or standard—that is, a publication picturing skeletal development at many levels, each of which is assigned a skeletal age. The most common bones used for this purpose are the hand and wrist bones (figure 9.7). Thus, from an X ray of a person's hand and wrist, we could determine a skeletal age by finding the picture in the atlas closest to the individual's X ray. For example, a boy might have a skeletal age of 8.5 years because the extent of ossification in his hand and wrist X ray is most similar to that in the standard for 8.5 years. If his chronological age is under 8.5, we would know he is an early maturer; if it is over 8.5, we would know he is a late maturer. Skeletal age can easily be a year ahead of or behind chronological age, emphasizing how much variation is possible in maturation status even among those born on the same day.

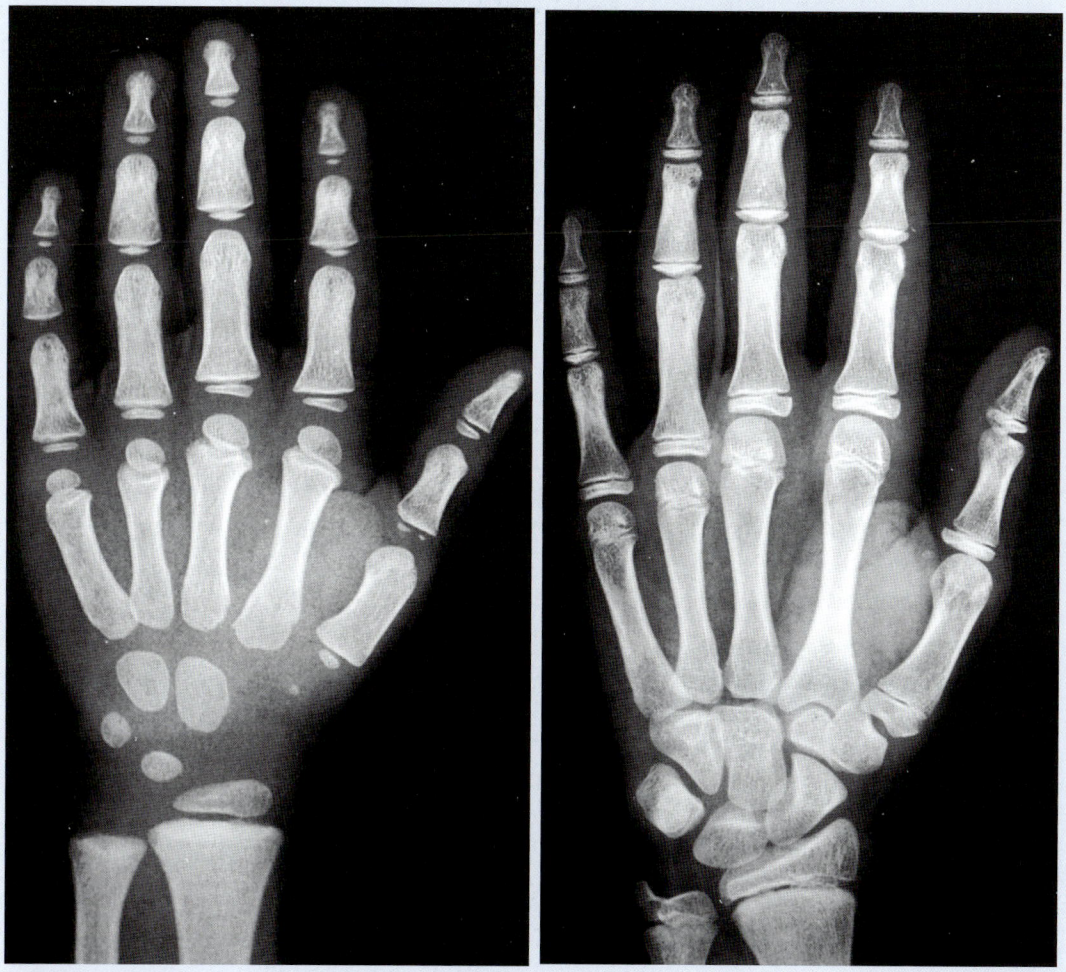

FIGURE 9.7 Hand and wrist X rays are often used to assess skeletal age. The numerous hand and wrist bones provide multiple sites for comparison of a child's X ray with the numerous standard X rays found in an assessment atlas. Here are two X rays from an atlas: *(a)* the standard for boys 48 months old and girls 37 months old, and *(b)* the standard for boys 156 months old and girls 128 months old. Note in the latter image how much more ossification (hardening) has occurred in the small wrist bones and the larger ossified area at the epiphyseal plates of the hand bones and the forearm bones.

Copyright Bolton-Brush Growth Study—B.H. Broadbent D.D.S.

Imagine you are the parent of a young boy who is the pitcher on his youth baseball team. He already practices once a week and plays a weekly game. The coach wants him to join a second baseball team so that he can get more pitching experience. Would you consent to this? Why or why not?

The Muscular System

During the first postnatal year the number of undifferentiated fibers decreases, and by 1 year of age the distribution of muscle fiber types is similar to that in adults (Malina et al., 2004). The exact proportions of fiber types for any given muscle vary among individuals (Simoneau & Bouchard, 1989).

Sex differences in muscle mass are minimal during childhood; muscle mass constitutes a slightly greater proportion of body weight in boys. During and after adolescence, however, sex differences become marked. Muscle mass increases rapidly in boys up to about age 17 and ultimately accounts for 54% of men's body weight. In sharp contrast, girls add muscle mass only until age 13, on average, and muscle mass makes up 45% of women's body weight (Malina, 1978). The large sex differences in muscle mass involve upper body musculature more than leg musculature. For example, the rate of growth in arm musculature is nearly twice as high for males as for females, but the difference in calf muscle growth is relatively small. These sex differences in the addition of muscle mass are related to hormonal influences.

The heart is muscle tissue too. Like skeletal muscle, it grows by hyperplasia and hypertrophy. The right ventricle (lower chamber) is larger than the left ventricle at birth, but the left ventricle catches up after birth by growing more rapidly than the right, and the heart soon reaches adult proportions (figure 9.8). The heart generally follows the sigmoid pattern of whole-body growth, including a growth spurt in adolescence, such that the ratio of heart volume to body weight remains approximately the same throughout growth. One of the Generation R studies (de Jonge et al., 2011) noted that left ventricular mass was already greater in overweight and obese children than in normal-weight children at 2 years. Future research will focus on whether this greater mass is related to a greater risk of cardiovascular disease in later life.

Early in the 20th century, some researchers thought that the large blood vessels around the heart developed more slowly than the heart itself, which implied that children who engaged in vigorous activity might be at risk. Later, it was shown that this myth had resulted from a misinterpretation of measurements taken in the late 1800s. In fact, blood vessel growth is proportional to the growth of the heart (Karpovich, 1937).

The Adipose System

A rapid increase of fat occurs in the first 6 months after birth, and the highest peak weight velocity occurs in the first month. Greater-than-average peak weight velocities were associated with increased risk of overweight and obesity at age 4 years in the Generation R Study (Mook-Kanamori et al., 2011). After this rapid increase in the first 6 months, fat mass increases gradually until age 8 in both boys and girls. Girls tend to have slightly more fat mass than boys at age 2 (Ay et al., 2008). In the Generation R Study, individual children tended to maintain their relative position in the group for the amount of subcutaneous fat mass, especially in the trunk, throughout the first 2 years of life. In boys, adipose tissue continues to increase gradually throughout adolescence, but girls experience a more dramatic increase. As a result, adult women have more fat weight than adult men, with averages of 14 kg (30.9 lb) and 10 kg (22 lb), respectively. Fat weight during growth increases by both hyperplasia and hypertrophy, but cell size does not increase significantly until puberty.

Individual fatness varies widely during infancy and early childhood. A fat baby will not necessarily become a fat child. After 7 to 8 years of age, though, it is more likely that individuals maintain their relative fatness. An overweight 8-year-old has a high risk of becoming an overweight adult.

The distribution of fat in the body changes during growth. During childhood, internal fat (fat around the viscera) increases faster than subcutaneous fat (fat under the skin), which actually

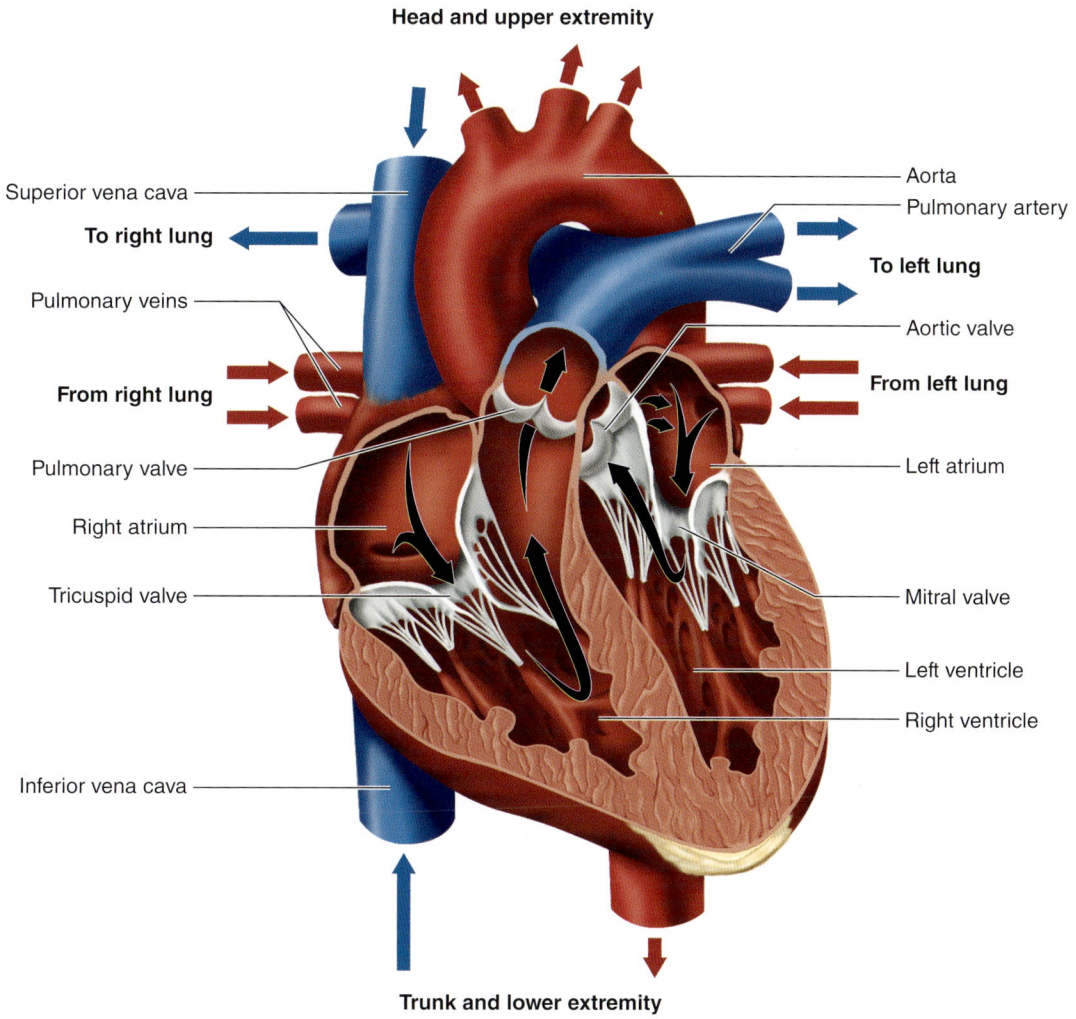

FIGURE 9.8 The human heart. The left ventricle is relatively smaller at birth and must catch up in growth in the early postnatal weeks.

decreases until age 6 or 7. Boys and girls then show an increase in subcutaneous fat until they are 12 or 13. This increase in subcutaneous fat continues in girls, but boys typically lose subcutaneous fat in midadolescence. Adolescent boys also tend to add more subcutaneous fat to their trunks than to their limbs, whereas girls have increased subcutaneous fat at both sites. Note that in figure 9.9, skinfold measurements for boys' extremities (top blue line) actually decrease, except during the growth spurt. Trunk skinfolds tend to hold steady but also increase during the growth spurt. Girls' skinfold measurements (purple lines) increase steadily for both trunk and limbs, especially after age 7. Girls usually add more subcutaneous fat to their legs than to their arms.

What are the life span implications of individuals adding too much fat during the periods of increase in fat tissue?

There is much we don't know about adipose tissue development and obesity. Researchers are currently examining many topics, including maternal weight gain during pregnancy, early infant feeding, and genetic factors. Of particular interest are the two periods when the number of adipose cells increases—during the first 6 postnatal months and around puberty. Increases in cell number are significant because adipose cells persist once they are formed, even with malnutrition; that is, the cells may be empty of fat, but they still exist. Therefore, these two periods may be critical in the control of obesity.

The Endocrine System

The endocrine system's regulation of growth is a complex and delicate interaction of hormones, genes, nutrients, and environmental factors. In fact, hormone levels must be delicately balanced. Either an excess or a deficiency of hormones may disturb the normal process of growth and development. A detailed discussion of how the hormones influence growth and maturation is beyond the scope of this text, so we will just mention three types of hormones here. All three promote growth in the same way: They stimulate protein anabolism (constructive metabolism), resulting in the retention of substances needed to build tissues. There are specific times in the growth period when one of these hormones may play a critical role in growth.

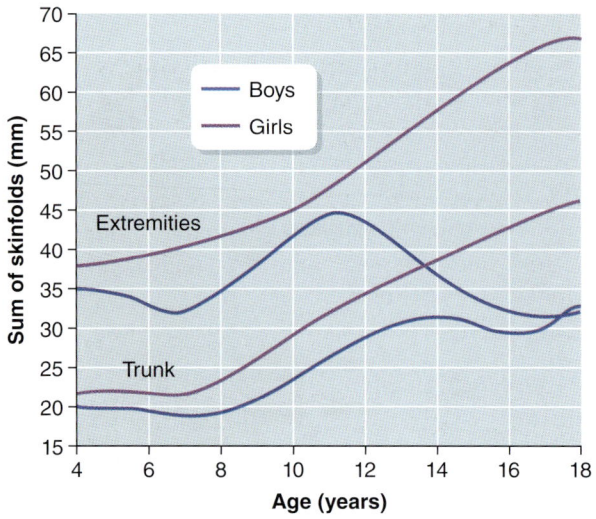

FIGURE 9.9 Changes in fat distribution during growth are illustrated by plotting the sum of five trunk skinfold measurements and five extremity skinfold measurements. Note the increase in both types of measurement in girls, contrasting with a decrease in extremity subcutaneous fat in boys during adolescence.

Reprinted by permission from Malina and Bouchard (1988).

Growth Hormone

Growth hormone (GH) influences growth during childhood and adolescence by stimulating protein anabolism so that new tissue can be built. Under the control of the central nervous system, GH is secreted by the anterior pituitary gland (figure 9.10). The body needs this hormone for normal growth after birth. A deficiency or absence of GH results in growth abnormalities and in some cases the cessation of linear growth.

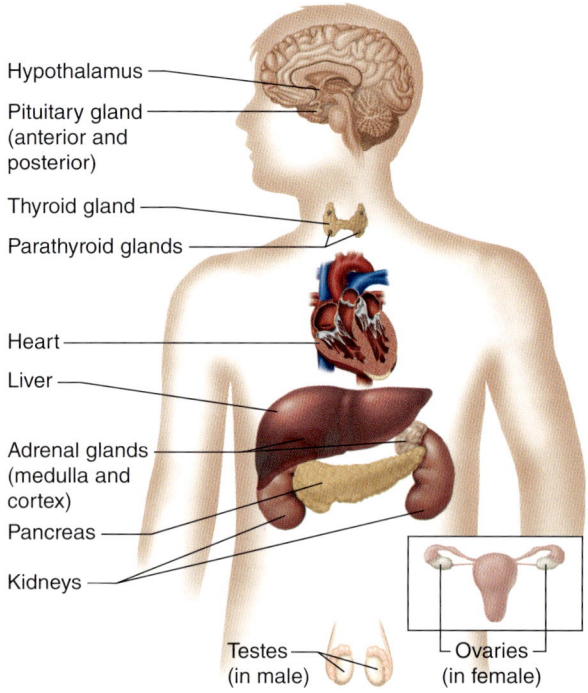

FIGURE 9.10 Location of the various endocrine glands.

Thyroid Hormones

The thyroid hormones are secreted by the thyroid gland, located in the anterior neck region. Two types of thyroid hormones influence whole-body growth after birth, and a third plays a role in skeletal growth.

The pituitary gland secretes a thyroid-stimulating hormone that regulates the hormones secreted by the thyroid gland. Thyroid-stimulating hormone excretion is, in turn, increased by a releasing factor found in the brain's hypothalamus. Thus, two systems act in concert: a pituitary–thyroid system and a nervous system–thyroid system. This is one example of how the nervous system and endocrine system work together.

Gonadal Hormones

The gonadal hormones affect growth and sexual maturation, particularly during adolescence, by stimulating development of the secondary sex characteristics and the sex organs. The androgens, specifically testosterone from the testes and androgens from the cortex of the adrenal glands, hasten fusion of the epiphyseal growth plates in the bones. Thus, these hormones promote skeletal maturation (fusion) at the expense of linear growth; this explains why early maturers tend to be shorter in stature than later maturers.

Androgens also play a role in the adolescent growth spurt of muscle mass by increasing nitrogen retention and protein synthesis. This spurt is more pronounced in young men than in young women because men secrete both testosterone and adrenal androgens whereas women produce only the adrenal androgens. In women, the ovaries and the adrenal cortex secrete estrogens. Increased estrogen secretion during adolescence, as with androgens, speeds epiphyseal closure, but estrogen also promotes fat accumulation, primarily in the breasts and hips. Men and women both have estrogen and testosterone but in very different proportions.

Teenage boys sometimes take steroid supplements in order to add muscle mass and look older. Increased secretion of androgen (a steroid) at puberty, though, hastens fusion at the epiphyseal plates. What unintended effect might these supplements have on growing boys?

Insulin

The hormones we have discussed up to this point all play a major and direct role in growth and development. Another familiar hormone, insulin, has an indirect role in growth. Produced in the pancreas, insulin is vital to carbohydrate metabolism, stimulating the transportation of glucose and amino acids through membranes. Its presence is also necessary for the full functioning of GH. A deficiency of insulin can decrease protein synthesis, which is detrimental at any time in life but especially during growth.

The Nervous System

At birth the brain is about 25% of its adult weight. Brain growth increases rapidly after birth and reaches 80% of adult weight by age 4. Then it enters a period of steady growth through adolescence, reaching an adult weight of approximately 3 pounds by adulthood. The rapid early growth reflects an increase in the size of the neurons, further branching to form synapses, and an increase in **glia** and **myelin**. The first postnatal year is one of prolific synaptic formation, and each neuron can establish 1,000 to 100,000 connections. Although axons are generally developed early in postnatal development, the process of brain development continues throughout childhood and adolescence, and potentially beyond that into adulthood (Arain et al., 2013; Stiles & Jernigan, 2010).

Glia are the cells of the nervous system that support and nourish the neurons.

Myelin is an insulating sheath around the axons.

At the same time, major changes in both structure and function occur within childhood and adolescence (Arain et al., 2013; Giedd et al., 1999). During that time, changes occur not only from maturation but also from neural pruning.

▶ **KEY POINT** The brain demonstrates enormous plasticity during all phases of the life span, and its 100 trillion connections change constantly.

This rapid growth of the early postnatal period continues to make neurological development very susceptible to extrinsic factors. Poor nutrition, for example, could stunt the growth of the brain, a deficit from which the individual might never recover. Injury to the left side of the **cerebral cortex** (figure 9.11) early in life leads to deficits in language ability (Witelson, 1987). Increasing evidence also shows that an infant's early life experiences influence development of the nervous system. Greenough and colleagues (Comery, Shah, & Greenough, 1995; Comery, Stamoudis, Irwin, & Greenough, 1996; Greenough et al., 1993; Wallace, Kilman, Withers,

The **cerebral cortex** is the wrinkled surface of the brain containing millions of neurons and regulating many human functions and behaviors.

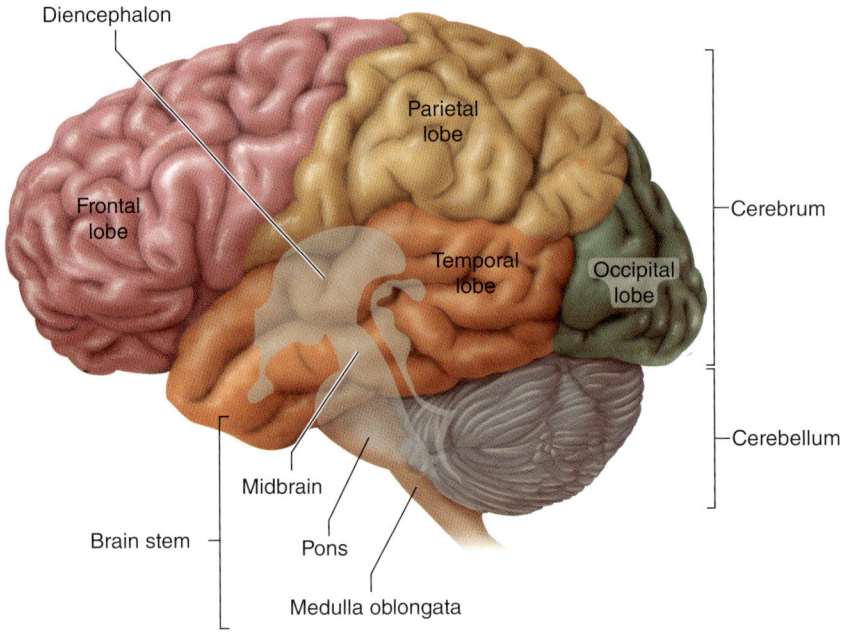

FIGURE 9.11 The human brain. The cerebral cortex consists of the frontal, parietal, temporal, and occipital lobes.

& Greenough, 1992) found that rats raised with much stimulation grew significantly more synapses than those raised without stimuli. The same pattern holds for humans (Tierney & Nelson, 2009). Learning is one of the most significant extrinsic factors influencing postnatal development of the nervous system. We now know that the brain restructures itself with learning. Magnetic resonance imaging (MRI) documents that areas of the brain corresponding to frequently used body parts expand as the synaptic connections in those areas expand. From the early weeks of life and continuing over the life span, neural connections and pathways that are stimulated are strengthened whereas those not used are weakened.

Although a significant portion of neural development occurs early in postnatal life, it continues throughout childhood and adolescence as well (Stiles & Jernigan, 2010). In fact, several longitudinal MRI studies indicate that a second surge of neuronal growth occurs just before puberty (Baird et al., 1999; Giedd et al., 1999). After this production of new neurons, connections within the brain are modified up until about 25 years old, particularly in the prefrontal cortex, through the processes of neural pruning (removal of unused synapses) as well as continued myelination (Arain et al., 2013; Stiles & Jernigan, 2010).

The Genome Project has determined that 30,000 to 50,000 of the 100,000 genes in the human genome are designated for the brain. Even that number probably does not fully control our 100 trillion synapses; there is room for variation resulting from experience, and most of our traits reflect the interaction of genes and our environment.

Brain Structures

The spinal cord and lower brain structures are more advanced at birth than are the higher brain structures. Lower brain centers involved in vital tasks, such as respiration and food intake, are relatively mature. Lower brain centers also mediate many reflexes and reactions. These automatic movement responses dominate the fetus' and newborn's movements, so it makes sense that lower brain centers are relatively more advanced than higher brain centers at this time.

For many years, researchers have interpreted the onset of goal-directed movements in infants as evidence that higher brain centers are maturing. The cortex is involved in purposeful, goal-directed movement. The first clear evidence of successful goal-directed, intentional movement (reaching) occurs at 3 to 5 postnatal months (Bushnell, 1982; Corbetta, Thurman, Wiener, Guan, & Williams, 2014; Williams & Corbetta, 2016). Hence, early researchers assumed this behavior signaled the first functioning of the cortex at about 4 months of age, even though the cerebral hemispheres are formed at birth.

In the 20th century, researchers used positron emission tomography (PET) scans to study the infant brain. The scans show little activity in the frontal cortex at 5 days of age, increased activity at 11 weeks, and adult levels at 7 to 8 months (Chugani & Phelps, 1986). More recently, researchers have used a variety of noninvasive brain imaging techniques to examine prefrontal cortex activity in infancy, such as functional near infrared spectroscopy (fNIRS; Pinti et al., 2018). Because infants can move at the same time they are being scanned with fNIRS, it is a good tool for understanding infant brain development. Recently, researchers at Brown University supported the notion that the prefrontal cortex is active during infancy, showing that infants use this region of the brain to learn hierarchical rules about relationships among faces, voices, toys, and words (Werchan, Collins, Frank, & Amso, 2016). At the same time, the frontal cortex continues to develop throughout childhood and adolescence and will not reach full maturity until approximately 25 years of age (Arain et al., 2013; Sowell et al., 2003).

The development of myelin in the nervous system contributes to speedy conduction of nerve impulses. Myelin cells, comprising mostly fat, wrap themselves around the outgoing neuron cell process, or axon (refer to figure 9.4). Myelinated axons can fire nerve impulses at higher frequencies for longer periods than those not myelinated (Kuffler, Nicholls, & Martin, 1984).

Axons that are as yet unmyelinated in the newborn are probably functional, but **myelination** improves the speed and frequency of firing. The function of the nervous system in movements requiring or benefiting from speedy conduction of nerve impulses, such as a series of rapid movements or postural responses, might be related to the myelination process during development. The importance of myelin is evident in multiple sclerosis, a disease that strikes young adults and breaks down the myelin sheath, resulting in tremor, loss of coordination, and possibly paralysis. Myelination continues through childhood into adolescence.

Myelination is the process whereby the axons of the neural cells are insulated when insulating myelin sheaths formed by Schwann (glial) cells wrap themselves around the axon.

The spinal cord is relatively small and short at birth. A cross-sectional view of the spinal cord (figure 9.12) shows a central horn-shaped area of gray matter and a surrounding area of white matter. The central area contains tightly packed neuron cell bodies. Note the roots that lie just outside the cord; they contain the axons of the cord's neurons and, in the case of the sensory roots, nerve cell bodies. Fibers from the dorsal and ventral roots merge to form the peripheral

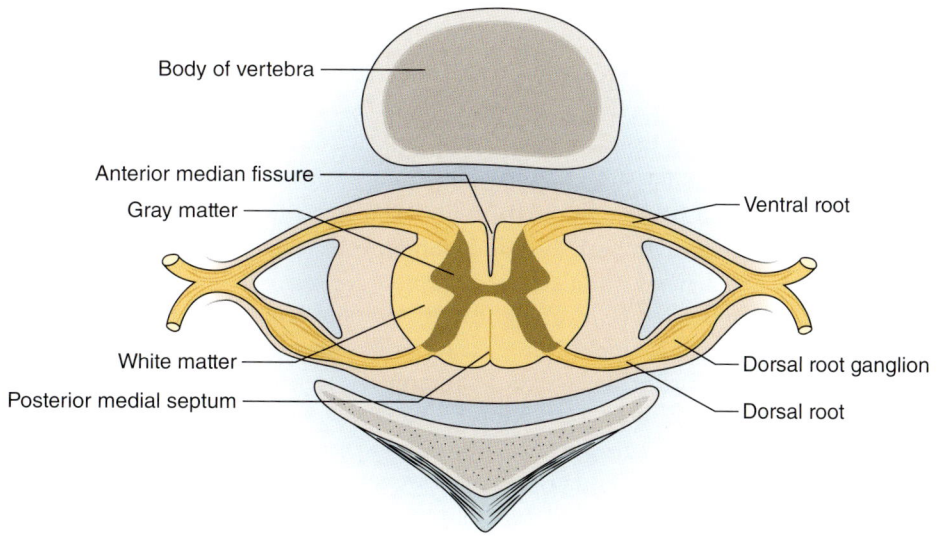

FIGURE 9.12 A cross section of the spinal cord.

Nerve tracts are major neurological pathways. There are two major motor tracts: the **extrapyramidal** and the **pyramidal**.

(spinal) nerves outside the cord. A marked increase in the myelination of these peripheral nerves occurs 2 to 3 weeks after birth, and this process continues through the second or third year of life.

Two major motor nerve pathways, or **nerve tracts**, carry impulses from the brain down the spinal cord to various parts of the body. One pathway, the **extrapyramidal tract**, is probably involved in delivering the commands for both the random and the postural movements made by the infant in the first days after birth. The other, the **pyramidal tract**, myelinates after birth; it is functioning by 4 to 5 months and controls the muscles for finger movements.

The myelination pattern that the spinal cord and nerve pathways undergo might have implications for motor development. Myelination proceeds in two directions in the cord: first in the cervical portion, followed by the progressively lower portions, and then in the motor (ventral) horns, followed by the sensory (dorsal) horns. The direction of myelination tends to be away from the brain in the motor tracts. In contrast, the direction of myelination is toward the brain in sensory tracts, occurring first in the tactile and olfactory pathways, then in the visual pathways, and finally in the auditory pathways. Sensory pathways mature slightly faster than motor pathways, except in the motor roots and cerebral hemispheres. Higher-level functioning might be possible only when the neurons involved in a behavior are myelinated, allowing faster and more frequent conduction of nerve signals.

Systems Development During Adulthood and Older Adulthood

After adolescence, maturational processes are complete and as a result, systems development occurs at a slower rate. In addition, for much of adulthood, changes in systems occur because of environmental factors (e.g., diet, exercise). As individuals reach old age, changes in hormone levels related to the aging process (menopause in women results in decreasing levels of estrogen, for example) are associated with changes in other systems (e.g., thinning of bones).

The Skeletal System

The skeletal structure itself changes little in young adulthood, but bone undergoes remodeling throughout the life span. Old bone is replaced by new bone. In youth, new bone is formed faster than older bone is resorbed, allowing for growth. In adulthood, though, bone formation begins to slow and eventually cannot keep pace with resorption. The result is a loss of bone tissue, starting as early as the mid-20s and averaging about 1% of bone mass per year (Boskey & Coleman, 2010; Smith, Sempos, & Purvis, 1981). These result in changes in bone morphology or shape, increasing the risk of breakage (Tommasini, Nasser, Schaffler, & Jepsen, 2005; Yates, Karasik, Beck, Cupples, & Kiel, 2007).

Bone composition also changes over the life span. Children have essentially equal amounts of inorganic and organic components in their bone tissue, but older adults have seven times more inorganic material, making the bone more brittle and subject to microfracture (Åstrand & Rodahl, 1986; Boskey & Coleman, 2010; Exton-Smith, 1985).

Bone loss with aging occurs in both men and women and is related to changes in certain hormone levels, dietary deficiencies, and decreased exercise. In postmenopausal women, decreased levels of estrogen are implicated in more significant losses of bone mass because estrogen hormones stimulate osteoblastic (bone forming) activity. Prolonged deficiency of calcium in the diet is another major factor in bone loss, as is shortage of vitamins and minerals (Borer, 2005; Boskey & Coleman, 2010; Ritchie, Joshipura, Hung, & Douglass, 2002). Before menopause, calcium supplementation does not appear to modify bone mineral density in women (Uusi-Rasi et al, 1998). During and after menopause, however, adequate calcium intake becomes increasingly important (Borer, 2005). For example, Cumming (1990) demonstrated the importance of dietary calcium by finding that women in early menopause who took a calcium supplement lost less than half the bone mass of women who took no supplement.

Both weight bearing and non-weight-bearing physical activity have an effect on the maintenance of bone by increasing bone formation, whereas calcium and estrogen supplementation lower bone resorption (Borer, 2005). When a person engages in physical activity, the mechanical forces applied to the bones help maintain bone thickness and density (Borer, 2005; Iwamoto, 2017). In fact, significant increases in bone mass are seen when older adults initiate exercise programs. When reviewing a large number of studies, Warburton, Nicol, & Bredin (2006) determined that exercise training programs for women either prevented or reversed the 1% of bone loss per year in key bones in both pre- and postmenopausal women.

Many older adults suffer from a major bone mineral disorder, osteoporosis, which is characterized by a bone mineral density significantly below the average for young adults and, consequently, by a loss of bone strength. The bone becomes abnormally porous through the enlargement of the canals, or the formation of spaces in the bone. This condition greatly increases the risk of fractures, especially at the hip, and adds to the difficulty of fracture repair (Pesce et al, 2009; NIH Osteoporosis and Related Bone Diseases National Resource Center, 2017). Osteoporosis can also lead to microfractures of the vertebrae in the spine. Vertebrae eventually may even collapse, resulting in a dramatic change of skeletal structure (refer to figure 8.11) in which the rib cage collapses forward, with the lower edge resting on the pelvis, so that the posture becomes stooped and standing height is notably reduced. The incidence of osteoporosis is higher in older adult women than in men.

It is likely that extrinsic factors, including hormone level, diet, and exercise, work in combination to influence the extent of bone loss and that we do not fully understand how these factors interact. However, it is clear that we can implement certain strategies to minimize the loss of bone tissue in adulthood. Women, for example, can maintain adequate calcium intake during adulthood so that they enter menopause with the highest bone mineral density possible. Widespread attention to the factors that can be manipulated and to early detection and treatment of osteoporosis changes the outlook for many in regard to maintaining bone tissue over the life span.

The Muscular System

Body composition begins changing in young adulthood. The proportion of lean body weight decreases, most often as a result of fat weight increasing. The change in muscle mass during adulthood is small. Only 10% of skeletal muscle mass is lost on average between the mid-20s and age 50. Changes in diet and physical activity level are probably responsible for this shift in body composition; poor diet promotes increased fat weight, and lack of physical activity leads to decreased muscle weight.

After age 50, individuals begin to lose muscle mass at a greater rate. The extent of loss varies greatly. Individuals who maintain a good diet and participate in resistance exercise lose far less muscle than others do, but on average an additional 30% of muscle mass is lost by age 80. By very old age, sedentary individuals with poor nutrition can lose as much as 50% of the muscle mass they possessed in young adulthood.

Both the number and the diameter (size) of muscle fibers appear to decrease (Green, 1986; Lexell, Henriksson-Larsen, Wimblad, & Sjostrom, 1983). The loss in number of fibers is small before the 50s—only about 5% of the adult number (Arabadjis, Heffner, & Pendergast, 1990)—but more rapid thereafter, amounting to approximately 35% (Lexell, Taylor, & Sjostrom, 1988). Fibers do not seem to decrease in size until the 70s (McComas, 1996). Recent research looked at the relationship between decline in muscle size and fiber size and type. In 2013, Nilwik and associates examined a group of 25 younger (average age 23.1 years) and older (average age 70 years) men and measured quadriceps cross-sectional area as well as type I and II fiber size. The older group had a significantly smaller quadriceps cross section ($p < .001$) as well as a 29% smaller type II fiber size ($p < .001$), with type I fibers tending toward smaller size. The older adult group went through a 6 month exercise intervention focusing on resistance training, and then both groups were measured again. The researchers determined that the older group increased type II muscle size by almost 25%, which accounted for all the increase in cross-sectional area as well as the difference in cross-sectional area between the groups.

In relation to cardiac muscle, in old age, the heart's ability to adapt to an increased workload declines. This might relate in part to degeneration of the heart muscle, a decrease in elasticity, and changes in the fibers of the heart valves (Lakatta & Levy, 2003a, 2003b; Strait & Lakatta, 2012). The major blood vessels also lose elasticity (Strait & Lakatta, 2012).

Bone and muscle mass are related to one another throughout the life span. Use of the muscles probably stimulates the bones to respond with increased bone formation, but many other factors certainly contribute to this relationship. Decline in bone and muscle mass is a constraint in the movement of older adults, and any loss of muscle strength accompanying decreases in muscle mass with aging can lead to a decrease in physical activities that are important to cardiovascular health or that the individual finds enjoyable. Such a loss also places an older individual at risk of falls, which increases the risk of bone fracture. We discuss muscle strength more extensively in chapter 11.

▶ **KEY POINT** It has been difficult for researchers to distinguish the changes that are an inevitable result of age from those that reflect the average older adult's lack of fitness or poor diet.

The Adipose System

Both sexes tend to gain fat weight during the adult years, reflecting changes in nutrition and activity level. This has become a critical issue worldwide; as of 2016, the World Health Organization found that more than 1.9 billion adults were considered overweight, which included 650 million categorized as obese (WHO fact sheet on obesity and overweight, www.who.int). Among U.S. adults, the average weight gain from adipose tissue is 1.1 to 2.2 pounds per year from early to middle adulthood for an average of 22 pounds for women and 19 pounds for men (Zheng et al., 2017). Total body weight begins to decline after age 50, but this reflects loss of bone and muscle, as body fat continues to increase.

Body fat redistributes with aging. Subcutaneous fat on the limbs tends to decrease, whereas internal fat in the abdomen tends to increase (Kuk, Saunders, Davidson, & Ross, 2009). This pattern is significant because abdominal obesity has been associated with a higher risk of cardiovascular disease as well as other health conditions (Cho et al., 2018; Kuk et al., 2009).

Although gains in adipose tissue may not be inevitable, most older adults add some fat weight as they age (Gill, Bartels, & Batsis, 2015). Active older adults add less than their sedentary peers, and physical activity interventions can help at any age (Gill et al., 2015). Overweight and obesity can be a constraint to movement at any age. Movement takes more effort with greater weight, joint movement can be restricted, and social pressure related to body image and self-esteem can discourage participation in physical activities.

The Endocrine System

Earlier, we acknowledged that the nervous system and the endocrine system work in concert to regulate cellular functions and organ systems. It is no surprise, then, that the continued functioning of these integrating systems is important for good health throughout the life span. In fact, one group of theories about the cause of aging, called gradual imbalance theories, suggests that over time the nervous system, endocrine system, and immune system gradually fail to function (Spirduso, Francis, & MacRae, 2005). This gradual failure might occur at different rates in the three systems, leading to imbalances between them. Imbalances and reduced effectiveness within systems leave older individuals at increased risk of disease.

Thyroid function is an example; it tends to decline with aging, and thyroid disorders are more prevalent among older adults. A long-term increase in thyroid hormone levels can be related to congestive heart failure. It is therefore important for older adults to be screened for hyperthyroidism. On the other hand, insufficiency of thyroid hormone, or hypothyroidism, is associated with acceleration of aging systems.

Gonadal hormone levels also decrease with age. Hormone replacement therapy may counteract many of the effects of aging. For example, prescribing androgen supplements has been successful in countering muscle wasting and osteoporosis. We need more information about the side effects of hormone replacement therapies, as evidenced by the eventual finding that women receiving hormone replacement therapy at menopause were unfortunately at increased risk of some types of cancers (Chlebowski et al., 2009).

Older adults maintain secretion levels of insulin comparable with those of younger adults, but the incidence of type 2 diabetes (non-insulin-dependent diabetes mellitus, which is caused by insulin deficiency) increases markedly with age. It is possible that older adults do not utilize insulin as effectively as younger adults to promote glycogen storage, thus delaying the mobilization of fuel for exercise. All these examples show that gradual declines or imbalances in the nervous, endocrine, and immune systems can lead to increased risk of disabilities or diseases that in turn can both threaten good health and serve as constraints to physical activity.

The Nervous System

The traditional view of the nervous system has been that after adolescence the only changes in the system would be losses, including a loss of neurons, thinning of the dendritic branches, a decline in the number of synapses, changes in the neurotransmitters, and reductions of myelin. This traditional view was based largely on observing behavior, especially slowing motor responses to stimuli as aging proceeds. Now, however, with the use of new imaging techniques that allow researchers to better see what is actually happening to brain tissue, we know there are significant exceptions to the trend of losses. Our new picture is one of enormous plasticity. **Neurogenesis** has been observed in some areas of the brain (Verret, Trouche, Zerwas, & Rampon, 2007), and the 100 trillion connections among the neurons are constantly changing over the life span.

Neurogenesis is the division and propagation of neurons.

The repercussions of age-related losses in the nervous system are widespread. Slowing of responses can affect movements in recreational activities as well as activities of daily living. Response slowing also affects the performance of cognitive tasks. Several theories have been advanced to explain how physiological changes result in slowing of responses. One of these theories is the neural network model. In this model, the nervous system is seen as a neural network of links and nodes. To respond to a stimulus, a signal begins at the input end of the individual's nervous system and travels through the network to the output end. With aging, links in the network are thought to break at random so that the neural signal must detour, increasing the time before the response is made. With advancing age, more links break and the processing time for a signal gets longer and longer (Cerella, 1990). Clearly, the losses of neurons, dendrites, and synapses, as well as the decline in neurotransmitters, are physiological changes that would result in broken links in the neural network. While not inevitable, these changes may result in conditions such as short-term memory loss and dementia, which have been on the rise worldwide as the population ages (Brayne & Miller, 2017).

▶ **KEY POINT** Regular vigorous exercise can play a key role in minimizing the loss of neurons and synapses with aging.

As in young people, extrinsic factors play a role in nervous system changes, and one of the most important factors is exercise. The very same exercise that benefits the cardiorespiratory system has positive effects on the nervous system, including reduced risk of stroke, increased branching of dendrites, and maintenance of the neurons' metabolism. Regular vigorous exercise maintains the level of blood flow to the brain, lessens the loss of dendrites, stimulates neurogenesis, and promotes new synaptic connections. These effects can result in improved cognitive function in older adulthood (Weuve et al., 2004).

Summary and Synthesis

A major theme in this discussion of body systems is that systems do not develop and age independently of one another; rather, they develop in concert, with one system often stimulating change in another. For example, growth of the long bones may stimulate the muscles to grow in length. In addition, the neurological system directs secretion of the pituitary hormones, which have their own effects (decreasing estrogen levels, for instance, affect bone strength in older women). Thus, a system can have its own timing or pattern of development but also interact with other systems in the bigger picture of the individual's development. Even when we want to focus on the development or aging of one body system, we should do so in the context of the other systems changing as well.

In addition, there are periods when change in a system is more rapid. These are often referred to as sensitive periods because we expect extrinsic factors to be more influential in times of greater change than in times of gradual change. Of course, the extrinsic influence could be positive (facilitating growth or slowing aging) or negative (slowing growth or accelerating aging).

Last, extrinsic factors can influence development at any point in the life span but have more influence in development as individuals move through the life span. Genes are also influential throughout the life span but have their greatest influence in transforming a tiny embryo of a few cells to a complex individual, all in less than 20 years. Extrinsic factors can affect a fetus, but the fetus is protected in the womb from many extrinsic factors. After birth, though, numerous extrinsic factors can influence many aspects of development at the levels of cell, system, and organism. These extrinsic factors can have transient or long-lasting effects. For example, resistance exercise promotes muscle strength, but when an individual stops exercising, the muscles begin losing strength. On the other hand, an active lifestyle in preadolescence may promote bone density that provides a lifelong benefit. This accumulating effect of extrinsic factors explains the great variation in health status we observe across individuals toward the end of the life span.

The structural constraints influencing movement can operate at the system level. So when we consider how the changing individual interacts with the task and environment to give rise to movement, it will most often be in the context of change in a system. We now know more about changes in the systems that make up an individual's structure. Of course, other characteristics of the individual change with growth and aging; vision, hearing, and self-confidence are just a few examples. Our knowledge of change in structural constraints, however, allows us to consider the course of motor development.

The model of constraints offers a deeper understanding of motor development than simply a description of the interaction of changing individual, task, and environmental factors. It also explains why certain movements can arise when they do. This is so because often a particular structural constraint shapes movement at a particular point in the life span. For example, consider a 4-month-old who can hold his head up but can't sit or stand on his own. Why not? We might suggest that the infant needs to undergo an improvement in balance, an increase in trunk muscle strength, an increase in leg muscle strength, an increase in bone density, an increase in leg length to offset the large size of the upper body, or other changes. Which system is the limiting one? The balance system? The muscle system? The skeletal system? That is, which system is the rate limiter, or the system limiting the rate of development?

We have come a long way in knowing more about some of the structural changes that accompany growth and aging. We can better predict how specific changes might influence movement, and because we know more about the course of physical development we can better predict when structural changes might change the movement. We also know more about when an individual is subject to greater or lesser influence from extrinsic factors. This knowledge can inform us about changes in extrinsic factors that could bring about changes in movement.

Reinforcing What You Have Learned About Constraints

TAKE A SECOND LOOK

Did Nerlens Noel's fractured growth plate result in a predisposition to knee injuries later in his career? Some medical professionals speculated that it did, and predicted additional knee issues across his career. Others, such as Dr. Ryan Goodwin, argue that it did not: "I can tell you that growth-plate injuries are, in fact, very common in children, and children can be big children all the way up through high school age," said Goodwin. "The good news is the vast majority of growth-plate injuries heal without consequence. Children heal and they go on to grow" (Silverman, 2013). Noel hasn't let the debate stop him from playing professional basketball. Since 2013, he's played more than 200 professional games, and it doesn't look as if he will stop anytime soon.

TEST YOUR KNOWLEDGE

1. What is the epiphyseal growth plate? What is the difference between a pressure epiphysis and a traction epiphysis? Why would an injury to the growth plate in a young child be of concern?
2. What is osteoporosis? Who does it affect, and what are the repercussions for health and for participation in activities?
3. Discuss sex differences in the growth of muscle tissue. How does the growth of cardiac muscle compare with that of skeletal muscle?
4. Do adults necessarily gain fat tissue as they age? What is the evidence for your answer?
5. How does the distribution of fat change over the growth period? How does the amount and distribution of fat change in adulthood? What distribution pattern in adulthood is associated with greater risk of cardiovascular disease?
6. What are the major types of hormones involved in growth? How do the hormones influence growth?
7. What contributes to the rapid gains in brain weight during the first year after birth? What part of the brain is most advanced at birth?
8. How has the view of what happens in the nervous system with aging changed with the use of new imaging techniques? What lifestyle factors could spur changes in the nervous system, and how?
9. Choose one extrinsic or environmental factor and describe how it might influence the growth of various systems.

LEARNING EXERCISE 9.1

System Changes in Older Adults

Throughout our discussion, we describe the average or typical course of aging for each system. It is often useful to consider how a particular person either matches or varies from the typical. Locate an adult who is 60 years of age or older and willing to discuss what he or she remembers about changes in his or her skeletal structure, muscle tissue, and adipose tissue. You might ask, for example, about osteoporosis screenings, changes in body weight during middle and older adulthood, and changes in fat versus muscle weight as the person changed body shape. Write a short paper summarizing your conversation, indicating what matched and what varied from the norm described in this chapter.

LEARNING EXERCISE 9.2

Human Growth Hormone

Human growth hormone, or GH (or a releasing factor that stimulates GH secretion), is available for sale on the Internet. Yet the use of GH is banned by many sport governing bodies, some of which test their athletes for use of GH as a supplement. Research the use of GH, and then answer the following questions.

1. Why would athletes want to use GH? What effect does it have on individuals who have reached maturity? How does it produce these effects?
2. Are there known risks of using GH supplements? If yes, explain your findings.
3. Even if little research has been conducted on the long-term effects of using GH as a supplement, what are some of the suspected risks of long-term GH supplementation?
4. Based on your findings, what would you recommend to a teenage athlete who is tempted to use GH? Why?

IV

Development of Physical Fitness

The theme of our study of motor development is that movement arises from the interaction of individual, environmental, and task constraints. We also note repeatedly that within each type of constraint, multiple systems interact. For example, chapter 9 examines individual structural systems that interact with growth and aging, such as the skeletal, muscular, and neurological systems. In part IV, we explore how physical fitness emerges from the interaction of physical activity with other constraints.

Physical fitness involves many systems and has many components, such as flexibility and strength. A person who is fit in one component is not necessarily fit in another. For example, an individual may be very strong but not very flexible. This part of the book discusses cardiorespiratory endurance (chapter 10) and strength and flexibility (chapter 11) as components of fitness, then explores relationships among fitness, activity level, motor competence, and body composition (chapter 12).

Some writers view fitness as including additional components, such as agility and power, but cardiorespiratory endurance, muscular strength, flexibility, and body composition are four of the essential ones. Potentially, a person can improve physical fitness through a systematic program of exercise aimed at these four components. An individual's fitness level in each of the four components—along with the interaction of the systems involved—can either permit or restrain movements over the life span. Fitness is important in every part of the life span, but older adulthood is the period when fitness may have the greatest influence on quality of life, through the movements permitted and the positive effect on all the body's systems.

Suggested Reading

Cattuzzo, M.T., dos Santos Henrique, R., Ré, A.H.N., de Oliveira, I.S., Melo, B.M., de Sousa Moura, M., et al. (2016). Motor competence and health related physical fitness in youth: A systematic review. *Journal of Science and Medicine in Sport, 19*(2), 123–129.

Leite, T., de Souza Teixeira, A., Saavedra, F., Leite, R.D., Rhea, M.R., & Simão, R. (2015). Influence of strength and flexibility training, combined or isolated, on strength and flexibility gains. *Journal of Strength and Conditioning Research, 29*(4), 1083–1088.

Rodrigues, L.P., Stodden, D.F., & Lopes, V.P. (2016). Developmental pathways of change in fitness and motor competence are related to overweight and obesity status at the end of primary school. *Journal of Science and Medicine in Sport, 19*(1), 87–92.

Sigmundsson, H., & Haga, M. (2016). Motor competence is associated with physical fitness in four-to six-year-old preschool children. *European Early Childhood Education Research Journal, 24*(3), 477–488.

VanVrancken-Tompkins, C., Sothern, M.S., & Bar-Or, O. (2016). Weaknesses and strengths in the response of the obese child to exercise. In M.S. Sothern, S.T. Gordon, & T.K von Almen (Eds.), *Handbook of pediatric obesity: Clinical management* (pp. 67–75). Boca Raton, FL: Taylor and Francis.

10

Development of Cardiorespiratory Endurance

CHAPTER OBJECTIVES

This chapter

- examines the body's response to short-term vigorous exercise and how this response changes over the life span,
- reviews the effects of short-term exercise over the life span,
- studies the body's response to prolonged exercise and how this response changes over the life span, and
- reviews the effects of endurance training over the life span.

Motor Development in the Real World

Never Leave Your Living Room

It is now common to see reasonably priced virtual reality headsets advertised to youths and adults alike. These headsets provide a realistic simulation of activities such as flying a jet, racing a car, or walking through a prehistoric forest. It makes one wonder whether people of the future will ever leave their living rooms to engage in the real activity! When time spent gaming is added to the hours spent watching television and using computers, tablets, or smartphones, it is easy to see why concern about the fitness level of people, including children, is worldwide.

Components of physical fitness can act as individual constraints to most activities; some components are more important for some kinds of physical activities than others. A lack of fitness can easily be a rate limiter to the performance of motor skills and the physical activities of everyday living. Indeed, fitness is related to one's very quality of life. Of course, a relationship exists between the growth and aging of the body and of its systems (structural constraints) and the fitness components, and a relationship exists between functional constraints and training for the maintenance or improvement of fitness. It is important to understand how these various structural and functional individual constraints interact in the performance of skills.

Cardiorespiratory endurance reflects one's ability to sustain vigorous activity. It is important for two broad reasons. First, participation in many physical activities demands sustained vigorous exertion. Second, the health of the cardiac, vascular, and respiratory systems is related to endurance level, largely because training that improves endurance makes these systems more efficient.

Of all the fitness components, cardiorespiratory endurance has the greatest implications for lifelong health. It is easy to assume that children automatically get enough exercise to become and remain fit. Yet studies conducted in the 2000s began to detect a worldwide trend toward reduced fitness in children (Tomkinson & Olds, 2007; Tomkinson, Olds, Kang, & Kim, 2007). The sedentary lifestyle that many of today's adults have adopted has spilled over to the lives of their children. A high percentage of children and teenagers are unable to sustain vigorous physical activity and already exhibit one or more of the risk factors for coronary heart disease, and far too many are obese. Children in poor physical condition are likely to maintain that status throughout their adult lives. Educators and exercise leaders must thoroughly understand the role of cardiorespiratory endurance in attaining and maintaining an appropriate level of fitness for vigorous activity. In this chapter we review the body's basic physiological responses to both short-term and long-term vigorous activities. We also discuss the changes that occur in these responses with growth and aging and the impact of training.

Physiological Responses to Short-Term Exercise

Vigorous physical activity can be a short burst of intense exercise, a long period of submaximal or maximal work, or a combination of these types. Our bodies meet the differing demands of brief, intense activity and of longer, more moderate activity with different physiological responses. During a brief period (10 seconds) of intense activity, the body responds by depleting local reserves of oxygen and sources of energy stored in the muscles, thus creating a deficit of oxygen that must eventually be replenished. These are **anaerobic** (without oxygen) systems. Anaerobic system performance can be reflected in measurements of **anaerobic power** and **anaerobic capacity**. Anaerobic power can be expressed as the highest value, **peak power**, or the average output for a test, **mean power**.

As the period of exercise demand grows longer, the anaerobic systems contribute less to the body's response. Respiration and circulation increase to bring oxygen to the muscles. Ninety seconds into an exercise bout, anaerobic and **aerobic** (with oxygen) energy systems contribute about equally. After 3 minutes, aerobic processes meet the demands of exercise. The types of training that promote anaerobic performance, then, are vigorous but of short duration, whereas those that promote aerobic performance are sustained and consequently less vigorous or intense.

Anaerobic power is the rate at which a person's body can meet the demand for short-term, intense activity.

Anaerobic capacity is the maximum oxygen deficit a person can tolerate.

Anaerobic Development and Training in Youth

At any age, anaerobic performance is related to

- body size, particularly fat-free muscle mass and muscle size;
- the ability to metabolize fuel sources in the muscles; and
- quick mobilization of oxygen delivery systems.

Some of these factors change as a person grows (Malina, Bouchard, & Bar-Or, 2004). We start with their status in childhood and adolescence.

Young children have smaller absolute quantities of energy reserves than adults do because they have less muscle mass (Eriksson, 1978; Shephard, 1982). Therefore, children attain less output of absolute anaerobic power than adults do. As children grow their muscle mass increases, as do their energy reserves. They also can better tolerate the by-products of the metabolic process. Thus, mean and peak anaerobic power improve steadily as a person ages (Duche et al., 1992; Falgairette, Bedu, Fellmann, Van Praagh, & Coudert, 1991; Inbar & Bar-Or, 1986). Total work output scores also improve, over the entire adolescent period in boys but only until puberty in girls, perhaps reflecting the patterns of muscle growth in the sexes (figure 10.1, *a* and *b*) or differences in the typical lifestyles of boys and girls.

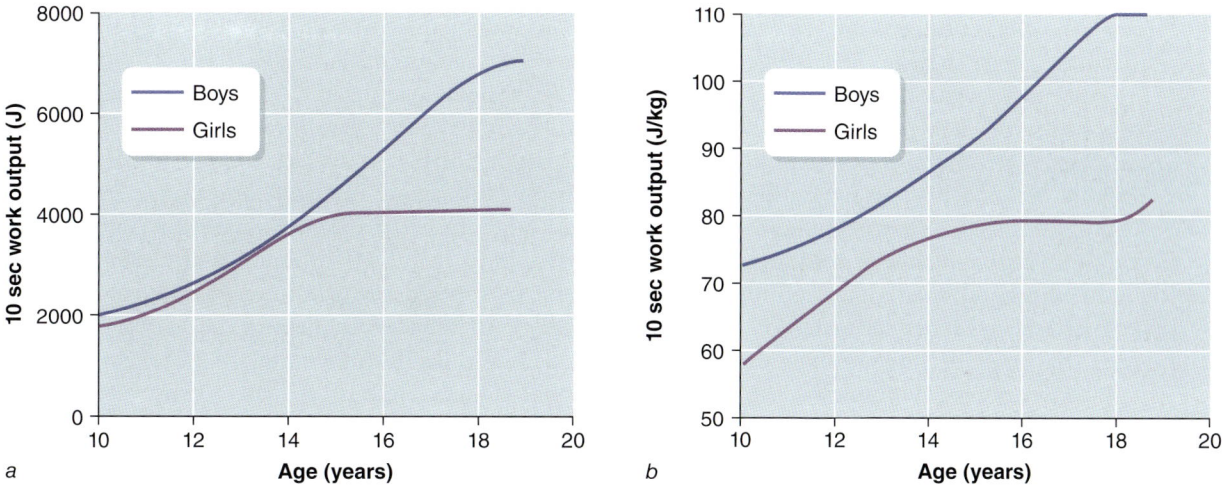

FIGURE 10.1 Anaerobic performance. *(a)* Change in total work output (measured in Joules) on a 10-second all-out bicycle ergometer ride with advancing age. Bouchard and Simoneau (unpublished data) measured a cross-sectional group of French Canadian youths on this task. When anaerobic performance scores are divided by body weight, as in *(b)*, scores still improve with age.

Reprinted by permission from Malina, Bouchard, and Bar-Or (2004, pg. 259).

Although body size and muscle mass greatly influence the increase in anaerobic power with growth, maturity also has a small effect (Carvalho et al., 2011). Undoubtedly, better neuromuscular coordination and skill contribute to improved anaerobic performance as children grow older and the capacity for energy production improves with age (Rowland, 1996). More mature children can be expected to show better anaerobic performance than less mature children even if they are similar in body size (Armstrong, Welsman, & Kirby, 1997; Tomkinson, Hamlin, & Olds, 2006). Mikulic (2011) determined that anaerobic power differences between early- and late-maturing 12- and 13-year-old boys were greatly reduced as the boys reached 17 to 18 years of age, although early maturers maintained a slight edge that seemed related to higher lean body mass.

▶ **KEY POINT** Anaerobic fitness improves with growth but at a faster rate than can be explained by growth alone.

Anaerobic Training in Youth

Children and adolescents of both sexes have higher peak power and mean power measures after training than do untrained counterparts (McNarry & Jones, 2014). One study even documented a decrease in peak and mean power after detraining, further illustrating the association between anaerobic performance and training (Ingle, Sleap, & Tolfrey, 2006). The extent of the differences between trained and untrained youths is variable, reflecting numerous factors such as length of training, similarity of the training and testing activities, increased muscle mass with training, and neurological adaptations (McNarry & Jones, 2014).

Imagine you are a physical education teacher. Which games that students play provide anaerobic training at the elementary school level? At the middle school level?

Anaerobic Development and Training in Adulthood

Once individuals attain adult body size, their anaerobic performance remains stable throughout young adulthood (Inbar & Bar-Or, 1986). Any improvement in anaerobic power and capacity is achieved through training alone. Starting around the age of 35 years, anaerobic capacity declines 6% to 8% per decade until approximately 70 years of age, after which the decline is much sharper. This decline is found in both nontraining and training adults, although an analysis of best performance times in short-distance cycling by male masters athletes found the decline to start later, in the late 40s (Capelli, Rittveger, Bruseghini, Calabria, & Tam, 2016).

Anaerobic performance is related to a large number of factors in adults, including muscle mass and fiber type, gender, and training (see Reaburn & Dascombe, 2009, for a review). Age-related changes in any of these factors would contribute to a decline in anaerobic performance. In fact, muscle mass declines and type II muscle fibers atrophy with aging in both nontraining and training adults. Yet research indicates that muscle mass might be better maintained with strength training, especially heavy resistance training and high-power exercise (Korhonen et al., 2006).

In adulthood, men maintain their edge in anaerobic performance over women in both laboratory tests and sport performance. Although both men and women decline more sharply after age 70, women decline significantly faster. This greater rate of decline in women might reflect a greater rate of type II muscle fiber atrophy and hormonal changes (Reaburn & Dascombe, 2009).

▶ **KEY POINT** Declines in anaerobic performance in older adults are associated with a loss of muscle mass and type II muscle fiber atrophy.

Anaerobic Training in Adulthood

Few studies have examined the effects of anaerobic training on sedentary older adults, but Makrides, Heigenhauser, and Jones (1990) had sedentary 60- to 70-year-old men engage in

Assessing Anaerobic Performance

No direct, noninvasive methods of measuring anaerobic fitness exist, so it is typically studied through short-duration tasks. The Quebec 10-second and the Wingate 30-second all-out rides on a bicycle ergometer and the Margaria step-running test are common laboratory tests that provide scores in total work output, mean power, or peak power. Total work output indicates how much absolute work an individual can do in 10 or 30 seconds. In contrast, power indicates the rate at which individuals can produce energy (i.e., the work they can do per a specific unit of time). Mean power is the average power individuals achieve during the 10- or 30-second period, whereas peak power is the highest rate they achieve. The 50-yard dash and sprinting a flight of stairs are common field tests. Participants must be willing and able to give an all-out effort in order to provide an accurate measure of anaerobic performance. Taking anaerobic measurements can be difficult or even dangerous with older adults, especially those who have been inactive.

high-intensity endurance training and noted an increase in work output during a 30-second anaerobic capacity test. In two studies that trained masters athletes with anaerobic or resistance training (Cristea et al., 2008; Reaburn, Logan, & Mackinnon, 1994), results suggest resistance training plus speed training improved their anaerobic performance. Although specific training is generally considered the most beneficial (i.e., use of anaerobic training to improve anaerobic performance), resistance training to increase muscle mass appears to be important for improving anaerobic performance in adulthood and older adulthood. Resistance training is discussed in more detail in the next chapter.

▶ **KEY POINT** Anaerobic training improves the anaerobic performance of preadolescent children and resistance training improves anaerobic performance of masters athletes.

Physiological Responses to Prolonged Exercise

How do our bodies sustain submaximal physical activity for prolonged periods? Unlike in short-term exercise, the energy for prolonged exercise is derived from aerobic systems—the oxidative breakdown of food stores—in addition to the local reserves depleted in the first few minutes of exercise. The success with which we meet the needs of prolonged activity can be indicated by measurements of **aerobic power** and **aerobic capacity**.

Aerobic power is the rate at which long-term oxygen demand is met during prolonged activity.

Aerobic capacity is the total energy available to meet the demands of prolonged activity.

Sustained, prolonged activity depends on the transportation of sufficient oxygen to the working muscles for longer periods. The needed oxygen is delivered through increases in heart and respiratory rates, cardiac output, and oxygen uptake. An increased respiratory rate brings more oxygen to the lungs, making it available for diffusion into the bloodstream. Increased cardiac output (the amount of blood pumped into the circulatory system) allows more oxygen to reach the muscles. The body achieves this increased cardiac output through increased heart rate or increased stroke volume. Changes in stroke volume during exercise are relatively small, but one of the long-term benefits of training is greater stroke volume.

The limiting factor to continued vigorous activity is the heart's ability to pump enough blood to meet the oxygen needs of the working muscles. When individuals engage in very heavy activity, their heart rates increase throughout the session until exhaustion ends the activity. When they stop vigorous activity, their heart rates decrease quickly for 2 to 3 minutes and then more gradually for a time related to the duration and intensity of the activity. Fit individuals regain their resting heart rates more quickly than unfit individuals.

This description is only a brief summary of the physiological responses to exercise. A more detailed treatment is available in exercise physiology textbooks.

Aerobic Development and Training in Youth

How do children respond physiologically to prolonged activity? Children tend to have hypokinetic circulation (Bar-Or, Shephard, & Allen, 1971); that is, their cardiac output is less than an adult's (cardiac output is the product of stroke volume and heart rate). Children have a smaller stroke volume than adults, reflecting their smaller hearts. They compensate in part with higher heart rates than adults at a given level of exercise, but their cardiac output is still somewhat lower than an adult's. Children also have lower blood **hemoglobin** concentrations than do adults; hemoglobin concentration is related to the blood's ability to carry oxygen.

Hemoglobin is the protein in the blood that carries oxygen.

You might assume that these two factors in children, hypokinetic circulation and low hemoglobin concentration, result in an oxygen transport system that is less efficient than that in adults. However, children can extract relatively more of the oxygen circulating to the active muscles than adults can (Malina & Bouchard, 1991; Shephard, 1982), which seems to compensate for these factors. The result is a comparably effective oxygen transport system. Children also mobilize their aerobic systems faster than adults do (Bar-Or, 1983).

▶ **KEY POINT** Children's physiological response to endurance activity is very efficient, but children cannot exercise as long as adults can.

Children do have a lower tolerance than adults for extended periods of exercise, perhaps because of smaller energy reserves in the muscles. As children grow, their hypokinetic circulation is gradually reduced and their response becomes increasingly similar to the adult response.

Longitudinal and cross-sectional studies demonstrate that absolute **peak oxygen uptake ($\dot{V}O_2$)** increases linearly in children throughout childhood and adolescence (Armstrong & McManus, 2016; Armstrong & Welsman, 2007; Krahenbuhl, Skinner, & Kohrt, 1985; Mirwald & Bailey, 1986; Shuleva, Hunter, Hester, & Dunaway, 1990). Peak $\dot{V}O_2$ in girls tends to plateau after 13 years of age. Boys begin with a slight edge over girls that widens during adolescence (see figure 10.2*a*). Peak $\dot{V}O_2$ and body mass are strongly correlated, so boys' greater muscle mass contributes to these sex differences because the larger muscle mass facilitates oxygen utilization. Peak oxygen uptake is the most common measure of fitness for endurance activities. The terms *peak oxygen uptake, maximal oxygen consumption, maximal oxygen uptake,* and *maximal aerobic capacity* are often used interchangeably, but there are differences among the terms. Determinations of *maximal* oxygen use require an intense measurement test wherein the oxygen used reaches a plateau. Much research with youth and older adults estimates this value with a submaximal test; hence, peak oxygen uptake is used in the context of this text.

Peak oxygen uptake ($\dot{V}O_2$) is the highest rate that oxygen can be consumed by the muscles during aerobic work.

▶ **KEY POINT** Peak $\dot{V}O_2$ increases in boys throughout childhood and adolescence and in girls until age 13, after which it plateaus. If peak $\dot{V}O_2$ is expressed relative to body weight, it is stable in boys and declines slightly in girls.

Because of the strong relationship between peak $\dot{V}O_2$ and body mass, researchers have divided peak $\dot{V}O_2$ by body mass, yielding a ratio. As figure 10.2*b* shows, peak $\dot{V}O_2$ relative to body weight stays about the same throughout childhood and adolescence in boys. It declines in girls, probably because adipose (fat) tissue increases. Although peak $\dot{V}O_2$ is related to fat-free

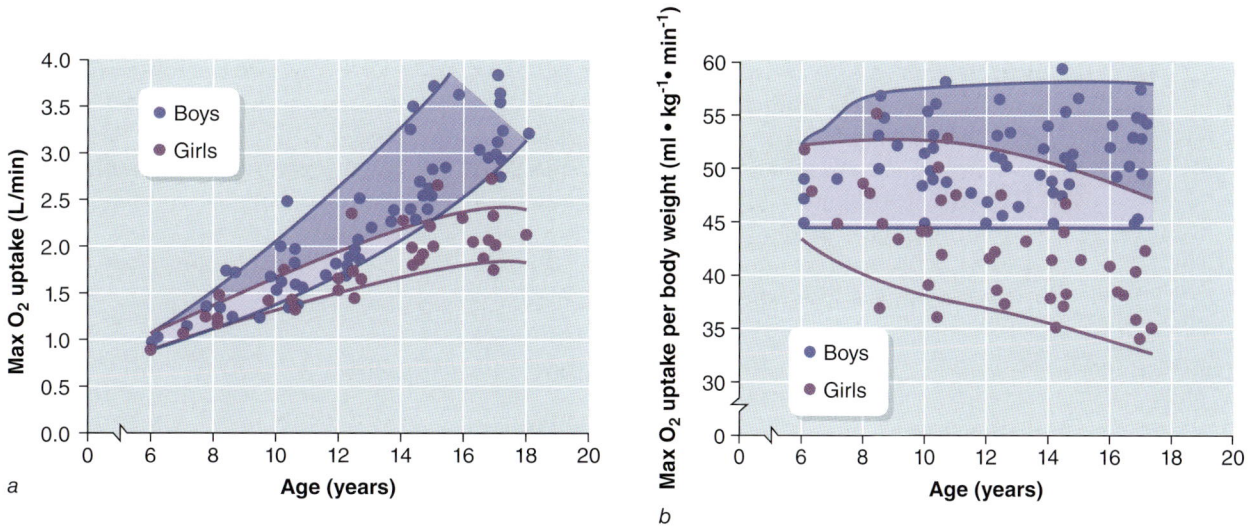

FIGURE 10.2 The relationship between maximal oxygen uptake and age. *(a)* Absolute scores. *(b)* Peak $\dot{V}O_2$ values relative to kilograms of body weight. The boys' scores are centered in the shaded area, and the girls' scores are centered in the unshaded area.

Reprinted by permission of Bar-Or (1983).

mass, scores reflecting fat-free mass show a slight decline during and after puberty, and small sex differences remain. Peak $\dot{V}O_2$–body mass ratios demonstrate the correlation between these two measures, but the ratio likely penalizes more mature or heavier individuals, so use of the ratio for any other purpose is limited.

Body mass tends to increase slightly faster than peak $\dot{V}O_2$ around puberty (Malina & Bouchard, 1991). Peak $\dot{V}O_2$ might depend somewhat on maturity in addition to body size; comparisons of peak $\dot{V}O_2$ with age show a relationship in adolescents who vary in age but are identical in size (Sprynarova & Reisenauer, 1978). Two adolescents identical in size could differ in peak $\dot{V}O_2$ if one was more physiologically mature than the other.

▶ **KEY POINT** Peak $\dot{V}O_2$ is related to body size, especially lean body mass, as well as to maturity status.

It is important to recognize the relationship between children's increasing body size and their improving ability to sustain exercise during growth. With body growth come increases in lung volume, heart and stroke volume, total hemoglobin, and lean body mass. These factors foster improved cardiac output and, subsequently, improved exercise capacity. Because children vary in size despite their chronological age, evaluations of exercise capacity among children should relate to body size rather than chronological age alone. In the past, educators frequently based evaluation only on age.

Average exercise capacity and average body size of groups of children and adolescents generally increase with age, but exercise capacity is also related to maturation rate. As noted in chapter 8, the relationship between chronological age and maturation status is imperfect. Therefore, each child's unique size *and* maturity level should be considered when establishing expectations for endurance performance.

In children, body size is a far better predictor of endurance than the child's sex. After puberty, however, boys on average attain a considerable edge over girls and have the potential to retain this edge throughout life. Several factors contribute to this sex difference. One is body composition. The average man gains more lean body mass and less adipose tissue during adolescence than does the average woman. Women are similar to men in peak $\dot{V}O_2$ per kilogram of fat-free body mass, but when adipose tissue is included, women have a lower peak $\dot{V}O_2$. Another factor in sex differences in oxygen consumption is that women tend to have lower hemoglobin concentrations than men do (Åstrand, 1976).

Imagine you are an administrator for the youth sports program at a community center. If maximal oxygen uptake is related to body composition and physical maturity, what would this mean for how you group children in teams? What should be the criteria when grouping children into teams for contact or combative sports? For noncontact sports?

By the time the average male reaches late adolescence, he has an edge over the average female in both oxygen consumption and working capacity (figure 10.3). It must be remembered that environmental factors, especially training, influence the endurance capacities of individual men and women throughout their lives. Thus, it would not be surprising to find that a well-trained woman has a higher peak $\dot{V}O_2$ than a sedentary man.

Aerobic Training in Youth

The result of aerobic training is predictable in adults. An adult improves peak $\dot{V}O_2$ by training at least three times a week for at least 20 minutes at an intensity of 60% to 90% of maximum heart rate. Stroke volume increases, and maximal cardiac output subsequently increases. Oxygen is better extracted from the blood at muscle sites. Maximal ventilation per minute rises. Inactive adults who begin training typically increase peak $\dot{V}O_2$ by 25% to 50% (Hartley, 1992). Therefore, appropriate training yields benefits. Let's consider whether the same is true for children.

To assess whether children and adolescents can improve their aerobic fitness with training, researchers must consider several things. First, they must distinguish any increase in peak $\dot{V}O_2$ due to growth from that due to training. It is absolutely necessary to include a control group that does not train but is measured over the same time as the training group. Moreover, as noted in chapter 8, children mature at different rates. Comparing a group that contains many early maturers with a group that contains many late maturers can certainly bias an investigation of training effects. In fact, one research group noted that when they sought to compare inactive and active groups of children, late maturers more often fell into the inactive category (Mirwald, Bailey, Cameron, & Rasmussen, 1981). Thus, maturation level must be assessed in research studies.

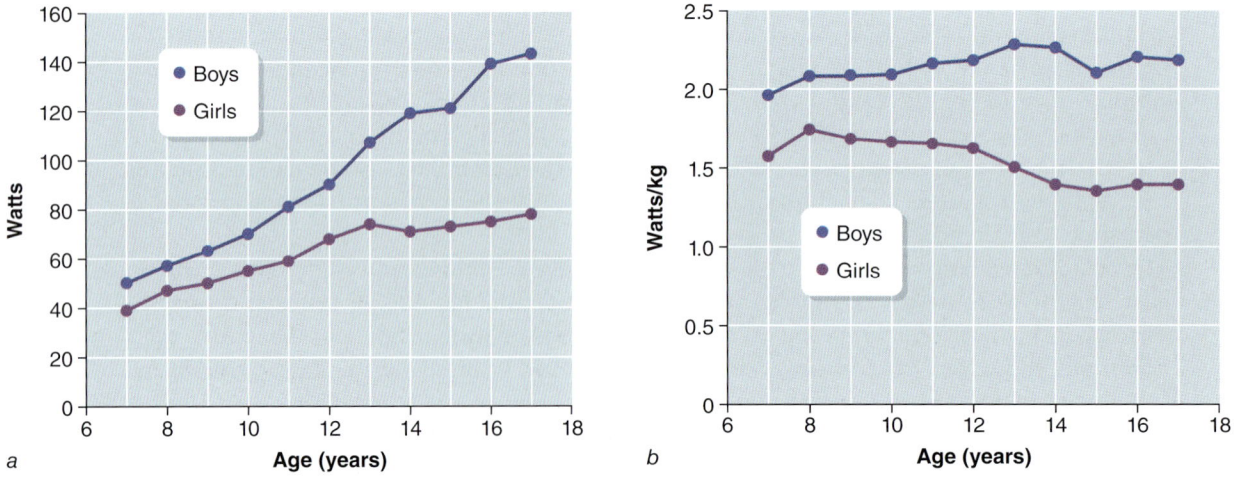

FIGURE 10.3 Physical working capacity with advancing age in childhood and adolescence. Measurements were made in school classrooms (without habituation of the Canadian subjects) at a heart rate of 170 beats per minute. Readings would probably be up to 10% higher given climatic control (20–22 °C) and some familiarization with experimental procedures. Measurements are in (*a*) watts (1 watt = 6 $kg \cdot m^{-1} \cdot min^{-1}$) and (*b*) watts per kilogram of body weight.
Data from Shephard (1982, pg. 70).

Early studies of aerobic training in prepubescent children were equivocal. Zwiren (1989) reviewed seven studies. Three found a significant increase in peak $\dot{V}O_2$ by the training group over a control group, and four found no significant difference after training. In a few longitudinal studies, training did not result in differences between active and inactive groups until the children reached peak height velocity (Kobayashi et al., 1978; Mirwald et al., 1981; Rutenfranz, 1986). This led Gilliam and Freedson (1980) to suggest the existence of a maturational threshold before which children are unable to respond to training. Later, Katch (1983) proposed the trigger hypothesis, that until the results of the hormones that initiate puberty are realized, the effects of aerobic training on peak $\dot{V}O_2$ are minimal at best.

To date there is little empirical evidence to support either the maturational threshold or the trigger hypothesis. Intensity of training appears to be a major consideration in explaining the mixed results of early studies. Studies using a sufficiently intense training program show an increase in peak $\dot{V}O_2$ regardless of age, stage of maturation, or sex (Armstrong & Barker, 2011). McNarry, Mackintosh, and Stoedefalke (2014) supported this conclusion in a study that measured boys over three years, starting at age 10. Two groups were measured, one that participated in swimming training and one that was untrained. Every year the trained group had a significantly higher peak $\dot{V}O_2$ and cardiac output. None of the pulmonary or cardiovascular measures interacted with maturational status, so training seemed to have a positive effect regardless of maturational status. Studies using constant-intensity exercise training have shown increases in children's peak $\dot{V}O_2$. Those using high-intensity interval training show increases in adolescents, but the benefit in children is uncertain because of the limited number of studies on this age group (Costigan, Eather, Plotnikoff, Taaffe, & Lubans, 2015). More research is needed on the intensity of training and the types of training programs required to improve peak $\dot{V}O_2$ in children.

Imagine you are a physical education teacher serving on a district-wide committee charged with revising the physical education curriculum. How much activity that is characterized as aerobic training would you favor at each grade level from kindergarten through 12th grade? What about anaerobic training activities? Would you advocate having high school students complete their physical education requirement as sophomores?

Peak $\dot{V}O_2$ might not be the best measure of training effects in children, even though it is widely used (Armstrong & Welsman, 2007). Studies of adults using constant-intensity and high-intensity interval training show improved pulmonary oxygen uptake ($p\dot{V}O_2$) kinetics, but few studies have used these measures in children, and those that did were cross-sectional. As more researchers consider using $p\dot{V}O_2$ measures, more could be learned about training effects in childhood.

▶ **KEY POINT** The effect of growth and maturation on peak $\dot{V}O_2$ must be distinguished from the effect of training.

Adolescents after puberty respond to aerobic training much as adults do. Heart size and volume, total blood volume, total hemoglobin, stroke volume, and maximal cardiac output all increase in adolescents who train (Costigan et al., 2015; Ekblom, 1969; Eriksson & Koch, 1973; Koch & Rocker, 1977; Lengyel & Gyarfas, 1979; Unnithan, Roche, Garrard, Holloway, & Marwood, 2015), whereas submaximal heart rate for a given level of exercise decreases (Brown, Harrower, & Deeter, 1972). Kobayashi et al. (1978) found a 15.8% increase in aerobic power with training between ages 14 and 17. A 15-year longitudinal study of males and females from ages 13 through 27 showed that those who reported being physically active, but not necessarily training, were 2% to 5% higher in aerobic fitness than those who did not (Kemper, Twisk, Koppes, van Mechelen, & Post, 2001). Sedentary university students who report high cell phone use were found to have low cardiorespiratory fitness (Lepp, Barkley, Sanders, Rebold, & Gates, 2013). A sedentary lifestyle is associated with poor aerobic fitness; while an active lifestyle contributes modestly to aerobic fitness, it is endurance training that greatly improves it.

Training is specific even in adolescents. Santos, Marinho, Costa, Izquierdo, and Marques (2012) noted that strength training in adolescent boys between 12 and 14 years did not improve aerobic capacity, but programs concurrently providing resistance and endurance training led to an improvement in both fitness components.

Web Study Guide **Analyze children's scores on a test of prolonged moderate activity and note sex differences in Lab Activity 10.1, Changes in Youth Endurance Performance, in the web study guide.**

Aerobic Development and Training in Adulthood

Average maximal oxygen uptake per kilogram of body weight peaks in the 20s, then decreases throughout the adult years. The loss is approximately 1% per year of life. The decline is found in both cross-sectional and longitudinal research and among athletic, active, and sedentary

Assessing Aerobic Performance

The most common activities used to assess aerobic performance in a laboratory are cycling on an ergometer or walking or running on a treadmill. The effort asked of the individual can be submaximal or maximal. Measurements of aerobic power and capacity tend to be specific to the task performed (e.g., cycling, running), so caution must be used in comparing scores on different tasks.

Aerobic exercise tests are usually graded; that is, they increase workload in stages. There is no standard protocol for any age group, but intensity should always be appropriate for the fitness level and size of those tested.

Many physiological responses can be measured during sustained activity. One of the most important measures of aerobic fitness is peak oxygen uptake (peak $\dot{V}O_2$), the highest rate oxygen can be consumed by the muscles during vigorous activity to exhaustion. The more efficiently a person's body uses oxygen (i.e., the less oxygen consumed for the same amount of work performed), the more fit the individual. Endurance exercise performance is too complex to be represented by one value, but peak $\dot{V}O_2$ is regarded as the best single measure, especially for youths (Armstrong & McNarry, 2016).

In tests assessing peak $\dot{V}O_2$, you can measure or estimate the amount of oxygen consumed during activity. This score is also expressed as oxygen consumed per minute per kilogram of body weight. Peak $\dot{V}O_2$ is a common measure of endurance in studies of children and older adults because it can be estimated from a submaximal test, thus avoiding the need for exercise to exhaustion. Direct measures of oxygen use require more sophisticated and expensive equipment than is needed for estimates from submaximal tests.

Another measure of physiological response to prolonged exercise is maximal working capacity, which means the highest work, or exercise, load a person can tolerate before reaching exhaustion (Adams, 1973). Because this test requires maximal effort, it requires motivating individuals to work to exhaustion. Although it is unlikely, an individual may have a heart attack during such a test. For this reason, this measure is not often used with children or older adults.

adults (Spirduso, 1995). Athletic and active adults, however, maintain a higher peak $\dot{V}O_2$ than sedentary adults. An analysis of cycling performance times in male masters athletes from 30 to 80 years of age noted that the decline did not start until age 45 (Capelli, Rittveger, Bruseghini, Calabria, & Tam, 2016). This section discusses the structural and functional changes in the cardiovascular and respiratory systems that contribute to this decline.

Cardiovascular Structure and Function

Cardiovascular function is related to the structure of the heart and blood vessels. The major structural changes in a nondiseased heart with aging include a progressive loss of cardiac muscle, a loss of elasticity in cardiac muscle fibers, a thickening of the left ventricular wall (Lakatta & Levy, 2003b), and fibrotic changes in the valves (Pomerance, 1965). The major blood vessels also thicken and stiffen (Lakatta & Levy, 2003a). It remains unclear whether these changes are unavoidable in aging or reflect a chronic lack of oxygen. The effects of these structural changes on cardiovascular function are numerous.

A measure of aerobic fitness that has gained recent attention is pulmonary oxygen uptake ($p\dot{V}O_2$) kinetics at the onset of exercise, or the rate and magnitude of respiratory gas exchange responses to a given metabolic demand (Armstrong & McNarry, 2016). This is potentially a better measure of aerobic fitness for youths, who tend to engage in intermittent periods of exercise with rapid changes in intensity. Maximum oxygen uptake is defined in terms of an exercise bout to exhaustion, and few children experience such an event. Rather, they tend to engage in start–stop activities varying in intensity. So $p\dot{V}O_2$ kinetics responses to step changes in exercise intensity might better describe children's aerobic fitness (Armstrong & McNarry, 2016). To date, the number of well-controlled studies using $p\dot{V}O_2$ is limited, but future research is more likely to use this measure.

Several research investigators attempted to identify field tests for children that estimate endurance nearly as reliably as when it is measured in a laboratory. Such field tests allow educators to measure aerobic performance without laboratory equipment. The investigators compared peak $\dot{V}O_2$ scores from laboratory tests against performance in 800-meter, 1,200-meter, and 1,600-meter runs for 83 children in the first, second, and third grades. Performance on the 1,600-meter run was a better predictor of peak $\dot{V}O_2$ for boys and girls than performance on the 800-meter or 1,200-meter runs. An average velocity score on the 1,600-meter run had a slightly higher correlation with peak $\dot{V}O_2$ than a total time score. We can conclude that a 1,600-meter run is a better field test of endurance in children than shorter runs. This test proved to have high test–retest reliability (Krahenbuhl, Pangrazi, Petersen, Burkett, & Schneider, 1978). In young trained runners, the correlation between peak $\dot{V}O_2$ and race time is high (Cunningham, 1990; Unnithan, 1993).

- **Maximum heart rate.** Whereas resting heart rate values of older adults are comparable with those of young adults, the maximum achievable heart rate with physical exertion gradually declines with aging (Lipsitz, 1989). Decreased maximum heart rate may be the major factor in reduced peak $\dot{V}O_2$ with aging (Hagburg et al., 1985).
- **Stroke volume.** The stroke volume of older adults may or may not decline with aging; research studies have yielded both results (see Stamford, 1988, for a review). Asymptomatic ischemic heart disease (affecting blood supply to the heart) may account for the equivocal results. Investigators using rigorous screening for heart disease may find no decrease in stroke volume, whereas researchers whose studies include participants with undetected disease may find a decrease (Safar, 1990).
- **Cardiac output.** Recall that cardiac output is the product of heart rate and stroke volume. Cardiac output at rest or with submaximal work is unchanged with aging. Healthy older adults experience a decline in cardiac output during heavy activity with a decline in peak $\dot{V}O_2$, and those with ischemic heart disease experience even greater decline as maximum heart rate and stroke volume both decrease. Cardiac output is much higher in adults who train aerobically than in sedentary adults.
- **Blood pressure.** Older adults reach their peak cardiac output at a lower intensity of work than do younger adults (Brandfonbrener, Landowne, & Shock, 1955; Shephard, 1978a). Older adults' more rigid arteries resist the volume of blood the heart pumps into them. This resistance is even greater if the person has atherosclerosis (the buildup of plaque on the artery walls). In turn, this resistance raises resting pulse pressure (the difference between systolic and diastolic blood pressure) and systolic blood pressure. Whether blood pressure increases or decreases during exercise also depends on the health of the cardiac muscle fibers and their ability to tolerate an increased workload. A lifestyle that includes regular physical activity is associated with lower systolic blood pressure (Reaven, Barrett-Connor, & Edelstein, 1991).
- **Blood flow and hemoglobin content.** For activity to be sustained, oxygen must be delivered to the working muscles by the blood. Peripheral blood flow is apparently well maintained in older adulthood. Hemoglobin is also maintained in older adulthood (Timiras & Brownstein, 1987), but the incidence of anemia increases. This condition is associated with reduced hemoglobin values.

▶ **KEY POINT** Peak $\dot{V}O_2$ declines throughout adulthood, a trend that is related to a decrease in maximum heart rate and in muscle mass. Active older adults maintain an edge in peak $\dot{V}O_2$ over those who are sedentary.

Respiratory Structure and Function

Forced vital capacity is the maximum volume of air the lungs can expel after maximal inspiration.

Elasticity of the lung tissue and chest walls declines with aging (Turner, Mead, & Wohl, 1968). Therefore, older adults expend more effort in breathing than young adults. Of interest is the lung volume, especially the volume termed **forced vital capacity**. A large vital capacity reflects a large inspiratory capacity of the lungs and results in better alveolar ventilation. Because the greatest part of oxygen diffusion to the capillaries takes place at the alveoli (figure 10.4), better alveolar ventilation contributes to increased amounts of oxygen circulating in the blood and reaching the working muscles.

A decreased vital capacity with aging is well established; the average decrease is 4% to 5% per decade (Norris, Shock, Landowne, & Falzone, 1956; Shephard, 1987). The loss is more dramatic in smokers than in nonsmokers, and well-trained persons in their 40s are known to maintain the vital capacity of their 20s (Shephard, 1987).

The oxygen and carbon dioxide exchange in the lungs loses some efficiency with aging, and this decline is not offset by training (Dempsey, Johnson, & Saupe, 1990). Generally, though, the pulmonary systems of older adults do well at rest and during moderate activity. Moreover, the pulmonary system is not the major limiting factor in exercise capacity.

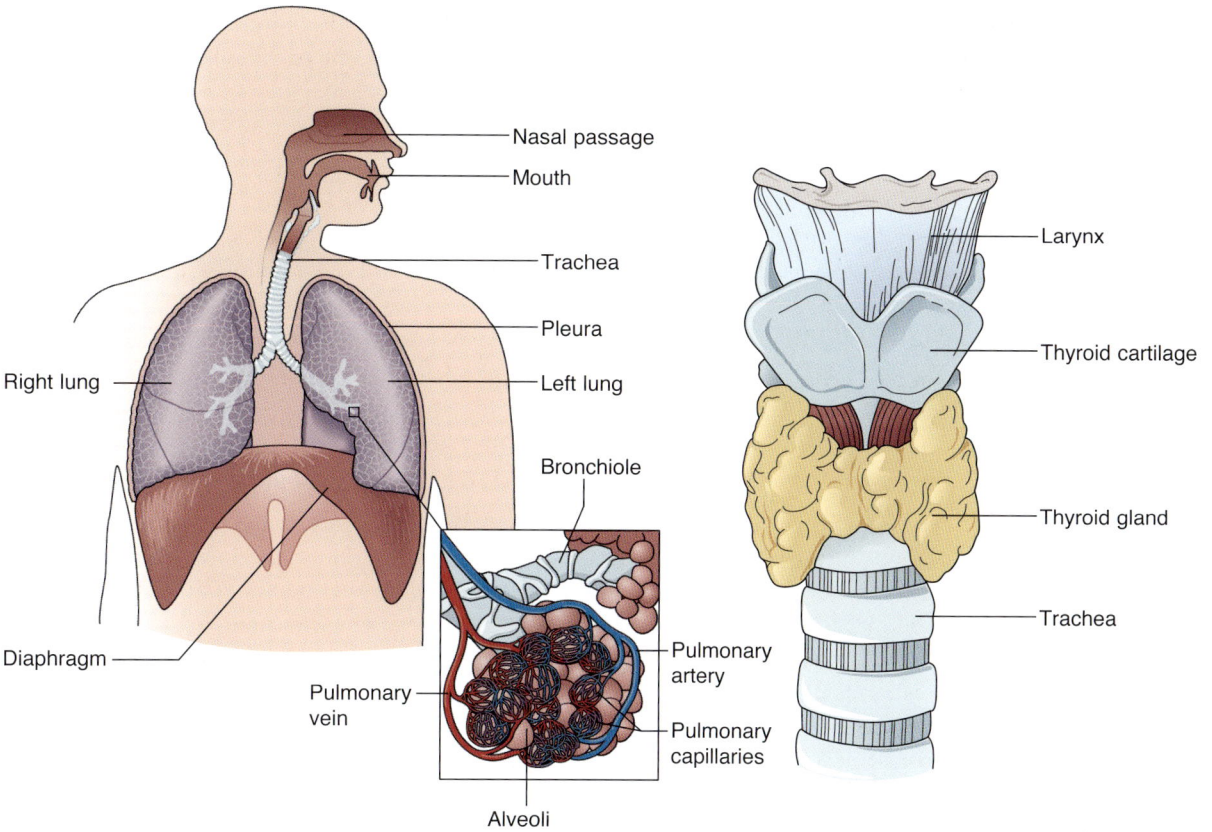

FIGURE 10.4 The respiratory system. Oxygen diffusion to the capillaries takes place at the alveoli, enlarged in the figure.

▶ **KEY POINT** Cardiovascular factors are a greater limitation to older adults' aerobic performance than are pulmonary factors.

Changes in Muscle Mass

The decline in peak $\dot{V}O_2$ is probably related to loss of muscle mass and the ability of muscles to use oxygen as well as to cardiovascular and respiratory changes. Recall that peak $\dot{V}O_2$ measures the amount of oxygen delivered to and used by the muscles. So the more muscle mass, the more likely that peak $\dot{V}O_2$ is greater. In fact, when peak $\dot{V}O_2$ is related to the kilograms of muscle (rather than kilograms of body weight) in older adults, declines shrink from 60% to 14% in men and 50% to 8% in women (Spirduso, 1995). Thus, maintenance of muscle mass is a factor in minimizing the loss of endurance performance. The addition of adipose tissue with aging works against maintenance of peak $\dot{V}O_2$.

The end result of cardiac and pulmonary changes and of the loss of muscle mass is that maximum exercise capacity and peak $\dot{V}O_2$ (whether absolute or relative to body weight) decline as an adult ages, and the recovery period after vigorous activity lengthens. The results of both longitudinal and cross-sectional studies are plotted in figure 10.5, and a decline with advancing age is evident. A lifetime of negative environmental factors, such as smoking or poor nutrition, can contribute to or accelerate the changes. Conversely, a lifetime of exposure to positive environmental factors, such as healthful exercise, can better maintain endurance levels.

If you were a personal trainer with older adult clients, what types of training activities would you plan in order to help them improve their aerobic performance?

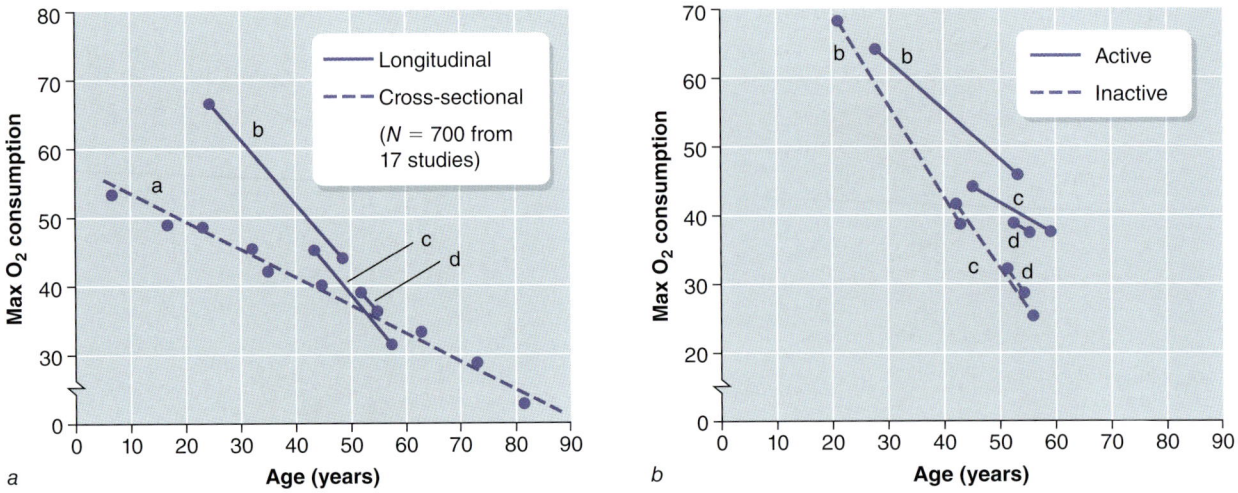

FIGURE 10.5 Maximal oxygen uptake declines as a person ages. *(a)* Cross-sectional studies and longitudinal studies show declines in adulthood. *(b)* The decline is not as rapid in active adults. The dotted lines represent the change in inactive adults, and the solid lines represent the change in active adults. Data plotted are from *(a)* Dehn and Bruce (1972), *(b)* Dill et al. (1967), *(c)* Hollman (1965), and *(d)* Dehn and Bruce (1972) (all cited in Dehn & Bruce, 1972).

Reprinted by permission from Stamford (1986, pg. 344).

Changes with growth and aging dramatically affect endurance performance throughout the life span. Various systems can constrain the potential for vigorous, sustained activity. It is important for everyone to have some knowledge of how the various systems influence aerobic activity because of the health implications of regular participation in aerobic activity. Moreover, educators and therapists must understand these influences thoroughly in order to promote training that yields significant health benefits.

Training Programs in Adulthood

Peak $\dot{V}O_2$ declines with aging, even in those who train, yet training and active adults have higher peak $\dot{V}O_2$ values than do sedentary adults (Hollenberg, Yang, Haight, & Tager, 2006) (figure 10.6). This finding shows that training programs for adults yield benefits. Let's consider two groups: (1) adults who maintain an active lifestyle and (2) sedentary adults who take up training.

First, evidence exists (Dehn & Bruce, 1972; Drinkwater, Horvath, & Wells, 1975; Kasch, Boyer, Van Camp, Verity, & Wallace, 1990; Shephard, 1978b; Smith & Serfass, 1981) that declines are not as dramatic in older adults who remain active as in those who become sedentary. Figure 10.5*b* shows that the decline in peak $\dot{V}O_2$ is steeper in inactive (dotted line) than in active (solid line) adults with advancing age. Vigorous training can even keep peak $\dot{V}O_2$ steady for a time in older adults (figure 10.6; Kasch & Wallace, 1976). Prolonged training can sharply reduce the decline in peak $\dot{V}O_2$. In a 28-year longitudinal study, Kasch et al. (1995) observed only a 5% per decade decline in men between 43 and 71 years of age who maintained exercise training compared with a 19% per decade decline in nonexercisers. Capelli et al. (2016) recorded a decrease of approximately 16% per decade in the cycling times of masters athletes.

Second, older adults can significantly increase their peak $\dot{V}O_2$ with a good training program (Posner, Gorman, Klein, & Woldow, 1986; Shephard, 1978b), even if they had undertaken little training earlier in their lives and even into their 70s (Hagburg et al., 1989; Stamford, 1973). Improvements range from 10% to 25% (Blumenthal et al., 1991; Shephard, 1987). These gains are not as high in absolute terms as those in younger people who begin training but are similar to those gains in the young in relative terms. Even low-intensity training can be very effective for older adults early in their exercise programs. Inactive older adults taking up aerobic training also improve in other strength and mobility tasks (Kalapotharakos, Michalopoulos, Strimpakos, Diamantopoulos, & Tokmakidis, 2006) and improve their blood lipids (Ring-Dimitriou et al., 2007).

▶ **KEY POINT** Adults benefit from aerobic training because it minimizes the decline in performance that would otherwise accompany aging.

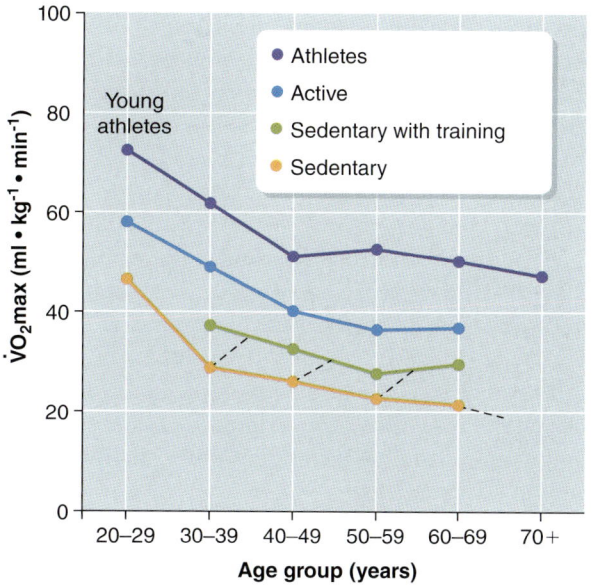

FIGURE 10.6 These average peak $\dot{V}O_2$ values for the adult years show that activity is associated with higher values, although all groups (active and inactive) experience decline. The dotted lines represent improvement in sedentary adults with training.

Reprinted by permission from Spirduso, Francis, and MacRae (2005, pg. 108).

What mechanisms are involved in the improvements in older adults with training? Undoubtedly, training maintains or improves muscle mass. As mentioned previously, more muscle mass is associated with higher peak $\dot{V}O_2$. Fit older adults also have larger vital capacity than sedentary older adults (Shephard, 1993). Information about the cardiovascular system is available from a case study of Clarence DeMar, who ran 12 miles a day throughout his life and competed in marathons at age 65. The autopsy performed after his death from cancer at age 70 showed well-developed cardiac muscle, normal valves, and coronary arteries two to three times the size normally seen in individuals of his age (Brandfonbrener et al., 1955).

Although the benefits of endurance training even at low intensity are well established for the older adult, vigorous work can still overwhelm the diseased heart. Older adults with cardiovascular disease should participate in programs designed specifically for this population. The guiding principle in designing training programs for older adults as well as for children is a gradual increase in exercise intensity and duration.

Web Study Guide **Compare age group records for aerobic and anaerobic events and identify trends in performance among older adults in Lab Activity 10.2, Aerobic and Anaerobic Performance in Older Adulthood, in the web study guide.**

Long-Term Training Effects

Despite the body's favorable response to training at any age, the question arises of whether active youths have an advantage over their sedentary counterparts in maintaining endurance into older adulthood. Ideally, researchers would address this question through long-term longitudinal studies; however, the difficulties involved in obtaining longitudinal data (necessary time and expense and subject attrition) make such research scarce.

In the absence of longitudinal research, consider a few cross-sectional studies that suggest an answer to the question. Trappe et al. (2013) identified nine lifelong endurance athletes—cross-country skiers—over 80 years of age. To be included in the study, these octogenarians must have trained consistently a minimum of 50 years. The men were age-matched to a group of men who were healthy but untrained. All participants wore a pedometer for two weeks to verify that the endurance athletes recorded significantly more steps per day than the untrained men. When the study participants were tested on a maximal cycle test to assess aerobic capacity, the lifelong endurance athletes had a significantly higher aerobic capacity and a higher final workload. In fact, the measurements were the highest recorded at that time in humans over 80 years of age. At the very least, this hints that lifelong endurance exercise has a positive influence on endurance levels in older adulthood, possibly through maintenance of the plasticity of physiological systems, benefiting overall health while reducing risk of disability and mortality.

Trudeau, Laurencelle, Tremblay, Rajic, and Shephard (1998) followed up with participants 20 years after their participation in a semi-longitudinal study. The treatment group in the original study took a 1-hour specialized physical education class five times per week during their 6 years of elementary school. The control group performed just 40 minutes of exercise per week during that time. As adults, women from the treatment group exercised three or more times per week more often than women from the control group. The men did not differ. More men and women from the treatment group than the control group self-reported their health to be very good to excellent.

Telama, Yang, Laakso, and Viikari (1997) also followed up on participants 9 and 12 years after they initially answered a questionnaire about their leisure activities (at the ages of 9, 12, 15, and 18 years). The correlations between youth and adult activity were low but significant. A line of longitudinal studies also shows that persistent participation in organized youth sports programs and competitions predicted physical activity levels in young adulthood (Telama, Yang, Hirvensalo, & Raitakari, 2006).

Despite the limitations of these studies, the evidence suggests that regular activity in youth has positive lifelong benefits. Promoting an active lifestyle among children and youths could predispose them to be more active as adults (figure 10.7). Nevertheless, the most important factor for endurance is the individual's current activity level. At all ages, the capacity for prolonged, vigorous work tends to be transitory. People maintain (or improve) endurance if they are currently training for endurance; conversely, endurance capacity decreases when people discontinue their training programs.

FIGURE 10.7 Endurance capacity is positively related to training, especially after puberty. Moreover, regular activity in childhood might predispose individuals to be more active in adulthood. Perhaps functional constraints such as a positive attitude toward exercise persist over the life span.

Think ahead to your own potential lifestyle 20 years from now. What is your plan for staying active? What physical activities do you plan to include in your life?

Summary and Synthesis

Endurance for vigorous activities, whether short or long term, improves as the body grows. In addition, an individual can increase endurance by training, although the effects are transitory. A person must maintain training in order to preserve higher levels of endurance and reap the associated benefits.

After the adolescent growth spurt, sex

differences in working capacity are apparent. The causes of these differences are still open to discussion, but body size, body composition, and hemoglobin levels are at least partially responsible. Many people still do not engage in regular exercise. It remains to be seen whether messages about the importance of an active lifestyle will result in more individuals at every age becoming more active or whether advances in technologies such as virtual reality will lead individuals to be even more sedentary.

Reinforcing What You Have Learned About Constraints

TAKE A SECOND LOOK

Our discussion of cardiorespiratory endurance helps us appreciate the interaction between this component of physical fitness and the performance of motor skills. Endurance is necessary for the performance of many skills and physical activities of daily living. In addition, appropriate training for endurance supports growth and maintenance of the body's systems such that participants are in better overall health and enjoy a better quality of life. However, the availability of technology in Westernized countries, including computers and gaming systems, tempts people to be more and more sedentary. Sedentary lifestyles at any age lead to a decline in the cardiac, respiratory, and vascular systems. This decline eventually results in a performance decrement and, with advancing age, greater risk of threats to good health. Other body systems, such as the neurological system, also can suffer from a sedentary lifestyle, which in turn can lead to a reduced quality of life.

Other components of physical fitness include muscular strength and flexibility, and performance of many sport and everyday living activities depends on a minimal level of strength and flexibility. Chapter 11 examines these two fitness components, which interact with task and environmental constraints in giving rise to movements.

TEST YOUR KNOWLEDGE

1. How do anaerobic endurance and aerobic endurance change with growth in childhood? How do they change with aging?
2. Can prepubescent children improve anaerobic endurance with training? Aerobic endurance? Explain your answers.
3. What are the sex differences in anaerobic and aerobic endurance over the life span? To what factors might these differences be attributed?
4. At what points in the life span can individuals improve aerobic endurance with training? Do those who build higher endurance in youth realize a lifelong benefit? What types of studies best answer this question? Why?
5. How is anaerobic endurance measured? Aerobic endurance? What is the difference between power and capacity in the measurement of anaerobic and aerobic endurance?
6. Do we know whether being active as a child or teen makes a difference in fitness levels in adulthood? On what do you base your answer?
7. How does maturity affect anaerobic and aerobic endurance in youth?
8. If you wanted to predict a youth's endurance level, would you base your prediction on age, size, maturity, or some combination of these? Why?
9. What factors tend to limit the aerobic endurance of older adults? The anaerobic endurance?

LEARNING EXERCISE 10.1

Testing Children and Teens for Endurance

Locate five research articles on endurance or aerobic performance in children and teens. You can use articles referenced in this text, perform an electronic search, or check a journal such as *Pediatric Exercise Science*. Once you have located the articles, read about the methods the authors used to conduct their research (typically described in a section titled Methods). Note the age and sex of the participants, and summarize how endurance performance was tested. What was similar and what was different about how each set of researchers tested endurance? What accommodations, if any, were made for the ages of the participants?

11

Development of Strength and Flexibility

CHAPTER OBJECTIVES

This chapter

- explores the relationship between muscle mass and strength and how these change in relation to each other over the life span,
- reviews the effects of strength training over the life span,
- describes changes in flexibility over the life span, and
- reviews the effects of flexibility training by individuals of any age.

Motor Development in the Real World

Super Athletes

It is not uncommon to hear about athletes who have been suspended or banned from their sport or who have been stripped of medals or championships because a drug test was positive. Despite clear rules in most organized sports against the use of supplements such as anabolic steroids, some athletes feel pressured to gain an edge over their competition by using these substances. Many of these supplements help athletes increase muscle mass quickly by allowing them to recover sooner from strenuous training. Because muscle mass is related to strength, these athletes gained a strength advantage over other competitors. The importance of strength, as well as flexibility, to performance of motor skills and tasks is widely recognized today, as we see by the risks some performers are willing to take in order to reach higher levels of strength and flexibility.

Strength and flexibility are obvious constraints to skilled performance; sometimes, in fact, skills can be performed only if one has sufficient strength. You might recall that we suspect leg strength is a rate limiter for infant standing. You also might know older adults who have difficulty climbing stairs after they have lost leg strength. Flexibility is also a necessity for many activities. Gymnasts and high jumpers work on their flexibility to perform skills. Senior golfers sometimes exhibit swings that reflect a loss of flexibility.

Today's coaches have come to realize that strength and flexibility are related. Athletes are at their best when they are strong *and* supple. Training that promotes increased muscle mass at the expense of flexibility puts athletes at risk of injury. Muscle balance is a goal of training today. Muscle strength should be built for all directions of joint movement (e.g., flexion and extension), and flexibility through the appropriate and full range of motion should be fostered. This chapter considers changes over the life span as well as the effects of training throughout the life span, first in strength and then in flexibility.

Muscle Mass and Strength

As noted in chapter 8, muscle mass follows a sigmoid growth pattern, and this growth is largely the result of an increase in muscle fiber diameter. Sex differences are minimal until puberty, when boys add significantly more muscle mass than girls do, especially in the upper body. Loss of muscle is small from young adulthood until the age of 50, but thereafter the average loss can be pronounced. The loss is greater for sedentary individuals with poor nutrition.

Strength is the ability to exert force.

What about muscle **strength**? Does it simply parallel the changes in muscle mass? Strength-training programs are promoted for individuals of all ages. What effect does resistance training have on strength and muscle mass, especially before the adolescent growth spurt? What about in older adulthood, when muscle mass is typically lost?

These are important questions to answer. Many skills require a certain level of strength, such as the gymnastics skills performed on parallel bars. Some skills can be performed better with more strength, such as baseball batting. Even activities of daily living can become difficult without sufficient strength. Older adults who have lost much of their strength have difficulty with everyday tasks, such as getting out of the bathtub or climbing the stairs, and they are often at greater risk of falling.

If you were a therapist, what activities of daily living would you include in the clinic that might be difficult or even risky for an individual who has lost strength because of disease, disability, or aging?

The amount of force a muscle group exerts depends on the fibers (muscle cells) that are neurologically activated and on leverage (the mechanical advantage the muscle fibers gain based on where force is applied in relation to an axis of rotation). In turn, the fibers activated depend on the cross-sectional area of the muscle and on the degree of coordination in activating the fibers (i.e., the nervous system's pattern and timing in innervating the various motor units to bring about the desired movement). The cross-sectional area of muscle increases with growth in youth, which means that strength increases as muscles grow, but muscle mass is not the only factor in strength. Neurological factors are also involved, and neurological changes over the life span influence muscle strength. Therefore, we cannot assume that strength changes simply as muscle mass changes. Keeping this in mind, let's see how strength changes over the life span.

▶ **KEY POINT** Muscle strength is related to muscle size, but changes in strength do not always parallel changes in muscle size.

Development of Strength

Strength is certainly one of the individual structural constraints that change with growth and aging. We know that body systems, especially the muscular system, also change with growth and aging, so we examine changes in strength and the impact of training over periods of the life span, starting with youth.

Development of Strength in Youth

Strength increases steadily as children grow older (figure 11.1). Boys and girls have similar strength levels until they are about 13 years old, although boys are very slightly stronger than girls of the same height during childhood. During adolescence, the number of girls who can equal boys on strength measures declines, and by 16 years of age, few girls can match an average measure for boys (Malina, Bouchard, & Bar-Or, 2004).

We know that muscle mass also increases steadily as children grow older, so how is strength related to muscle mass in childhood? Wood, Dixon, Grant, and Armstrong (2006) measured the elbow flexor strength, muscle size, and moment arm length (the perpendicular distance between the joint center, or axis of rotation, and the muscle tendon's point of attachment to the bone) of 38 boys and girls around 10 years of age. The latter two values

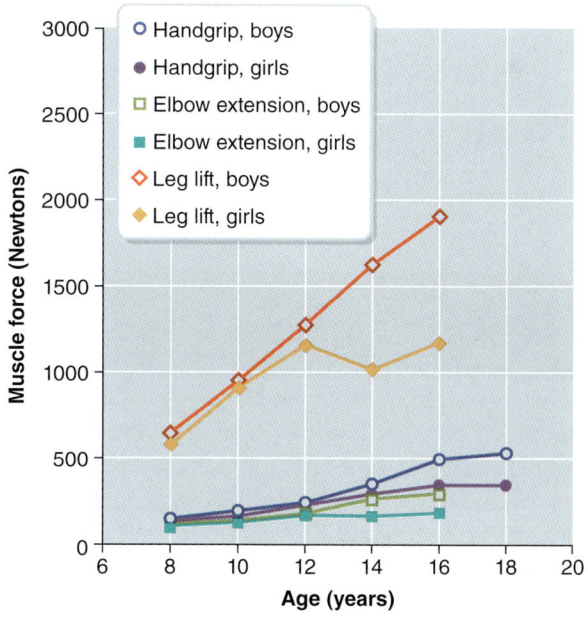

FIGURE 11.1 Development of isometric strength. Boys (open symbols) continue to steadily improve in isometric strength throughout adolescence whereas girls (filled symbols) tend to plateau. Graph is based on data accumulated by Shephard (1978b) for handgrip and on unpublished results of Howell, Loiselle, and Lucas (1966) for other measures. Based on Shepard (1982).

Assessing Strength

Isotonic strength is the exertion of force against constant resistance through the range of motion at a joint.

Isokinetic strength is the exertion of force at a constant limb velocity through the range of motion at a joint.

Isometric strength is the exertion of force without a change in muscle length (i.e., without movement of a limb).

In strength assessments, individuals typically exert maximal force against resistance. They might move their limbs, as in an **isotonic** test (constant resistance, as in lifting a barbell) or **isokinetic** test (constant speed of movement, as with a Cybex machine), or they might exert force against an immovable resistance, as in an **isometric** test. To compare results between individuals, those conducting the assessment must report several kinds of information:

- The muscle group, such as knee flexors or elbow extensors
- The movement, such as knee flexion or elbow extension
- The speed of movement, usually in degrees per second

For isometric tests, the angle of the joint (in degrees) as force is exerted must also be recorded because a muscle group can exert different levels of force at different joint angles.

A common isotonic strength test is a 1-repetition maximum (1RM) lift of a free weight such as a barbell. As a limb moves through a range of motion, force production is maximal at one point and thus submaximal at other points. The 1RM test therefore indicates forces that can be sustained at the weaker ranges of joint motion. If an isokinetic exercise machine is used, movement speed is kept constant and the device automatically provides an adjusted counterforce. A force–velocity curve is generated, and the peak on that curve indicates the maximal strength achieved at the strongest joint angle. Because the 1RM test is difficult (and potentially dangerous) for novices, scales have been developed that estimate 1RM weight based on the maximum number of lifts at a given lower weight.

Several devices assess isometric strength. The spring-loaded dynamometer requires individuals to compress a handle, and their exertion is registered. Alternatively, the individual can pull on an anchored cable with a handle. A tensiometer is placed on the cable and registers the force of exertion. Dynamometers and tensiometers usually measure in Newtons, a measurement unit for force.

In school settings, functional tests of strength are often used with children. Among these are chin-ups, the flexed-arm hang, and rope climbing. Note that body weight is used as the resistance in these tasks, so body weight is a factor in performance levels. Some of these tasks also require skills, such as rope climbing, and the skill factor must be considered in interpreting test results.

were assessed using MRI. The largest contribution to strength was the cross-sectional area of the elbow flexor muscles. In children, then, strength is greatly related to muscle mass. In fact, Barrett and Harrison (2002) found that children matched adults in the functional ability of muscle per unit of muscle volume, implying that muscle size plays a large factor in child–adult strength differences.

Other factors might be involved in strength levels. Consider the age at which individuals reach peak gains in muscle mass and strength. As noted in chapter 8, peak gain (the peak in the velocity curve) indicates the point of the fastest increase. If strength development directly follows muscle mass development, the peak gain in strength would coincide with the peak gain in muscle mass. In turn, teachers and coaches could predict children's strength levels by simply measuring their muscle mass, which can be estimated from weight measurements or by subtracting a child's estimated fat weight from body weight.

However, these peak gains do not coincide with each other in most adolescents. For example, Rasmussen, Faulkner, Mirwald, and Bailey (1990) conducted a longitudinal study with boys and found that peak muscle mass velocity occurred at an average age of 14.3 years, but peak strength velocity occurred at 14.7 years. This sequence of peak muscle mass velocity followed by peak strength velocity probably reflects increasing hormone levels and their effect on the protein structure and enzyme systems of the muscle fibers. Thus, the endocrine system plays a role in strength increase with growth.

Another way to examine muscle growth and strength development is to relate measures of muscle strength to various body sizes in children and determine whether strength increases at the same rate as body size. In a well-known study from the 1950s, Asmussen and Heeboll-Nielsen (1955, 1956) divided boys of the same height into two age groups, one younger and one older by approximately 1.5 years. The older group showed greater arm and leg strength by about 5% to 10% per year of age. This experiment also demonstrates that strength is not related to muscle size alone. Neural influences that change with maturation can influence strength. These influences might include myelination of nerve fibers, improved muscle coordination (movement requires a contraction of some muscles and a coordinated relaxation of the muscles on the opposite aspect of the body), and improved extent of motor unit activation (Blimkie, 1989; Kraemer, Fry, Frykman, Conroy, & Hoffman, 1989; Sale, 1989). Only one of these neural influences—improved motor unit activation—has been examined experimentally. Blimkie (1989) found some support for the suggestion that older children can activate a greater proportion of motor units to exert force.

The studies mentioned thus far typically measured isometric strength directly with a cable tensiometer or a dynamometer. The benefit of measuring strength with this equipment is that the effects of skill, practice, and experience are minimized. However, these factors do influence the performance of sports skills, making studies of the development of functional muscle strength very useful.

▶ **KEY POINT** Functional strength tasks have a strength component and a skill component.

Two skills that involve functional muscle strength are vertical jumping and sprinting. Practice and experience, as well as leg strength, influence children's performance on both tasks. Asmussen and Heeboll-Nielsen (1955, 1956) measured performance on these two skills in successive height groups of Danish children. They found that functional muscle strength, just as isometric strength, increased at a faster rate than one would anticipate from muscle growth alone. Further, the rate of gain in functional muscle strength was even greater than the rate of gain in isometric strength, emphasizing again the role of neurological factors in improved muscle strength as children mature. More recent studies confirmed these findings (Parker, Round, Sacco, & Jones, 1990; Kanehisa, Yata, Ikegawa, & Fukunaga, 1995; Froberg & Lammert, 1996).

Web Study Guide **Plot data and analyze changes in functional strength in preadolescence in Lab Activity 11.1, Examining Trends in Strength Development, in the web study guide.**

▶ **KEY POINT** Strength increases gradually throughout childhood; boys experience a spurt of increased strength in adolescence, whereas strength increases steadily in girls.

As noted in chapter 9, boys gain more muscle mass in adolescence than girls do, largely as a result of higher levels of androgen secretion. It is no surprise, then, that boys undergo a spurt of increased strength at about age 13. Girls continue a steady increase in strength during adolescence before reaching a plateau. Fraser et al. (2017) were able to repeat strength and power measures of youths aged 9, 12, or 15 years some 20 years later. The measures remained relatively stable from youth to young adulthood.

Strength Training in Youth

Strength is often an individual constraint in the performance of motor tasks. The strength level of an individual interacts with the task and environment either to permit a task or not or to influence how a movement is performed. If strength training can change an individual's level of strength in a relatively short time, then clearly it becomes a means to help individuals perform tasks. It can change the point at which strength becomes a rate limiter for a given task or skill. Educators and therapists can intervene to change motor performance over a matter of weeks. Hence, we should take great interest in how strength training can change strength at any point in the life span. This section examines strength training in youth.

Research has documented that boys and girls as young as 6 or 7 years can increase their strength with a variety of resistance-training methods (figure 11.2). (Faigenbaum, Lloyd, & Myer, 2013; Shenouda, Wilson, & Fletcher, 2016). For example, Pfeiffer and Francis (1986) compared the strength of 14 prepubescent boys with that of a control group before and after a 9-week, 3-day-a-week training program. The boys trained on a Universal machine and with free weights, completing 3 sets of 10 repetitions in each session. Strength improved significantly in the young boys. In fact, the percentage increase was greater in the young boys than in the pubescent and postpubescent boys Pfeiffer and Francis also tested (figure 11.3). Others have confirmed that although postpubertal individuals gain more absolute strength with training, prepubertal individuals gain more strength expressed as a percentage change from their starting strength (Sale, 1989).

Fritz, Rosengren, Dencker, Karlsson, and Karlsson (2016) demonstrated the impact of increased physical education time on strength. They started with children 6 to 9 years of age and

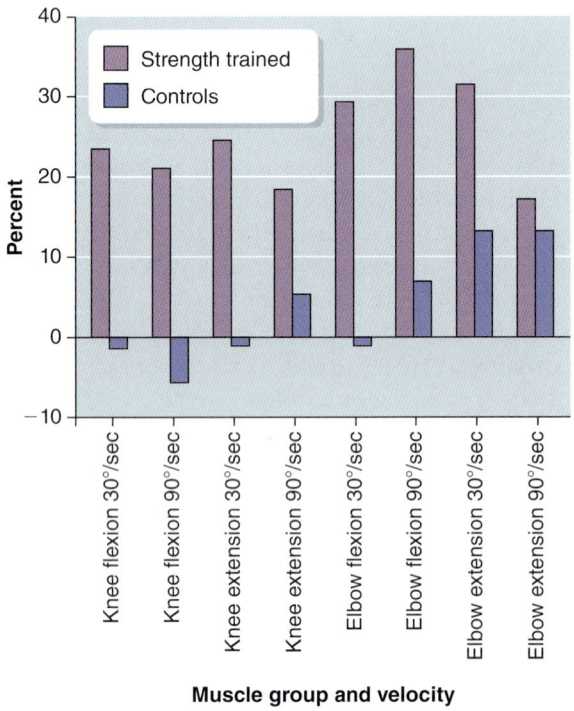

FIGURE 11.2 Muscle strength increases with training. Compared with their nontraining counterparts, prepubescent boys achieved larger relative increases in the strength of four muscle groups at two speeds of movement.

Reprinted by permission from Malina, Bouchard, O. Bar-O (2004, pg. 495).

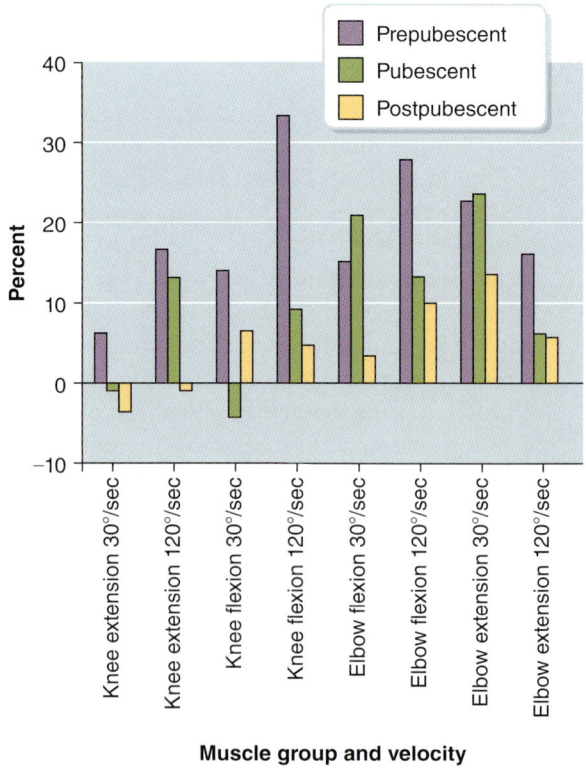

FIGURE 11.3 Percentage increases in strength with training. Prepubescent boys generally achieved larger relative increases in the strength of four muscle groups at two speeds of movement with 9 weeks of training than did pubescent or postpubescent boys.

Reprinted by permission from Malina, Bouchard, O. Bar-O (2004, pg. 498).

increased their time in physical education to 200 minutes per week for 7 years. Compared with children receiving only 60 minutes per week, the intervention group had significantly higher knee flexion strength and more tibia cortical thickness at the end of the 7 years. Girls also had more spine bone mass, so this increased training had a favorable impact on both strength and the skeletal system.

Faigenbaum, Milliken, Moulton, and Westcott (2005) considered whether low- or high-repetition-maximum resistance training is better. Although boys and girls increased their strength with either approach far more than a control group did, the high-repetition group demonstrated gains in muscle endurance and flexibility as well. Behm et al. (2017) conducted a meta-analysis of studies comparing strength and power training. There was evidence that each type of training had the greatest impact on like performance—strength training for strength measures and power training for power measures. A benefit to introducing strength training before power training was noted. The importance of continued strength training in youth was observed in both pre- and early pubertal boys (Ingle, Sleap, & Tolfrey, 2006). An increase in strength was observed after a 12-week training program, but strength gains were lost when the boys stopped training.

Several investigators found that increased muscle size did not accompany increased strength in prepubescents (Ramsay et al., 1990; Sale, 1989; Weltman et al., 1986). What, then, accounts for the strength increase? As noted previously, strength is related both to muscle size and to the central nervous system's ability to fully activate muscles. Improvement in prepubescents with training likely results from their improved ability to exert force in the intended direction as they are better able to activate the agonist (contracting) muscles and coordinate the antagonist (lengthening) muscles (Sale, 1989).

▶ **KEY POINT** Prepubescent children can increase strength with training, even without an accompanying increase in muscle size.

Even if prepubescent children can improve their strength with training, does such training involve negative effects? Children's bones are still growing and could be susceptible to injury at both traction and pressure epiphyses. Weight training could potentially cause a single traumatic injury or chronic injury from repeated lifts. Also, some professionals who work with children are concerned that a loss of flexibility or even stature may accompany strength training. Research studies have found no damage to bones or muscles due to training (Falk & Eliakim, 2003; Gunter, Almstedt, & Janz, 2012) and little risk of injury (Faigenbaum & Myer, 2010). In one study in which 27 prepubescent boys were observed over 2 years of a twice-weekly resistance-training program, only one minor injury occurred, and there were no differences in height compared with a nontraining group (Sadres, Eliakim, Constantini, Lidor, & Falk, 2001). All the prepubescents in these studies were closely monitored, so close supervision of training programs is prudent, especially programs using free weights. Researchers find no loss of flexibility with resistance training (Rians, et al., 1987; Servedio et al., 1985; Sewall & Micheli, 1986; Siegel, Camaione, & Manfredi, 1989). With the benefits of resistance exercise for prepubescent children firmly established, resistance exercise has become a common part of curricula in elementary school physical education (figure 11.4).

Imagine you are a middle school physical education teacher who is planning resistance-training activities. What are some important constraints to consider when implementing a training program for children? Think of individual structural and functional constraints as well as task and environmental constraints.

Developmentalists generally accept that strength training also has beneficial effects for adolescents. Pfeiffer and Francis (1986) demonstrated that pubescent and postpubescent boys improved their strength with training. Other training methods yield the same result, including isometric training (Nielsen, Nielsen, Hansen, & Asmussen, 1980) and plyometric training (Steben & Steben, 1981). Compared with adults undertaking the same training, adolescents have shown a higher recovery capacity between sets (Tibana et al., 2012) and greater gains in explosive power (Pesta et al., 2014). Adolescents, like children, should be closely supervised when using weight training to improve strength. Their bones are still growing, and they are susceptible to a variety of musculoskeletal injuries if unsupervised (Risser & Preston, 1989).

Imagine you are a physical education teacher. What activities not typically labeled "resistance training" might still improve leg strength? Upper body strength? Are any of these typically gender stereotyped?

FIGURE 11.4 Increasing muscle mass with growth—a structural constraint—leads to increased strength, but resistance training also increases strength over the life span.

After puberty, muscle **hypertrophy** can accompany regular strength training. As noted previously, adolescent boys add far more muscle mass than do adolescent girls during the growth spurt. Do the sexes also differ in their response to training? Cureton, Collins, Hill, and McElhannon (1988) placed young adult men and women on a weight-training program in which the resistance level was 70% to 90% of the individual's maximum. Men and women gained strength at identical levels in terms of percentage increase, but men gained more strength in terms of absolute increase for two of four tests. For example, men and women might increase 5%, but if the men were stronger at the start, their increase was greater in absolute terms. Both men and women experienced muscle hypertrophy in their upper arms, again by an identical percentage increase, although one measure yielded a greater absolute increase in men. After puberty, then, both improved coordination in recruiting the muscle units needed to exert force and muscle hypertrophy response to strength training appear to be similar in males and females in relative terms. Muscle hypertrophy is more noticeable in adolescent boys and men in that a percentage increase of a larger muscle mass yields greater absolute dimensions.

▶ **KEY POINT** Adolescents can increase strength and muscle mass with training.

Year-to-year comparisons of strength measurements taken between ages 7 and 17 years show that the strongest children are not necessarily the strongest adolescents (Rarick & Smoll, 1967), correlations being low to only moderately high (Malina, 1996). The weakest 7-year-olds might be late maturers who eventually catch up to or pass their peers. Also, weaker children who initiate participation in physical activity or even resistance training can increase strength and surpass children who become or remain sedentary.

Development of Strength in Adulthood

As a result of differential growth of muscle mass during adolescence the average adult man is stronger than the average adult woman. Women can produce only 60% to 80% of the force that men can exert, although most of these differences can be attributed to differences in arm and shoulder strength rather than in trunk or leg strength (Asmussen, 1973). As noted in chapter 9, sex differences in muscle mass are more pronounced in the arms and shoulders than in the trunk and legs.

However, the average difference in body or muscle size accounts for only half the difference in strength between men and women. Cultural norms probably play a role when the sexes are measured for strength. These norms, of course, begin to exert their influence very early in life. For example, Shephard (1982) noted the effect of repeating strength measures on boys and girls who have never been tested for strength. Whereas the boys showed no tendency to improve over three visits, the girls improved on each subsequent visit in almost every case and improved significantly on two of the eight strength measures (figure 11.5). It is possible that the task gained acceptability to the girls as they became more familiar with it. The boys may have been more used to all-out demonstrations of strength. Girls at that time were probably not encouraged to go all out and might even have been discouraged from doing so, which would have limited their experience in exerting strength. Neither should motivation be discounted as a major factor in strength measurement. Certainly, if Shephard had recorded only the first set of scores, he would have concluded that the sex differences in strength were much greater than what he found after comparing the third set of scores. Clearly, cultural norms can be influenced by exposure, in this case experience with activities. Media can be influential in changing cultural norms. So, even women who did not participate in strength training as girls can begin training in young, middle, and older adulthood as they see strength training gain acceptability and participation increase among their peers. If measured for strength, these women might be more likely to feel comfortable giving a maximal effort.

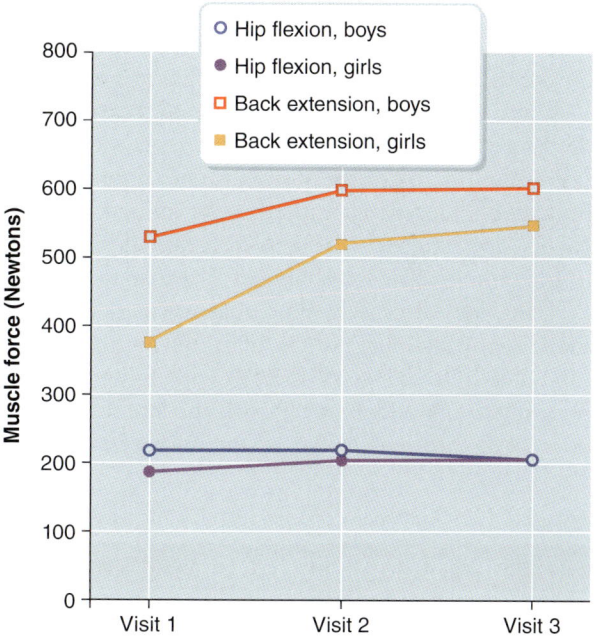

FIGURE 11.5 The effect of test repetition on muscle force measurement. When repeated visits were measured, girls improved on these strength measures whereas boys showed little or no change.

Based on Shepard (1982).

If you were a coach or personal trainer of young girls, how might you work to overcome any stigmas associated with weight training in order to help them improve their strength?

Some research has hinted that sex differences exist in muscle fiber composition—that is, that men and women do not have the same proportions of type I (slow-twitch) and type II (fast-twitch) muscle fibers. If so, part of the sex differences in strength might be attributed to muscle fiber composition. Animal studies indicate that muscle composition is related to isometric strength (see Komi, 1984, for a review). On the other hand, Davies, White, and Young (1983) could find no relationship between strength and muscle fiber composition in boys and girls 11 to 14 years of age. Much more research is needed on this topic with individuals of all ages.

Strength levels generally are maintained throughout the 20s and 30s. For the average adult, both isometric and isotonic strength decline thereafter. McKay et al. (2017) established the normative reference values for strength and flexibility of 1,000 healthy children and adults stratified into age groups of 3 to 9, 10 to 19, 20 to 59, and 60+ years. The norms for isometric strength in 12 muscle groups increased with age in childhood and adolescence. Norms decreased for some muscle groups in adulthood but for all muscle groups in older adulthood. From 10 years of age on, the norms were higher for males than females.

We see several trends in the overall decline of strength with aging; table 11.1, from Spirduso (1995), summarizes these trends. On the left are the better-maintained aspects of strength and on the right are the aspects that decline more in the general population.

These losses are what we would expect from the loss of muscle mass in older adulthood, yet the loss of strength might be larger than the loss of muscle mass. Young, Stokes, and Crowe (1985) found a 39% loss of strength but only a 25% loss in cross-sectional area in the quadriceps muscles of older men compared with younger men. Aniansson, Hedberg, Henning, and Grimby (1986) documented a 10% to 22% loss of strength (figure 11.6) but a 6% loss of muscle mass in the same muscle group over a 7-year span.

Thus, loss of muscle mass does not parallel loss of strength in older adulthood. Spirduso, Francis, and MacRae (2005) identified a number of factors, in addition to muscle atrophy, that can contribute to loss of strength with aging (figure 11.7). As illustrated, a decrease in activity, poor nutrition, and an increase in the likelihood of disease contribute to loss of strength either directly or through changes in the body systems.

TABLE 11.1 Summary of Strength Changes With Aging

BETTER MAINTENANCE	GREATER DECLINE
Muscles used in daily activities	Muscles used infrequently in specialized activities
Isometric strength	Dynamic strength
Eccentric contractions	Concentric contractions
Slow-velocity contractions	Rapid-velocity contractions
Repeated low-level contractions	Power production
Strength using small joint angles	Strength using large joint angles
Males' strength	Females' strength

Reprinted by permission from Spirduso (1995, pg. 127).

The nervous system might be involved because of a loss of motor neurons in the spinal cord with aging, resulting in a loss of motor units (Green, 1986; Grimby, 1988). Other units reinnervate some of the fibers of the lost motor neurons, such that the number of fibers per motor neuron increases (Campbell, McComas, & Petito, 1973; Fitts, 1981). The result would be a loss of muscular coordination, especially fine motor coordination. The vascular system also might be involved in the loss of strength. The number of capillaries per muscle fiber seems to decline with aging, but this is almost assuredly related to a trend toward inactivity (Cartee, 1994). In older adults who undertake aerobic exercise, the number of capillaries actually increases and muscle blood flow improves.

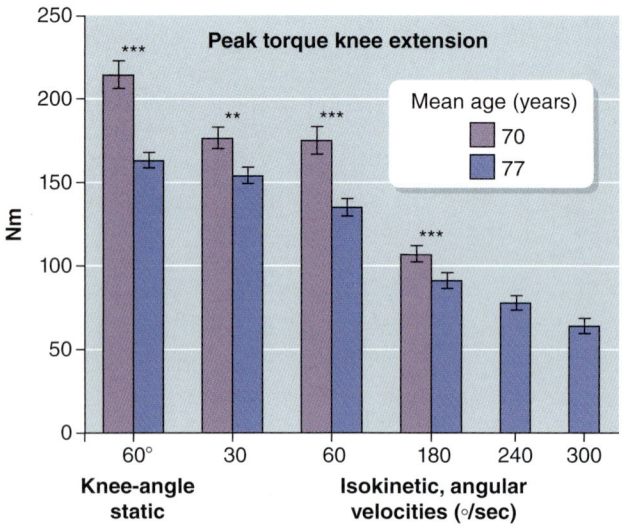

FIGURE 11.6 Changes in strength with aging. The average force (torque measured in Newton meters, Nm) exerted in a stationary knee position and at several speeds of knee extension decreased for 23 men over a 7-year interval. Changes are significant at the confidence levels of $p < .01$ (**) or $p < .001$ (***).

Reprinted from Aniansson et al. (1986, pg. 588).

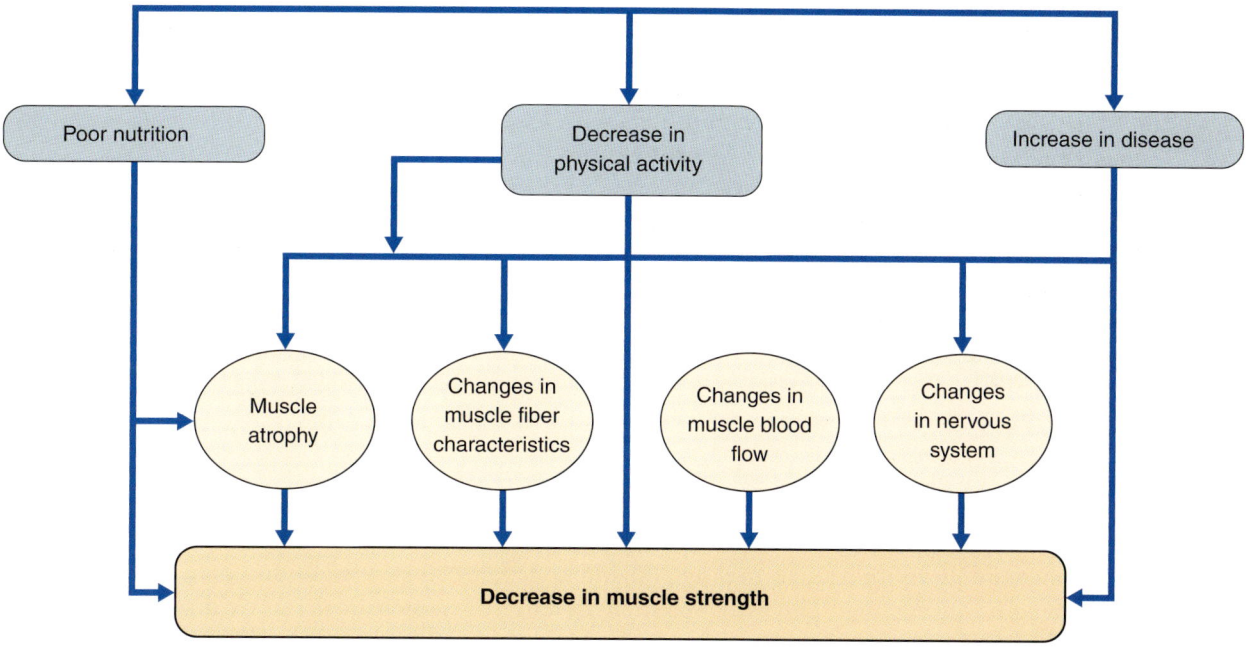

FIGURE 11.7 Factors contributing to the loss of muscle strength with aging.
Reprinted by permission from Spirduso, Francis, and MacRae (2005, pg. 112).

▶ **KEY POINT** In the absence of training, adults lose strength at a greater rate than would be expected based strictly on loss of muscle mass.

As with so many other aspects of aging, it is difficult to distinguish whether loss of muscle mass and strength in older adults is related to aging of tissues or disuse. We know that strength is better maintained in frequently used muscles than in infrequently used muscles (Kauffman, 1985; Wilmore, 1991). Kallman, Plato, and Tobin (1990) demonstrated how variable the loss of strength is among older adults. They observed young, middle-aged, and older adults over a 10-year period. Many of the older adults lost *less* strength than middle-aged and young adults lost during the 10 years, and some lost no strength at all. This variability most likely reflects extrinsic factors among these adults, especially exercise and activity levels, reminding us that significant loss of strength with aging is not a foregone conclusion. Next, we consider strength training in adulthood.

▶ **KEY POINT** Strength and muscle mass share the same five general phases of change over the life span (early increase, steady advancement, adolescent spurt, maintenance in adulthood, possible decline in older adulthood), yet the timing of those changes can be distinct, as can the degree of change.

Strength Training in Adulthood

An adult can increase muscle strength with strength training, which also results in a noticeable increase in muscle size. The effect is most noticeable in postpubescent men; hence, circulating testosterone was initially considered the stimulus for such increases in muscle size. In the past, this view probably led many to think that resistance, or weight, training was of limited use to other groups. The thinking has changed dramatically. Numerous online articles and television segments feature older adults who are taking up weight training. Rehabilitation programs focus on regaining strength after injury, even when the patient is not a professional athlete.

If you were a therapist, why would restoring the strength of someone not participating in sport be as important as restoring the strength of an athlete after disease or injury?

Young and middle-aged adults can maintain or even increase their strength through resistance training. Male soldiers improved push-up performance and leg power with just a 12-week resistance-training program (Kraemer et al., 2004). Even obese women not dieting increased their muscle strength with a 12-week training program (Sarsan, Ardic, Ozgen, Topuz, & Sermez, 2006). Women who had just gone through menopause improved muscle strength with a resistance-training program (Asikainen et al., 2006).

▶ **KEY POINT** Middle-aged and older adults can increase strength and muscle mass with training.

But what about older adulthood, when strength levels decline? Can older adults prevent or reverse losses in muscle mass and strength through training? Mayer et al. (2011) examined more than 1,500 articles published between 2005 and 2010 that addressed the effectiveness of resistance training in individuals over age 60 and concluded that older adults could increase their strength with training. This increased strength reflected an increase in muscle mass and an improved recruitment of motor units along with an increase in motor unit firing rate. Overall, these articles demonstrated that older adults could increase muscle mass by training at 60% to 85% of their maximum voluntary strength. Older adults could improve the rate of force development, but, just as with the young adults, this required a training intensity greater than 85%. Three to four training sessions per week yielded the best results.

Imagine you are a recreation leader who would like to increase the participation of older adults in fitness classes—especially classes that would increase strength—at a recreation center. How would you promote participation to the area's citizens? What activities would you schedule? How would you minimize the risk of injury for participants?

On the other hand, both low- and high-volume training improved muscle quality for older adults (Radaelli et al., 2013), and a short 6 weeks of training yielded improvement in older adults (Scanlon et al., 2014). Silva, Oliveira, Fleck, Leon, and Farinatti's (2014) meta-analysis of dose–response relationship studies indicates that many combinations of training variables improve strength, but the longer the training program duration for older adults, the greater the strength gains. Mayer et al. (2011) found no evidence that older adults need to train at relatively lighter loads than do young adults in order to avoid injury. Older adults benefitted from and tolerated classic training regimens of 3 or 4 sets of about 10 repetitions at 80% of 1RM, done three times per week for 8 to 12 weeks. Older adults at high risk for cardiac catastrophe or with osteoporosis (skeletal atrophy) or arthritis should train with light resistance and under the supervision of a knowledgeable professional.

After the growth period, increases in muscle mass are associated with resistance training. Some drugs used in conjunction with training can increase muscle mass at a rate greater than training alone, but most have unhealthy side effects. Electromyographic measurements of muscle activation in strength tasks show that improved strength in adults who are engaged in resistance training is related to improved neurological activation and increased muscle size. In fact, in the early weeks of training, most strength improvements are related to neurological factors because muscle has not yet increased in size (Moritani & DeVries, 1980). Some drugs used in conjunction with training can increase muscle mass at a rate greater than training alone, but they tend to have unhealthy side effects. This is one reason sport organizations usually ban their use among competitors.

▶ **KEY POINT** Resistance training is beneficial for increasing strength throughout the life span.

Summary of the Development of Strength

The typical pattern of strength change over the life span has five phases. In childhood, strength steadily increases. In adolescence, girls continue this steady increase but boys have a spurt of growth in strength. In the 20s and 30s, strength levels are relatively stable. After this, strength gradually declines until sometime in the 50s, when the loss becomes more dramatic.

This typical pattern can be changed by resistance training at any point in the life span. Parents, teachers, and therapists can change the movement that arises from the interaction of person, task, and environment by introducing resistance training to those in their care, thus changing an individual structural constraint.

Changes in strength tend to parallel changes in muscle mass. However, muscle mass is not the only factor involved in increased strength. Neurological factors play a large role; in fact, strength improvements in childhood with resistance training are largely related to neurological factors.

Development of Flexibility

Although muscle strength is important for the performance of skills, so is suppleness, or flexibility. Individuals must be able to move through full ranges of motion and position their limbs to undertake movements in sport and dance as well as in daily living. Optimal **flexibility** often benefits maximal performance at any age. On the other hand, limited flexibility is a factor in sport injuries and in restricted mobility; that is, flexibility can be a rate limiter. Young athletes sometimes overlook this important aspect of physical fitness, emphasizing endurance and strength at the expense of flexibility. Exceptions to this generalization are dancers and gymnasts, who have long realized the importance of flexibility in their activities. People typically view lack of flexibility as a problem only for older adults, whose movement limitations are more readily apparent, especially when individuals need help to perform activities of daily living. This section describes first the typical pattern of change in flexibility over the life span and then the effects of training and how it alters the typical pattern.

Flexibility is the ability to move joints through a full range of motion.

The range of motion possible at any joint depends on that joint's bone structure and on the soft tissues' resistance to movement. The soft tissues include muscles, tendons, joint capsules, ligaments, and skin. The belief that flexibility is related to limb length is incorrect. Habitual use and exercise preserve the elastic nature of the soft tissues, whereas disuse is associated with a loss of elasticity. To improve poor flexibility, a person must move the joint regularly and systematically through an increasingly larger range of motion to modify the soft tissues. Athletes, then, tend to increase the flexibility of joints they use in their sports, whereas laborers who spend much of their time in one posture may lose flexibility in some joints. It is likely that people who do not exercise fully lose flexibility because everyday activities rarely require movement through a full range of motion. Thus, at any age, flexibility reflects the normal range of movement to which an individual subjects specific joints.

An important characteristic of flexibility is its specificity to each joint. An individual can be relatively flexible at one joint and inflexible at another. In addition, genetic factors play a role. Schutte, Nederend, Hudziak, de Geus, and Bartels (2016) conducted a meta-analysis of studies testing the flexibility of identical and nonidentical twins and their siblings. The studies analyzed generally included individuals aged 10 years to early adulthood. Shutte et al. found that genetic factors play a large role in individual differences in flexibility.

Development of Flexibility in Youth

As mentioned in chapter 2, the 1950s, 1960s, and 1970s were a period of normative description in motor development. Researchers of this time measured flexibility of children and adolescents to describe any age-related differences. For example, Hupprich and Sigerseth (1950) administered 12 flexibility measures to 300 girls aged 6, 9, 12, 15, and 18 years. Most of the flexibility measurements improved across the 6-, 9-, and 12-year-old groups but declined in the older groups. After reviewing the information available in 1975, Clarke (1975) concluded that boys tend to lose flexibility after age 10 years and girls after age 12 years. Krahenbuhl and Martin (1977) found that flexibility in both boys and girls declined between ages 10 and 14, but Milne, Seefeldt, and Reuschlein (1976) reported that second graders in their study already had poorer flexibility than kindergartners. Girls as a group are usually more flexible than boys (Beunen, Malina, Renson, & Van Gerven, 1988; DiNucci, 1976; Phillips et al., 1955; Simons et al., 1990).

As the normative descriptive period waned, few comprehensive studies of age-related changes in flexibility were done, but recently two groups of researchers have sought to establish normative reference values for flexibility measures across the life span (McKay et al., 2017; Soucie et al., 2011). Soucie and colleagues determined the mean range of motion for four age groups: 2 to 8 years, 9 to 19 years, 20 to 44 years, and 45 to 69 years. They generally found that across all the joints they measured, the youngest age group had a greater range of motion than the oldest age group (figure 11.8). Women typically were more flexible than men, although the difference was not great in some joints.

McKay et al. (2017) measured a sample of 1,000 from Australia, divided into four age groups: 3 to 9 years, 10 to 19 years, 20 to 59 years, and 60+ years. They also found a gradual

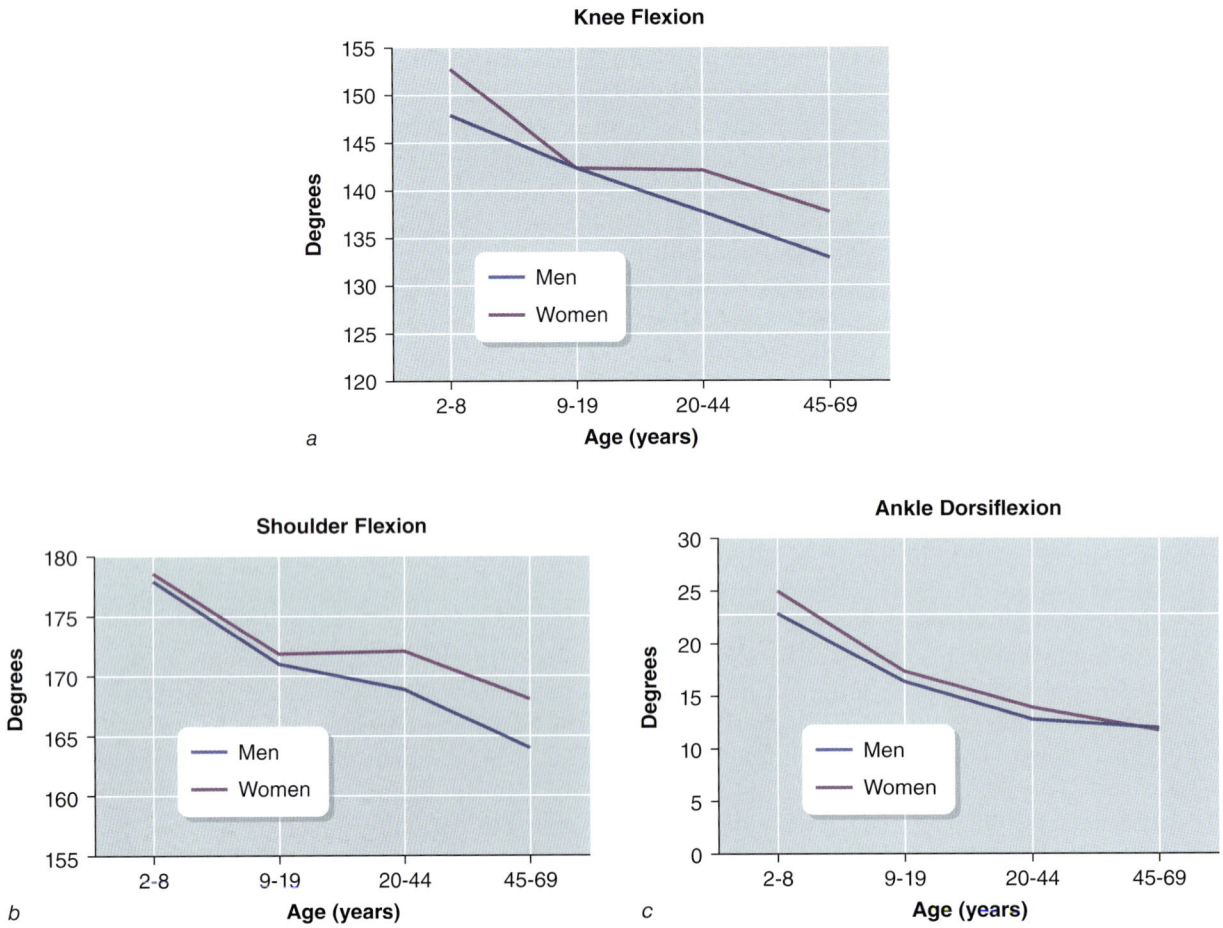

FIGURE 11.8 Reference values obtained in a cross-sectional study of life span passive range of motion (Soucie et al., 2011). Overall, flexibility declines over the life span for these motions, and women are somewhat more flexible than men.
Data from Soucie et al. (2011).

decrease with age, but in contrast to Soucie et al. found very few differences between boys and girls or men and women. These equivocal results could indicate that stretching exercises in some cultures are more socially acceptable for girls, and higher proportions of girls than boys participate in gymnastics and dance, both of which emphasize flexibility. Too, the sex differences found in the normative descriptive period could reflect these factors. It is certainly the case today that participation in exercise programs emphasizing flexibility is a far better predictor of flexibility than is sex (figure 11.9).

FIGURE 11.9 Flexibility becomes more variable in adolescence as some individuals exercise and others become sedentary. It is unclear how the changing structural constraints of skeletal system growth and muscle system growth influence flexibility.

The Soucie et al. findings broadly agree with the studies done in the normative descriptive period. The decrease in range of motion observed around puberty and then in postpubescence likely reflects the increase of body mass. Obviously, the addition of fat weight could reduce range of motion, but so too could the addition of muscle mass (Bini et al., 2000; Parker & James, 1985). Greater flexibility in adolescent girls compared with boys could reflect greater joint laxity in adolescent girls after they enter puberty (Quatman, Ford, Myer, Paterno, & Hewett, 2008). Too much laxity can be a factor in injuries.

▶ **KEY POINT** Flexibility tends to decline from childhood values starting by adolescence and reflecting age-related changes in joint laxity and body mass.

The sit-and-reach test (figure 11.10) is of particular interest because it has been used as the representative measure of flexibility in fitness test batteries. This use continues today. Some researchers are concerned that the sit-and-reach test reflects body proportions as well as flexibility because it measures flexibility relative to a point even with the feet. A small number of individuals with unusually long legs, short arms, or both are at a disadvantage. A modified sit-and-reach test corrects for limb length bias by measuring flexibility relative to an individual's fingertips when sitting up straight (Hoeger et al., 1990).

Norms developed in the National Children and Youth Fitness Study II project (Ross et al., 1987) for children aged 6 to 9 reflect generally stable sit-and-reach performance during childhood. In an extensive cross-sectional study of Flemish girls aged 6 to 18 years, the sit-and-reach scores of girls in the upper percentiles were stable until age 12 and then improved. The scores of girls in the lower percentiles declined from 6 to 12 years, improved somewhat in midadolescence, and then declined again at 17 and 18 (figure 11.11). Thus, the range of scores was wider in successively older age groups (Simons et al., 1990). Belgian boys measured longitudinally improved their sit-and-reach performance from 12 to 18 years of age at a rate of about 1 cm per year (Beunen et al., 1988). Abdominal strength might be a factor in sit-and-reach perfor-

Assessing Flexibility

Because flexibility is specific to a joint, one or two flexibility measures cannot accurately represent one's overall flexibility. To know the flexibility in a specific joint in a particular individual, it must be measured. Most flexibility measures are made with a goniometer, which is a protractor with two long arms. The axis of the goniometer is centered over the joint to be measured. The limb is positioned at one end of the range of motion, and one arm of the goniometer is aligned with it. The limb is moved to the other end of the range, and the second arm is aligned with it. The degrees between the two arms on the goniometer represent the range of motion at the joint.

It is often impractical to give a battery of flexibility measures at various joints, especially if strength, endurance, and body composition are all being assessed at the same time. Fitness test batteries such as Physical Best (American Alliance for Health, Physical Education, Recreation and Dance, 1988), Fitnessgram (Meredith & Welk, 1999), and that used in the National Children and Youth Fitness Study II (Ross, Pate, Delpy, Gold, & Svilar, 1987) employ a single representative measure of flexibility. The sit-and-reach test (figure 11.10) was chosen because trunk and hip flexibility are thought to be important in the prevention and care of low back pain in adults (Hoeger, Hopkins, Button, & Palmer, 1990).

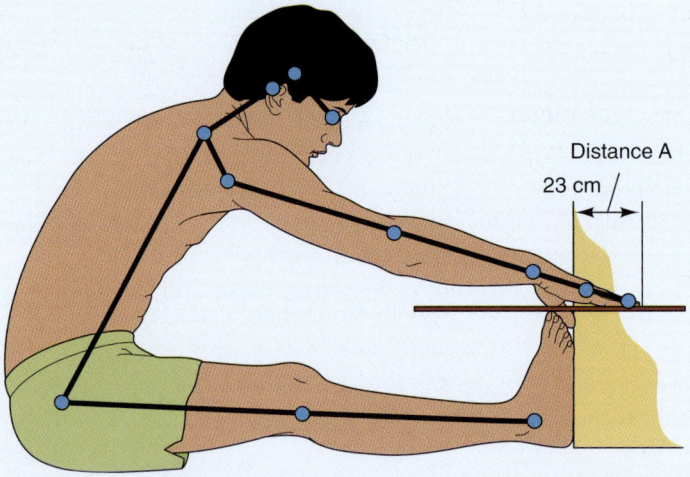

FIGURE 11.10 The sit-and-reach test. The individual sits with the feet against a box corresponding to the 23 cm point along the ruler. Upon reaching forward as far as possible, the individual receives a score of 23 cm plus or minus the distance reached measured at the fingertips (distance A).

Reprinted by permission from Hoeger et al. (1990).

mance (Beunen et al., 1988) because individuals with strong abdominal muscles can pull the trunk forward to a greater degree of flexion.

▶ **KEY POINT** In adolescence, flexibility becomes more variable with advancing age, and some individuals in the lower percentiles lose a significant degree of flexibility.

Researchers, then, document both declines and improvements in flexibility during the growing years. It is possible that because the bones grow in length and then stimulate muscles to grow in length, a temporary loss of flexibility occurs during growth, especially in early adolescence (Micheli, 1984), as muscle growth lags behind bone growth. However, it is not clear that this would result in a measurable decline in flexibility, even over a short period of time.

Although some changes might be particular to the joint or joints measured, overall it is apparent that children and adolescents can lose their flexibility if they do not train to maintain or improve it. Flexibility becomes more variable in groups of adolescents because some adolescents train whereas others abandon exercise programs and physical activities. Most of us think of arthritis as a disease of older adulthood, but approximately 1 out of every 250 children in the United States has a form of arthritis and associated joint pain. Expertise in treatment is required because the traditional adult therapy of steroids can stunt children's growth.

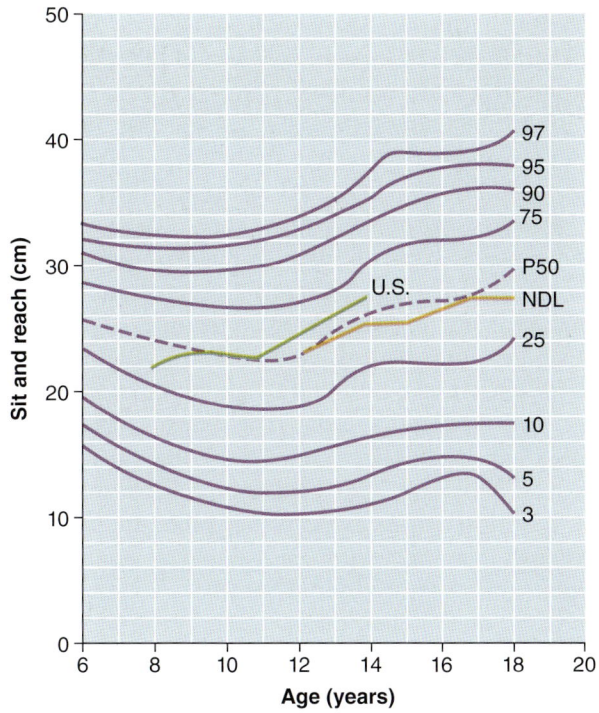

FIGURE 11.11 Changes in sit-and-reach test performance over age. Flemish girls at the upper percentiles maintained their flexibility during childhood and then improved in adolescence. Girls at the lower percentiles declined and then only slightly improved in midadolescence. The median scores of girls from the United States (U.S.) and the Netherlands (NDL) are superimposed on the graph.

Reprinted by permission from Simons et al. (1990, pg. 118).

Think about your own fitness regimen. Does it include activities that can maintain your flexibility over the next 30 or 40 years? Do you need to add to your personal workout plan?

Web Study Guide **Plot data and examine trends in flexibility over time in Lab Activity 11.2, Examining Trends in Sit-and-Reach Performance, in the web study guide.**

Flexibility Training in Youth

Few studies of flexibility training in childhood or adolescence have been done, but Rodríguez, Santonja, López-Miñarro, Sáinz de Baranda, and Yuste (2008) studied both elementary and secondary school children who participated in a hamstring stretching program twice a week for 32 weeks in their physical education classes. Both age groups significantly improved their flexibility as measured by the sit-and-reach test. Control groups that did not stretch tended to lose flexibility. Mayorga-Vega, Merino-Marban, Sanchez-Rivas, and Viciana (2014) demonstrated that children 9 to 10 years of age could improve their hamstring flexibility as measured by the sit-and-reach test with an 8-week stretching program. Yet they found that after 5 weeks of no training, flexibility measures returned to the level they were before the training program. These results demonstrate the importance of training to maintain and improve flexibility. The typical patterns of decline discussed earlier are likely related to an absence of training for flexibility.

Another study (Notarnicola et al., 2017) used five different forms of stretching with 15- to 18-year-old basketball players over a 5-month period, with a different type of stretching each month. The researchers found that flexibility improved, but the effectiveness of the different stretching methods depended on the body area. Dynamic stretching seemed best for increasing flexibility of the hamstrings, and postural protocol stretching seemed best for increasing trunk flexibility. Zakas (2005) asked adolescent soccer players to do one stretch for 30 seconds, or two stretches for 15 seconds, or six stretches for 5 seconds. All improved their flexibility, but there was no difference among the three protocols. Specificity of training is likely necessary because Milanovic et al. (2014) found that speed, agility, and quickness training had no effect on four different measures of flexibility. In general, flexibility training must be maintained in order to maintain improved levels of flexibility, and stretches must be done for all the joints where improved flexibility is desired.

Development of Flexibility in Adulthood

Unfortunately, adolescence does not mark the end of a person's trend toward reduced flexibility. Holland, Tanaka, Shigematsu, and Nakagaichi (2002) reviewed the research literature on flexibility and older adults. From the mid- to late 20s, maximum range of motion declines; it does so faster in some joints than in others (Bell & Hoshizaki, 1981). For example, the decreases in spinal extension and shoulder flexion are relatively large compared with smaller decreases in hip extension and knee flexion (Einkauf, Gohdes, Jensen, & Jewell, 1987; Germain & Blair, 1983; Roach & Miles, 1991). Both upper and lower extremities showed declines in flexibility (Rikli & Jones, 1999).

The work of McKay et al. (2017) was mentioned earlier. In addition to strength, they established normative references values for flexibility in 13 joints of the same 1,000 children and adults. The flexibility norms of 8 of the 13 joints decreased with aging over adolescence and adulthood but in 12 of the 13 joints over older adulthood. They found little difference in this decrease between males and females.

Osteoarthritis is a chronic degenerative disease of the joints.

Various factors contribute to decreases in flexibility, including degeneration of musculoskeletal and soft tissues as well as diseases, especially **osteoarthritis** and **osteoporosis**. Collagen increases and elastin degenerates with advancing age, and both of these changes lead to increased joint stiffness (Alnaqeeb, Al-Zaid, & Goldspink, 1984; Gosline, 1976). Disuse magnifies all of these changes, though we do not know how disuse influences the rate of decline. The research studies of range of motion in adulthood have used the cross-sectional design. Longitudinal studies would be needed to determine how much of the decline is due to age-related tissue change and how much is due to disuse. The learning exercise at the end of this chapter gives you an opportunity to observe flexibility in some older adults.

▶ **KEY POINT** Flexibility declines in adulthood, especially in little-used joints.

Flexibility Training in Adulthood

Researchers generally agree that both specialized stretch training and general exercise interventions moderately improve range of motion in older adults, including frail elderly persons. Germain and Blair (1983) documented improved shoulder flexibility in adults aged 20 to 60 who participated in a stretching program for shoulder flexion. Geremia, Iskiewicz, Marchner Lehnen, and Lehnen (2015) used Pilates to train healthy older adults around 70 years of age for 10 weeks. Almost 20 various measurements of joint flexibility significantly improved. Carneiro et al. (2015) studied the effects of resistance training 2 versus 3 days per week on the flexibility of women 60 years and over. In two of three measures, flexibility improved regardless of frequency. For the third measurement, three training days per week yielded significantly more improvement in flexibility. Low-impact aerobics, Tai Chi, rhythmic stretching, and general fitness interventions have all yielded improvements (Hubley-Kozey, Wall, & Hogan, 1995; Lan, Lai, Chen, & Wong, 1998; McMurdo & Rennie, 1993; Rikli & Edwards, 1991).

▶ **KEY POINT** An individual's flexibility decreases without training at any point in the life span, but specific training can reverse a loss of flexibility at any age.

Summary of the Development of Flexibility

The range of motion possible in a joint reflects a person's activity and training more than it reflects his or her age per se. Flexibility declines in the average adolescent and adult as a result of increases in body mass, limited daily activity, and lack of exercise. Flexibility training can bring about an improvement in the range of motion at any age, but it must be consistent because gains are lost if an individual stops training. For many individuals, then, if flexibility limits a desired movement, appropriate training can change this structural constraint.

Summary and Synthesis

Muscle strength and flexibility are discussed separately in this chapter, but their interrelationship as individual structural constraints should be noted. Individuals can improve strength or flexibility at any time in the life span with an appropriate training program. Ideally, though, individuals train for both. Having strong muscles to move a joint in one direction such that the joint cannot move through its appropriate range in the opposite direction can limit movement just as much as a lack of strength can. Training for strength and flexibility is not just for athletes; to the contrary, if reasonable levels of strength and flexibility are not maintained, many movements needed for daily living can be difficult if not impossible. Therapists routinely help individuals regain lost strength and flexibility after accidents, injuries, and surgery.

We should not forget that endurance is also related to strength and flexibility. Many activities promote improvement in all three components. Swim training, for example, can promote endurance, strength, and flexibility at the same time. Our perspective of the importance of physical fitness at various points of the life span, then, should include all the components of fitness. Training programs above all should strive for balance.

Weight status is another important factor in health-related physical fitness. A body composition that is high in lean muscle mass and low in fat tissue enhances cardiorespiratory endurance, is associated with increased strength, and permits flexibility as long as the muscles are balanced. In contrast, a high proportion of body fat puts an individual at risk of disease and death. The role of training in promoting good weight status is an important area of study. Too, we are interested in how the development of motor skill is related to the development of fitness. Is a high level of motor skill required to engage in the sufficiently intense activities that promote fitness? We will consider these topics in the next chapter.

Reinforcing What You Have Learned About Constraints

TAKE A SECOND LOOK

Being strong and flexible is an advantage to performance, whereas being weak and inflexible can limit performance. In other words, the musculoskeletal systems can be rate-limiting systems for movement. Training for strength and flexibility can be a healthy activity, and greater muscle mass can make a positive contribution to health. For example, greater muscle mass is associated with expending more calories and maintaining healthy body composition. Greater muscle mass is also associated with greater cardiorespiratory endurance. Yet as we have seen so often, the musculoskeletal system does not function in isolation. Individuals who try to enhance their strength and flexibility training with drugs often risk damage to other systems, especially the endocrine system with the use of anabolic steroids. This fact reminds us that the interaction of all systems must be considered when examining the effect of changing a system to give rise to certain movements.

TEST YOUR KNOWLEDGE

1. How does the rate of increase in strength with growth compare with the rate of increase in muscle mass? How do the rates of decrease in strength and muscle mass compare in aging?
2. Can strength and flexibility improve with training? How?
3. What are the sex differences in the development of strength and flexibility in children and adolescents?
4. Consider the older adults in your society. Can you think of constraints (individual, environmental, and task) that might lead to a loss of strength in the older years?
5. How is maturation related to strength in children and teens?
6. What factors are involved in the loss of strength in older adulthood? What effect does resistance training have on these factors?
7. What factors are important to consider in assessing strength? In assessing flexibility?
8. How does the change in functional muscle strength compare with the change in isometric muscle strength during the growing years?
9. How can cultural norms differentially affect assessment of strength and flexibility of the sexes?
10. How does flexibility change with growth and with aging? What is responsible for the change in childhood?

Learning Exercise 11.1

OLDER ADULT FLEXIBILITY

Observe the following in two or three older adults and report your findings.

1. When seated on the floor with his back against a wall, can the individual keep the knee of the extended leg flat on the floor as he draws the lower portion of his other leg up against the thigh?
2. Can she raise her arms overhead, fingers pointing to the ceiling, to be even with or behind the ears?
3. When standing facing you, can he keep his elbows tucked in and turn his palms to face you?
4. In a standing position, can she link her hands behind her back and raise them up away from her back to a level even with her waist?

Did the individuals pass or fail all four items? Ask individuals about their favorite activities, and see if you can account for the maintenance of flexibility by matching body areas to those activities.

12

Weight Status, Fitness, and Motor Competence

CHAPTER OBJECTIVES

This chapter

- reviews the effects of exercise on body composition over the life span,
- discusses the effects of obesity on health, and
- explores the interrelationships among health-related fitness, physical activity, weight status, and motor competence.

Motor Development in the Real World

Naya Rivera, Oprah Winfrey, Dennis Quaid, Lady Gaga, Katie Couric, Elton John, Kate Beckinsale, Audrey Hepburn, Victoria Beckham, Jane Fonda, Adam Rippon, Princess Diana—this is just a subset of a long list of actors and actresses, musicians, athletes, and public figures over recent generations who have dealt with an eating disorder. Although many factors contribute to an individual's eating disorder, feeling pressured to conform to a thin body type likely plays a part. If these accomplished professionals feel the pressure, those young people who seek to be like them feel that pressure. The paradox is that the media sources simultaneously promote lifestyles that make a desirable weight harder to achieve. Fast foods that are deficient in nutrients and high in calories are pushed to young people, as are screen-time activities, such as cell phone use, social media use, and electronic gaming, which all increase time being sedentary. These push aside desirable influences, such as developing motor competence and engaging in physical activities, that burn calories and promote a healthy cardiorespiratory system.

The extremely thin body is the dominant advertising image. It would be easy to conclude from watching media that the less fat we have, the better. Although excess fat weight is associated with a number of health challenges, some fat tissue is needed for insulation, protection, and energy storage. The more healthy perspective is to think of the body as composed of lean tissue (bones, organs, and muscles) and an optimal amount of fat tissue. It is important to understand how motor competence and active lifestyles contribute to a healthy weight status.

Body composition is the composition of tissue making up the body as divided into lean tissues or fat (adipose) tissues.

Motor competence is proficiency in common foundational movement skills that enable participation in a variety of everyday activities, sports, and dance.

Body composition and weight status are two other aspects of health-related fitness. Compared with the other fitness components, more myths surround body composition and weight status than any other. Many people try to simplify maintenance of a healthy weight status. Late in the 20th century, it became popular to use running as a path to both cardiorespiratory endurance and a lean weight. School curricula started to emphasize running and other vigorous exercise at the expense of skill development. Yet this is a case where many factors are interrelated, and it is important to understand these multiple relationships before deciding how to help individuals achieve good health.

A Model of Interrelationships

Individuals can have much control over their body composition and weight status through diet and exercise. A complete discussion of diet is beyond the scope of this text, but we will explore the role of physical activity in maintaining a healthy **body composition** and weight status. Generally, the more active an individual of any age, the more likely fat and lean tissue are optimal, unless excessive exercise drives fat levels too low. However, the relationship between activity level and body composition is bidirectional: Body composition also influences levels of physical activity. Individuals who are overweight or obese can find it uncomfortable and difficult to be physically active. Those closer to an optimal body composition find it easier to be active and exercise.

Further, a person's level of motor skill proficiency, or **motor competence**, could influence his or her level of physical activity. Skilled movers use their energy efficiently when they are physically active, allowing them to sustain activity long enough to realize the health benefits of being active. Inefficient movers in effect waste energy and have difficulty sustaining activity. It is also possible to see how overweight can make it difficult to achieve motor competence. Either excess weight can discourage a person from practicing enough to become proficient, or excess weight can impede certain movements. In this case, body composition is a structural constraint. It can also be a functional constraint if individuals who are overweight believe they can't exercise sufficiently to lose fat weight.

A body composition high in muscle mass and low in adipose tissue contributes to optimal performance. The muscle mass can be used to exert force, and low adipose tissue means a performer does not have extra weight to move, both of which constitute advantages in many physical activities. In contrast, a body composition that is high in adipose tissue can make it difficult to move the body, especially for extended times, and difficult to achieve certain body positions. In addition to the health repercussions, overweight status can be a rate limiter to performance of motor skills, but the relationship works both ways. An individual who lacks skills finds it difficult to move vigorously enough to maintain a healthy body composition and fitness level. Motor skill competence is both a precursor to and a consequence of body composition (Robinson et al., 2015).

Figure 12.1 illustrates the interrelationships among the factors discussed here and adds perceived motor competence to the model. Perception of motor competence can influence the choice to engage in motor skills, and that in turn can influence physical activity level and health-related fitness. Individuals who perceive themselves as having little motor competence might avoid physical activity. On the other hand, the perception of being competent in motor skills tends to make physical activities pleasant and might cause individuals to seek out opportunities to be active. We will discuss perceived motor competence in more detail in a later chapter, but it clearly should join the other interrelated factors. Let us begin our discussion of these interrelationships by first reviewing what is known about body composition over the life span and how exercise affects body composition.

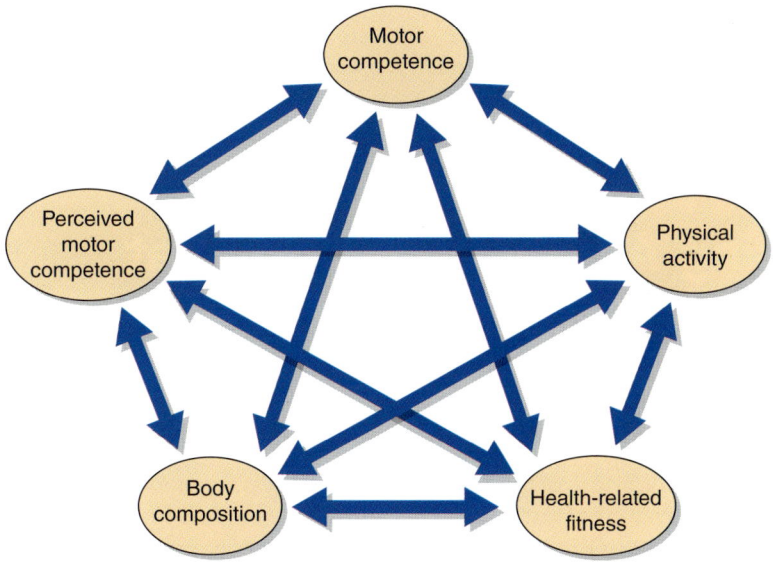

FIGURE 12.1 The model of interrelationships related to motor competence and health.

Body Composition

Body mass can be divided into two types of tissue: **lean tissue**—which includes muscle, bone, and organs—and fat, or **adipose tissue**. The relative percentages of fat-free and fat tissues that make up the body mass give a measure of body composition. As mentioned in our opening, many people care about body composition because it is related to appearance and it can influence individuals' feelings about themselves. Many societies value a lean body appearance. Obesity may contribute to a negative body concept and negative self-concept, thus making it difficult for an obese person to relate to others.

Aside from appearance, body composition is important in a variety of health issues:

- Higher proportions of lean body mass show a positive link to working capacity, and higher proportions of fat tissue show a negative link.
- Excess fat weight adds to the workload whenever the body is moved.
- Excess fat can limit an individual's range of motion.
- Obesity places a person at increased risk of suffering coronary heart and artery disease, stroke, diabetes, and hypertension.

As noted earlier, everyone has some fat tissue, which is needed for insulation, protection, and energy storage. Women need a certain level of fat tissue (approximately 12% of body weight) to support functions of reproduction. Only *excess* fat weight is negatively related to fitness and health. Attempts to reduce fat tissue to excessively low levels are equally a health concern.

Basal metabolic rate is the amount of energy needed to sustain the body's vital functions in the waking state.

Genetic and environmental factors affect body composition. People can manipulate two major environmental factors—diet and exercise—to manage the relative amounts of lean and adipose tissue in their bodies. Maintaining body composition is in part a matter of balancing the calories consumed against the **basal metabolic rate**—the amount of energy used to keep the body functioning—and the amount of physical exertion. Rates vary among individuals; some burn more calories than others just to keep the body running. The basal metabolic rate is under the control of various hormones, and it cannot be easily altered in the short term. In

Assessing Amounts of Body Fat

There are many ways to measure the amount of adipose tissue in the body. These measurements can be used directly to track changes with growth and aging, or they can be used to estimate the percentage of the body's weight that is fat. We also have several methods for measuring lean body mass; they allow an estimation of body fat as well:

- Measuring the thickness of the skin and underlying (subcutaneous) fat with skinfold calipers. The amount of total body fat can be estimated from skinfold measurements taken at specified sites. This is one of the most common ways of estimating fat weight, especially in children.
- Weighing a person underwater and contrasting that value with normal body weight. This method estimates body density and, subsequently, the proportion of lean versus fat weight. It is difficult to take this measurement on young children and adults who are afraid of being underwater.
- Analyzing the intensity of reemitted infrared light emitted by a probe into the biceps brachii muscle with a near-infrared interactance device. This is an easy measurement method to use with children but may not be as accurate as other methods (especially underwater weighing) (Smith et al., 1997).

contrast, an individual can control exercise level on a daily basis. This discussion focuses on the relationship between body composition and exercise.

Recall from chapter 9 that fat tissue increases rapidly during two periods: the first 6 months after birth and again in early adolescence. In girls, this increase continues throughout adolescence, whereas in boys the gain stops and may even reverse for a time. Muscle tissue also grows rapidly in infants, followed by a steady period of increase during childhood; it again increases rapidly during the adolescent growth spurt, more dramatically in boys than in girls. This typical pattern may be altered through either diet or exercise. Overeating results in excess fat weight, and starvation can lead to levels of fat so low that the body obtains energy by muscle wasting (breaking down muscle tissue to use as energy). Exercise, of course, burns calories, thus potentially altering a person's body composition. Resistance training can increase muscle mass, especially after puberty.

In middle age, the average adult loses fat-free body mass and gains fat such that body weight increases and the portion of body weight that is fat increases. Of particular concern is an accumulation of upper body fat, which is associated with increasingly poor cardiovascular health (Lee et al., 2017). In old age, fat-free body mass and fat mass decline. It is important to remember that this is the typical profile and that individuals are extremely variable. Also, obese individuals often die before reaching older adulthood (Faeh, Braun, Tarnutzer, & Bopp, 2011), which can change average measurements taken on groups of older adults.

As mentioned earlier, both diet and exercise influence body composition. A discussion of diet is beyond the scope of this text, but the influence of exercise on body composition is a vitally important aspect of our discussion of motor development.

- Measuring soft tissue composition with a dual-energy X-ray absorptiometer (DEXA), which allows a direct measure of body density but requires expensive equipment (Steinberger et al., 2005; Sutton & Miller, 2006).
- Measuring air displacement (rather than water displacement) by air-displacement plethysmography. This measure requires a Bod Pod chamber but allows measurement of infants and obese individuals (Dioum, Gartner, Maire, Delpeuch, & Wade, 2005).

Another common indicator of body fat is body mass index (BMI), the ratio of body weight (kg) to height squared (m). A healthy BMI is considered to range from 18.5 to 24.9. This is a convenient measure because one needs only height and weight in order to calculate BMI. Yet body weight reflects both lean and adipose tissue, so the BMI might be misleading for some individuals with above-average lean muscle weight.

Web Study Guide **Evaluate changes in body mass index in a group of children over a period of 4 years in Lab Activity 12.1, Body Composition in Childhood, in the web study guide.**

Body Composition and Exercise

Longitudinal studies are particularly valuable in the study of interrelationships between body composition and physical activity levels. Though conducted a number of years ago, Parizkova's longitudinal studies (1968a, 1977) provide an insight into this relationship, so we will begin with them.

Childhood and Adolescence

Parizkova conducted a series of studies on body composition and activity levels of boys and girls in the former Czechoslovakia (now the Czech Republic). First, he divided nearly 100 boys into four groups by their activity level. Boys in the most active group (group I) were involved in basketball or track for at least 6 hours a week. Boys in the least active group (group IV) participated only in unorganized and unsystematic activity. The boys in the other two groups had intermediate activity levels.

Parizkova first tested the boys at an average age of 10.7 years, then followed them in successive years until they were 14.7 years old. Over the 4 years, the children in the most active group significantly increased in body mass while their absolute level of fat weight remained the same; hence, the fat proportion of their total weight decreased and the increase in lean body mass *alone* accounted for the increase of body weight with growth (figure 12.2, *a* and *b*). In contrast, the boys in the inactive group increased significantly in absolute fat weight. Physical activity had a beneficial effect on body composition in these boys.

▶ **KEY POINT** Physical activity has a favorable effect on boys during the growing years in that it increases lean body mass and minimizes addition of fat weight.

Parizkova (1972) then followed 41 of these boys for another 3 years, and the body composition trends of the first 4 years continued. The most active and least active groups differed in total weight by the time they reached age 16.7. The active group was heavier in total body weight because the boys' lean body mass was greater. The active boys had less total fat weight than the inactive boys, and their fat weight actually declined in some years. Parizkova determined that

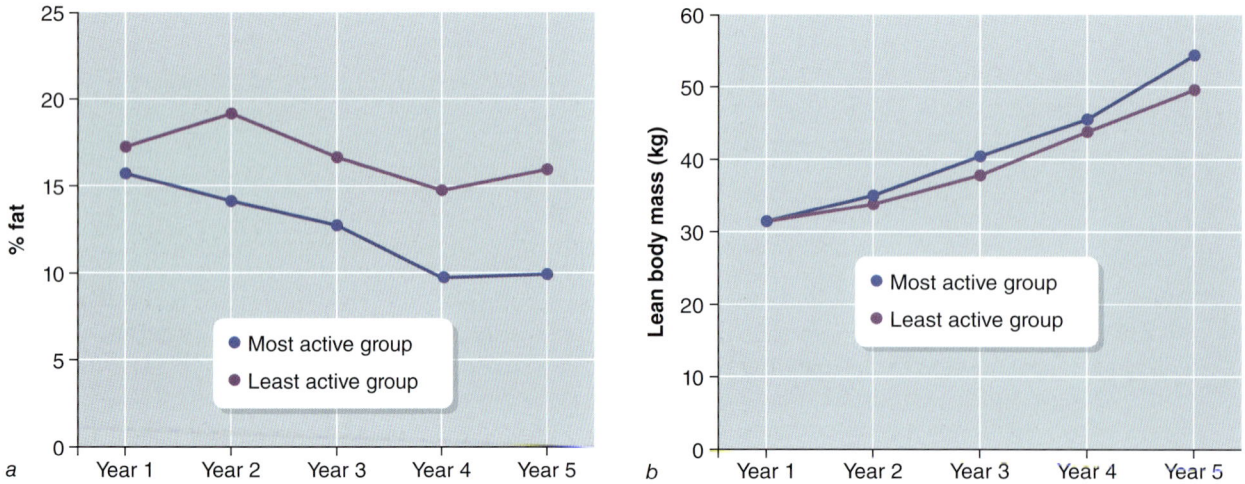

FIGURE 12.2 *(a)* Relative percentage body fat in the most and least active groups of boys followed by Parizkova from an average age of 10.7 years to 14.7 years. *(b)* Lean body mass of the same groups in Parizkova's study.

Reprinted by permission from Parizkova (1977).

the groups did not differ in average skeletal age, so the differences noted in body composition cannot be attributed to maturational differences. He also noted that the boys maintained their relative position in the group in both distribution and absolute amount of subcutaneous fat. This means the relative amount of fat weight and its pattern of distribution in the body were relatively stable over the years of the study.

▶ **KEY POINT** Physically active boys can be heavier than inactive boys because they have more lean body mass, even with less total fat weight.

Parizkova followed 16 of these 41 young men for yet another 6 years. Although this number was too small for a reliable analysis by activity level, Parizkova (1977) noted that percentage body fat declined in the group until age 21.7 years, then varied widely among individuals, probably reflecting changes in lifestyle. The Parizkova studies, then, indicate that physical activity has a favorable influence on boys' body composition during the growing years.

If you were a high school principal, what implications would you see in the Parizkova studies for the physical education curriculum at your school?

The growth of adipose and lean muscle tissue differs dramatically between the sexes during adolescence. Girls gain proportionately more fat than muscle compared with boys. Even so, the beneficial effect that activity has on body composition in boys also occurs in active girls. Over a span of 5 years, Parizkova (1963, 1977) studied 32 girls who belonged to a gymnastics school and 45 girls who were not engaged in any type of training. The girls were first measured at the age of 12 or 13 years. The gymnasts followed a regular yearly cycle of training in which they attended a rigorous camp in the summer, stopped training in the early fall, and resumed a heavy training schedule from October to December.

These cycles are shown (for 11 of the gymnasts) in figure 12.3 as black-outlined bars; the higher the bar, the more intense the training. Measurements of the girls' fat weight paralleled Parizkova's findings with boys. The gymnasts remained at the same level of subcutaneous fat during the 5 years, and the total skinfold thickness showed no trend, even though it increased or decreased for short periods. In contrast, the control group gained a significant amount of fat weight. Height and body weight trends in the two groups were similar throughout the 5 years, so the differences were truly in body composition.

▶ **KEY POINT** Teenage girls in training can increase lean body mass and decrease subcutaneous fat, even when they eat more calories in response to training.

The cyclic nature of the gymnasts' training schedule provided information about their weight and skinfold thicknesses. During periods of inactivity the gymnasts gained in both total body weight and skinfold thickness (including subcutaneous fat tissue), but during training they increased in total body weight while their skinfold thicknesses declined. (Note that in figure 12.3, total skinfold thickness goes down when the intensity of training goes up, and total skinfold thickness goes up when training stops for a time.) Total height and weight keep increasing with age. Therefore, the weight increases during the various activity periods resulted from changing ratios of fat and lean body weight. Parizkova also recorded the gymnasts' caloric intake and found that even though they consumed more calories during periods of intense training, fat deposits decreased and lean body mass increased.

If you were a physical education teacher, what results from the Parizkova studies could you use to counsel your teenage girl students on diet and exercise?

Parizkova (1973, 1977) also simultaneously followed 12 boys and 12 girls engaged in swimming training from ages 12 to 16. At age 12, the average height, weight, lean body mass, and fat

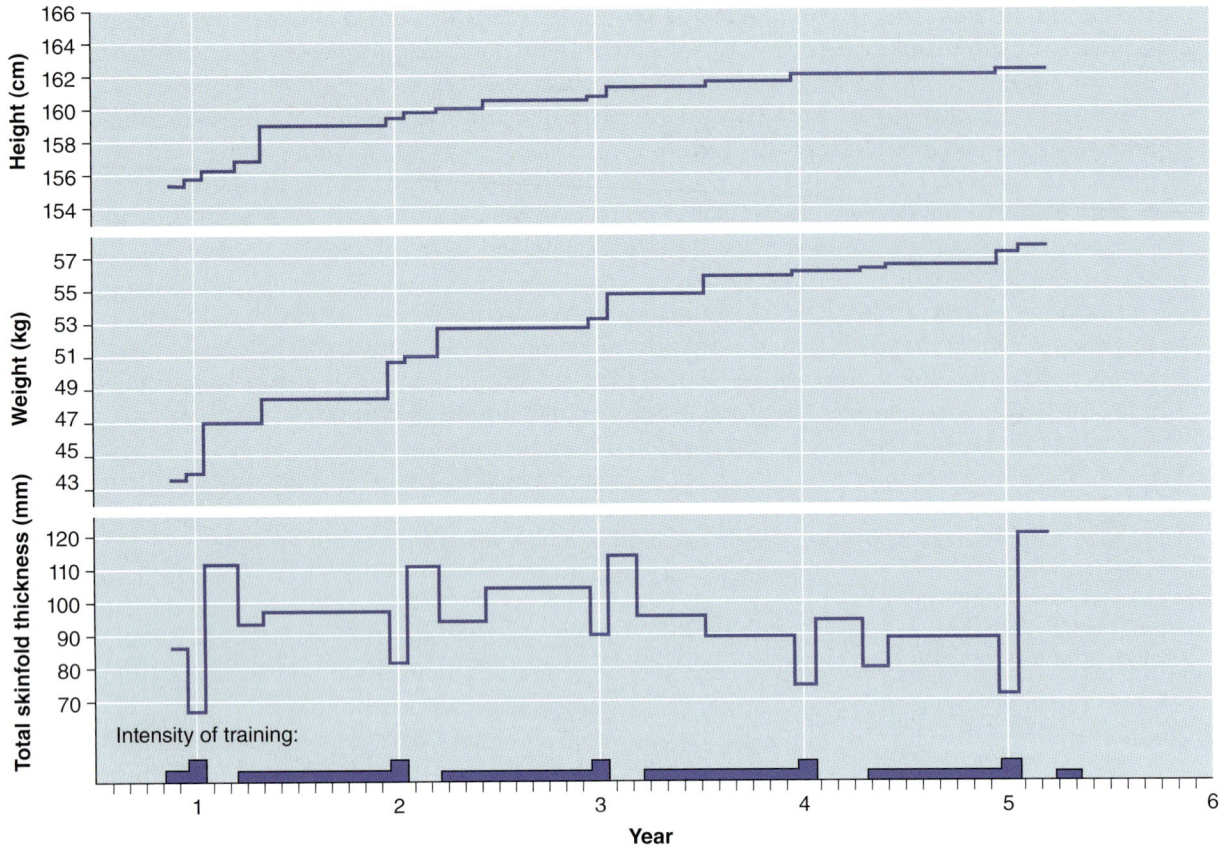

FIGURE 12.3 Changes in height, weight, and subcutaneous fat (sum of 10 skinfold measurements) in a group of regularly training female gymnasts (n = 11) during a 5-year period of varying intensity of training (see bottom scale).
Reprinted by permission from Parizkova (1977).

weight of the two groups were about the same. Lean body mass values for the swimmers were higher than the average levels for teens not in training. By age 15, the boys were significantly taller, heavier, and leaner than the girls, but both sexes showed an increased proportion of lean body mass at the expense of fat weight over the years of training.

How has your body composition changed throughout your life span? What do you think contributed to that change? How might you use your experience in working with others?

More recent research has confirmed many of Parizkova's findings. A longitudinal investigation of cardiovascular disease risk factors was conducted among the residents of Muscatine, Iowa. Participants were measured for fitness, body composition, blood pressure, heart mass, and maturation level in youth. Janz, Burns, and Mahoney (1995) reported on a 2-year follow-up with more than 120 children who were 10 years old at the first set of measurements. They found that increased systolic blood pressure was associated with increased body fatness and decreased physical fitness. A 5-year follow-up of participants in the Muscatine Study (Janz, Dawson, & Mahoney, 2002) led investigators to conclude that promoting physical fitness reduced the prevalence of obesity.

As part of the Iowa Bone Development Study, 379 children were tracked for activity patterns and body composition over 3 years between an average age of 5.6 to 8.6 years (Janz, Burns, & Levy, 2005). Activity patterns were measured by accelerometry and survey while body fat was measured by DEXA. The children who maintained a high level of physical activity but low levels of screen time over the years were less likely to be in the upper quartile of percent body fat. Alarmingly, levels of sedentary behavior were stable within the group over this time span; that is, those sedentary at 5 years tended to be sedentary at 8 years.

Jones, Hinkley, Okely, and Salmon (2013) searched the research literature for 11 studies tracking physical activity and sedentary behavior over time. Their summary of the studies' findings noted a moderate tendency for levels of physical activity to be stable from early to middle childhood and a somewhat stronger tendency for sedentary behaviors to be stable from early to middle childhood.

In summary, these investigations show that involvement in training programs favorably affects body composition. Although children and adolescents who engage in active training exhibit the general growth trend of increased weight, this increase represents the addition of relatively more lean body mass and less fat weight than in their nontraining peers. Unfortunately, it appears that lifestyles containing more or less physical activity and more or less sedentary behavior tend to persist in youth, so active lifestyles need to be adopted in early childhood.

▶ **KEY POINT** Appropriate levels of exercise in youths are associated with a healthier body composition.

Adulthood

Exercise in young and older adulthood might favorably influence body composition in two ways: It could increase fat-free mass or decrease fat. The increase in fat-free mass could be an increase in muscle mass, an increase in bone density, or both. Some studies, discussed in this section, have tracked these changes in exercising adults.

It was established a number of years ago that middle-aged and older adult athletes who were regular exercisers tended to maintain their muscle and fat masses, and many compared favorably with younger adult populations (Asano, Ogawa, & Furuta, 1978; Kavanagh & Shephard, 1977; Pollock, 1974; Saltin & Grimby, 1968; Shephard, 1978b). However, we cannot assume from these observations that the same would be true of the population at large or of sedentary older adults who begin training. It is possible that healthier older adults are more able to be active and that what is being observed is good health status rather than the benefits of exercise. For this reason, it is important to longitudinally study older adults for exercise effects. The current number of longitudinal studies is tiny, however, so we often must rely on short-term studies for information.

Studies of changes in muscle mass with exercise have used computed tomography to document changes in muscle area. Without exercise, older adults in their 70s lose muscle mass, strength, and muscle quality (Goodpaster et al., 2006). Binder et al. (2005) compared frail older adults in their 70s who engaged in 3 months of low-intensity exercise followed by 3 months of progressive resistance training against a control group. The exercisers significantly increased their knee extension strength and their fat-free mass compared with the control group. Resistance training, though, did not change their fat mass. Studies on resistance training, even high-intensity interval resistance training, are equivocal on whether resistance training reduces fat mass (Moro et al., 2017).

Studies of young athletes have concluded that regular exercise promotes bone growth, but whether or not exercise improves bone mass in older adults depends on the type of exercise program. Gomez-Cabello, Ara, Gonzalez-Aguero, Casajus, & Vicente-Rodriguez (2012) reviewed studies on how training affected bone mass in older adults. They concluded that strength training improved or maintained bone mass, while walking exercise was not very effective. Exercise programs that combine strength training, aerobic training, high-impact or weight-bearing training, and whole-body vibration also were effective in increasing bone mass, or at least in preventing further decline, in older adults. This included postmenopausal women, a group at risk of bone fractures. Another meta-analysis (Marques, Mota, & Carvalho, 2012) concluded that low-impact and resistance exercise studies tend to find improved bone mineral density specifically in the lumbar spine and neck of the femur in older adults.

Schwartz et al. (1991) placed 15 men between 60 and 82 years of age on a 6-month endurance-training program. Their training intensity gradually increased so that eventually they were walking or jogging 45 minutes per session, 5 days per week, at 85% of heart rate reserve. Over the 6 months, their body fat decreased 2.3% and their waist circumferences decreased 3.4%. Although the loss of body fat overall was small, the loss of fat in specific trunk locations was more dramatic, which is significant because of the association between trunk fat and increased cardiovascular risk. Paillard, Lafont, Costes-Salon, Riviere, and Dupui (2004) found that a relatively short-term walking program of 12 weeks for men between 63 and 72 years of age brought about a decrease of fat weight. No increase occurred in lean body mass or bone mineral density, though, for an intervention of this length.

▶ **KEY POINT** Adults can increase muscle mass and bone density with resistance training and lose fat weight with endurance training, but individuals are variable in their amount of change.

Think about your own diet and fitness routines. Do you have habits that will keep your body composition similar to what it is now as you get older, or would a change be warranted?

Although more longitudinal research on adults in the area of body composition and exercise is needed, there are clear indications that physical activity has a favorable effect on body composition. Observation of those engaged in vigorous activity over the life span demonstrates at the very least that a decline in fat-free mass and an increase in fat mass is not a foregone conclusion for everyone.

Web Study Guide **Measure skinfolds, height, and weight in Lab Activity 12.2, Comparing Body Composition Measures, in the web study guide.**

If you were a teacher or a doctor, what would be your strategy for reversing the trend of declining fitness in today's youths?

Obesity

The prevalence of **obesity** has increased around the world, especially in industrialized countries, in all age categories for the past several decades. According to the World Health Organization (2017), the prevalence of obesity tripled between 1975 and 2016 (see table 12.1). The most common definition for obesity is having a body mass index (BMI) of more than 30.0 (Kotz, Billington, & Levine, 1999; see table 12.2). A healthy BMI is defined as the range from 18.5 to 24.9. It is challenging to define obesity for children because of ongoing growth, but one frequently used criterion is a weight-for-height measurement over the 95th percentile; another is a triceps skinfold over the 95th percentile (Rudloff & Feldmann, 1999).

Obesity is most commonly defined as a body mass index of more than 30.0.

Obesity in Childhood and Adolescence

Obesity is a concern at any point in the life span, yet chances are great that obese children will remain obese into adulthood, and obesity tends to be stable over young, middle, and older adulthood. Between 9% and 13% of children are obese (Flegal & Troiano, 2000; Fredriks, van Buuren, Wit, & Varloove-Vanhorick, 2000). Hence, there is a sense of urgency about addressing obesity in children even while recognizing its medical and social repercussions at any age.

Parents often believe their child's obesity is caused by a metabolic or thyroid disorder. In fact, these disorders account for less than 1% of obesity in children (Dietz & Robinson, 1993). What, then, is the typical cause? Obesity is a good example of the interaction between genetic and extrinsic factors. Genetic factors are certainly related to obesity. BMI is highly correlated in twins, even if they are raised apart, but is poorly correlated in parents and adopted children.

TABLE 12.1 Prevalence of Obesity in the World

NUMBER OF CHILDREN UNDER 5	NUMBER OF CHILDREN 5–19	NUMBER OF ADULTS (%)	
Overweight or obese	Overweight or obese	Overweight	Obese
41 million	340 million	1.9 billion (39%)	650 million (13%)

Data from World Health Organization Fact Sheet, October 2017. Available at http://www.who.int/mediacentre/factsheets/fs311/en/.

TABLE 12.2 Criteria for Overweight and Obesity

AGE GROUP	OVERWEIGHT	OBESE
Adults	BMI ≥ 25	BMI ≥ 30
Children between 5 and 19	BMI for age > 1 sd above WHO growth reference median	BMI for age > 2 sd above WHO growth reference median
Children under 5	Weight for height > 2 sd above WHO child growth standards median	Weight for height > 3 sd above WHO child growth standards median

Note: WHO = World Health Organization; sd = standard deviation.

Source: World Health Organization Fact Sheet, October 2017. Available at http://www.who.int/mediacentre/factsheets/fs311/en/.

However, no single genetic factor is related to obesity in all individuals. Various factors under genetic influence include basal metabolic rate, dietary **thermogenesis**, appetite control and satiety, and lipid metabolism and storage (Rudloff & Feldmann, 1999).

Thermogenesis is the production of heat in the body.

The increase in obesity over the past several decades demonstrates the strong influence of extrinsic factors on obesity because genetic influences could not change the incidence rate so rapidly (Rosenbaum & Leibel, 1998). Increasing modernization reduces energy expenditure as laborious tasks are taken over by machines (figure 12.4) and time spent sitting in front of screens (television, computer, tablet, gaming, and smartphone) increases. A Westernized diet, high in fat and sugar, is also a major factor in obesity (Kotz et al., 1999). Because genetic predispositions are fixed in individuals, manipulation of energy intake and expenditure is the most available means for addressing obesity over the life span.

▶ **KEY POINT** The trends in extrinsic factors that lead to obesity are problematic on two counts: (1) People are less active, and (2) diets increasingly consist of high levels of fat and sugar.

Restricting caloric intake in children is challenging because sufficient energy must be provided to support growth (Braet, Tanghe, De Bode, Franckx, & Van Winckel, 2003). The associations between overweight and various aspects of nutrition such as fruit and vegetable consumption, soft drink consumption, and skipping breakfast are inconsistent (Haug et al., 2009). Yet a relatively modest adjustment of calories with good nutritional balance in diet can be very effective (Faith, Carnell, & Kral, 2013). However, reduced motor activity is a common characteristic of obese children (Haug et al., 2009), and increasing calorie expenditure through exercise has multiple benefits in altering body fat. First, it can offset the decrease in basal metabolic rate that accompanies caloric restriction. Second, it can promote the growth of muscle tissue, which requires more calories for maintenance than fat tissue requires (Bar-Or, 1993). This difference is significant because without exercise, 30% to 40% of the weight lost with caloric restriction in adults is from lean body mass (Harris, 1999); this is likely the trend with children, too. Finally, Schwartz, King, Perreira, Blundell, and Thivel (2017) conducted a meta-analysis on nine studies and concluded that physical activity interventions were associated with reduced food intake in obese adolescents.

FIGURE 12.4 An increase in screen time causes more people to be sedentary rather than active. These environmental and task constraints interact with body systems to decrease lean body mass, increase fat tissue, and increase the risk of cardiovascular disease.

Hesketh and Campbell (2010) reviewed 23 studies on interventions for preventing obesity in toddlers and young children up to 5 years of age. Most of the studies reviewed were conducted in preschool or child-care settings and home settings, and about half of the studies were done with disadvantaged participants. Researchers tended to use multiple modes of intervention, such as improved diet, increased physical activity, and reduced sedentary behavior. The nature of the intervention programs was varied and the success of the programs was mixed, but overall the studies demonstrated that interventions could positively affect obesity in early childhood, especially if parents were involved.

A synthesis of reviews and meta-analyses (Khambalia, Dickinson, Hardy, Gill, & Baur, 2012) on obesity interventions in school-age children suggests that intervention programs were more likely to yield a significant weight reduction in children if they were long term rather than short term. Additionally, programs tended to be successful if they combined improved diet, increased physical activity, and family involvement. Hens et al. (2017) conducted a meta-analysis on studies that tracked types of adipose tissue during diet or exercise interventions. They found that both diet and exercise reduced the adipose tissue in and around the skeletal muscles and organs in children and adolescents.

There is also research on types of exercise. Kelley, Kelley, and Pate (2017) conducted a meta-analysis on 34 studies and found that both aerobic exercise and aerobic exercise combined with strength training, but not strength training alone, were associated with a reduction in BMI. Although the research conducted on intervention programs thus far has been helpful, more research is needed on programs that measure both weight-related outcomes and health-related outcomes.

▶ **KEY POINT** Exercise is an important strategy in altering obesity because it expends calories and offsets a decrease in basal metabolic rate that accompanies caloric restriction.

It is well established that obese children do not perform as well as lean children do on a variety of physical fitness and motor skills tests. Malina et al. (1995) selected a group of Belgian girls between 7 and 17 years of age. At each age, the leanest 5% outperformed the fattest 5% on arm-strength and endurance tasks, trunk-strength tasks, the vertical jump, an agility shuttle run, and a balance task. Adolescent boys show the same performance differences (Beunen et al., 1983). This supports the bidirectional relationship between motor competence and weight status as well as fitness. Motor competence facilitates the active lifestyle that promotes healthy weight and fitness. A healthy weight status allows individuals to be active and practice skills sufficiently to become proficient.

If you were a middle school physical education teacher, how might you intervene with your obese students to put them on a path toward improved health?

▶ **KEY POINT** Motor competence facilitates an active lifestyle, in turn promoting a healthy weight status and fitness.

Obesity in Adulthood

The incidence of obesity increases in men and women from early adulthood to middle adulthood (figure 12.5). Obesity puts individuals at risk for hypertension, cardiovascular disease, diabetes, gallstones, osteoarthritis, and some forms of cancer; hence, the obese are at greater risk of early mortality. In fact, a decrease in the prevalence of obesity in the late 60s and beyond might reflect the shortened life span of the obese. The association of obesity and mortality is stronger among those whose increased fatness is particularly concentrated in the abdomen (Kotz et al., 1999).

As at younger ages, genetic and extrinsic influences play a role in adult obesity, though the relative contributions of each can vary in an individual over the life span (Rosenbaum & Leibel, 1998). It is well known that activity levels are low among adults in Westernized countries. In the United States, individuals 6 years and older spend almost 55% of their waking time in sedentary behaviors (Matthews et al., 2008). As with children and teens, a combination of caloric restriction and increased activity is the most effective strategy for altering body fatness among adults. Research studies show that progress is greater with a combination than with exercise alone or caloric restriction alone. Even a modest 10% loss of body weight can have a substantial benefit for cholesterol levels, fasting blood glucose levels, and blood pressure (Harris, 1999).

Body composition is an important component of physical fitness and is related to physical performance. Although genetic factors influence body composition, the extrinsic factors of diet and exercise can greatly affect an individual's relative levels of fat and lean body mass. A

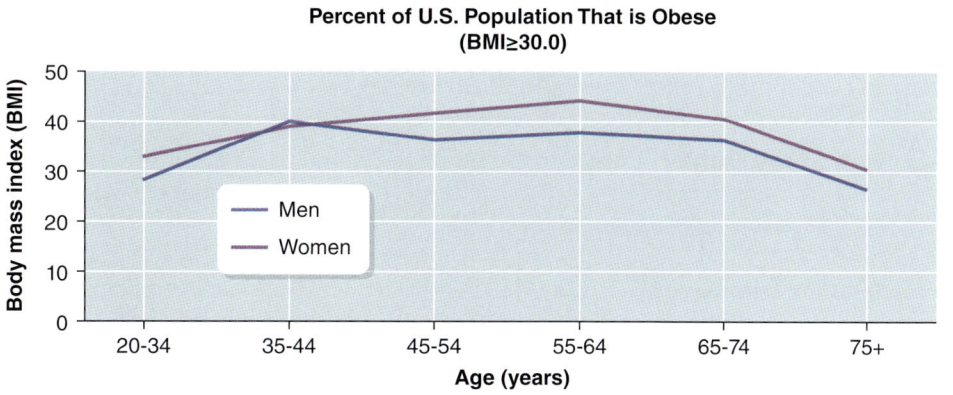

FIGURE 12.5 The prevalence of obesity over adulthood in the United States, 2011–2014. Declines in the later years reflect the greater risk of early mortality in the obese; that is; many obese individuals died at younger ages than their normal or overweight counterparts.

Data from the U.S. Department of Health and Human Services (2016).

person of any age who wishes to change his or her body fatness can manipulate both diet and exercise. Miller et al. (2013) reviewed 14 intervention studies that featured a control group and randomly assigned obese adult participants to groups. They concluded that an intervention of energy restriction plus exercise was more effective for improving cardiorespiratory fitness and muscle strength, promoting fat loss, and preserving lean body mass than energy restriction alone. Regular exercise can play a large and favorable role in altering body composition because it promotes muscle mass and an increase in basal metabolic rate. In turn, a body composition higher in lean mass and lower in fat mass makes exercise and physical performance easier.

Motor Competence, Activity, Fitness, and Body Composition

Although a few publications before 2008 spoke to the interrelationships among motor competence, activity, fitness, and body composition, it was an article published by leaders in the field of motor development, Stodden, Goodway, Langendorfer, Roberton, Rudisill, Garcia, and Garcia (2008), that gave impetus to the study of these interrelated factors. Stodden et al. made a case for the importance of proficiency in common foundational movement skills, generally referred to as motor competence, to levels of physical activity, health-related fitness, and weight status. Their conceptual model of the relationships among these factors accounts for the strengthening of relationships through early childhood, middle childhood, and late childhood. Further, the model illustrates that those lacking an adequate foundation in motor competency might not engage in sufficient levels of physical activity to attain an adequate level of health-related fitness and optimal body composition and weight status. This would put such individuals at greater risk of obesity and low fitness levels over the life span.

If motor competence is related to levels of physical activity and fitness, this has important implications for programming in childhood and adolescence. For example, if you are concerned about the trends toward increased overweight and declining fitness levels in youths, would the answer be to focus physical education programs solely on fitness activities, or would there be value in focusing on developing both motor competence and fitness?

Many structured and unstructured games, sports, and activities, including dance, build on the fundamental motor skills. For example, baseball requires running, throwing, catching, and striking. A dance might require walking, running, and hopping as well as balance and body awareness. Being competent in fundamental skills permits students to become proficient movers during physical activity. As we mentioned earlier, proficient movers are efficient and can sustain vigorous activity. Think of two tennis players. If they are proficient in moving and striking, they can play long rallies and therefore expend high levels of energy. Alternatively, if they are not proficient, the action might stop after one or two strikes so that errant balls can be retrieved. Exercise and concomitant energy expenditure are limited.

Web Study Guide **Consider the emphasis given to physical fitness and skill development in Lab Activity 12.3, The Curriculum in Elementary School Physical Education, in the web study guide.**

Children do not automatically acquire skill proficiency. Instructional programs and opportunities for practice are vital for achieving motor competence. Obviously, it is important for both researchers and practitioners to know if there is a link between motor competence and physical activity level, health-related fitness status, and weight status. Further, individuals who achieve motor competence when young are positioned to engage in enjoyable and vigorous physical activity for a lifetime.

Motor Competence and Level of Physical Activity

Robinson et al. (2015) published a narrative review on the relationships among motor competency, physical activity, health-related fitness, perceived motor competence, and weight status from a developmental perspective. They located two articles (Lubans, Morgan, Cliff, Barnett, & Okely, 2010; Holfelder & Schott, 2014) that reviewed research on the relationship between motor competence, as assessed by both product and process measures, and physical activity in children and adolescents. Twelve of 13 studies in the first article found a positive association; in the second, 12 of 23 studies, which also included measures of motor ability and coordination, found a positive association. A review paper that included only process assessments of motor competency (Logan, Webster, Getchell, Pfeiffer, & Robinson, 2015) also found a positive association in 12 of 13 studies. They found low to moderate relationships between fundamental motor skill competence and physical activity in early childhood (r = .16 to .48; R^2 = 3%–23%, four studies), low to high relationships in middle to late childhood (r = .24 to .55; R^2 = 6%–30%, seven studies), and low to moderate relationships in adolescence (r = .14 to .35; R^2 = 2%–12.3%, two studies).

Two longitudinal studies were also supportive. One (Barnett, Zask, Rose, Hughes, & Adams, 2009) found that object control competency in children explained a small but significant portion of moderate to vigorous physical activity level. The second (Lopes, Santos, Pereira, & Lopes, 2012) found that children at the age of 6 years with high motor competence self-reported higher levels of motor activity than children with low or moderate motor competency when measured 3 years later.

Figueroa and An (2017) also reviewed studies on the motor competency and physical activity levels of preschoolers. Eight of the 11 studies, conducted in five different countries, reported a significant relationship between motor competency and physical activity. Henrique et al. (2016) found that in children between 3 and 5 years of age, locomotor skill competency and sports participation predicted sports participation two years later. There is strong emerging evidence of a positive association between motor competency and physical activity over the growing years.

Robinson et al. hoped to draw a conclusion about the changes in the association between motor competency and physical activity over childhood and adolescence, but more research, especially research using the same measures, is needed. It might be hypothesized that early in life, higher levels of physical activity drive acquisition of motor competence and thereafter the relationship is reciprocal. Loprinzi, Davis, and Fu (2015) suggested a conceptual model delineating the potential for motor competency to mediate physical activity in childhood and adulthood, perhaps indirectly through increased enjoyment of physical activity. They found consistent evidence that motor competency is associated with increased physical activity in early, middle, and late childhood and adolescence. Lloyd, Saunders, Bremer, and Tremblay (2014) provided preliminary information about adulthood. They analyzed questionnaires about physical activity levels completed by 17 participants who had been assessed on motor competency 20 years earlier, at age 6 years. Motor competency at age 6 was positively associated with leisure time physical activity in females 20 years later. Much more research on motor competency and adult physical activity levels is needed to address this aspect of Loprinzi et al.'s conceptual model.

▶ **KEY POINT** Youths who are highly competent in motor skills tend to be more active than less competent youths.

Web Study Guide **Observe the interaction of activity level and skill level as children play in Lab Activity 12.4, Skill and Activity Level, in the web study guide.**

A study by Vedul-Kjelsås, Sigmundsson, Stendsdotter, and Haga (2011) is a reminder that self-perception in children is related to motor competence and physical fitness. They found this relationship in all aspects of self-perception measured by Harter's Self-Perception Profile for Children: social acceptance, athletic competence, physical appearance, and general self-worth. The authors suggested that these aspects of self-perception facilitate participation in physical activity. We will discuss perceived motor competence in more detail in a later chapter.

Motor Competence and Health-Related Fitness

What about the association between motor competency and health-related fitness? Barnett, van Beurden, Morgan, Brooks, and Beard (2008) measured youths approximately 8 to 12 years old on fundamental motor skills and a shuttle run–type cardiorespiratory test. They then repeated the tests 5 years later. They found that some of the fundamental motor skills—interestingly, the object-control skills rather than locomotor skills—predicted adolescent cardiorespiratory fitness. This was true for both boys and girls. Perhaps the youths with good object-control skills were more likely to participate in physical activities. Hands (2008) took a similar approach but included children who were classified as either low or high in motor competence. She also repeated her measures every year for 5 years. The two competency groups were different in all measures (the high competency group was better) except body mass index, for which no difference was found. The differences remained over the 5 years but widened on the shuttle run test for aerobic fitness and narrowed on a sprint run and a balance test. The children with low motor competency improved over the 5 years but never caught up with the children with high competency. Better motor skill was associated with greater cardiorespiratory endurance.

Cattuzzo et al. (2016) reviewed 44 cross-sectional and longitudinal studies of children and adolescents published between 1990 and 2013. A positive association between motor competency and cardiorespiratory fitness was found in 12 of 12 studies and between motor competence and musculoskeletal fitness in 7 of 11 studies. Higher motor competence was associated with lower weight status in 27 of 33 studies. The reviewers concluded that motor competence was directly and indirectly associated with health-related fitness.

Very little research exists on the motor competence of adults and its impact on fitness, but Stodden, Langendorfer, and Roberton (2009) did examine this relationship in young adults 18 to 25 years old. They assessed motor competence on maximum kicking and throwing speed and maximum jumping distance. They also recorded percent body fat, grip strength, and maximum leg press as well as performance on the 12-minute run/walk and the curl-up test. The motor competency scores were highly related to the variability in fitness among the adults, suggesting that motor competence is important for attaining and maintaining fitness in adulthood.

▶ **KEY POINT** Higher motor competence is associated with better cardiorespiratory fitness, greater strength, and healthier weight status.

Motor Competence and Weight Status

Finally, let us consider the relationship between motor competence and weight status. It is possible that overweight impedes motor development in infancy. Low motor competence makes movement more difficult for children, and lower physical activity ultimately contributes to higher levels of overweight and obesity. Robinson et al. (2015) found a number of studies that showed an inverse relationship between motor competence and weight status (high motor competence with lower weight and low motor competence with higher weight) emerging in early childhood (Logan, Scrabis-Fletcher, Modlesky, & Getchell, 2011; Nervik, Martin, Rundquist, & Cleland, 2011; Saraiva, Rodrigues, Cordovil, & Barreiros, 2013) and strengthening in childhood (D'Hondt et al., 2011; Lopes, Santos, Pereira, & Lopes, 2012). In adolescence and adulthood the studies they reviewed were mixed.

A longitudinal study provides interesting information about this relationship. D'Hondt et al. (2014) measured height and weight to calculate BMI z-scores and motor coordination on the KörperkoordinationsTest für Kinder (KTK) for over 2,500 children between 5 and 13 years of age. Two years later over 750 were tested again. A low motor competence score at baseline significantly predicted an increased BMI z-score two years later. At the same time, a higher BMI z-score at baseline significantly predicted a decrease in the motor competency score. Thus, a reciprocal relationship between motor competency and BMI was demonstrated.

▶ **KEY POINT** Motor competence and weight status have a reciprocal relationship.

Our discussion of motor competency, health-related fitness, physical activity, and body composition and weight status has provided much evidence of the interrelationships among these factors. While more research evidence is needed, especially from long-term longitudinal studies, there is much support for programs that develop motor competency at young ages. Not only does motor competency appear to have a positive association in childhood and adolescence with the other factors, there is reason to hypothesize it has a positive association throughout the life span.

Summary and Synthesis

There is strong evidence that motor competence, health-related physical fitness, physical activity, and body composition are interrelated. Many of these factors influence the others and vice versa. For educators and health professionals who desire to improve the health of individuals at any point in the life span, understanding these interrelationships is vital. Simple interventions are not likely to be successful if the complexity of these relationships is overlooked. Approaches that are global in promoting motor competence and physical activity are most likely to realize an impact on health-related fitness and healthy weight status.

Reinforcing What You Have Learned About Constraints

TAKE A SECOND LOOK

The obesity issue highlights the interactive nature of the body's structural constraints and movement. Physical activity can alter the structural constraints over time and thus permit movements requiring fitness. In the case of obesity, being physically active contributes to reduction of body weight, thus making movement easier and more proficient. A lack of activity can alter the structural constraints over time. Not only is the body heavier, but the eventual effect on the body systems contributes to restriction of activities and movements, especially those requiring a certain level of fitness. Individuals can change their fitness levels and body composition with training, although age-related differences exist in the effect of training. The media messages that pressure individuals from all walks of life to want to look ultra-thin present a false goal. That goal, rather, should be a healthy body with modest levels of fat tissue, and we know that is best attained through an active lifestyle. Motor competence allows individuals to enjoy various physical activities with enough vigor that a balance of calories consumed and calories expended can be achieved.

TEST YOUR KNOWLEDGE

1. How does regular participation in physical activity affect body composition in children and adolescents?
2. What are the sex differences in body composition? Does exercise affect the body composition of males and females similarly or differently? How so?
3. What are the best weight-management strategies for obese children?
4. What are the favorable effects of exercise on the body composition of older adults?
5. What negative effects does obesity have on children? On middle-aged and older adults?

6. How is body composition assessed? What are the advantages and disadvantages of specific techniques at various points in the life span?
7. How does motor competence influence levels of physical activity? Health-related fitness? Body composition?
8. How could engagement in physical activity impact motor competence?
9. Explain the reciprocal relationship between motor competency and weight status.
10. Select three of the research studies or research reviews mentioned in this chapter, and identify which arrow and direction(s) in the model of interrelationships are supported by the research.

LEARNING EXERCISE 12.1

Children and Obesity

The increase in the number of children around the world who are obese is of great concern to all of us. In the past few years this topic has received much attention in the popular press, and many people have tried to identify the causes and suggest interventions in order to reverse the trend. Conduct an Internet search and find three solutions that have been proposed to reverse the trend of increased obesity in children. Do the writers present evidence that would lead you to believe the solutions would work based on what you have read here? Explain. Are you persuaded that there is one solution that would work, or do you believe that multiple solutions are necessary? Why?

LEARNING EXERCISE 12.2

The Stodden Model

Look up the citation for the Stodden et al. (2008) paper and obtain a copy of this paper. Find the illustration of the model discussed in this chapter. Examine the model and identify three relationships among the factors of motor competence, physical activity, weight status, and physical fitness. Are the relationships represented as unidirectional or bidirectional (reciprocal)? Give an example of each relationship. How does the model represent development? Explain.

V

Perceptual-Motor Development

Infants and toddlers experience dramatic changes in perception. Infants learn, for example, the names and locations of their body parts, as well as the relationships between objects, such as "in front of" or "behind." Such changes play a large part in the cognitive and physical skills infants and toddlers can execute. There is no doubt that the perceptual systems, as individual structural constraints, interact with the task and environment to give rise to movement; in fact, the interactions between the perceptual systems and the environment are very rich.

The study of perception and its relationship to movement, or action, has been at least as controversial as any aspect of motor development. Certainly, professionals have adopted varying perspectives on the role of perception in motor development. Perhaps the most recent and significant debate involves the notion that movement drives perceptual development as much as perceptual development permits new movements. On the horizon, too, is a research frontier concerned with how movement and exercise facilitate growth in the neurological system over the life span. For both these areas of research, the model of constraints is useful because it highlights the interaction of individual, environment, and task in giving rise to movement. We begin our discussion by reviewing the age-related changes in sensation and perception within the vision, kinesthetic, and audition systems.

Suggested Reading

Bornstein, M.H. (2017). Perceptual development: Stability and change in feature perception. In M.H. Bornstein & W. Kessen (Eds.), *Psychological development from infancy* (pp. 37–81). New York: Routledge.

Corbetta, D., DiMercurio, A., Weiner, R.F., Connell, J.P., & Clark, M. (2018). How perception and action fosters exploration and selection in infant skill acquisition. *Advances in Child Development and Behavior, 55*, 1–29.

de Klerk, C.C., Johnson, M.H., Heyes, C.M., & Southgate, V. (2015). Baby steps: Investigating the development of perceptual-motor couplings in infancy. *Developmental Science, 18*(2), 270–280.

Kay, B.A., & Kelso, J.A.S. (2016). Information and control: A macroscopic analysis of perception-action coupling. In H. Heuer & A. Sanders (Eds.), *Perspectives on perception and action* (pp. 17–46). New York: Routledge.

Lynch, A., & Getchell, N. (2010). Using an ecological approach to understand perception, cognition, and action coupling in individuals with autism spectrum disorder. *International Public Health Journal, 2*(1), 7–16.

Witt, J.K., & Riley, M.A. (2014). Discovering your inner Gibson: Reconciling action-specific and ecological approaches to perception–action. *Psychonomic Bulletin & Review, 21*(6), 1353–1370.

13

Sensory-Perceptual Development

CHAPTER OBJECTIVES

This chapter

- reviews developmental changes in the vision, audition, and kinesthetic systems;
- discusses changes in visual, auditory, and kinesthetic sensation that occur with aging;
- traces the development of visual perception—in particular, perception of space, objects, and motion;
- provides an overview of the development of kinesthetic perception, especially perception of tactile location, the body, limb movements, spatial orientation, and direction;
- describes the development of auditory perception; and
- studies the process whereby environmental objects and events perceived in different modalities are perceived as the same object or event.

Motor Development in the Real World

Your Environment

Most of us have had the opportunity to see an IMAX movie on a large surround screen. In recent years, there has been an upsurge in the number of three-dimensional IMAX theaters, and Hollywood filmmakers have embraced the IMAX experience. Many of these movies include the view seen as if flying from the cockpit of an airplane. The visual information is so rich that oftentimes people who tend to get airsick or seasick cannot watch such movies without getting sick. These movies serve as a reminder that sensory and perceptual information—especially visual information—is an important part of our experience in, and interaction with, our environment. We exist only in an environment. How we operate in that environment is a function of how we sense and perceive it.

In many ways, almost every motor act can be considered a perceptual-motor skill. Human movement is based on information about the environment and one's position or location in it. For example, a softball infielder sees the location of the pitch, the batter striking the ball, and the ball bouncing on the ground; hears the hit and perhaps sees a runner on the base path; and feels the position of her body and arms. The infielder uses this information to decide where and when she can intercept the ball, where to move, and how to position her body. It might seem that not all movements are so dependent on sensing and perceiving the environment. Yet even an experienced platform diver, blindfolded and wearing earplugs, must feel how gravity pulls his body and know where his trunk and limbs are relative to one another to execute his dive.

As the motion sickness effect of a three-dimensional movie demonstrates, sensory information and perceptual information are highly integrated. We typically experience events in multiple sensory systems. We are uncomfortable if the information from one sense contradicts the information from another—we stagger, fall, or feel sick. If we are denied information from one sense we can compensate by attending to information from another, but we might not be as accurate in our perceptions. Moreover, our sensory-perceptual selves and the environment are interactive systems. We do not simply receive information from the environment; rather, we act to obtain information. For example, we turn our ears toward a sound or reach to feel the texture of a surface. Thus, we must keep in mind the highly integrative nature of **sensation**, **perception**, and movement even as we discuss individual systems or types of perceptual discrimination.

Sensation is the neural activity triggered by a stimulus that activates a sensory receptor and results in sensory nerve impulses traveling along the sensory nerve pathways to the brain.

Perception is a multistage process that takes place in the brain and includes selecting, processing, organizing, and integrating information received from the senses.

Individuals with normally functioning sensory receptors can attach different meanings to the same stimulus, and even the same individual can interpret a single stimulus in different ways. You might remember seeing in a general psychology class some visual displays that have this effect. Figure 13.1 can be seen as two facial profiles or as a vase. Thus, perception is the process whereby we attach meaning to sensory stimuli. How individuals interpret sensory stimuli is the fascinating topic of perceptual development. For individuals to move or act in an environment, they must perceive that environment. In fact, some views of perception and action see them as so interactive as to be inseparable. The environment influences what movements are possible or efficient, and moving through the environment informs us about the nature of the environment and our interactions with it. No study of motor development is complete without the study of the relationship between perception and action.

The sensory-perceptual systems are, of course, individual structural constraints to movement and to other activities such as reading. Earlier chapters discussed the development of many of the structural systems, such as the skeletal and muscular systems. This chapter discusses the development of visual, auditory, and kinesthetic sensation and perception.

Visual Development

Vision plays a major role in most skill performance. To better understand this role, we need to examine age-related changes in visual sensation and visual perception.

Visual Sensation

Several aspects of vision determine how clearly one can see objects (figure 13.2). Here, we confine our discussion to visual **acuity**. During the first month of life, the visual system provides the infant with functionally useful but unrefined vision at a level approximately 5% of eventual adult acuity, or 20/400 on the Snellen scale of visual acuity (20/20 is desirable) (figure 13.3). The newborn's resolution of detail is such that she can differentiate facial features from a distance of 20 inches; beyond this, she probably cannot see objects clearly (Kellman & Arterberry, 1998).

Acuity is sharpness of sight.

At about 6 months of age, as infants' motor systems are ready to begin self-propelled locomotion, their visual systems perceive adequate detail to assist them in the task. From the ecological perspective, vision is another system that must develop to an adequate level to facilitate locomotion.

Visual sensation continues to improve during childhood. Five-year-olds have visual acuity of about 20/30, and by age 10 children without a visual anomaly score at the desired level of 20/20. It is likely that visual experience is necessary for the development of vision because deprivation of vision during development is known to induce refractive errors in animals (Atkinson & Braddick, 1981).

As a person ages, changes in the visual system occur naturally, and some conditions and diseases become more prevalent, especially in older adults. These changes may affect the quality of the visual information that reaches the central nervous system and may have implications for the performance of skills as well as tasks of everyday living.

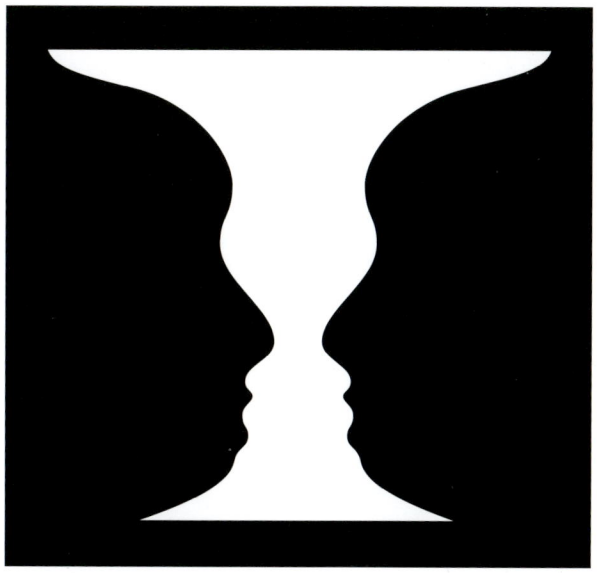

FIGURE 13.1 This drawing can be seen as two facing facial profiles or as a vase.

Reprinted from WikiCommons.

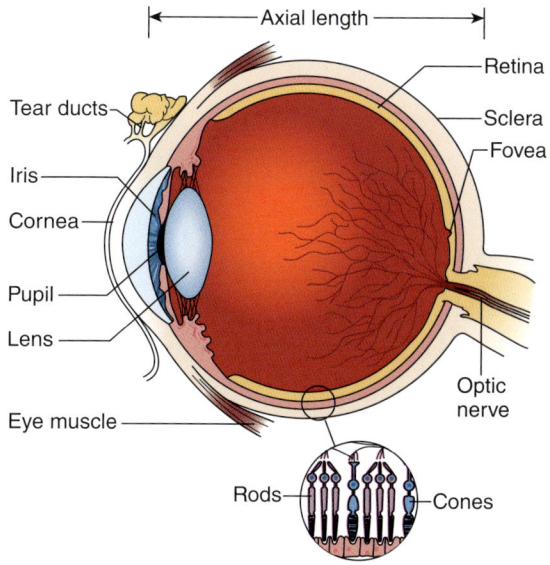

FIGURE 13.2 The human eye. An axial length that is too short or too long results in farsightedness or nearsightedness, respectively. An imperfect curvature of the cornea also causes blurred vision, a condition known as astigmatism.

▶ **KEY POINT** Vision reaches adult levels around 10 years of age, but any refractive errors resulting from imperfections in the axial length of the eye can be corrected with glasses or contacts.

Presbyopia is the gradual loss of accommodation power to focus on near objects. It accompanies advancing age.

For example, the condition termed **presbyopia** (from *presbys* for "old man" and *ops* for "eye") becomes clinically significant at around age 40. It affects the ability to see nearby images clearly. The resting diameter of the pupil also decreases with aging, typically reducing retinal illuminance (the amount of light reaching the retina) in a 60-year-old to one-third of that in a young adult. The lens also yellows with age, further reducing the amount of illuminance reaching the eye and making glare a problem for older adults.

Visual disturbances that are more prevalent in older adults include the following:

- Cataracts
- Glaucoma
- **Age-related maculopathy**

Age-related maculopathy is a disease affecting the central area of the retina that provides detailed vision.

People who work with children or older adults can look for certain signs that may indicate a visual problem. These include

- squinting,
- under- or overreaching for objects, and
- performing unusual head movements to align one's gaze with a particular object.

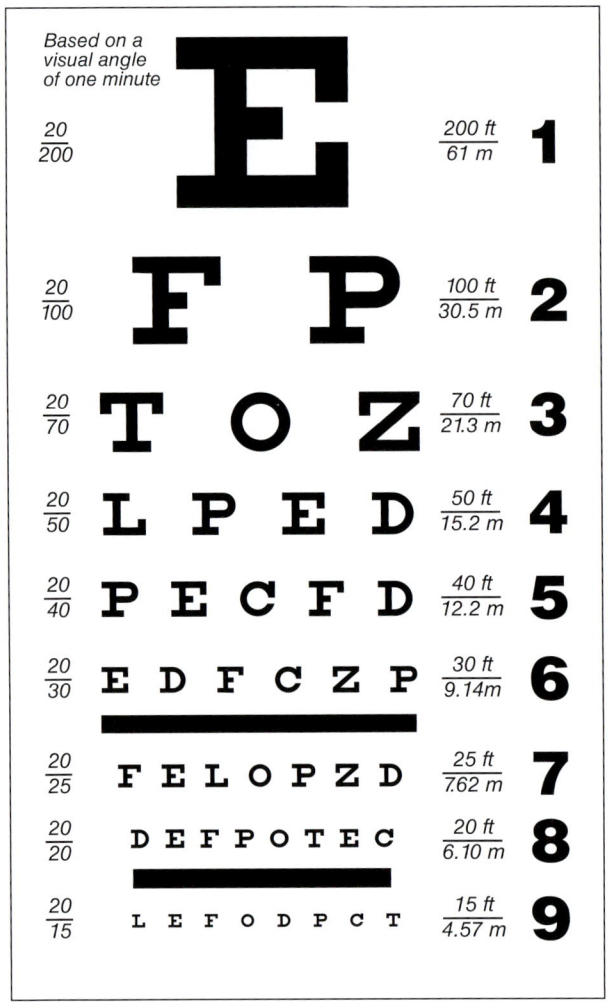

FIGURE 13.3 A Snellen chart. Sharpness of sight is measured by whether observers can distinguish letters that differ only by whether a small gap is filled, such as *F* and *P*, or *C* and *O*. Children must know letters to be measured in this manner. Alternative methods are available for testing infants and toddlers.

Activity leaders should make sure that activity areas are well lit but without glare, and they should encourage performers to wear any corrective lenses prescribed for them (Haywood & Trick, 1990). Because vision provides so much of the perceptual information that people need in order to perform skills successfully, efforts to enhance the visual information that the central nervous system receives should also enhance visual perception and thus skill performance. An excellent way to remind ourselves of how much we rely on sensory information is to close our eyes while trying to perform a routine activity.

Visual Perception

People depend heavily on visual perception in the performance of most skills. The development of visual perception is a topic for texts in and of itself, so only major aspects of visual perception are highlighted here.

Perception of Space

One of the fundamental perceptions is that of three-dimensional space. Almost all movements—reaching and grasping, locomotion, and complex skills such as driving a car or piloting a plane—depend on a perception of three-dimensional space. Visual sensations are received by sensory receptors in the retina in approximately a two-dimensional format. So how do people interpret the world in three dimensions?

To perceive space in three dimensions, individuals must perceive depth and distance. The visual system has numerous sources of information about distance and **depth perception**. One source is **retinal disparity**. Because an individual's two eyes are in different locations, each eye sees the visual field from a slightly different angle (figure 13.4). The information needed for judging depth comes from a comparison of the two slightly different pictures. Depth perception is aided by good visual acuity because a sharper picture from each eye provides more information for the comparison.

Viewers have other sources of information about depth. By moving the head or moving through space, they receive depth cues from **motion parallax**. Objects in space change locations on our retinas, and nearer objects overlap more distant objects as the head moves. Gibson (1966) suggested that this transformation of the optical array, which he called **optic flow**, provides much information about the three-dimensional nature of our environment. This direct means of perceiving the environment likely guides locomotion, controls posture, and helps us anticipate contact with objects and surfaces (Crowell & Banks, 1993; Johansson, von Hofsten, & Jansson, 1980; Warren & Wertheim, 1990).

Viewers with experience in the world also use an assumption of physical equality to judge depth. That is, when two like objects can be expected to have the same size but project different relative sizes on the retina, we assume that the object with the larger retinal size is closer to us. Similarly, if we look down a roadway, we assume it is the same width across even though the curbs appear to get closer to one another (the curbs form converging lines).

Depth perception is a person's judgment of the distance from self to an object or place in space.

Retinal disparity is the difference in the images received by the two eyes as a result of their different locations.

Motion parallax is the change in optical location for objects at different distances during viewer motion.

Optic flow is change in the pattern of optical texture, a transformation of the optic array, as a viewer moves forward or backward in a stable environment.

If you were a physical education teacher, what types of activities might you teach that would require depth perception?

Infants have functional vision and, therefore, the mechanics for retinal disparity and motion parallax as sources of depth perception. From about 1 month of age, infants blink more often when shown a display that appears to be approaching than when shown a display that does not (Nanez & Yonas, 1994), demonstrating that they perceive the object to be moving toward them, not merely increasing in size. In the well-known visual cliff experiments of Walk and Gibson (1961; Gibson & Walk, 1960; Walk, 1969), infants between 6 and 14 months of age, placed on one side of an apparent drop-off

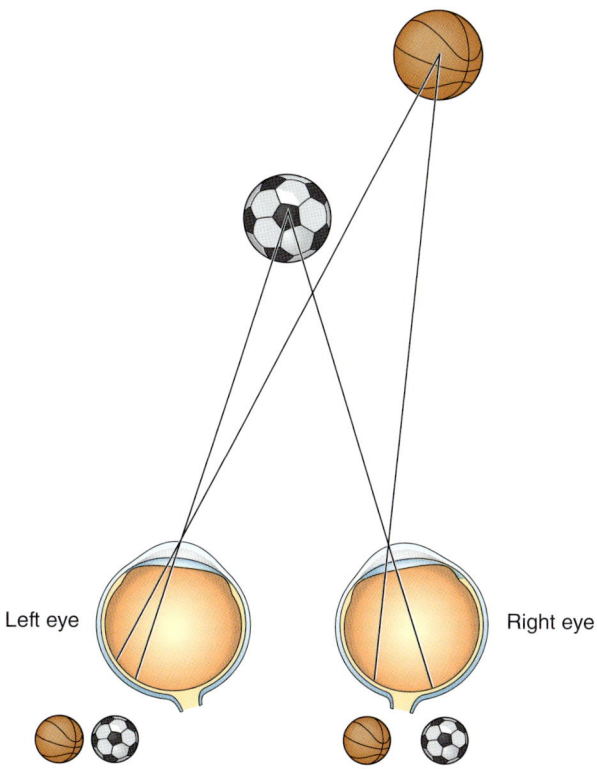

FIGURE 13.4 Retinal disparity: Each eye sees the visual field from a slightly different angle

(a piece of glass over the drop-off prevented it from being a real cliff), stopped at the edge even though their mothers beckoned them from the other side. These studies demonstrate that even young infants have some level of depth perception. Yet, children may err in judging depth until near-adult levels are reached in early adolescence (Williams, 1968).

▶ **KEY POINT** Cues about depth and distance in our environment are often derived from the two eyes being in different locations or from movement of the head.

Behavioral experiments on depth perception are consistent with work on maturation of the visual cortex of the cerebrum. At birth, the cells in layer four of the cortex receive neural input from both eyes. By 6 months of age, these neural inputs separate into alternating columns, receiving input from the right and left eyes, respectively (Held, 1985, 1988; Hickey & Peduzzi, 1987). Disparity information would depend on knowing which eye is sending what information, so this aspect of neurological maturation might well be crucial in the onset of depth perception through retinal disparity.

More older adults than younger adults fail depth perception tests, but thresholds for distinguishing depth change little if at all (Wright & Wormald, 1992; Yekta, Pickwell, & Jenkins, 1989). Higher failure rates probably reflect an increase with advancing age in the number of viewers with visual problems.

Although perception of space is an important aspect of visual perception, our environment also includes objects. Thus, it is equally important to perceive objects, their attributes, and their relationships to oneself and to others.

Perception of Objects

Among the important attributes of objects are size, shape, and motion. The concept of "object" is relative. An airplane pilot might consider a runway to be an object, whereas a person standing on the runway considers it a surface. With growth, what infants initially perceive as a surface might become an object. For example, the floor of a playpen is a surface to an infant, whereas the playpen is an object to an adult, who can fold it and carry it away. Adults use a variety of diverse sources of information in perceiving objects (Kellman & Arterberry, 1998). For example, it is likely that we detect edges (discontinuities in the visual display) and decide whether they are object boundaries. If we see a person standing in front of a car, we assume that the nearer object (in this case, the person) has a boundary and that the car continues behind the person. We do not think the car stops at one edge of the person and then starts again at the other edge. Depth and motion cues help in these perceptions.

The perception of edges and boundaries helps us extract an object or figure from the background environment (figure 13.5). You might recall doing puzzle pages of embedded figures. In these pages, an artist embeds familiar objects such as a ball or candy cane in a line drawing. The type of perception that allows us to find the embedded objects is **figure-and-ground perception**. The perception of edges and boundaries also helps us distinguish whole objects from parts of an object, called **whole-and-part perception**. For example, if you are driving down the street and see half a bicycle tire protruding from a row of parked cars and a child's head above it, you are not puzzled. You immediately perceive that a child on a bicycle is pulling into your path, and you slow down.

Figure-and-ground perception is the ability to see an object of interest as distinct from the background.

Whole-and-part perception is the ability to discriminate parts of a picture or an object from the whole, yet integrate the parts into the whole, perceiving them simultaneously.

We know little of infant perception of edges and boundaries. Some research indicates that infants rely more on depth and motion cues than on edges in perceiving objects (Granrud et al., 1984; von Hofsten & Spelke, 1985). Children improve in figure-and-ground perception tasks between 4 and 6 years of age (Williams, 1983) and again between 6 and 8 years (Temple, Williams, & Bateman, 1979).

Very young children have difficulty integrating objects that form a whole. For example, you might recall seeing sculptures comprising familiar objects, such as a stick person constructed from nuts and bolts. Pictures of this nature are used to assess whole-and-part perception (figure 13.6).

Children under 9 years of age typically report seeing only the person, only the nuts and bolts, or both but at different times. After 9, most children can integrate parts and the whole into the total picture (Elkind, 1975; Elkind, Koegler, & Go, 1964). Realize, though, that adult levels of sensitivity to object perception cues far exceed what is necessary to perceive objects in typical environments (Kellman & Arterberry, 1998). So infants may still perceive objects fairly well, even though not at adult levels.

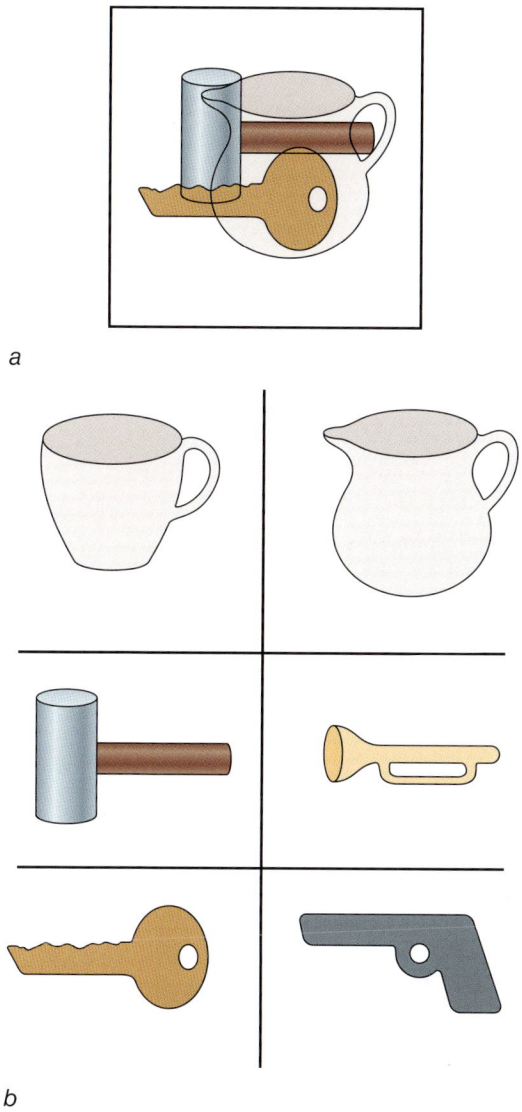

FIGURE 13.5 A test plate from the Figure-Ground Perception Test of the Southern California Sensory Integration Test. A child must identify which of the six objects in *(b)* are present, or embedded, in picture *(a)*.

Reprinted by permission from Ayres (1972).

Think about driving a car around a busy city. When and how often are space perception and object perception involved in your actions?

The perception of distances influences our perception of objects in the environment and their properties. We must perceive that an object has constant size even though it might vary in distance from us (figure 13.7). Slater, Mattock, and Brown (1990) showed that newborns have **size constancy**. They demonstrated first that infants look more at objects with a larger projection size on the retina. Next they familiarized the infants with cubes (large and small) whose size remained constant but whose distance from the infants was varied. When a familiar object with constant size was shown to the infants along with an object of novel size (at distances to make both projected sizes equal), they looked more at the novel-sized object, indicating that they detected the difference in size (see the sidebar Assessment of Infant Perception).

Evidence of newborn sensitivity to shape or form (i.e., **shape constancy**) has also been found through the **habituation** method. If a newborn is habituated to one shape and is then presented that shape along with a new one, the newborn will spend more time looking at the new shape if shape differences are perceived. One type of form perception is **face perception**, and even 4-day-old infants spend a longer time looking at their mothers' faces than at a female stranger's (Bushnell, 1998; Bushnell, Sai, & Mullin, 1989). They probably use the outer contour of faces to perceive patches of light and dark as faces. To perceive form, viewers must either attend to or ignore the **spatial orientation** of objects, depending on whether this information is relevant to the task at hand. In some cases, it is crucial to recognize that two objects are identical even if one is tipped to one side, upside down, or rotated. In other situations, the differing orientation of an object or symbol is critical to its meaning; such is the case with the letters *d* and *b*.

Size constancy is the perception of actual object size despite the size of its image as projected on our retinas.

Shape constancy is the perception of actual object shape despite its orientation to a viewer.

Habituation is the state of having adapted to a stimulus.

Spatial orientation is the orientation or position of objects as they are located in space or in a two-dimensional drawing.

Imagine you are an early childhood teacher. Identify all the letters that can become another letter if their orientation is changed.

▶ **KEY POINT** Infants are sensitive to the size and shape of objects.

Children seem better able to attend to spatial orientation of an object than to ignore it (Gibson, 1966; Pick, 1979). Children at 3 and 4 years of age can learn directional extremes such as high and low, over and under, and front and back, but they often call intermediate orientations the same as the nearest extreme. By age 8, most children have learned to differentiate obliques (various angles) and diagonals (45°) but may still confuse left and right (Naus & Shillman, 1976; Williams, 1973).

FIGURE 13.6 A typical picture that could be used to assess whole-and-part perception. Very young children typically report seeing a face or the pieces (e.g., banana, strawberry, pumpkin). Older children and adults typically report seeing a face made from pieces of fruit.

Perception of Motion

Motion perception is of particular interest in the study of motor development. We know that dedicated neurological mechanisms exist for detecting motion. Specifically, individual corti-

Assessment of Infant Perception

Preferential looking is a research technique in which two stimuli are presented to a subject, who turns to look toward the preferred stimulus.

Because infants are not able to describe what they perceive, researchers must devise other ways to discover what infants perceive through observing their actions and responses. One of the clever ways this is done is through **preferential looking**. Infants tend to look at objects or events that are new, surprising, or different from those they are familiar with. Similarly, the attention of an infant tends to wander away from objects and events to which they are exposed continuously or repeatedly. In the latter case, we say the infant has habituated to the object or event.

To determine what infants perceive with this method, researchers first expose an infant to an object or event, typically for a certain length of time or number of presentations. When the infant habituates to this stimulus and becomes so used to it that the infant's attention wanders elsewhere, the researcher presents another object or event that is different in some dimension. For example, the researcher changes the size of the object if she is interested in perception of size, or the shape if she is interested in perception of shape. The infant

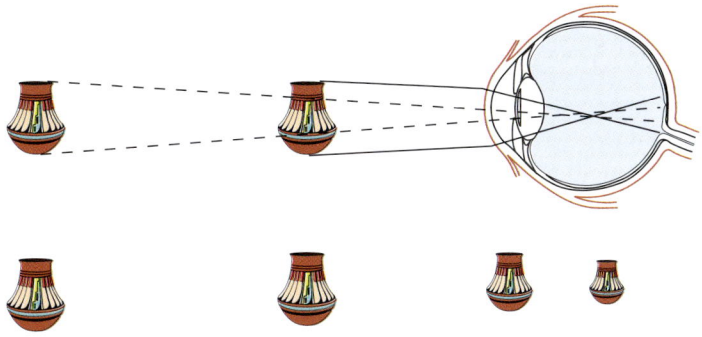

FIGURE 13.7 Size constancy. The image of an object halves in size with each doubling of the distance of the object from the eye, but the object does not appear to shrink. We assume that the object is constant in size and is changing distance from us rather than changing in size and remaining at a constant distance.

cal cells fire according to the direction, location, and speed of an object on the retina, and the medial temporal area of the visual cortex is dedicated to processing motion signals (Kellman & Arterberry, 1998). Therefore, it is not surprising that infants perceive motion.

Early in infancy, however, infants lack adult sensitivity to motion. Direction of motion is not well perceived until 8 weeks of age (Wattam-Bell, 1996a, 1996b). Thresholds for detecting velocity are higher in newborns than in adults; however, by 6 weeks of age, only extremely slow velocities of nearby objects are difficult for the infant to perceive (Aslin & Shea, 1990; von Hofsten, Kellman, & Putaansuu, 1992). Older adults have difficulty perceiving motion at the **detection thresholds** (Elliott, Whitaker, & Thompson, 1989; Kline, Culham, Bartel, & Lynk, 1994). It is not clear whether this has practical significance in real-world conditions; further research is needed.

A **detection threshold** is the point on a continuum at which the energy level is just sufficient for one to register the presence of a stimulus.

attends to the new stimulus if he perceives it as different. The infant shows little interest if the object is perceived to be the same as the familiar one. The researcher could vary the amount of change to see how much difference the infant perceives.

Researchers also habituate an infant to an object and then present it along with a novel object. Usually, one object is placed on the infant's right and the other on the left. The researcher, positioned directly in front of the infant, records the amount of time the infant looks at each object. The infant presumably prefers the object that is novel, if indeed the infant perceives a difference, hence the term *preferential looking*. If much more time is spent looking at the novel object, the researcher concludes that the infant perceives the new object as different from the familiar one. If there is no difference in looking time, the researcher concludes that the difference is not perceived. To learn more about this method, see Bornstein (1985).

This discussion of visual perception has been necessarily brief. Overall, however, the evidence discussed here indicates that basic visual perceptions provide even infants with a great deal of information about the environment. As a child grows, perception at thresholds of detection improves to adult levels. It is likely that attention plays a role in the performance of visual perception tasks and that performance is improved by attention to the important parts of the environment (Madden, Whiting, & Huettel, 2005). However, perception at thresholds will most likely show decrements in older adulthood. Far more information is needed on what significance performance at thresholds has for daily tasks in the real world.

▶ **KEY POINT** Infants perceive motion, but direction and velocity are better perceived with advancing age.

Kinesthetic Development

The kinesthetic system gives us "body sense." It is vital to our ability to position ourselves, move in our environment, and identify the objects we contact. Kinesthesis also provides our sense of force, heaviness, and effort. To know the importance of kinesthesis you need only recall walking through a fun house at a fair or circus, where your visual system and your kinesthetic system are given conflicting information.

Kinesthetic Sensation

The kinesthetic, or proprioceptive, system is important to skill performance because it yields information about the

- relative position of the body parts in relation to each other,
- position of the body in space,
- body's movements, and
- nature of objects that the body comes into contact with.

Proprioceptor is the collective name of the various kinesthetic receptors located in the periphery of the body; the two types of proprioceptors are the somatosensors and the vestibular apparatus.

Unlike the visual system, which relies on the eyes as sensory receptors, kinesthetic information comes from various types of receptors throughout the body called **proprioceptors** (table 13.1). Those proprioceptors located in the muscles, at the muscle–tendon junctions, in joint capsules and ligaments, and under the skin are called **somatosensors**; those located in the inner ear are called the **vestibular apparatus** (figure 13.8). Sometimes we are unaware that kinesthetic receptors are providing information; for example, we automatically perform postural adjustments that help us maintain an upright stance.

The somatosensors located in the muscles, called muscle spindles, play a major role in position and movement sense, with skin receptors playing a secondary role (Proske & Gandevia, 2012).

Somatosensors are the receptors located under the skin, in the muscles, at muscle–tendon junctions, and in joint capsules and ligaments.

The **vestibular apparatus** houses the receptors located in the inner ear.

TABLE 13.1 Kinesthetic Receptors and Their Locations

KINESTHETIC RECEPTOR	LOCATION
Muscle spindles	Muscles
Golgi tendon organs	Muscle–tendon junctions
Joint receptors Spray-type Ruffini endings Golgi-type receptors Modified Pacinian corpuscles	Joint capsule and ligaments
Vestibular semicircular canals	Inner ear
Cutaneous receptors	Skin and underlying tissues

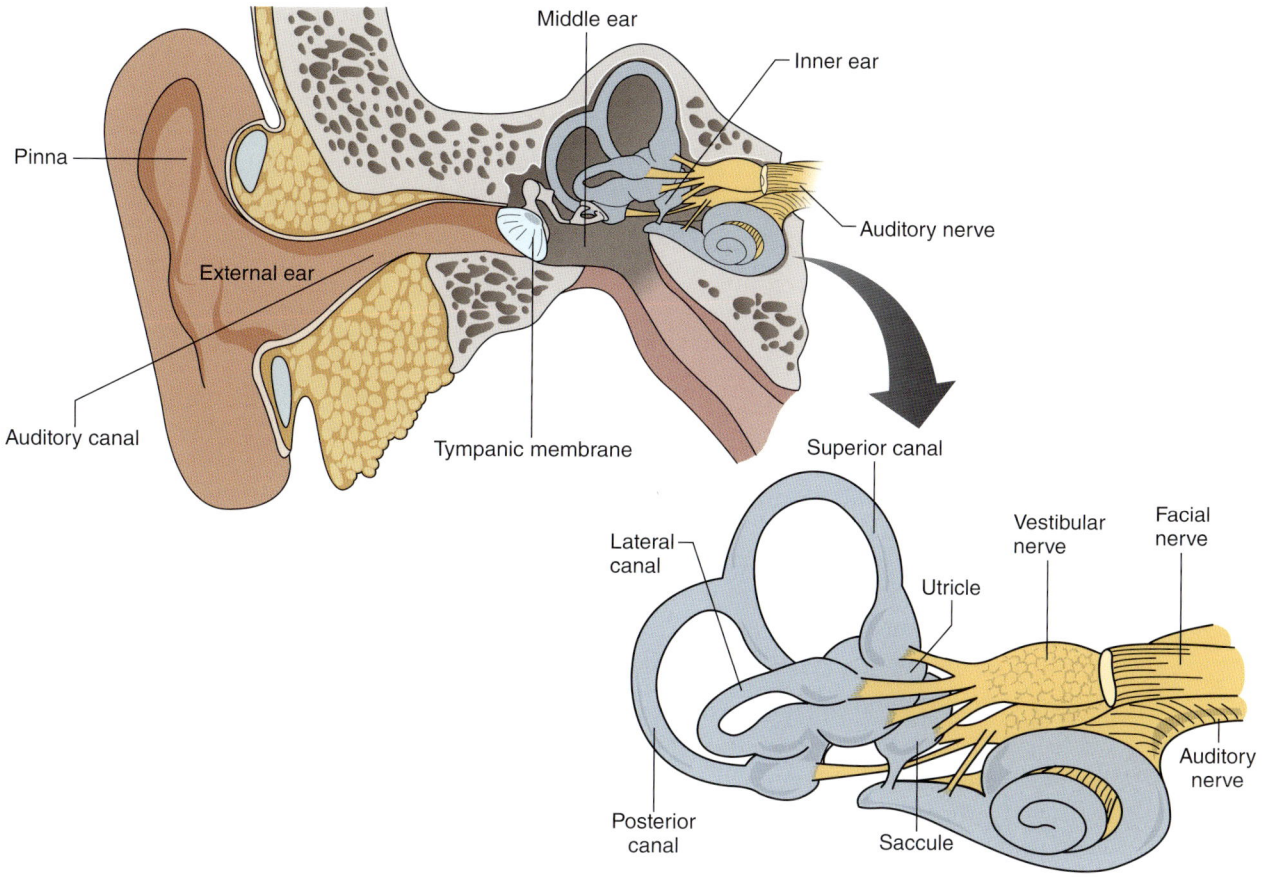

FIGURE 13.8 Structures of the inner ear. Sensory receptors are located in the utricle and saccule.

Receptors at the muscle–tendon junctions provide a sense of force and heaviness. The kinesthetic system provides both feed*back* about body position and feed*forward* information to help us maintain our body position, even when a perturbation (disruption) to that position occurs.

Many infantile reflexes are stimulated through kinesthetic receptors. Therefore, the onset of a reflex indicates that the corresponding kinesthetic receptor is functioning. The first prenatal reflex that can be elicited is opposite-side neck flexion through tactile stimulation around the mouth at just 7.5 weeks after conception.

▶ **KEY POINT** Kinesthetic sensation comes from a variety of sensory receptors throughout the body.

Researchers have used tactile stimulation of other body parts to determine that cutaneous receptor development proceeds in an oral, genital–anal, palmar, and plantar (sole of foot) sequence. This developmental sequence follows the cephalocaudal and proximodistal growth directions we discuss in chapter 8.

At birth, infants clearly respond to touch. They can also identify the location of touches, especially in the region of the mouth and the face (Kisilevsky, Stach, & Muir, 1991). We know, too, that the vestibular apparatus is anatomically complete at approximately 9 to 12 weeks of prenatal life, but its functional status before birth is unclear. The labyrinthine righting reflex appears around the second postnatal month (Timiras, 1972), and that fact provides some evidence of vestibular function. By 3 years of age the muscle spindles are mature, and by 7 years of age spinal nerve circuits for the somatosensory system are mature. Therefore, the system for kinesthetic sensation is functional in early life, and at least some parts of the system mature in midchildhood.

What are some ways parents might use touch to communicate with their infants?

Kinesthetic Perception

Although the kinesthetic receptors are functional in early life, improvements in kinesthetic perception continue through adolescence and into young adulthood (Cignetti et al., 2017). Both the ability to detect a proprioceptive stimulus (sensitivity) and to discriminate between stimuli (precision, or acuity) improve. Children improve substantially in kinesthetic sensitivity between 6 and 7 years and then gradually improve from 7 to 11 years of age (Li, Su, Fu, & Pickett, 2015). Yet young adolescents around 12.5 years were not at adult levels in sensitivity to passive limb motion (Pickett & Konczak, 2009). Visser and Geuze (2000) used a sequential research design to observe kinesthetic acuity in adolescents. Acuity improved over the age range of 11.5 to 16.5 years. Generally, then, large improvements in sensitivity and acuity come in childhood, with gradual improvements continuing over the preadolescent and adolescent years and variability decreasing with age (Holst-Wolf, Yeh, & Konczak, 2016). There can be variations from this pattern within specific aspects of kinesthetic perception. Types of kinesthetic perception can be grouped in several ways. Here we discuss localization, manipulation, and movement and then body awareness.

Tactile Localization, Manipulation, and Movement

Tactile localization is the ability to identify without sight the exact spot on the body that has been touched.

Although newborns feel touches, an individual must know where on the body a touch occurs as well as the nature of that touch; this knowledge is termed **tactile localization**. Making fine discriminations about where one has been touched, sight unseen, and whether the touch involves one point or two in close proximity, is an ability that develops in childhood. Children are less accurate at 4 years of age than at 6 to 8 years in locating a touch on the hands and forearms; performance on this type of task does not improve significantly between ages 6 and 8 (Ayres, 1972; Temple et al., 1979). Based on this limited data, then, the perception of tactile localization on the hands and arms seems to be relatively mature by age 6.

Threshold discrimination—detecting the smallest gap between two points that touch the skin—varies in different areas of the body (figure 13.9); we do not know whether it also varies with age (Van Duyne, 1973; Williams, 1983). Ayres (1966) reported that only half of a group of 5-year-olds could consistently discriminate a touch on different fingers, though average performance improved through 7.5 years of age (the oldest age tested).

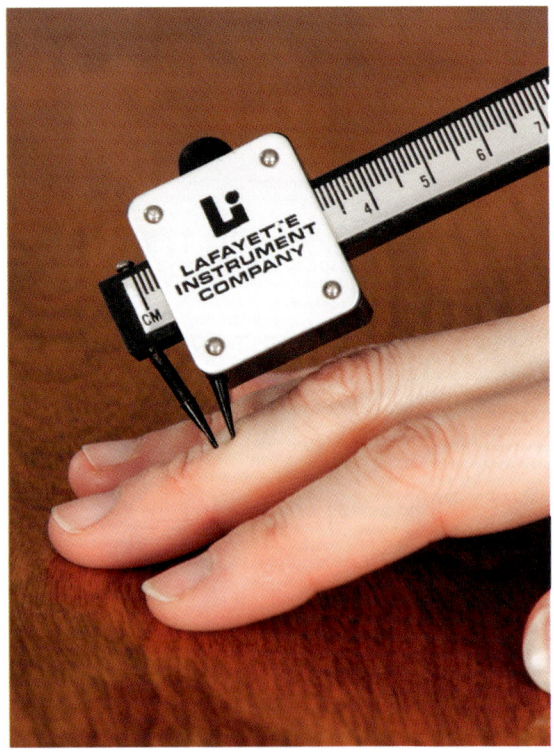

FIGURE 13.9 Tactile point perception includes accurate judgment of the number of simultaneous touches on the skin. As two touch points get closer together, it is more difficult to discriminate between a single touch and two touches.

▶ **KEY POINT** Children improve in their ability to locate touches, but little is known about threshold discriminations for touch.

Recognizing unseen objects and their characteristics by manipulation is the kinesthetic perception parallel to the visual perception of objects. In infants, such manipulation is often more accidental than purposeful. Yet by age 4, the average child can handle objects purposefully, and by age 5 a child can explore the objects' major features. Manual exploration becomes systematic—that is, children become more methodical—at about age 6 (Van Duyne, 1973), and in the next 2 years, haptic (cutaneous) memory and object recognition also improve (Northman & Black, 1976). Research by Temple et al. (1979) indicates that children also increase their speed of tactile recognition during this time.

Perception of movement is another form of kinesthetic perception. You can assess a child's perception of the extent of movement at a joint by asking the child to accurately reproduce a limb movement or to relocate a limb position without looking. Children improve in this task between ages 5 and 8; little improvement is noted after age 8 (Ayres, 1972; Williams, 1983).

Perception of the Body (Body Awareness)

To carry out everyday activities and to perform complex skills, it is necessary to have a sense of the body, its various parts, and its dimensions. Aspects of **body awareness** include identification of body parts, awareness of self, laterality, lateral dominance, side preference, spatial orientation, and directionality.

Body awareness is the recognition, identification, and differentiation of the location, movement, and interrelationships of body parts and joints; it also refers to a person's awareness of the spatial orientation and perceived location of the body in the environment.

Identification of Body Parts

As children get older, more of them can label the major body parts correctly (DeOreo & Williams, 1980), and they can name more detailed body parts (Cratty, 1979). The rate at which an individual child learns body part labels is largely a function of the amount of time parents or other adults spend practicing with the child. Probably two-thirds of 6-year-olds can identify the major body parts, and mistakes are rare in all typically developing children after age 9.

Imagine you are a youth sports coach in one of your favorite activities. What skills in this activity rely at least in part on body awareness? What cues can you use to draw a beginner's attention to body position?

Children also need a sense of the body's spatial dimensions, such as up and down. They usually master the up–down dimension first, followed by front–back, and finally side. A high percentage of 2.5- to 3-year-olds can place an object in front of or behind their bodies, but more of them have difficulty placing an object in front of or behind something else. By about age 4, most children can do the latter task as well as place an object to the side of something (Kuczaj & Maratsos, 1975).

Web Study Guide **Observe children's positioning of objects in relation to their own bodies in Lab Activity 13.1, Development of Spatial Dimensions, in the web study guide.**

Awareness of Self

Young children develop an objective awareness of self during their second year (Moore, Mealiea, Garon, & Povinelli, 2007), as demonstrated by mirror recognition tasks. Yet up to age 30 months they tend to make "scale errors," such as trying to fit their bodies into spaces that are too small (DeLoache, Uttal, & Rosengren, 2004). These errors gradually decrease, but some aspects of own-body perception develop over childhood. An example is provided by the rubber hand illusion in which a fake hand is seen being stroked synchronously with stroking on an individual's hidden real hand. This illusion can make even adults feel as if the fake hand is theirs. The illusion is stronger in 4- to 9-year-olds than in adults, but early adolescents 10- to 11-years of age demonstrate adult levels (Cowie, Sterling, & Bremner, 2016).

Laterality is a component of body awareness—specifically, the awareness that one's body has two distinct sides that can move independently.

Laterality

Although children typically master up–down and front–back awareness before age 3, they develop an understanding that the body has two distinct sides, or **laterality**, at approximately 4 to 5 years of age (Hecaen & de Ajuriaguerra, 1964). The child comes to realize that even though his two hands, two legs, and so on are the same size and shape, he can position them differently and move them independently. Eventually, the child is able to discriminate right and left sides (i.e., to label or identify these dimensions).

An age-related improvement in the ability to make right–left discriminations occurs between age 4 or 5 and age 10; most children respond almost perfectly by age 10 (Ayres, 1969; Swanson & Benton, 1955; Williams, 1973). However, children can be taught to label right and left at younger ages, too, even as young as 5 (Hecaen & de Ajuriaguerra, 1964). Young children also have difficulty executing a task when a limb must cross the midline of the body, such as writing on a chalkboard from left to right. Ofte and Hugdahl (2002) asked 7- to 8-year olds, 12- to 13-year-olds, and adults to label right and left hands on front and back views of a person. Some pictures had arms crossing over the body's midline. Performance improved over the entire age range tested.

Imagine you are an early childhood educator. What activities could you use to help children learn to discriminate between left and right?

Lateral dominance is the consistent preference for use of one eye, ear, hand, or foot instead of the other, although the preference for different anatomical units is not always on the same side.

Lateral Dominance

Interest in **lateral dominance**, especially hand dominance, dates back to Aristotle. Hand dominance was part of a nature versus nurture debate in the 1960s as behavioral scientists considered whether hand dominance reflected a naturally occurring emergence of the brain on the side of the body opposite the dominant hand becoming dominant over the other side of the brain and whether environmental influences could disturb brain dominance.

Asymmetries in hand use have been widely observed in infants. Infants younger than 3 months of age grasp objects longer, make a fist longer, and are more active with one hand than the other (Hawn & Harris, 1983; Michel & Goodwin, 1979; Michel & Harkins, 1986). These asymmetries are not consistently predictive of adult hand dominance (Michel, 1983, 1988), but a link may exist between early asymmetries and later hand dominance because the asymmetries tend to follow orientation. Infants who prefer to turn their heads to the right seem to prefer reaching with their right hands, and vice versa. These self-generating experiences may facilitate eye–hand coordination of one hand more than the other (Bushnell, 1985; Michel, 1988).

When infants begin to reach after 3 months, they also demonstrate a hand preference (Hawn & Harris, 1983). Unimanual manipulation appears at approximately 5 months, and by 7 months infants show a preference for manipulating with a particular hand (Ramsay, 1980; table 13.2). A hand preference is evident approximately 1 month after bimanual manipulation first appears, even as both hands hold an object (Ramsay, Campos, & Fenson, 1979). Infants typically prefer the same hand in unimanual and bimanual handling; that is, they use either the right or left hand in both types of manipulation (Ramsay, 1980). Although these early preferences might change, usually the hand that

TABLE 13.2 Infant Hand Preferences

NATURE OF HAND PREFERENCE	APPROXIMATE AGE
Fisting and longer grasps	Before 3 mo
Unimanual reaching	After 3 mo
Unimanual manipulation	By 7 mo
Bimanual manipulation	Within 1 mo of emergence of unimanual manipulation
Hand dominance	By 4 yr

emerges as preferred in early childhood, most often by age 4, remains the dominant hand in youth and adulthood (Sinclair, 1971). It is important to remember that in certain environmental situations children might find it convenient to use their nonpreferred limbs (Connolly & Elliott, 1972). By adulthood, individuals typically use their dominant limbs even if it is more awkward to do so.

Think about your daily activities and the instruments you use. Do any of them favor right-handedness or left-handedness?

Side Preference

In addition to hand preferences, we come to favor one of our eyes, ears, and feet over the other. If the favored parts are all on one side of the body, the dominance is termed pure; otherwise, it is called mixed. In the past, developmentalists have suggested that pure dominance is preferable, the implication being that one side of the brain is clearly dominant (Delacato, 1966). Research has never shown this to be the case. Studies have failed to show any real cognitive advantage for individuals with more lateralized brains (Kinsbourne, 1988, 1997).

▶ **KEY POINT** Although some developmentalists have suggested that pure dominance is necessary for proper neurological organization, no objective evidence indicates that this is true.

Spatial Orientation

Kinesthetic spatial orientation involves perception of the body's location and orientation in space, independent of vision. Temple et al. (1979) tested this perception by asking children to walk a straight line while blindfolded and measuring their deviation from the straight path. Performance improved between 6 and 8 years of age; 8-year-olds were the oldest age group included in the study. Investigations of spatial orientation over a wider age range are necessary.

Direction

Directionality is the ability to project the body's spatial dimensions into surrounding space and to grasp spatial concepts about the movements or locations of objects in the environment. For example, knowing the body's spatial dimension of "left," one can project that dimension into surrounding space to say, "That object is on my left" or "The car is passing on my left."

Directionality is often linked to laterality, an awareness of the body's two distinct sides. Children with a poor sense of laterality typically also have poor directionality. Although this relationship seems intuitively logical, deficiencies in laterality are not known to be the cause of deficiencies in directionality (Kephart, 1964).

Individuals obtain most information for directional judgments through vision, so these judgments rely on integration of visual and kinesthetic information. Long and Looft (1972) suggested that children improve their sense of directionality between ages 6 and 12. By age 8, children typically can use body references to indicate direction. They are able to say correctly, "The ball is on my right" and "The ball is to the right of the bat." At age 9, children can change the latter statement to "The ball is to the left of the bat" when they walk around to the opposite side of the objects. They can also identify right and left for a person opposite them. Such improvements in directional references continue through age 12. Long and Looft noted that some refinement of directionality must take place in adolescence because many 12-year-olds are unable to transpose left and right from a new perspective, such as when looking in a mirror.

Kinesthetic Changes With Aging

We have known for some time that some, but not all, older adults lose cutaneous sensitivity, vibratory sensitivity, and sensitivity to temperature and pain (Kenshalo, 1977). More recent research has documented a deterioration in proprioceptive acuity for both static positions and movements. Proprioceptive impairment in the lower limbs is concerning because of its role in loss of balance in older adults. Age differences between young and old widen as position-matching tasks increase in complexity and movement extent and when they involve contralateral limbs (Schaap, Gonzales, Janssen, & Brown, 2015). Improvements in proprioception, though, were noted with electrical noise stimulation and rapid, repetitive passive joint movement interventions (Ju, Lin, Cheng, Cheng, & Wong, 2013; Toledo, Barela, & Kohn, 2017).

Also, older adults could match young adults in discriminating the curvature of a touched surface sight unseen when using dynamic touch (active feeling) but not static touch. This suggests that when additional proprioceptive information is added to cutaneous information, older adults could make more accurate judgments (Norman et al., 2013). More research on age-related changes in kinesthetic perception is needed, especially regarding proprioception in the lower limbs because of the connection to maintaining balance and avoiding falls.

Auditory Development

Although it is not as important to skill performance as vision or kinesthesis, auditory information is still valuable for accurate performance. People often use sounds as critical cues to initiate or time their movements.

Auditory Sensation

Hearing involves the external ear, the middle ear, and the cochlea of the inner ear. The inner ear develops first and is close to adult form by the third prenatal month. By midfetal life, the external ear and middle ear are formed as well (Timiras, 1972). Fetuses reportedly respond to loud sounds, but perhaps this response is actually to tactile stimuli (i.e., vibrations) (Kidd & Kidd, 1966).

Absolute threshold is the minimal detectable sound a hearer can sense at least half of the time a signal is sounded.

Differential threshold is the closest that two sounds can be yet still allow the hearer to distinguish them at least 75% of the time.

A newborn's hearing is imperfect partly because of the gelatinous tissue filling the inner ear. The **absolute threshold** is about 60 decibels higher for a newborn than for an adult. So a newborn can detect only an average speaking voice when an adult can detect a whisper (Kellman & Arterberry, 1998). Newborns also do not discriminate changes in the intensity of sounds (**differential threshold**) or in sound frequencies as well as adults can.

The gelatinous material in the inner ear is reabsorbed during the first postnatal week so that hearing improves rapidly (Hecox, 1975; Timiras, 1972). By 3 months, infants hear low-frequency sounds (500–1,000 Hz) very well but do not hear high-frequency sounds (4,000 Hz) quite as well. Because human speech generally is under 5,000 Hz, this level of hearing permits the infant to sense speech. In fact, infants might be predisposed to listen to speech (Vouloumanos & Werker, 2007) and process their own mother's voice faster than that of others as early as 4 months of age (Purhonen, Kilpelainen-Lees, Valkonen-Korhonen, Karhu, & Lehtonen, 2005). The infant can hear low- to mid-pitched voices better than high-pitched voices. By 6 months, however, infants' hearing is similar to that of adults, including hearing of high-frequency sounds (Spetner & Olsho, 1990).

▶ **KEY POINT** Infants can hear human speech.

Presbycusis is a loss of hearing sensitivity.

More older adults than younger adults suffer from **presbycusis** (from *presbys* for "old man" and *okousis* for "hearing"), but the source of this loss varies among individuals. Some hearing loss might result from physiological degeneration, but hearing loss often results from exposure to environmental noise. In fact, exposure in childhood to loud and chronic noise can cause hearing loss for life (Harrison, 2008). Individuals are born with a fixed number of cochlear hair cells that do not regenerate. Hair cells killed by excessive noise exposure at any point in the life span results in a permanent loss.

The absolute threshold for hearing pure tones and speech increases in older adults, meaning that sounds must be louder for older adults to hear them. Differential thresholds also increase for pitch and speech discrimination (Corso, 1977). As a person ages, the ability to hear high-frequency sounds is particularly affected. One result is that older adults cannot hear certain consonant sounds well; they might report that they hear someone talking but cannot understand the message. Older adults are also at a distinct disadvantage in adverse listening situations, such as attempting to listen to one person in a room crowded with talking people (Stine, Wingfield, & Poon, 1989).

Think of your older relatives and acquaintances. What activities of daily living can present difficulties for seniors with presbycusis?

Auditory Perception

It is easy to overlook the amount of information we get from sound. For example, we can determine the location of an event by sound, whether something or someone is leaving or approaching, who or what made a sound, and even the material from which an object is made. Although we think of vision and kinesthesis as more important to skill performance, auditory perception gives us much information about the environment in which we move. The aspects of auditory perception that we discuss here are location, differences between similar sounds, patterns, and auditory figure and ground. Notice that several of these aspects are parallel to types of visual and kinesthetic perception.

Location

We locate a sound by determining its direction and distance from us (figure 13.10). Newborns turn in the direction of a sound, and they rapidly improve in their ability to locate sound during the first year. When presented two sounds, each in a different location, the minimum angle between the two locations that 6- and 7-month-olds can detect as being two different locations is in the range of 12° to 19° (Ashmead, Clifton, & Perris, 1987; Morrongiello, 1988b), compared with 1° to 2° in adults. Infants determine the direction of nearby sounds better than that of distant sounds, but improvement is continuous such that by age 3 children can determine the direction of even distant sounds (Dekaban, 1970). Infants between 4 and 10 months also can distinguish temporal patterns in sounds (Lewkowicz & Marcovitch, 2006).

Think of your living routines. What are some tasks that involve localizing sound?

It is more difficult to determine how well infants perceive the distance of a sound. Clifton, Perris, and Bullinger (1991) found that 7-month-olds reached for an object that was the source of a sound significantly more often when it was within reach than when it was out of reach. It is possible they choose not to reach because they know it is out of reach. It seems that from birth, individuals have some sense of the location of sounds in the environment and rapidly improve in determining both the direction and distance of sounds.

Older adults with presbycusis show a notable decrement in the ability to localize sound (Nordlund, 1964). This is not surprising given that localization depends on accurate auditory sensations related to the time at which sounds arrive at the two ears and on the intensity differences in sound. In fact, older adults who demonstrate good speech discrimination abilities also show normal sound localization, whereas those with poor speech discrimination show poor sound localization (Hausler, Colburn, & Marr, 1983).

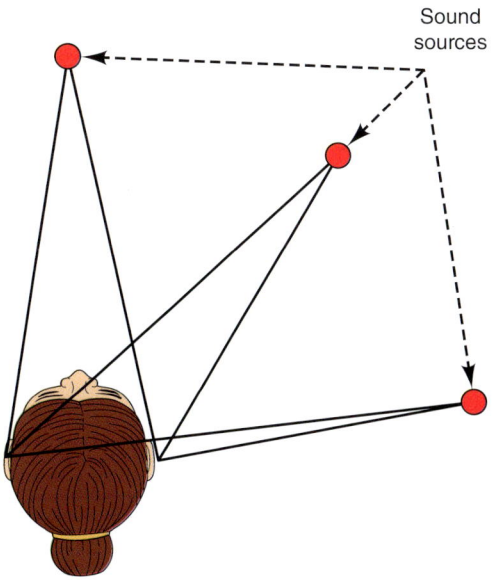

FIGURE 13.10 Sound localization. The more a sound deviates from the straight-ahead position, the greater the time difference in the arrival of the sound at each ear.

Reprinted from Bower (1977).

▶ **KEY POINT** Auditory acuity is not as good in infants as in adults.

Differences in Sounds

The perception of sound differences by children is often studied by means of discrimination tasks. For example, children are asked to distinguish two sounds that are similar in pitch, loudness, or speech sound, such as *d* and *t* or *b* and *p*. Infants as young as 1 to 4 months can discriminate between basic speech sounds, such as *p*, *b*, and *m* (Doty, 1974), but children between 3 and 5 years old experience increasing accuracy in recognizing differences in sounds (DiSimoni, 1975). Temple et al. (1979) found a further improvement in auditory discrimination between 6 and 8 years, as did Birch (1976) between 7 and 10 years, in an auditory matching task. A similar trend apparently exists for discrimination of pitch (Kidd & Kidd, 1966). In general, it appears that by 8 to 10 years of age, children have greatly improved their ability to detect differences in similar sounds, but they continue to refine their auditory discrimination skills until they are at least 13.

If we could set aside age-related changes in sensitivity for hearing pure tones, the deficits in hearing speech sounds among older adults would be minimal (Helfer, 1992; Lutman, 1991; van Rooij & Plomp, 1992). Therefore, age deficits in speech perception are largely a function of decline in pure-tone sensitivity. Interestingly, older adults often make better use of context cues to help their recognition of speech than young adults do (Craig, Kim, Rhyner, & Chirillo, 1993; Holtzman, Familant, Deptula, & Hoyer, 1986).

Patterns

For speech and music to be more than just noises, individuals must perceive relationships between sounds. Of course, we perceive patterns in other senses. Visual pattern perception has long interested developmentalists, but attention to auditory pattern perception is more recent.

Auditory patterns are nonrandom, temporally (time-) ordered sound sequences. Three properties of sound give rise to auditory patterns:

1. Time
2. Intensity
3. Frequency (Morrongiello, 1988a)

Speech and music have a temporal pattern, an intensity (loudness or softness) pattern, and a frequency (high pitch or low pitch) pattern simultaneously. Developmentalists usually study one characteristic at a time.

Infants as young as 2 to 3 months old react to changes in the temporal pattern of a tone sequence, showing that they perceive temporal patterns (Demany, McKenzie, & Vurpillot, 1977). Young infants, however, perceive only pattern changes involving the number of groups of tones (e.g., changing nine tones from three groups of three to two groups, one of five and one of four) (Morrongiello, 1984). At 12 months, infants can perceive changes in the number of groups and in the number of tones in each group (figure 13.11). Thus, by the end of the first year, infants can perceive sound on the basis of temporal pattern, which is probably a prerequisite for language development.

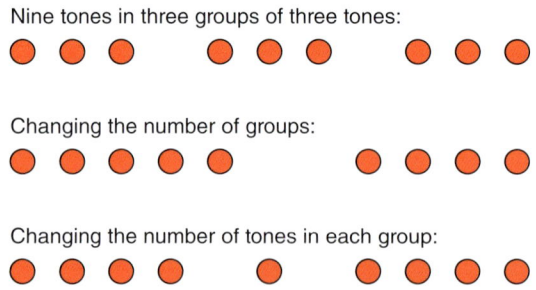

FIGURE 13.11 Auditory stimulus patterns presented to infants. Young infants can detect a change in the number of groups from what is familiar to them, but it is not until they are 12 months old that they can detect changes in both the number of groups and the number of tones in a group. Time between tones in a group was 0.2 seconds, and time between groups was 0.6 seconds.

Based on B.A. Morrongiello (1988a).

Infants between 5 and 11 months can discriminate intensity changes for vowels in a syllable (Bull, Eilers, & Oller, 1984), but we know little else about infants' intensity perception. Infants younger than 6 months can discriminate frequency relationships in a short, simple sequence. Not until the end of their first year, though, can infants perceive frequency relationships between the tones in a long, complex sequence (Morrongiello, 1986; Trehub, Bull, & Thorpe, 1984). The same is true of speech patterns. Children between 4 and 6 years can discriminate the frequency features of six-tone melodies played at normal speed (Morrongiello, Trehub, Thorpe, & Capodilupo, 1985). Infants progress rapidly in auditory pattern perception during their first year. These advances probably are prerequisites to language development. Preschool children make further progress in perceiving patterns in increasingly longer and more complex contexts.

What systems might limit the development of auditory pattern perception? Obviously, the auditory system must be developed, and, as mentioned earlier, auditory sensation is quite mature within days of birth. The sensory cortex of the brain, however, is still maturing rapidly over the first few years of life. With continuing development, it probably permits conceptualization of patterns and of the identity of transformed patterns (Morrongiello, 1988a)—for example, the same rhythmic pattern played at different tempos. Cognition also must advance because in order to perceive patterns, an individual must be able to remember and process information, especially for long and complex sequences.

In addition, the environment in which infants develop might "tune" the developing auditory system to recognize certain features of language and music. In this way, we might learn to prefer the perceptual patterns prevalent in our native language and the music of our culture (Morrongiello, 1988a; Swingley, 2005; Trehub & Hannon, 2006).

Auditory Figure and Ground

Often a person must attend to certain sounds while ignoring other irrelevant sounds in the background. In this auditory parallel to visual figure-and-ground perception, the figure is the sound of interest and the ground is distracting noises in the background. For example, try listening to someone talk to you on the telephone (figure sounds) while music is playing and several people in your room are talking (background sounds). Young infants can detect sounds amid ambient noise (Morrongiello & Clifton, 1984), but some children have more difficulty than others in separating auditory figures from the background. We would benefit from more research on the processes underlying these differences.

Think about driving an automobile. What clues for driving safely might you miss if music is playing loudly or you are wearing earphones?

Older adults commonly report difficulty with hearing amid background noise (see Tun & Wingfield, 1993, for a review). It is possible that this problem reflects changes in the sensory system or in parts of the neurological system related to hearing. It may also reflect changes in attention mechanisms—that is, older adults might have more difficulty attending to a particular sound source in the midst of other sounds.

As noted previously, development of auditory perception is rapid. Not long after birth, infants can already perceive the location of and differences in sounds. An individual's ability to make fine discriminations improves in childhood. Perceptions of auditory events in the environment in adulthood are likely disturbed only when age-related changes in sensation, including injury and disease, affect detection of sounds.

Web Study Guide **Administer a hearing test to older adults in Lab Activity 13.2, Auditory Sensation in Adulthood, in the web study guide.**

Summary of Sensation, Perception, and Perceptual-Motor Development

It is clear that some aspects of visual, kinesthetic, and auditory perception exist in infancy. Developmental trends continue throughout childhood, especially in the finer discriminations. By the time children are 8 to 12 years old, aspects of their visual perception have developed to near-adult levels. It seems that kinesthetic perception typically develops to near-adult levels somewhat earlier, usually by about age 8, although this generalization is based on limited research. Young children can perceive the location of sound, and by age 10 they perform at near-adult levels on many auditory discrimination tasks. Refinement of auditory skills continues through the early teens. Some aspects of auditory perception have not been studied in children.

In general, children between the ages of 8 and 12 approach adult levels of performance on many perceptual tasks, and only small refinements in perceptual skills are yet to be made. Assessments of perceptual-motor development have been designed, and educators and therapists sometimes use these to screen young children for deficits in perceptual-motor development.

Some aspects of perceptual development are not well documented; further research is needed. In addition, little is known about what causes changes in perceptual processes as people age, but it is known that decremental changes in the sensory systems reduce the quality of the sensory information reaching the central nervous system, potentially affecting perception. At any age, limited sensory information could serve as a rate limiter to performance by influencing perception of needed information.

The perceptual systems do not operate in isolation of one another. To complete this discussion of perceptual development, the following section explores how information perceived in one sense, or modality, is related to that perceived in other modalities.

Intermodal Perception

Events occur in the environment and are often sensed and, therefore, perceived in different modalities, or senses. If a jar slips from our hands while we are trying to open it, we feel it slipping, we see it falling, we hear it hit the floor and break, and we might even smell the released contents. This event can be perceived through vision, kinesthesis, and audition. Developmentalists have considered perception through different modalities from two very different perspectives. From the first, or integrational, perspective, the energy reaching the different senses is of different forms—light, sound, temperature, and so on—and each sensory system yields a unique sensation. The task of a developing infant, then, is to learn how to integrate the separate systems (i.e., to learn how those unique sensations are related to one another).

The second, or unified, perspective sees the senses as united in bringing information about events, but through different modalities. The nervous system is structured for multimodal perception so that, from the start, perceptions are coherent in time and space (Damasio, 1989; Stein & Meredith, 1993). The perceptual systems extract patterns; many patterns are similar across the modalities. For example, events occur at a point in time, so the temporal properties of an event are not unique to any one modality. In a sense, these patterns are **amodal invariants**. We see a drummer strike a drum and we hear the drum's sound, but we also perceive the rhythmic pattern that existed across vision and audition. In this model, the central task of development is to learn about events in the world from the information coming through various sensory systems (Kellman & Arterberry, 1998). During the 1980s and 1990s, research in neurophysiology identified areas of the brain containing neurons that receive input from different modalities (Stein, Meredith, & Wallace, 1994); this encouraged researchers to adopt a unified perspective of intermodal perception. The view of the sensory-perceptual systems as distinct and separate waned, and the unified view gradually became the more dominant view after the turn of the century.

Amodal invariants are patterns in space or time that do not differ across the sensory-perceptual modalities.

The unified perspective is more consistent with the ecological perspective of perception and action. The integration perspective is more consistent with an information processing perspective. Earlier chapters acknowledge that much of the research on perception has been done from the information processing perspective. Keep this in mind as we review research in the following areas of intermodal perception:

- Auditory-visual
- Visual-kinesthetic
- Auditory-kinesthetic
- Spatial-temporal

▶ **KEY POINT** One view of intermodal perception emphasizes the development of infants' abilities to integrate separate perceptual systems. The other emphasizes the perception of patterns about an environment unified across the systems.

Auditory-Visual Intermodal Perception

Newborn infants have been observed to move their eyes in the direction of a sound. Morrongiello, Fenwick, Hillier, and Chance (1994) played a 20-second recording of a rattle to newborns. They placed the loudspeaker at varying angles from each infant's midline. The farther the speaker from the midline, the farther the newborns turned their heads. In some trials, the investigators also shifted the sound from one loudspeaker to another, and the infants adjusted their heads correspondingly. Although this is a rudimentary response, it appears that even newborns seek to match their visual fixation to the spatial origin of a sound.

Four-month-olds were found to integrate auditory and visual information based on harmonicity (pleasing combination of sounds). Infants heard an in-tune tone perceived by adults as one sound or a mistuned tone perceived by adults as two sounds and watched either video of one bouncing ball or video of two bouncing balls, in various combinations that were either congruent or incongruent. Measuring look time, researchers found that infants looked longer at the video display with the mismatched or incongruent audio track (Smith, Folland, Martinez, & Trainor, 2017). Also, 5-month-olds matched the vocal expressions of other infants with their facial expressions (Vaillant-Molina, Bahrick, & Flom, 2013), and 6-month-olds matched at least an approximate number of sounds with an approximate number of seen objects (Feigenson, 2011). Hence infants demonstrate some level of visual-auditory integration early in their first year.

▶ **KEY POINT** Newborns link visual and auditory events, and children improve in finer visual-auditory intermodal discriminations.

More challenging auditory-visual perceptions show a developmental trend in childhood (see figure 13.12). Goodnow (1971b) tapped out a sequence [* ***], then asked children to write the sequence using dots and spaces to picture where the taps occurred. She also reversed the auditory-visual (A-V) task by asking children to tap out a pictured sequence (V-A). Children around age 5 did not perform the A-V sequence as well as children at age 7. A trend toward improved performance on the V-A task was also found in children between ages 6.9 and 8.5 years. This and similar studies indicate that visual and auditory intermodal perception improves between ages 5 and 12 (Williams, 1983). Young children find A-V tasks more difficult than V-A tasks, but this difference diminishes after age 7 (Rudel & Teuber, 1971).

Imagine you are a youth coach in your favorite sport. Is the integration of auditory and visual information involved in any part of the sport? How about kinesthetic and visual information? What might you do to help beginners use this information to improve performance?

FIGURE 13.12 Musicians play notes in the rhythm notated in their sheet music to create sounds corresponding to the notated pattern.
Jose Luis Pelaez Inc/DigitalVision/Getty Images

Visual-Kinesthetic Intermodal Perception

Visual-kinesthetic perception is the coordination between seen and felt properties of objects. Because infants do not reach for and manipulate objects before 4 to 5 months of age, the study of visual-kinesthetic perception at young ages centers on mouthing of objects. Meltzoff and Borton (1979) found that 1-month-olds looked longer at the type of pacifier they had mouthed but had not seen, either one that was a cube with nubs or one that was a smooth sphere. At some level, then, infants relate oral and visual information.

Visual-kinesthetic perception involving manipulation of objects has been explored at later stages of infancy, and research study outcomes have been variable. Goodnow (1971a) studied visual and kinesthetic integration in children. She presented five shapes (Greek and Russian letters) by either sight or feel to three age groups (5.0- to 5.5-year-olds, 5.6- to 6.8-year-olds, and 9.0- to 10.0-year-olds). She then presented these five shapes, along with five new ones, again by sight or feel, and challenged the children to identify the familiar shapes. Four presentation patterns were possible:

1. Visual presentation–visual recognition (V-V)
2. Kinesthetic presentation–kinesthetic recognition (K-K)
3. Visual presentation–kinesthetic recognition (V-K)
4. Kinesthetic presentation–visual recognition (K-V)

Goodnow found that children, especially the youngest ones, had more difficulty in the K-K pattern than in the V-V pattern. This performance discrepancy narrowed in the older age groups. The K-V task proved more difficult for the children than the V-K task. Goodnow noted that the scores of the youngest group in the kinesthetic conditions were extremely variable. This study and others using similar tasks and different age groups lead us to the conclusion that a developmental trend exists in visual-kinesthetic intermodal perception during childhood. When the kinesthetic task involves active manipulation of an object, 5-year-olds can recognize the shapes relatively well, but slight improvement continues until age 8. If passive movements are involved, performance is not as advanced, and improvements continue through age 11 (Williams, 1983).

▶ **KEY POINT** Children have more difficulty in intermodal visual and kinesthetic perception if their initial exposure is through the kinesthetic system.

Auditory-Kinesthetic Intermodal Perception

The amount of research conducted on auditory-kinesthetic integration is small compared with that involving vision. Tanaka, Kanakogi, Kawasaki, & Myowa (2018) used electroencephalogram and event-related potential recordings on 7- to 8-month-old infants to obtain evidence that audio and tactile information is integrated in infants' brains. Experience might be important to this integration. Temple et al. (1979) included the Witeba Test of Auditory-Tactile Integration in a test battery administered to 6- and 8-year-olds. In this test, an experimenter twice tells a child the name of an object or shape. The child then feels a number of objects or shapes, attempting to select the one that matches the auditory label. The investigators found that 8-year-olds performed this task much better than 6-year-olds did.

This experimental method is based on children understanding the label given to the object or shape. Thus, it is possible that this age-related difference in performance resulted from younger children not knowing, misunderstanding, or not remembering the auditory label in addition to, or instead of, their auditory-kinesthetic intermodal perception. With this limitation in mind, we can tentatively conclude that auditory-kinesthetic integration improves in childhood.

Spatial-Temporal Intermodal Perception

You may recall the earlier discussion of amodal invariants—patterns that might be invariant across modalities—such as space and time. For example, when children viewed the dot pattern in Goodnow's experiment, they were dealing with a spatial stimulus—the arrangement of dots in space. When they listened to an auditory pattern, they were attending to a temporal (time-based) stimulus. They were perceiving, then, a pattern that crossed space and time as well as vision and audition.

Sterritt, Martin, and Rudnick (1971) devised nine tasks that varied the number of perceptual integrations to be made as well as the type of integration, including spatial-temporal characteristics. For example, a child must integrate a short pause between two tones (temporal) with a short space between two dots (spatial). They presented the nine tasks to 6-year-olds. The easiest task for the children was the V-V spatial (intramodality) task. Children had some difficulty with tasks that required them to integrate visual-spatial stimuli with visual-temporal or auditory-temporal stimuli. They had more difficulty integrating two temporal patterns, whether the task was intra- or intermodal. While progressing in intermodal perception, then, children also improve their ability to integrate spatial and temporal stimuli as well as their ability to integrate two sets of temporal stimuli.

▶ **KEY POINT** Temporal patterns are more difficult than spatial patterns for children to integrate.

Difficult or subtle aspects of intermodal perception might continue to develop during adolescence. Intermodal perception most likely is stable in adulthood and older adulthood. Any decrements are probably a function of changes in the sensory-perceptual systems—changes that affect the amount of information available. For example, if cataracts cause a viewer to miss seeing the details of an object, the visual information for an integration may not be available. On the other hand, older adults might be able to use their experience as a compensatory mechanism and use information from one modality to compensate for information not available in another because of age-related change in the sensory or neurological systems. Certainly, more research is needed on this topic.

Web Study Guide Observe children's intermodal perception of small objects seen and manipulated in Lab Activity 13.3, Development of Intermodal Perception, in the web study guide.

Intermodal Development Summary

Intermodal coordination begins at birth, but there appears to be a developmental trend in childhood and adolescence for tasks that involve matching and subtle aspects of integration. The accuracy of children's performance is related to the order of presentation. That is, presenting the visual pattern or object first yields better performance than presenting the auditory information first. Also, children first master spatial-spatial integration tasks, followed by mixed spatial and temporal tasks, and finally temporal-temporal tasks.

Summary and Synthesis

The visual, kinesthetic, and auditory systems function at birth and continue to improve throughout infancy and childhood. The level of function in infancy appears adequate for the learning tasks facing infants, and the rate of improvement seems consistent with the learning tasks facing toddlers. By late childhood, the senses function at levels similar to those of adults. Detecting stimuli, however, is not the same as knowing what they mean; sensation is not the same as perception. In chapter 14 we consider the advancement of perception and perceptual-motor behavior.

Aging is accompanied by change in the sensory systems, although we know more about the changes in vision than about those in kinesthesis or audition. Decrements tend to vary widely among older adults. Compensation for some of these losses is possible; for example, seniors can wear eyeglasses or hearing aids. Conditions that accentuate differences are also helpful to older adults. Examples include the provision of good lighting and the reduction of background noise. Of course, a decrement in sensation can make for difficulty in perception, so just as with the early portion of the life span, it is important to study age-related change in perception.

Traditionally, much of the study of perceptual and perceptual-motor development has focused on the changing capacity of each individual system regardless of the environment. Even study of how the perceptual systems put together information received by each system about the same object or event assumed that integration was a step that followed perceptual processing. More ecological views of perception have been around for some time, but the difficulty of studying a perceptual system and the environment as an ecosystem has limited the data available to inform this perspective.

Reinforcing What You Have Learned About Constraints

TAKE A SECOND LOOK

When we watch an IMAX movie, the visual sensations and perceptions can be so real that even the kinesthetic system responds as if we were having the real experience. Those inclined to get airsick or carsick might actually do so while watching. The interactions of the sensory-perceptual systems are demonstrated even in the somewhat artificial experience of an IMAX movie. The model of constraints we use throughout our discussion of motor development stresses interactions. Thus, the ecological viewpoint is a better fit with our model of constraints. If we extend the ecological viewpoint a step further, perceptual and motor or perception–action become inseparable. Each continually informs the other so that there is a continuous interaction of perceiving the world and moving in it. We can see how important it is for teachers, therapists, coaches, and trainers to understand sensory and perceptual systems and how these systems might change over the life span. As the final part of this discussion of perceptual-motor development, chapter 14 explores perception–action from this viewpoint.

TEST YOUR KNOWLEDGE

1. What changes in visual sensation occur during infancy? During childhood?
2. Describe how humans perceive depth in the space around them.
3. Describe the various aspects of visual object perception.
4. What changes in kinesthetic sensation occur during infancy? During childhood?
5. What are the various aspects of kinesthetic perception, and at what age does each likely reach near-adult levels?
6. What changes in auditory sensation occur during infancy? During childhood?
7. What are the various aspects of auditory perception, and what information about the sound source does each provide?
8. What changes occur in the visual, kinesthetic, and auditory receptors in older adulthood?
9. What is the typical method for studying intermodal perception?
10. What are amodal invariants?

Learning Exercise 13.1

LIMITED SENSATION

We can gain an appreciation of the information that comes to us through our sensory-perceptual systems by artificially limiting that information. Working with a partner, try these activities:

1. Play catch in an old pair of sunglasses with tape covering one lens.
2. Walk down a hallway while blindfolded (with your partner guiding you for safety).
3. Facing away from your partner, carry on a conversation while wearing a pair of earplugs as your partner slowly increases the distance between the two of you.

Afterward, discuss what tasks were difficult or impossible and what the implications would be for daily living—for example, attending a university, driving a car, or playing intramural sports.

14

Perception and Action in Development

CHAPTER OBJECTIVES

This chapter

- reviews historical perspectives on the role of action in perceptual development;
- surveys contemporary views on perceptual-motor programs and the links between the cognitive, perceptual, and motor systems;
- examines differences in perception between infants with and without experience in self-produced movement;
- reviews the interdependence of the perceptual and cognitive systems and action; and
- studies the interaction between perception and action in maintaining balance after infancy.

Motor Development in the Real World

Redshirt Your Kindergartener?

The term *redshirt* was borrowed from a practice in athletics in which first-year college players are held out of athletic participation for a year in order to give them additional time to grow and mature. The practice has been particularly popular in sports such as football. In a similar vein, some parents delay their children's entry into kindergarten for a year (termed an academic redshirt), especially if their children would otherwise be among the youngest starting in a given year. Parents have always been concerned about their children's readiness to start school. They want their children to reach a maturity level that will enable them to succeed in school once they start rather than risk them being behind the majority of their classmates.

Throughout this text, we have emphasized that individuals are made up of systems at various levels. At the global level we can think of individuals consisting of multiple developmental systems: motor, perceptual, cognitive, and social. These developmental systems are intertwined. Perception and cognition are required to carry out actions, while actions generate perceptions, provide knowledge, and promote social interaction (Adolph & Franchak, 2017). To assess whether an individual is ready for a challenge, it is necessary to consider all the developmental systems. Chapter 13 reviews the sensory and perceptual systems used in motor skills. But might movement actually play a significant role in the development of sensory-perceptual systems, or for that matter the cognitive system? Are perception, cognition, and movement more tightly coupled than our discussion thus far has acknowledged? Although past thinking considered developmental systems to be independent, we have evolved today to a more contemporary view of interdependent systems.

This chapter focuses on the interrelationship between perception and movement actions. It begins with the notion that movement has a role in, and perhaps is even necessary for, perceptual development. The chapter then examines an aspect of everyday life in which perception and action are linked: maintenance of posture and balance. Later chapters explore the role of social systems.

The Role of Action in Perception

Developmentalists have long suspected that movement is extremely important to the development of perception. That is, they suspect that movement through the environment is vital for the coupling of perceptions and purposeful movements in the environment. The exact role of motor activity in the development of perception is difficult for researchers to study. The ideal experiment on this topic, of course, would be to deprive some individuals of movement and compare them with others who were allowed to move through the environment. Because this isn't possible, our information tends to come from animal studies and other research situations with humans in which movement experiences vary through naturally occurring circumstances. Advancements in technology have also opened new research frontiers.

Historical Views

Historically, motor development, perceptual development, and cognitive development were studied separately and treated as distinct systems. Their conceptualization mimicked a belief that the brain centers for thought and the brain centers for controlling movement were more separate than, as we now know, they really are. In part, this view of distinct systems harks back to mind–body dualism as outlined by Descartes in the 17th century. Mind–body dualism holds that the mind and the body are distinct natures. Although thinking has been colored by this separatist view, developmentalists in the 1960s pointed out how important perceptual development was to both motor development and cognitive development, and they began to explore interrelationships of the systems. They proposed a number of perceptual-motor theories, screening tools, and remedial programs.

Many of these developmentalists were interested in perceptual-motor activity because they realized that perceptual development is as important to the development of cognition as it is to the development of skilled movement. For example, individuals must perceive the difference in spatial orientation between a circle and a line when they are arranged to form the letter *d* and when they are arranged to form the letter *b*. If individuals cannot perceive this difference, they will have difficulty reading. Some earlier developmentalists saw perception as a precursor to both movement and cognition, and they proposed that children with learning disabilities had deficits in perceptual development. Further, they hypothesized that perceptual-motor activity programs could remediate deficits. By practicing to improve perceptual-motor responses, children would overcome perceptual deficiencies, and cognitive activities reliant on perception would benefit as much as motor activities.

Among the more popular theories in the mid-20th century were the neurological organization theory of Delacato (1959, 1966); the physiological optics program of Getman (1952, 1963); the visual perception tests and program of Frostig, Lefever, and Whittlesey (1966); the sensory-integration tests of Ayres (1972); the movigenics theory of Barsch (1965); and the perceptual-motor theory of Kephart (1971). Early on, there appeared to be empirical support for these theories and programs as children placed in the remedial programs showed improved classroom performance. The evaluations of these programs, however, were often flawed because they did not account for other factors that could contribute to improvement, such as the increased attention that children received in the remedial programs. Eventually, sufficient information from well-designed evaluations failed to show that participation in a perceptual-motor program produced improvements in readiness skills, intelligence, classroom achievement, or language (Goodman & Hamill, 1973). Perceptual-motor programs did help in the development of motor skills.

Piaget (1952) also recognized the importance of movement. He proposed that reality is constructed by relating action to sensory information in well-defined developmental stages during infancy, childhood, and adolescence. For Piaget, neither perception nor action is well organized in infancy.

Contemporary Views

Today, educators and therapists are cautious about claims that participation in a perceptual-motor program can remediate learning deficiencies. Yet they realize that such participation is beneficial for children with and without learning difficulties. Perceptual-motor programs at least provide valuable experience in performing skills based on key perceptual characteristics of a task. As such, they can contribute to a positive outlook on one's ability to perform. Perceptual-motor activities can also reinforce concepts needed for motor and cognitive tasks, such as shapes and directions. Most current physical education curricula for young children devote significant time to perceptual-motor activities. In addition, supplemental perceptual-motor programs are frequently offered to special groups. A recent hypothesis posits that physical activity triggers brain activity, which facilitates learning for a time after the period of activity (Ratey, 2008).

Perceptual-motor programs can be either comprehensive or focused on certain aspects of perception. They can also be designed for young children in general, for groups with a characteristic deficiency, or for individuals (based on their particular deficits). Table 14.1 illustrates this variability among perceptual-motor programs. Parents and educators alike must act as critical consumers in assessing the value of any program and its claim for success. Until we understand more about the links between perception, cognition, and action, the most realistic claims for perceptual-motor programs are those focused on the development of motor skills. The best programs do not advocate a single approach to the exclusion of others.

Advancements in technology have opened new frontiers for investigating the links among perception, cognition, and action. For example, scanning techniques that allow imaging of the

TABLE 14.1 Stated Features of Various Contemporary Perceptual-Motor Programs

FACTOR	TYPICAL FEATURES
Purpose of the program	Develops the ability to remember patterns of movement, sequences of sounds, and the look and feel of objects via training of the nervous system Enhances brain development by stimulating the 5 senses through movement Helps children become efficient movers and enhances learning readiness Develops gross motor skills and fine motor skills Improves self-esteem through success at play Replicates early movement experiences required to establish wiring of the brain
Intended participants	Preschool and primary school children Preschool children with speech and motor development delays Normally developing 2-, 3-, and 4-year-olds Special needs students Children with neurodevelopmental delays (learning difficulties, attention disorders, behavior problems)
Instructors	Teachers Professional-preparation students Physiotherapists Occupational and speech therapists
Context	Regular school offering Fee-based weekend programs Fee-based after-school programs
Location	Preschool Elementary school University Clinic
Activities	Gross motor skills Fine motor skills Swimming skills Rhythmic skills Visual-spatial skills (tracking objects, matching shapes) Ocular control activities (converging, tracking, fixating) Eye–hand coordination activities Eye–foot coordination activities Crossing the midline of the body Body awareness activities Spatial awareness activities Establishment of a preferred hand Balance activities Directionality activities Laterality activities Localizing touch Body concept activities Body image activities Clapping to rhythms Recognizing sound rhythms and patterns Locating a sound source Musical games Auditory discrimination and figure-and-ground activities

brain and its specific areas have given rise to new viewpoints. Diamond (2000) reviewed evidence of brain function and development and suggests that motor development and cognitive development may be more interrelated than previously thought, even to the extent of being fundamentally intertwined.

Other research work has focused on a group of brain proteins called factors, especially brain-derived neurotrophic factor (BDNF), which is involved in building and maintaining the infrastructure of the nervous system. It both stimulates growth of neurons and protects against neuron loss. Moreover, BDNF strengthens connections between neurons. Animal studies have demonstrated increases in BDNF in rodents that exercised; the increase was in the hippocampus, an important center in the brain for learning and memory processes (Cotman & Berchtold, 2002). In addition, hormones called growth factors are released when circulation increases, as with exercise. These factors work with BDNF, and one of them stimulates capillary growth in the brain (Ratey, 2008). These growth factors and BDNF have a role in neurogenesis and in strengthening connections between neurons, which in turn is necessary for memory. Production of BDNF and growth factors declines with aging. Recall that chapter 10 discussed a link between aerobic exercise and cognitive function in older adults.

▶ **KEY POINT** Exercise increases metabolic substances in the brain that can help build new neurons, especially in brain areas that are important for learning and memory.

All these observations indicate greater interdependence of the brain in cognitive and motor tasks than was previously emphasized. Both thinking patterns and movement, once learned, are stored in primitive areas of the brain that were once thought to control only movement. This process allows higher brain centers to continue adapting to new experiences. Ivry and Keele (Ivry, 1993; Ivry & Keele, 1989; Keele & Ivry, 1990) also proposed that the lateral hemispheres of the cerebellum are involved in critical timing functions that are crucial to sensory, cognitive, and motor tasks. It is interesting to note that children with dyslexia have difficulty with bimanual tasks requiring timing precision (Wolff, Michel, Ovrut, & Drake, 1990). Several contemporary educators report success in promoting active learning for both normally developing and exceptional learners. Active learning is the notion that movement activates the brain and facilitates learning, in contrast to passive learning environments that require learners to sit quietly, watching and listening to a teacher (Hannaford, 1995; Jackson, 1993, 1995, 2000). Finally, Sibley and Etnier (2003) conducted a meta-analysis of studies on the relationship between physical activity and cognition in children; these studies included a variety of physical activities and a variety of cognitive assessments. A significant positive relationship was found between physical activity and cognitive functioning; the largest effects for cognitive assessment were seen specifically with perceptual skills tests.

Imagine you are a teacher. As we learn more about the connection between movement and learning, would your approach to instruction include teacher-centered activities that require students to simply follow directions or more student-centered activities such as movement exploration? Why?

Momentum is building to approach the study of the cognitive, perceptual, and motor systems in more integrated ways, and we hope this approach will allow us to one day better understand the nature of the links between them. For now, the ecological view of development embraces the notion of a close link between perception and action (Kellman & Arterberry, 1998). Ecological developmentalists believe that the task of starting with very little perception and poor motor control and matching them through trial and error is too monumental for infants to achieve in a matter of months. Instead, the ecological view holds that the newborn infant perceives the environment and many of its properties before the onset of purposeful movements. Thus, the infant has a somewhat limited perception, which guides a movement, which in turn generates additional perceptions. The cycle is repeated and the infant eventually refines perception. This sequence is termed a perception–action loop (Gibson, 1966, 1979). The difficulty with this view is that we don't observe behaviors in infants that appear to be perception–action loops. Developmentalists do not yet know whether we simply have not found a way to measure the behavior or whether these loops do not exist.

Thinking back to our discussion of recent research in perceptual development, a slightly different view emerges: Perception develops ahead of movement skills. In infancy, new motor skills are acquired with guidance from the information obtained through perception. New actions in turn make new information available, and perceptual exploration now extracts more information. The infant is more sensitive, and more perceptual information is extracted from the environment. (Kellman & Arterberry, 1998; Kellman & Garrigan, 2009; von Hofsten, 1990). With this current perspective in mind, we now examine self-produced locomotion and its role in the refinement of perceptual abilities.

▶ **KEY POINT** Motor development, perceptual development, and cognitive development appear to be fundamentally interwoven.

Web Study Guide **Gain some experience with perceptual-motor activities in Lab Activity 14.1, Testing Perceptual-Motor Development, in the web study guide.**

Self-Produced Locomotion

If action facilitates perceptual development, then some types of perception would be evident only after an infant has begun performing a specific action. Researchers typically have observed perception in infants of the same age but with varying locomotor experience so that differences would be related to experience and not age. As mentioned earlier, researchers must use research paradigms in which experience varies naturally or use animal studies in which they can control conditions. In 1963, Held and Hein studied early motor activity in kittens. These researchers restricted the movements of some newborn kittens and permitted others to move. They kept the visual experience identical for all the kittens by placing them in pairs in a merry-go-round apparatus. One of the pair was harnessed but could walk around (active kitten), whereas the other was restricted to riding in a gondola (passive kitten) (figure 14.1). The passive kittens later failed to accurately judge depth and failed to exhibit paw placing or eye blinking when an object approached. Evidently, self-produced movement is related to the development of behavior depending on visual perception. There is also evidence of more brain growth and more efficient nervous system functioning in young animals when researchers provided them with perceptual-motor stimulation over and above the norm (Williams, 1986).

The visual cliff studies described in chapter 13 suggest that depth perception is present early in life. Other studies have suggested that avoidance of heights develops between 6 months and 1 year as a result of self-produced locomotor experience. Bertenthal, Campos, and Barrett (1984) found that prelocomotor infants given artificial locomotor experience by use of a baby walker (a seat in a frame that has wheels) responded to heights, whereas infants of the same age but without this artificial locomotor experience did not. In addition, one infant whose locomotor skills were delayed as a result of wearing a heavy cast did not respond to the visual cliff until self-produced locomotion began. Finally, infants who averaged 41 days of creeping experience were much more likely to avoid the visual cliff than were infants with 11 days of experience, even at identical ages. Thus, self-produced locomotion appears to facilitate development of depth perception. Once infants learn to avoid the visual cliff drop-off when crawling, they maintain the avoidance when learning to walk (Witherington, Campos, Anderson, Lejeune, & Seah, 2005).

Imagine you're a therapist working with a toddler for whom walking is not physically possible. What activities could you do that would facilitate the child's perceptual development?

FIGURE 14.1 The apparatus Held and Hein used for equating motion and consequent visual feedback for an actively moving (A) and a passively moved (P) animal.
Reprinted by permission from Held and Hein (1963).

Kermoian and Campos (1988) also investigated the link between infants' self-produced locomotion and their perception of spatial relationships by studying the infants' strategies in searching for objects. They gave infants a set of progressively more difficult searching tasks (called object permanence tasks) ranging from retrieving a half-hidden object to retrieving objects under one of several cloths after the passage of time. Three groups of 8.5-month-old infants performed the tasks:

1. Prelocomotor infants
2. Prelocomotor infants with walker experience
3. Locomotor (creeping) infants

The more locomotor experience infants had, the better they scored. Other studies support the suggestion that locomotor experience facilitates development of **spatial perception**. Lockman (1984) found that a basic ability to detour around a barrier is present in 12-month-old infants. By testing infants longitudinally starting at age 8 months, Lockman identified a sequence of improvements in spatial perception:

- Infants first learn to retrieve an object hidden behind a cloth; they become aware that objects still exist even if they are hidden behind a barrier.
- Some weeks after developing this ability, infants can reach around a barrier to obtain their goal.
- Infants can move themselves around a barrier to obtain their goal. On average, several weeks pass between success in reaching around a barrier and success in traveling around it.
- Most infants can successfully detour around an opaque barrier before they can travel around a transparent barrier. Transparent barriers initially puzzle infants because visual and kinesthetic (tactile) cues conflict.

Spatial perception is the perception that enables one to deal effectively with spatial properties, dimensions, and distances of objects and object relations in the environment.

Thus, infants are able to deal with spatial relationships at increasing distances from their bodies. McKenzie and Bigelow (1986) further demonstrated that infants become more efficient by taking the shortest path around a barrier (figure 14.2) and that they can better adapt to a relocated barrier by 14 months of age. Hence, with increasing movement experience in the environment, infants perceive spatial relationships even at a distance from their bodies.

Web Study Guide **Observe the development of spatial relationships in an infant in Lab Activity 14.2, Development of Spatial Relationships and Object Permanence, in the web study guide.**

Another line of research involves perception of surfaces. In these studies, researchers were interested in how locomotor experience influences the actions of infants when presented with different surfaces. For example, Gibson et al. (1987) presented infants with crawling experience and walking experience with a rigid surface (cloth over plywood) and a "deforming" surface (cloth over a waterbed). All the infants traversed the surfaces, but the walkers hesitated to cross the deforming surface. They first stopped to explore the deforming surface, through both vision and touch, and eventually crossed the deforming surface by crawling. When presented the opportunity to cross either surface (rigid or deforming), the crawlers showed no preference but the walkers chose the rigid surface.

▶ **KEY POINT** Locomotor experience facilitates depth perception, spatial perception, surface texture, and slope perception, so it may be necessary for normal perceptual development.

Adolph, Eppler, and Gibson (1993) also noted that walkers were more sensitive than crawlers to surface slopes. Crawlers, with less locomotor experience, almost always attempted to crawl up and down slopes even if the slopes were too steep for them. Walkers again tended to explore the surface, by patting it with their hands or feet or by stepping onto the sloped surface and rocking back and forth over their ankles. All walked up slopes of 10°, 20°, 30°, or 40°. They often refused steep descending slopes or used another form of locomotion, such as crawling down backward. Thus, the walkers had enough experience with surface slopes that they could

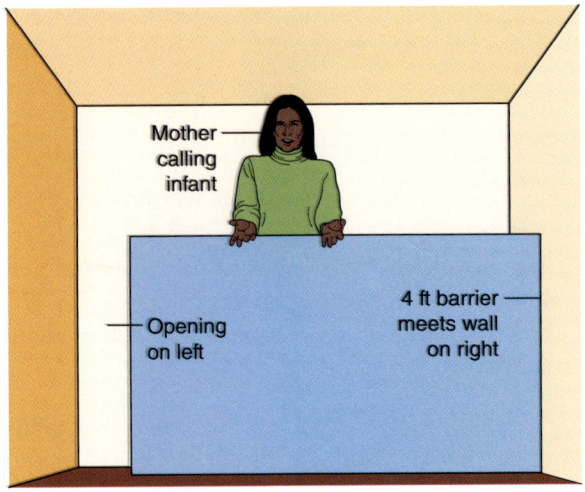

FIGURE 14.2 Room layout for a detour task. Infants can take the most efficient route around a barrier to their mothers (whom they can see over the barrier) by 14 months of age. By this age, they can also adapt when the barrier is relocated against the left wall. Younger infants usually take less efficient routes, such as approaching the barrier, then traveling along it, sometimes turning the wrong way and backtracking, or going to where the opening was before the barrier was relocated.

immediately perceive which slopes did not afford walking. They quickly chose another form of locomotion appropriate for the surface slope.

Locomotor experience leads infants to make better judgments and avoid risky behaviors beyond their abilities. Through movement, infants generate perceptual information about their bodies and the environment (Adolph & Franchak, 2017). As development proceeds, exploratory movement allows infants to calibrate environmental parameters and their bodies and to perceive affordances.

Perception of Affordances and Body Scaling

Recall that the ecological view of perception and action is based on direct perception of the environment rather than indirect perception. Indirect perception is derived from an assessment of environmental characteristics, cognitive calculations, and projections based on those characteristics. Consistent with the notion of direct perception, developmentalists with an ecological perspective believe that we directly perceive what the objects and surfaces in the environment permit us to do, given our own capabilities. That is, we perceive **affordances** (see chapter 2).

Affordances are the actions or behaviors provided for or permitted to an individual by the places, objects, and events in and of an environment.

▶ **KEY POINT** Affordances incorporate our body scale, which is our size relative to the environment.

Stair climbing provides a good example of an affordance. A set of stairs with an 8-inch (20 cm) rise between steps does not afford alternate-step climbing for an 18-month-old, as it does for an adult. A 24-inch (61 cm) rise does not afford alternate-step climbing for the average adult. As an individual grows and develops, her perception of affordances might change as her action capabilities change, even though an object's physical properties remain the same. Taking action, then, is a critically important aspect of the development of the perception–action system. Interaction with the environment is valuable for the perception of affordances.

If we perceive affordances rather than object characteristics, then individuals must be sensitive to the scale of their bodies. For example, perhaps individuals must be sensitive to their leg length in order to judge the "climbability" of any set of stairs. Warren (1984) tested this notion with adults and found that individuals perceived stairs with a riser height of more than 88% to 89% of their leg length to be "unclimbable" by means of alternate stepping. This model did not apply to older adults, whose affordances for stair climbing related more to strength and flexibility than to leg length (Konczak, Meuwssen, & Cress, 1988, cited in Konczak, 1990). Nor did the model apply to infants and toddlers. Infants in a study chose smaller step heights than did toddlers, but no anthropometric measurements related to the choice of step height (Ulrich, Thelen, & Niles, 1990).

Imagine you are a parent or a therapist in an average home environment. Aside from stairs, what actions do certain objects or structures afford? How do these differ for older children, older adults, or individuals with disabilities?

▶ **KEY POINT** If we perceive affordances rather than object characteristics, then the size of one's body in relation to environmental objects plays a role in that perception.

Conversely, the work of Gibson et al. (1987) and Adolph et al. (1993), described earlier, indicates that infants can perceive affordances. Infants seem to remember the results of their own previous actions with surfaces and slopes. Also, Bushnell and Boudreau (1993) found that infants can perceive the properties of objects in the following order: size and temperature, texture and hardness, and weight and shape. These findings are consistent with infants' manual abilities to explore objects. Perception of size and temperature requires only clutching, whereas perception of texture and hardness requires rubbing and poking, and perception of weight and shape requires finger, hand, and arm movement. This is the same order in which these manipulations are acquired, suggesting perception and the action proceed together.

Lockman (2000) suggested that infant tool use has its origins in perception–action routines repeatedly used by infants during the first year (figure 14.3). Through trial and error, infants gradually explore forms of tool use, relating objects to other objects and surfaces. In so doing, infants detect affordances. These are not affordances of individual tools, but affordances of the relationships between objects. Infants use tools differently on different surfaces, even when the area is small (Fontenelle, Kahrs, Neal, Newton, & Lockman, 2007). The notion that infants perceive affordances between tools and surfaces is a marked contrast with previous perspectives that tool use reflects advances in cognitive abilities (Lockman & Kahrs, 2017). Tool use depends on properties of both the tool and the surface or another object. Trial-and-error tool use can be viewed as self-generated movement opportunity for perceptual learning (Lockman, 2000). Early movements might be building blocks for later tool use such as in hammering and pounding. That is, early arm movements such as banging objects become tuned for later percussive tool use (Kahrs, Jung, & Lockman, 2012).

FIGURE 14.3 The ability to reach, grasp, control, and bang objects provides an infant with the opportunity to detect affordances between objects and surfaces.

Individuals may use many types of body scales, and the important scales may change throughout life. Perhaps changes in a person's various body systems influence which scale he or she uses. Our sensitivity to body scaling has implications for skill instruction. For example, if a child cannot swing a big, heavy adult tennis racket with one hand, the child cannot use adult technique in the sport. The large racket does not afford the adult style of movement. Either the racket must be scaled down to fit the child or the child might need to use two hands to swing the racket. Indeed, scaling task constraints for children playing a racket sport facilitates their performance (Fitzpatrick, Davids, & Stone, 2018). Gagen, Haywood, and Spaner (2005) found that strength as well as size might be an important consideration in scaling equipment for such ballistic tasks.

Ishak, Franchak, and Adolph (2014) studied the development of the affordance for reaching through openings of various sizes. Of course, hand size varied over their age range of 16 months to 20 years, so hand size predicted the affordance for fitting the hand through the opening. Accuracy of decisions about whether the hand would fit improved with age beginning at 7 years of age. Yet every age group was sensitive to changes in the opening size by scaling their reaching attempts. So infants and young children were systematic, even when inaccurate. Perhaps they were more inclined to explore body–environment relationships near the threshold of what openings were big enough for their hands than were older children and adults.

Body scaling helps us appreciate how important it is for those interested in motor development to understand the course of growth and aging. Continued research is necessary to determine the reference scales that individuals use for particular tasks. Such research would help determine whether it is indeed an affordance or individual characteristics of objects that are perceived.

If you were an early childhood or elementary physical education teacher, how would you use knowledge of body scales to select equipment for your students?

We have reviewed evidence that movement facilitates continued perceptual development. Recall the earlier discussion of neurological development. Greenough, Black, and Wallace (1987) hypothesized that, initially, an excess number of synapses forms among neurons. With continued development, some survive whereas others do not. Connections that are activated by sensory and motor experience survive; unused connections are lost. Synaptic proliferation prepares an organism for experiences—presumably the experiences common to all members of a species. Undergoing experiences during this sensitive period of development both promotes survival of the synaptic connections and strengthens those connections (Ratey, 2008).

▶ **KEY POINT** A neurological basis exists for positing the necessity of movement experience to perceptual development.

These theories need more experimental verification, but they provide a plausible explanation for the role of action in perceptual development (Bertenthal & Campos, 1987). They also imply that deprivation of action experience puts an individual at risk of deficient perceptual development.

Another way of looking at the interplay of perception and action is to examine the development of postural control and balance. Action must be coupled with perception so that individuals can deal with events or movements that disturb their posture and balance.

Postural Control and Balance

Postural control and balance are perfect examples of perception and action as an ecosystem. To control our posture in order to sit, stand, or assume any desired position, we must continually change our motor response patterns according to the perceptual information that specifies the environment and our bodies' orientation in it. Several perceptual systems are involved in maintaining posture and balance. Vision tells us how our bodies are positioned relative to the environment. Kinesthetic input from our bodies' proprioceptors tells us how our limbs and body parts are positioned relative to each other. Kinesthetic input from the vestibular system provides information about our head position and movement. Even the auditory system can contribute information about balance (Horak & MacPherson, 1995).

We must maintain posture and balance in an almost infinite number of situations. Sometimes we balance when stationary (static balance) and sometimes when moving (dynamic balance). We must also balance on a variety of body parts, not just two feet. Think of all the body parts on which gymnasts must balance in their various events. Sometimes we need to balance on surfaces other than the ground, such as a ladder. We might even have to balance without all the information we would like—for example, when we have to walk in the dark.

Given the number of perceptual systems involved in balance and the wide range of environmental and task constraints that are possible for any given balance task, the triangular model of constraints provides a good perspective on the development of balance. A developmental trend for a certain set of task and environmental constraints might differ from the trend for another set of constraints. In fact, movement scientists recognized some time ago that performance levels on various types of balancing tasks are specific to that task (Drowatzky & Zuccato, 1967). We discussed postural control and balance in infants in chapter 9. Now let's consider the development of balance in childhood through older adulthood.

▶ **KEY POINT** The timing of developmental trends in balance is related to the type of balance task under consideration.

Balance in Childhood

It has long been established that performance improves on a variety of balance tasks from 3 to 19 years of age (Bachman, 1961; DeOreo & Wade, 1971; Espenschade, 1947; Espenschade, Dable, & Schoendube, 1953; Nougier, Bard, Fleury, & Teasdale, 1998; Seils, 1951; Shumway-Cook & Woollacott, 1985; Winterhalter, 1974; Woollacott, Shumway-Cook, & Williams, 1989), with the exact nature of the improvement trend depending on the task.

Since these improvement trends are well established, more recent research has focused on what strategies children use to maintain equilibrium in various contexts, as well as how the strategies change over the life span.

Balancing during locomotion is a challenging task. When we walk or run, for example, we must maintain our stability yet propel the body forward in order to travel. To do so, we probably use two frames of reference. One is the supporting surface, and the other is gravity. Another challenge is to control the degrees of freedom of movement at the various body joints. On one hand, individuals might stabilize the head on the trunk in order to minimize the movement they must control. On the other hand, they might stabilize head position in space and use the orientation of the head and trunk to control their equilibrium. Investigating frame of reference, Roncesvalles, Schmitz, Zedka, Assaiante, and Woollacott (2005) observed manual tasks and trunk manipulations in four age groups: 2 to 3 years, 4 to 6 years, 7 to 9 years, and adults. The two younger groups used the trunk or support surface as a reference, while older groups could use gravity as their frame of reference.

The strategy to maintain quiet stance is likely to use sensory feedback, with vision being particularly important for children. In contrast, a dynamic balance strategy likely requires feedforward control of body segments (i.e., anticipatory postural adjustments). Disturbances to balance require fast motor responses to maintain stability (Hatzitaki, Zisi, Kollias, & Kioumourtzoglou, 2002).

▶ **KEY POINT** To maintain dynamic balance, anticipatory postural adjustment requiring fast motor responses is often needed.

Assaiante and Amblard (1995; Assaiante, 1998) proposed a model to explain the development of balance in locomotion over the life span. The model describes four important periods. The first covers birth to the onset of standing and is characterized by a cephalocaudal (head to toe) direction of muscle control. The second includes the achievement of upright stance to about 6 years of age; during this time, coordination of the lower and upper body must be mastered. The third period, from about age 7 to sometime in adolescence, is characterized by the refinement of head stabilization in balance control. The head can be stabilized on the trunk or it can be stabilized in space. The fourth and last period, which begins in adolescence and extends through adulthood, is characterized by refined control of the degrees of freedom of movement in the neck. Thus, the task in childhood is to learn how the different frames of reference complement one another during movement. This is an intriguing model that generated additional research on the development of dynamic balance.

One aspect of postural control studied was the adjustment necessary as one initiates walking. Assaiante, Woollacott, and Amblard (2000) observed 1- to 4- and 9- to 17-month-olds, 4- to 5-year-olds, and adults and saw anticipatory postural adjustments in all ages. Yet with aging, the adjustments were more consistent and body segments were better coordinated. Further, older individuals could make the adjustments with the lower body alone, not needing upper body adjustments.

When experiencing a large enough balance perturbation, adults can take a step or two to regain balance. Roncesvalles, Woollacott, and Jensen (2000) observed infants with varying amounts of walking experience (independent standers, walking <2 weeks, walking 1 to 3 months, and walking >3 months) as their balance was perturbed. New walkers rarely stepped to regain balance, whereas infants with 3 months' experience or more could use a step effectively to remain balanced and never fell.

Think of your own experience in visiting an amusement park attraction or fun house that used visual displays to confuse you. How did the visual display conflict with your other senses? Which of your systems were put into conflict? How did you maintain your balance (if you did)?

Balance Changes With Aging

In adulthood, individuals standing on a force platform (see the sidebar Assessing Balance) show a minimal amount of sway. If the platform is moved repetitively back and forth, adults use visual information to stabilize the head and upper body, and the muscle response to movement occurs in the ankles (Buchanan & Horak, 1999). When adults stand on such a platform and it is moved slightly or slowly but unexpectedly, they use an ankle strategy to regain balance. That is, they use lower leg muscles that cross the ankle joint to bring themselves upright once again. When the movement is larger or faster, a hip strategy is used; muscles crossing the hip and knee joints bring the center of gravity back over the base of support (Horak, Nashner, & Diener, 1990; Kuo & Zajac, 1993).

FIGURE 14.4 Declines in balance with aging make tasks such as descending stairs more challenging.
wanderluster/iStock/Getty Images

Older adults experience a decline in the ability to balance (figure 14.4). Those over 60 sway more than younger adults when standing upright, especially if they are in a leaning position (Hasselkus & Shambes, 1975; Hellebrandt & Braun, 1939; Perrin, Jeandel, Perrin, & Bene, 1997; Sheldon, 1963). Age-related changes in balance are also seen with older adults on movable platform tests. In comparison with young adults, slightly more time passes before an older adult's leg muscles respond after a perturbation in order to maintain balance, and sometimes the upper leg muscles respond first instead of the lower leg muscles, a pattern opposite that found in young adults. The strength of the muscles' response is more variable among repetitions in older adults (Perrin et al., 1997; Woollacott, Shumway-Cook, & Nashner, 1982, 1986).

Age-related changes in balance ability could be related to a variety of changes in the body's systems, especially in the nervous system. As mentioned previously, some older adults experience changes in the kinesthetic receptors, and these changes might be more extreme in the lower limbs than in the upper ones. This could lead to an overreliance on vision to maintain balance (Yeh, Cluff, & Balasubramaniam, 2014), yet older adults might also be placed at a disadvantage because of vision changes as well as the changes in the vestibular receptors and nerves in adults over 75 (Bergstrom, 1973; Johnsson & Hawkins, 1972; Rosenhall & Rubin, 1975). A decrease in fast-twitch muscle fibers or a loss of strength could hamper an older adult's quick response to changes in stability, as might arthritic conditions in the joints. The prevalence of falls increases in older adults with pain (Patel et al., 2014), and giving older adults motor or cognitive tasks while balancing decreases their performance (Sertel et al., 2017). As with children, balance performance in older adults is task specific (Dunsky, Zeev, & Netz, 2017).

Perrin et al. (1997) recorded electromyograph activity in older adults during a backward tilt of a movable force platform. They observed some of the reflexes in the lower legs that were not involved in balance control, as well as the responses necessary for regaining balance. By comparing the time from the balance perturbation with the onset of each of these muscle responses in young and older adults, the investigators determined that nerve conduction speed in both the peripheral and central nervous systems was slower in the older adults. Thus, the declines in balance performance with aging most likely are associated with age-related changes in a variety of systems.

▶ **KEY POINT** The difficulties that older adults experience with balance most likely reflect changes in more than one system.

Web Study Guide **Test several people on balance tasks and rate the balance tasks in Lab Activity 14.3, Development of Balance, in the web study guide.**

Falls are a significant concern in older adults. In fact, falls are the leading cause of accidental death for people over 75 years old. A common result of falling, especially among older adults with osteoporosis, is fracture of the spine, hip (pelvis or femur), or wrist. Complications of such a fracture can result in death. Even when older adults recover, they experience heavy health care costs, a period of inactivity, and dependence on others. A fear of falling again can make them change their lifestyles or be overly cautious in subsequent activities.

Woollacott (1986) studied the reaction of older adults when a movable platform tipped forward or backward to perturb their balance unexpectedly. Half the older adults she observed lost their balance the first time, but these adults learned to keep their balance after a few more tries. Thus, older adults are more liable to fall on a slippery surface than young adults but are capable of improving their stability with practice. Campbell et al. (1997) and Campbell, Robertson, Gardner, Norton, and Buchner (1999) compared the number of falls over a 1-year period in women over 80 years of age who participated in an individualized exercise program stressing strength and balance with the number of falls in women over 80 who did not participate in an exercise program. The number of falls in the exercise group (88) was significantly lower than the number of falls in the other group (152). Research since has firmly established the benefit of balance training for older adults (Ruffieux, Mouthon, Keller, Wälchli, & Taube, 2017). Prevention and rehabilitation programs, then, are useful in reducing the risk of falls in older adults, but they must be ongoing. Recall that in chapter 10, we discussed the role of aerobic exercise in maintaining the speed of cognitive processes.

▶ **KEY POINT** Exercise programs focused on improving strength and balance can reduce the risk of falls in older adults.

Assessing Balance

Balance can be assessed in many ways, both in field settings and in laboratories. Different assessments are used for static balance and dynamic balance. A device used in many laboratory settings is a force plate or force platform. A simple force plate consists of two square plates positioned one over the other, with four pressure gauges in between the plates and at the four corners. The device is placed on the floor, or even set into the flooring to be level with the surface, so that individuals can stand on, walk across, or even jump on or off the plate.

The most basic force plate simply measures vertical force applied in the geometric center of the top plate. More complicated force plates can measure force at, and the location of, a center of pressure. Think about an individual standing on a force plate on one leg. As he or she sways and the body varies from perfect vertical, the center of pressure exerted on the force plate moves. The force plate can detect the location of the center of pressure, how far it moves, and when. The most advanced force plates can break the vector of the force exerted on the force plate into three spatial components. So force plates can measure changing pressures under the feet as someone stands on or moves across the platform.

Imagine you have a grandparent who comes to live with you. What types of surfaces and conditions around your house could be more likely to lead to falls for him or her than for a young adult? What steps could you take to reduce the chances of a fall?

Summary and Synthesis

Perception and action are an ecosystem. Actions are coupled to perceptions, as shown by postural and balance responses. There is some disagreement about the exact role of action in the development of perception but little disagreement over its importance. Experience with movement has been shown to facilitate perception of space—including depth, surfaces, and slopes—and perception of affordances.

Perception–action coupling for posture and balance is evident in young infants. However, it appears that a developmental trend determines which perceptual system gets priority. Young infants depend more on visual information when it conflicts with kinesthetic information. With advancing development, this finding is reversed. Older children, youths, and young adults rarely fall when placed in an environment in which vision and kinesthesis conflict. They have learned to rely more on kinesthetic information. Older adults show changes in their responses to balance perturbations. An overreliance on vision resulting from changes in the perceptual systems could affect these responses, but the changes seem to occur more in the timing and pattern of the muscle responses to perceptual information.

Thelen (1995) summed up the relationship of perception and action: "People perceive in order to move and move in order to perceive. What, then, is movement but a form of perception, a way of knowing the world as well as acting on it?"

When researchers are interested in static balance, they can ask individuals to stand on a force plate and measure both how far the individual sways and the velocity of sway. Individuals can stand on one foot or two feet and in any kind of stance, such as side stride or split stride. Researchers also can ask individuals to lean as far as possible without losing balance to quantify the ability to control the body or the maximum limits of stability.

Computerized dynamic posturography assessments incorporate a force plate. These devices are used to study the reaction of individuals to being slightly thrown off balance by virtue of the force plate tilting. By controlling the surrounding visual field with a three-sided enclosure around the participant, researchers can present conditions with normal vision or no vision and with a surround that is stable or that moves as the individual sways. Researchers can also control whether the force plate moves, and in what direction, by rotating or translating. This allows them to study the visual, vestibular, and somatosensory systems and their interactions in balance, including when balance is perturbed and the person must react to regain or maintain balance. Electromyographs can be used in conjunction with systems such as this to record how the muscles are activated to regain balance.

Reinforcing What You Have Learned About Constraints

TAKE A SECOND LOOK

Think about the dilemma presented at the beginning of this chapter. It has always been hard for parents and teachers to know when to push children to take on certain learning tasks and when to allow children to put off those challenges. On one hand they want their children to be successful, but on the other they are afraid their children will be behind others in their development. Recent research appears to show that cognitive, perceptual, and motor systems develop together. If development in one system falls behind development in the others, we know from the model of constraints that it can become a rate-limiting system that holds back the others. Hopes for artificially controlling the rate of development are generally met with failure. What parents and professionals can do is manipulate the environment and manipulate task goals to set the stage for advances in development when individuals are ready to make those advances.

TEST YOUR KNOWLEDGE

1. What are some reasons that contemporary researchers think cognitive and motor development are more intertwined than previously thought?
2. What seems to be the role of experience with self-produced locomotion in the development of perception? Which aspects of perception are most affected?
3. Considering your answer to the preceding question, what would be the repercussions for perceptual and motor development of depriving an infant of locomotor experience?
4. How did views of perceptual-motor development change in the 20th century?
5. What is an affordance? What does the notion of affordance have to do with adapting equipment size to the size of a performer (scaling)?
6. Is there a developmental trend in the perception of affordances? (Justify your answer.)
7. On what perceptual systems do children rely for balance, and how does this change with development?
8. What changes in various body systems might lead to a higher frequency of falls in older adults? What might reduce the risk of falling?

LEARNING EXERCISE 14.1

Cognitive and Motor Deficits

Choose one of the following disorders: autism, dyslexia, developmental coordination disorder, or attention-deficit/hyperactivity disorder. Research the characteristics of the disorder to determine whether both cognitive and motor deficits are commonly associated with it. Describe specific characteristics of deficits in each area (cognitive and motor), as appropriate. What accommodations would be necessary for a child with this disorder in a regular physical education class offered at the elementary school level?

VI

Functional Constraints in Motor Development

Part VI focuses on the effect of the sociocultural environment—for example, those constraints that exist as a function of family influences or cultural belief systems—on individual functional constraints. Functional constraints can include motivation, attitude, self-concept, perception of a gender role, and knowledge about a topic. Especially when working with children, we must wait for individual *structural* constraints to undergo change through growth and maturation. In contrast, *functional* constraints can change more quickly. For example, a teacher could set a task goal that interacts with motivation to bring about a rather rapid change in motor behavior. Not all functional constraints, however, change quickly. Self-concept is shaped over many years and is influenced by social interactions, and knowledge about a sport is often acquired over several years of experience in playing that sport.

Functional constraints and environmental constraints interact richly. For example, sociocultural norms strongly influence perceived gender roles; in turn, one's perceived gender role influences the types of physical activity that one views as appropriate. Even the popularity of certain sports or dance forms in a culture can influence the knowledge that someone living in the culture possesses about that sport or dance.

This part of the text examines functional constraints and the changes they undergo over the life span. Chapter 15 considers the role of society and culture in influencing individuals' choice of physical activities and play environments. Chapter 16 discusses how environmental constraints influence the functional constraints of self-esteem and motivation and how that interaction influences choices about physical activities. The chapter also looks at developmental changes in perceived and actual motor competence. Chapter 17 provides an overview of the processes of motor learning and how they change across the life span. In Chapter 18, we summarize and synthesize concepts used throughout the textbook.

Suggested Reading

Coyne, S.M., Linder, J.R., Rasmussen, E.E., Nelson, D.A., & Birkbeck, V. (2016). Pretty as a princess: Longitudinal effects of engagement with Disney princesses on gender stereotypes, body esteem, and prosocial behavior in children. *Child Development, 87*(6), 1909–1925.

Dinella, L.M., & Weisgram, E.S. (2018). Gender-typing of children's toys: Causes, consequences, and correlates. *Sex Roles, 79*(5/6), 253–259.

Estevan, I., & Barnett, L.M. (2018). Considerations related to the definition, measurement and analysis of perceived motor competence. *Sports Medicine,* 1–10. doi:10.1007/s40279-018-0940-2

Rudisill, M.E., & Johnson, J.L. (2018). Mastery motivational climates in early childhood physical education: What have we learned over the years? *Journal of Physical Education, Recreation & Dance, 89*(6), 26–32.

Slykerman, S., Ridgers, N.D., Stevenson, C., & Barnett, L.M. (2016). How important is young children's actual and perceived movement skill competence to their physical activity? *Journal of Science and Medicine in Sport, 19*(6), 488–492.

Sullivan, K.J., Kantak, S.S., & Burtner, P.A. (2008). Motor learning in children: Feedback effects on skill acquisition. *Physical therapy, 88*(6), 720–732.

Wulf, G. (2013). Attentional focus and motor learning: A review of 15 years. *International Review of Sport and Exercise Psychology, 6*(1), 77–104.

15

Social and Cultural Constraints in Motor Development

The Effects of Environmental Constraints

CHAPTER OBJECTIVES

This chapter

- discusses the role of sociocultural constraints in motor development;
- defines the role of specific social agents, such as parents and schools, in individual development; and
- explains the socialization process and how it differs for various groups.

Motor Development in the Real World

Gender Stereotypes in Lacrosse

"The women of the Massachusetts College of Liberal Arts (MCLA) lacrosse team are standing on the field, the sun turning their cheeks a bright shade of pink. Their skirts flip behind them as they run. A few players near the goal are adjusting their skirts back down to their rightful place, but they keep riding up. If you watch closely you can catch each player tug casually on their skirt every few minutes.

"Despite their ladylike uniform, women's lacrosse players are eager to participate in a more aggressive game. But women's rules don't give female players that right. The rules of person-to-person contact are one of the main differences between the men's and women's games, along with lack of padding, shallower stick pockets, and the traditional uniforms.

"Some of these differences are frustrating to MCLA team members. Players don't want the same rules as men's lacrosse, but would appreciate rules that don't suggest women players are weak.

"'They don't let us have body-to-body contact in women's lacrosse, but men's lacrosse is allowed to have it. It's not fair because the rule is suggesting that we are weak and just because we're girls we can't handle contact,' Mackenzie Cutler, sophomore lacrosse player, said.

"According to uslacrosse.org there are many differences between men's and women's rules. Women aren't allowed to have a deep pocket. Men must wear helmets, mouth guards, and padding where women must wear mouth guards and protective eye wear. Aggressive checking and body contact are illegal in the women's game, while they are legal in men's.

"'In some ways the women's game is harder than the men's game. To master the stick skills definitely takes a lot more work,' Coach Bartini, the women's lacrosse head coach, said. 'We have incorporated some of the rules of the men's game while limiting some of the brute force that I don't really see as athleticism anyway.'"

Reprinted by permission from Wiese (2016).

When selecting sports in which to participate, people are influenced by the culturally specific gender associations of some sports. In the preceding example, both men and women play lacrosse, but the rule system for women is different from that of men to reduce the amount of body contact and aggression. No physiological reasons exist for these differences; the differences emerged long ago to keep the sport "ladylike" for females. Field hockey is another illustrative example. No one would think twice if a boy played field hockey in Europe; in the United States, however, very few boys play the sport. When we think of this phenomenon in terms of constraints, we can see that no individual constraints discourage or prevent boys (as a group) from playing field hockey, just as no constraints keep girls from playing lacrosse using the rule structure for men's lacrosse. The constraints have more to do with the social or cultural environment.

Society as a whole influences the activity choices that individuals make, and girls and boys alike benefit from the addition of new athletic role models. When social or cultural factors influence the types of physical activity in which people get involved, those factors act as sociocultural constraints. You might not have considered sociocultural constraints as important to motor development, but in this chapter you will discover that these ever-present constraints can have a great influence on motor behavior throughout the life span.

The idea that social and cultural aspects can influence motor development may come as a surprise to a maturationist. If you believe that genetics determines development, then you would be hard pressed to think of society as a developmental agent. However, those who follow an ecological perspective believe that social and cultural influences (in the form of environmental constraints) may greatly influence and interact with individual and task constraints. This means that media coverage of events such as women's wrestling and ice hockey may encourage participation in these sports by changing some of the social and cultural stereotypes associated with females in sport.

Social and Cultural Influences as Environmental Constraints

In chapter 1, we introduce the idea of sociocultural influences as environmental constraints—the idea that sociocultural attitudes of groups of people either encourage or discourage certain motor behaviors. These factors are considered environmental constraints because they reflect a general attitude or belief system present either in society at large or in certain subcultures. If such attitudes are pervasive enough, they can modify someone's behavior. They may not be obvious at all, yet they may still exert a powerful influence on how individuals move. Just as temperature and ambient light can fill a room, field, or community, so can attitudes, values, norms, and stereotypes envelop us. Even as late as the 1970s girls were not expected, or in some cases even allowed, to participate in some organized sports, such as baseball and ice hockey. This attitude about girls in sport meant the opportunity to play organized and even pickup sports was limited. In essence, this attitude discouraged sport participation for many girls, especially after puberty. However, the passage of Title IX (requiring equal opportunity for girls and women in sport) in 1972 drastically changed the landscape of sport in the United States, making it more possible and, in time, socially acceptable for girls and women to participate in sport.

Society and culture can have a profound effect on an individual's movement behaviors, particularly in the area of sport and physical activity (Clark, 1995). Sociocultural elements such as gender, race, religion, and national origin can all direct one's future movement behavior (Lindquist, Reynolds, & Goran, 1998). Even the media encourage and promote different types of physical activities (e.g., those that are gender specific) to mass audiences (Cooky & Messner, 2018; Koivula, 2000; Musto, Cooky, & Messner, 2017), although that has changed somewhat in recent years with the rise of the World Wide Web and Internet-based news as well as social media (Bruce, 2016).

A simple example illustrates how sociocultural constraints work: Think about who the most successful American athlete was during the past 10 years. Many athletes may come to mind, such as LeBron James, Carson Wentz, or Alex Morgan. Most likely, you imagine a trim, muscular individual who plays a professional sport in the United States. However, if we asked this question of someone from Japan, he or she might picture a sumo wrestler (figure 15.1). Most Americans would not even know the names of sumo wrestlers. More important, in the context of motor development, most American children would not aspire to become sumo wrestlers, and most American adults would not attempt to participate in sumo wrestling, regardless of individual constraints such as body type (which may actually encourage participation in some cases). In the United States, sumo wrestling is not encouraged as a sport. Thus, society and culture influence the choice of sport or physical activity in which one participates; that is, they act as environmental constraints, encouraging certain movement activities while discouraging others. The chances that a young American boy or girl would pursue a career in sumo wrestling are slim. As a result, an entire group of movements (those associated with sumo wrestling) are discouraged and may never be performed; over time, this constraint interacts with individual constraints to limit or even prevent the emergence of these movements.

▶ **KEY POINT** Societal and cultural beliefs, attitudes, and stereotypes can encourage or discourage motor behaviors. These are ever-present environmental constraints.

Participating in physical activities contributes to motor development. The benefits of experience in physical activity are well known and include improved physical and emotional health. In addition, sport may influence the behavioral patterns of participants (e.g., by teaching leadership and other skills). Thus, it makes sense to provide opportunities for all people to participate in sport and physical activity from an early age and throughout the life span. However, decisions to participate in sport or maintain a physically active lifestyle can have as much to do with the social milieu as with individual constraints. For example, the individual constraints of most typically developing American children allow them to participate in a wide variety of activities, yet many choose computer and video games and television over playing outdoors. Why?

What are some of the most important social and cultural elements (people, places, and so on) that have influenced you during your life? How have these influences changed from the time you were an infant to the present?

An individual's early socialization in sport and physical activity is a key factor in motor development and the likelihood of later participation. People and situations continue to influence individuals in their choice of activities throughout their lives. For example, your peers influence your recreational activities and lifestyle choices. These activities can be physical (pickup basketball versus online games), academic (library versus study group), and social (movies versus barhopping), among others. The **socialization process**—as related to sport and physical activities, including the individuals who are influential in the process—deserves attention as a major environmental constraint in one's motor development.

The process by which one learns a social role in groups with certain values, morals, and rules is one's **socialization process**.

Three major elements of the socialization process lead an individual to learn a societal role, as shown in figure 15.2 (Greendorfer, 1992; Kenyon & McPherson, 1973):

FIGURE 15.1 Although quite popular in Asian countries, sumo wrestling is not followed intently in the United States.

Buddhika Weerasinghe / Contributor/Getty Images News/Getty Images AsiaPac

1. Significant others (influential or important people, called socializing agents)
2. Social situations (places where socialization takes place—schools, home, playgrounds)
3. Personal attributes (individual constraints)

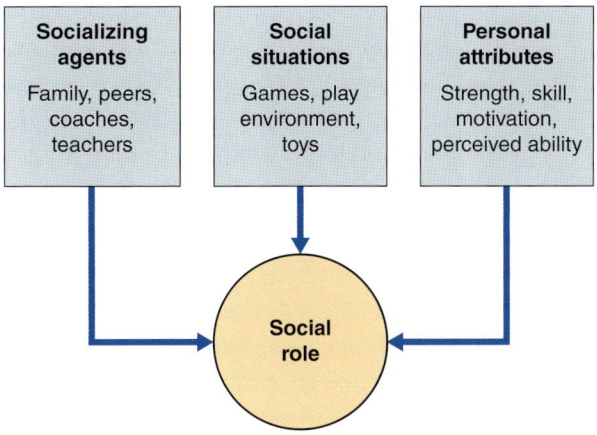

FIGURE 15.2 The three major elements of the socialization process that lead to the learning of a societal role for participation in physical activity.
Based on Kenyon and McPherson (1973).

We examine the first two of these elements to see their influence and importance in the process of socialization into sport and physical activity. Of course, the third element, personal attributes, represents an interaction between environmental constraints (socializing agents and situations) and individual constraints. Among the socializing agents are family members, peers, teachers, and coaches. This section examines the influences these people provide—and how they might encourage or discourage certain motor behaviors. First, however, we examine a cultural phenomenon that cuts across many contexts: gender typing in sport and physical activities.

▶ **KEY POINT** Significant others (e.g., parents and friends) and social situations (e.g., school or sports teams) contribute to an individual's socialization process.

Sociocultural Constraints in Action: Gender-Specific Stereotyped Behaviors

Significant others enter any context with socially and culturally prescribed notions of how they and others should act. Examination of one such notion, that of gender-specific stereotyping, shows just how potent sociocultural constraints can be. In general, people are born physiologically either male or female; their biological characteristics determine their **sex**. In contrast, **gender** is a culturally determined sociological construct that differentiates between men ("masculine") and women ("feminine") (Eitzen & Sage, 2015).

Sex refers to biological characteristics used to determine whether individuals are classified as male or female.

Gender refers to culturally defined sociological characteristics used to differentiate between males and females.

Parents and other significant socializing agents often encourage children toward what they perceive as gender-appropriate behaviors, based on each child's biological characteristics (Fagot & Leinbach, 1996; Fagot, Leinbach, & O'Boyle, 1992; Lorber, 1994). In terms of developing motor skills, significant others steer boys toward "masculine" and girls toward "feminine" sports and physical activities (Royce, Gebelt, & Duff, 2003; Shakib & Dunbar, 2004). This practice is often termed **gender typing**, or gender-role stereotyping. Children begin to learn these gender roles early, perhaps as early as their first year (Fagot & Leinbach, 1996).

Gender typing, or gender-role stereotyping, occurs when a parent or significant other encourages activities that are deemed "gender appropriate."

Traditionally, Western societies gender-type participation in sport and physical activities. Certain sports (e.g., football, baseball, and wrestling) are identified as masculine, and others (e.g., figure skating, gymnastics, and field hockey) are identified as feminine. In addition, Westerners consider sport to be important and appropriate for boys; however, that attitude doesn't always carry through for girls. Therefore, adults often permit and encourage vigorous, outgoing, rough-and-tumble play for toddler boys whereas they may be more likely to discourage girls from (or even punish them for) running, climbing, or venturing away from parents (Bosacki, Woods, & Copeland, 2015; Campbell & Eaton, 2000; Storli & Sandseter, 2015, 2017). Although the number of girls participating in high school sports in the United States has drastically increased since the inception of Title IX, from just over 294,000 in 1971–1972 to over 3.4 million in 2016–2017, girls still lag behind boys' participation by almost 2 million athletes (National Federation of State High School Associations, 2017). Furthermore, girls are more likely to drop out of sport and activity participation after high school.

Why is the issue of gender typing important for girls and boys? For girls, such limited involvement and practice may not allow them to develop their motor skills to their full potential. Even girls who do participate may feel that all-out effort and skilled performance are gender inappropriate. This, in turn, could affect a girl's or woman's motivation for participating, for training, or for striving for high achievement standards that rival those of boys and men. At the same time, boys may feel forced into participating in gender-appropriate sports they dislike. Worse yet, they may drop out of physical activity altogether rather than be subjected to participating in an undesired but gender-typed sport. Thus, this pervasive societal influence on boys' and girls' sport participation may factor into measurements of skill and fitness that compare the sexes. This is an important consideration in the context of an integrated model of interacting constraints. What appear to be fitness or skill differences in boys and girls based on physiological makeup (sex) may in fact be related to a lifetime of stereotyped influences (gender) (Campbell & Eaton, 2000).

Despite a growing awareness during the 1970s and 1980s that these societal roles might limit girls' opportunities to enjoy the many benefits of sport participation, parents did not seem to change their contact patterns with their children. Research studies in the mid-1980s confirmed that parents still tended to interact differently with sons and daughters in play environments (Power, 1985; Power & Parke, 1983, 1986; see Williams, Goodman, & Green, 1985, on "tomboys"). For example, parents tended to direct their girls' play but allowed boys more opportunities for independent, exploratory play (Power, 1985).

Can Laws Change Constraints? Effects of Title IX on Girls' and Women's Sport Participation

Before the passage of Title IX, far more boys than girls participated in high school athletics. In 1971, fewer than 300,000 female athletes participated in high school sports compared with almost 4 million male athletes (Reith, 2004). Some argued that boys were biologically predisposed to sport participation; that is, more boys participate in sport because their sex is an individual constraint that encourages athletics. This argument provided a biological rationale for providing boys with more athletic opportunities than were provided for girls. But was biology the reason for the vast difference in participation numbers, or was this difference socially constructed? Title IX, passed in 1972, provided a unique chance to examine this question. Title IX states, "No person in the United States shall, on the basis of sex, be excluded from participation in, be denied the benefits of, or be subjected to discrimination under any education program or activity receiving federal financial assistance." In terms of its effect on sport, the law mandated that educational programs strive for more gender equity. (For a full description of Title IX and its effect on sport, see Acosta & Carpenter, 2014, or Gregg & Gregg, 2017.)

Although many changes seemed to occur during the 1990s, research indicates that boys and girls still received stereotypical messages about participation in physical activity well into the 21st century (Heinze et al., 2017; Eitzen & Sage, 2015), suggesting that societal roles have not yet changed. In a 2003 study by McCallister, Blinde, and Phillips, middle-school-age girls were surveyed on their beliefs about and attitudes toward girls and boys in physical activity and sport. The girls in the study associated being an athlete with being a male and perceived boys as more athletic and physically capable; further, they perceived athleticism as a negative trait in a girl. Overall, the researchers found that traditional, stereotypical beliefs held true in this sample. For example, Heinze et al. (2017) surveyed 814 parents about the benefits and types of sports their daughters play. They found that gender still played a small but statistically significant role in shaping parents' beliefs about girls' involvement in sports. Some research indicates that times are changing: In a sample of 565 university-age students, Royce et al. (2003) found that both men and women perceived female athletes as respected. Overall, the sample studied did not see being feminine and being an athlete as mutually exclusive, suggesting a change in negative stereotypes related to women in sport.

What happens to girls who defy gender-role stereotypes? Giuliano, Popp, and Knight (2000) studied 84 Division III female college students, both athletes and nonathletes. They found that as children the athletes tended to play with "masculine" toys and games, were considered "tomboys," and played primarily with boys or mixed-gender groups, whereas the nonathletes did not. This finding suggests that, rather than harming the females in any way, these early "masculine" experiences may have encouraged them to participate in athletics and physical activities throughout college—and perhaps beyond. Given the importance of a physically active lifestyle, then, parents may wish to avoid rigid adherence to gender-typed behaviors for their daughters.

Times have changed since 1971. Almost 8 million high school students participated in athletics between 2016 and 2017. Of these, 3.4 million were girls and 4.5 million were boys (National Federation of State High School Associations, 2017). These numbers show that participation in high school sports has expanded for both genders. What trends have appeared since 1972 in the types of sports high school students select? It appears that more high school athletes—both boys and girls—select gender-neutral sports, whereas participation in highly gendered sports has tended to increase more slowly (football is the major exception to this trend; Stevenson, 2007). In 1972, boys played football more than any other sport, followed by basketball and track. In 2017, football's popularity dropped to number 5 (basketball and track were number 1 and 2, respectively). The most popular sports for girls were basketball, track and field, and volleyball. The overall increase in athletic participation and the specific increase in participation among girls suggest that the constraints discouraging participation were not individual but rather were related to the sociocultural environment.

Web Study Guide Examine television commercials and the packaging of toys for evidence of gender-role stereotyping in Lab Activity 15.1, Examining Gender-Role Stereotyping, in the web study guide.

Significant Others: People's Values Acting as Constraints

Significant others, or **socializing agents**, are family members, peers, teachers, coaches, and others who are involved in the socialization process of an individual.

Significant others, or **socializing agents**, are the people most likely to play a role in an individual's socialization process—family members, peers, teachers, and coaches (figure 15.3). People who act as socializing agents should be considered constraints because they will encourage or discourage certain motor behaviors. This section examines how each of these groups might influence participation in sport and physical activity.

The roles that parents, peers, teachers, and coaches play in the socialization of children can vary with the gender of a child. In addition, the gender of the person serving as a model for behavior may differentially influence the child's internalization of the behavior. The result of such socialization can constrain a child to very specific types of physical activities and virtually eliminate others.

Family Members

A person's family has a major influence in the process of socialization into physical activities, as well as other pursuits, in part because the family's influence begins so early in a child's life (Kelly, 1974; Pargman, 1997; Snyder & Spreitzer, 1973, 1978; Weiss & Barber, 1996). In fact, the family may be the only source of social interaction that an infant has—and therefore the primary source of social constraints. From their very first interactions, family members expose their infants to certain experiences and attitudes. They reinforce the behaviors deemed appropriate through their gestures, praise, and rewards; at the same time, they punish inappropriate behaviors. The process is systematic, but at times it is so subtle that family members may hardly realize what and how they communicate to the infant.

FIGURE 15.3 Significant others such as coaches may influence the socialization process throughout childhood.

Jose Luis Pelaez Inc/DigitalVision/Getty Images

Parents

When someone participates in physical activities after early childhood, he probably reflects his parents' interest and encouragement during the early years. Parents can encourage children to engage in either physical or sedentary activities. This may relate to the participation habits of the parent (DiLorenzo, Stucky-Ropp, Vander Wal, & Gotham, 1998). As children become physically active, parents can encourage or discourage games and, eventually, specific sports or physical activities. Parents' early involvement could lead to a lifetime of participation in physical activities for a child (Weiss & Barber, 1996). About 75% of eventual sport participants become involved in sport by age 8 (Greendorfer, 1979; Snyder & Spreitzer, 1976). In fact, the best predictor of adult sport involvement is participation during childhood and adolescence (Greendorfer, 1979; Loy, McPherson, & Kenyon, 1978; Snyder & Spreitzer, 1976). It follows, then, that a parent's early bias toward or away from physical activities can have lasting consequences. Although Title IX may be opening new doors for girls in terms of parental expectations for gendered activity, things may not have changed much for boys. In a 2007 study, Kane determined that parents perceived gender nonconformity in their preschool children as primarily positive—but only within a limited range for sons. At the same time, the parents in this study reported that it was important for their sons to conform to normative standards of masculinity.

Individual parents may play different roles in socializing children into physical activity. Snyder and Spreitzer (1973) proposed that a child's same-sex parent is most influential in the extent of that child's sport involvement. Further, McPherson (1978) suggested specifically that mothers serve as sport role models for their daughters. This notion was supported by DiLorenzo et al. (1998), who found that for eighth- and ninth-grade girls, their mothers' physical activity and support were predictors for physical activity. Some researchers believe that fathers more strictly reinforce gender-appropriate behavior, which would include sport participation for boys (Lewko & Greendorfer, 1988). Greendorfer and Lewko (1978) identified fathers rather than mothers as a major influence in the sport involvement of both boys and girls. In contrast, Lewko and Ewing (1980) found that fathers influenced boys between the ages of 9 and 11 years who were highly involved in sport and that mothers influenced highly involved girls. In order to become involved, girls seemed to need a higher level of encouragement from their families than boys did, and they needed it from many members of the family. A similar pattern was found in Japanese children (Ebihara, Ikeda, & Miyashita, 1983).

Although the research does not definitively indicate a differential role for mothers and fathers, parents clearly influence and affect the choices their children make in physical activities. Recently, Yao and Rhodes (2015) performed a meta-analysis on research related to the impact of parental modeling and support on physical activity in children and adolescents. They synthesized the results of 115 studies and found that father–son modeling was significantly higher than mother–son modeling ($p < .05$), but parental gender did not moderate the relationship between parental modeling and girls' physical activity. In other words, girls did not change their level of physical activity differently through modeling either their mother's or their father's physical activity. Sterdt, Liersch, and Walter (2014) also performed a systematic review of 10 systematic reviews of correlates of physical activity in children and adolescents and found a consistently positive association between physical activity and parental support for both age groups, regardless of gender.

During the 1980s and 1990s, girls' and women's participation in sport and physical activity became more recognized and widespread. Furthermore, it has become far more socially acceptable for women to participate in sports that have been gender-typed as male in the past, such as soccer and ice hockey. For example, in 2016 and 2017, more than 14,500 high school girls participated in wrestling, and more than 9,500 participated in ice hockey (National Federation of State High School Associations, 2017). Sports leagues for both genders have begun to include divisions for adults of different ages and skill levels, reflecting an increased interest in sport past high school and college. In addition, more opportunities exist for women and men to participate in nonsport physical activities ranging from SoulCycle to yoga to boot camp.

These increased opportunities for parents will likely have a positive effect on the socialization of their children into physical activity.

Siblings

Siblings form an infant's first playgroup and thus may act as important socialization agents into physical activity. Both brothers and sisters can influence girls' sport and physical activity participation (Blazo & Smith, 2017; Blazo, Czech, Carson, & Dees, 2014). Prior research has suggested that African American boys see athletes as their role models and that their male siblings shape their idea of a role model (Assibey-Mensah, 1998). On the other hand, some children and teens report that older siblings were not important in their sport involvement (Greendorfer & Lewko, 1978; Patriksson, 1981). Thus, it is possible that for most children, siblings merely reinforce the socialization pattern into physical activity established by parents rather than act as a major socializing force in themselves (Lewko & Greendorfer, 1988).

How Do Race, Ethnicity, and Other Factors Affect the Role of the Family in Physical Activity Socialization?

Various investigators have reached different conclusions about the influence of family members on socialization into physical activity. Greendorfer and Lewko (1978) attempted to clarify these various conclusions by questioning children from a broad range of social backgrounds. They found some differences in the patterns of significant influences. The significant other who exerted the most influence on socialization into physical activity varied somewhat among children according to sex, social background, race, and geographic location. For example, fathers were influential in socializing Caucasian American but not African American boys into sport (Greendorfer & Ewing, 1981). In contrast, Lindquist et al. (1998) found few differences in children's physical activity based on ethnicity when they controlled for social class and family background. This finding suggests that the roles of race, ethnicity, social background, and other factors in family socialization are more complex and difficult to characterize on a group basis. In fact, this complexity supports our notion of motor development: Socially and culturally specific agents constrain motor behaviors of individuals in different ways, leading to the emergence of different motor behaviors. We should not generalize about social agents but rather keep in mind that diverse patterns of influence may exist. More recent research in this area has not been done.

Peers

A child's peers have the potential to reinforce or counteract the sport socialization process begun in the family (Bigelow, Tesson, & Lewko, 1996; Brown, Frankel, & Fennell, 1990; Greendorfer & Lewko, 1978; Weiss & Barber, 1996). If a peer group tends to participate in active play or sport, its individual members are drawn to such activities. If the group prefers passive activities, its individual members tend to follow that lead. Adult athletes typically report that peer groups or friends influenced the extent of their sport participation when they were in school, although the strength of this influence varies by sport. The first peer group a child encounters is typically a playgroup. Children typically become involved in such groups from a very young age (some playgroups begin when children are still in infancy) and continue in them during their early school years.

Boys and girls from several countries, including the United States, Japan, and Canada, have reported that peers influenced their childhood sport participation (Ebihara et al., 1983; Greendorfer & Ewing, 1981; Greendorfer & Lewko, 1978; Yamaguchi, 1984). During preadolescence, children enter more formalized peer groups, such as cliques. These peers continue to be influential during adolescence (Brown, 1985; Brown et al., 1990; Butcher, 1983, 1985; Higginson, 1985; Patrick et al., 1999; Patriksson, 1981; Schellenberger, 1981; Smith, 1979; Weiss & Barber, 1996; Yamaguchi, 1984). In fact, among the women she questioned, Greendorfer (1976) found that the peer group was the only socializing agent that influenced sport involvement throughout all phases of the life cycle studied: childhood, adolescence, and young adulthood. Other socializing agents were important at some ages but not at others. For example, the family, so important to young children, probably is less influential for adolescents.

Peers often provide a stronger influence for participation in team sports than for participation in individual sports during childhood and adolescence (Kenyon & McPherson, 1973). Children's and adolescents' supportive peer groups are usually made up of others of the same sex. For adults, especially women, and particularly after marriage, spouses and friends of the opposite sex become more influential in either encouraging or discouraging involvement in certain activities (Loy et al., 1978). As individuals leave school and enter new social environments as members of the workforce, they often leave their peer groups. If a peer group was sport oriented, a reduction in sport involvement might follow. On the other hand, new peer groups at the workplace could stimulate sport involvement; the individual might, for example, join a team in a recreational sport league or perhaps participate in company-sponsored exercise and recreational programs (Loy et al., 1978). Recent research continues to indicate the importance of peers for promoting physical activity, particularly in girls. For example, Laird, Fawkner, Kelly, McNamee, and Niven (2016) performed a systematic review and meta-analysis of 84 published research articles and determined that social support from peers and friends had a small but positive relationship to physical activity participation in adolescent girls.

▶ **KEY POINT** An individual's peer group may either encourage or discourage physical activities. As socializing agents, peer groups can be as important as family.

It is likely that the typical middle-aged adult, even one who was involved in sport as a young adult, reduces sport involvement. A study by Ebrahim and Rowland (1996) found that of 704 women aged 44 to 93 years, only 25% took part in vigorous activity during the week before the study. This trend might be due in part to a lack of programs aimed specifically at middle-aged and older adults. However, this has been changing in recent years as the emphasis on fitness that began in the late 1970s has led to greater availability of exercise and recreation programs for members of these age groups. In addition, adult participation in sport and exercise programs has become acceptable and even desirable in Western societies. Peer groups appear to be essential for adherence to exercise, so they may be part of the initial reason for joining a recreational group. Once involved, adults keep participating to be part of a peer group.

Despite the strong influence of peer groups on sport participation and physical activity throughout life, it is still not clear whether membership in a sport-oriented peer group always precedes participation (i.e., that a person is drawn to an activity because of a desire to associate with peers). It is possible that individuals first select groups that fit their interests, including an interest in sport (Loy et al., 1978). Although it is unclear which comes first, the interest in sport and the desire to be part of a peer group make it likely that an individual will continue to participate and to select membership in active groups. Research in the 1980s indicated that peers play just as important a role in sport socialization as the family plays (Lewko & Greendorfer, 1988). Current research suggests that no individual source of social support stands out as being a strong predictor of physical activity levels, but a variety of different sources (peers, friends, parents, family) all have small, positive influences on promoting physical activity (Laird et al., 2016; Sterdt et al., 2014).

Coaches and Teachers

Coaches and teachers can also influence an individual's involvement in sport and physical activity (Greendorfer & Lewko, 1978; Laird et al., 2016). Male athletes consistently report that coaches and teachers influenced both their participation in and their selection of sports, particularly when they were adolescents and young adults (Ebihara et al., 1983; Kenyon & McPherson, 1973). Female athletes report that teachers and coaches influenced them during childhood (Greendorfer & Ewing, 1981; Weiss & Knoppers, 1982) and adolescence (Greendorfer, 1976,

1977). In contrast, Yamaguchi (1984) found that schoolteachers and coaches were not influential. Participants rarely name teachers and coaches as the most influential agents in their sport involvement. Perhaps the role of teachers and coaches is to strengthen the sport socialization process begun earlier by family and friends. Clearly, this area of study needs additional research for us to understand the role of coaches and teachers in the 21st century.

Adults who dislike physical activity often report that they had poor movement experiences, particularly in physical education, when they were children. Keeping this in mind, how could you, as a physical educator, manipulate different types of constraints to make the gymnasium a more positive learning environment?

Assessing Youth Sports Coaching Behaviors: Coaches as Socializing Agents

Participation in youth sports has grown steadily over the past several decades (Smoll & Smith, 2001), with 60% of boys and 47% of girls in the United States participating on teams by the age of 6 years (Sabo & Veliz, 2008). This growth has led to a demand for coaches who understand the needs of young participants. Remember, coaches can act as socializing agents for young children. Many of the feelings, values, and behaviors people have in terms of physical activity come from their experiences in youth sports. A good coach can facilitate a lifetime of positive experiences, just as a poor coach can drive young people away from sport and physical activity.

Frank Smoll and Ron Smith (2001) suggested that youth sports coaches adopt a four-part philosophy to enhance the enjoyment and benefits of children's participation in sport. They posit that the primary objective of youth sports is to have fun. Here are the four points:

1. Winning isn't everything, nor is it the only thing.
2. Failure is not the same thing as losing.
3. Success is not synonymous with winning.
4. Children should be taught that success is found in striving for victory; that is, success is related to effort.

How do coaches evaluate their ability to make physical activity a fun, positive experience for kids? Coaches can understand their own coaching behaviors better through self-monitoring. To aid in this process, Smoll and Smith developed the Coaching Self-Report Form, which the coach should complete soon after each practice or game (Smoll & Smith, 2001). This form helps coaches assess the frequency of desired behaviors in sport situations. Along with providing feedback from knowledgeable sources such as other coaches or teachers, the form can enhance a coach's ability to be a positive socializing agent for participants in youth sports.

Nevertheless, teachers and coaches should not overlook their potential to influence their students' sport involvement. They can introduce children and adolescents to exciting new activities and stimulate them to learn the skills and attitudes associated with sport. Conversely, teachers and coaches must also recognize the potential they have to turn their students away from sport and physical activity. Bad experiences in school can have lifelong consequences for a person's overall lifestyle (Snyder & Spreitzer, 1973). Such negative experiences, known as **aversive socialization**, can occur when teachers or coaches embarrass children in front of their peers, overemphasize performance criteria at the expense of learning and enjoyment, or plan class activities that result in overwhelming failure rather than success. Children who experience aversive socialization naturally avoid physical activities and fail to learn skills well; consequently, any attempts they make to participate frustrate and discourage them.

Coaching Self-Report Form

Complete this form as soon as possible after a practice or game.

For items 1, 2, and 3, think not only about what you did but also about the kinds of situations in which the actions occurred and the kinds of athletes who were involved.

1. Approximately what percentage of the time did you respond to good players' actions with reinforcement?
2. Approximately what percentage of the time did you respond to players' mistakes or errors with each of the following communications?
   a. Encouragement only
   b. Corrective instructions given in an encouraging manner
   (Sum of *a* and *b* should not exceed 100%)
3. About how many times did you reinforce athletes for showing effort, complying with team rules, encouraging teammates, showing team spirit, and exhibiting other good behaviors?
4. How well did your team play tonight? (Circle one.)
   very poorly not very well average quite well very well
5. How positive an experience *for the kids* was this practice or game?
   very negative somewhat negative neutral somewhat positive very positive
6. How positive an experience *for you* was this practice or game?
   very negative somewhat negative neutral somewhat positive very positive
7. Is there anything you might do differently if you had a chance to coach this practice or game again? (If so, briefly explain.)

Reprinted by permission from J. Williams, *Applied Sport Psychology: Personal Growth to Peak Performance*, 4th ed. (New York: McGraw-Hill Companies, 2001). © McGraw-Hill Companies, Inc.

▶ **KEY POINT** It is essential that coaches and teachers understand their potential influence in promoting or deterring physical activity participation among their athletes and students.

Web Study Guide **Reflect on how your life was shaped by socializing agents in Lab Activity 15.2, Significant People in Your Life, in the web study guide.**

Social Situations

The situations in which children spend their formative years are a part of the socialization process. Play environments, games, and the toys children use can all influence their later activities.

Play Environments and Games

An adequate environment for play, such as a backyard or playground, can provide the social situation and environment a child needs in order to begin involvement in sport and physical activity. Play spaces probably also influence activity selection. A child who lacks an adequate play space has a diminished opportunity to get involved in activities and to practice skills. These environmental constraints thus discourage participation in sport and gross motor activities. Children who grow up in urban areas with limited play space are typically exposed to sports and activities that require little space and equipment, such as basketball. Colder climates provide children with an opportunity to learn ice skating; warmer climates encourage swimming.

Play environment may also act as a sociocultural constraint, especially if the play space has gender-associated values, which can influence boys and girls to participate in gender-typed activities. For example, double-dutch rope jumping falls in the "feminine" domain; a boy might be labeled a "sissy" for rope jumping and thus be discouraged from participating in that activity. A girl might be told that a certain sport (e.g., football) is inappropriate for girls or labeled a "tomboy" if she does participate. Western society has traditionally considered certain types of games appropriate for boys but not for girls and vice versa. This labeling is particularly apparent as children enter adolescence.

The pressure to participate in gender-appropriate games has implications for children's opportunities to practice skills. Traditional boys' games are typically complex and involve the use of strategy; participants are encouraged to work hard in pursuit of specific goals and to use negotiation to settle disputes over rules. In the past, traditional girls' games were typically noncompetitive, and rather than encouraging interdependence among group members, they involved waiting for turns to perform simple repetitive tasks, such as jumping rope or playing hopscotch. Such games rarely gave girls opportunities to increase game complexity or to develop increasingly more difficult skills. In fact, the games often ended because the participants lost interest, not because they achieved a goal (Greendorfer, 1983).

These days, more and more children are participating in activities that are not "gender appropriate" (Giuliano et al., 2000). Further, some sports and activities, such as soccer and aerobics, are losing their gender-specific associations. Gender typing of sports and activities still exists, however, and it acts as a strong constraint on movement activities. Educators should keep in mind that a play environment that channels boys and girls into gender-typed games perpetuates a situation in which boys can better develop complex motor skills but girls cannot.

Play With Toys

Imagine you are a child walking into a toy store. What do you experience? Bright colors and loud sounds beckon you toward toys that promise to enlighten, engage, and excite. As a child (or even an adult), you may not realize that these toys act as part of the socialization process. That's right—even toys are constraints! Toys can encourage children to be active or inactive. For example, a Frisbee or Nerf ball encourages a child to throw, catch, and develop an accurate shot. On the other hand, a board game or doll encourages sedentary play. Toys can also stimulate children to emulate sports figures; among others, you can find basketball, soccer, and cheerleader Barbies as well as UFC action figures. Video and computer games may simulate sport without promoting any physical activity at all (e.g., EA FIFA or Axis Football), or they may promote some physical activity (such as the Wii Fit Plus or EA Sports Active 2). Each kind of toy has its advantages, but certain toys facilitate children's socialization into sport and physical activity more than others do.

Consider a toy that is popular today, such as LEGO Boost Creative Toolbox or Hatchimals. How might these toys encourage certain behaviors and discourage other behaviors in a child?

Toys are also a means by which gender typing can occur in the socialization process (Auster & Mansback, 2012; Cherney & London, 2006; Murnen, Greenfield, Younger, & Boyd, 2016). For example, toys marketed to boys tend to be more complex, develop spatial skills, and encourage more vigorous activity than those marketed to girls (Jirout & Newcombe, 2015). The typical girls' toy, such as a doll or kitchen set, promotes quiet indoor play (Coyne et al., 2016; Greendorfer, 1983; Liss, 1983). Gender typing through toys is well entrenched in society and, in fact, has not improved recently despite strides made toward gender equality in other areas (Paoletti, 2012), and even young children may be aware of the gender associations of toys (Levy, 2000; Weisgram, Fulcher, & Dinella, 2014). In a series of studies published in 2005, Blakemore and Centers interviewed undergraduates to determine their perceptions of the gender suitability of certain toys and to find out how they rated the characteristics of the toys. The participants associated girls' toys with physical attractiveness, nurturance, and domestic skill and associated boys' toys with violence, competition, excitement, and, to some degree, danger (Blakemore & Centers, 2005). Manufacturers often use gender-typed strategies to advertise their products. For example, commercials or packaging for sports equipment, racing-car sets, and action-oriented video games feature boys, and those for dolls picture girls (figure 15.4). Watch carefully for television advertisements during daytime television—most target either boys or girls but not both. These marketing ploys influence children as well as their parents.

Parents also enjoy giving their children the same kinds of toys they played with as children, thus tending to perpetuate traditional gender typing. For example, a father might buy a Lincoln Logs set for his son, remembering the hours he spent with one as a child—despite the more modern, complex, and potentially less gender-typed toys on the market. Moreover, parents can promote gender typing by negatively reinforcing play with toys they judge to be gender inappropriate (Fagot, 1978), such as telling boys not to play with dolls. In a study of gender typing, toys, and preschoolers, Raag and Rackliff (1998) found that many of the boys thought their fathers would perceive cross-gender-typed toys as "bad." Raag (1999) also found that children who had a parent or significant other who viewed gender-neutral toys as "bad" were somewhat influenced by gender-typed toy labels. Such gender typing through toys is slow to change, and there is little evidence of change over the past several decades (Blakemore & Centers, 2005; Campenni, 1999; Eisenberg, Welchick, Hernandez, & Pasternack, 1985; Lloyd

FIGURE 15.4 Advertising for children's toys is often gender typed.

& Smith, 1985; Marcon & Freeman, 1999). In a unique study, Pennell (1999), disguised as Santa's head elf, questioned 359 males and 417 females of various ages and ethnic backgrounds about their toy choices. Pennell found that both girls and (to a greater extent) boys had strong gender-typed toy preferences.

In recent years, society has become more aware of the many ways in which children are gender typed and the implications of this process. Yet there is little evidence of any substantial change away from gender typing (Banerjee & Lintern, 2000; Blakemore & Centers, 2005; Pennell, 1999; Turner & Gervai, 1995; Turner, Gervai, & Hinde, 1993; Weisner, Garnier, & Loucky, 1994). Teachers must realize that they influence this aspect of socialization (Fagot, 1984). Again, the evidence shows that teachers still behave differently toward the play of boys than toward that of girls (Fagot, 1984; Oettingen, 1985; Smith, 1985). They can reinforce early gender typing by continuing to label certain activities as more important or appropriate for one sex than for the other. They can choose different activities for boys' and girls' achievements. Or they can make every attempt possible to eliminate such distinctions and allow each individual to explore his or her full potential. It is likely that such day-to-day decisions and expectations accumulate over time to reduce differences in boys' and girls' motor development by channeling their practice opportunities (Brown et al., 1990; Brundage, 1983; Giuliano et al., 2000; Greendorfer & Brundage, 1984).

Other Sociocultural Constraints: Race, Ethnicity, and Socioeconomic Status

Earlier in this chapter, we describe some constraints related to gender as socially constructed rather than biologically defined. For example, the notion that girls are weaker than boys is firmly established in Western culture even though little biological evidence backs it up. (Recall that few physiological differences exist between boys and girls before puberty.) Socially constructed notions also go beyond gender differences into the realms of race, ethnicity, and socioeconomic status (SES). Oftentimes, it's difficult to distinguish between sociocultural constraints (e.g., prevailing cultural attitudes) and individual constraints (e.g., physiological functioning) because research may not be completely clear-cut on how race, class, or ethnicity is defined. For example, race and ethnicity are often used together, but they are not equivalent. Racial characteristics are biologically based and relate to genetic similarities within groups, whereas ethnic characteristics are culturally based and relate to cultural similarities that connect groups. Race and ethnicity can coincide (biologically similar individuals who live in a particular geographic locale likely share culture), which makes their independent study very difficult.

Consider ways in which low socioeconomic status might encourage certain behaviors and discourage others.

Furthermore, social class and SES are associated with certain characteristics that may cut across race and ethnicity. Given that all these factors interrelate, it is hard to identify constraints as strictly sociocultural or individual when considering SES. It may be best to consider the relationship of SES to other factors when looking for the influence of constraints. For example, children who come from a lower SES background may have less access to organized sports and physical activities, particularly those that require expensive equipment (e.g., ice hockey) or lessons (e.g., figure skating or tennis) and extensive time commitments from at least one parent. As a result, these children may not gain experiences and practice related to these particular activities.

We should consider the research on race, ethnicity, and SES from a slightly different point of view—one that examines differences among groups without suggesting a priori that differences are biological in nature. This approach allows us to examine the potential influence of a variety of constraints without limiting our interpretation to "biological fact" (which might actually be a cultural assumption). Malina, Bouchard, and Bar-Or (2004) provide an extensive review of historical and contemporary research related to physical differences based on race, ethnicity, and SES.

Another sociocultural constraint that can affect motor skill development across the life span is called stereotype threat (Chalabaev et al., 2013; Heidrich & Chiviacowsky, 2015). **Stereotype threat** occurs in situations where a stigmatized group feels pressured by the possibility of conforming to a negative stereotype related to their racial, ethnic, gender, or other cultural group, and as a result, they perform motor skills at levels below their actual capabilities. For example, boys may perceive dancing as "feminine" or "for girls" and therefore may downplay their ability in order to avoid that negative stereotype.

Stereotype threat is the experience of being at risk of conforming to stereotypes, usually negative, related to a racial, ethnic, gender, or cultural group.

Summary and Synthesis

Humans are social beings. That is, individuals constantly interact with and depend on others as a part of everyday life. People form groups that can be small (family), medium (sports teams, town membership), or large (United States citizens). These groups often feature distinct values, morals, rules, and other factors that create a social atmosphere in which group members live. Thus, different groups and group members act as socializing agents who, along with social situations, encourage what is viewed as socially and culturally appropriate motor development. As you might expect, these sociocultural constraints interact with functional individual constraints to influence motivation, self-esteem, and feelings of competence for a task. Such constraint interactions are explored in chapter 16.

Reinforcing What You Have Learned About Constraints

TAKE A SECOND LOOK

We should not overlook the effects of the social and cultural environment, or the influence of gender typing, on motor development. Societal beliefs about gender can create different sets of rules for men and women, like the example provided of the MCLA women's lacrosse team. This can disadvantage both genders. Back in the early 1970s, boys participated in sports such as field hockey, gymnastics, volleyball, and softball in far greater numbers than they do today. After Title IX passed, girls began to participate in these sports in large numbers. Perhaps the increase in girls' participation led to gender typing of these sports as "feminine" and, in turn, to a drop in boys' participation. However, with the renewed participation of men in gender-typed sports such as field hockey, sociocultural constraints will likely change again, eventually encouraging a broader range of individuals to play more sports.

TEST YOUR KNOWLEDGE

1. Who are the socializing agents most likely to influence children's socialization into sport and physical activity?
2. How might gender-role stereotyping result in fewer women participating in sport and physical activity?
3. How might stereotype threat act as a constraint for boys interested in female gender-typed physical activities?
4. Describe how toys are part of the socialization process.
5. What is the difference between sex and gender, and why does this distinction matter in the context of motor development?

6. Describe the changing roles of significant others across childhood and adolescence.
7. How do sociocultural constraints work in regard to our model of motor development? Provide specific examples.

LEARNING EXERCISE 15.1

Observing Sociocultural Constraints on the Internet

Have you ever wondered what your motor development might be like if you had grown up in a different country? One of the benefits of the Internet is that we have immediate access to information from around the world. After a little web browsing, it becomes clear that various societies and cultures promote varying activities for their members—sports, for example, or the age at which a certain activity is deemed appropriate, or the roles viewed as proper for males and females, and so on. In this learning activity you will use the Internet to explore several countries and identify sociocultural constraints specific to those places.

1. Imagine in turn that you are a college-age individual from each of six continents: Africa, Asia, Australia, Europe, North America, and South America. To get started, select a country from each continent. Do not choose the country in which you reside.
2. Next, visit at least two websites *from* each country as well as two websites *about* each country (e.g., from a travel guide). Remember to record the URLs of these websites for future reference. The more websites you visit, the more information you will have to work with.
3. For each country, identify sociocultural constraints specific to that society or culture.
4. For each country you choose, develop a biographical portrait of yourself as you might be if you had been born and raised there. Focus on sociocultural constraints. What would you be like? How would your life and motor development differ from country to country? How might your motor development there compare with your actual motor development in your real home country? Would similarities exist between your lives in the various countries? Describe those.

16

Psychosocial Constraints in Motor Development

Individual–Environmental Constraints

CHAPTER OBJECTIVES

This chapter

- examines associations between perceived and actual motor competency as they change throughout childhood,
- explores the relationship between social influences and an individual's feeling of self-esteem,
- discusses the effect of self-esteem on motivation to participate in sport and physical activity,
- investigates why individuals continue participation or drop out of sport, and
- examines children's attributions of success or failure in physical activity.

Motor Development in the Real World

Project ACES and the World's Largest Exercise Class

On the first Wednesday in May of each year, millions of schoolchildren all over the globe exercise at the same time (10 a.m. in each locality) in a symbolic gesture of fitness and unity. It's called Project ACES (All Children Exercise Simultaneously), and it has been celebrated for 30 years! This noncompetitive program has proven to be educational, motivational, and fun. When Len Saunders created Project ACES in 1989, he had no idea it would reach the magnitude and success it enjoys today. The program has been praised by U.S. presidents, state governors, senators, and sports and entertainment celebrities. It has been endorsed by groups such as the American College of Sports Medicine and the President's Council on Sports, Fitness, and Nutrition. Project ACES has reached millions of children, parents, and teachers all over the world, including participants from more than 50 countries. Visit the project's website at www.lensaunders.com/aces/index.html.

The goal of Project ACES is to motivate children to participate in physical activity on a daily basis. The belief is that good experiences with physical activity in childhood lead to continued participation throughout the life span, which in turn allows a lifetime of improved health. In the United States, a government focus on health and physical activity (e.g., Healthy People 2020) may have helped increase the number of citizens who choose to exercise. During the past 20 years, more people reported that they exercised on a regular basis. However, Healthy People 2020 fell far short of the targeted 50% of adults engaging in at least 150 minutes a week of moderate to vigorous aerobic physical activity (MVPA) along with twice weekly resistance training. As of 2016, only 22.5% of persons aged 18 years and over met the current federal age-adjusted physical activity guidelines, and only 32% reached either 150 minutes of MVPA or twice weekly resistance training (Blackwell & Clark, 2018). Clearly, the U.S. population has a long way to go in terms of incorporating physical activity into daily life.

Why do some individuals participate in physical activities on a regular basis whereas others avoid them? We spend much of this text describing motor behaviors that most typically developing individuals exhibit. However, we have yet to discuss one type of constraint—the individual functional constraint—that can drastically alter type and amount of personal physical activity and affect the emergence of movement over time. An individual functional constraint is not a specific anatomical structure but rather a psychological construct, such as motivation, self-efficacy, or emotion. Often, socializing agents such as parents or peers play a strong role in developing an individual's functional constraints. Therefore, we consider the interaction between sociocultural constraints and individual functional constraints.

As noted in the previous chapter, the social or cultural environment can encourage or discourage specific behaviors. Of course, these environmental constraints have different effects on different individuals. One person may not participate in an activity because of parental influences that discourage sport; another person may participate *because of* these same influences, as an act of rebellion. This chapter explores the interaction between social factors and functional constraints such as emotions, perceived ability, motivation, and other personal attributes. One key functional constraint related to physical activity is self-esteem.

Self-Esteem

All individuals evaluate themselves in various areas, such as physical ability, physical appearance, academic ability, and social skills. These self-judgments are called by many names, including self-esteem, self-concept, self-image, self-worth, and self-confidence. This chapter uses the term **self-esteem** to mean the degree to which individuals value themselves, or their personal judgment of their own capability, significance, success, and worthiness; it is conveyed to others in words and actions (Biddle & Asare, 2011; Coopersmith, 1967; Lindwall, Asci, & Crocker, 2014). Whether your self-evaluations are accurate is not as important to your self-esteem as is your *belief* that they are accurate (Weiss, 1993). Others can identify your level of self-esteem through what you say to them as well as through your nonverbal behaviors in joining or avoiding certain activities. For example, someone with high self-esteem for physical activity is not likely to avoid physical activity. Self-esteem is important because it influences one's motivation to join and sustain particular activities. Researchers have found a range of positive associations between physical activity and self-esteem, from large (McAuley, 1994; Sonstroem, 1997) to moderate small (Ekeland, Heian, Hagen, Abbott, & Nordheim, 2004; Spence, McGannon, & Poon, 2005).

Self-esteem is an individual's personal judgment of his or her own capability, significance, success, and worthiness; it is conveyed to others through words and actions. It involves self-evaluation both in general and in specific areas.

Self-esteem is not just a general sense. It is also specific to **domains** (i.e., areas or situations) (Fox & Corbin, 1989). For example, a certain teenage boy may evaluate himself as high in the physical and social domains but low in the academic domain. In each domain, individuals may differentiate their abilities at even more specific levels (Fox & Corbin, 1989). Academic ability may be perceived in terms of ability in mathematics, writing, foreign languages, and so on. This chapter focuses on self-evaluations in the physical domain related to physical skills.

A **domain** is an independent area or sphere of influence, such as the social, physical, or academic.

▶ **KEY POINT** Self-esteem influences participation in sport and physical activity; it also influences skill mastery. It becomes more accurate as a person ages. Over time, an individual's self-esteem in a given domain more closely matches his or her actual abilities.

Professionals interested in motivating people to be active must understand self-esteem and the factors that influence people's judgments of their capabilities. Those working with children should know how self-esteem develops, and those working with people of any age should be aware of the criteria that people use as a basis for their evaluations and whether these criteria change as individuals grow older.

Development of Self-Esteem

Children's self-esteem is greatly influenced by verbal and nonverbal communications from those who are significant to them, including parents, siblings, friends, teachers, and coaches (figure 16.1). Verbal comments such as "Good" or "Why can't you do better?" are sources of information, as are facial expressions and gestures (Weiss, 1993). Children are likely to compare themselves with other children as well, and the results of these evaluations influence self-esteem. These appraisals and comparisons do not, however, exert equal influence throughout life. This section examines how the pattern of influence can change.

Imagine you are a physical therapist. Should improving patients' self-esteem be a primary concern in your work? Why or why not?

Social Interactions

Children as young as age 5 can compare themselves with others (Scanlan, 1988), but under the age of 10 they depend more on parental appraisals and outcomes of contests than on direct comparisons (Horn & Hasbrook, 1986, 1987; Horn & Weiss, 1991). Young children are not as accurate as teenagers in their evaluations of their physical competence. The level of intrinsic motivation and the extent to which children believe they control their lives influence the accuracy of children's perceptions of their physical ability. Children older than 10 rely on comparisons with and appraisals given by their peers. Perceived competence is important: Those with high perceptions of competence tend to have more positive reactions in sport and physical activity than do those who feel less competent (Weiss & Ebbeck, 1996).

Feedback and appraisal from teachers and coaches also contribute to the development of self-esteem in the physical domain (Smoll & Smith, 1989). For example, male athletes aged 10 to 15 years show high self-esteem when they play for coaches who give frequent encouragement and corrective feedback (figure 16.2), especially if the athletes begin with somewhat low self-esteem (Smith, Smoll, & Curtis, 1979). Coaches' appraisals and self-perceptions of improvement also influence teenage girls, but the pattern of coaches' influence is interesting. In a study by Horn (1985), self-esteem did not increase when girls received reinforcement from coaches after successful performances. Instead, an increase in perceived competence was associated with criticism. Apparently, the coaches' positive comments were general and did not relate specifically to the girls' performance whereas the criticisms were associated with a skill error and often included a suggestion for improvement. Therefore, teachers and coaches cannot expect global praise to automatically raise a child's self-esteem. Feedback should relate to performance (Horn, 1986, 1987).

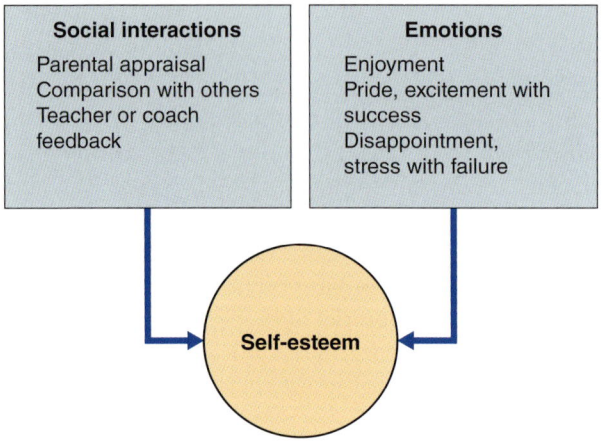

FIGURE 16.1 Emotions and social interactions influence the development of self-esteem for physical performance. Interactions are verbal and nonverbal.

Based on Horn (1987).

Measuring Self-Esteem in Children

It would seem much easier for developmentalists to measure running and jumping, or strength and flexibility, than self-esteem in children. Susan Harter (1985) uses a question format ("Some kids . . . BUT other kids . . .") to measure children's self-perceptions. For example, one pair of statements is "Some kids feel that they are better than other kids their age at sports BUT other kids don't feel they can play as well." Next to each statement are two boxes, one labeled *really true for me* and one labeled *sort of true for me*. Children check one of the boxes, indicating which kids they perceive as being like themselves and to what extent. In 1983, Harter & Pike created a pictorial scale of perceived competence for young children that included physical competence as one of four domains (Harter & Pike, 1984). Because the Harter and Pike scale did not include fundamental motor skills as part of the motor domain, Barnett and associates (2015, 2016, 2018) created a new pictorial scale based on the Test of Gross Motor Development (TGMD-2), so that children's perceptions of motor competence could be aligned with measures of actual motor competence derived from the TGMD test. Since 2015, they have established the validity and reliability of their instrument, the Pictorial Scale of Perceived Movement Skill Competence (PMSC), in

Emotions

The development of self-esteem is also related to emotions associated with participation. The pride and excitement associated with success, as well as the disappointment and stress associated with failure, influence a person's self-esteem and motivation to sustain participation (Weiss, 1993). This, of course, relates not just to sport but to physical activity in general. Enjoyment leads to higher levels of self-esteem and motivation to participate. In turn, perceptions of high ability and mastery, low parental pressure, and greater parent or coach satisfaction lead to enjoyment in preadolescents and young adolescents (Brustad, 1988; Scanlan & Lewthwaite, 1986; Scanlan, Stein, & Ravizza, 1988).

FIGURE 16.2 Feedback from a teacher or coach can contribute to the development of an important individual constraint: self-esteem.
© Rainer Martens

Relationship Between Causal Attributions and Self-Esteem

Self-esteem can influence behavior because people tend to act in ways that confirm their beliefs of themselves; that is, people tend to be self-consistent. If you have low perceived competency and low self-esteem surrounding your ability to perform a skill, then you tend to perform the skill with low competency. These beliefs are often evident in the reasons people give for their successes and failures. These reasons are called **causal attributions**. People of any age with high self-esteem tend to make attributions that are

Causal attributions are the reasons to which people credit their successes and failures. These differ for people with high and low self-esteem.

a variety of countries including Australia (Barnett, Ridgers, Zask, & Salmon, 2015; Barnett, Robinson, Webster, & Ridgers, 2015), Brazil (Valentini et al., 2017), Spain (Estevan et al., 2018), Portugal (Lopes et al., 2016), and Greece (Venetsanou et al., 2018).

Harter's Self-Perception Profile for Children contains 36 statements for five specific domains (scholastic competence, athletic competence, social acceptance, physical appearance, and behavioral conduct) and a global score for self-worth. This profile is appropriate for children aged 8 through early adolescence. For children under age 8, Harter and Pike (1984) designed a pictorial scale. Instead of two statements, two pictures are presented: One shows a competent or accepted child and the other shows an unaccepted child or a child who is unable to do the task. Children say whether they are a lot or a little like the child in the picture. Hence, the scale is made more concrete for young children and can be given to children who cannot read or understand written statements. The pictorial scale assesses four domains: cognitive competence, physical competence, peer acceptance, and maternal acceptance. Scales available for adolescents and adults typically cover many more domains.

1. *internal* (believing that they influence outcomes through their own behavior),
2. *stable* (believing that the factors influencing outcomes are consistent from situation to situation), and
3. *controllable* (believing that they personally control the factors influencing outcomes).

For example, competitors with high self-esteem attribute their success to their talent (internal), think they can win again (stable), and believe they are responsible for their successes rather than merely lucky (controllable). They view their failures as temporary and meet them with renewed effort and continued practice to improve skills.

In contrast, people with low self-esteem attribute success to factors that are

1. *external* (believing that they could not change outcomes),
2. *unstable* (believing that outcomes are a product of fluctuating influences such as good and bad luck), and
3. *uncontrollable* (believing that nothing they do could result in different outcomes).

Competitors with low self-esteem often attribute losing to a lack of ability and attribute winning to luck or to a task so easy that anybody could win.

Examining causal attributions can help us understand adult behavior, but few researchers have studied the causal attributions of children in sport and physical activity. This information is particularly important because children are in the process of developing self-esteem. We have seen that children use various factors in judging themselves as they develop. Therefore, we must be concerned with the accuracy of their self-estimates and the roles that adults play in helping children make appropriate attributions.

Children's Attributions

The sparse information available on age-related changes in children's attributions indicates that children aged 7 to 9 years attribute outcomes to both effort and luck more than older children and teens do (Bird & Williams, 1980). These factors are unstable. The children in this study, however, reacted to stories provided by the researchers rather than to actual outcomes they experienced, and a later study failed to find age differences in attributions after actual participation (Weiss, McAuley, Ebbeck, & Wiese, 1990). Because young children might not be able to distinguish between ability and effort very well, more information is needed on age differences.

Differences do exist in the attributions made by children who differ in their perceived physical competence (Weiss et al., 1990). As expected, children with high physical self-esteem give internal, stable, and controllable reasons for their successes. Their attributions for success are more stable and their future expectations for success are higher than those of children with low physical self-esteem. Again, children vary in the accuracy of their physical estimates (Weiss & Horn, 1990), and girls who underestimate (rather than accurately estimate or overestimate) their physical abilities typically choose less challenging skills and attribute outcomes to external factors. Boys who underestimate their physical abilities report little understanding of what is responsible for their successes or failures. Children who both perceive their physical abilities as low and tend to underestimate their abilities probably make inaccurate attributions about the outcomes of their efforts. Their behavior is characterized by

- an unwillingness to try challenging tasks,
- a lack of effort to do well, and
- avoidance of participation.

▶ **KEY POINT** Children who perceive their physical abilities as low are not likely to persist in physical activities, therefore missing out on the associated health and psychosocial benefits (Weiss, 1993).

Parents, teachers, and coaches can help children, especially those with low self-esteem, give proper credit to the reasons for success or failure. Adults can help children with low self-esteem retrain their attributions (Horn, 1987; figure 16.3). Rather than let children attribute failure to lack of ability and attribute success to luck, adults can emphasize improvement through effort and continued practice. They can also encourage children to set goals and can provide accurate feedback about the children's progress. Children who come to think their situations are hopeless (i.e., those with learned helplessness) need challenges that are accurately matched to their abilities and in which difficulty is increased in steps much smaller than those presented to other children. Children with high self-esteem for physical competence probably possess high levels of intrinsic motivation to participate in physical activity. If children with low self-esteem are ever to enjoy physical activity and ultimately realize the benefits of participation, adults must make special efforts to improve their self-esteem (Weiss, 1993).

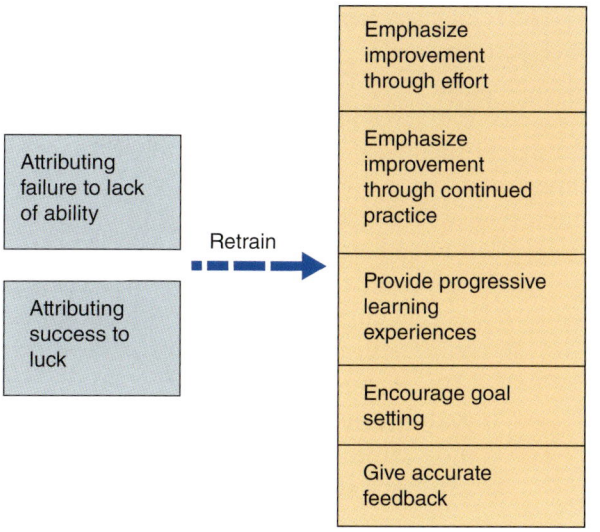

FIGURE 16.3 Adults must help children with low self-esteem for physical performance improve their self-esteem. Retraining can change causal attributions.

Adults' Attributions

Self-esteem also influences the motivation of adults. Like children, adults tend to behave according to their beliefs about themselves. Recall that children obtain the information on which they base their self-judgments largely from their significant others and their own comparisons. Adults obtain information from four sources (Bandura, 1986):

1. Actual experiences (previous accomplishments or failures)
2. Vicarious experiences (observing a model)
3. Verbal persuasion from others
4. Their physiological state

▶ **KEY POINT** An adult's level of self-esteem affects motivation for physical activity. Like children, adults behave according to their beliefs about themselves, which are acquired from actual and vicarious experiences, others' opinions, and their physiological state.

An individual's actual experiences are particularly influential, and changing physiological status is a reality for most older adults. For example, failing eyesight lowers an older adult's confidence for participating in racket sports. In contrast, verbal persuasion is a much weaker influence. The models available to older adults vary considerably. Some have opportunities to see others like themselves participating in a wide range of activities; others do not, especially on a personal basis rather than in a magazine or on television. Given these influences, it is clear that a person's self-esteem in physical activity can increase or decrease throughout life.

A few investigators have related adults' physical self-esteem and their motivation to maintain or improve their fitness. Ewart, Stewart, Gillilan, and Kelemen (1986) involved men with coronary artery disease, aged 35 to 70, in either a walk or jog plus a circuit weight-training program or a walk or jog plus volleyball program for 10 weeks. They measured self-esteem, arm and leg strength, and treadmill-running performance before and after the program.

The researchers found that those with higher pretraining self-esteem improved more in arm strength than those with lower self-esteem, even when accounting for beginning strength level, type of training, and frequency of participation. Self-esteem did improve with training but only when participants received information indicating that their performance was improving. For example, the weight-training group improved their self-esteem for lifting weights but not for jogging, even though they improved on both tests in a postprogram assessment. They could monitor their improvements in weight training during the program but their jogging distance remained constant, so they had no indication they were improving. Hogan and Santomeir (1984) also observed an increase in self-esteem for swimming in older adults after a 5-week swimming class. Thus, older adults' self-esteem can influence how much improvement they realize in a program, and participation can raise self-esteem when participants have information about their actual improvements.

Web Study Guide **Interview sport participants to obtain information about their attributions for success and failure in Lab Activity 16.1, Identifying Causal Attributions in Sport Participants, in the web study guide.**

The Link Between Perceived and Actual Motor Competence

There is an old saying that "perception is reality"; in our context, this suggests there is a connection between what individuals perceive their motor capabilities are and how they actually move. In fact, perceived motor competence is an important source of achievement-related behaviors such as participation in physical activity (Ryan & Deci, 2000), as was discussed in chapter 12. Benefits of high perceived competence can include higher self-esteem and increased performance effort and engagement (Robinson, 2011). Recent findings suggest that a developmental relationship exists between actual and perceived motor competence (Barnett, Morgan, van Beurden, & Beard, 2008; De Meester et al., 2016; LeGear et al., 2012; Robinson, 2011).

During early childhood, children tend to inaccurately perceive their actual motor abilities, interpreting increased effort as higher levels of motor skill competence (Goodway & Rudisill, 1997; Harter & Pike, 1984; Gabbard, Caçola, & Cordova, 2009). At the same time, the association between perceived and actual motor competence tends to be positive, such that young children with higher perceived competence tend to have higher actual motor competence (Barnett et al., 2008). In 2010, Robinson tested 119 preschool children on the TGMD-2 (Ulrich, 2000) and the Pictorial Scale of Perceived Competence and Social Acceptance (Harter & Pike, 1984), then correlated the results. She found moderate positive relationships between the measures that were stronger for locomotor skills than object control skills as well as stronger for girls than boys. Other studies have found moderate positive correlations between these measures in young children—in particular, in object control skills—in countries such as Canada (LeGear et al., 2012), Denmark (Toftegaard-Stoeckel, Groenfeldt, & Andersen, 2010), and Australia (Barnett, Ridgers, & Salmon, 2015; Liong, Ridgers, & Barnett, 2015).

▶ **KEY POINT** How young children perceive or comprehend their motor competence generally does not match their actual motor competence.

As children move into middle childhood, they improve in their ability to accurately perceive their actual motor competence (Harter, 1999). However, gender differences persist. In their study of 58 children between the ages of 8 and 10 years, Clark, Moran, Drury, Venetsanou, and Fernandes (2018) also had children perform the TGMD-2 and the Pictorial Scale of Perceived Movement Skill Competence for young children. They had three key findings. First, although there were no significant differences between boys and girls in actual motor skills, gender differences existed in their perceived motor skills, with boys perceiving higher motor competence than girls in both locomotor and object control skills. Second, girls perceived locomotor skills to be significantly lower than their actual locomotor skills. Finally, boys perceived their object control skills to be significantly higher than their actual object control skills. This mismatch by genders has been noted in other research as well (Masci et al., 2017).

As children become adolescents, it has been hypothesized that their perceptions should come in line with their actual movement abilities (Harter, 1999; Stodden et al., 2008). Interestingly, research has found several distinct patterns. De Meester et al. (2016) used the KörperkoordinationsTest für Kinder (KTK) to measure actual motor competence and used validated questionnaires to measure perceived motor competence (among other measures) in 215 adolescents (average age: 13.64 ± 0.58 years). Although actual and perceived motor competence were only moderately correlated, when the researchers performed a cluster analysis—a statistical test that groups similar variables into the same cluster—they found four distinct clusters. They classified the first group of subjects as "low – accurate" estimators; their low perceptions accurately reflected their low abilities. The next cluster consisted of adolescents described as "low overestimators." Despite their actual motor abilities being lower than all other groups, they perceived their abilities to be much better, even better than the "average – accurate" estimators, who matched perceived and actual ability fairly well. The last group were average in terms of motor performance but overestimated their ability. Undoubtedly, the relationship between perceived and actual competence changes over time in a nonlinear fashion.

Web Study Guide See Lab Activity 16.2, Comparing Perceived and Actual Motor Competence in Locomotor Skills and Lab Activity 16.3, Comparing Perceived and Actual Motor Competence in Object Control Skills.

Since Stodden and colleagues published their paper in 2008, several studies have looked at the relationship between motor skill competency and physical activity, finding positive associations between the two that change developmentally (Barnett, Van Beurden, Morgan, Brooks, & Beard, 2009; Lopes, Santos, Pereira, & Lopes, 2012; see Holfelder & Schott [2014] and Lubans, Morgan, Cliff, Barnett, & Okely [2010] for systematic reviews). Researchers have hypothesized that perceived motor competence acts as a mediator between actual motor competence and physical activity (Barnett et al., 2008; De Meester et al., 2016; Stodden et al., 2008; see chapter 2). A mediator variable explains the relationship between two other variables. Stated simply, the relationship between individuals' actual motor competence and how physically active they are depends, in part, on how competent they perceive themselves to be (Barnett, Ridgers, & Salmon, 2015; Barnett, Lubans, Timpeiro, Salmon, & Ridgers, 2018; Bardid et al., 2016).

In a longitudinal study over 6 years, Barnett et al. (2008) found perceived competence mediated children's object control competence and self-reported physical activity during the adolescent years. In this study, 928 children were assessed for motor skill proficiency as part of a school-based physical activity intervention. Six years later, 276 participants completed assessments for perceived sports competence (Physical Self-Perception Profile), physical activity (Adolescent Physical Activity Recall Questionnaire), and cardiorespiratory fitness (multistage fitness test). These data were analyzed using structural equation modeling. The results found that perceived competence acted as a mediator between object control skill proficiency developed in early childhood and later fitness and physical activity during adolescence. In other words, object control skill proficiency as a child (regardless of gender) appears important in developing a positive perception of competence in sports and seems to increase physical activity and fitness outcomes as an adolescent. Within the literature, there is increasing support that perceived motor competence mediates the relationship between actual motor competence and physical activity, although more experimental and longitudinal studies need to be performed to confirm this (Robinson et al., 2015).

Motivation

The **motivation** to participate in activities of a certain type involves many factors, including those that lead people to initiate or join an activity (figure 16.4). Other factors encourage people

FIGURE 16.4 Motivation is an important component of persistence in sport.
Hero Images/Getty Images

to persist in an activity and to exert effort in order to improve. Still other factors lead people to end their involvement. In the previous chapter, we discuss factors that encourage children's initial sport involvement or the sport socialization process. Let's turn now to factors that keep children in physical activity and sport or lead them to drop out. We also consider how the factors that motivate people to participate in physical activities change over the life span.

Persistence

Researchers have focused quite a bit of attention on the reasons that children and teens continue to participate in sport and physical activity (Efrat, 2016; Weiss, 1993). In general, the reasons include the following:

- A desire to be competent by improving skills or attaining goals
- A desire to affiliate with or make new friends
- A desire to be part of a team
- A desire to undertake competition and be successful
- A desire to have fun
- A desire to increase fitness

McAuley (1994) and Sonstroem (1997) found that girls most often cited fun (followed by health benefits) as the reason they participate in physical activity. Most individuals cite not just one or two but several reasons for participating. Harter (1978, 1981) proposed a competence motivation theory to explain this. According to the theory, children are motivated to demonstrate their competency and therefore seek out mastery attempts, or opportunities to learn and demonstrate skills. Those who perceive that they are competent and believe that they control situations have more intrinsic motivation to participate than others.

Membership in subgroups can also influence a person's motivation to persist in sport. Examples of subgroups include age groups, starters versus benchwarmers, elite athletes versus recreational participants, and so on. Consider age groups. Brodkin and Weiss (1990) studied varying age groups of competitive swimmers: ages 6 to 9, 10 to 14, 15 to 22, 23 to 39, 40 to 59, and 60 to 74. They found that children cited wanting to compete, liking the coaches, and pleasing family and friends as reasons to participate. The 15- to 22-year-olds listed social status, as did young children to an extent, and fitness motives were important to the young and middle adults. Children and older adults did not consider fitness as important. Young children and older adults named fun as the most important reason to participate.

Another investigation of children involved in swimming found that those younger than 11 years were motivated to participate by external factors: encouragement from family and friends, liking the coaches, social status, and activities they enjoyed (Gould, Feltz, & Weiss, 1985). Teenagers in this study cited more internal factors: competence, fitness, and the excitement of swimming. Thus, different age groups may have different reasons for participating, but more research is needed on other activities and with participants of varying skill levels (Weiss, 1993).

Dropping Out

Withdrawal from sport programs is a very real aspect of youth involvement in physical activity. Changing from one type of activity to another might be part of one's development or might reflect a person's changing interests or desire to try something new, but withdrawing from activity altogether has serious repercussions for health at any point in life. It is often difficult for surveys and research studies to distinguish between participants who switch activities and those who withdraw from activity altogether. In addition, dropouts do not always quit by choice; injuries or high monetary costs, for instance, might force some to withdraw. Thus, the reasons participants give for quitting deserve further attention.

Some young dropouts cite very negative experiences, such as the following, as reasons for withdrawing from sport (McPherson, Marteniuk, Tihanyi, & Clark, 1980; Orlick, 1973, 1974):

- Dislike for the coach
- Lack of playing time
- Too much pressure
- Too much time required
- Overemphasis on winning
- Lack of fun
- Lack of progress
- Lack of success

Such negative reactions come from a small number of dropouts (Feltz & Petlichkoff, 1983; Gould, Feltz, Horn, & Weiss, 1982; Klint & Weiss, 1986; Sapp & Haubenstricker, 1978). The majority of dropouts withdraw to pursue other interests, to try different sport activities, or to participate at lower intensity levels. Teens often report dropping out to take jobs. Many plan to reenter their sport later. Thus, much of the attrition in youth sports reflects shifting interests and involvement levels rather than negative experiences. Nonetheless, professionals should be concerned about negative experiences because they can be detrimental to a person's psychological development and can lead to a lifelong avoidance of healthful activities.

Recently, Crane and Temple (2015) performed a systematic review of research related to children's and adolescents' dropout from organized sport. From the 43 studies that met their inclusion criteria, they found five major areas associated with dropping out: (1) lack of enjoyment, (2) low perceptions of physical competence, (3) social pressures, (4) competing priorities, and (5) physical factors (maturation and injuries). It is interesting to note that many of the reasons given for dropping out in studies from the 20th century persist two decades later.

▶ **KEY POINT** Not all children and adolescents cite negative reasons for leaving sport and physical activity. Often, individuals simply want to pursue different activities that may or may not include physical activity.

Web Study Guide **Reflect on activities in your life and what influenced you to persist or end involvement in those activities in Lab Activity 16.4, Motivation to Participate, in the web study guide.**

Teacher-Centered Versus Student-Centered Approaches

What motivates a child to learn motor skills? When teaching fundamental motor skills to young children, instructors often attempt to promote change in movement through teacher-centered methods. That is, the instructor designs and presents developmentally appropriate activities in class and then chooses when to progress students to the next task. As a motor skills intervention, the teacher-centered approach has proven successful in various research studies (Goodway & Branta, 2003; Sweeting & Rink, 1999). However, to date, it is unknown whether teacher-centered approaches are the most effective way to improve children's motor skills.

As an alternative to the teacher-centered approach, a group of researchers have examined a different method for teaching motor skills to young children. It is called mastery motivational climate (see Rudisill, 2016, for a more complete description). Fundamental to this approach is the notion that effort and outcome are related; that is, when the learner's environment is both mastery oriented and highly autonomous, children achieve and learn (in this case, improve in fundamental motor skills; Ames, 1992). Several research studies show that this approach to teaching and learning leads to improvement in motor skills (Valentini & Rudisill, 2004a, 2004b, 2004c) and in physical activity levels (Wadsworth, Rudisill, Hastie, Irwin, & Rodriguez-Hernandez, 2017; Parish, Rudisill, & St. Onge, 2007).

How would an instructor develop a mastery motivational climate for young children? Researchers at Auburn University provided a model that follows the principles presented by Ames (1992); they call it HAPPE (high autonomy physical play environment) and describe it as follows (Parish & Rudisill, 2006):

- Toddlers (and young children) engage in a variety of authentic and meaningful tasks that match their skills and abilities. The tasks allow children to make choices according to individual interests and abilities.
- The primary authority in the classroom rests with the teacher, who serves as a facilitator of learning. Toddlers and young children are actively involved in decision making, self-management, and self-monitoring, and they have opportunities to develop leadership roles.
- Teachers offer recognition to individual children in response to their effort and engagement in learning. Teachers give feedback and encourage toddlers' attempts to learn a skill.
- Groupings emerge naturally as toddlers and young children choose to play alone or with another child and as they decide which skill they want to practice. More experienced toddlers may choose to play in small groups.
- Toddlers are encouraged to evaluate their own performance, and teachers guide toddlers as they solve problems typically encountered during physical play.
- Toddlers have plenty of time to fully explore and practice physical play.

Teachers can apply these principles to older children as well.

Researchers have found that motivational climates help young children improve in fundamental motor skills and physical activity (e.g., Goodway & Branta, 2003; Goodway, Crowe, & Ward, 2003; Hastie, Johnson, & Rudisill, 2018; Parish, Rudisill, & St. Onge, 2007). A recent systematic review (Bandeira, Santayana de Souza, Zanella, & Valentini, 2017) looked across six studies that used mastery motivational climates and determined that these intervention programs led to positive outcomes in terms of the development of motor skills. Still, more research needs to be done in order to determine how and why teacher-centered and student-centered approaches differ as well as the amount and rate at which they enhance motor skill development (e.g., Hastie et al., 2018; Rudisill & Johnson, 2018; Logan, Webster, Getchell, Pfeiffer, & Robinson, 2015; Wadsworth et al., 2017).

Adult Activity Levels

Both the amount and the intensity level of physical activity decrease as adults grow older, especially among women (Boothby, Tungatt, & Townsend, 1981; Curtis & White, 1984; Ebrahim & Rowland, 1996; McPherson, 1983; Rudman, 1986). In 2008, the U.S. Department of Health and Human Services reported that even when adding together all the different types of exercise in which individuals participate, more than 60% of adults aged 50 and older did not achieve recommended levels (U.S. Department of Health and Human Services, 2008). This withdrawal from and reduction in physical activity does not result from changes in physiological health alone (Spreitzer & Snyder, 1983). Psychosocial factors also influence adults' activity levels (McPherson, 1986). These factors include the following:

- Stereotypes of appropriate activity levels
- Limited access to facilities and programs
- Childhood experiences
- Concerns over personal limitations on exercise
- Lack of role models
- Lack of knowledge about appropriate exercise programs
- Belief that exercise is harmful or is ineffective in preventing disease (Duda & Tappe, 1989a)

However, indications exist that adults, especially older ones, are becoming more actively interested in health and in the influence of physical activity on health status (Howze, DiGilio, Bennett, & Smith, 1986; Maloney, Fallon, & Wittenberg, 1984; Prohaska, Leventhal, Leventhal, & Keller, 1985). In fact, the number of participants in the National Senior Games increased from 2,500 in its inaugural year to over 10,500 in 2017 (National Senior Games, 2018).

Duda and Tappe (1988, 1989a, 1989b) proposed that adult exercise participation reflects three interrelated factors (figure 16.5):

1. Personal incentives, such as a desire to demonstrate mastery, compete, be with others, receive recognition, maintain health, cope with stress, or improve physical fitness
2. A sense of self, particularly in regard to one's self-esteem for physical activity
3. Perceived options, or the opportunities a person has in a given situation, such as transportation to various sites where adult programs are offered

If you were to design a physical activity program for older adults, what could you do to encourage your participants first to join and then to continue with the program?

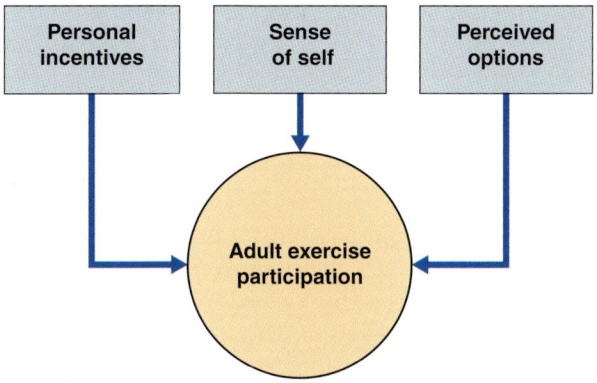

FIGURE 16.5 Three interrelated factors can influence the level of adults' exercise participation.

Personal incentive values and self-esteem can change throughout life. For example, as an adult ages, the desire to compete might decrease while the desire to be with others might increase. Older adults can also come to perceive that their physical abilities have declined over time. Duda and Tappe surveyed 144 adults in three age groups (25–39, 40–60, and 61-plus years) who were participating in an exercise program. Personal incentives differed among the age groups and between men and women. Middle-aged and older adults placed more value on the health benefits of exercise than did young adults. For example, figure 16.6 shows the extent to which men and women in each age group valued the stress-reducing benefits of exercise. Young adult men put little emphasis on this exercise benefit, as shown by their low average on the Personal Incentives for Exercise Questionnaire. Men also valued competitive activities more than women did. Exercise leaders, then, might help older adults stick to their exercise programs by emphasizing social interaction, health benefits, and stress reduction (Duda & Tappe, 1989b).

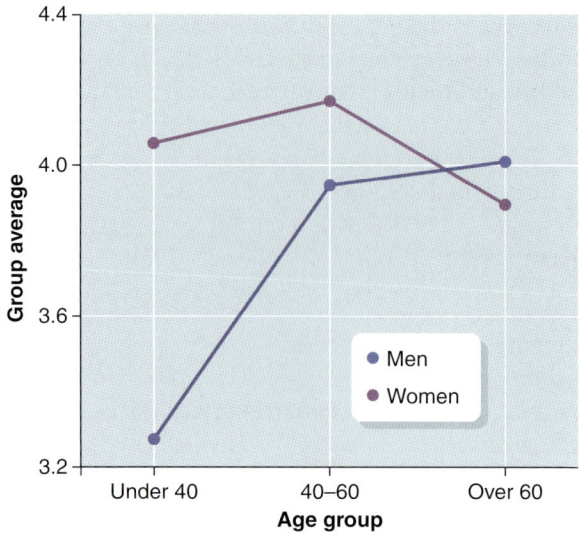

FIGURE 16.6 Personal incentives for adults to exercise differ between age groups and between the sexes. Group averages on the "coping with stress" category of the Personal Incentives for Exercise Questionnaire (a 5-point Likert-type scale) are plotted here.

Reprinted from Duda and Tappe (1989, pg. 246, 248).

No age group differences in self-esteem were apparent among these older adults, but differences did exist between men and women. The women had lower physical self-esteem and less feeling of control over their health status than the men did. These beliefs are typically associated with less involvement, but the women felt they had more social support for their involvement than did the men, and they continued to participate.

Exercise leaders who adopt strategies targeted at adults who might have low physical self-esteem can improve participants' self-esteem and exercise involvement (Duda & Tappe, 1989b). Another group of adults might not have the same characteristic incentives and perceptions as those Duda and Tappe surveyed. Yet exercise leaders can encourage older adults to persist in their exercise programs by being aware of the incentives and perceptions of their particular groups. They can then emphasize the aspects and benefits of exercise that are most important to those participants.

Summary and Synthesis

Individuals' perceptions of their physical abilities can change dramatically across the life span and do not always mirror individuals' actual motor competence. In turn, these perceptions can affect self-esteem. Maintaining high levels of self-esteem seems to enhance performance as well as perceived competence, which motivates an individual to continue participating in physical activity. This set of dynamics offers an example of how constraints can interact to encourage movement. For example, older adults who desire social interactions with friends, as well as improved fitness levels, may join an exercise program for older adults. This program may involve activities that facilitate both socialization and fitness, which help individuals improve their self-esteem. The higher levels of self-esteem and perceived competence then help motivate the older adults to return to the program, which continues to foster self-esteem, and so on.

At the same time, these constraint interactions can discourage behavior. Consider children who begin participating in a sport such as soccer. They may have joined to be with friends and have fun. Perhaps, however, the coach wants to win and provides criticism and negative feedback to the players if they make a mistake. The players may begin to attribute losses to their lack of ability and believe that they lack competence in that activity. In turn, their self-esteem begins to decrease. Eventually, they may drop out of the sport altogether.

These two examples demonstrate the powerful interplay between sociocultural and individual functional constraints. We all live in a social context and are subject to social opinions. These opinions help fashion and reinforce our beliefs about ourselves. Eventually, we act as we believe. Keeping this in mind, it is essential for those who work with others in physical activity and sport to look beyond the activity to the individuals themselves.

Reinforcing What You Have Learned About Constraints

TAKE A SECOND LOOK

Think back to project ACES, discussed at the beginning of the chapter. Imagine you are exercising and that, at the very same moment, millions of other people are doing the exact same thing. Does the thought of all those people joined in simultaneous physical activity motivate you to exercise? Len Saunders designed Project ACES to motivate children to exercise by bringing them together at one point in time. Motivation (an individual functional constraint) can be greatly enhanced by creating a learning environment designed to motivate, such as Project ACES or HAPPE at Auburn University. This interaction of constraints (motivated individuals in a motivational climate) should encourage positive and progressive change in motor skill over time.

TEST YOUR KNOWLEDGE

1. What is self-esteem? Is it general or specific? How is it developed?
2. People tend to attribute their successes and failures to various causes. What are the differences in the causal attributions made by those with high self-esteem and those with low self-esteem? To what do children tend to attribute their performance?
3. What factors are associated with persisting in sport and physical activity? With dropping out?
4. How does perceived competence change with children's causal attributions?

Learning Exercise 16.1

EXPLORING MOTIVATIONS FOR PHYSICAL ACTIVITY AND EXERCISE

What motivates you and other students to be involved in sport and physical activities? If you evaluate a group of students, you will likely discover a diverse array of reasons to participate—or not participate.

1. First, determine your own motivations.
   - Do you participate in sport and physical activities now? Look at the list of reasons for persisting in sport participation in the Persistence section of this chapter. Write down those reasons that apply to you and add any others not included in the list.
   - Have you dropped out of a physical activity? Look at the list of reasons for dropping out of a sport in the Dropping Out section of this chapter. Do any of the reasons listed apply to you?

- Have you persisted in some activities and dropped out of others? What factors are related to these choices?

2. Compare your notes from question 1 with a group of other students.

- What are the factors most commonly associated with persistence?
- What are the factors most commonly associated with dropping out?
- Calculate percentages for easy interpretation (e.g., "Seventy percent of my group dropped out because of lack of time").
- Reflect on these factors and offer some generalizations about motivational factors and the students in your class.

17

Developmental Motor Learning

CHAPTER OBJECTIVES

This chapter

- defines motor learning,
- explains how motor learning can be developmental,
- describes stages of motor learning,
- explains how different practice conditions affect learning,
- describes the effect of augmented feedback on learning, and
- explains how speed of information processing and memory change over the life span.

Motor Development in the Real World

You *Can* Teach an Old Dog New Tricks!

For many years, people have been concerned about the loss of fluid intelligence, the ability to think quickly and recall information. Prior research indicated that fluid intelligence reaches a pinnacle at around age 20, suggesting a long, slow downhill voyage from there as individuals age, dampening enthusiasm for one's 21st birthday. Fortunately, recent research out of several laboratories in Massachusetts has enabled people to put their party hats back on. In this study, researchers overcame a limitation of previous research examining cognitive changes over time related to participant demographics. Although many studies examined college-age students (college professors' favorite population to study) and adults over 65 years, no studies examined a large sample of participants *in between* those ages. Hartshorne and Germine (2015) changed this. By creating free websites (testmybrain.org and gameswithwords.org), they were able to collect data and examine 30 different types of intelligence in a large group of participants (50,000 for this study) across a broad range of ages.

What they found was surprising. Although information processing speed did reach a peak at almost 20 years old, other cognitive skills did not. For example, short-term memory continued to improve until age 25 and then plateaued for about 10 years before beginning to slowly decline. Other skills peaked in the 40s or even later—they found that crystallized intelligence peaked into the 60s and 70s! One of the authors, Joshua Hartshorne, put it best: "At any given age, you're getting better at some things, you're getting worse at some other things, and you're at a plateau at some other things. There's probably not one age at which [you] peak on most things, much less all of them" (Trafton 2015).

In chapter 1 of this textbook, we describe three related concepts (motor learning, motor development, and motor control) that fall within the discipline of motor behavior. The focus of this book is on motor development, but that doesn't mean the remaining areas of study exclude a developmental perspective. In fact, both motor learning and motor development share one important characteristic: changes in the way individuals move over time (Newell, Liu, & Mayer-Cress, 2001). In this chapter, we discuss the intersection of motor learning and motor development, aptly described as developmental motor learning (Wade, 1976). Recall that motor learning is defined as the relatively permanent gains in motor skill capability associated with practice or experience (Schmidt & Lee, 2014). Central to this definition is the idea that change in motor performance occurs because a learner either practices or has experiences that drive change, including when directed by a teacher. By adding the word *developmental* before *motor learning*, we acknowledge that individuals learn differently at different points across the life span. In other words, effective practice that promotes motor skill learning in a 15-year-old may not be effective for a 5- or a 65-year-old. This chapter introduces terminology and topics related to the acquisition of motor skills, then describes what we know about them across the life span.

Motor skill capability is a person's potential for skilled motor performance under favorable conditions.

Unpacking the Definition of Motor Learning

To better understand what motor learning is, it is helpful to look more deeply at its definition. Let's start with what changes, which is **motor skill capability**. Don't assume that capability is synonymous with ability. An ability is an innate, underlying trait that doesn't change as a function of practice (Schmidt & Lee, 2014). On the other hand, a capability is a potential for skilled performance under favorable conditions. Different abilities may underlie certain motor skill capabilities (which explains why some people may pick up a new skill more easily than others), but the capability to perform a specific skill comes through effective practice. Further, an individual's performance on any given day may fluctuate (e.g., a baseball batter may be 0 for 4 in the first game of a doubleheader and 4 for 4 in the second) depending on different conditions that can be intrinsic (fatigue, stress, motivation) or extrinsic (weather, equipment, pitch speed). In sum, an individual's motor skill capability is his or her potential for adeptly performing a motor skill.

Critical to the notion of motor learning is that changes in capability occur as a result of **practice** of a specific or similar skill. Sometimes used synonymously with the word *experience*, practice can be defined as repeated performance of a motor skill, with the goal of improving that motor skill. Although other factors such as growth, maturation, or increased strength may improve motor performance, these factors alone do not improve motor skill capabilities. Throughout this textbook, we describe ways in which development can affect motor skill performance. Back in chapter 3, when discussing the principles of motion and stability, we describe the relationship between mass and force and note that children can produce more forceful kicks or throws simply by growing bigger, which increases limb length as well as overall body mass. Clearly, these changes do not come as a result of practice; they may result in improved product measures (e.g., ball speed) but will not likely result in improving a person's potential for skilled performance. On the other hand, if children receive quality instruction on optimal coordination patterns for the overarm throw and then practice the skill repeatedly while receiving error feedback from a teacher or coach, they will learn better throwing mechanics and consistently produce more accurate and forceful throws.

Practice is repeated attempts to perform a motor skill as a means of skill acquisition.

▶ **KEY POINT** Motor skill capability changes with effective practice or experience with related activities.

The final important term in the definition of motor learning is ***relatively permanent***, which relates to changing capabilities. Remember the saying "You never forget how to ride a bike"? The fact that you can still ride a bicycle even after many years of not riding indicates that something inside of your nervous system was permanently changed during the process of learning. In motor learning research, whether relatively permanent changes occur or not are established through the use of retention and/or transfer tests. After a skill is **acquired**, or learned, researchers have performers stop practice to allow for any temporary effects to dissipate. Then, after a designated time, either (1) the learned skill is performed again (called a **retention test**) or (2) a similar but more complex form of the skill is performed (called a **transfer test**). The retention or transfer test results are compared against performance at the end of the acquisition period. If learning has occurred, performance on the retention test should be similar to peak performance at the end of the acquisition period, or if a transfer test is given, performance would be better than if trying the new skill for the first time.

A **retention test** is used to see if participants retain the ability to produce a specific motor skill after practice has been removed for a period of time.

A **transfer test** is used to see if participants can transfer aspects of a motor skill learned through practice to a new skill.

Figure 17.1 shows a hypothetical learning curve and two hypothetical outcomes from a motor learning study where the objective of the study was to achieve the highest score possible on a novel throwing task (e.g., throwing a rope ball at a target). In this example, throwing practice is provided in blocks of trials during the motor skill acquisition phase. Throwing scores improve over time as a result of those experiences. After the acquisition phase ends, there is a break with no throwing practice (washout phase). This is followed by a retention test, where the skill is repeated, and a transfer test, where a similar skill is introduced. The solid lines at the top represent instances where the skill has been learned, because performance stays the same as it was after acquisition. The dotted lines represent instances where the skill has not been learned, since performance declines significantly after acquisition ends.

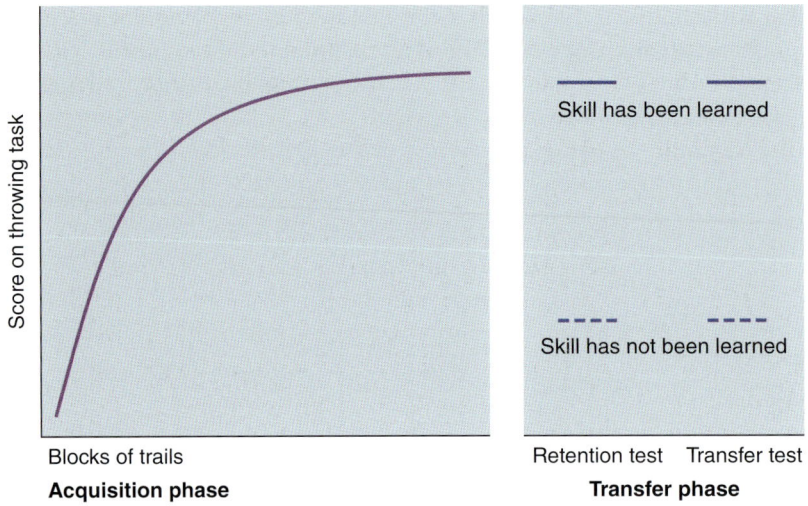

FIGURE 17.1 A hypothetical learning curve and hypothetical outcomes. If the skill has been learned, performance stays the same as it was after acquisition. If the skill has not been learned, performance declines after acquisition ends.

Enter the words *motor learning* into your Internet search engine. What results do you get? How do these differ from the results you get if you search for *motor development*?

Now that the term *motor learning* has been operationally defined, we can add the notion of *developmental* to it. In chapter 1, we discuss the developmental litmus test put forth by Roberton in 1988, where we differentiate between motor learning and development by suggesting that only motor development is interested in past, present, and future motor behavior. This still holds true. It is also true that studies of motor learning and development focus on different time scales during the life span (e.g., Newell, Liu, & Mayer-Cress, 2001) and use very different research methodologies. The time scale for motor learning is short, more likely hours or days, whereas the time scale for motor development is long, perhaps weeks, months, or even years. Motor learning addresses the process of skill acquisition as a function of relatively short-term practice. Therefore, developmental motor learning focuses on how this skill acquisition process differs at different points in the life span (Wade, 1976). For example, someone interested in developmental motor learning may ask, "Will the amount and timing of feedback when learning a novel motor skill have a different effect in children than in adults?"

▶ **KEY POINT** In motor learning research, the learning of a skill is established by performance on a retention or transfer test.

Stages of Learning and the Development of Expertise

Learning new motor skills takes practice. Does this mean there is a linear relationship between practice and performance? In other words, does the amount someone practices always lead to the same amount of change? Many different research studies have indicated that this is not the case; the same amount of practice produces different amounts of performance change at different points in time. Therefore, researchers have theorized that the acquisition of motor skills occurs in distinct stages. Several models have been proposed, and here we discuss Fitts and Posner's and Bernstein's three-stage models.

Web Study Guide Learn about the Stages of Learning firsthand as fellow students practice writing with their non-dominant hand in Lab Activity 17.1, Observing Stages of Learning in a Handwriting Task, in the web study guide.

Fitts and Posner's Model

One of the best known stage models is that of Fitts and Posner (1967). This three-stage model focuses on the perceptual and cognitive characteristics of the learner. When individuals first learn a motor skill, they are in the **cognitive stage**. In this stage, new learners expend a significant amount of time and cognitive energy processing information in order to understand what they are supposed to do. In other words, they approach the motor skill with their brains, trying to understand the objectives of the movement and how to coordinate their limbs in order to solve the movement problem in its most basic form. At this stage of learning, learners have little or no experience in producing the desired movements, making it difficult for them to know when they are producing incorrect movements or how to correct them. Picture a child swinging a tennis racket for the first time. Without any previous experience, she may grasp and swing the racket with two hands in an effort to figure out a movement strategy that allows her to hit the ball. She may not be able to interpret the ball velocity as it moves toward her, so she swings too late to connect with the ball.

During the cognitive stage of learning a movement, learners often rely on instructions and feedback from an instructor, coach, or rehabilitation specialist. In our previous example, a coach or physical education teacher would provide instruction and feedback on when to swing at the appropriate time in order to help the child improve. During the cognitive stage of learning, learners will demonstrate many large errors in their performances, which tend to be variable and inconsistent (Magill & Anderson, 2017). Yet basic skill acquisition comes relatively quickly with practice and instruction, with rapid gains in performance.

Learners advance to the **associative stage** of learning after they have mastered the basic form of the movement and begin to refine performance of the skill. This may take hours or days if the motor skill is simple, or it may take weeks or longer if the skill is complex. The term *associative* describes the way the learner begins to associate particular environmental cues with specific skill-related movements required to successfully perform the motor skill. The attentional demands required to produce the skill therefore begin to decline. Learners no longer use trial and error to find a movement solution that works. They find an acceptable solution and then use practice to hone their performance. As a result, movement variability decreases from one performance of the skill to the next. Learners also improve their ability to detect and correct their own errors.

According to Fitts and Posner, the final stage of learning is the **autonomous stage**. Individuals must practice the skill for a long time before reaching this movement stage, and some people never reach this stage. Let's think about what movement in this stage is like. The word *autonomous* means having the freedom to act independently. In the case of performing a motor skill autonomously, individuals do not have to allocate conscious attention to the skilled movement. Rather, the movement occurs fairly automatically. In other words, the mind is free to focus on other things, such as strategy, and not on production of the movement. This becomes very useful in sporting situations such as basketball, where a player may dribble the ball down the court automatically while paying attention to the position of teammates around the court.

Think about both sports and activities of everyday living. What are some movements you perform automatically, without thinking specifically about where and when to move your limbs?

Let's look at an example of moving through the three stages of learning. Remember when you first began using a computer? During the cognitive stage, you began to learn how to type on a keyboard. You had to look at the keyboard carefully to determine the location of specific keys and then pressed each key individually (a procedure known as "hunt and peck"). Typing out words was a slow and arduous process filled with many errors and miscues. Your attention was focused entirely on matching your fingers to the correct keys. After some practice, you began to associate certain finger movements with specific letters and positions on the keyboard, and you moved into the associative stage. Your keyboard typing still was not perfect, but you didn't have to stare down at the keyboard all the time to find individual keys, and you made far fewer errors. In fact, you began putting together combinations of letters you used frequently, such as *th*. You began to refine your typing skills. As you continued to practice typing on your computer, you may have reached the autonomous stage of learning. In this stage, you no longer have to think about finger placement; you can allocate your attention to what someone is saying (such as during a lecture class) or what you are thinking (if writing an essay or an e-mail to a friend). You can automatically produce a single letter, combinations of letters, or whole words without focusing on your fingers at all (in fact, if you start to pay attention to your finger placement, you may actually type more slowly, with more errors).

▶ **KEY POINT** Fitts and Posner's three-stage model of motor learning—the cognitive, associative, and autonomous stages—is compatible with the information processing perspective.

Bernstein's Model

Fitts and Posner focused on perceptual and cognitive elements when describing stages of movement; this model emerged from the information processing theoretical perspective. By comparison, Bernstein (1967) described the stages of skill acquisition from a dynamical systems perspective, which focuses on the progression in solving the problem of degrees of freedom (Vereijken, Whiting, & Beek, 1992; Vereijken, van Emmerik, Whiting, & Newell, 1992). Within a human body, **degrees of freedom** are the number of independent variables (e.g., joints, muscles, motor units) that must be controlled when individuals complete a movement. For example, just think of two joints involved in an arm reach. The elbow has two degrees of freedom because it flexes and extends. The shoulder has six because it flexes, extends, abducts, adducts, internally rotates, and externally rotates. And this covers only the joints involved in the movement! Simply stated, in the process of acquiring the ability to make an efficient and effective movement, individuals must learn to coordinate actions with many different degrees of freedom.

Degrees of freedom are the number of independent variables (e.g., joints, muscles, motor units) that must be controlled when individuals complete a movement.

Bernstein's model also includes three stages of learning. In stage 1, individuals exhibit control through **freezing degrees of freedom**, or limiting the number of joints that move independently (figure 17.2 *photo sequence 1*). Look back at the developmental sequences in chapters 5, 6, and 7. Many of the early developmental levels provide evidence of freezing degrees of freedom. For example, in the arm action of throwing, new throwers limit their movement to flexion and extension of the elbow; in the leg action, they do not take a step. Both are examples of minimizing movement, of locking out, or freezing, nonessential joints in order to reduce the number of moving parts. The body functions more like one unit, and the action seems more singular than sequential.

Freezing degrees of freedom occurs when novices lock joints that are not specifically used in producing a movement.

Stage 2 represents **releasing degrees of freedom** (figure 17.2 *photo sequence 2*). After learners can successfully perform the basic motor skill, they no longer need to isolate body segments. Rather, they begin to release tightly locked joints to allow for more fluid movements and transfer of energy among the different segments. Movements become actions; that is, segments work together in a coordinated fashion. This can be seen within developmental sequences as well. In throwing, developmental level 2 of arm action adds movement at the shoulder, and developmental level 2 of leg action includes an ipsilateral step.

The final stage in Bernstein's model is **exploiting degrees of freedom** (figure 17.2 *photo sequence 3*), where learners begin to exploit reactive forces and passive dynamics of the body and environment (we discuss this in detail in relation to the principles of motion and stability in chapter 3). The learners reorganize degrees of freedom in a way that allows them to move efficiently and effectively by adjusting their bodies to the environment. In general, this occurs after learners have had many practice experiences over a long period. For throwing, the most

FIGURE 17.2 The overarm throw at different learning stages according to Bernstein. *(1)* Freezing degrees of freedom. Notice that arm movement is restricted to flexion and extension of the elbow and shoulder and that there is no trunk rotation. *(2)* Releasing degrees of freedom. Notice that there is more movement of the legs and trunk, which improves ability to produce force. The motion of the arm is still primarily flexion and extension. *(3)* Exploiting degrees of freedom. Here, the thrower takes advantage of reaction forces and the passive dynamics of his body to optimize force generation.

advanced developmental profile is a series of movements of many body segments perfectly timed to transfer momentum and create a whipping action.

▶ **KEY POINT** Bernstein's three-stage model focuses on controlling the degrees of freedom in an action to make a movement.

Web Study Guide **Do children differ from adults in the way in which they pass through Stages of Learning? Find out in Lab Activity 17.2, Developmental Differences in Stages of Learning, in the web study guide.**

Practice and Motor Learning

One of the fundamental principles of motor learning is that it comes as a result of practice. This leads to an important consideration: How do different practice conditions affect motor learning? For practitioners, this is a critical question, since they want to use the most efficient and effective strategies to promote motor skill learning in their clients, patients, or students. It is their job to select and plan the best practice strategies.

Practice schedules can have a number of characteristics. Consider how to structure practice when learning a single skill: Is it better to practice the same skill over and over until perfected (called constant practice) or to practice variations of the skill (called varied or variable practice) in order to promote the best motor learning? The second question relates to learning multiple skills: Should a single skill be practiced repetitively before moving to the next skill (called blocked practice), or should practice of different skills be mixed (called random practice) in order to gain the greatest learning benefit? Inherent in both of these questions is the same idea: Does practice variability enhance or detract from motor learning?

Think of a tennis instructor faced with teaching the forehand stroke, the backhand stroke, the serve, and the volley in a 4-week unit. How would the teacher's instruction plan look if she implemented blocked practice? If she implemented random practice?

Learning a Single Motor Skill: Constant Versus Varied Practice Schedules

Consider a scenario where a physical education instructor wants to teach overarm throwing to a group of children. One simple way to go about this is to break the children up into pairs and have them throw a ball back and forth to each other from a set distance numerous times without changing task conditions. However, is this the most effective way to teach throwing skills? Another way to teach the skill would be to provide practice with a number of intentional variations. In this scenario, students might alternate throws from three or four distances, use balls of different sizes or weights, or aim at targets of different sizes.

Varied Practice and Schema Learning in Adults

According to Schmidt (1975), varied practice promotes schema learning. The learner acquires a set of rules, called the schemas, that relate the surface features of an action (e.g., distances, speeds of throwing) to the parameter values necessary to produce those actions. Whenever a movement is made, the learner notes the result as well as the parameters that were used. For example, "I didn't throw hard and the ball bounced in front of my target." Eventually these relationships are generalized into a schema. Learners acquire schemas when they practice; varied practice enhances their development, allowing more effective performance of a new task in the future. The change of the task's parameters is known as variability of practice (Shapiro & Schmidt, 1982). Researchers have posited the importance of introducing variability during motor learning so that people do not rely on a particular set of answers, which will ultimately reduce their chances for transfer and generalization of learning skills (Kazdin, 1975; Shute & Gawlick, 1995).

Think about a teacher working on the overhand throw with his young students. He decides to set up four stations and use varied practice. What might the activity at each of the four stations be?

Effect of Variable Practice in Children

Several studies have tried to determine whether introducing variation has the same benefit for children as it does for adults. One of the earliest studies to examine the effect of variable practice in young children was performed by Pigott and Shapiro in 1984. In this experiment, children tossed a weighted beanbag to a fixed target in one of four conditions for a total of 24 practice **trials**. The first group practiced the toss at only one weight (constant practice). The second group tossed four beanbags of varying weights (3, 4, 5, and 6 ounces; 1 oz = 30 g) that were randomized from one trial to the next. The third group tossed bags of the same weight for **blocks** of three trials, and the fourth group performed blocked practice of six trials per block for each weight. After the practice trials, all participants performed a transfer test of three trials at one of two possible test weights (2 ounces or 7 ounces). In this experiment, although the groups learning with variable practice all outperformed the constant practice group on the transfer test, the group practicing with blocks of three trials at each variation performed better in the transfer test than the two other variable practice groups, suggesting that complete randomization is not necessarily the best approach for children either.

A **trial** in an experiment is one performance of the task under study.

A **trial block** is a set number of trials that have been grouped into one unit (e.g., blocked). Trial blocks are often followed by rest periods.

In 1991, Wulf wanted to determine if variable practice was more effective than constant practice for helping children develop schemas and learn motor skills, as is the case with adults. For this study, 86 children with an average age of 11.3 years performed a throwing task. These participants were split into four experimental groups and a control group that didn't practice. Three experimental groups learned with different types of variable practice (different target distances and ball weights). The fourth experimental group received constant throwing practice. After the practice trials, all groups were required to perform in a novel condition (novel target distance and weight) without knowledge of their results. Compared with constant practice, variable practice, in general, enhanced performance of a novel movement variation. The results supported the variability-of-practice hypothesis in children, in that variable practice in general facilitated recall and recognition on a novel task.

In a more recent study, Zetou et al. (2014) wanted to determine the effect of variable practice on learning how to head a soccer ball (header skill) in a group of 39 children between the ages of 10 and 12 years. Children were divided into either a variable or constant practice group, then both participated in an 8-week header training program three times a week for 20 minutes. The variable practice group practiced one block of 10 trials of one parameter (e.g., heading "near"), then practiced another parameter in the next block (e.g., heading high balls), then practiced a third block with the first parameter. The constant group practiced just one parameter for the header skill, using in each drill only one parameter for all three blocks within a session. They all received a pretest, posttest, and retention test. After the training and testing were complete, the researchers found that a significant interaction occurred between measures and groups, indicating that the variable group benefited from variable practice more than the constant group benefited from practicing just one skill at a time.

▶ **KEY POINT** Children generally learn better with variable than constant practice, although not all degrees of variability are more effective.

The results of these three studies suggest that adding variability to practice of a specific skill appears to enhance motor learning in children. At the same time, the findings of Pigott and

Shapiro (1984) suggest that all types of variability are not necessarily good. This was also the conclusion of Zipp & Gentile (2010), who looked at the impact of practice variability when learning a Frisbee throwing task to three different distance targets in 8- to 10-year-old children and adults (a visual representation of their study is provided in figure 17.3). Results indicate that, contrary to earlier studies, throwing accuracy was better after blocked practice than random practice for both children and adults in the retention tests. Further, children trained under random conditions performed poorer than all other groups in one of the two transfer tests. In the other, adults outperformed children.

▶ **KEY POINT** Variability of practice might be a better strategy for learners in the associative stage of motor learning.

In another study, Van den Tillaar and Marques (2013) also looked at the effect of practice variability on the acquisition of overhead throwing in children. They practiced throwing with

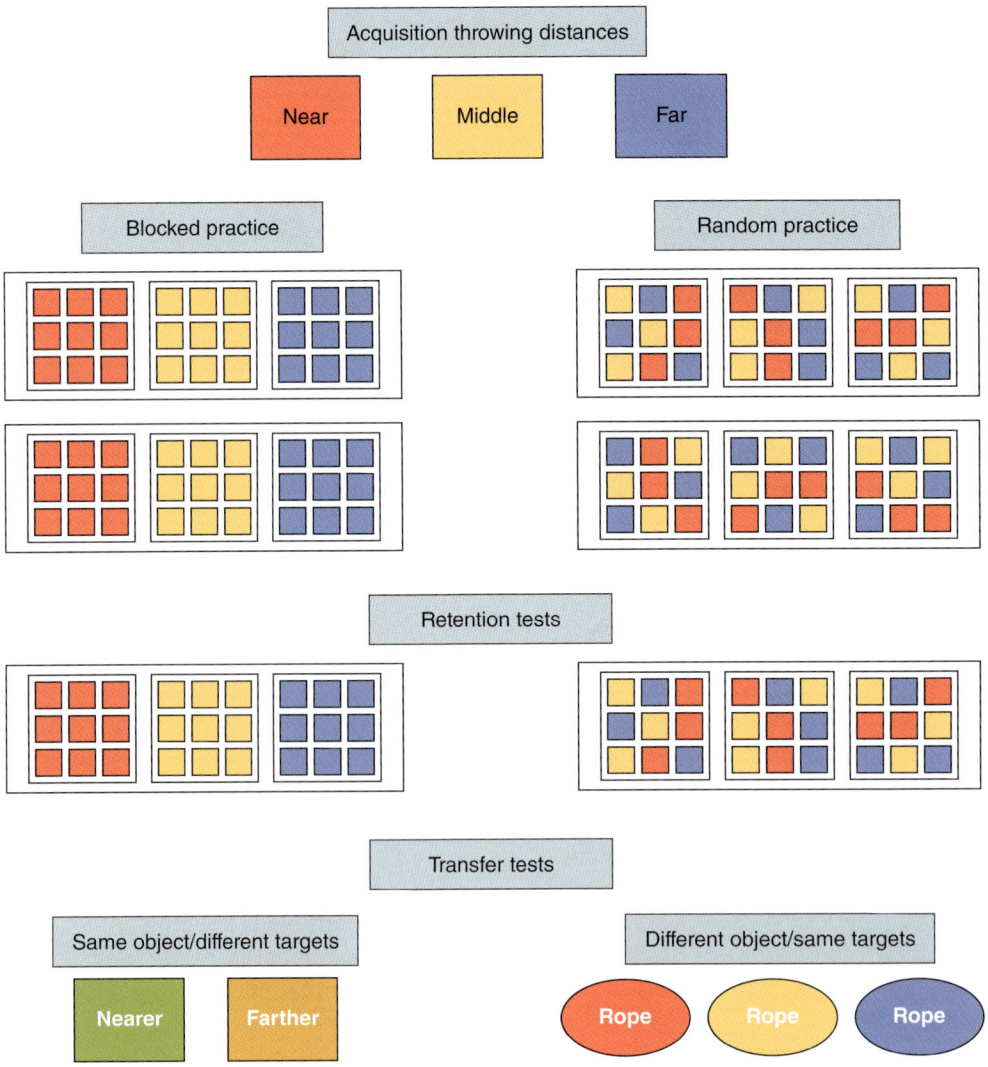

FIGURE 17.3 A visual representation of Zipp & Gentile's study examining the effect of variability in practice schedules. In their study, participants practiced three different throwing distances (represented at the top of the figure). During acquisition, the blocked group (left) practiced each throwing distance repetitively for a specific number of trials, whereas the random group (right) mixed throwing distances throughout the trial blocks. These were followed by retention tests similar to acquisition conditions and several different transfer tests.

three groups (a total of 41 children with an average age of 7.7 ± 0.5 years) twice per week for six weeks. The first two groups used constant practice. One group threw a soccer ball and the other a 1 kg (2.2 lb) ball. The third group used variable practice with 0.35, 0.45, 0.5, and 1 kg balls. Throwing speed and distance with different balls were measured before and after the practice period. All three groups significantly improved performance from pretest to posttest. At the same time, there were no significant differences among the groups, indicating that both constant and variable practice led to similar improvements in performance.

When looking at the results across all these studies, it appears that the effect of variable practice is not consistent in children. This may be a developmental effect or relate to which stage of learning an individual is in when receiving practice. Researchers have suggested that during the initial learning of a skill (the cognitive stage), constant practice may benefit both adults and children while they learn the fundamentals of how to produce the skill in a way that allows for some success (Gentile, 1972). Before this point, introducing variability may lead to frustration and lack of motivation on the part of the learner. Once learners begin to become more consistent in their performances (e.g., enter the associative stage), variability can be gradually introduced in the process of skill acquisition.

Augmented Feedback and Motor Learning

Researchers have explored another area of motor learning, the role of augmented feedback in skill acquisition. When individuals move, they receive sensory feedback from the various receptors in their bodies (see chapter 13 for a more complete discussion of the development of sensation). This feedback, coming as a result of movement, is termed intrinsic because it comes from the body's internal sensory receptors (Schmidt & Lee, 2014). For example, when a softball player throws a ball, cutaneous receptors provide information about the texture of the ball, proprioceptors indicate muscle length and tension of the throwing arm, and visual receptors provide visual information regarding the trajectory and end position of the ball. In addition to this naturally occurring feedback, other performance-related feedback can come from external sources. This is called extrinsic, or augmented, feedback. A simple example is a coach giving the softball player information about the position of her arm during the backswing when she throws the ball. The term *augmented* means the feedback comes from an external, or supplementary, source. In other words, augmented feedback enriches naturally occurring intrinsic feedback, perhaps to aid the performance of motor skills. The coach's feedback to the softball player provides extra information about her arm that she may not have been able to detect on her own, and the result could be a more forceful, accurate throw.

Now consider a softball pitcher who is practicing her fastball pitch. Her coach can provide augmented feedback about the outcome of the pitch ("Your pitch was low and outside") or about her technique during the pitch ("You released the ball too early"). Each of these represents a different type of augmented feedback. Within the field of motor learning, these two types of augmented feedback are named **knowledge of results (KR)** and **knowledge of performance (KP)**.

Knowledge of results consists of verbal or verbalizable information about the outcome of a motor performance (Magill & Anderson, 2017). This can be related specifically to a task goal.

Knowledge of performance is information about how a person moved. It can be delivered verbally or by technology, such as a video clip.

An example of KR might be that a softball pitcher wants to pitch a strike (task goal) but misses, and her coach describes her pitch as low and outside (information about performance in relation to goal). KR can also be related to success or failure in reaching a target goal, such as an umpire yelling, "Strike!" when the pitch is within the strike zone. There are clinical applications for KR as well. A physical therapist may provide KR such as walking speed or force output to a stroke patient trying to improve his gait. The key characteristic of KR is that it provides information about performance outcome in relation to the task goal; KR does not provide information about the actual motor pattern produced by the mover.

The type of augmented feedback that provides information about the movement pattern (i.e., characteristics of how the person moved while performing a skill) is KP (Magill & Anderson, 2017; Schmidt & Lee, 2014). In our previous example of a softball pitcher, when the coach tells the pitcher that she "released the ball too early," the coach has provided KP to the player.

KP provides information about the kinematics or movement pattern but does not provide information about the success or failure (i.e., outcome) of the movement itself.

What type of feedback is best? An important consideration for anyone who wishes to provide augmented feedback for learners is this: Which type provides for more efficient and effective motor learning? First, both types of feedback work. Various studies have shown that KR is effective for motor learning (e.g., Liu & Wrisberg, 1997; Masters, Maxwell, & Eves, 2009; Sharma, Chevidikunnan, Khan, & Gaowgzeh, 2016). Other studies have found KP effective (e.g., Zubiuar, Oña, & Delgado, 1999). But what if the two types of feedback are compared with each other? Studies in the 1990s suggested that KP was better at facilitating motor skill acquisition. In their 1992 study examining throwing with the nondominant arm, Kernodle and Carlton (1992) found that providing verbal information about technique resulted in greater throwing distance than providing KR about throwing distance. These were also the findings of Zubiaur et al. (1999), who examined the differences in volleyball serving between groups receiving KP (information about technique) and KR (outcome of serve). In a more recent study, Sharma et al. (2016) compared throwing performance (distance) in groups of adults who were given either KR or KP during 4 weeks of practice. Both groups significantly improved their throwing distance. However, the KP group outperformed the KR group, showing greater improvement in distance thrown over the course of practice. In sum, it appears that although both types of augmented feedback enhance motor learning, KP may be more influential than KR.

▶ **KEY POINT** Both KR and KP can benefit learners of a motor skill, but KP may be somewhat better, especially during the skill acquisition stage.

Given that augmented feedback enhances learning, how much feedback should be given? The literature related to adult motor learning is fairly unequivocal on this point: More augmented feedback is not necessarily better, and reducing the amount of feedback can, in fact, improve motor learning (e.g., Anderson, Magill, Sekiya, & Ryan, 2005; Winstein & Schmidt, 1990; Wulf & Schmidt, 1989). Is the same true for children?

Goh, Kantak, and Sullivan (2012) examined two groups (children and adults) who practiced 200 trials of an arm movement task. Half of each group received feedback on 100% of the trials, while the other half received feedback on 62%; both groups then performed retention and reacquisition trials. The researchers found that the adult group with reduced feedback performed with increased consistency during the retention test compared with those who practiced with 100% feedback. In contrast, children who received reduced feedback during practice performed with *less* accuracy and consistency during the retention test than those who received 100% feedback. During the reacquisition trials, the reduced feedback group of children improved their performance so that it was comparable to the 100% feedback group. The results of this study suggest that children differ from adults in the way they use feedback, and they may require more practice with higher amounts of feedback for longer periods of time than adults do.

▶ **KEY POINT** Children may benefit from more feedback for longer periods compared with adults.

What about older adults? Research appears to be mixed on the effect of reducing feedback in older adults. Several studies have shown that older adults perform better on retention tests when augmented feedback is provided less frequently (e.g., Carnahan, Vandervoort, & Swanson, 1996; Swanson & Lee, 1992), while others have shown no benefit of decreasing the amount of feedback (e.g., Behrman, Vander Linden, & Cauraugh, 1992; Wishart & Lee, 1997). More research needs to be performed before we understand the effect of amount of augmented feedback in older adults.

Other Factors That Influence Motor Learning

In addition to practice and augmented feedback, several other characteristics influence the acquisition of motor skills. One is how quickly learners can make decisions related to executing a skill, including selecting a response. Another is how effectively learners can focus their attention on the factors more important to skill execution. Memory capacity and retrieval also play a role. Let us consider how these factors change over the life span.

Information Processing Speed

From an information processing perspective, one of the key questions about motor performance is related to decision making: How fast can individuals process and act on a single stimulus? This would be more pertinent when participating in activities requiring quick decisions and responses. For example, slower cognitive function would not be an issue in deciding how to pick up a spare in bowling because there is sufficient time between deliveries. It would be an issue, however, in the middle of a tennis point when deciding whether a lob is an appropriate shot for the situation.

Most of the research on cognitive speed has been undertaken from an information processing perspective. From this viewpoint, short-term and long-term memory and information retrieval play a major role in movement responses. In contrast, ecological perspectives downplay the role of knowledge and cognitive processes in movement responses. From this perspective, affordances in the environment are directly perceived. Experience might influence whether an affordance is perceived, but the affordance is always available in the environment. With this in mind, let's first consider the role of cognitive speed in children's motor performance.

Speed of Cognitive Processing in Children

Children take longer than adults to process cognitive information to be remembered. As children get older, they can eventually process either the same amount of information faster or more information in the same amount of time. This trend is apparent in even the simplest of motor responses, **simple reaction time (SRT)**. Reaction time, an indicator of information processing speed, is the amount of time between the onset of stimuli and the initiation of motor response; with simple reaction time, there is just one stimulus and one response, and they represent the most basic unit of cognitive processing speed. Simple reaction time improves over the course of childhood and adolescence, which reflects improvements in information processing speed (Lambert & Bard, 2005; Iida, Miyazaki, & Uchida, 2010; Kiselev, Espy, & Sheffield, 2009). The slower processing speed exhibited in children appears related to central processes (processes of the central nervous system, or CNS) rather than peripheral ones (Kiselev, 2015). Among these central processes are attention, working memory, and fluid and crystalized intelligence (Fry & Hale, 2000; Tourva, Spanoudis, & Demetriou, 2016).

Simple reaction time is the time between the onset of a stimulus (e.g., a light or buzzer) and the beginning of a movement response (e.g., lifting a finger from a button).

The speed with which an individual can select motor responses changes as a function of age, which can be measured by observing **choice reaction time (CRT)**. In choice reaction-time tasks, there is more than one stimulus–response pair, and participants must choose the correct response based on the specific stimulus presented. The introduction of choices adds to the overall information processing time, which in turn results in slower response times. Several researchers have found improvements with age until approximately 15 years, particularly between the ages of 6 and 9 years, in choice reaction-time tasks and more complex activities (Bucsuhazy & Semela, 2017; Favilla, 2006; Lambert & Bard, 2005). In a more complex task, Clark (1982) manipulated the spatial stimulus–response compatibility of a reaction-time task when testing 6-year-olds, 10-year-olds, and adults. In the compatible condition, participants pressed a key on the right if the right stimulus light came on and a key on the left if the left stimulus light came on. In the incompatible condition, participants pressed a key opposite the direction of the light. Spatial compatibility, then, affects the participant's response selection. Clark found that processing time decreased (performance improved) in the older groups tested in the incompatible condition.

Choice reaction time is when participants must select the appropriate motor response when suddenly presented with one of several stimuli.

▶ **KEY POINT** Speed of initiating a response increases throughout childhood and youth and is faster when the response is compatible with the stimulus signal.

Although central factors such as working memory and attention influence children's slower processing speeds, peripheral factors do not. For example, nerve impulse conduction speed in the peripheral nerves does not contribute substantially to the speed differences between children and adults. Motor and sensory nerve conduction velocity at birth is about half that of a normal adult's, increases very quickly during the first year of life, and reaches adult values between 3 and 5 years of age (García-García & Calleja-Fernández, 2004). Young children can process information faster as they mature most likely because of improvements in central factors such as response selection and speed of the memory process (Bucsuhazy & Semela, 2017).

How could slower cognitive processing affect children in sports such as soccer, basketball, and tennis? If you were a coach, how might you structure their tasks for increased success given this limitation?

Speed of Cognitive Processing in Adults

As people age, they tend to slow down, and as is the case with young children, older adults exhibit limitations in the processing of information (Tun & Lachman, 2009; Reimers & Maylor, 2005). Simple reaction time appears to be fairly stable throughout early and middle adulthood, with minimal slowing until after the 50s and declines thereafter (Alfred & Rice, 2012; Der & Deary, 2006; Dykiert, Der, Starr, & Deary, 2012). On the other hand, choice reaction time declines more consistently across adulthood, as do increases in variability of the measure (Dykiert et al., 2012; Der & Deary, 2017). These limitations are also apparently related to central rather than peripheral processes. However, researchers have found important differences between performers at opposite ends of the life span. Der and Deary (2017) examined the relationship between reaction time and intelligence and how it changes as a function of aging. They analyzed a large data sample of 2,196 participants in three cohorts (30, 50, and 69 years old), which included measures of SRT, CRT (four choices), and the AH4 test of general intelligence. They found strong negative correlations between IQ and both SRT and CRT in all age groups with stronger correlations to CRT and the association growing stronger as a function of increasing age. This suggests a complex relationship among aging, processing speed, and intelligence.

▶ **KEY POINT** Reaction time declines as people age. This occurs earlier in adulthood in choice reaction time than in simple reaction time.

As people age, does their capacity to learn new motor skills decrease? Research on this point is mixed, with some studies showing reduced capacity and others enhanced (Ehsani, Abdollahi, Mohseni Bandpei, Zahiri, & Jaberzadeh, 2015). Researchers have hypothesized that these differences result from research paradigms that tap into either online components of learning (learning processes occurring *during* the acquisition phase or skill practice) or offline components of learning (learning processes occurring *after* the acquisition phase and *before* the retention test) (Vahdat, Albouy, King, Lungu, & Doyon, 2017; Yan, Abernethy, & Li, 2010). It appears that online motor learning is better maintained (although gradually declines) during aging and can result in significant performance improvements during training (Ehsani et al., 2015; Shea, Park & Braden, 2006). On the other hand, offline learning shows much greater deficits as people age. For example, Ehsani et al. (2015) examined younger (18–35 years) and older (60–80 years) adults as they performed a color-matching test for eight blocks of 10 trials each. The participants implicitly learned—that is, they were not explicitly told what to learn—a pattern of stimulus–response choices based on four colors. In this study, although younger adults showed greater overall learning, older adults demonstrated a significantly higher amount of online learning than did younger adults, as measured by their serial reaction time. At the same time, the older adults did not improve whereas the younger adults showed significant differences in offline learning.

Web Study Guide **Observe changes in reaction time that occur at different ages in Lab Activity 17.3, Age-Related Reaction Times, in the web study guide.**

Besides processing speed and offline learning, attentional factors also play a role in the slowing behavioral performance of older adults, because attentional resources decline as a function of age (Glisky, 2007; Godefroy et al., 2010). Selective, divided, and switching attention all appear to decline as individuals age (Ruthruff & Lein, 2015).

▶ **KEY POINT** At any point in the life span, CNS factors play a much larger role in speed of cognitive processing than do peripheral factors.

Many older adults are more easily distracted and attend less well to critical stimuli than when they were younger. The cause of this decline in performance might be a lowered signal-to-noise ratio in the CNS. The neural impulses of the CNS take place against a background of random neural noise such that the effectiveness of a neural signal depends on the ratio between the signal strength and the background noise—the signal-to-noise ratio. As a person ages, signal levels in the CNS decrease because of changes in the sense organs, loss of brain cells, and factors affecting brain cell functioning; at the same time, noise level increases (Rizzo, Anderson, & Fritzsch, 2018). Older adults can compensate for this lower signal-to-noise ratio if they are given extra time to complete a task, but they are at a disadvantage if they must perform a series of movements or make a series of decisions rapidly.

CNS factors also influence the slower speed of processing in older adults. Researchers have consistently documented a slowing of reaction time with aging. Although a slight slowing of neural impulse conduction velocity is associated with aging, it is not great enough to account for the magnitude of lengthened reaction times.

Choice reaction time slows in older adults even more than does simple reaction time. Making a task more complex by increasing the number of signals or by designating responses that are less logical (e.g., pressing the left button in response to the right signal light) disproportionately increases older adults' reaction time when compared with that of younger adults (Dykiert et al., 2012; Der & Deary, 2017).

Older adults' movement time has long been known to slow very slightly (Singleton, 1955), but older adults maintain the speed of planned, repetitive movements such as tapping (Earles & Salthouse, 1995; Fieandt, Huhtala, Kullberg, & Saarl, 1956; Jagacinski, Liao, & Fayyad, 1995). Because almost all behaviors mediated by the CNS slow down as an adult ages, central factors are assumed to be largely responsible for slower information processing speed (Birren, 1964). However, the schemata of older adults can be particularly complete and refined for skills the adult has had a lifetime of experience with. This experience is particularly helpful when accuracy is more important than speed. When older adults are not pressed to perform as quickly as possible, they demonstrate very accurate performance on well-practiced tasks.

Factors Affecting Changes in Adulthood

In our discussion to this point, you may have noticed that older adults have been discussed as if they form a homogeneous group. No distinction has been made between subgroups such as healthy adults and clinical populations, or active and inactive adults. Since the 1970s, however, researchers have become more interested in performance differences between active and inactive adults. Active older adults typically perform more like young adults in simple and choice reaction-time tasks than do inactive older adults (Rikli & Busch, 1986; Spirduso, 1975, 1980). In 2003, Colcombe and Kramer published a meta-analysis of 18 aerobic fitness intervention studies with older adults. They found that fitness training improved performance on a variety of cognitive tasks. The greatest effect was for executive tasks (those involving planning, inhibition, and scheduling of mental processes), but speed, visual-spatial, and controlled-process (e.g., choice reaction time) tasks also improved (figure 17.4). The benefits of training were greater if the intervention was a combined aerobic and strength program as compared with aerobic training alone, if the program lasted more than 6 months, if sessions lasted more than 30 minutes, and if exercisers were "young-old" (55–65 years) or "mid-old" (66–70) rather than "old-old" (71–80). An additional review (Voss, Nagamatsu, Liu-Ambrose, & Kramer, 2011) found that both aerobic and resistance training are beneficial for maintaining cognitive and brain health in older adults.

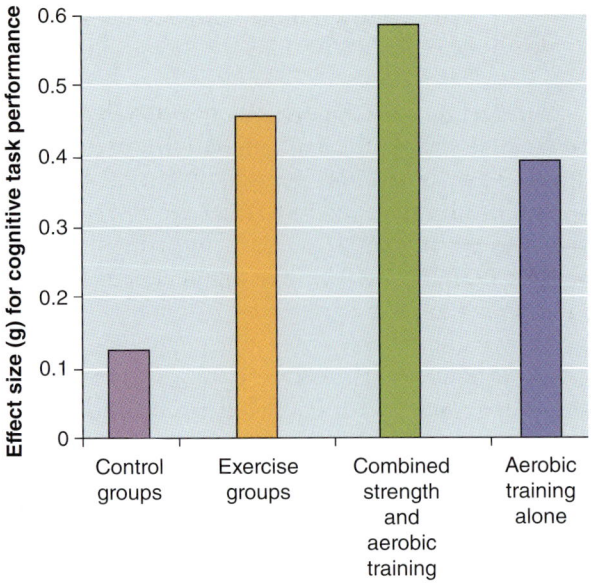

FIGURE 17.4 Improvements in cognitive task performance after exercise. The cognitive tasks tested were speed, visual-spatial, controlled processing, and executive control. The greatest effect was on executive control tasks, but improvement occurred on all cognitive tasks. Data are from Colcombe and Kramer (2003).

Great interest exists in learning how exercise exerts its favorable effect on cognitive functions, and researchers in this area can now take advantage of more widely available advanced imaging techniques, such as functional magnetic resonance imaging (fMRI). Colcombe et al. (2003) used MRI scans to show that aerobic fitness levels moderated loss of nervous system tissue with aging, and Colcombe et al. (2006) used MRI scans to find that brain volume increased in 60- to 79-year-olds who started an aerobic exercise program. So aerobic fitness has a favorable effect on the brain structure of older adults. Is the same true of brain function? Colcombe et al. (2004) used functional MRI scans to see that fit adults showed greater activity in involved areas of the brain during a cognitive task compared with unfit adults (see also McAuley, Kramer, & Colcombe, 2004). This finding, along with those on training older adults to perform specific tasks (Erickson et al., 2007), suggests that the older adult brain retains more plasticity in functioning than was previously thought. A number of other factors could be involved in the beneficial effect of exercise, including improved vascular health in the brain and beneficial effects on insulin resistance and glucose intolerance (Weuve et al., 2004).

Memory

Learning and memory are two sides of the same coin, where learning represents a process and memory the product of that process. Learning results in memories, so the more memories individuals have, the more they have learned. Furthermore, motor learning results in motor memories. Sutherland, Pipe, Schick, Murray, and Gobbo (2003) found that providing children with prior information about an event improved their recall of the event and their learning in the event, both soon after the event and 4 months later. So new experiences are integrated with our existing base of meaning.

The question asked most often about memory development is whether memory capacity changes with development. Yet how much we remember, no matter what our age, depends on what we already know about a topic. Knowledge is organized or structured in specific content domains (Kuhn, 2000), such as chess, dinosaurs, or baseball. Memorizing, then, is a process of revising our knowledge of a topic. Although much research has been carried out on the topic of memory capacity, the answer to whether it increases with development has been elusive. This probably reflects researchers' approaching the study of memory without regard to one's knowledge context. That is, memory has been studied in isolation. The answer to the question of capacity awaits new research approaches that study memory in the broader context of the developing cognitive system.

▶ **KEY POINT** Memories are knowledge structures resulting from our efforts to understand and know.

People of all ages remember more when they have a reason to do so. Very young children first remember when adults engage them in recounting experiences. With advancing age, children internalize this remembering activity and carry it out on their own. Eventually they remember purposively, for their individual benefit or that of their social group. Again, laboratory research on memory often has involved memorizing items for no particular reason other than completing the research task. Future researchers must study memory in the context of information that is important to people.

Young children typically do not employ strategies for remembering, but they can be taught to use strategies such as rehearsal, labeling, and grouping. Thomas, Thomas, and Gallagher (1981) demonstrated that teaching children a rehearsal strategy along with a skill enhanced their skill acquisition. Gallagher and Thomas (1980) also found that grouping arm movements in an organized order helped children recall and duplicate movements. The difficulty is that children won't necessarily apply the strategies learned in one context to another context. Perhaps the use of memory strategies is related to a broader issue—the development of cognitive strategies such as inference and problem solving—and needs to be studied in that context. Van Duijvenvoorde, Jansen, Bredman, and Huizenga (2012) found that when the demands of long-term and working memory were reduced, children, adolescents, and young adults were all capable of making advantageous decisions. Explicitly providing the pros and cons of options helped children and adolescents make advantageous decisions even in complex situations. Because this research used a cognitive task, additional research in movement settings is needed to see whether the same results are obtained.

Research on memory in adults and older adults tends to find a decline in performance on memory tasks. Yet as with the research involving children, researchers have tended to study memory in isolation and without regard to adults' knowledge of a topic or motivation to remember. Moreover, a host of environmental factors might affect performance of older adults on memory tasks. Diseases (e.g., hypertension) might impair memory performance. Highly fit older adults have been observed to perform better than unfit adults on memory tasks (Stones & Kozma, 1989), and memory performance has been linked to self-reported health status (Perlmutter & Nyquist, 1990). Improvements on memory tasks have also been noted after exercise interventions, so exercise probably has a small but positive effect on memory performance (Clarkson-Smith & Hartley, 1990; Colcombe et al., 2005).

Alzheimer's disease is devastating for individuals and their families. Late-onset Alzheimer's disease, the most common form, is characterized by confusion, memory loss, and behavioral problems. As the number of individuals living into older adulthood increases, so too will the number of older adults who develop Alzheimer's. The cause of late-onset Alzheimer's disease is likely a combination of genetic, lifestyle, and environmental factors. Some research has focused on specific genes that may be responsible for the condition, but to date, no specific gene has been found. However, at least one genetic risk factor (the apolipoprotein E [APOE] gene on chromosome 19) has been associated with higher rates of developing the disease (National Institute on Aging, 2016).

Although performance on memory tests might show improvement through childhood and decline in older adulthood, it is most important to acknowledge that memory is related to current knowledge and understanding of information in a specific context as well as to the motivation to remember information.

Summary and Synthesis

Throughout this text, we examine aspects of motor learning over the life span. In the short term, though, skills are learned and refined through practice. The conditions that promote learning might not be the same at every phase of the life span. The subdiscipline of developmental motor learning studies practice schedules, such as constant versus varied practice and blocked versus random practice, and augmented feedback, including how their benefit varies over the life span. Practitioners might not only implement different characteristics of their instructional plan for different ages but might also take into account the learners' stage of learning. Other characteristics of the learner that might be considered are processing speed, level of attention, and memory. Although older adults typically experience a slowing of processing speed, exercise training seems to offset much of this decline.

Reinforcing What You Have Learned About Constraints

TAKE A SECOND LOOK

Does becoming an adult mean the ability to process, retain, and learn motor skills has to decline after 21? Not at all! Many components of information processing plateau or even improve with age, such as crystallized intelligence, which may improve into the seventh decade. In addition, the characteristics of the learning environment are very important to the learning of motor skills. What works well for children is not always the same as what works well for adults or for older adults. Parents, teachers, coaches, and therapists can construct the environmental and task constraints in a learning context. If they think about the interaction of these constraints with the learner's individual constraints (speed of processing, attention level, memory), they can construct instructional plans that maximize the learning of motor skills.

TEST YOUR KNOWLEDGE

1. What are Fitts and Posner's three stages of learning? What is a characteristic of each stage?
2. What are Bernstein's three stages of learning? What is a characteristic of each stage?
3. What is the difference between constant and varied practice? Is one better for children? Explain.
4. What is the difference between blocked and random practice? Is one better for children? Explain.
5. What is the difference between KR and KP? Is one better for children? Is one better for learners early in the skill acquisition process? Explain your responses.
6. Define simple and choice reaction time. What does research on reaction time tell us about differences in processing speed between children, adults, and older adults? Why?
7. How does aerobic training affect cognitive functioning in older adults? What are the implications for activities of daily living and sport performance?

Learning Exercise 17.1

INSTRUCTIONAL PLAN WITH CONSTANT OR VARIED PRACTICE

Assume you are teaching primary-school-age children the basics of tennis in a 6-week, 3 days-per-week summer recreational program. You will teach the forehand stroke, backhand stroke, and serve. Create an instructional plan that uses either constant or varied practice, specifying the activities for each of the 18 days. Write a rationale for your choice of constant or varied practice, and indicate how the activities implement your choice of practice schedules.

18

Conclusion: Interactions Among Constraints

Applications to Movement

CHAPTER OBJECTIVES

This chapter

- allows you to examine, all at one time, the individual, task, and environmental constraints and their interactions affecting an individual;
- encourages you to see each individual as unique;
- demonstrates how you can use the model to manipulate constraints for a specific educational or therapeutic purpose;
- gives you practice in structuring developmentally appropriate learning environments and designing developmentally appropriate learning tasks;
- provides a framework for charting constraints to both enhance developmentally appropriate teaching and track and assess progress; and
- provides case studies so that you have the opportunity to apply your knowledge of motor development to real-life situations.

Motor Development in the Real World

The Paralympic Games

The following quote is from the official website of the 2004 Athens Paralympic Games: "The Paralympic Games is the top sports event in the life of every Paralympic athlete . . . . In the Paralympic Games, athletes engage in obstinate, noble, and sustained competition to achieve the highest sports distinction. Their efforts are guided and shaped by a unique strength and determination. Their strength and ability to overcome hardship becomes a shining flame, a pole of attraction for everyone who values sports as the highest expression of humanity."

The Paralympic Games have been held the same year as the Olympic Games since 1960 and in the same city since 1988. They are held in both summer and winter. At the 2016 Summer Paralympics, held in Rio de Janeiro, Brazil, 4,342 athletes representing 159 countries competed in 22 sports. The events included four wheelchair sports, sitting volleyball, swimming, powerlifting, judo, and, of course, track and field. In 2018, the Winter Paralympics were held in Pyeongchang, South Korea, where 569 athletes representing 49 countries participated in sports such as alpine skiing, para ice hockey, and wheelchair curling.

What does this description of the Paralympics mean to you now that you have finished reading this text on life span motor development? We hope you view Paralympians as people who have unique sets of constraints along with many others that are common to all humans. The structural and functional individual constraints of these Paralympians do not stop them from participating in physical activity at the highest levels. Their constraints allow them to move in activities of daily living and compete at a high level of athletics. These interacting constraints include high levels of strength (structural), strong motivation (functional), a supportive environment (sociocultural), and high-tech equipment (task), among others. Put these elements into the context of a sporting event and the results are elite, record-breaking athletes.

Years ago, Paralympians might have been labeled *disabled*, just as special needs children once were. We hope you now see individuals not as labels but rather as unique persons who possess unique combinations of individual functional and structural constraints. Those individual constraints interact with the environmental and task constraints to provide both possibilities and challenges in moving.

Not everyone can be—or wants to be—an elite athlete, but everyone moves constantly, every day. All movement occurs in a context and results from an interaction of constraints. Certain constraints may influence movement behavior more at a particular time than others do, and some can change drastically over the course of the life span. But all exist and interact, allowing movement to emerge. Why have we spent so much time emphasizing this point?

Throughout this text, we use a developmental perspective in discussing the different types of constraints that affect motor development across the life span. To conceptualize how constraints work, we separate them into individual, environmental, and task constraints. It is important to realize, however, that although one type of constraint may be more influential at any given time, all are present and constantly interacting. In fact, something can act as a constraint only when it interacts with an individual in a movement context, which means you must understand how constraints affect each other. At first glance, this may seem somewhat confusing. However, assessing the influence of constraints on each other is what we have been doing all along. Remember the news article in chapter 8 noting that teenagers experience a period of awkwardness during their adolescent growth spurt? The significance of the story is related to individual, environmental, and task constraints all acting together to produce movement. In this case, rapid changes in individual constraints changed emergent movement and motor development for a period of time.

Looking at the interaction of constraints is helpful in understanding life span motor development. The most important message of this text is that manipulating constraints can be useful in influencing movement and motor development (figure 18.1). Manipulating a constraint at any given time may produce a functional change in movement. However, in motor development, we are most concerned with changes in movements over time, particularly ones that become more permanent or structural. We emphasize this point: If short-term change in a constraint leads to a short-term change in the interaction among constraints, it can lead to long-term change in motor behavior. In other words, we can influence our own motor behavior and that of others by manipulating constraints to make them more developmentally appropriate. Isn't that the point of teaching and rehabilitation?

Using Constraints to Enhance Learning in Physical Activity Settings

In everyday life, people frequently modify constraints in order to change movements. These adjustments can enable movements that otherwise might have been difficult or impossible. For example, individuals using wheelchairs can perform activities of daily living more easily if their household appliances (e.g., sinks, stoves, and countertops) are scaled to their relative (seated) height. Sometimes without even thinking, an individual alters something in the relationships between himself or herself, the environment, and the task at hand. For example, we would probably slide a heavy book across the table and closer to us before picking it up rather than attempt

FIGURE 18.1 By manipulating task constraints—in this case, providing a prosthetic limb—a person with unique individual constraints can participate in many different physical activities in the same capacity as a person with typical individual constraints.

Josie Gealer/Photodisc/Getty Images

to lift it at arm's length. Or consider children learning to play the violin: Because children have small hands and arms, music teachers often provide them with smaller instruments, scaled to their body size, so they can succeed in learning to play skillfully. These examples illustrate that modifying a task or environmental constraint can allow for a more developmentally appropriate, functional motor skill. For movement educators, it is important to consider all types of constraints and how they interact. As you might expect, interaction is a dynamic process and may result in a change in one or all of the interacting constraints. Movement educators, therefore, must attempt to manipulate constraints to allow their students or clients to perform skills more proficiently or to achieve a certain goal (Gagen & Getchell, 2004, 2018; Getchell & Gagen, 2006).

▶ **KEY POINT** Constraints can often be manipulated to make a movement developmentally appropriate.

Physical educators often manipulate constraints when designing play experiences for students in their classes. Let's use the example of basketball. Thinking of Newell's triangle, imagine a child in a movement setting with the structural constraint of being short, the environmental constraint of an indoor basketball court, and the task constraint of the goal of shooting the ball into the basket, which is, in relation to the child, pretty high. Most of the situations in teaching and rehabilitation can be even more complicated than this. Let's adapt Newell's model by moving away from the triangle and using another shape to represent a larger number of the most relevant constraints, keeping in mind that in any context, there can be more important constraints in any constraint category and fewer in another. In figure 18.2, a hexagon is used to illustrate two structural constraints (being short and possessing moderate strength), one environmental constraint (the indoor basketball court), and three task constraints (shooting the ball through the basket, the height of the basketball hoop, and the weight of the basketball). Clearly, this combination of constraints is not likely to result in a movement of successfully shooting the basketball through a basket at the regulation height of 10 feet (3 m). Movement educators can adjust this play experience by altering one or more constraints.

Theoretically, one can manipulate all constraints—individual, environmental, and task. Practically speaking and on a day-to-day basis, however, educators cannot change children's structural constraints. Over the course of a semester, individual constraints such as height and weight may change very little, and changing functional constraints such as fear or motivation may require a longer time. Therefore, teachers must accept that individual constraints cannot be easily manipulated on a given day in the gym. However, by modifying environmental or task constraints, movement educators manipulate the *interactions* between the constraints and thereby facilitate change to allow and encourage more proficient or desired movements.

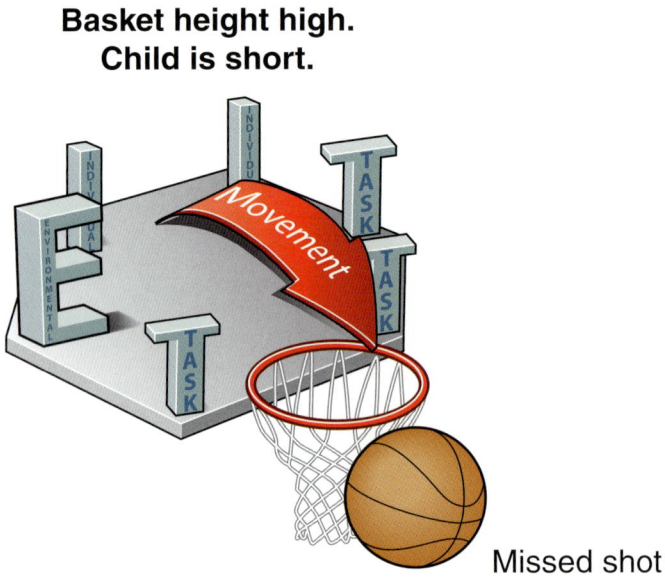

FIGURE 18.2 Using a hexagon instead of a triangle allows a model of constraints to represent more than one individual, environmental, and task constraint.

Returning to our basketball example, a teacher or coach realizes that the structural constraints cannot be changed in the short term and that the overall goal of shooting a basket into the hoop is fundamental to the game. A potentially easy fix that will result in successful motor performance is to adjust a different task constraint. Figure 18.3 depicts the basket height. In the original scenario the hoop was at the standard 10-foot height, but if the instructor lowers the hoop, the movement arising from the interaction of the constraints pictured might be the desired one. Another practical constraint change that may be easier than lowering the height of the basket is that the instructor could provide a ball that is slightly smaller and somewhat lighter, making the desired movement even more likely to result from the interaction of these constraints (see figure 18.4). In addition, the children will be more successful, which will keep them engaged and excited about movement experiences.

Of course, structural constraints change over time and with growth, maturation, and experiences of individuals. Individuals get taller and stronger (see figure 18.5). As they do, basketball teachers and coaches can adjust the basket height, eventually to that established in rules for mature players, and can provide bigger and heavier basketballs until players again use a standard-size ball. Adjusting the environmental constraints in relation to the changes in structural constraints permits the same movement outcome. When teaching a learner over a time of growth and maturation, an instructor who keeps the environmental constraints developmentally appropriate permits the desired movement outcome to arise from the interaction of all the constraints. If the instructor stubbornly maintains an environment intended for bigger and stronger movers, the movement outcome will be very different.

Therapists take a similar approach. They adapt environmental and task constraints to an individual's current structural constraints. As individuals improve by increasing their range of motion or strength, therapists adjust the constraints in concert. The relationship remains approximately the same among the constraints, but with small adjustments in environmental and task con-

FIGURE 18.3 Changing one task constraint, basketball basket height, while the other constraints remain the same changes the interaction of this constraint with all the others.

FIGURE 18.4 Changing other constraints, size and weight of the basketball, instead of changing basket height again changes the interactions among the constraints.

straints, structural constraints that are limiting gradually improve to—or even surpass—the level before an injury or surgery.

▶ **KEY POINT** Although children's structural constraints cannot be altered in the short term, environment and task can be manipulated so that the resulting movement is developmentally appropriate. They can be continually adjusted as an individual's structural constraints change.

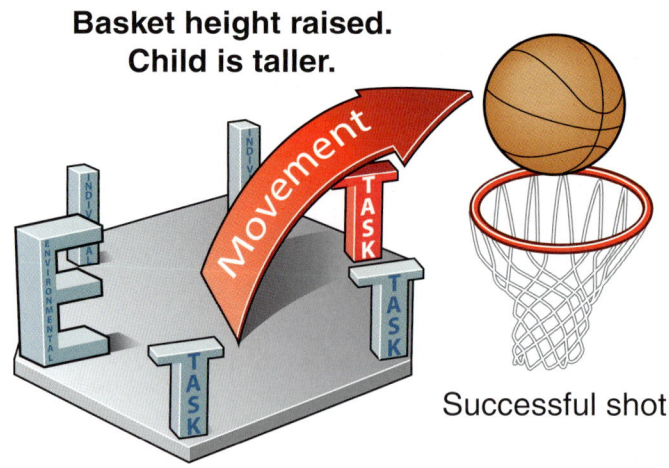

FIGURE 18.5 Young persons' individual constraints clearly change with experience, growth, and maturation. This model represents an increase in height and an increase in strength. Teachers and coaches can change environmental and task constraints at a rate consistent with the change in individual constraints so that the movement outcome is the same. That is, the basket height and ball size and weight are scaled up (e.g., moved toward regulation dimensions) as the individual constraints change. This way the movement (task goal) of shooting a one-hand basketball set shot can be attained throughout the period of growth and maturation.

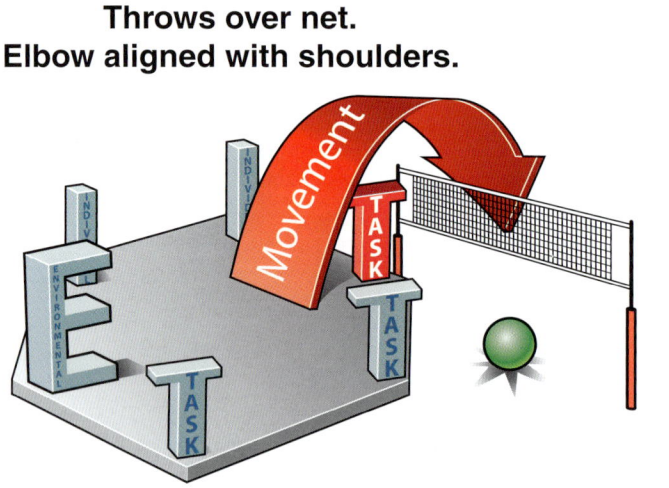

FIGURE 18.6 The expanded model of constraints can help teachers and coaches identify ways to create a new movement outcome. In this figure, the constraints are set to encourage young throwers to align the upper arm and elbow with the shoulders (arm step 2 in the throwing for force developmental sequence).

In Paralympians, environmental and task constraints are often changed in concert with the athletes' structural constraints to permit the same sport movements that can be executed by other athletes. In archery, a bow can be adapted so that an individual missing an arm can draw the bow with his or her teeth. This is an adjustment to equipment. In sitting volleyball, adjustments are made to equipment and to the rules. The net is lowered to be slightly over 1 meter high, and the rules require that some part of a player's body between the buttocks and shoulders remain in contact with the floor when a ball is played. In other cases, a prosthetic, as an additional piece of equipment, allows a desired movement.

Constraints can also be adjusted to help push movers to different movement patterns. Recall the developmental sequence for upper arm action in the overhead throw. Imagine that a teacher observes many children in her class using a step 1 movement pattern: throwing with the elbow pointing downward rather than aligned with the shoulders. The teacher wants students to perform a throwing motion with an aligned upper arm. The teacher designs a task (i.e., structures a learning environment) that is more likely to result in a step 2 movement pattern (see figure 18.6).

The instructor designs a game called "clean house" in which players throw small balls up and over a volleyball net until all the balls in play are on the other team's side of the net. The teacher provides small balls that the children can throw with one hand and puts a volleyball net at a height that requires them to throw up and over but not so high that they cannot get balls to the other side. It is difficult to throw over the net with the elbow pointing down, so the environmental and task constraints encourage the children to use a movement pattern that brings the upper arm closer to parallel. This is another way that movement instructors can manipulate constraints in a developmentally appropriate way and encourage a new movement. With time, the new movement pattern becomes the preferred pattern for throwing.

Web Study Guide **Use the model of constraints to assess a playground space in Lab Activity 18.1, Assessing a Play Space, in the web study guide.**

Structuring the Learning Environment

In this textbook, you have read about many developmental changes that occur across the life span. Movement educators should keep these changes in mind as they structure their learning environments. For example, it's easy to consider a gymnasium a static environment. However, factors such as wall color can influence how proficiently a child catches a ball. Remember, younger children have greater difficulty discriminating objects from the environment and benefit from more salient visual cues. To provide these cues, a physical educator can purchase equipment that is multicolored or distinct from the wall color. What if new equipment is not an option? Why not tape white paper to the wall as a backdrop? In a rehabilitation setting, the environment can be structured to be more ecologically valid, or more like the real world. The setting could be restructured to resemble a home or work environment, which would facilitate movement in that context.

When young children run at play, the running surface dictates how fast they run and how well they can remain on their feet. Long, clumpy grass presents different problems to running children than do blacktop playground surfaces or slippery tile gym floors. Weather is another environmental aspect that may influence activities. Running a mile on a hot, humid day, when breathing is difficult for most anyone, will be nearly impossible for some. Planning more strenuous activities for days when the temperature is cooler, the humidity is lower, and the air is clearer of pollen or pollutants (e.g., after a rain) will allow students to be more successful (Gagen & Getchell, 2004, 2018).

Let's not forget the sociocultural environment. When selecting activities and games, teachers can choose games that do not promote success based on sex, race, ethnicity, or socioeconomic status. For example, when activities are gender neutral, both boys and girls feel comfortable playing and succeeding. Some new games promote the same movement skills as traditional games but do not have particular sociocultural associations—two examples are team handball and sepak (a sport in which players kick a ball over a volleyball-type net). This approach opens opportunities to children who otherwise might not participate in a more traditional American sport that has been stereotyped. Different types of environmental constraints influence the structure of the learning environment. Manipulating the environment—or at the very least, being mindful of its influence—will allow movement educators in many fields to create a setting that promotes movement proficiency.

▶ **KEY POINT** More proficient movement might emerge when environmental and task constraints are adjusted for an individual's structural and functional constraints.

Designing the Learning Task

No matter what the setting, movement educators *design* learning and rehabilitation tasks. The model of constraints provides a methodical means for designing the tasks. Consider how the interaction of relevant constraints encourages particular movement skills, keeping in mind that making changes can make skills easier or more difficult to achieve. How do the goals and rules of the task, as well as the equipment used in a task, interact with students' unique individual constraints in the class environment to allow the children to perform a desired, successful movement?

Task goals are the behavioral outcomes of the lesson. Teachers choose the goal of a task to encourage certain desired movements. Consider the task of throwing a ball. How a child throws depends on the goal of the task: to throw the ball as far as possible, as high as possible, as accurately as possible, or as quickly as possible. The throwing movements that result from each of these different task goals will differ substantially.

If children are young, small, or not very strong, some task goals are developmentally inappropriate and will not result in the practice of good throwing technique. For example, competitive games such as pickle (a game that simulates a baseball runner caught between two bases while two throwers attempt to get the runner out) encourage children to throw quickly but may inhibit the use of appropriate throwing technique. When children focus on competition, they may simply pick up the throwing objects and use any method to propel them in the interest of speed. This does not encourage children to set their feet and use an appropriate backswing or aiming technique, nor does it promote correct use of all the body parts that should be sequentially involved in applying force and direction to the throw. In this example, then, if the task goal is proficient throwing technique, competitive games should be avoided with young children.

Movement educators can carefully manipulate the task goals so that children achieve an intended skill without being conscious of the intent. If a teacher places large pieces of paper against a wall and asks her students to "make the biggest noise possible," the students will throw harder without any potentially negative comparisons with their classmates for not throwing as far as another child. In this case, throwing harder without throwing farther will often encourage children to use better technique; throwers will get feedback from the noise of the paper targets as the balls hit them, but the students need to control the throw in order to hit the target. The game "clean house" described previously is an example of encouraging a specific movement by using a manipulation of a learning task in the form of a game rather than direct instruction.

Teachers can also modify the rules of a task to elicit a desired movement behavior. Teachers often modify games (change the rules) to encourage different movements or levels of participation. Playing three-on-three soccer on small fields is a game modification that allows shorter, more controlled kicking and receiving of the ball and more participation by each child, thus changing the focus of the game from running and chasing to movement technique. Playing volleyball with rules that allow the ball to bounce once will often give children the time to move into a better striking position, thus allowing them to use more appropriate striking technique. Requiring three passes before a shot in basketball promotes team play and cooperation. Such modifications can also be made so that children with disabilities can participate with their typically developing peers (Getchell & Gagen, 2006). For example, volleyball can be played from a seated position similar to the Paralympic sport, allowing for the inclusion of children who have a disability involving the lower limbs (e.g., certain types of cerebral palsy or spina bifida). The game can be enjoyable for a class of students, even those capable of playing standing volleyball!

Body scaling is a relatively easy way to manipulate task constraints by modifying the equipment and play spaces in proportion to the physical size or strength of the movers. Movement educators and rehabilitation specialists often scale equipment and play spaces to assist movers who have smaller stature or less strength. Bats, rackets, golf clubs, and balls designed for women are often smaller and lighter than those designed for men, and those designed for children are smaller and lighter still. Soccer fields and base paths for children's leagues are often shortened to better match the shorter legs of younger children. Shorter volleyball nets and 6- and 8-foot basketball standards are thought to promote more effective ball skills in younger performers (Chase, Ewing, Lirgg, & George, 1994; Davis, 1991). Thus, when teaching, coaching, or rehabilitating people, movement educators should very carefully think through the process of choosing equipment to match physical size and strength. Smaller balls that fit into smaller hands are easier to throw, *but* larger balls are easier to catch (Payne & Koslow, 1981). Therefore, the overall goal of the task (e.g., throwing or catching) must always be kept in mind.

► **KEY POINT** Body scaling the equipment and the play spaces used in an activity is a way to modify task and environmental constraints to permit certain movements.

Let's consider the example of a striking task for children, that of batting a ball. A range of bat characteristics must be considered in relation to the child: the weight of the bat (the child's strength interacting with gravity to allow her to swing the bat using correct technique), the length of the bat (the child's ability to judge where the barrel of the bat will be relative to the ball and his own body), the grip size of the bat (so that the child's hands can fit around the grip to hold it well), and perhaps the size of the barrel of the bat (a wider barrel provides more surface area and perhaps a greater chance of contacting the ball). Certain choices can allow the child to swing the bat easily, whereas other choices can lead to difficulty in swinging it. A good bat choice for very young children might be lightweight with a small grip, and short but with a wider barrel. When educators work with a group of children, they should expect a wide range of size, strength, and maturation levels. Providing bats with a wide range of characteristics gives each child the opportunity to select a bat that he or she can succeed with (Gagen & Getchell, 2004, 2006, 2018).

Ecological Task Analysis: Charting Constraints to Enhance Developmentally Appropriate Teaching

Imagine you are coaching for the first time a volleyball team made up of 10-year-olds. Height, weight, and skill level vary widely in the group. How do you approach coaching this team? You could simply teach the skills they need to learn by showing them the correct form, then making them practice over and over again. This approach might or might not provide results over the long run, but it will probably prove to be frustrating or boring for all involved. Is there a better way to teach motor skills?

By using ecological task analysis (Burton & Davis, 1996; Davis & Broadhead, 2007; Davis & Burton, 1991), you can create developmentally appropriate lesson plans and assess movement ability. In general, a task analysis is exactly what it sounds like—an analysis of how a particular task or skill is accomplished, focusing on critical components that influence movement. This analysis is usually performed by a teacher, therapist, or coach who is interested in developing motor proficiency in children performing the task or skill. Once a task analysis is developed, it can be used as a guide to help advance motor performance in that task in small, sequential steps.

When someone uses traditional task analysis to teach or coach, he compares the movement pattern of an individual with the correct form; in that way, traditional task analysis provides an error model. Each person moves somewhere on the continuum of incorrect to correct. The instructor teaches skills by interceding in the production of the skill wherever it deviates from the ideal performance and correcting that portion of the movement.

What could be improved in this approach to teaching movement skills? For one thing, the traditional task analysis doesn't account for the different individual constraints each person might have. Second, no real consideration is given to the ways in which the environmental and task constraints might act in conjunction with individual constraints. Ecological task analysis, in contrast, does both of these things. The term *ecological* is a nod to the theoretical overview from which it was developed, the ecological perspective (see chapter 2). As we have discussed throughout this text, the ecological perspective acknowledges that action does not happen in a vacuum; rather, movement is influenced by the mover's environment as well as the goals and rules of the task. Ecological task analysis acknowledges the confluence of constraints and uses them to the advantage of the teacher or coach so that a developmentally appropriate, or skill level appropriate, challenge can be provided to students (Newell & Jordan, 2007). Furthermore, each person moves on a developmental continuum, which enhances the current ability of the performer rather than labels it as correct or incorrect.

Creating a Developmentally Appropriate Ecological Task Analysis

Burton and Davis (1996) outline four steps involved in creating an ecological task analysis. The initial step involves establishing the task goal through structuring the environmental constraints. Next, the movement educator should allow the mover to solve the movement task in a variety of ways. In other words, don't provide one "solution" to the movement task (e.g., "Throw like this"); instead, let the mover pick from a variety of available movements. In the next step, which comes into play after the individual moves, the educator manipulates the mover, environment, or task in a way that allows more proficient movement to emerge. Finally, the movement educator should provide instruction to assist in a more proficient performance.

What does a first-time teacher who has never attempted to make a constraints-based task analysis do? Here is a practical method of working through the process using a constraints perspective. Essentially, teaching any given skill involves three steps. Begin by considering the most important individual constraints related to that skill. Of course, there may be many, but try to narrow the list to the two or three that seem most important or influential. Consider the skill of kicking a ball. Three important individual constraints include balance (an individual must balance on one foot while striking the ball with the other), coordination (an individual must sequence and time the action within and between legs), and strength (an individual must strike the ball with sufficient power). Now consider ways to change the environment or task to make the skill easier or more difficult in relation to the individual constraints. This is the basis of the constraints-based task analysis. If coordination is an important individual constraint to kicking, what changes can be made to the task to make it easier or more difficult? How about changing the movement of the ball? Kicking a stationary ball is easier, and kicking a moving ball is more difficult. This change in task constraint is also related to balance. To account for strength, changing the distance to be kicked changes the individual–task constraint interaction.

To develop an ecological task analysis, systematically scale environmental and task constraints to accommodate individual constraints in a developmentally appropriate manner. To summarize, the process is as follows:

1. Pick out a skill or task to teach.
2. Determine the individual constraints that are most important for this skill.
3. Pick several environmental or task constraints for this particular task that can be manipulated in relation to each individual constraint.
4. For each environmental or task constraint, determine a practical range (from easy to hard) for the learner. When scaling, keep in mind that small changes in a constraint can lead to large changes in performance.

The finished product is an ecological task analysis for a particular skill (figures 18.7 and 18.8). There are two ways to use your task analysis. First, you can use it to structure lesson plans or teaching progressions. If an individual or group has difficulty with the task as initially designed, the task analysis suggests changes in task and environmental constraints to make the challenge more appropriate. As individuals progress in skill level within a particular profile, the task analysis suggests ways to make the task more difficult by scaling up one or more of the constraints. This keeps the task interesting, rewarding, and challenging for learners. Individuals are more likely to succeed when a new challenge is slightly more difficult than what they can achieve easily, so it is best to be conservative in the number of constraints made more difficult at any one time. Building success on success through small steps in difficulty contributes to confidence. Varying combinations of constraints also creates many practice activities, which keeps the learning process interesting and challenging.

How do the model of constraints and ecological task analysis relate to one another? Imagine that the columns of a task analysis chart represent various constraints and show how each constraint could be scaled for a particular individual or group of individuals with a common characteristic. Figure 18.9 illustrates this relationship. The constraints placed on the hexagonal model can be entered as column headings on a task analysis chart. The easiest relevant level of a

Factors	Size of the object being thrown	Distance object must be thrown	Weight of the object being thrown	Accuracy required of the throw	Speed at which target being thrown at is moving	Acceleration and deceleration characteristics of the target being thrown at	Direction in which target being thrown at is moving
Levels: Simple	Small	Short	Light	None	Stationary	No movement	No movement
			Moderately light	Little	Slow	Steady speed	Left to right of thrower
							Right to left of thrower
	Medium	Medium					
				Moderate	Moderate	Decelerating	Toward thrower
Complex	Large	Long	Heavy	Much	Fast	Accelerating	Away from thrower

FIGURE 18.7 General task analysis for throwing behavior.
Reprinted by permission from Herkowitz (1978, pg. 141).

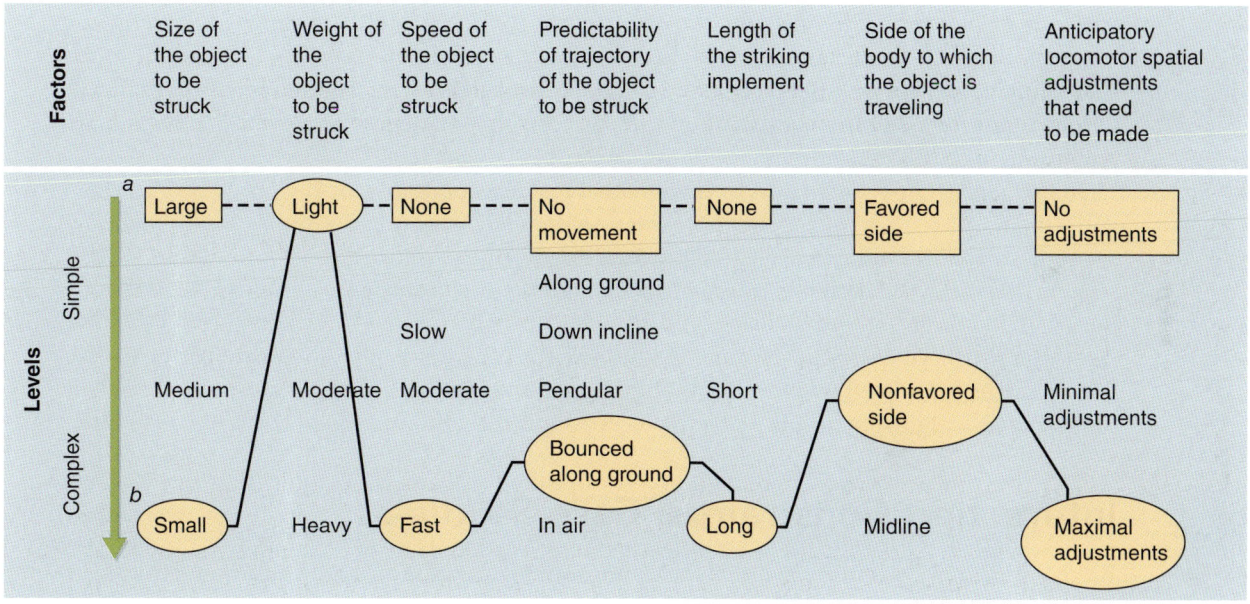

FIGURE 18.8 General task analysis for striking behavior. *(a)* Profile of a general task analysis for a relatively simple striking task (dotted line). *(b)* Profile of a general task analysis for a relatively complex striking task (solid line).
Reprinted by permission from Herkowitz (1978, pg. 149).

constraint can be written at the top of the column, the most difficult relevant level at the bottom of the column, and intermediate levels in between. The task analysis chart helps an individual identify changes to the constraints that scale to the other constraints so that the desired movement outcome arises from their interaction.

The ecological task analysis also provides a way to standardize a test environment so performers can easily be compared with each other (or with themselves on different occasions). In this case, select a particular profile and set up an assessment environment accordingly. Using these

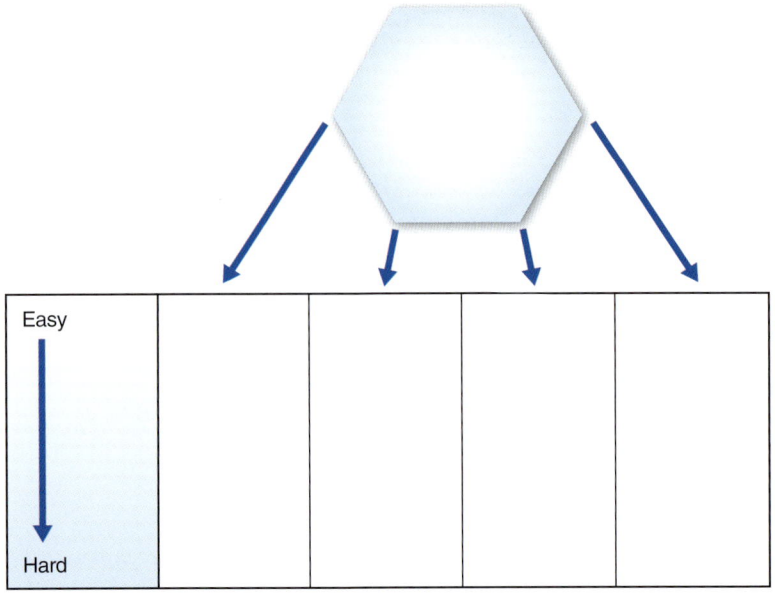

FIGURE 18.9 A hexagonal model of constraints can be converted to an ecological task analysis table by using the constraints as column headings. The levels along the continuum of change for each constraint are then entered into the table in order from easy (at the top of the column) to difficult (at the bottom of the column).

standard task and environmental constraints, assess students' developmental levels for that skill within that profile. This approach allows for a more systematic assessment between students and over a set period of time.

In many programs, instructors or therapists are held accountable for the progress of learners and patients. Task analysis charts can provide a written record of how an initial developmentally appropriate task was progressively made more difficult. It can indicate the combination of constraints that yielded a successful performance outcome, perhaps to some criterion such as four out of five attempts, at a particular point in time. If instructors and therapists prepare the task analysis chart ahead of time, they can quickly circle the constraints for a successful performance. Charts can be completed for individuals or groups and can both suggest an adjustment based on performance and document the performance for a specific combination of levels of constraints.

Interacting Constraints: Case Studies

By manipulating constraints we can make immediate, short-term, and long-term changes in motor development and behavior. Often, knowing what changes to make is simply an issue of understanding the varying degrees of influence exerted by different constraints. Sometimes, even small changes in one constraint will allow a wide variety of behaviors to emerge. For example, providing an infant with support can account for both strength and posture, allowing for many different upright movements. With this in mind, read the following case studies; try to determine the most important constraints and what you can change to allow certain motor behaviors to appear. After identifying the constraints to be changed, analyze how these constraints interact with one another (if they do) and whether the interaction helps achieve the goal or works against it.

Case Study A: Gender Typing of Physical Activities

You are the movement educator for a class of 25 fourth graders. During your first class, you attempt to teach gymnastic skills. The boys in your class show an obvious dislike for the activities, and one exclaims, "Gymnastics is for girls!" What can you do to modify the task so the children learn the skills you want but are not put off by gender typing?

Case Study B: Older Adults

AB is a 76-year-old man who recently lost his spouse of 45 years. He lives in a suburb of a large metropolitan area. Since the death of his spouse, AB has not gone on the daily strolls they used to take together. He is losing strength and flexibility, and his arthritis is flaring up. How can you reintroduce physical activity into AB's life?

Case Study C: Teaching Fundamental Motor Skills

You are coaching an under-10-year-old soccer team. You've noticed a wide diversity of individual constraints (height, weight, skill level) among the players. How can you make practices challenging for all the players?

Case Study D: Cerebral Palsy

You are teaching an 11th-grade physical education class. In your class is an individual with cerebral palsy. He can walk, but he has some muscle spasticity and rigidity. You would like your class to participate in an activity or game in which everyone can be equally involved without having to change or modify the rules. What kind of activity could you play?

Case Study E: Middle-Aged Adults

CW is a 50-year-old woman who plays doubles on a tennis team. Women from their 20s to their 60s participate in this tennis program. CW weighs about 15 pounds more than she did in her 20s, but she does walk for a half hour each day. CW's team has one match per week and one practice per week for 8 months of the year. The top teams qualify for a series of playoffs—district, sectional, then national—in which the winning team advances to the next level. CW's team lost in the semifinals of the sectional tournament last year and has established the goal of getting to and winning the finals of the sectional tournament for the upcoming year. CW wants to be a major contributor to the team's success. What constraints could prove to be a challenge to CW's success, and how would you recommend that she address those constraints?

Case Study F: Age Grouping

MF was born at the end of August, just before the cutoff date for her parents to be able to delay school entry for a year. Therefore, she is the youngest girl in her elementary school class. A youth sports program is available at the school, and children participate with their grade level. This means MF is one of the youngest players on her team every year and for every sport. MF listens to her coach and works hard in practices, but she doesn't have the coordination required to be among the better performers in her elementary school years. If you were MF's parent, how would you talk with her about her youth sports experiences? On which constraints would your conversation center?

Case Study G: Grade-Level Expectations

You are a physical education teacher about to start a new school year, and you have just received documents identifying the grade-level expectations for each of the six levels of physical education classes you teach. Grade-level expectations indicate what skills or knowledge a student should have upon completing a particular grade. What tools could you use to ensure that your students progress to the expected level by the end of the school year? A sample grade-level expectation for the fifth grade is "Demonstrate ability to follow rules, cooperate with teammates, and apply a simple strategy in a variety of sport-specific lead-up games." How could you use the tools you identified to plan a sequence of activities over the year to achieve this expectation?

Web Study Guide Apply the model of constraints to examine the interaction of players in a soccer game in Lab Activity 18.2, Examining Constraints in a Context: Soccer, in the web study guide.

Summary and Synthesis

The challenge confronting motor developmentalists, teachers, coaches, and parents is to tailor goals and expectations to individual capabilities and characteristics. Optimal motor development is likely related to the degree to which practice opportunities and insightful instruction are matched with individual constraints. It is complex and time consuming to individualize motor development goals and instruction in most institutional settings, but findings from motor development research at various stages of the life span point in this direction. Continued research and observation of motor development will undoubtedly yield a better understanding of developmental processes, but our task remains to find ways of using our knowledge to foster optimal motor development in every individual.

Reinforcing What You Have Learned About Constraints

TAKE A SECOND LOOK

The Paralympic Games are an excellent example of a program that changes task and environmental constraints in conjunction with individual structural constraints to provide an appropriate challenge for those who would like to compete. Individuals with disabilities can be tested at the highest level by competing with and against like individuals. People with disabilities affecting their locomotion can play wheelchair basketball or sitting volleyball. Individuals with the use of only one arm can hold a bowstring with their teeth to compete in archery. An important realization for all of us is that although Paralympic athletes might have obvious and permanent disabilities, all of us have individual characteristics that can influence our ability to move in a certain way. Those characteristics might exist because we are still growing, because we are aging, because we are injured, because we lack confidence in our ability, or because we don't have much experience with an activity. Whatever the reason, adapting environmental and task constraints to those individual constraints can allow us to move in a way that is enjoyable and healthful.

TEST YOUR KNOWLEDGE

1. How might a teacher or coach use either a model of constraints or an ecological task analysis to design a sequence of lesson or practice plans?
2. How might a teacher or community program leader use a model of constraints or an ecological task analysis to allow for the involvement of a disabled child in a group activity?
3. Teachers are charged with providing a challenging learning task for students whose physical growth and maturation status, level of coordination, and experience with a task vary. How could a teacher use a model of constraints to plan four stations of varying difficulty levels for the class?

LEARNING EXERCISES

The case studies in the Interacting Constraints: Case Studies section of this chapter serve as the learning exercises for chapter 18.

APPENDIX: Skinfold, Body Mass Index, and Head Circumference Charts

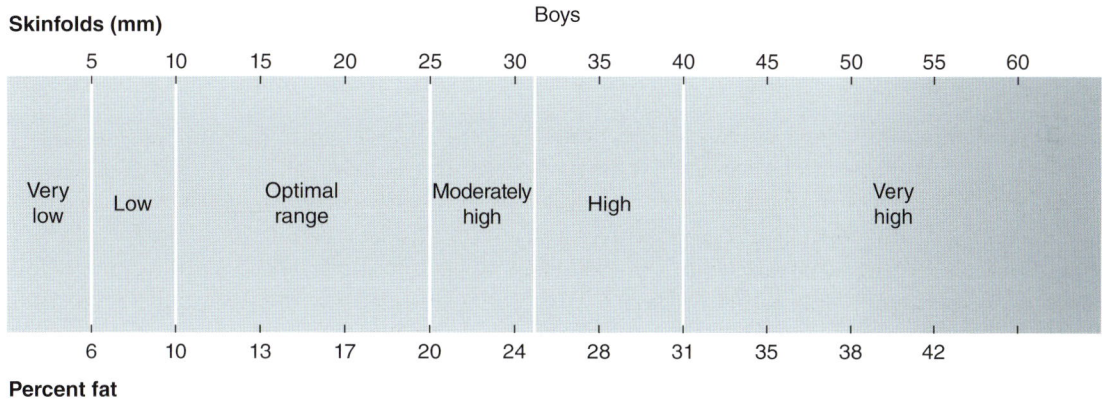

FIGURE A.1 Calf plus triceps skinfolds: boys.

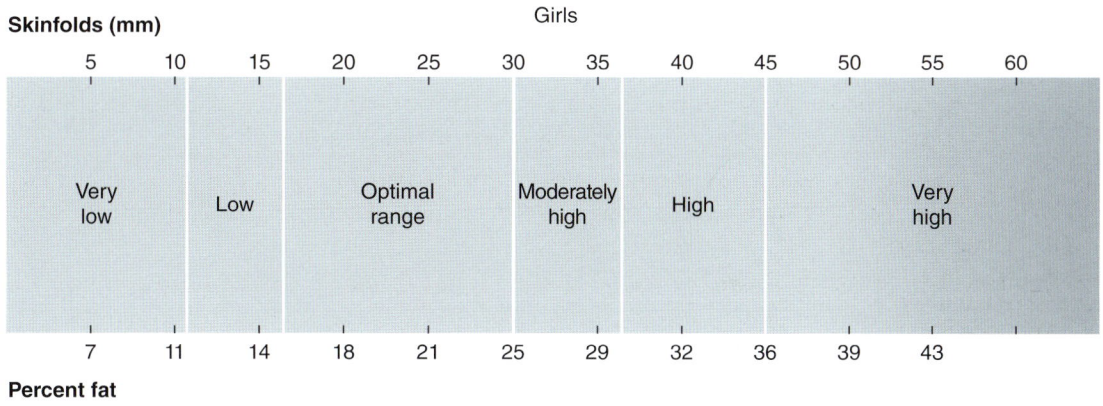

FIGURE A.2 Calf plus triceps skinfolds: girls.

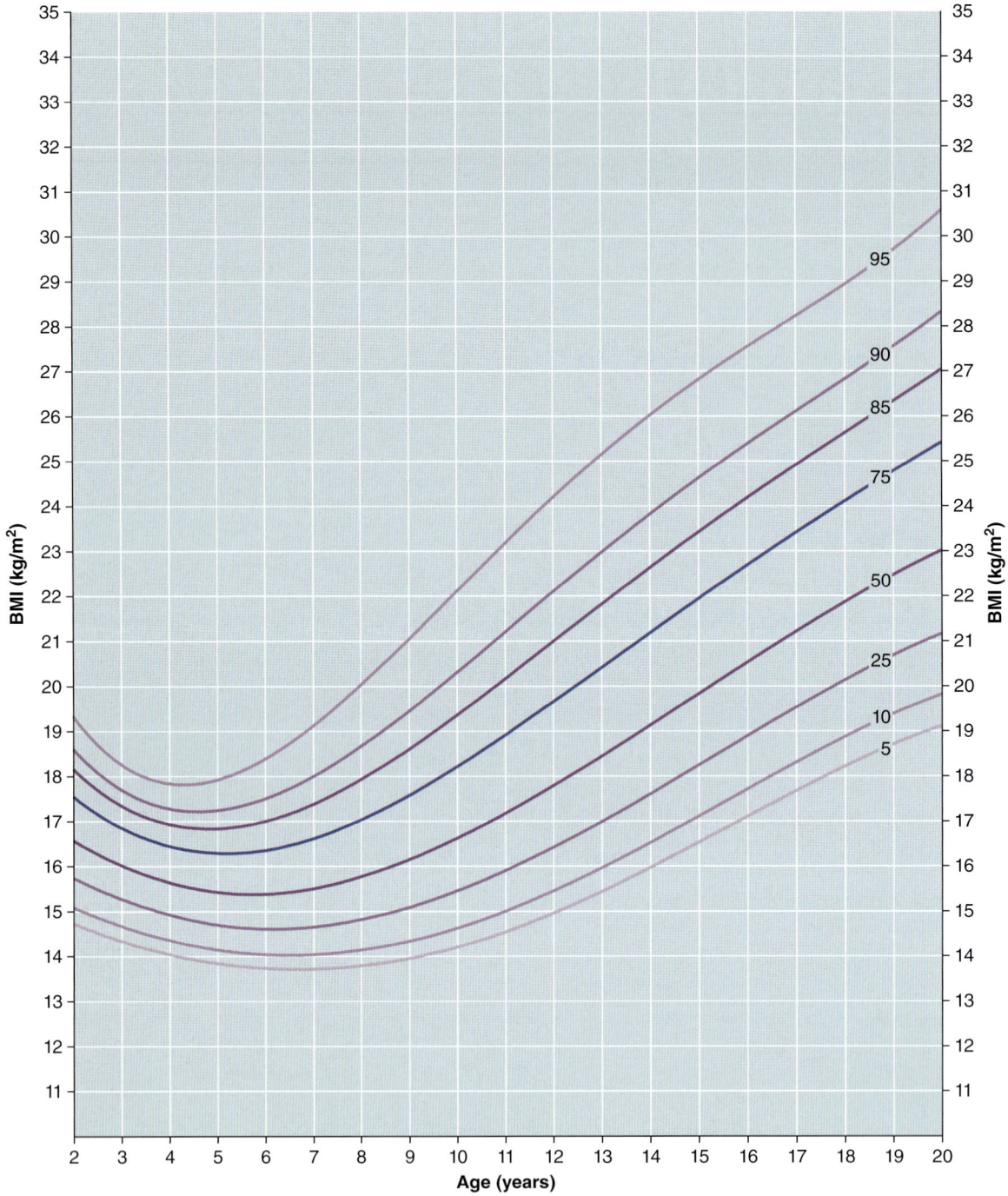

FIGURE A.3A Body mass index for age percentiles for boys aged 2 to 20 years.

Adapted from National Center for Health Statistics in collaboration with the National Center for Chronic Disease Prevention and Health Promotion (2000).

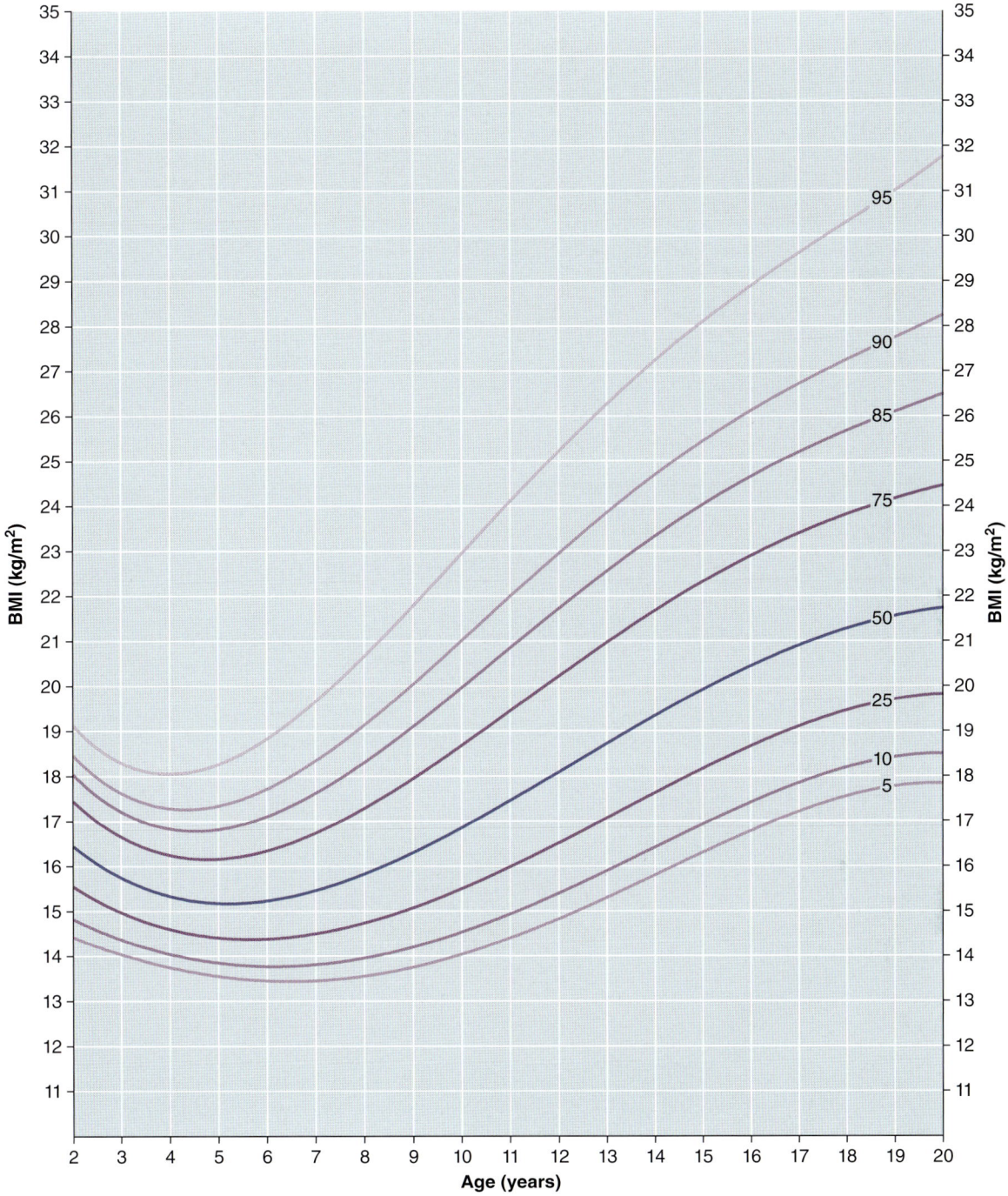

FIGURE A.3B Body mass index for age percentiles for girls aged 2 to 20 years.
Adapted from CDC 2000.

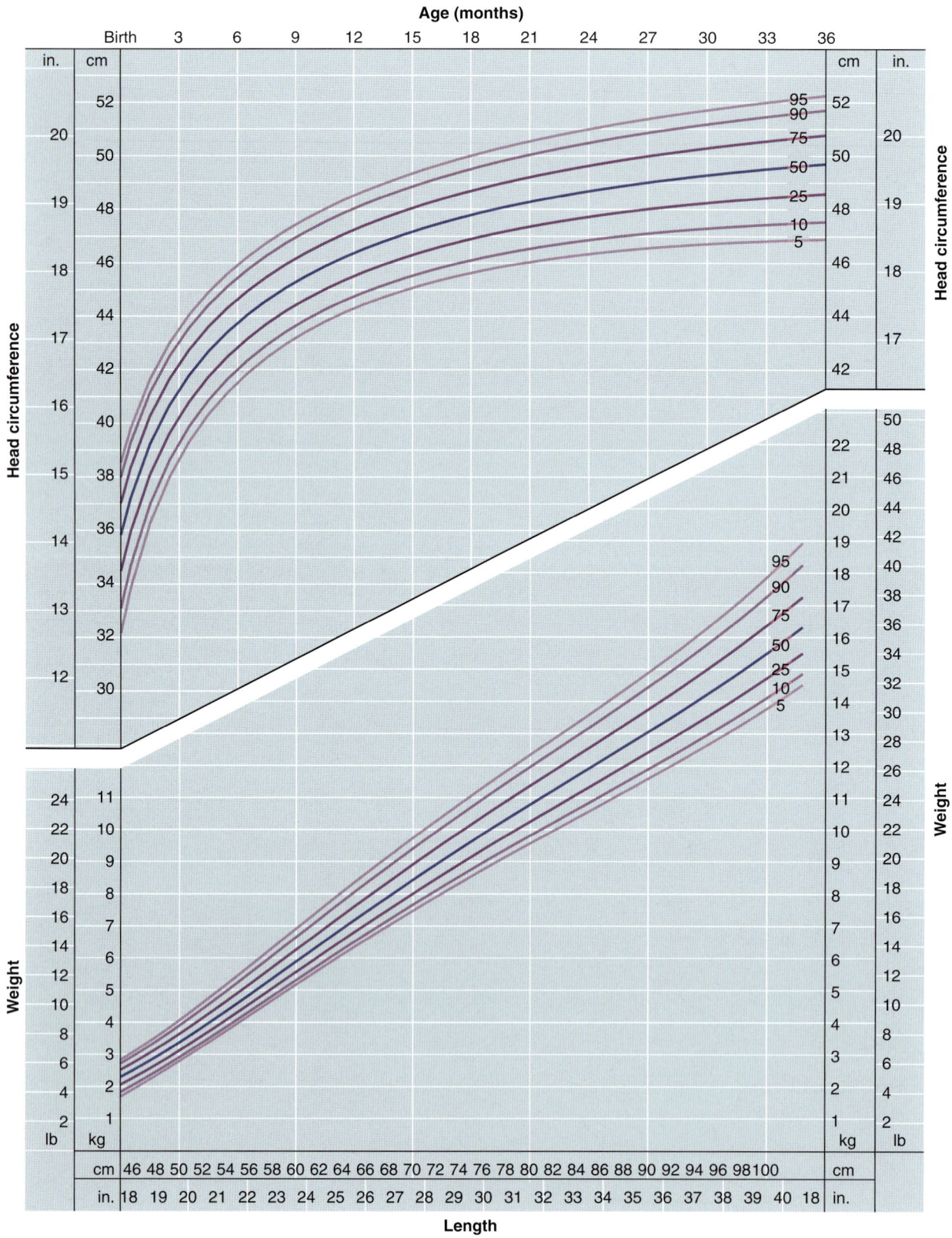

FIGURE A.4A Head circumference-for-age and weight-for-length percentiles for boys, birth to 36 months.
Adapted from CDC 2000.

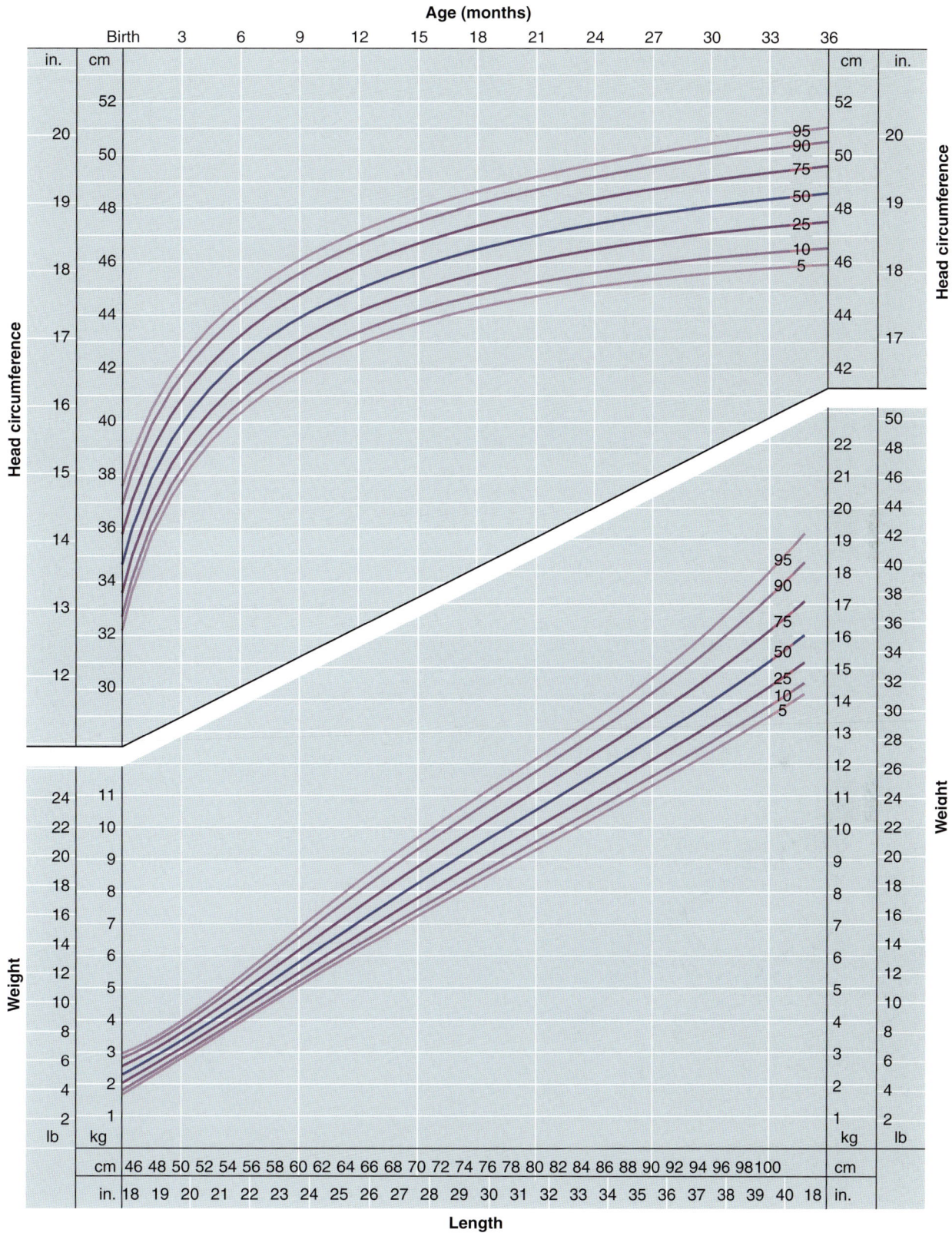

FIGURE A.4B Head circumference-for-age and weight-for-length percentiles for girls, birth to 36 months.
Adapted from CDC 2000.

REFERENCES

Abernethy, B., Wood, J.M., & Parks, S. (1999). Can the anticipatory skills of experts be learned by novices? *Research Quarterly for Exercise and Sport, 70,* 313–318.

Acosta, R.V., & Carpenter, L.J. (2014). Women in intercollegiate sport: A longitudinal, national study. Thirty-seven year update (1977–2014). Retrieved from www.acostacarpenter.org

Adams, F.H. (1973). Factors affecting the working capacity of children and adolescents. In G.L. Rarick (Ed.), *Physical activity: Human growth and development* (pp. 80–96). New York, NY: Academic Press.

Adolph, K. (1997). Learning in the development of infant locomotion. *Monographs of the Society for Research in Child Development, 62*(3), 1–162.

Adolph, K.E. (2018). Motor development. In M. Bornstein & M. Arterberry (Eds.). *The SAGE encyclopedia of lifespan human development* (pp. 1450–1453). Thousand Oaks, CA: Sage.

Adolph, K., Cole, W., Komati, M., Garciaguirre, J., Badaly, D., Lingeman, J., et al. (2012). How do you learn to walk? Thousands of steps and dozens of falls per day. *Psychological Science, 23*(11), 1387–1394. doi:10.1177/0956797612446346

Adolph, K., Vereijken, B., & Shrout, P.E. (2003). What changes in infant walking and why. *Child Development, 74*(2), 475–497.

Adolph, K.E., Cole, W.G., & Vereijken, B. (2015). Intra-individual variability in the development of motor skills in childhood. In M. Diehl, K. Hooker, & M. Sliwinski (Eds.), *Handbook of intra-individual variability across the lifespan* (pp. 59–83). New York, NY: Routledge/Taylor & Francis Group.

Adolph, K.E., Eppler, M.A., & Gibson, E.J. (1993). Crawling versus walking in infants' perception of affordances for locomotion over sloping surfaces. *Child Development, 64,* 1158–1174.

Adolph, K.E., & Franchak, J.M. (2017). The development of motor behavior. *WIREs Cognitive Science, 8,* e1430. doi:10.1002/wcs.1430

Adolph, K.E., & Hoch, J.E. (2019). Motor development: Embodied, embedded, enculturated, and enabling. *Annual Review of Psychology, 70,* 141-164.

Adolph, K.E., Rachwani, J., & Hoch, J.E. (2018). Motor and physical development: Locomotion. In *Neuroscience and biobehavioral psychology reference module* (pp. 1-17). Elsevier. Retrieved from https://www.elsevier.com/solutions/sciencedirect/content/reference-modules/neuroscience-and-biobehavioral-psychology-module

Adolph, K.E., & Robinson, S.R. (2013). The road to walking: What learning to walk tells us about development. In P. Zelazo (Ed.), *Oxford handbook of developmental psychology* (Vol. 1, pp. 403–443). New York, NY: Oxford University Press.

Adolph, K.E., & Robinson, S.R. (2015). Motor development. In R.M. Lerner (Series Eds.) & L. Liben & U. Muller (Vol. Eds), *Handbook of child psychology and developmental science: Vol. 2: Cognitive processes* (7th ed., pp. 114–157). New York, NY: Wiley.

Adolph, K.E., & Tamis-LeMonda, C.S. (2014). The costs and benefits of development: The transition from crawling to walking. *Child Development Perspectives, 8,* 187–192.

Adrian, M.J. (1982, April). *Maintaining movement capabilities in advanced years.* Paper presented at the American Alliance for Health, Physical Education, Recreation and Dance, Houston.

Alfred, P.E., & Rice, V.J. (2012). Age differences in simple and procedural reaction time among healthy military personnel. *Proceedings of the Human Factors and Ergonomics Society Annual Meeting, 56,* 1809–1813.

Allen, K.A., Bredero, B., Van Damme, T., Ulrich, D.D., & Simons, J. (2017). Test of Gross Motor Development-3 (TGMD-3) with the use of visual supports for children with autism spectrum disorder: Validity and reliability. *Journal of Autism and Developmental Disorders, 47,* 813. doi:10.1007/s10803-016-3005-0

Allen, M., & Alexander, G. (1994). Screening for cerebral palsy in preterm infants: Delay criteria for motor milestone attainment. *Journal of Perinatology, 14,* 190–193.

Alnaqeeb, M.A., Al-Zaid, N.S., & Goldspink, G. (1984). Connective tissue changes and physical properties of developing and aging skeletal muscle. *Journal of Anatomy, 189*(4), 677–689.

American Alliance for Health, Physical Education, Recreation and Dance. (1988). *Physical best.* Reston, VA: Author.

Ames, C. (1992). Classroom: Goals, structures, and student motivation. *Journal of Educational Psychology, 84,* 409–414.

Anderson, D.I., Magill, R.A., Sekiya, H., & Ryan, G. (2005). Support for an explanation of the guidance effect in motor skill learning. *Journal of Motor Behavior, 37*(3), 231–238.

Aniansson, A., Hedberg, M., Henning, G.B., & Grimby, G. (1986). Muscle morphology, enzymatic activity and muscle strength in elderly men: A follow-up study. *Muscle and Nerve, 9,* 585–591.

Arabadjis, P.G., Heffner, R.R., & Pendergast, D.R. (1990). Morphologic and functional alterations in aging rat muscle. *Journal of Neuropathology and Experimental Neurology, 49,* 600–609.

Arain, M., Haque, M., Johal, L., Mathur, P., Nel, W., Rais, A., et al. (2013). Maturation of the adolescent brain. *Neuropsychiatric Disease and Treatment, 9,* 449–461. doi:10.2147/NDT.S39776

Armstrong, N., & Barker, A.R. (2011). Endurance training and elite young athletes. In M. Armstrong & A.M. McManus (Eds.), *The elite young athlete* (pp. 59–83). Basel: Karger.

Armstrong, N., & McManus, A.M. (Eds.) (2011). *The elite young athlete.* Basel: Karger.

Armstrong, N., & McNarry, M. (2016). Aerobic fitness and trainability in healthy youth: Gaps in our knowledge. *Pediatric Exercise Science, 28,* 171–177. doi:10.1123/pes.2015-0251

Armstrong, N., & Welsman, J.R. (2007). Aerobic fitness: What are we measuring? *Medicine and Sport Science, 50,* 5–25.

Armstrong, N., Welsman, J.R., & Kirby, B.J. (1997). Performance on the Wingate Anaerobic Test and maturation. *Pediatric Exercise Science, 9,* 253–261.

Aruin, A.S., Kanekar, N., Lee, Y.-J., & Ganesan, M. (2015). Enhancement of anticipatory postural adjustments in older adults as a result of a single session of ball throwing exercise. *Experimental Brain Research, 233,* 649–655. doi:10.1007/s00221-014-4144-1

Asano, K., Ogawa, S., & Furuta, Y. (1978). Aerobic work capacity in middle- and old-aged runners. In F. Landry & W.A.R. Orban (Eds.), *Proceedings of the International Congress of Physical Activity Sciences: Vol. 4. Exercise physiology.* Quebec: Symposia Specialists.

Ashmead, D.H., Clifton, R.K., & Perris, E.E. (1987). Precision of auditory localization in human infants. *Developmental Psychology, 23*(5), 641–647.

Asikainen, T.M., Suni, J.H., Pasanen, M.E., Oja, P., Rinne, M.B., Miilunpalo, S.I., et al. (2006). Effect of brisk walking in 1 or 2 daily bouts and moderate resistance training on lower-extremity muscle strength, balance, and walking performance in women who recently went through menopause: A randomized, controlled trial. *Physical Therapy, 86,* 912–923.

Aslin, R.N., & Shea, S.L. (1990). Velocity thresholds in human infants: Implications for the perception of motion. *Developmental Psychology, 26*(4), 589–598.

Asmussen, E. (1973). Growth in muscular strength and power. In G.L. Rarick (Ed.), *Physical activity: Human growth and development* (pp. 60–79). New York, NY: Academic Press.

Asmussen, E., & Heeboll-Nielsen, K. (1955). A dimensional analysis of physical performance and growth in boys. *Journal of Applied Physiology, 7,* 593–603.

Asmussen, E., & Heeboll-Nielsen, K. (1956). Physical performance and growth in children: Influence of sex, age, and intelligence. *Journal of Applied Physiology, 8,* 371–380.

Assaiante, C. (1998). Development of locomotor balance control in healthy children. *Neuroscience and Biobehavioral Reviews, 22*(4), 527–532.

Assaiante, C., & Amblard, B. (1995). An ontogenetic model for the sensorimotor organization of balance control in humans. *Human Movement Science, 14,* 13–43.

Assaiante, C., Woollacott, M., & Amblard, B. (2000). Development of postural adjustment during gait initiation: Kinematic and EMG analysis. *Journal of Motor Behavior, 32,* 211–226.

Assibey-Mensah, G. (1998). Role models and youth development: Evidence and lessons from the perceptions of African-American male youth. *Western Journal of Black Studies, 21,* 242–252.

Åstrand, P. (1976). The child in sport and physical activity: Physiology. In J.G. Albinson & G.M. Andrew (Eds.), *Child in sport and physical activity* (pp. 19–33). Baltimore, MD: University Park Press.

Åstrand, P.O., & Rodahl, K. (1986). *Textbook of work physiology.* New York, NY: McGraw-Hill.

Atkinson, J., & Braddick, O. (1981). Acuity, contrast sensitivity, and accommodation in infancy. In R. Aslin, J. Alberts, & M. Peterson (Eds.), *Development of perception* (pp. 245–277). New York, NY: Academic Press.

Atun-Einy, O., Berger, S.E., Ducz, J., & Sher, A. (2014). Strength of infants' bimanual reaching patterns is related to the onset of upright locomotion. *Infancy, 19,* 82–102. doi:10/1111/infa.12030

Auster, C.J., & Mansbach, C.S. (2012). The gender marketing of toys: An analysis of color and type of toy on the Disney store website. *Sex Roles, 67*(7/8), 375–388. doi:10.1007/s11199-012-0177-8.

Ay, L., Hokken-Koelega, A.C.S., Mook-Kanamori, D.O., Hofman, A., Moll, H.A., Mackenbach, J.P., et al. (2008). Tracking and determinants of subcutaneous fat mass in early childhood: The Generation R study. *International Journal of Obesity, 32,* 1050–1059.

Ay, L., Jaddoe, V.W.V., Hofman, A., Moll, H.A., Raat, H., Steegers, E.A.P., et al. (2011). Foetal and postnatal growth and bone mass at 6 months: The Generation R study. *Clinical Endocrinology, 74,* 181–190.

Ayres, A.J. (1966). *Southern California sensory-motor integration tests.* Los Angeles, CA: Western Psychological Services.

Ayres, A.J. (1969). *Southern California perceptual-motor tests.* Los Angeles, CA: Western Psychological Services.

Ayres, A.J. (1972). *Southern California sensory-motor integration tests manual.* Los Angeles, CA: Western Psychological Services.

Babik, I., Galloway, J.C., & Lobo, M.A. (2017). Infants Born Preterm Demonstrate Impaired Exploration of Their Bodies and Surfaces Throughout the First 2 Years of Life. *Physical therapy, 97*(9), 915-925.

Bachman, J.C. (1961). Motor learning and performance as related to age and sex in two measures of balance coordination. *Research Quarterly, 32,* 123–137.

Baird, A.A., Gruber, S.A., Fein, D.A., Maas, L.C., Steingard, R.J., Renshaw, P.F., et al. (1999). Functional magnetic resonance imaging of facial affect recognition in children and adolescents. *Journal of the American Academy of Child and Adolescent Psychiatry, 38*(2):195–199.

Baldwin, K.M. (1984). Muscle development: Neonatal to adult. In R.L. Terjung (Ed.), *Exercise and sport science reviews* (Vol. 12, pp. 1–19). Lexington, MA: Collamore.

Bandeira, P.F.R., Santayana de Souza, M., Zanella, L.W., & Valentini, N.C. (2017). Impact of motor interventions oriented by mastery motivational climate in fundamental motor skills of children: A systematic review. *Motricidade, 13*(Supl. 1), 50–61.

Bandura, A. (1986). *Social foundations of thought and action: A social cognitive theory.* Englewood Cliffs, NJ: Prentice Hall.

Banerjee, R., & Lintern, V. (2000). Boys will be boys: The effect of social evaluation concerns on gender-typing. *Social Develop-*

ment, 9(3), 397–408.

Bar-Or, O. (1983). *Pediatric sports medicine for the practitioner.* New York, NY: Springer-Verlag.

Bar-Or, O. (1993). Physical activity and physical training in childhood obesity. *Journal of Sports Medicine and Physical Fitness, 33*(4), 323–329.

Bar-Or, O., Shephard, R.J., & Allen, C.L. (1971). Cardiac output of 10- to 13-year-old boys and girls during submaximal exercise. *Journal of Applied Physiology, 30,* 219–223.

Bard, C., Fleury, M., Carriere, L., & Bellec, J. (1981). Components of the coincidence-anticipation behavior of children aged 6 to 11 years. *Perceptual and Motor Skills, 52,* 547–556.

Bard, C., Fleury, M., & Gagnon, M. (1990). Coincidence-anticipation timing: An age-related perspective. In C. Bard, M. Fleury, & L. Hay (Eds.), *Development of eye-hand coordination across the life span* (pp. 283–305). Columbia: University of South Carolina Press.

Bardid, F., De Meester, A., Tallir, I., Cardon, G., Lenoir, M., & Haerens, L. (2016). Configurations of actual and perceived motor competence among children: Associations with motivation for sports and global self-worth. *Human Movement Science, 50,* 1–9.

Bardid, F., Lenoir, M., Huyben, F., De Martelaer, K., Seghers, J., Goodway, J.C., & Deconinck, F.J.A. (2017). The effectiveness of a community-based fundamental motor skill intervention in children aged 3-8 years: Results of the "Multimove for Kids" project. *Journal of Science and Medicine in Sport, 20,* 184–189. doi:10.1016/j.jsams.2016.07.005

Barela, J.A., Jeka, J.J., & Clark, J.E. (1999). The use of somatosensory information during the acquisition of independent upright stance. *Infant Behavior and Development, 22*(1), 87–102.

Barnett, L.M., Lubans, D., Timperio, A., Salmon, J., & Ridgers, N.D. (2018). What is the contribution of actual motor skill, fitness, and physical activity to children's self-perception of motor competence? *Journal of Motor Learning and Development, 6,* S461-S473, 1–21. doi:10.1123/jmld.2016-0076

Barnett, L.M., Morgan, P.J., van Beurden, E., & Beard, J.R. (2008). Perceived sports competence mediates the relationship between childhood motor skill proficiency and adolescent physical activity and fitness: A longitudinal assessment. *International Journal of Behavioral Nutrition and Physical Activity, 5,* 40.

Barnett, L.M., Ridgers, N.D., & Salmon, J. (2015). Associations between young children's perceived and actual ball skill competence and physical activity. *Journal of Science and Medicine in Sport, 18*(2), 167–171.

Barnett, L.M., Ridgers, N.D., Zask, A., & Salmon, J. (2015). Face validity and reliability of a pictorial instrument for assessing fundamental movement skill perceived competence in young children. *Journal of Science and Medicine in Sport, 18*(1), 98–102. doi:10.1016/j.jsams.2013.12.004

Barnett, L.M., Robinson, L.E., Webster, E.K., & Ridgers, N.D. (2015). Reliability of the Pictorial Scale of Perceived Movement Skill Competence in 2 diverse samples of young children. *Journal of Physical Activity and Health, 12*(8), 1045–1051. doi:10.1123/jpah.2014-0141

Barnett, L.M., van Beurden, E., Morgan, P.J., Brooks, L.O., & Beard, J.R. (2008). Does childhood motor skill proficiency predict adolescent fitness? *Medicine and Science in Sports and Exercise, 40,* 2137–2144.

Barnett, L.M., Van Beurden, E., Morgan, P.J., Brooks, L.O., & Beard, J.R. (2009). Childhood motor skill proficiency as a predictor of adolescent physical activity. *Journal of adolescent health, 44*(3), 252-259.

Barnett, L.M., Vazou, S., Abbott, G., Bowe, S.J., Robinson, L.E., Ridgers, N.D., & Salmon, J. (2016). Construct validity of the Pictorial Scale of Perceived Movement Skill Competence. *Psychology of Sport and Exercise, 22,* 294–302.

Barnett, L.M., Zask, A., Rose, L., Hughes, D., & Adams, J. (2015). Three-year follow-up of an early childhood intervention: What about physical activity and weight status? *Journal of Physical Activity and Health, 12,* 319–321. doi:10.1123/jpah.2013-0419

Barnett, L.M., Lubans, D.R., Timpeiro, A., Salmon, J., & Ridgers, N.D. (2018) What is the Contribution of Actual Motor Skill, Fitness, and Physical Activity to Children's Self-Perception of Motor Competence? *Journal of Motor Learning and Development,* 6 Issue: s2 Pages:S461-S473 doi: 10.1123/jmld.2016-0076

Barrett, K.R. (1979). Observation for teaching and coaching. *Journal of Physical Education and Recreation, 50,* 23–25.

Barrett, T.M., Davis, E.F., & Needham, A. (2007). Learning about tools in infancy. *Developmental Psychology, 43,* 352–368.

Barrett, U., & Harrison, D. (2002). Comparing muscle function of children and adults: Effects of scaling for muscle size. *Pediatric Exercise Science, 14,* 369–376.

Barsch, R.H. (1965). *Achieving perceptual-motor efficiency.* Seattle: Special Child.

Bartlett, D. (1997). Primitive reflexes and early motor development. *Journal of Developmental and Behavioral Pediatrics, 18,* 151–157.

Bayley, N. (1936). The development of motor abilities during the first three years. *Monographs of the Society for Research in Child Development, 1*(1), 1–26.

Bayley, N. (1969). *Manual for the Bayley Scales of Infant Development.* New York, NY: Psychological Corp.

Beck, M. (1966). *The path of the center of gravity during running in boys grades one to six.* Unpublished doctoral dissertation, University of Wisconsin, Madison.

Behm, D.G., Young, J.D., Whitten, J.H., Reid, J.C., Quigley, P.J., Low, J. . . . Granacher, U. (2017). Effectiveness of traditional strength vs. power training on muscle strength, power and speed with youth: A systematic review and meta-analysis. *Frontiers in Physiology, 8,* 423. DOI: 10.3389/fphys.2017.00423

Behrman, A.L., Vander Linden, D.W., & Cauraugh, J.H. (1992). Relative frequency knowledge of results: Older adults learning a force-time modulation task. *Journal of Human Movement Studies, 23,* 233–250.

Bell, R., & Hoshizaki, T. (1981). Relationships of age and sex with joint range of motion of seventeen joint actions in humans. *Canadian Journal of Applied Sport Sciences, 6,* 202–206.

Bennett, S., Button, C., Kingsbury, D., & Davids, K. (1999).

Manipulating visual informational constraints during practice enhances the acquisition of catching skill in children. *Research Quarterly for Exercise and Sport, 70*(3), 220–232.

Bergenn, V.W., Dalton, T.C., & Lipsett, L.P. (1992). Myrtle B. McGraw: A growth scientist. *Developmental Psychology, 28,* 381–395.

Bergstrom, B. (1973). Morphology of the vestibular nerve: II. The number of myelinated vestibular nerve fibers in man at various ages. *Acta Oto-Laryngologica, 76,* 173–179.

Bernstein, N. (1967). The co-ordination and regulation of movement. Oxford, UK: Pergamon Press.

Bertenthal, B., Campos, J., & Barrett, K. (1984). Self-produced locomotion: An organizer of emotional, cognitive and social development in infancy. In R. Emde & R. Harmon (Eds.), *Continuities and discontinuities in development* (pp. 175–210). New York, NY: Plenum Press.

Bertenthal, B., & von Hofsten, C. (1998). Eye, head, and trunk control: The foundation for manual development. *Neuroscience and Biobehavioral Reviews, 22*(4), 515–520.

Bertenthal, B.I., & Bai, D.L. (1989). Infants' sensitivity to optical flow for controlling posture. *Developmental Psychology, 25,* 936–945.

Bertenthal, B.I., & Campos, J.J. (1987). New directions in the study of early experience. *Child Development, 58,* 560–567.

Bertenthal, B.I., Rose, J.L., & Bai, D.L. (1997). Perception-action coupling in the development of visual control of posture. *Journal of Experimental Psychology: Human Perception and Performance, 23*(6), 1631–1643.

Beunen, G., & Malina, R.M. (1988). Growth and physical performance relative to the timing of the adolescent spurt. *Exercise and Sport Sciences Reviews, 16,* 503–540.

Beunen, G., Malina, R.M., Ostyn, M., Renson, R., Simons, J., & Van Gerven, D. (1983). Fatness, growth and motor fitness of Belgian boys 12 through 17 years of age. *American Journal of Physical Anthropology, 59,* 387–392.

Beunen, G., Malina, R.M., Renson, R., & Van Gerven, D. (1988). *Adolescent growth and motor performance: A longitudinal analysis of Belgian boys.* Champaign, IL: Human Kinetics.

Biddle, S.J.H., & Asare, M. (2011). Physical activity and mental health in children and adolescents: A review of reviews. *British Journal of Sports Medicine, 45,* 886–895.

Bigelow, B., Tesson, G., & Lewko, J. (1996). *Learning the rules: The anatomy of children's relationships.* New York, NY: Guilford Press.

Binder, E.F., Yarasheski, K.E., Steger-May, K., Sinacore, D.R., Brown, M., Schechtman, K.B., & Holloszy, J.O. (2005). Effects of progressive resistance training on body composition in frail older adults: Results of a randomized controlled trial. *Journals of Gerontology: Series A, 20,* 1425–1431. doi:10.1093/gerona/60.11.1425

Bini, V., Celi, F., Beriolli, M.G., Bacosi, M.L., Stella, P., Giglio, P., et al. (2000). Body mass index in children and adolescents according to age and pubertal stage. *European Journal of Clinical Nutrition, 54,* 214–218.

Birch, L.L. (1976). Age trends in children's timesharing performance. *Journal of Experimental Child Psychology, 22,* 331–345.

Bird, A.M., & Williams, J.M. (1980). A developmental-attributional analysis of sex-role stereotypes for sport performance. *Developmental Psychology, 16,* 319–322.

Biro, F.M., & Kiess, W. (2016). Contemporary trends in onset and completion of puberty, gain in height and adiposity. In J.-P. Bourguignon & A-.S. Parent (Eds), *Puberty from bench to clinic* (Vol. 29, pp. 122–133). Basel, Switzerland: Karger.

Biro, F.M., Pajak, A., Wolff, M.S., Pinney, S.M., Windham, G.C., Galvez, M.P., et al. (2018). Age of menarche in a longitudinal US cohort. *Journal of Pediatric and Adolescent Gynecology, 31*(4), 339–345.

Birren, J.E. (1964). The psychology of aging in relation to development. In J.E. Birren (Ed.), *Relationships of development and aging* (pp. 99–120). Springfield, IL: Charles C Thomas.

Bisi, M.C., & Stagni, R. (2016). Development of gait motor control: What happens after a sudden increase in height during adolescence? *BioMedical Engineering OnLine, 15,* 47.

Blackwell, D.L. & Clarke, T.C. (2018). State variation in meeting the 2008 federal guidelines for both aerobic and muscle-strengthening activities through leisure-time physical activity among adults aged 18–64: United States 2010–2015. National Health Statistics Reports; no 112. Hyattsville, MD: National Center for Health Statistics

Blakemore, J.E.O., & Centers, R.E. (2005). Characteristics of boys' and girls' toys. *Sex Roles, 53,* 619–633.

Blazo, J.A., Czech, D., Carson, S., & Dees, W. (2014). A qualitative investigation of the sibling sport achievement experience. *The Sport Psychologist, 28,* 36–47. doi:10.1123/tsp.2012-0089

Blazo, J.A., & Smith, A.L. (2018). A systematic review of siblings and physical activity experiences. *International Review of Sport and Exercise Psychology, 11*(1), 122–159. doi:10.1080/1750984X.2016.1229355.

Blimkie, C.J.R. (1989). Age- and sex-associated variation in strength during childhood: Anthropometric, morphological, neurologic, biomechanical, endocrinologic, genetic, and physical activity correlates. In C.V. Gisolfi & D. R. Lamb (Eds.), *Youth, exercise, and sport* (Vol. 2, pp. 99-164). Indianapolis: Benchmark Press.

Blumenthal, J.A., Emergy, C.F., Madden, D.J., Coleman, R.E., Riddle, M.W., Schniebolk, S., et al. (1991). Effects of exercise raining on cardiorespiratory function in men and women >60 years of age. *American Journal of Cardiology, 67,* 633–639.

Boothby, J., Tungatt, M., & Townsend, A. (1981). Ceasing participation in sports activity: Reported reasons and their implication. *Journal of Leisure Research, 13,* 1–14.

Boren, C. (2018, March 20). Watch: 102- and 100-year-old runners set world records. *The Washington Post.* Available: www.pressherald.com/2018/03/20/102-and-100-year-old-runners-set-world-records-because-they-can/.

Borer, K.T. (2005). Physical activity in the prevention and amelioration of osteoporosis in women. *Sports Medicine, 35,* 779–830. doi:10.2165/00007256-200535090-00004

Bornstein, M.H. (1985). Habituation of attention as a measure of visual information processing in human infants: Summary, systematization, and synthesis. In G. Gottlieb & N.A. Krasnegor (Eds.), *Measurement of audition and vision in the first year of postnatal life: A methodological overview* (pp. 253–300). Norwood, NJ: Ablex.

Bosacki, S., Woods, W., & Coplan, R. (2015). Canadian female and male early childhood educators' perceptions of child aggression and rough-and-tumble play. *Early Child Development and Care, 185*(7): 1134–1147. doi:10.1080/03004430.2014.980408.

Boskey, A.L., & Coleman, R. (2010). Aging and bone. *Journal of Dental Research, 89*(12), 1333–1348. doi:10.1177/0022034510377791

Bouquet, J. (2016). *Concurrent validity of TGMD-2 and TGMD-3 in children with Down syndrome.* Unpublished thesis.

Bower, T.G.R. (1977). *A primer of infant development.* San Francisco: Freeman.

Bower, T.G.R., Broughton, J.M., & Moore, M.K. (1970). The co-ordination of visual and tactual input in infants. *Perception and Psychophysics, 8,* 51–53.

Braet, C., Tanghe, A., De Bode, P., Franckx, H., & Van Winckel, M. (2003). Inpatient treatment of obese children: A multicomponent programme without stringent calorie restriction. *European Journal of Pediatrics, 162,* 391–396. doi:10.1007/s00431-003-1155-5

Brandfonbrener, M., Landowne, M., & Shock, N.W. (1955). Changes in cardiac output with age. *Circulation, 12,* 557–566.

Branta, C., Haubenstricker, J., & Seefeldt, V. (1984). Age changes in motor skill during childhood and adolescence. In R.L. Terjung (Ed.), *Exercise and sport science reviews* (Vol. 12, pp. 467–520). Lexington, MA: Collamore.

Brayne, C., & Miller, B. (2017). Dementia and aging populations—A global priority for contextualized research and health policy. *PLoS Medicine, 14*(3), e1002275. doi:10.1371/journal.pmed.1002275

Brian, A., Taunton, S., Liebermain, L.J., Haibach-Beach, P., Forley, J., & Santarossa, S. (2018). Psychometric properties of the Test of Gross Motor Development-3 for children with visual impairments. *Adaptive Physical Activity Quarterly, 35*(2), 145–158.

Brodkin, P., & Weiss, M.R. (1990). Developmental differences in motivation for participation in competitive swimming. *Journal of Sport and Exercise Psychology, 12,* 248–263.

Brouwer, W.H., Waterink, W., Van Wolffelaar, P.C., & Rothengartter, T. (1991). Divided attention in experienced young and older drivers: Land tracking and visual analysis in a dynamic driving simulator. *Human Factors, 33,* 573–582.

Brown, B., Frankel, G., & Fennell, M. (1990). Hugs or shrugs: Parental and peer influences on continuation of involvement in sport by female adolescents. *Sex Roles, 20,* 397–412.

Brown, B.A. (1985). Factors influencing the process of withdrawal by female adolescents from the role of competitive age group swimmers. *Sociology of Sport Journal, 2,* 111–129.

Brown, C.H., Harrower, J.R., & Deeter, M.F. (1972). The effects of cross-country running on pre-adolescent girls. *Medicine and Science in Sports, 4,* 1–5.

Brown, K.A., Patel, D.R., & Darmawan, D. (2017). Participation in sports in relation to adolescent growth and development. *Translational Pediatrics, 6*(3), 150–159.

Brownell, C.A., Zerwas, S., & Ramani, G.B. (2007). "So big": The development of body self-awareness in toddlers. *Child Development, 78,* 1426–1440.

Bruce, T. (2016). New rules for new times: Sportswomen and media representation in the third wave. *Sex Roles, 74,* 361–376.

Brundage, C.L. (1983). *Parent/child play behaviors as they relate to children's later socialization into sport.* Unpublished master's thesis, University of Illinois, Urbana–Champaign.

Bruner, J.S. (1970). The growth and structure of skill. In K.J. Connolly (Ed.), *Mechanisms of motor skill development* (pp. 63–94). London: Academic Press.

Bruner, J.S. (1973). Organization of early skilled action. *Child Development, 44,* 1–11.

Bruner, J.S., & Koslowski, B. (1972). Visually pre-adapted constituents of manipulatory action. *Perception, 1,* 3–12.

Brustad, R.J. (1988). Affective outcomes in competitive youth sport: The influence of intrapersonal and socialization factors. *Journal of Sport and Exercise Psychology, 10,* 307–321.

Buchanan, J.J., & Horak, F.B. (1999). Emergence of postural patterns as a function of vision and translation frequency. *Journal of Neurophysiology, 81*(5), 2325–2339.

Bucsuhazy, K., & Semela, M. (2017). Case study: Reaction time of children according to age. *Transbaltica 2017: Transportation Science and Technology, 187*(Suppl. C), 408–413.

Bull, D., Eilers, R., & Oller, K. (1984). Infants' discrimination of intensity variation in multisyllabic stimuli. *Journal of the Acoustical Society of America, 76,* 13–17.

Burnett, C.N., & Johnson, E.W. (1971). Development of gait in childhood, part II. *Developmental Medicine and Child Neurology, 13,* 207–215.

Burton, A.W. (1999). Hrdlicka (1931) revisited: Children who run on all fours. *Research Quarterly for Exercise and Sport, 70,* 84–90.

Burton, A.W., & Davis, W.E. (1996). Ecological task analysis: Utilizing intrinsic measures in research and practice. *Human Movement Science, 15,* 285–314.

Bushnell, E.W. (1982). The ontogeny of intermodal relations: Vision and touch in infancy. In R. Walk & H. Pick (Eds.), *Intersensory perception and sensory integration* (pp. 5–36). New York, NY: Plenum Press.

Bushnell, E.W. (1985). The decline of visually guided reaching during infancy. *Infant Behavior and Development, 8,* 139–155.

Bushnell, E.W., & Boudreau, J.P. (1993). Motor development and the mind: The potential role of motor abilities as a determinant of aspects of perceptual development. *Child Development, 64,* 1005–1021.

Bushnell, I.W.R. (1998). The origins of face perception. In F. Simion & G. Butterworth (Eds.), *The development of sensory, motor and cognitive capacities in early infancy: From perception to cognition* (pp. 69–86). Hove, UK: Psychology Press.

Bushnell, I.W.R., Sai, F., & Mullin, J.T. (1989). Neonatal recognition of the mother's face. *British Journal of Developmental*

Psychology, 7, 3–15.

Butcher, J. (1983). Socialization of adolescent girls into physical activity. *Adolescence, 18,* 753–766.

Butcher, J. (1985). Longitudinal analysis of adolescent girls' participation in physical activity. *Sociology of Sport Journal, 2,* 130–143.

Butterworth, G., & Hicks, L. (1977). Visual proprioception and postural stability in infancy. *Perception, 6,* 255–262.

Butterworth, G., Verweij, E., & Hopkins, B. (1997). The development of prehension in infants: Halverson revisited. *British Journal of Developmental Psychology, 15*(2), 223–236.

Campbell, A.J., Robertson, M.C., Gardner, M.M., Norton, R.N., & Buchner, D.M. (1999). Falls prevention over 2 years: A randomized controlled trial in women 80 years and older. *Age and Ageing, 28*, 513–518.

Campbell, A.J., Robertson, M.C., Gardner, M.M., Norton, R.N., Tilyard, M.W., & Buchner, D.M. (1997). Randomised controlled trial of a general practice programme of home based exercise to prevent falls in elderly women. *British Medical Journal, 315,* 1065–1069.

Campbell, D., & Eaton, W. (2000). Sex differences in the activity level of infants. *Infant and Child Development, 8,* 1–17.

Campbell, M.J., McComas, A.J., & Petito, F. (1973). Physiological changes in aging muscles. *Journal of Neurology, Neurosurgery, and Psychiatry, 36,* 174–182.

Campenni, C.E. (1999). Gender stereotyping of children's toys: A comparison of parents and nonparents. *Sex Roles, 40,* 121–138.

Capelli, C., Rittveger, J., Bruseghini, P., Calabria, E., & Tam, E. (2016). Maximal aerobic power and anaerobic capacity in cycling across the age spectrum in male master athletes. *European Journal of Applied Physiology, 116*, 1395–1410. doi:10.1007/s00421-016-3396-9

Carnahan, H., Vandervoort, A.A., & Swanson, L.R. (1996). The influence of summary knowledge of results and aging on motor learning. *Research Quarterly for Exercise and Sport, 67*, 280–287.

Carnahan, H., Vandervoort, A.A., & Swanson, L.R. (1998). The influence of aging and target motion on the control of prehension. *Experimental Aging Research, 24*(3), 289–306.

Carr, G. (1997). *Mechanics of sport.* Champaign, IL: Human Kinetics.

Carneiro, N.H., Ribeiro, A.S., Nascimento, M.A., Gobbo, L.A. Schoenfeld, B.J., Achour, J.A. . . . Cyrino, E.S. (2015). Effects of different resistance training frequencies on flexibility in older women. *Clinical Interventions in Aging, 10*, 531-538.

Cartee, G.D. (1994). Aging skeletal muscle: Response to exercise. *Exercise and Sport Sciences Reviews, 22*, 91–120.

Carvalho, H.M., Coelho-e-Silva, M.J., Goncalves, C.E. Philippaerts, R.M., Castagna, C., & Malina, R.M. (2011). Age-related variation of anaerobic power after controlling for size and maturation in adolescent basketball players. *Annals of Human Biology, 38*, 721–727. doi:10/3109/03014460.2011.613852

Cattuzzo, M.T., dos Santos Henrique, R., Re, A.H.N., Oliveira, I.S., Melo, B.M., dos Santos Moura, M., et al. (2016). Motor competence and health related physical fitness in youth: A systematic review. *Journal of Science and Medicine in Sport, 19*, 123–129. doi:10.1016/j.jsams.2014.12.004

Cerella, J. (1990). Aging and information-processing rate. In J.E. Birren & K.W. Schaie (Eds.), *Handbook of the psychology of aging* (3rd ed., pp. 201–221). New York, NY: Academic Press.

Cesqui, B., Russo, M., Lacqauniti, F., & d'Avella, A. (2016). Grasping in one-handed catching in relation to performance. *PLoS ONE, 11*, e0158606. doi:10.1371/journal.pone.0158606

Chalabaev, A., Brisswalter, J., Radel, R., Coombes, S.A., Easthope, C., & Clément-Guillotin, C. (2013). Can stereotype threat affect motor performance in the absence of explicit monitoring processes? Evidence using a strength task. *Journal of Sport and Exercise Psychology, 35*, 211–215.

Chase, M.A., Ewing, M.E., Lirgg, C.D., & George, T.R. (1994). The effects of equipment modification on children's self-efficacy and basketball shooting performance. *Research Quarterly for Exercise and Sport, 65*(2), 159–168.

Chen, L.C., Jeka, J., & Clark, J.E. (2016). Development of adaptive sensorimotor control in infant sitting posture. *Gait and Posture, 45*, 157–163.

Chen, L.-C., Metcalfe, J.S., Jeka, J.J., & Clark, J.E. (2007). Two steps forward and one back: Learning to walk affects infants' sitting posture. *Infant Behavior and Development, 30, 16–25.*

Cherney, I.D., & London, K. (2006). Gender-linked differences in the toys, television shows, computer games, and outdoor activities of 5-to 13-year-old children. *Sex Roles, 54*(9/10), 717–726. doi:10.1007/s11199-006-9037-8

Chlebowski, R.T., Kuller, L.H., Prentice, R.L., Stefanick, M.L., Manson, J., Gass, M., et al. (2009). Breast cancer after use of estrogen plus progestin in postmenopausal women. *New England Journal of Medicine, 360*(6), 573–587.

Cho, G.J., Yoo, H.J., Hwang, S.Y., Choi, J., Lee, K.M., Choi, K.M., et al. (2018). Differential relationship between waist circumference and mortality according to age, sex, and body mass index in Koreans with age of 30–90 years: A nationwide health insurance database study. *BMC Medicine, 16*, 131.

Chugani, H.T., & Phelps, M.E. (1986). Maturational changes in cerebral function in infants determined by 18FDG positron emission tomography. *Science, 231,* 840–843.

Cignetti, F., Fontan, A., Menant, J., Nazarian, B., Anton, J-L., Vaugoyeau, M., & Assainte, C. (2017). Protracted development of the proprioceptive brain network during and beyond adolescence. *Cerebral Cortex, 27*, 1285-1296. doi: 10.1093/cercor/bhv323

Clark, C.C.T., Moran, J., Drury, B., Venetsanou, F., & Fernandes, J.F.T. (2018). Actual vs. perceived motor competence in children (8–10 years): An issue of non-veridicality. *Journal of Functional Morphology and Kinesiology, 3*, 20.

Clark, J.E. (1982). Developmental differences in response processing. *Journal of Motor Behavior, 14,* 247–254.

Clark, J.E. (1995). On becoming skillful: Patterns and constraints. *Research Quarterly for Exercise and Sport, 66,* 173 183.

Clark, J.E. (2005). From the beginning: A developmental perspective on movement and mobility. *Quest, 57,* 37–45.

Clark, J.E. (2017). Pentimento: A 21st century view on the canvas of motor development. *Kinesiology Review, 6*, 232–239. doi:10.1123/kr.2017-0020

Clark, J.E., & Phillips, S.J. (1985). A developmental sequence of the standing long jump. In J. Clark & J. Humphrey (Eds.), *Motor development: Vol. 1. Current selected research* (pp. 73–85). Princeton, NJ: Princeton Book.

Clark, J.E., & Phillips, S.J. (1993). A longitudinal study of intralimb coordination in the first year of independent walking. *Child Development, 64,* 1143–1157.

Clark, J.E., Phillips, S.J., & Petersen, R. (1989). Developmental stability in jumping. *Developmental Psychology, 25,* 929–935.

Clark, J.E., & Whitall, J. (1989a). What is motor development? *Quest, 41,* 183–202.

Clark, J.E., & Whitall, J. (1989b). Changing patterns of locomotion: From walking to skipping. In M.H. Woollacott & A. Shumway-Cook (Eds.), *Development of posture and gait across the life span* (pp. 128–151). Columbia: University of South Carolina Press.

Clark, J.E., Whitall, J., & Phillips, S.J. (1988). Human interlimb coordination: The first 6 months of independent walking. *Developmental Psychobiology, 21,* 445–456.

Clarke, H.H. (Ed.). (1975). Joint and body range of movement. *Physical Fitness Research Digest, 5,* 16–18.

Clarkson-Smith, L., & Hartley, A.A. (1990). Structural equation models of relationships between exercise and cognitive abilities. *Psychology and Aging, 5,* 437–446.

Clifton, R.K., Muir, D.W., Ashmead, D.H., & Clarkson, M.G. (1993). Is visually guided reaching in early infancy a myth? *Child Development, 64*, 1099–1110.

Clifton, R.K., Perris, E.E., & Bullinger, A. (1991). Infants' perception of auditory space. *Developmental Psychology, 27*(2), 187–197.

Clouse, F. (1959). *A kinematic analysis of the development of the running pattern of preschool boys.* Unpublished doctoral dissertation, University of Wisconsin, Madison.

Cobb, K., Goodwin, R., & Saelens, E. (1966). Spontaneous hand positions of newborn infants. *Journal of Genetic Psychology, 108,* 225–237.

Colcombe, S., & Kramer, A.F. (2003). Fitness effects on the cognitive function of older adults: A meta-analytic study. *Psychological Science, 14*, 125–130.

Colcombe, S.J., Erickson, K.I., Raz, N., Webb, A.G., Cohen, N.J., McAuley, E., et al. (2003). Aerobic fitness reduces brain tissue loss in aging humans. *Journal of Gerontology: Series A: Biological Sciences and Medical Science, 55*, 176–180.

Colcombe, S.J., Erickson, K.I., Scalf, P.E., Kim, J.S., Prakash, R., McAuley, E., et al. (2006). Aerobic exercise training increases brain volume in aging humans. *Journal of Gerontology: Series A: Biological Sciences and Medical Sciences, 61A*, 1166–1170.

Colcombe, S.J., Kramer, A.F., Erickson, K.I., Scalf, P., McAuley, E., & Cohen, N.J. (2004). Cardiovascular fitness, cortical plasticity, and aging. *Proceedings of the National Academy of Science, 101*, 3316–3321.

Colcombe, S., Wadwha, R., Kramer, A., McAuley, E., Scalf, P., Alvarado, M., et al. (2005). *Cardiovascular fitness training improves cortical recruitment and working memory in older adults: Evidence from a longitudinal fMRI study.* Presented at the *Annual Meeting of the Cognitive Neuroscience Society*, New York.

Coleman, S. (2013, February 20). Nerlens Noel injury: High school ailment linked to ACL tear. *SBNation.* Retrieved from www.sbnation.com/college-basketball/2013/2/20/4007340/nerlens-noel-injury-kentucky

Colling-Saltin, A.S. (1980). Skeletal muscle development in the human fetus and during childhood. In K. Berg & B.O. Eriksson (Eds.), *International congress on pediatric work physiology: Children and exercise IX* (pp. 193–207). Baltimore, MD: University Park Press.

Comery, T.A., Shah, R., & Greenough, W.T. (1995). Differential rearing alters spine density on medium-sized spiny neurons in the rat corpus striatum: Evidence for association of morphological plasticity with early response gene expression. *Neurobiology of Learning and Memory, 63*(3), 217–219.

Comery, T.A., Stamoudis, C.X., Irwin, S.A., & Greenough, W.T. (1996). Increased density of multiple-head dendritic spines on medium-sized spiny neurons of the striatum in rats reared in a complex environment. *Neurobiology of Learning and Memory, 66*(2), 93–96.

Composite Tissue Allotransplantation. (2012). Hand transplant: Matthew Scott. Retrieved from www.handtransplant.com/ThePatients/MatthewScott/tabid/83/Default.aspx

Connolly, K.J., & Elliott, J.M. (1972). The evolution and ontogeny of hand function. In N. Blurton-Jones (Ed.), *Ethological studies of child behavior* (pp. 329–383). Cambridge: Cambridge University Press.

Contreras-Vidal, J.L., Teulings, H.L., & Stelmach, G.E. (1998). Elderly subjects are impaired in spatial coordination in fine motor control. *Acta Psychologica, 100,* 25–35.

Cooky, C., & Messner, M.A. (2018). *No slam dunk: Gender, sport and the unevenness of social change.* New Brunswick, NJ: Rutgers University Press.

Coopersmith, S. (1967). *The antecedents of self-esteem.* San Francisco: Freeman.

Corbetta, D., & Bojczyk, K.E. (2002). Infants return to two-handed reaching when they are learning to walk. *Journal of Motor Behavior, 34*(1), 83–95.

Corbetta, D., & Mounoud, P. (1990). Early development of grasping and manipulation. In C. Bard, M. Fleury, & L. Hay (Eds.), *Development of eye-hand coordination across the life span* (pp. 188–216). Columbia: University of South Carolina Press.

Corbetta, D., & Thelen, E. (1996). The developmental origins of bimanual coordination: A dynamic perspective. *Journal of Experimental Psychology: Human Perception and Performance, 22,* 502–522.

Corbetta, D., Thurman, S.L., Wiener, R.F., Guan, Y., & Williams, J.L. (2014). Mapping the feel of the arm with the sight of the object: On the embodied origins of infant reaching. *Frontiers in Psychology, 5*, 576. doi:10.3389/fpsygf.2014.00576

Corso, J.F. (1977). Auditory perception and communication. In

J.E. Birren & K.W. Schaie (Eds.), *Handbook of the psychology of aging* (pp. 535–553). New York, NY: Van Nostrand Reinhold.

Costigan, S.A., Eather, N., Plotnikoff, R.C., Taaffe, D.R., & Lubans, D.R. (2015). High-intensity interval training for improving health-related fitness in adolescents: A systematic review and meta-analysis. *British Journal of Sports Medicine, 49,* 1253–1261. doi:10.1136/bjsports-2014-094490

Cotman, C.W., & Berchtold, N.C. (2002). Exercise: A behavioral intervention to enhance brain health and plasticity. *Trends in Neurosciences, 25,* 295–301.

Cowie, D., Sterling, S., & Bremner, A.J. (2016). The development of multisensory body representation and awareness continues to 10 years of age: Evidence from the rubber hand illusion. *Journal of Experimental Child Psychology, 142,* 230–238. doi:10.1016/j.jecp.2015.10.003

Coyne, S.M., Linder, J.R., Rasmussen, E.E., Nelson, D.A., & Collier, K.M. (2014). It's a bird! It's a plane! It's a gender stereotype!: Longitudinal associations between superhero viewing and gender stereotyped play. *Sex Roles, 70*(9/10), 416–430. doi:10.1007/s11199-014-0374-8

Craig, C.H., Kim, B., Rhyner, P.M.P., & Chirillo, T.K.B. (1993). Effects of word predictability, child development, and aging on time-gated speech recognition performance. *Journal of Speech and Hearing Research, 36,* 832–841.

Craik, R. (1989). Changes in locomotion in the aging adult. In M.H. Woollacott & A. Shumway-Cook (Eds.), *Development of posture and gait across the life span* (pp. 176–201). Columbia: University of South Carolina Press.

Crane, J., & Temple, V. (2015). A systematic review of dropout from organized sport among children and youth. *European Physical Education Review, 21*(1), 114–131.

Cratty, B.J. (1979). *Perception and motor development in infants and children* (2nd ed.). Englewood Cliffs, NJ: Prentice Hall.

Cristea, A., Korhonen, M.T., Hakkinen, K., Mero, A., Alen, M., Sipila, S., et al. (2008). Effects of combined strength and sprint training on regulation of muscle contraction at the whole-muscle and single-fibre levels in elite master sprinters. *Acta Physiologica, 193,* 275–289.

Crowder, C., & Austin, D. (2005). Age ranges of epiphyseal fusion in the distal tibia and fibula of contemporary males and females. *Journal of Forensic Science, 50*(5), 1001–1007.

Crowell, J.A., & Banks, M.S. (1993). Perceiving heading with different retinal regions and types of optic flow. *Perception and Psychophysics, 53,* 325–337.

Cumming, R.G. (1990). Calcium intake and bone mass: A quantitative review of the evidence. *Calcified Tissue International, 47,* 194–201.

Cunningham, L.N. (1990). Relationship of running economy, ventilatory threshold, and maximum oxygen consumption to running performance in high school females. *Research Quarterly for Exercise and Sport, 61,* 369–374.

Curcton, K.J., Collins, M.A., Hill, D.W., & McElhannon, F.M. (1988). Muscle hypertrophy in men and women. *Medicine and Science in Sports and Exercise, 20,* 338–344.

Curtis, J.E., & White, P.G. (1984). Age and sport participation: Decline in participation with age or increased specialization with age? In N. Theberge & P. Donnelly (Eds.), *Sport and the sociological imagination* (pp. 273–293). Fort Worth: Texas Christian University Press.

Darrah, J., Bartlett, D., Maguire, T.O., Avison, W.R., & Lacaze-Masmonteil, T. (2014). Have infant gross motor abilities changed in 20 years? A re-evaluation of the Alberta Infant Motor Scale normative values. *Developmental Medicine and Child Neurology, 56*(9):877–881.

Damasio, A.R. (1989). The brain binds entities and events by multiregional activation from convergence zones. *Neural Computation, 1,* 123–132.

Davies, C.T.M., White, M.J., & Young, K. (1983). Muscle function in children. *European Journal of Applied Physiology, 52,* 111–114.

Davis, B.E., Moon, R.Y., Sachs, H.C., & Ottolini, M.C. (1998). Effects of sleep position on infant motor development. *Pediatrics, 102*(5), 1135-1140.

Davis, C.I. (1991). The effects of game modification on opportunities to respond in elementary volleyball classes. *Dissertation Abstracts International, 52*(2), 465.

Davis, W.E., & Broadhead, G. (Eds.) (2007). *Ecological task analysis and movement.* Champaign, IL: Human Kinetics.

Davis, W.E., & Burton, A.W. (2007). Ecological task analysis: Translating movement behavior theory into practice. *Adapted Physical Activity Quarterly, 8,* 154–177.

Dehn, M.M., & Bruce, R.A. (1972). Longitudinal variations in maximum oxygen intake with age and activity. *Journal of Applied Physiology, 33,* 805–807.

de Jonge, L.L., van Osch-Gevers, L., Willemsen, S.P., Steegers, E.A.P., Hofman, A., Helbing, W.A., et al. (2011). Growth, obesity, and cardiac structures in early childhood: The Generation R study. *Hypertension, 57,* 934–940.

Dekaban, A. (1970). *Neurology of early childhood.* Baltimore, MD: Williams & Wilkins.

Delacato, C.H. (1959). *Treatment and prevention of reading problems.* Springfield, IL: Charles C Thomas.

Delacato, C.H. (1966). *Neurological organization and reading.* Springfield, IL: Charles C Thomas.

DeLoache, J.S., Uttal, D., & Rosengren, K. (2004). Scale errors offer evidence for a perception-action dissociation early in life. *Science, 304,* 1027–1029. doi:10.1126/science.1093567

Demany, L., McKenzie, B., & Vurpillot, E. (1977). Rhythmic perception in early infancy. *Nature, 266,* 718–719.

De Meester, A., Maes, J., Stodden, D., Cardon, G., Goodway, J., Lenoir, M., & Haerens, L. (2016). Identifying profiles of actual and perceived motor competence among adolescents: Associations with motivation, physical activity, and sports participation. *Journal of Sports Sciences, 34,* 21, 2027–2037. doi:10.1080/02640414.2016.1149608

Dempsey, J.A., Johnson, B.D., & Saupe, K.W. (1990). Adaptations and limitations in the pulmonary system during exercise. *Chest, 97*(3 Suppl.), 81S–87S.

de Onis, M., Garza, C., Victora, C.G., Onyango, A.W., Frongillo,

E.A., & Martines, J., (2004). The WHO Multicentre Growth Reference Study: Planning, study design, and methodology. *Food Nutrition Bulletin, 25*, S15–S26.

de Onis, M., Onyango, A.W., Borghi, E., Siyam, A., Nishida, C., & Siekmann, J. (2007). Development of a WHO growth reference for school-aged children and adolescents. *Bulletin of the World Health Organization 2007, 85,* 660–667.

DeOreo, K., & Keogh, J. (1980). Performance of fundamental motor tasks. *A textbook of motor development*, 76-91.

DeOreo, K., & Wade, M.G. (1971). Dynamic and static balancing ability of preschool children. *Journal of Motor Behavior, 3,* 326–335.

DeOreo, K.L., & Williams, H.G. (1980). Characteristics of kinesthetic perception. In C.B. Corbin (Ed.), *A textbook of motor development* (2nd ed., pp. 174–196). Dubuque, IA: Brown.

Der, G., & Deary, I.J. (2006). Age and sex differences in reaction time in adulthood: Results from the United Kingdom Health and Lifestyle Survey. *Psychology and Aging, 21*(1), 62–73.

Der, G., & Deary, I.J. (2017). The relationship between intelligence and reaction time varies with age: Results from three representative narrow-age age cohorts at 30, 50 and 69 years. *Intelligence, 64*, 89–97. doi:10.1016/j.intell.2017.08.001

D'Hondt, E., Deforche, B., Gentier, I., Verstuyf, J., Vaeyens, R., De Bourdeaudhuij, I., et al. (2014). A longitudinal study of gross motor coordination and weight status in children. *Obesity, 22,* 1505–1511. doi:10.1002/oby.20723

D'Hondt, E., Deforche, B., Vaeyens, R., Vandorpe, B., Vandendriessche, J., Pion, J., et al. (2011). Gross motor coordination in relation to weight status and age in 5- to 12-year-old boys and girls: A cross-sectional study. *International Journal of Pediatric Obesity, 6*, e556–e564.

Diamond, A. (2000). Close interrelation of motor development and cognitive development and of the cerebellum and prefrontal cortex. *Child Development, 71,* 44–56.

Dietz, W.H., & Robinson, T.N. (1993). Assessment and treatment of childhood obesity. *Pediatric Review, 14*, 337-343.

DiLorenzo, T., Stucky-Ropp, R., Vander Wal, J., & Gotham, H. (1998). Determinants of exercise among children: II. A longitudinal analysis. *Preventive Medicine, 27,* 470–477.

DiNucci, J.M. (1976). Gross motor performance: A comprehensive analysis of age and sex differences between boys and girls ages six to nine years. In J. Broekhoff (Ed.), *Physical education, sports, and the sciences.* Eugene, OR: Microform.

Dioum, A., Gartner, A., Maire, B., Delpeuch, F., & Wade, S. (2005). Body composition predicted from skinfolds in African women: A cross-validation study using air-displacement plethysmography and a black-specific equation. *British Journal of Nutrition, 93*, 973–979.

DiSimoni, F.G. (1975). Perceptual and perceptual-motor characteristics of phonemic development. *Child Development, 46,* 243–246.

Dittmer, J. (1962). *A kinematic analysis of the development of the running pattern of grade school girls and certain factors which distinguish good from poor performance at the observed ages.* Unpublished master's thesis, University of Wisconsin, Madison.

Dorfman, P.W. (1977). Timing and anticipation: A developmental perspective. *Journal of Motor Behavior, 9,* 67–80.

Doty, D. (1974). Infant speech perception. *Human Development, 17,* 74–80.

Drillis, R. (1961). The influence of aging on the kinematics of gait. *The Geriatric Amputee, 919, 134–145.*

Drinkwater, B.L., Horvath, S.M., & Wells, C.L. (1975). Aerobic power of females, age 10–68. *Journal of Gerontology, 30,* 385–394.

Drowatzky, J.N., & Zuccato, F.C. (1967). Interrelationship between static and dynamic balance. *Research Quarterly, 38,* 509–510.

Duche, P., Falgairette, G., Bedu, M., Fellmann, N., Lac, G., Robert, A., et al. (1992). Longitudinal approach of bioenergetic profile in boys before and during puberty. In J. Coudert & E. Van Praagh (Eds.), *Pediatric work physiology: Methodological, physiological and pathological aspects* (pp. 43–45). Paris: Masson.

Duda, J.L., & Tappe, M.K. (1988). Predictors of personal investment in physical activity among middle-aged and older adults. *Perception and Motor Skills, 66,* 543–549.

Duda, J.L., & Tappe, M.K. (1989a). Personal investment in exercise among middle-aged and older adults. In A.C. Ostrow (Ed.), *Aging and motor behavior* (pp. 219–238). Indianapolis: Benchmark Press.

Duda, J.L., & Tappe, M.K. (1989b). Personal investment in exercise among adults: The examination of age and gender-related differences in motivational orientation. In A.C. Ostrow (Ed.), *Aging and motor behavior* (pp. 239–256). Indianapolis: Benchmark Press.

Duijts, L., Jaddoe, V.W.V., Hofman, A., & Moll, H.A. (2010). Prolonged and exclusive breastfeeding reduces the risk of infectious diseases in infancy. *Pediatrics, 126*, e18.

Dunham, P. (1977). Age, sex, speed and practice in coincidence-anticipation performance of children. *Perceptual and Motor Skills, 45,* 187–193.

Dunsky, A., Zeev, A., & Netz, Y. (2017). Balance performance is task specific in older adults. *BioMed Research International, 2017*, 6987017. doi:10.1155/2017/6987017

DuRandt, R. (1985). Ball catching proficiency among 4-, 6-, and 8-year-olds. In J.E. Clark & J.H. Humphrey (Eds.), *Motor development: Current selected research* (pp. 35–44). Princeton, NJ: Princeton Book.

Dykiert, D., Der, G., Starr, J.M., & Deary, I.J. (2012). Sex differences in reaction time mean and intraindividual variability across the life span. *Developmental Psychology, 48*(5), 1262–1276.

Earles, J.L., & Salthouse, T.A. (1995). Interrelations of age, health, and speed. *Journal of Gerontology: Psychological Sciences, 50B,* P33–P41.

Ebihara, O., Ikeda, M., & Miyashita, M. (1983). Birth order and children's socialization into sport. *International Review of Sport Sociology, 18,* 69–89.

Ebrahim, S., & Rowland, L. (1996). Towards a new strategy for health promotion for older women: Determinants of physical activity. *Psychology, Health and Medicine, 1*(1), 29–40.

Efrat, M.W. (2016). Understanding factors associated with children's motivation to engage in recess-time physical activity. *Contemporary Issues in Educational Research, 9*(2), 77–86.

Ehl, T., Roberton, M.A., & Langendorfer, S.J. (2005). Does the throwing "gender gap" occur in Germany? *Research Quarterly for Exercise and Sport, 76*, 488–493.

Ehsani, F., Abdollahi, I., Mohseni Bandpei, M.A., Zahiri, N., & Jaberzadeh, S. (2015). Motor learning and movement performance: Older versus younger adults. *Basic and Clinical Neuroscience, 6*(4), 231–238.

Einkauf, D.K., Gohdes, M.L., Jensen, G.M., & Jewell, M.J. (1987). Changes in spinal mobility with increasing age in women. *Physical Therapy, 67,* 370–375.

Eisenberg, N., Welchick, S.A., Hernandez, R., & Pasternack, J.F. (1985). Parental socialization of young children's play: A short-term longitudinal study. *Child Development, 56,* 1506–1513.

Eitzen, D.S., & Sage, G.H. (2015). *Sociology of North American sport* (10th ed.). Madison, WI: WCB McGraw-Hill.

Ekblom, B. (1969). Effect of physical training on oxygen transport system in man. *Acta Physiologica Scandinavica Supplementum, 328,* 1–76.

Ekeland, E., Heian, F., Hagen, K.B., Abbott, J.M., & Nordheim, L. (2004.) Exercise to improve self esteem in children and young people. *Cochrane Database of Systematic Reviews, 1*, CD003683. doi:10.1002/14651858.CD003683.pub2

Elkind, D. (1975). Perceptual development in children. *American Scientist, 63,* 533–541.

Elkind, D., Koegler, R., & Go, E. (1964). Studies in perceptual development: Whole-part perception. *Child Development, 35,* 81–90.

Elliott, C.B., Whitaker, D., & Thompson, P. (1989). Use of displacement threshold hyperacuity to isolate the neural component of senile vision loss. *Applied Optics, 28,* 1914–1918.

Erickson, K.I., Colcombe, S.J., Wadhwa, R., Bherer, L., Peterson, M.W., Scalf, P.E., et al. (2007). Training-induced plasticity in older adults: Effects of training on hemispheric asymmetry. *Neurobiology of Aging, 28*, 272–283.

Eriksson, B., & Koch, G. (1973). Effect of physical training on hemodynamic response during submaximal exercise in 11–13 year old boys. *Acta Physiologica Scandinavica, 87,* 27–39.

Eriksson, B.O. (1978). Physical activity from childhood to maturity: Medical and pediatric considerations. In G. Landry & W.A.R. Orban (Eds.), *Physical activity and human well-being.* Miami, FL: Symposia Specialists.

Espenschade, A.S. (1947). Development of motor coordination in boys and girls. *Research Quarterly, 18,* 30–44.

Espenschade, A.S., Dable, R.R., & Schoendube, R. (1953). Dynamic balance in adolescent boys. *Research Quarterly, 24,* 270–274.

Estevan, I., Molina-García, J., Abbott, G., Bowe, S., Castillo, I., & Barnett, L. (2018). Evidence of reliability and validity for the Pictorial Scale of Perceived Movement Skill Competence in Spanish children. *Journal of Motor Learning and Development, 0*(0), 1–27. doi:10.1123/jmld.2016-0065

Estevan, I., Molina-García, J., Queralt, A., Álvarez, O., Castillo, I., & Barnett, L. (2017). Validity and reliability of the Spanish version of the Test of Gross Motor Development-3. *Journal of Motor Learning and Development, 5*, 69-81. doi: 10.1123/jmld.2016-0045

Ewart, C.K., Stewart, K.J., Gillilan, R.E., & Kelemen, M.H. (1986). Self-efficacy mediates strength gains during circuit weight training in men with coronary artery disease. *Medicine and Science in Sports and Exercise, 18,* 531–540.

Exton-Smith, A.N. (1985). Mineral metabolism. In C.E. Finch & E.L. Schneider (Eds.), *Handbook of the biology of aging* (2nd ed., pp. 511–539). New York, NY: Van Nostrand Reinhold.

Faeh, D., Braun, J., Tarnutzer, S., & Bopp, M. (2011). Obesity but not overweight is associated with increased mortality risk. *European Journal of Epidemiology, 26*, 647–655. doi:10.1007/s10654-011-9593-2

Fagard, J. (1990). The development of bimanual coordination. In C. Bard, M. Fleury, & L. Hay (Eds.), *Development of eye-hand coordination across the life span* (pp. 262–282). Columbia: University of South Carolina Press.

Fagard, J., Spelke, E., & von Hofsten, C. (2009). Reaching and grasping a moving object in 6-, 8-, and 10-month-old infants: Laterality and performance. *Infant Behavior and Development, 32*, 137–146. doi:10.1016.j.infbeh.2008.12.002

Fagot, B., & Leinbach, M. (1996). Gender knowledge in egalitarian and traditional families. *Sex Roles, 32,* 513–526.

Fagot, B., Leinbach, M., & O'Boyle, C. (1992). Gender labeling, gender stereotyping, and parenting behaviors. *Developmental Psychology, 28*(2), 225–230.

Fagot, B.I. (1978). The influence of sex of child on parental reactions to toddler children. *Child Development, 49,* 459–465.

Fagot, B.I. (1984). Teacher and peer reactions to boys' and girls' play styles. *Sex Roles, 11,* 691–702.

Faigenbaum, A.D., Lloyd, R.S., & Myer, G.D. (2013). Youth resistance training: Past practices, new perspectives, and future directions. *Pediatric Exercise Science, 25*, 591–604.

Faigenbaum, A.D., Milliken, L., Moulton, L., & Westcott, W.L. (2005). Early muscular fitness adaptations in children in response to two different resistance training regimens. *Pediatric Exercise Science, 17,* 237–248.

Faigenbaum, A.D., & Myer, G. (2010). Resistance training among young athletes: Safety, efficacy and injury prevention effects. *British Journal of Sports Medicine, 44*, 56–63. doi:10.1136/bjsm.2009.068098

Faith, M.S., Carnell, S., & Kral, T.V.E. (2013). Genetics of food intake self-regulation in childhood: Literature review and research opportunities. *Human Heredity, 75*, 80–89. doi:10.1159/000353879

Falgairette, G., Bedu, M., Fellmann, N., Van Praagh, E., & Coudert, J. (1991). Bio-energetic profile in 144 boys aged from 6 to 15 years. *European Journal of Applied Physiology, 62,* 151–156.

Falk, B., & Eliakim, A. (2003). Resistance training, skeletal muscle and growth. *Pediatric Endocrinology Review, 1*, 120–127.

Farley, C. (1997). Just skip it. *Nature, 394,* 721–723.

Favilla, M. (2006). Reaching movements in children: Accuracy and reaction time development. *Experimental Brain Research, 169*, 122–125.

Feigenson, L. (2011). Predicting sights from sounds: 6-month-olds' intermodal numerical abilities. *Journal of Experimental Child Psychology, 110*, 347–361. doi:10.1016/j.jecp.2011.04.004

Feldkamp, M.L., Botto, L.D., & Carey, J.C. (2015). Reflections on the etiology of structural birth defects: Established teratogens and risk factors. *Birth Defects Research Part A: Clinical and Molecular Teratology, 103*(8), 652–655.

Feltz, D.L., & Petlichkoff, L. (1983). Perceived competence among interscholastic sport participants and dropouts. *Canadian Journal of Applied Sport Sciences, 8,* 231–235.

Fieandt, K.V., Huhtala, A., Kullberg, P., & Saarl, K. (1956). *Personal tempo and phenomenal time at different age levels* (Report no. 2). Helsinki: Psychological Institute, University of Helsinki.

Figueroa, R., & An, R. (2017). Motor skill competence and physical activity in preschoolers: A review. *Maternal and Child Health Journal, 21*, 136–146. doi:10.1007/s10995-016-2102-1

Filatova, S., Koivumaa-Honkanen, H., Khandaker, G.M., Lowry, E., Nordström, T., Hurtig, T., et al. (2018). Early motor developmental milestones and schizotypy in the Northern Finland Birth Cohort Study 1966. *Schizophrenia Bulletin, 44*(5), 1151–1158.

Fink, P.W., Foo, P.S., & Warren, W.H. (2009). Catching fly balls in virtual reality: A critical test of the outfielder problem. *Journal of Vision, 9*(14), 1–8. doi:10.1167/9.13.14

Fitts, P.M., & Posner, M.I. (1967). *Human performance.* Belmont, CA: Brooks/Cole.

Fitts, R.H. (1981). Aging and skeletal muscle. In E.L. Smith & R.C. Serfass (Eds.), *Exercise and aging: The scientific basis* (pp. 31–44). Hillside, NJ: Enslow.

Fitzpatrick, A., Davids, K., & Stone, J.A. (2018). Effects of scaling task constraints on emergent behaviours in children's racquet sports performance. *Human Movement Science, 58*, 80–87. doi:10.1016/j.humov.2018.01.007

Flegal, K.M., & Troiano, R.P. (2000). Changes in the distribution of body mass index of adults and children in the US population. *International Journal of Obesity, 24*, 807–818.

Fontenelle, S.A., Kahrs, B.A., Neal, S.A., Newton, A.R., & Lockman, J.J. (2007). Infant manual exploration of composite substrates. *Journal of Experimental Child Psychology, 98*, 153–167.

Forssberg, H., & Nashner, L. (1982). Ontogenetic development of postural control in man: Adaptation to altered support and visual conditions during stance. *Journal of Neuroscience, 2,* 545–552.

Fox, K.R., & Corbin, C.B. (1989). The physical self-perception profile: Development and preliminary validation. *Journal of Sport and Exercise Psychology, 11,* 408–430.

Frankenburg, W.K., & Dodds, J.B. (1967). The Denver Developmental Screening Test. *Journal of Pediatrics, 71,* 181–191.

Fraser, B.J., Schmidt, M.D., Huynh, Q.L., Dwyer, T., Venn, A.J., & Magnussen, C.G. (2017). Tracking of muscular strength and power from youth to young adulthood: Longitudinal findings from the Childhood Determinants of Adult Health Study. *Journal of Science and Medicine in Sport, 20*, 927-931. doi:10.1016/j.jsams.2017.03.021

Fredriks, A.M., van Buuren, S., Wit, J.M., & Verloove-Vanhorick, S.P. (2000). Body index measurements in 1996–1997 compared with 1980. *Archives of Disease in Childhood, 82*, 107–112.

French, K.E., & Thomas, J.R. (1987). The relation of knowledge development to children's basketball performance. *Journal of Sport Psychology, 9,* 15–32.

Fritz, J., Rosengren, B.E., Dencker, M., Karlsson, C., & Karlsson, M.K. (2016). A seven-year physical activity intervention for children increased gains in bone mass and muscle strength. *Acta Paediatrica, 105*, 1216-1224. doi:10.1111/apa.13440

Froberg, K., & Lammert, O. (1996). Development of muscle strength during childhood. In O. Bar-Or (Ed.), *The child and adolescent athlete* (pp. 25-41). Cambridge, MA: Oxford.

Frostig, M., Lefever, W., & Whittlesey, J. (1966). *Administration and scoring manual for the Marianne Frostig Developmental Test of Visual Perception.* Palo Alto, CA: Consulting Psychologists Press.

Fry, A.F., & Hale, S. (2000). Relationships among processing speed, working memory, and fluid intelligence in children. *Biological Psychology, 54*, 1–34.

Fryar, C.D., Gu, Q., & Ogden, C.L. (2012). Anthropometric reference data for children and adults: United States, 2007–2010. National Center for Health Statistics. *Vital Health Stat 11*(252).

Gabbard, C., Caçola, P., & Cordova, A. (2009). Is perceived motor competence a constraint in children's action planning? *Journal of Genetic Psychology, 170*(2), 151–158.

Gabel, R.H., Johnston, R.C., & Crowninshield, R.D. (1979). A gait analyzer/trainer instrumentation system. *Journal of Biomedical Engineering, 12,* 543–549.

Gabell, A., & Nayak, U.S.L. (1984). The effect of age on variability of gait. *Journal of Gerontology, 39,* 662–666.

Gagen, L., & Getchell, N. (2004). Combining theory and practice in the gymnasium: "Constraints" within an ecological perspective. *Journal of Physical Education, Recreation and Dance, 75,* 25–30.

Gagen, L., & Getchell, N. (2006). Using "constraints" to design developmentally appropriate movement activities for early childhood education. *Early Childhood Education Journal, 34,* 227–232.

Gagen, L., & Getchell, N. (2008). Applying Newton's apple to elementary physical education: An interdisciplinary approach. *Journal of Physical Education, Recreation, and Dance, 79*, 43–51.

Gagen, L., & Getchell, N. (2018). Using "constraints" to design developmentally appropriate movement activities for early childhood education. In H. Brewer & M. Ranck Jalongo (Eds.), *Physical activity and health promotion in the early years: Effective strategies for early childhood educators* (pp. 57-74). New York, NY: Springer.

Gagen, L.M., Haywood, K.M., & Spaner, S.D. (2005). Predicting the scale of tennis rackets for optimal striking from body dimensions. *Pediatric Exercise Science, 17,* 190–200.

Gallagher, J.D., & Thomas, J.R. (1980, April). *Adult-child differences in movement reproduction: Effects of kinesthetic sensory storage and organization of memory.* Paper presented at the annual convention of the American Alliance for Health, Physical Education, Recreation and Dance, Detroit.

Galloway, J.C., Rhu, J., & Agrawal, S. (2008). Babies driving robots: Self-generated mobility in very young infants. *Journal of Intelligent Service Robotics, 1*, 123–134.

García-García, A., & Calleja-Fernández, J. (2004). Neurophysiology of the development and maturation of the peripheral nervous system. Revista de neurologia, 38(1), 79–83.

Geerdink, J.J., Hopkins, B., Beek, W.J., & Heriza, C.B. (1996). The organization of leg movements in preterm and full-term infants after term age. *Developmental Psychobiology, 29,* 335–351.

Gentile, A.M. (1972). A working model of skill acquisition with application to teaching. *Quest, 17*, 3–23.

Geremia, J.M., Iskiewicz, M.M., Marschner, R.A., Lehnen, T.E., & Lehnen, A.M. (2015). Effect of a physical training program using the Pilates method on flexibility in elderly subjects. *Age, 37*, 119. doi:10.1007/s11357-015-9856-z

Germain, N.W., & Blair, S.N. (1983). Variability of shoulder flexion with age, activity, and sex. *American Corrective Therapy Journal, 37,* 156–160.

Gesell, A. (1928). *Infancy and human growth.* New York, NY: Macmillan.

Gesell, A. (1954). The ontogenesis of infant behavior. In L. Carmichael (Ed.), *Manual of child psychology* (2nd ed.). New York, NY: Wiley.

Gesell, A., & Amatruda, C.S. (1949). *Gesell Developmental Schedules.* New York, NY: Psychological.

Getchell, N., & Gagen, L. (2006). Interpreting disabilities from a "constraints" theoretical perspective: Encouraging movement for *all* children. *Palaestra, 22,* 20–53.

Getchell, N., & Roberton, M.A. (1989). Whole body stiffness as a function of developmental level in children's hopping. *Developmental Psychology, 25,* 920–928.

Getman, G.N. (1952). *How to develop your child's intelligence: A research publication.* Lucerne, MN: Author.

Getman, G.N. (1963). *The physiology of readiness experiment.* Minneapolis: P.A.S.S.

Gibson, E.J., Riccio, G., Schmuckler, M.A., Stoffregen, T.A., Rosenberg, D., & Taormina, J. (1987). Detection of the traversability of surfaces by crawling and walking infants. Special issue: The ontogenesis of perception. *Journal of Experimental Psychology: Human Perception and Performance, 13*(4), 533–544.

Gibson, E.J., & Walk, R.D. (1960). The "visual cliff." *Scientific American, 202*(4), 64–71.

Gibson, J.J. (1966). *The senses considered as perceptual systems.* Boston, MA: Houghton Mifflin.

Gibson, J.J. (1979). *An ecological approach to visual perception.* Boston, MA: Houghton Mifflin.

Giedd, J.N., Blumenthal, J., Jeffries, N.O., Castellanos, F.X., Liu, H., Zijdenbos, A., et al. (1999). Brain development during childhood and adolescence: A longitudinal MRI study. *Nature Neuroscience, 2*(10), 861.

Gieysztor, E.Z., Choi ska, A.M., & Paprocka-Borowicz, M. (2018). Persistence of primitive reflexes and associated motor problems in healthy preschool children. *Archives of Medical Science, 4*(1), 167–173.

Gill, L.E., Bartles, S.J., & Batsis, J.A. (2015). Weight management in older adults. *Current Obesity Reports, 4*(3), 379–388.

Gilliam, T.B., & Freedson, P.S. (1980). Effects of a 12-week school physical fitness program on peak $\dot{V}O_2$ body composition and blood lipids in 7 to 9 year old children. *International Journal of Sports Medicine, 1*, 73–78.

Giuliano, T., Popp, K., & Knight, J. (2000). Football versus Barbies: Childhood play activities as predictors of sport participation by women. *Sex Roles, 42,* 159–181.

Glisky, E.L. (2007). Changes in cognitive function in human aging. In D.R. Riddle (Ed.), *Brain aging: Models, methods, and mechanisms* (chapter 1). Boca Raton, FL: CRC Press/Taylor & Francis. Retrieved from www.ncbi.nlm.nih.gov/books/NBK3885

Goggin, N.L., & Keller, M.J. (1996). Older drivers: A closer look. *Educational Gerontology, 22,* 245–256.

Goggin, N.L., & Stelmach, G.E. (1990). A kinematic analysis of precued movements in young and elderly participants. *Canadian Journal on Aging, 9,* 371–385.

Goh, H., Sullivan, K., & Kantak, S. (2012). Movement pattern and parameter learning in children: Effects of feedback frequency. *Research Quarterly for Exercise and Sports, 83*(2), 346–352.

Goldfield, E.C., & Michel, G.F. (1986). The ontogeny of infant bimanual reaching during the first year. *Infant Behavior and Development, 9,* 81–89.

Gomez-Cabello, A., Ara, I., Gonzalez-Aguero, A., Casajus, J.A., & Vicente-Rodriguez, G. (2012). Effects of training on bone mass in older adults: A systematic review. *Sports Medicine, 42,* 301–325.

Goodale, M.A. (1988). Modularity in visuomotor control: From input to output. In Z. Pylyshyn (Ed.), *Computational processes in human vision: An interdisciplinary perspective* (pp. 262–285). Norwood, NJ: Ablex.

Goodman, L., & Hamill, D. (1973). The effectiveness of the Kephart Getman activities in developing perceptual-motor and cognitive skills. *Focus on Exceptional Children, 4,* 1–9.

Goodnow, J.J. (1971a). Eye and hand: Differential memory and its effect on matching. *Neuropsychologica, 9,* 89–95.

Goodnow, J.J. (1971b). Matching auditory and visual series: Modality problem or translation problem? *Child Development, 42,* 1187–1201.

Goodpaster, B.H., Park, S.W., Harris, T.B., Kritchevsky, S.B., Nevitt, M., Schwartz, A.V., et al. (2006). The loss of skeletal muscle strength, mass, and quality in older adults: The Health, Aging and Body Composition Study. *Journal of Gerontology: Medical Sciences, 61A*, 1059–1064.

Goodway, J.D., & Branta, C.F. (2003). Influence of motor skill intervention on fundamental motor skill development of disadvantaged pre-school children. *Research Quarterly for Exercise and Sport, 74,* 36–46.

Goodway, J.D., & Rudisill, M.E. (1997). Perceived physical competence and actual motor skill competence of African American preschool children. *Adapted physical activity quarterly, 14*(4), 314-326.

Goodway, J.D., Crowe, H., & Ward, P. (2003). Effects of motor skill instruction on fundamental motor skill development. *Adapted Physical Activity Quarterly, 30,* 298–314.

Gosline, J.M. (1976). The physical properties of elastic tissue. In D.A. Hull & D.S. Jackson (Eds.), *International review of connective tissue research* (Vol. 7, pp. 184–210). New York, NY: Academic Press.

Gould, D., Feltz, D., Horn, T., & Weiss, M.R. (1982). Reasons for attrition in competitive youth swimming. *Journal of Sport Behavior, 5,* 155–165.

Gould, D., Feltz, D., & Weiss, M.R. (1985). Motives for participating in competitive youth swimming. *International Journal of Sport Psychology, 6,* 126–140.

Granrud, C.E., Yonas, A., Smith, I.M., Arterberry, M.E., Glicksman, M.L., & Sorknes, A.C. (1984). Infants' sensitivity to accretion and deletion of texture as information for depth at an edge. *Child Development, 55,* 1630–1636.

Green, H.J. (1986). Characteristics of aging human skeletal muscles. In J.R. Sutton & R.M. Brock (Eds.), *Sports medicine for the mature athlete* (pp. 17–26). Indianapolis: Benchmark Press.

Greendorfer, S.L. (1976, September). *A social learning approach to female sport involvement.* Paper presented at the annual convention of the American Psychological Association, Washington, DC.

Greendorfer, S.L. (1977). Role of socializing agents in female sport involvement. *Research Quarterly, 48,* 304–310.

Greendorfer, S.L. (1979). Childhood sport socialization influences of male and female track athletes. *Arena Review, 3,* 39–53.

Greendorfer, S.L. (1983). Shaping the female athlete: The impact of the family. In M.A. Boutilier & L. Sangiovanni (Eds.), *The sport woman* (pp. 135–155). Champaign, IL: Human Kinetics.

Greendorfer, S.L. (1992). Sport socialization. In T.S. Horn (Ed.), *Advances in sport psychology* (pp. 201–218). Champaign, IL: Human Kinetics.

Greendorfer, S.L., & Brundage, C.L. (1984, July). *Sex differences in children's motor skills: Toward a cross-disciplinary perspective.* Paper presented at the 1984 Olympic Scientific Congress, Eugene, OR.

Greendorfer, S.L., & Ewing, M.E. (1981). Race and gender differences in children's socialization into sport. *Research Quarterly for Exercise and Sport, 52,* 301–310.

Greendorfer, S.L., & Lewko, J.H. (1978). Role of family members in sport socialization of children. *Research Quarterly, 49,* 146–152.

Greenough, W.T., Black, J.E., & Wallace, C.S. (1987). Experience and brain development. *Child Development, 58,* 539–559.

Greenough, W.T., Wallace, C.S., Alcantara, A.A., Anderson, B.J., Hawrylak, N., Sirevaag, A.M., et al. (1993). Development of the brain: Experience affects the structure of neurons, glia, and blood vessels. In N.J. Anatasiow & S. Harel (Eds.), *At-risk infants: Interventions, families, and research* (pp. 173–185). Baltimore, MD: Brookes.

Gregg, E.A., & Gregg, V.H. (2017). Women in sport: Historical perspectives. *Clinics in Sports Medicine, 36*(4), 603–610.

Grimby, G. (1988). Physical activity and effects of muscle training in the elderly. *Annals of Clinical Research, 20,* 62–66.

Gunter, K.B., Almstedt, H.C., & Janz, K.F. (2012). Physical activity in childhood may be the key to optimizing lifespan skeletal health. *Exercise and Sport Science Review, 40,* 13–21. doi:10.1097/JES/0b013e318236e5ee

Gutteridge, M. (1939). A study of motor achievements of young children. *Archives of Psychology, 244,* 1–178.

Hagburg, J.M., Allen, W.K., Seals, D.R., Hurley, B.F., Ehsani, A.A., & Holloszy, J.O. (1985). A hemodynamic comparison of young and older endurance athletes during exercise. *Journal of Applied Physiology, 58,* 2041–2046.

Hagburg, J.M., Graves, J.E., Limacher, M., Woods, D.R., Leggett, S.H., Cononie, C., et al. (1989). Cardiovascular responses of 70- to 79-year-old men and women to exercise training. *Journal of Applied Physiology, 66,* 2589–2594.

Hall, S.J. (2019). *Basic biomechanics* (5th ed.). Dubuque, IA: McGraw-Hill.

Halverson, H.M. (1931). An experimental study of prehension in infants by means of systematic cinema records. *Genetic Psychology Monographs, 10,* 107–286.

Halverson, L.E. (1983). *Observing children's motor development in action.* Paper presented at annual convention of the American Alliance for Health, Physical Education, Recreation and Dance, Eugene, OR.

Halverson, L.E., Roberton, M.A., & Langendorfer, S. (1982). Development of the overarm throw: Movement and ball velocity changes by seventh grade. *Research Quarterly for Exercise and Sport, 53,* 198–205.

Halverson, L.E., & Williams, K. (1985). Developmental sequences for hopping over distance: A prelongitudinal screening. *Research Quarterly for Exercise and Sport, 56,* 37–44.

Hands, B. (2008). Changes in motor skill and fitness measures among children with high and low motor competence: A five-year longitudinal study. *Journal of Science and Medicine in Sport, 11,* 155–162.

Hannaford, C. (1995). *Smart moves: Why learning is not all in your head.* Arlington, VA: Great Ocean.

Hansman, C.F. (1962). Appearance and fusion of ossification centers in the human skeleton. *American Journal of Roentgenology, 88,* 476–482.

Harris, J.E. (1999). The role of physical activity in the management of obesity. *Journal of the American Osteopathic Association, 99*(4), S15–S19.

Harrison, R.V. (2008). Noise-induced hearing loss in children: A "less than silent" environmental danger. *Paediatric Child Health, 13,* 377–382.

Harter, S. (1978). Effectance motivation reconsidered: Towards a developmental model. *Human Development, 21,* 34–64.

Harter, S. (1981). A model of intrinsic mastery motivation in children: Individual differences and developmental change. In W.A. Collins (Ed.), *Minnesota Symposium on Child Psychology*

(Vol. 14, pp. 215–225). Hillsdale, NJ: Erlbaum.

Harter, S. (1985). *Manual for the self-perception profile for children.* Denver: University of Denver.

Harter, S., & Pike, R. (1984). The pictorial scale of perceived competence and social acceptance for young children. *Child Development, 55,* 1969–1982.

Hartley, L.H. (1992). Cardiac function and endurance. *Endurance in sport* (pp. 72-79). Oxford: Blackwell Scientific Publications.

Hartley, A.A. (1992). Attention. In F.I.M. Craig & T.A. Salthouse (Eds.), *The handbook of aging and cognition* (pp. 3–49). Hillsdale, NJ: Erlbaum.

Hartshorne, J.K., & Germine, L.T. (2015). When does cognitive functioning peak? The asynchronous rise and fall of different cognitive abilities across the lifespan. *Psychological Science, 26*(4), 433–443. doi:10.1177/0956797614567339

Hasselkus, B.R., & Shambes, G.M. (1975). Aging and postural sway in women. *Journal of Gerontology, 30,* 661–667.

Hastie, P.A., Johnson, J.L., & Rudisill, ME. (2018). An analysis of the attraction and holding power of motor skill stations used in a mastery motivational physical education climate for preschool children. *Physical Education and Sport Pedagogy, 23*(1), 37–53, doi:10.1080/17408989.2017.1341476

Hatakenaka, Y., Ninomiya, H., Billstedt, E., Fernell, E., & Gillberg, C. (2017). ESSENCE-Q—used as a screening tool for neurodevelopmental problems in public health checkups for young children in south Japan. *Neuropsychiatric Disease and Treatment, 13,* 1271–1280.

Hatzitaki, V., Zisi, V., Kollias, I., & Kioumourtzoglou, E. (2002). Percpetual-motor contributions to static and dynamic balance control in children. *Journal of Motor Behavior, 34,* 161–170.

Haubenstricker, J.L., Branta, C.F., & Seefeldt, V.D. (1983). *Standards of performance for throwing and catching.* Paper presented at the annual conference of the North American Society for Psychology of Sport and Physical Activity, Asilomar, CA.

Haubenstricker, J.L., Seefeldt, V.D., & Branta, C.F. (1983, April). *Preliminary validation of a developmental sequence for the standing long jump.* Paper presented at the American Alliance for Health, Physical Education, Recreation and Dance, Houston.

Haug, E., Rasmussen, M., Samdal, O., Ionnotti, R., Kelly, C., Borraccino, A., et al. (2009). Overweight in school-aged children and its relationship with demographic and lifestyle factors: Results from the WHO-Collaborative Health Behaviour in School-aged Children (HBSC) Study. *International Journal of Public Health, 54,* S167–S179. doi:10.1007/s00038-009-5408-6

Hausler, R., Colburn, S., & Marr, E. (1983). Sound localization in subjects with impaired hearing: Spatial discrimination and discrimination tests. *Acta Oto-Laryngologica (Suppl.), 40C,* 6–62.

Hawn, P.R., & Harris, L.J. (1983). Hand differences in grasp duration and reaching in two- and five-month old infants. In G. Young, S. Segalowitz, C.M. Carter, & S.E. Trehub (Eds.), *Manual specialization and the developing brain* (pp. 331–348). New York, NY: Academic Press.

Haywood, K., & Trick, L. (1990). Changes in visual functioning and perception with advancing age. *Missouri Journal of Health, Physical Education, Recreation and Dance,* 51–73.

Haywood, K.M. (1977). Eye movements during coincidence-anticipation performance. *Journal of Motor Behavior, 9,* 313–318.

Haywood, K.M. (1980). Coincidence-anticipation accuracy across the life span. *Experimental Aging Research, 6*(3), 451–462.

Haywood, K.M. (1982). Eye movement pattern and accuracy during perceptual-motor performance in young and old adults. *Experimental Aging Research, 8,* 153–157.

Haywood, K.M. (1989). A longitudinal analysis of anticipatory judgment in older adult motor performance. In A.C. Ostrow (Ed.), *Aging and motor behavior* (pp. 325–335). Indianapolis: Benchmark Press.

Haywood, K.M., Greenwald, G., & Lewis, C. (1981). Contextual factors and age group differences in coincidence-anticipation performance. *Research Quarterly for Exercise and Sport, 52,* 458–464.

Haywood, K.M., & Williams, K. (1995). Age, gender, and flexibility differences in tennis serving among experienced older adults. *Journal of Aging and Physical Activity, 3,* 54–66.

Haywood, K.M., Williams, K., & VanSant, A. (1991). Qualitative assessment of the backswing in older adult throwing. *Research Quarterly for Exercise and Sport, 62,* 340–343.

Healthy People 2020 [Internet]. Washington, DC: U.S. Department of Health and Human Services, Office of Disease Prevention and Health Promotion [cited August 29, 2018]. Retrieved from www.healthypeople.gov

Hecaen, H., & de Ajuriaguerra, J. (1964). *Left-handedness: Manual superiority and cerebral dominance.* New York, NY: Grune & Stratton.

Hecox, K. (1975). Electro-physiological correlates of human auditory development. In L.B. Cohen & P. Salapatek (Eds.), *Infant perception: Vol. 2. From sensation to cognition* (pp. 151–191). New York, NY: Academic Press.

Heidrich, C., & Chiviacowsky, S. (2015). Stereotype threat affects the learning of sport motor skills. *Psychology of Sport and Exercise, 18,* 42–46. doi:10.1016/j.psychsport.2014.12.002

Heinze, J.E., Heinze, K.L., Davis, M.M., Butchart, A.T., Sincer, D.C., & Clark, S.J. (2017). Gender role beliefs and parents' support for athletic participation. *Youth & Society, 49*(5), 634–657.

Held, R. (1985). Binocular vision: Behavioral and neuronal development. In J. Mehler & R. Fox (Eds.), *Neonate cognition: Beyond the blooming buzzing confusion* (pp. 37–44). Hillsdale, NJ: Erlbaum.

Held, R. (1988). Normal visual development and its deviations. In G. Lennerstrand, G. Von Noorden, & E. Campos (Eds.), *Strabismus and amblyopia* (pp. 247–257). London: Macmillan.

Held, R., & Hein, A. (1963). Movement-produced stimulation in the development of visually guided behavior. *Journal of Comparative and Physiological Psychology, 56,* 872–876.

Helfer, K.S. (1992). Aging and the binaural advantage in reverberation and noise. *Journal of Speech and Hearing Research, 35,* 1394–1401.

Hellebrandt, F.A., & Braun, G.L. (1939). The influence of sex and age on the postural sway of man. *American Journal of Physical Anthropology, 24*(Series 1), 347–360.

Henrique, R.S., Re, A.H.N., Stodden, D.F., Fransen, J., Campos, C.M.C., Queiroz, D.R., & Cattuzzo, M.T. (2016). Association between sports participation, motor competence and weight status: A longitudinal study. *Journal of Science and Medicine in Sport, 19*, 825–829. doi:10.1016/j.jsams.2015.12.512

Hens, W., Vissers, D., Hansen, D., Peeters, S. Gielen, J., Van Gaal, L., & Taeymans, J. (2017). The effect of diet or exercise on ectopic adiposity in children and adolescents with obesity: A systematic review and meta-analysis. *Obesity Reviews, 18*, 1310–1322. doi:10.1111/obr.12577

Heriza, C.B. (1986). *A kinematic analysis of leg movements in premature and fullterm infants.* Unpublished doctoral dissertation, University of Southern Illinois, Edwardsville.

Herkowitz, J. (1978). Developmental task analysis: The design of movement experiences and evaluation of motor development status. In M.V. Ridenour (Ed.), *Motor development* (pp. 139–164). Princeton, NJ: Princeton Book.

Hesketh, K.D., & Campbell, K.J. (2010). Interventions to prevent obesity in 0-5 year olds: An updated systematic review of the literature. *Obesity, 18*, S27–S35.

Hickey, T.L., & Peduzzi, J.D. (1987). Structure and development of the visual system. In P. Salapatek & L.B. Cohen (Eds.), *Handbook of infant perception: From sensation to perception* (pp. 1–42). New York, NY: Academic Press.

Higginson, D.C. (1985). The influence of socializing agents in the female sport-participation process. *Adolescence, 20,* 73–82.

Hoeger, W.W.K., Hopkins, D.R., Button, S., & Palmer, T.A. (1990). Comparing the sit and reach with the modified sit and reach in measuring flexibility in adolescents. *Pediatric Exercise Science, 2,* 155–162.

Hogan, P.I., & Santomeir, J.P. (1984). Effect of mastering swim skills on older adults' self-efficacy. *Research Quarterly for Exercise and Sport, 55,* 294–296.

Hohlstein, R.E. (1982). The development of prehension in normal infants. *American Journal of Occupational Therapy, 36,* 170–176.

Holfeder, B., & Schott, N. (2014). Relationship of fundamental movement skills and physical activity in children and adolescents: A systematic review. *Psychology of Sport and Exercise, 15*, 382–391. doi:10.1-16/j.psychsport.2014.03.005

Holland, G.J., Tanaka, K., Shigematsu, R., & Nakagaichi, M. (2002). Flexibility and physical functions of older adults: A review. *Journal of Aging and Physical Activity, 10,* 169–206.

Hollenberg, M., Yang, J., Haight, T.J., & Tager, I.B. (2006). Longitudinal changes in aerobic capacity: Implications for concepts of aging. *Journal of Gerontology Series A: Biological Sciences and Medical Sciences, 61*, 851–858.

Holst-Wolf, Yeh, I-L., & Konczak, J. (2016). Development of proprioceptive acuity in typically developing children: Normative data on forearm position sense. *Frontiers in Human Neuroscience, 10*, 436. doi: 10.3389/fnhum.2016.00436

Holtzman, R.E., Familant, M.E., Deptula, P., & Hoyer, W.J. (1986). Aging and the use of sentential structure to facilitate word recognition. *Experimental Aging Research, 12,* 85–88.

Horak, F.B., & MacPherson, J.M. (1995). Postural orientation and equilibrium. In J. Shepard & L. Rowell (Eds.), *Handbook of physiology* (pp. 252–292). New York, NY: Oxford University Press.

Horak, F.B., Nashner, L.M., & Diener, H.C. (1990). Postural strategies associated with somatosensory and vestibular loss. *Experimental Brain Research, 82,* 167–177.

Horn, T.S. (1985). Coaches' feedback and changes in children's perceptions of their physical competence. *Journal of Educational Psychology, 77,* 174–186.

Horn, T.S. (1986). The self-fulfilling prophecy theory: When coaches' expectations become reality. In J.M. Williams (Ed.), *Applied sport psychology: Personal growth to peak performance* (pp. 59–73). Mountain View, CA: Mayfield.

Horn, T.S. (1987). The influence of teacher-coach behavior on the psychological development of children. In D. Gould & M.R. Weiss (Eds.), *Advances in pediatric sport science: Vol. 2. Behavioral issues* (pp. 121–142). Champaign, IL: Human Kinetics.

Horn, T.S., & Hasbrook, C.A. (1986). Information components influencing children's perceptions of their physical competence. In M.R. Weiss & D. Gould (Eds.), *Sport for children and youths* (pp. 81–88). Champaign, IL: Human Kinetics.

Horn, T.S., & Hasbrook, C.A. (1987). Psychological characteristics and the criteria children use for self-evaluation. *Journal of Sport Psychology, 9,* 208–221.

Horn, T.S., & Weiss, M.R. (1991). A developmental analysis of children's self-ability judgments in the physical domain. *Pediatric Exercise Science, 3,* 310–326.

Howell, M.L., Loiselle, D.S., & Lucas, W.G. (1966). *Strength of Edmonton schoolchildren.* Unpublished manuscript, University of Alberta Fitness Research Unit, Edmonton, Alberta.

Howze, E.H., DiGilio, D.A., Bennett, J.P., & Smith, M.L. (1986). Health education and physical fitness for older adults. In B. McPherson (Ed.), *Sport and aging* (pp. 153–156). Champaign, IL: Human Kinetics.

Hrdlicka, A. (1931). *Children who run on all fours: And other animal-like behaviors in the human child.* New York, NY: Whittlesey House.

Hubley-Kozey, C.L., Wall, J.C., & Hogan, D.B. (1995). Effects of a general exercise program on passive hip, knee, and ankle range of motion of older women. *Topics in Geriatric Rehabilitation, 10,* 33–44.

Hughes, S., Gibbs, J., Dunlop, D., Edelman, P., Singer, R., & Chang, R.W. (1997). Predictors of decline in manual performance in older adults. *Journal of the American Geriatrics Society, 45,* 905–910.

Hupprich, F.L., & Sigerseth, P.O. (1950). The specificity of flexibility in girls. *Research Quarterly, 21,* 25–33.

Iida, Y., Miyazaki, M., & Uchida, S. (2010). Developmental changes in cognitive reaction time of children aged 6–12 years. *European Journal of Sport Science, 10*, 151–158. doi:10.1080/17461390903515162

Inbar, O., & Bar-Or, O. (1986). Anaerobic characteristics in male children and adolescents. *Medicine and Science in Sports and Exercise, 18,* 264–269.

Ingle, L., Sleap, M., & Tolfrey, K. (2006). The effect of a complex training and detraining programme on selected strength and power variables in early pubertal boys. *Journal of Sports Sciences, 24*, 987–997. doi:10.1080/02640410511457117

Isaacs, L.D. (1980). Effects of ball size, ball color, and preferred color on catching by young children. *Perceptual and Motor Skills, 51,* 583–586.

Isaacs, L.D. (1983). Coincidence-anticipation in simple catching. *Journal of Human Movement Studies, 9,* 195–201.

Ishak, S., Franchak, J.M., & Adolph, K.E. (2014). Perception-action development from infants to adults: Perceiving affordances for reaching through openings. *Journal of Experimental Child Psychology, 117*, 92–105. doi:10.1016/j.jecp.2013.09.003

Ivry, R.B. (1993). Cerebellar involvement in the explicit representation of temporal information. In P. Tallal, A.M. Galaburda, R.R. Llinas, & C. von Euler (Eds.), *Temporal information processing in the nervous system: Special reference to dyslexia and dysphasia* (pp. 214–230). New York, NY: New York Academy of Sciences.

Ivry, R.B., & Keele, S.W. (1989). Timing functions of the cerebellum. *Journal of Cognitive Neuroscience, 1,* 136–152.

Iwamoto, J. (2017). Calcium and bone metabolism across women's life stages: Exercise and sport to increase bone strength in accordance with female lifecycle. *Clinical Calcium, 27*, 5, 715–721.

Jackson, T. (1993). *Activities that teach.* Cedar City, UT: Red Rock.

Jackson, T. (1995). *More activities that teach.* Cedar City, UT: Red Rock.

Jackson, T. (2000). *Still more activities that teach.* Cedar City, UT: Red Rock.

Jagacinski, R.J., Greenberg, N., & Liao, M. (1997). Tempo, rhythm, and aging in golf. *Journal of Motor Behavior, 29*(2), 159–173.

Jagacinski, R.J., Liao, M.J., & Fayyad, E.A. (1995). Generalized slowing in sinusoidal tracking in older adults. *Psychology and Aging, 10,* 8–19.

Jantz, J.W., Blosser, C.D., & Fruechting, L.A. (1997). A motor milestone change noted with a change in sleep position. *Archives of pediatrics & adolescent medicine, 151*(6), 565-568.

Janz, K.F., Burns, T.L., & Levy, S.M. (2005). Tracking of activity and sedentary behaviors in children: The Iowa Bone Development Study. *American Journal of Preventive Medicine, 28*, 171–178.

Janz, K.F., Burns, T.L., & Mahoney, L.T. (1995). Predictors of left ventricular mass and resting blood pressure in children: The Muscatine study. *Medicine and Science in Sports and Exercise, 27*(6), 818–825.

Janz, K.F., Dawson, J.D., & Mahoney, L.T. (2002). Increases in physical fitness during childhood improve cardiovascular health during adolescence: The Muscatine Study. *International Journal of Sports Medicine, 23*, 15-21. doi: 10.1055/s-2002-28456

Jensen, J. (2005). The puzzles of motor development: How the study of developmental biomechanics contributes to the puzzle solutions. *Infant and Child Development, 14*(5), 501–511.

Jensen, J.L., & Korff, T. (2005). Continuing the discourse on the contribution of biomechanics to understanding motor development: Response to the commentaries. *Infant and Child Development, 14*, 529–533.

Jensen, J.L., Thelen, E., Ulrich, B.B., Schneider, K., & Zernicke, R.F. (1995). Adaptive dynamics of the leg movement patterns of human infants: III. Age-related differences in limb control. *Journal of Motor Behavior, 27,* 366–374.

Jerome, G.J., Ko, S., Kauffman, D., Studenski, S.A., Ferrucci, L., & Simonsick, E.M. (2015). Gait characteristics associated with walking speed decline in older adults: Results from the Baltimore Longitudinal Study of Aging. *Archives of Gerontology and Geriatrics, 60*(2), 239–243. doi:10.1016/j.archger.2015.01.007

Jirout, J.J., & Newcombe, N.S. (2015). Building blocks for developing spatial skills: Evidence from a large, representative U.S. sample. *Psychological Science, 26*(3):302–310. doi:10.1177/0956797614563338.

Jobling, A., & Virji-Babul, N. (2004). *Down syndrome: Play, move and grow* (Vol. 1). Down Syndrome Research Foundation.

Johansson, G., von Hofsten, C., & Jansson, G. (1980). Event perception. *Annual Review of Psychology, 31,* 27–63.

Johnsson, L.G., & Hawkins, J.E., Jr. (1972). Sensory and neural degeneration with aging, as seen in micro-dissections of the inner ear. *Annals of Otology, Rhinology, and Laryngology, 81,* 179–193.

Johnston, I. (May 20, 2016). Some teenage boys are clumsy because their brains can't keep up with the speed they are growing. *Independent.* Retrieved from www.independent.co.uk/news/science/teenagers-boys-clumsy-awkward-gait-growth-spurt-growing-a7038486.html

Jones, R.A., Hinkley, T., Okely, A.D., & Salmon, J. (2013). Tracking physical activity and sedentary behavior in childhood: A systematic review. *American Journal of Preventive Medicine, 44*, 651–658.

Jouen, F. (1990). Early visual-vestibular interactions and postural development. In H. Bloch & B.I. Bertenthal (Eds.), *Sensory-motor organization and development in infancy and early childhood* (pp. 199–215). Dordrecht, the Netherlands: Kluwer.

Jouen, F., Lepecq, J.C., Gapenne, O., & Bertenthal, B.I. (2000). Optical flow sensitivity in neonates. *Infant Behavior and Development, 23*(3–4), 271–284.

Ju, Y.-Y., Lin, J.-K., Cheng, H.-Y.K., Cheng, C.-H., & Wong, A.M-K. (2013). Rapid repetitive passive movement promotes knee proprioception in the elderly. *European Review of Aging and Physical Activity, 10*, 133–139. doi:10.1007/s11556-013-0125-9

Kahrs, B.A., Jung, W.P., & Lockman, J.J. (2012). What is the role of infant banging in the development of tool use? *Experimental Brain Research, 218*, 315–320. doi:10.1007/s00221-012-3062-3

Kail, R., & Cavanaugh, J.C. (2017). *Essentials of human development: A life span view* (2nd ed.). Boston, MA: Cengage Learning.

Kalapotharakos, V.I., Michalopoulos, M., Strimpakos, N., Diamantopoulos, K., & Tokmakidis, S.P. (2006). Functional and neuromotor performance in older adults: Effect of 12 wks of aerobic exercise. *American Journal of Physical Medicine and Rehabilitation, 85*, 61–67.

Kallman, D.A., Plato, C.C., & Tobin, J.D. (1990). The role of muscle loss in the age-related decline of grip strength: Cross-sectional and longitudinal perspectives. *Journal of Gerontology: Medical Sciences, 45,* M82–M88.

Kane, E.W. (2007). "No way my boys are going to be like that!": Parents' responses to children's gender. *Gender Society, 20,* 149–176.

Kanehisa, H., Yata, H., Ikegawa, S., & Fukunaga, T. (1995). A cross-section study of the size and strength of the lower leg muscles during growth. *European Journal of Applied Physiology and Occupational Physiology, 72,* 150-156.

Karpovich, P.V. (1937). Textbook fallacies regarding the development of the child's heart. *Research Quarterly, 8,* 33–37. (Reprinted in 1991 in *Pediatric Exercise Science, 3,* 278–282.)

Kasch, F.W., Boyer, J.L., Van Camp, S., Nettl, F., Verity, L.S., & Wallace, J.P. (1995). Cardiovascular changes with age and exercise: A 28-year longitudinal study. *Scandinavian Journal of Medicine and Science in Sports, 5,* 147–151. doi:10.1111/j.1600-0838.1995.tb00028.x

Kasch, F.W., Boyer, J.L., Van Camp, S.P., Verity, L.S., & Wallace, J.P. (1990). The effects of physical activity and inactivity on aerobic power in older men (a longitudinal study). *The Physician and Sportsmedicine, 18,* 73-83.

Kasch, F.W., & Wallace, J.P. (1976). Physiological variables during 10 years of endurance exercise. *Medicine and Science in Sports, 8,* 5–8.

Katch, V.L. (1983). Physical conditioning of children. *Journal of Adolescent Health Care, 3,* 241–246.

Kauffman, T.L. (1985). Strength-training effect in young and aged women. *Archives of Physical Medicine and Rehabilitation, 65,* 223–226.

Kauranen, K., & Vanharanta, H. (1996). Influences of aging, gender, and handedness on motor performance of upper and lower extremities. *Perceptual and Motor Skills, 82,* 515–525.

Kavanagh, T., & Shephard, R.J. (1977). The effect of continued training on the aging process. *Annals of the New York Academy of Sciences, 301,* 656–670.

Kawai, K., Savelsbergh, G.J.P., & Wimmers, R.H. (1999). Newborns and spontaneous arm movements are influenced by the environment. *Early Human Development, 54*(1), 15–27.

Keele, S.W., & Ivry, R. (1990). Does the cerebellum provide a common computation for diverse tasks? A timing hypothesis. *Annals of the New York Academy of Sciences, 608,* 179–211.

Kelley, G.A., Kelley, K.S., & Pate, R.R. (2017). Exercise and BMI z-score in overweight and obese children and adolescents: A systematic review and network meta-analysis of randomized trials. *Journal of Evidence-Based Medicine, 10,* 108–128. doi:10.1111/jebm.12228

Kellman, P.J., & Arterberry, M.E. (1998). *The cradle of knowledge: Development of perception in infancy.* Cambridge, MA: MIT Press.

Kellman, P.J., & Garrigan, P. (2009). Perceptual learning and human expertise. *Physics of Life Reviews, 6,* 53–84. doi:10.1016/j.plrev.2008.12.001

Kelly, J.R. (1974). Socialization toward leisure: A developmental approach. *Journal of Leisure Research, 6,* 181–193.

Kemper, H.C.G., Twisk, J.W.R., Koppes, L.L.J., van Mechelen, W., & Post, G.B. (2001). A 15-year physical activity pattern is positively related to aerobic fitness in young males and females (13–27 years). *European Journal of Applied Physiology, 84,* 395–402.

Kenshalo, D.R. (1977). Age changes in touch, vibration, temperature, kinesthesis, and pain sensitivity. In J.E. Birren & K.W. Schaie (Eds.), *Handbook of the psychology of aging* (pp. 562–579). New York, NY: Van Nostrand Reinhold.

Kenyon, G.S., & McPherson, B.D. (1973). Becoming involved in physical activity and sport: A process of socialization. In G.L. Rarick (Ed.), *Physical activity: Human growth and development* (pp. 301–332). New York, NY: Academic Press.

Kephart, N.C. (1964). Perceptual-motor aspects of learning disabilities. *Exceptional Children, 31,* 201–206.

Kephart, N.C. (1971). *The slow learner in the classroom* (2nd ed.). Columbus, OH: Merrill.

Kermoian, R., & Campos, J.J. (1988). Locomotor experience: A facilitator of spatial cognitive development. *Child Development, 59,* 908–917.

Kernodle, M.W., & Carlton, L.G. (1992). Information feedback and the learning of multiple-degree-of-freedom activities. *Journal of Motor Behaviour, 24,* 187–196

Khambalia, A.Z., Dickinson, S., Hardy, L.L., Gill, T., & Baur, L.A. (2012). A synthesis of existing systematic reviews and meta-analyses of school-based behavioural interventions for controlling and preventing obesity. *Obesity Reviews, 13,* 214–233.

Khomut, B., & Warren, W. (2007). Catching fly balls in VR: A test of the OAC, LOT and trajectory prediction strategies. *Journal of Vision, 7,* 146 (abstract). doi:10.1167/7.9.146

Kidd, A.H., & Kidd, R.M. (1966). The development of auditory perception in children. In A.H. Kidd & J.L. Rivoire (Eds.), *Perceptual development in children* (pp. 113–142). New York, NY: International Universities Press.

Kim, R., Nauhaus, G., Glazek, K., Young, D., & Lin, S. (2013). Development of coincidence-anticipation timing in a catching task. *Perceptual and Motor Skills: Physical Development and Measurement, 117,* 319–338. doi:10.2466/10.23.PMS.117x17z9

Kinsbourne, M. (1988). Sinistrality, brain organization and cognitive deficits. In D.L. Molfese & S.J. Segalowitz (Eds.), *Brain lateralization in children: Brain implications* (pp. 259–280). New York, NY: Guilford.

Kinsbourne, M. (1997). The development of lateralization. In H.W. Reese & M.D. Franzen (Eds.), *Biological and neuropsychological mechanisms: Life span developmental psychology* (pp. 181 – 197). Hillsdale, NJ: Erlbaum.

Kinsella, K., & Velkoff, V.A. (2001). *An aging world: 2001* (U.S. Census Bureau, Series P95/01-1). Washington, DC: U.S. Government Printing Office.

Kiselev, S. (2015). Age-related differences in processing speed in preschool children. *Open Behavioral Science, 9*(Suppl. 1–M4), 23–31.

Kiselev, S., Espy, K.A., & Sheffield, T. (2009). Age-related differences in reaction time task performance in young children. *Journal of Experimental Child Psychology, 102*(2), 150–166. doi:10.1016/j.jecp.2008.02.002

Kisilevsky, B.S., Stach, D.M., & Muir, D.W. (1991). Fetal and infant response to tactile stimulation. In M.J.S. Weiss & P.R. Zelazo (Eds.), *Newborn attention: Biological constraints and the influence of experience* (pp. 63–98). Norwood, NJ: Ablex.

Kline, D.W., Culham, J., Bartel, P., & Lynk, L. (1994). Aging and hyperacuity thresholds as a function of contrast and oscillation rate. *Canadian Psychology, 35,* 14.

Klint, K.A., & Weiss, M.R. (1986). Dropping in and dropping out: Participation motives of current and former youth gymnasts. *Canadian Journal of Applied Sport Sciences, 11,* 106–114.

Knudson, D. (2013). *Fundamentals of biomechanics.* New York, NY: Springer-Verlag.

Ko, S., Ling, S.M., Winters, J., & Ferrucci, L. (2009). Age-related mechanical work expenditure during normal walking: The Baltimore Longitudinal Study of Aging. *Journal of Biomechanics, 42*(12), 1834–1839. doi:10.1016/j.jbiomech.2009.05.037

Ko, S.U., Stenholm, S., Metter, E.J., & Ferrucci, L. (2012). Age-associated gait patterns and the role of lower extremity strength—results from the Baltimore Longitudinal Study of Aging. *Archives of Gerontology and Geriatrics, 55*(2), 474–479. doi:10.1016/j.arch-ger.2012.04.004.

Kobayashi, K., Kitamura, K., Miura, M., Sodeyama, H., Murase, Y., Miyashita, M., et al. (1978). Aerobic power as related to body growth and training in Japanese boys: A longitudinal study. *Journal of Applied Physiology, 44,* 666–672.

Koch, G., & Rocker, L. (1977). Plasma volume and intravascular protein masses in trained boys and fit young men. *Journal of Applied Physiology, 43,* 1085–1088.

Koivula, N. (2000). Gender stereotyping in televised media sport coverage. *Sex Roles, 41,* 589–604.

Komi, P.V. (1984). Physiological and biomechanical correlates of muscle function: Effects of muscle structure and stretch-shortening cycle on force and speed. In R.L. Terjung (Ed.), *Exercise and sport science reviews* (Vol. 12, pp. 81–121). Lexington, MA: Collamore.

Konczak, J. (1990). Toward an ecological theory of motor development: The relevance of the Gibsonian approach to vision for motor development research. In J.E. Clark & J.H. Humphrey (Eds.), *Advances in motor development research* (Vol. 3, pp. 201–224). New York, NY: AMS Press.

Kooijman, M.N., Kruithof, C.J., van Duijn, C.M., Duijts, L., Franco, O.H., van IJzendoorn, M.H., et al (2017). The Generation R Study: Design and cohort update 2017. *European Journal of Epidemiology, 31*, 1243–1264.

Korhonen, M.T., Cristea, A., Alen, M., Hakkinen, K., Sipila, S., Mero, A., et al. (2006). Aging, muscle fiber type, and contractile function in spring-trained athletes. *Journal of Applied Physiology, 101*, 906–917. doi:10.1152/japplphysiol.002999.206

Kornatz, K.W., Christou, E.A., & Enoka, R.M. (2005). Practice reduces motor unit discharge variability in a hand muscle and improves manual dexterity in old adults. *Journal of Applied Physiology, 98*, 2072–2080. doi: 10.1152/japplphysiol.01149.2004

Kotz, C.M., Billington, C.J., & Levine, A.S. (1999). Obesity and aging. *Clinics in Geriatric Medicine, 15*(2), 391–412.

Kraemer, W.J., Fry, A.C., Frykman, P.N., Conroy, B., & Hoffman, J. (1989). Resistance training and youth. *Pediatric Exercise Science, 1,* 336–350.

Kraemer, W.J., Vescovi, J.D., Volek, J.S., Nindl, B.C., Newton, R.U., Patton, J.F., et al. (2004). Effects of concurrent resistance and aerobic training on load-bearing performance and the Army Physical Fitness Test. *Military Medicine, 169,* 994–999.

Krahenbuhl, G.S., & Martin, S.L. (1977). Adolescent body size and flexibility. *Research Quarterly, 48,* 797–799.

Krahenbuhl, G.S., Pangrazi, R.P., Petersen, G.W., Burkett, L.N., & Schneider, M.J. (1978). Field testing of cardiorespiratory fitness in primary school children. *Medicine and Science in Sports, 10,* 208–213.

Krahenbuhl, G.S., Skinner, J.S., & Kohrt, W.M. (1985). Developmental aspects of maximal aerobic power in children. *Medicine and Science in Sports and Exercise, 13,* 503–538.

Kretch, K.S., & Adolph, K.E. (2013). Cliff or step? Posture-specific learning at the edge of a drop-off. *Child Development, 84*, 226–240.

Kuczaj, S.A., II, & Maratsos, M.P. (1975). On the acquisition of front, back, and side. *Child Development, 46,* 202–210.

Kuffler, S.W., Nicholls, J.G., & Martin, A.R. (1984). *From neuron to brain* (2nd ed.). Sunderland, MA: Sinauer.

Kugler, P.N., Kelso, J.A.S., & Turvey, M.T. (1980). On the concept of coordinative structures as dissipative structures: I. Theoretical lines of convergence. In G.E. Stelmach & J. Requin (Eds.), *Tutorials in motor behavior* (pp. 3–47). New York, NY: North-Holland.

Kugler, P.N., Kelso, J.A.S., & Turvey, M.T. (1982). On the control and coordination of naturally developing systems. In J.A.S. Kelso & J.E. Clark (Eds.), *The development of movement control and coordination* (pp. 5–78). New York, NY: Wiley.

Kuhn, D. (2000). Does memory development belong on an endangered topic list? *Child Development, 71,* 21–25.

Kuhtz-Buschbeck, J.P., Stolze, H., Boczek-Funcke, A., Joehnk, K., Heinrichs, H., & Illert, M. (1998). Kinematic analysis of prehension movements in children. *Behavioural Brain Research, 93,* 131–141.

Kuk, J.L., Saunders, J.T., Davidson, L.E., & Ross, R. (2009). Age-related changes in total and regional fat distribution, *Ageing Research Reviews, 8*(4), 339–348.

Kuo, A.D., & Zajac, F.E. (1993). Human standing posture: Multi-joint movement strategies based on biomechanical constraints. *Progress in Brain Research, 97,* 349–358.

Kuo, Y.L., Liao, H.F., Chen, P.C., Hsieh, W.S., & Hwang, A.W. (2008). The influence of wakeful prone positioning on motor development during the early life. *Journal of Developmental & Behavioral Pediatrics, 29*(5), 367-376.

Laird, Y., Fawkner, S., Kelly, P., McNamee, L., & Niven, A. (2016). The role of social support on physical activity behaviour in adolescent girls: A systematic review and meta-analysis. *International Journal of Behavioral Nutrition and Physical Activity, 13*, 79

Lakatta, E.G., & Levy, D. (2003a). Arterial and cardiac aging: Major shareholders in a cardiovascular disease enterprises. Part I: Aging arteries: A "set up" for vascular disease. *Circulation,*

107, 139–146.

Lakatta, E.G., & Levy, D. (2003b). Arterial and cardiac aging: Major shareholders in cardiovascular disease enterprises. Part II: The aging heart in health: Links to heart disease. *Circulation, 107*, 346–354.

Lambert, J., & Bard, C. (2005). Acquisition of visuomanual skills and improvement of information processing capacities in 6 to 10 year old children performing a 2D pointing task. *Neuroscience Letters, 377*, 1–6

Lan, C., Lai, J.S., Chen, S.U., & Wong, M.K. (1998). 12-month tai chi training in the elderly: Its effects on health fitness. *Medicine and Science in Sports and Exercise, 30*(3), 345–351.

Lane, A.P., Molina, S.L., Tolleson, D.A., Langendorfer, S.J., Goodway, J.D., & Stodden, D.F. (2018). Developmental sequences for the standing long jump landing: A pre-longitudinal screening. *Journal of Motor Learning and Development, 6*, 114–129.

Langendorfer, S. (1980). *Longitudinal evidence for developmental changes in the preparatory phase of the overarm throw for force.* Paper presented at the annual convention of the American Alliance for Health, Physical Education, Recreation and Dance, Detroit.

Langendorfer, S. (1982). *Developmental relationships between throwing and striking: A prelongitudinal test of motor stage theory.* Unpublished doctoral dissertation, University of Wisconsin, Madison.

Langendorfer, S. (1987). Prelongitudinal screening of overarm striking development performed under two environmental conditions. In J.E. Clark & J.H. Humphrey (Eds.), *Advances in motor development research* (Vol. 1, pp. 17–47). New York, NY: AMS Press.

Langendorfer, S. (1990). Motor-task goal as a constraint on developmental status. In J.E. Clark & J.H. Humphrey (Eds.), *Advances in motor development research* (Vol. 3, pp. 16–28). New York, NY: AMS Press.

Langendorfer, S., & Roberton, M.A. (2002a). Individual pathways in the development of forceful throwing. *Research Quarterly for Exercise and Sport, 73,* 245–256.

Langendorfer, S.J., & Roberton, M.A. (2002b). Developmental profiles in overarm throwing: Searching for "attractors," "stages," and "constraints." In J. Clark & J. Humphrey (Eds.), *Motor development: Research and reviews* (Vol. 2, pp. 1–25). Reston, VA: National Association for Sport and Physical Education.

Lee, D.N., & Aronson, E. (1974). Visual proprioceptive control of standing in human infants. *Perception and Psychophysics, 15,* 529–532.

Lee, J.J., Pedley, A., Therkelsen, K.E., Hoffmann, U., Massaro, J.M., Levy, D., & Long, M.T. (2017). Upper body subcutaneous fat is associated with cardiometabolic risk factors. *American Journal of Medicine, 130*, 958–966. doi:10.1016/j.amjmed.2017.01.044

Lee, M., Liu, Y., & Newell, K.M. (2006). Longitudinal expressions of infant's prehension as a function of object properties. *Infant Behavior and Development, 29*, 481–493.

Lefebvre, C., & Reid, G. (1998). Prediction in ball catching by children with and without a developmental coordination disorder. *Adapted Physical Activity Quarterly, 15*(4), 299–315.

LeGear, M., Greyling, L., Sloan, E., Bell, R.I., Williams, B.-L., Naylor, P.-J., & Temple, V.A. (2012). A window of opportunity? Motor skills and perceptions of competence of children in kindergarten. *International Journal of Behavioral Nutrition and Physical Activity, 9*, 29. doi:10.1186/1479-5868-9-29

Leme, S., & Shambes, G. (1978). Immature throwing patterns in normal adult women. *Journal of Human Movement Studies, 4*, 85-93.

Lengyel, M., & Gyarfas, I. (1979). The importance of echocardiography in the assessment of left ventricular hypertrophy in trained and untrained school children. *Acta Cardiologica, 34,* 63–69.

Lenoir, M., Musch, E., Janssens, M., Thiery, E., & Uyttenhove, J. (1999). Intercepting moving objects during self-motion. *Journal of Motor Behavior, 31*(1), 55–67.

Lepp, A., Barkley, J.E., Sanders, G.J., Rebold, M., & Gates, P. (2013). The relationship between cell phone use, physical and sedentary activity, and cardiorespiratory fitness in a sample of U.S. college students. *International Journal of Behavioral Nutrition and Physical Activity, 10*, 79. doi:10.1186/1479-5868-10-79

Levy, G.D. (2000). Gender-typed and non-gender-typed category awareness in toddlers. *Sex Roles, 41,* 851–873.

Lew, A.R., & Butterworth, G. (1997). The development of hand-mouth coordination in 2- to 5-month-old infants: Similarities with reaching and grasping. *Infant Behavior and Development, 20*(1), 59–69.

Lewko, J.H., & Ewing, M.E. (1980). Sex differences and parental influences in sport involvement of children. *Journal of Sport Psychology, 2,* 62–68.

Lewko, J.H., & Greendorfer, S.L. (1988). Family influences in sport socialization of children and adolescents. In F.L. Smoll, R.A. Magill, & M.J. Ash (Eds.), *Children in sport* (3rd ed., pp. 287–300). Champaign, IL: Human Kinetics.

Lewkowicz, D.J., & Marcovitch, S. (2006). Perception of audiovisual rhythm and its invariance in 4- to 10-month-old infants. *Developmental Psychobiology, 48*, 288–300.

Lexell, J., Henriksson-Larsen, K., Wimblad, B., & Sjostrom, M. (1983). Distribution of different fiber types in human skeletal muscles: Effects of aging studies in whole muscle cross-sections. *Muscle and Nerve, 6,* 588–595.

Lexell, J., Taylor, C., & Sjostrom, M. (1988). What is the cause of ageing atrophy? Total number, size, and proportion of different fiber types studied in whole vastus lateralis muscle from 15- to 83-year-old men. *Journal of Neurological Sciences, 84,* 275–294.

Li, K.-Y., Su, W.-J., Fu, H.-W., & Pickett, K.A. (2015). Kinesthetic deficit in children with developmental coordination disorder. *Research in Developmental Disabilities, 38*, 125–133.

Lindquist, C., Reynolds, K., & Goran, M. (1998). Sociocultural determinants of physical activity among children. *Preventive Medicine, 29,* 305–312.

Lindwall, M., Asci, H., & Crocker, P. (2014). The physical self in motion: Within-person change and associations of change in self-esteem, physical self-concept, and physical activity in adolescent girls." *Journal of Sport and Exercise Psychology, 36*(6),

551–563. doi:10.1123/jsep.2013-0258

Liong, G.H.E., Ridgers, N.D., & Barnett, L.M. (2015). Associations between skill perceptions and young children's actual fundamental movement skills. *Perceptual and Motor Skills, 120*(2), 591–603

Lipsitz, L.A. (1989). Altered blood pressure homeostasis in advanced age: Clinical and research implications. *Journal of Gerontology: Medical Sciences, 44,* M179–M183.

Liss, M.B. (1983). Learning gender-related skills through play. In M.B. Liss (Ed.), *Social and cognitive skills: Sex roles and children's play* (pp. 147–166). New York, NY: Academic Press.

Liu, J., & Wrisberg, C.A. (1997). The effect of knowledge of results delay and the subjective estimation of movement form on the acquisition and retention of a motor skill. *Research Quarterly for Exercise and Sport, 68*(2), 145–151.

Lloyd, B., & Smith, C. (1985). The social representation of gender and young children's play. *British Journal of Developmental Psychology, 3,* 65–73.

Lloyd, M., Saunders, T.J., Bremer, E., Tremblay, & M.S. (2014). Long-term importance of fundamental motor skills: A 20-year follow-up study. *Adapted Physical Activity Quarterly, 31*, 67–78. doi:10.1123/apaq.2013-0048

Lobo, M.A., Kokkoni, E., de Campos, A.C., & Galloway, J.C. (2014). Not just playing around: Infants' object behaviors reflect ability, constraints, and object properties. *Infant Behavior and Development, 37*(3), 334–351.

Lockman, J.J. (1984). The development of detour ability during infancy. *Child Development, 55,* 482–491.

Lockman, J.J. (2000). A perception-action perspective on tool use development. *Child Development, 71,* 137–144.

Lockman, J.J., Ashmead, D.H., & Bushnell, E.W. (1984). The development of anticipatory hand orientation during infancy. *Journal of Experimental Child Psychology, 37*, 176–186.

Lockman, J.J., & Kahrs, B.A. (2017). New insights into the development of human tool use. *Current Directions in Psychological Science, 26*, 330–334. doi:10.1177/0963721417692035

Logan, S.W., Scrabis-Fletcher, K., Modlesky, C., & Getchell, N. (2011). The relationship between motor skill proficiency and body mass index in preschool children. *Research Quarterly for Exercise and Sport, 82*, 442–448.

Logan, S.W., Webster, E.K., Getchell, N., Pfeiffer, K.A., & Robinson, L.E. (2015). Relationship between fundamental motor skill competence and physical activity during childhood and adolescence: A systematic review. *Kinesiology Review, 4*, 416–426.

Long, A.B., & Looft, W.R. (1972). Development of directionality in children: Ages six through twelve. *Developmental Psychology, 6,* 375–380.

Lopes, L., Santos, R., Pereira, B., & Lopes, V.P. (2012). Associations between sedentary behavior and motor coordination in children. *American Journal of Human Biology, 24*, 746–752. doi:10.1002/ajhb.22310

Lopes, V.P., Barnett, L.M., Saraiva, L., Goncalves, C., Bowe, S.J., Abbott, G., et al. (2016). Validity and reliability of a pictorial instrument for assessing perceived motor competence in Portuguese children. *Child: Care, Health and Development, 42*(5), 666–674. doi:10.1111/cch.12359

Lopes, V.P., Stodden, D.F., Bianchi, M.M., Maia, J.A.R., & Rodrigues, L.P. (2012). Correlation between BMI and motor coordination in children. *Journal of Science and Medicine in Sport, 15*, 38–43. doi:10.1016/j.jsams.2011.07.005

Loprinzi, P.D., Davis, R.E., & Fu, Y.-C. (2015). Early motor skill competence as a mediator of child and adult physical activity. *Preventive Medicine Reports, 2*, 833–838. doi:10.1016/j.pmedr.2015.09.015

Lorber, J. (1994). Believing is seeing: Biology as ideology. *Gender and Society, 7,* 568–581.

Lorson, K.M., & Goodway, J.D. (2008). Gender differences in throwing form of children ages 6-8 years during a throwing game. *Research Quarterly for Exercise and Sport, 79*, 174–182.

Lorson, K.M., Stodden, D.F., Langendorfer, S.J., & Goodway, J.D. (2013). Age and gender differences in adolescent and adult overarm throwing. *Research Quarterly for Exercise and Sport, 84*, 239–244. doi:10.1080/02701367.2013.784841

Lowrey, G.H. (1986). *Growth and development of children* (8th ed.). Chicago: Year Book Medical.

Loy, J.W., McPherson, B.D., & Kenyon, G. (1978). *Sport and social systems.* Reading, MA: Addison-Wesley.

Lubans, D.R., Morgan, P.J., Cliff, D.P., Barnett, L.M., & Okely, A.D. (2010). Fundamental movement skills in children and adolescents. *Sports Medicine, 40*, 1019–1035.

Lutman, M.E. (1991). Degradations in frequency and temporal resolution with age and their impact on speech identification. *Acta Oto-Laryngologica (Suppl.), 476,* 120–126.

Lynch, A., Rhu, J., Agrawal, S., & Galloway, J.C. (2009). Power mobility training for a 7-month-old infant with spina bifida. *Pediatric Physical Therapy, 21*(4), 362–368.

Lyons, J., Fontaine, R., & Elliott, D. (1997). I lost it in the lights: The effects of predictable and variable intermittent vision on unimanual catching. *Journal of Motor Behavior, 29*(2), 113–118.

Madden, D.J., Whiting, W.L., & Huettel, S.A. (2005). Age-related changes in neural activity during visual perception and attention. In R. Cabeza, L. Nyberg, & D. Park (Eds.), *Cognitive neuroscience of aging: Linking cognitive and cerebral aging* (pp. 157–185). New York, NY: Oxford University Press.

Magill, R.A., & Anderson, D. (2017). *Motor learning and control: Concepts and applications* (11th ed.). New York: McGraw-Hill.

Makrides, L., Heigenhauser, G.J., & Jones, N.L. (1990). High-intensity endurance training in 20- to 30- and 60- to 70-yr-old healthy men. *Journal of Applied Physiology, 69*, 1792–1798. doi:10.1152/jappl.1990.69.5.1792

Mally, K.K., Battista, R.A., & Roberton, M.A. (2011). Distance as a control parameter for place kicking. *Journal of Human Sport and Exercise, 6*(1), 122–134.

Malina, R.M. (1978). Growth of muscle tissue and muscle mass. In F. Falkner & J.M. Tanner (Eds.), *Human growth: Vol. 2. Postnatal growth* (pp. 273–294). New York, NY: Plenum Press.

Malina, R.M. (1996). Tracking of physical activity and fitness across the lifespan. *Research Quarterly for Exercise and Sport, 67* (supplement), 48-57

Malina, R.M., Beunen, G.P., Claessens, A.L., Lefevre, J., Vanden Eynde, B., Renson, R., et al. (1995). Fatness and fitness of girls 7 to 17 years. *Obesity Research, 3,* 221–231.

Malina, R.M., & Bouchard, C. (1991). *Growth, maturation, and physical activity.* Champaign, IL: Human Kinetics.

Malina, R.M., Bouchard, C., & Bar-Or, O. (2004). *Growth, maturation, and physical activity* (2nd ed.). Champaign, IL: Human Kinetics.

Maloney, S.K., Fallon, B., & Wittenberg, C.K. (1984). *Aging and health promotion: Market research for public education, executive summary* (Contract no. 282-83-0105). Washington, DC: Public Health Service, Office of Disease Prevention and Health Promotion.

Marcon, R., & Freeman, G. (1999). Linking gender-related toy preferences to social structure: Changes in children's letters to Santa since 1978. *Journal of Psychological Practice, 2,* 1–10.

Marques, E.A., Mota, J., & Carvalho, J. (2012). Exercise effects on bone mineral density in older adults: A meta-analysis of randomized controlled trials. *Age, 34,* 1493–1515. doi:10.1007/s11357-011-9311-8

Marques-Bruna, P., & Grimshaw, P.N. (1997). 3-dimensional kinematics of overarm throwing action of children age 15 to 30 months. *Perceptual and Motor Skills, 84,* 1267–1283.

Marshall, W.A., & Tanner, J.M. (1969). Variations in pattern of pubertal changes in girls. *Archives of Disease in Childhood, 44,* 291–303.

Marshall, W.A., & Tanner, J.M. (1970). Variations in the pattern of pubertal changes in boys. *Archives of Disease in Childhood, 45,* 13–23.

Martorell, R., Malina, R.M., Castillo, R.O., Mendoza, F.S., & Pawson, I.G. (1988). Body proportions in three ethnic groups: Children and youth 2–17 years in NHANES II and HHANES. *Human Biology, 60,* 205–222.

Masci, I., Schmidt, M., Marchetti, R., Vannozzi, G., & Pesce, C. (2017). When children's perceived and actual motor competence mismatch: Sport participation and gender differences. *Journal of Motor Learning and Development, 0,* 1–33.

Masters, R.S., Maxwell, J.P., & Eves, F.F. (2009). Marginally perceptible outcome feedback, motor learning and implicit processes. *Consciousness and Cognition, 18,* 639–645.

Matthews, C.D., Chen, K.Y., Freedson, P.S., Buchowski, M.S., Beech, B.M., Pate, R.R., & Troiano, R.P. (2008). Amount of time spent in sedentary behaviors in the United States, 2003–2004. *American Journal of Epidemiology, 167,* 875–881. doi:10.1093/aje/kwm390

Mayer, F., Scharhag-Rosenberger, F., Carlsohn, A., Cassel, M., Müller, S., & Scharhag, J. (2011). The intensity and effects of strength training in the elderly. *Deutsches Ärzteblatt International, 108,* 359–364.

Mayorga-Vega, D., Merino-Marban, R., Sanchez-Rivas, E., & Viciana, J. (2014). Effect of a short-term static stretching training program followed by five weeks of detraining on hamstring extensibility in children aged 9-10 years. *Journal of Physical Education and Sport, 14,* 355–359. doi:10.7752/jpes.2014.03054

McAuley, E. (1994). Physical activity and psychosocial outcomes. In C. Bouchard & R. Shephard (Eds.), *Physical activity, fitness, and health: International proceedings and consensus statement* (pp. 551–568). Champaign, IL: Human Kinetics.

McAuley, E., Kramer, A.F., & Colcombe, S.J. (2004). Cardiovascular fitness and neurocognitive function in older adults: A brief review. *Brain, Behavior, and Immunity, 18,* 214–220.

McBeath, M.K., Shaffer, D.M., & Kaiser, M.K. (1995). How baseball outfielders determine where to run to catch fly balls. *Science, 268,* 569–573.

McCallister, S., Blinde, E., & Phillips, J. (2003). Prospects for change in a new millennium: Gender beliefs of young girls in sport and physical activity. *Women in Sports and Physical Activity Journal, 12,* 83–109.

McCarty, M.E., & Ashmead, D.H. (1999). Visual control of reaching and grasping in infants. *Developmental Psychology, 35,* 620–631.

McCaskill, C.L., & Wellman, B.L. (1938). A study of common motor achievements at the preschool ages. *Child Development, 9,* 141–150.

McComas, A.J. (1996). *Skeletal muscle: Form and function.* Champaign, IL: Human Kinetics.

McConnell, A., & Wade, G. (1990). Effects of lateral ball location, grade, and sex on catching. *Perceptual and Motor Skills, 70,* 59–66.

McGinnis, P. (2013). *Biomechanics of sport and exercise* (3rd ed.). Champaign, IL: Human Kinetics.

McGraw, M. (1935). *Growth: A Study of Johnny and Jimmy.* New York, NY: Appleton-Century-Crofts.

McGraw, M.B. (1943). *The neuromuscular maturation of the human infant.* New York, NY: Columbia University Press.

McKay, M.J., Baldwin, J.N., Ferreira, P., Simic, M., Vanicek, N., & Burns, J. (2017). Normative reference values for strength and flexibility of 1,000 children and adults. *Neurology, 88,* 36–43.

McKenzie, B.E., & Bigelow, E. (1986). Detour behavior in young human infants. *British Journal of Developmental Psychology, 4,* 139–148.

McLeod, P., & Dienes, Z. (1993). Running to catch the ball. *Nature, 362,* 23.

McLeod, P., & Dienes, Z. (1996). Do fielders know where to go to catch the ball or only how to get there? *Journal of Experimental Psychology: Human Perception and Performance, 22*(3), 531–543.

McMurdo, M.E., & Rennie, L. (1993). A controlled trial of exercise by residents of old people's homes. *Age and Ageing, 22,* 11–15.

McNarry, M., & Jones, A. (2014). The influence of training status on the aerobic and anaerobic responses to exercise in children: A review. *European Journal of Sport Science, 14,* S57–S68. doi:10.1080/17461391.2011.643316

McNarry, M.A., Mackintosh, K.A., & Steodefalke, K. (2014). Longitudinal investigation of training status and cardiopulmonary responses in pre- and early-pubertal children. *European Journal of Applied Physiology, 114,* 1573–1580. doi:10.1007/s00421-014-2890-1

McPherson, B.D. (1978). The child in competitive sport: Influence of the social milieu. In R.A. Magill, M.J. Ash, & F.L. Smoll (Eds.), *Children in sport: A contemporary anthology* (pp. 219–249). Champaign, IL: Human Kinetics.

McPherson, B.D. (1983). *Aging as a social process: An introduction to individual and population aging.* Toronto: Butterworths.

McPherson, B.D. (1986). Sport, health, well-being and aging: Some conceptual and methodological issues and questions for sport scientists. In B. McPherson (Ed.), *Sport and aging* (pp. 3–23). Champaign, IL: Human Kinetics.

McPherson, B.D., Marteniuk, R., Tihanyi, J., & Clark, W. (1980). The social system of age group swimmers: The perceptions of swimmers, parents, and coaches. *Canadian Journal of Applied Sciences, 5,* 143–145.

Meltzoff, A.N., & Borton, R.W. (1979). Intermodal matching by human neonates. *Nature, 282,* 403–404.

Meredith, M.D., & Welk, G.J. (1999). *Fitnessgram test administration manual* (2nd ed.). Champaign, IL: Human Kinetics.

Messick, J.A. (1991). Prelongitudinal screening of hypothesized developmental sequences for the overhead tennis serve in experienced tennis players 9–19 years of age. *Research Quarterly for Exercise and Sport, 62,* 249–256.

Metcalfe, J.S., McDowell, K., Chang, T.Y., Chen, L.-C., Jeka, J.J., & Clark, J.E. (2005). Development of somatosensory-motor integration: An event-related analysis of infant posture in the first year of independent walking. *Developmental Psychobiology, 46,* 19–35.

Michaels, C.F., & Oudejans, R.R.D. (1992). The optics and actions of catching fly balls: Zeroing out optical acceleration. *Ecological Psychology, 4,* 199–222.

Michel, G.F. (1983). Development of hand-use preference during infancy. In G. Young, S. Segalowitz, C.M. Carter, & S.E. Trehub (Eds.), *Manual specialization and the developing brain* (pp. 33–70). New York, NY: Academic Press.

Michel, G.F. (1988). A neuropsychological perspective on infant sensorimotor development. In C. Rovee-Collier & L.P. Lipsitt (Eds.), *Advances in infancy research* (Vol. 5, pp. 1–37). Norwood, NJ: Ablex.

Michel, G.F., & Goodwin, R.A. (1979). Intrauterine birth position predicts newborn supine head position preferences. *Infant Behavior and Development, 2,* 29–38.

Michel, G.F., & Harkins, D.A. (1986). Postural and lateral asymmetries in the ontogeny of handedness during infancy. *Developmental Psychobiology, 19,* 247–258.

Micheli, L.J. (1984). Sport injuries in the young athlete: Questions and controversies. In L.J. Micheli (Ed.), *Pediatric and adolescent sports medicine* (pp. 1–9). Boston, MA: Little, Brown.

Mikulic, P. (2011). Development of aerobic and anaerobic power in adolescent rowers: A 5-year follow-up study. *Scandinavian Journal of Medicine and Science in Sports, 21,* e143–e149. doi:10.111/j.1600-0838.2010.01200.x

Milani-Comparetti, A. (1981). The neurophysiologic and clinical implications of studies on fetal motor behavior. *Seminars in Perinatology, 5,* 183–189.

Milani-Comparetti, A., & Gidoni, E.A. (1967). Routine developmental examination in normal and retarded children. *Developmental Medicine and Child Neurology, 9,* 631–638.

Milanovic, Z., Sporis, G., Trajkovic, N., Sekulic, D., James, N., & Vuckovic, G. (2014). Does SAQ training improve the speed and flexibility of young soccer players? A randomized controlled trial. *Human Movement Science, 38,* 197–208. doi:10.1016/j.humov.2014.09.005

Miller, C.T., Fraser, S.F., Levinger, I., Straznicky, N.E., Dixon, J.B., Reynolds, J., & Selig, S.E. (2013). The effects of exercise training in addition to energy restriction on functional capacities and body composition in obese adults during weight loss: A systematic review. *PLoS ONE, 8,* e81692.

Milne, C., Seefeldt, V., & Reuschlein, P. (1976). Relationship between grade, sex, race, and motor performance in young children. *Research Quarterly, 47,* 726–730.

Milner, A.D., & Goodale, M.A. (1995). *The visual brain in action.* New York, NY: Oxford University Press.

Mirwald, R.L., & Bailey, D.A. (1986). *Maximal aerobic power: A longitudinal analysis.* London, Ontario: Sport Dynamics.

Mirwald, R.L., Bailey, D.A., Cameron, N., & Rasmussen, R.L. (1981). Longitudinal comparison of aerobic power in active and inactive boys aged 7.0 to 17.0 years. *Annals of Human Biology, 8,* 405–414.

Mohammadi, F., Bahram, A., Khalaji, H., & Ghadiri, F. (2017). Determining motor development status of 3-10 years old children in Ahvaz City using TGMD-3 test. *International Journal of Basic Science in Medicine, 2*(3),139–146

Molen, H.H. (1973). *Problems on the evaluation of gait.* Unpublished doctoral dissertation, Free University, Amsterdam.

Mook-Kanamori, D.O., Durmus, B., Sovio, U., Hofman, A., Raat, H., Steegers, E.A.P., et al. (2011). Fetal and infant growth and the risk of obesity during early childhood: The Generation R study. *European Journal of Endocrinology, 165,* 623–630.

Moore, C., Mealiea, J., Garon, N., & Povinelli, D.J. (2007). The development of body self-awareness. *Infancy, 11,* 157–174.

Moritani, T., & DeVries, H.A. (1980). Potential for gross muscle hypertrophy in older men. *Journal of Gerontology, 35,* 672–682.

Moro, T., Tinsley G., Biaco, A., Gottardi, A., Gottardi, G.B., Faggian, D., et al. (2017). High intensity interval resistance training (HIIRT) in older adults: Effects on body composition, strength, anabolic hormones and blood lipids. *Experimental Gerontology, 98,* 91–98. doi:10.1016/j.exger.2017.08.015

Morris, G.S.D. (1976). Effects ball and background color have upon the catching performance of elementary school children. *Research Quarterly, 47,* 409–416.

Morrongiello, B.A. (1984). Auditory temporal pattern perception in 6- and 12-month-old infants. *Developmental Psychology, 20,* 441–448.

Morrongiello, B.A. (1986). Infants' perception of multiple-group auditory patterns. *Infant Behavior and Development, 9,* 307–320.

Morrongiello, B.A. (1988a). The development of auditory pattern perception skills. In C. Rovee-Collier & L.P. Lipsitt (Eds.), *Advances in infancy research* (Vol. 6, pp. 135–172). Norwood,

NJ: Ablex.

Morrongiello, B.A. (1988b). Infants' localization of sounds along the horizontal axis: Estimates of minimum audible angle. *Developmental Psychology, 24*(1), 8–13.

Morrongiello, B.A., & Clifton, R.K. (1984). Effects of sound frequency on behavioral and cardiac orienting in newborn and five-month-old infants. *Journal of Experimental Child Psychology, 38,* 429–446.

Morrongiello, B.A., Fenwick, K.D., Hillier, L., & Chance, G. (1994). Sound localization in newborn human infants. *Developmental Psychology, 27*(8), 519–538.

Morrongiello, B.A., Trehub, S.E., Thorpe, L.A., & Capodilupo, S. (1985). Children's perceptions of melodies: The role of contour, frequency, and rate of presentation. *Journal of Experimental Child Psychology, 40,* 279–292.

Morrow, D., & Leirer, V. (1997). Aging, pilot performance, and expertise. In A.D. Fisk & W.A. Rogers (Eds.), *Handbook of human factors and the older adult* (pp. 199–230). San Diego: Academic Press.

Murnen, S.K., Greenfield, C., Younger, A., & Boyd, H. (2016). Boys act and girls appear: A content analysis of gender stereotypes associated with characters in children's popular culture. *Sex Roles, 74*(1/2), 78–91. doi:10.1007/s11199-015-0558-x.

Murray, M.P., Drought, A.B., & Kory, R.C. (1964). Walking patterns of normal men. *Journal of Bone and Joint Surgery, 46A,* 335–360.

Murray, M.P., Kory, R.C., Clarkson, B.H., & Sepic, S.B. (1966). Comparison of free and fast speed walking patterns of normal men. *American Journal of Physical Medicine, 45,* 8–24.5

Murray, M.P., Kory, R.C., & Sepic, S.B. (1970). Walking patterns of normal women. *Archives of Physical Medicine and Rehabilitation, 51,* 637–650.

Musto, M., Cooky, C., & Messner, M.A. (2017). From fizzle to sizzle: Televised sports news and the production of gender-bland sexism. *Gender & Society, 31,* 573–596.

Nagin, D.S. (1999). Analyzing developmental trajectories: A semiparametric, group-based approach. *Psychological Methods, 4,* 139–157.

Nanez, J., & Yonas, A. (1994). Effects of luminance and texture motion on infant defensive reactions to optical collision. *Infant Behavior and Development, 17,* 165–174.

National Federation of State High School Associations. (2017). Annual report 2016–17. Retrieved from www.nfhs.org/media/1018857/2016-17-annual-report.pdf

National Institute on Aging. (2016). Alzheimer's disease fact sheet. Retrieved from www.nia.nih.gov/health/alzheimers-disease-fact-sheet

Naus, M., & Shillman, R. (1976). Why a Y is not a V: A new look at the distinctive features of letters. *Journal of Experimental Psychology: Human Perception and Performance, 2,* 394–400.

Nelson, C.J. (1981). *Locomotor patterns of women over 57.* Unpublished master's thesis, Washington State University, Pullman.

Nelson, J., Thomas, J., & Nelson, J. (1991). Longitudinal change in throwing performance: Gender differences. *Research Quarterly for Exercise and Sport, 62,* 105–108.

Nervik, D., Martin, K., Rundquist, P., & Cleland, J. (2011). The relationship between body mass index and gross motor development in children aged 3 to 5 years. *Pediatric Physical Therapy, 23,* 144–148.

Newell, K., & Jordan, K.M. (2007). Task constraints and movement organization: A common language. In W. Davis & B.D. Broadhead (Eds.), *Ecological task analysis and movement* (pp. 5–23). Champaign, IL: Human Kinetics.

Newell, K.M. (1986). Constraints on the development of coordination. In M.G. Wade & H.T.A. Whiting (Eds.), *Motor development in children: Aspects of coordination and control* (pp. 341–361). Amsterdam: Nijhoff.

Newell, K.M., Liu, Y.-T., & Mayer-Kress, G. (2001). Time scales in motor learning and development. *Psychological Review, 108*(1), 57–82.

Newell, K.M., Scully, D.M., McDonald, P.V., & Baillargeon, R. (1989). Task constraints and infant grip configurations. *Developmental Psychobiology, 22,* 817–832.

Newell, K.M., Scully, D.M., Tenenbaum, F., & Hardiman, S. (1989). Body scale and the development of prehension. *Developmental Psychobiology, 22,* 11–13.

Nielsen, B., Nielsen, K., Hansen, M.B., & Asmussen, E. (1980). Training of "functional muscle strength" in girls 7–19 years old. In K. Berg & B.O. Eriksson (Eds.), *Children and exercise IX* (pp. 69–78). Baltimore, MD: University Park Press.

NIH Osteoporosis and Related Bone Diseases National Resource Center. (2017). Osteoporosis overview. Retrieved from www.bones.nih.gov/health-info/bone/osteoporosis/overview

Nilwik, R., Snijders, T., Leenders, M., Groen, B.B., van Kranenburg, J., Verdijk, L.B., & van Loon, L.J. (2013). The decline in skeletal muscle mass with aging is mainly attributed to a reduction in type II muscle fiber size. *Experimental Gerontology, 48*(5), 492–498. doi:10.1016/j.exger.2013.02.012

Nordlund, B. (1964). Directional audiometry. *Acta Oto-Laryngologica, 57,* 1–18.

Norman, J.F., Kappers, A.M.L., Cheeseman, J.R., Ronning, C., Thomason, K.E., Baxter, M.W., et al. (2013). Aging and curvature discrimination from static and dynamic touch. *PLoS ONE, 8,* e68577. doi:10.1371/journal.pone.0068577

Norris, A.H., Shock, N.W., Landowne, M., & Falzone, J.A. (1956). Pulmonary function studies: Age differences in lung volume and bellows function. *Journal of Gerontology, 11,* 379–387.

Northman, J.E., & Black, K.N. (1976). An examination of errors in children's visual and haptic-tactual memory for random forms. *Journal of Genetic Psychology, 129,* 161–165.

Notarnicola, A., Perroni, F., Campese, A., Maccagnano, G., Monno, A., Moretti, B., & Tafuri, S. (2017). Flexibility responses to different stretching methods in young elite basketball players. *Muscles, Ligaments and Tendons Journal, 7,* 582–589.

Nougier, V., Bard, C., Fleury, M., & Teasdale, N. (1998). Contribution of central and peripheral vision to the regulation of stance: Developmental aspects. *Journal of Experimental Child Psychology, 68,* 202–215.

Nyhan, N.L. (1990). Structural abnormalities. *Clinical Symposia, 42*(2), 1–32.

Oettingen, G. (1985). The influence of the kindergarten teacher on sex differences in behavior. *International Journal of Behavioral Development, 8,* 3–13.

Ofte, S.H., & Hugdahl, K. (2002). Right-left discrimination in male and female, young and old subjects. *Journal of Clinical and Experimental Neuropsychology, 24,* 82–92.

Olson, P.L., & Sivak, M. (1986). Perception-response time to unexpected roadway hazards. *Human Factors, 28,* 91–96.

Onyango, A.W., De Onis, M., & World Health Organization. (2008). Training course on child growth assessment: WHO child growth standards:. Retrieved from https://www.who.int/childgrowth/training/module_h_directors_guide.pdf

Orlick, T.D. (1973, January/February). Children's sport: A revolution is coming. *Canadian Association for Health, Physical Education, and Recreation Journal,* 12–14.

Orlick, T.D. (1974, November/December). The athletic drop-out: A high price for inefficiency. *Canadian Association for Health, Physical Education, and Recreation Journal,* 21–27.

Oudejans, R.R.D., Michaels, C.F., Bakker, F.C., & Dolne, M.A. (1996). The relevance of action in perceiving affordances: Perception of catchableness of fly balls. *Journal of Experimental Psychology, 22*(4), 879–891.

Paillard, T., Lafont, C., Costes-Salon, M.C., Riviere, D., & Dupui, P. (2004). Effects of brisk walking on static and dynamic balance, locomotion, body composition, and aerobic capacity in ageing healthy active men. *International Journal of Sports Medicine, 25,* 539–546.

Paoletti, J.B. (2012). *Pink and blue: Telling the boys from the girls in America.* Bloomington: Indiana University Press.

Pargman, D. (1997). *Understanding sport behavior.* Englewood Cliffs, NJ: Prentice Hall.

Parish, L.E., & Rudisill, M.E. (2006). HAPPE: Promoting physical play among toddlers. *Young Children, 61*(3), 32.

Parish, L.E., Rudisill, M.E., & St. Onge, P.M. (2007). Mastery motivational climate: Influence on physical play heart rate and intensity in African American toddlers. *Research Quarterly for Exercise and Sport, 78,* 171–178.

Parizkova, J. (1963). Impact of age, diet, and exercise on man's body composition. *Annals of the New York Academy of Sciences, 110,* 661–674.

Parizkova, J. (1968a). Longitudinal study of the development of body composition and body build in boys of various physical activity. *Human Biology, 40,* 212–225.

Parizkova, J. (1972). Somatic development and body composition changes in adolescent boys differing in physical activity and fitness: A longitudinal study. *Anthropologie, 10,* 3–36.

Parizkova, J. (1973). Body composition and exercise during growth and development. In G.L. Rarick (Ed.), *Physical activity: Human growth and development* (pp. 97–124). New York, NY: Academic Press.

Parizkova, J. (1977). *Body fat and physical fitness.* The Hague, the Netherlands: Nijhoff.

Parker, A.W., & James, B. (1985). Age changes in the flexibility of Down syndrome children. *Journal of Mental Deficiency Research, 29,* 207–218.

Parker, D.F., Round, J.M., Sacco, P., & Jones, D.A. (1990). A cross-sectional survey of upper and lower limb strength in boys and girls during childhood and adolescence. *Annals of Human Biology, 17,* 199-211. doi:10.1080/0301446900000096

Patel, K.V., Phelan, E.A., Leveille, S.G., Lamb, S.E., Missikpode, C., Wallace, R.B., et al. (2014). High prevalence of falls, fear of falling, and impaired balance in older adults with pain in the United States: Findings from the 2011 National Health and Aging Trends Study. *Journal of the American Geriatrics Society, 62,* 1844–1852.

Patrick, H., Ryan, A.M., Alfeld-Liro, C., Fredricks, J., Hruda, L., & Eccles, J. (1999). Adolescents' commitment to developing talent: The role of peers in continuing motivation for sports and the arts. *Journal of Youth and Adolescence, 28,* 741–763.

Patriksson, G. (1981). Socialization to sports involvement. *Scandinavian Journal of Sports Sciences, 3,* 27–32.

Payne, V.G. (1982). Simultaneous investigation of effects of distance of projection and object size on object reception by children in grade 1. *Perceptual and Motor Skills, 54,* 1183–1187.

Payne, V.G., & Koslow, R. (1981). Effects of varying ball diameters on catching ability of young children. *Perceptual and Motor Skills, 53,* 739–744.

Peiper, A. (1963). *Cerebral function in infancy and childhood.* New York, NY: Consultants Bureau.

Pennell, G. (1999). Doing gender with Santa: Gender-typing in children's toy preferences. *Dissertation Abstracts International, 59-8*(B), 4541.

Perlmutter, M., & Nyquist, L. (1990). Relationships between self-reported physical and mental health and intelligence performance across adulthood. *Journal of Gerontology: Psychological Sciences, 45,* P145–P155.

Perrin, P.P., Jeandel, C., Perrin, C.A., & Bene, M.C. (1997). Influence of visual control, conduction, and central integration on static and dynamic balance in healthy older adults. *Gerontology, 43,* 223–231.

Pesce, V., Speciale, D., Sammarco, G., Patella, S., Spinarelli, A., & Patella, V. (2009). Surgical approach to bone healing in osteoporosis. *Clinical Cases in Mineral and Bone Metabolism, 6*(2), 131–135.

Pesta, D., Thaler, A., Hoppel, F., Macek, C., Schocke, M., & Burtscher, M. (2014). Effects of a 10-week conventional strength training program on lower leg muscle performance in adolescent boys compared to adults. *The Journal of Sports Medicine and Physical Fitness, 54,* 147-153.

Petranek, L.J., & Barton, G.V. (2011). The overarm-throwing pattern among U-14 ASA female softball players: A comparative study of gender, culture, and experience. *Research Quarterly for Exercise and Sport, 82,* 220–228.

Pfeiffer, R., & Francis, R.S. (1986). Effects of strength training on muscle development in prepubescent, pubescent, and postpubescent males. *The Physician and Sportsmedicine, 14,* 134–143.

Phillips, M., Bookwalter, C., Denman, C., McAuley, J., Sherwin,

H., Summers, D., et al. (1955). Analysis of results from the Kraus-Weber test of minimum muscular fitness in children. *Research Quarterly, 26,* 314–323.

Piaget, J. (1952). *The origins of intelligence in children.* New York, NY: International Universities Press.

Pick, A.D. (Ed.). (1979). *Perception and its development: A tribute to Eleanor J. Gibson.* Hillsdale, NJ: Erlbaum.

Pick, H.L. (1989). Motor development: The control of action. *Developmental Psychology, 25,* 867–870.

Pickett, K., & Konczak, J. (2009). Measuring kinaesthetic sensitivity in typically developing children. *Developmental Medicine & Child Neurology, 51,* 711-716. doi: 10.1111/j.1469-8749.2008.03229.x

Piek, J.P., & Gasson, N. (1999). Spontaneous kicking in full term and preterm infants: Are there leg asymmetries? *Human Movement Science, 18,* 377–395.

Piek, J.P., Gasson, N., Barrett, N., & Case, I. (2002). Limb and gender differences in the development of coordination in early infancy. *Human Movement Science, 21,* 621–639.

Piéraut-Le Bonniec, G. (1985). Hand-eye coordination and infants' construction of convexity and concavity. *British Journal of Developmental Psychology, 3,* 273–280.

Pigott, R.E., & Shapiro, D.C. (1984). Motor schema: The structure of the variability session. *Research Quarterly for Exercise and Sport, 55,* 41–45.

Pin, T., Eldridge, B., & Galea, M.P. (2007). A review of the effects of sleep position, play position, and equipment use on motor development in infants. *Developmental Medicine & Child Neurology, 49*(11), 858-867.

Pinti, P., Tachtisidis, I., Hamilton, A., Hirsch, J., Aichelburg, C., Gilbert, S., et al. (2018). The present and future use of functional near infrared spectroscopy (fNIRS) for cognitive neuroscience. *Annals of the New York Academy of Sciences.* Advanced online publication. doi:10.1111/nyas.13948

Piper, M., & Darrah, J. (1994). *Motor assessment of the developing infant.* Philadelphia: Saunders.

Pollock, M.L. (1974). Physiological characteristics of older champion track athletes. *Research Quarterly, 45,* 363–373.

Pomerance, A. (1965). Pathology of the heart with and without failure in the aged. *British Heart Journal, 27,* 697–710.

Ponds, R.W., Brouwer, W.H., & Van Wolffelaar, P.C. (1988). Age differences in divided attention in a simulated driving task. *Journal of Gerontology: Psychological Sciences, 43,* P151–P156.

Pope, M., Liu, T., Breslin, C., & Getchell, N. (2012). Using constraints to design developmentally appropriate movement activities for children with autism spectrum disorders. *Journal of Physical Education, Recreation, and Dance, 83*(2), 35–41.

Pope, M.J. (1984). *Visual proprioception in infant postural development.* Unpublished doctoral dissertation, University of Southampton, Highfield, Southampton, UK.

Posner, J.D., Gorman, K.M., Klein, H.S., & Woldow, A. (1986). Exercise capacity in the elderly. *American Journal of Cardiology, 57,* 52C–58C.

Postma, D.B.W., Smith, J., Pepping, G.-J., van Andel, S., & Zaal, F.T.J.M. (2017). When a fly ball is out of reach: Catchability judgments are not based on optical acceleration cancelation. *Frontiers in Psychology, 8,* 535. doi:10.3389/psyg.2071.00535

Power, T.G. (1985). Mother- and father-infant play: A developmental analysis. *Child Development, 56,* 1514–1524.

Power, T.G., & Parke, R.D. (1983). Patterns of mother and father play with their 8-month-old infant: A multiple analyses approach. *Infant Behavior and Development, 6,* 453–459.

Power, T.G., & Parke, R.D. (1986). Patterns of early socialization: Mother- and father-infant interactions in the home. *International Journal of Behavioral Development, 9,* 331–341.

Prader, A., Tanner, J.M., & von Harnack, G.A. (1963). Catch-up growth following illness or starvation: An example of developmental canalization in man. *Journal of Pediatrics, 62,* 646–659.

Prohaska, T.R., Leventhal, E.A., Leventhal, H., & Keller, M.L. (1985). Health practices and illness cognition in young, middle aged, and elderly adults. *Journal of Gerontology, 40,* 569–578.

Proske, U., & Gandevia, S.C. (2012). The proprioceptive senses: Their roles in signaling body shape, body position and movement, and muscle force. *Physiology Review, 92,* 1651–1697. doi:10.1152/physrev.0048.2011

Pryde, K.M., Roy, E.A., & Campbell, K. (1998). Prehension in children and adults: The effects of size. *Human Movement Science, 17*(6), 743–752.

Pulito Runion, B., Roberton, M.A., & Langendorfer, S.J. (2003). Forceful overarm throwing: A comparison of two cohorts measured 20 years apart. *Research Quarterly for Exercise and Sport, 74,* 324–330.

Purhonen, J., Kilpelainen-Lees, R., Valkonen-Korhonen, M., Karhu, J., & Lehtonen, J. (2005). Fourth-month-old infants process own mother's voice faster than unfamiliar voices: Electrical signs of sensitization in infant brain. *Cognitive Brain Research, 24,* 627–633.

Quatman, C.E., Ford, K.R., Myer, G.D., Paterno, M.V., & Hewett, T.D. (2008). The effects of gender and pubertal status on generalized joint laxity in young athletes. *Journal of Science and Medicine in Sport, 11,* 257–263.

Quatman-Yates, C.C., Quatman, C.E., Meszaros, A.J., Paterno, M.V., & Hewett, T.E. (2012). A systematic review of sensorimotor function during adolescence: A developmental stage of increased motor awkwardness? *British Journal of Sports Medicine, 46*(9), 649–655. doi:10.1136/bjsm.2010.079616

Raag, T. (1999). Influences of social expectations of gender, gender stereotypes, and situational constraints on children's toy choices. *Sex Roles, 41*(11/12), 809–831.

Raag, T., & Rackliff, C.L. (1998). Preschoolers' awareness of social expectations of gender: Relationships to toy choices. *Sex Roles, 38*(9/10), 685–700.

Radaelli, R., Botton, C.E., Wilhelm, E.N., Bottaro, M., Lacerda, F., Gaya, A., . . . Pinto, R.S. (2013). Low- and high-volume strength training induces similar neuromuscular improvements in muscle quality in elderly women. *Experimental Gerontology, 48,* 710-716. doi: 10.1016/j.exger.2013.04.003

Ramsay, D.S. (1980). Onset of unimanual handedness in infants. *Infant Behavior and Development, 3,* 377–386.

Ramsay, D.S. (1985). Infants' block banging at midline: Evidence for Gesell's principal of "reciprocal interweaving" in development. *British Journal of Developmental Psychology, 3,* 335–343.

Ramsay, D.S., Campos, J.J., & Fenson, L. (1979). Onset of bimanual handedness in infants. *Infant Behavior and Development, 2,* 69–76.

Ramsay, J.A., Blimkie, C.J.R., Smith, K., Garner, S., MacDougall, J.D., & Sale, D.G. (1990). Strength training effects in prepubescent boys. *Medicine and Science in Sports and Exercise, 22,* 605–614.

Rarick, G.L., & Smoll, F.L. (1967). Stability of growth in strength and motor performance from childhood to adolescence. *Human Biology, 39,* 295–306.

Rasmussen, R.L., Faulkner, R.A., Mirwald, R.L., & Bailey, D.A. (1990). A longitudinal analysis of structure/function related variables in 10–16 year old boys. In G. Beunen, J. Ghesquiere, T. Reybrouck, & A.L. Claessens (Eds.), *Children and exercise* (pp. 27–33). Stuttgart: Verlag.

Ratey, J.J. (2001). *A user's guide to the brain: Perception, attention, and the four theaters of the brain.* New York, NY: Vintage Books.

Ratey, J.J. (2008). *Spark.* New York, NY: Little, Brown.

Reaburn, P., & Dascombe, B. (2009). Anaerobic performance in masters athletes. *European Review of Aging and Physical Activity, 6,* 39. doi:10.1007/s11556-008-0041-6

Reaburn, P., Logan, P., & Mackinnon, L. (1994). The effect of hypertrophy resistance training on anaerobic work capacity in veteran sprint runners. In *1994 The Year of the Coach: National coaching conference proceedings* (pp. 168–172). Canberra, Australia: Australian Coaching Council.

Reaven, P.D., Barrett-Connor, E., & Edelstein, S. (1991). Relation between leisure-time physical activity and blood pressure in older women. *Circulation, 83,* 559–565.

Reid, G., & Block, M.E. (1996). Motor development and physical education. *New approaches to Down syndrome,* 309-340.

Reimers, S., & Maylor, E.A. (2005). Task switching across the life span: Effects of age on general and specific switch costs. *Developmental Psychology, 41,* 661–671.

Reith, K.M. (2004). *Playing fair: A Women's Sports Foundation guide to Title IX in high school and college sports.* East Meadow, NY: Women's Sports Foundation.

Rians, C.B., Weltman, A., Cahill, B.R., Janney, C.A., Tippett, S.R., & Katch, F.I. (1987). Strength training for prepubescent males: Is it safe? *American Journal of Sports Medicine, 15,* 483–489.

Rikli, R.E., & Busch, S. (1986). Motor performance of women as a function of age and physical activity level. *Journal of Gerontology, 41,* 645–649.

Rikli, R.E., & Edwards, D.J. (1991). Effects of a 3 year exercise program on motor function and cognitive speed in older women. *Research Quarterly for Exercise and Sport, 62*(1), 61–67.

Rikli, R.E., & Jones, C.J. (1999). Functional fitness normative scores for community-residing older adults, ages 60–94. *Journal of Aging and Physical Activity, 7,* 162–181.

Ring-Dimitriou, S., von Duvillard, S.P., Paulweber, B., Stadlmann, M., Lemura, L.M., Peak, K., et al. (2007). Nine months aerobic fitness induced changes on blood lipids and lipoproteins in untrained subjects versus controls. *European Journal of Applied Physiology, 99,* 291–299.

Rintala, P.O., Sääkslahti, A.K., & Iivonen, S. (2017). Reliability assessment of scores from video-recorded TGMD-3 performances. *Journal of Motor Learning and Development, 5,* 59–68.

Risser, W.L., & Preston, D. (1989). Incidence and causes of musculoskeletal injuries in adolescents training with weights [Abstract]. *Pediatric Exercise Science, 1,* 84.

Ritchie, C.S., Joshipura, K., Hung, H.C., & Douglass, C.W. (2002). Nutrition as a mediator in the relation between oral and systemic disease: Associations between specific measures of adult oral health and nutrition outcomes. *Critical Reviews in Oral Biology and Medicine, 13,* 291–300.

Rivilis, I., Hay, J., Cairney, J., Klentrou, P., Liu, J., & Faught, B.E. (2011). Physical activity and fitness in children with developmental coordination disorder: A systematic review. *Research in Developmental Disabilities, 32,* 894–910.

Rizzo, M., Anderson, S.W., & Fritzsch B. (Eds.) *The Wiley handbook on the aging mind and brain.* Hoboken, NJ: Wiley.

Roach, K.E., & Miles, T.P. (1991). Normal hip and knee active range of motion: The relationship to age. *Physical Therapy, 70,* 656–665.

Roberton, M.A. (1977). Stability of stage categorizations across trials: Implications for the "stage theory" of overarm throw development. *Journal of Human Movement Studies, 3,* 49–59.

Roberton, M.A. (1978a). Longitudinal evidence for developmental stages in the forceful overarm throw. *Journal of Human Movement Studies, 4,* 167–175.

Roberton, M.A. (1978b). Stages in motor development. In M.V. Ridenour (Ed.), *Motor development: Issues and applications* (pp. 63–81). Princeton, NJ: Princeton Book.

Roberton, M.A. (1984). Changing motor patterns during childhood. In J.R. Thomas (Ed.), *Motor development during childhood and adolescence* (pp. 48–90). Minneapolis: Burgess.

Roberton, M.A. (1988). The weaver's loom: A developmental metaphor. In J.E. Clark & J.H. Humphrey (Eds.), *Advances in motor development research* (Vol. 2, pp. 129–141). New York, NY: AMS Press.

Roberton, M.A. (1989). Motor development: Recognizing our roots, charting our future. *Quest, 41,* 213–223.

Roberton, M.A., & DiRocco, P. (1981). Validating a motor skill sequence for mentally retarded children. *American Corrective Therapy Journal, 35,* 148–154.

Roberton, M.A., & Halverson, L.E. (1984). *Developing children: Their changing movement.* Philadelphia: Lea & Febiger.

Roberton, M.A., & Halverson, L.E. (1988). The development of locomotor coordination: Longitudinal change and invariance. *Journal of Motor Behavior, 20,* 197–241.

Roberton, M.A., & Konczak, J. (2001). Predicting children's overarm throw ball velocities from their developmental levels in throwing. *Research Quarterly for Exercise and Sport, 72,* 91–103.

Roberton, M.A., & Langendorfer, S. (1980). Testing motor

development sequences across 9–14 years. In D. Nadeau, W. Halliwell, K. Newell, & G. Roberts (Eds.), *Psychology of motor behavior and sport—1979* (pp. 269–279). Champaign, IL: Human Kinetics.

Robinson, L.E. (2011). The relationship between perceived physical competence and fundamental motor skills in preschool children. *Child: Care, Health and Development, 37*, 589–596. doi:10.1111/j.1365-2214.2010.01187.x

Robinson, L.E., Stodden, D.F., Barnett, L.M., Lopes, V.P., Logan, S.W., Rodrigues, L.P., & D'Hondt, E. (2015). Motor competence and its effect on positive developmental trajectories of health. *Sports Medicine, 45*, 1273–1284. doi:10.1007/s40279-015-0351-6

Rodríguez, P.L., Santonja, F.M., Lopez-Miñarro, P.A., Sáinz de Baranda, P., & Yuste, J.L. (2008). Effect of physical education stretching programme on sit-and-reach score in schoolchildren. *Science & Sports, 23*, 170-175.

Roncesvalles, M.N., Schmitz, C., Zedka, M., Assaiante, C., & Woollacott, M. (2005). From egocentric to exocentric spatial orientation: Development of posture control in bimanual and trunk inclination tasks. *Journal of Motor Behavior, 37*, 404–416.

Roncesvalles, M.N.C., Woollacott, M.H., & Jensen, J.L. (2000). The development of compensatory stepping skills in children. *Journal of Motor Behavior, 32*, 100–111. doi:10.1080/00222890009601363

Rosenbaum, M., & Leibel, R.L. (1998). The physiology of body weight regulation: Relevance to the etiology of obesity in children. *Pediatrics, 101*(3S), 525–539.

Rosenhall, V., & Rubin, W. (1975). Degenerative changes in the human sensory epithelia. *Acta Oto-Laryngologica, 79*, 67–81.

Ross, J.G., Pate, R.R., Delpy, L.A., Gold, R.S., & Svilar, M. (1987). New health-related fitness norms. *Journal of Physical Education, Recreation and Dance, 58*, 66–70.

Rowland, T.W. (1996). *Developmental exercise physiology.* Champaign, IL: Human Kinetics.

Rowland, T.W. (2012). Inferior exercise economy in children: Perpetuating a myth? *Pediatric Exercise Science, 24*, 501–506.

Roy, E.A., Winchester, T., Weir, P., & Black, S. (1993). Age differences in the control of visually aimed movements. *Journal of Human Movement Studies, 24*, 71–81.

Royce, W.S., Gebelt, J.L., & Duff, R.W. (2003). Female athletes: Being both athletic and feminine. *Athletic Insight, 5*, 1–15.

Rudel, R., & Teuber, H. (1971). Pattern recognition within and across sensory modalities in normal and brain injured children. *Neuropsychologica, 9*, 389–400.

Rudisill, M.E. (2016). Mastery motivational climates: Motivating children to move and learn in physical education contexts. *Kinesiology Review, 5*(3), 157–69.

Rudisill, M.E., & Johnson, J.L., (2018). Mastery motivational climates in early childhood physical education: What have we learned over the years? *Journal of Physical Education, Recreation & Dance, 89*(6), 26–32. doi:10.1080/07303084.2018.1476940

Rudloff, L.M., & Feldmann, E. (1999). Childhood obesity: Addressing the issue. *Journal of the American Osteopathic Association, 99*(4), S1–S6.

Rudman, W. (1986). Life course socioeconomic transitions and sport involvement: A theory of restricted opportunity. In B. McPherson (Ed.), *Sport and aging* (pp. 25–35). Champaign, IL: Human Kinetics.

Ruff, H.A. (1984). Infants' manipulative exploration of objects: Effects of age and objects' characteristics. *Developmental Psychology, 29*, 9–20.

Ruffieux, J., Mouthon, A., Keller, M., Wälchli, M., & Taube, W. (2017). Behavioral and neural adaptations in response to five weeks of balance training in older adults: A randomized controlled trial. *Journal of Negative Results in BioMedicine, 16*, 11. doi:10.1186/s12952-017-0076-1

Rutenfranz, J. (1986). Longitudinal approach to assessing maximal aerobic power during growth: The European experience. *Medicine and Science in Sports and Exercise, 15*, 486–490.

Ruthruff, E., & Lien, M.C. (2015). Aging and attention. *Encyclopedia of geropsychology*, 1-7.

Ryan, R.M., & Deci, E.L. (2000). Self-determination theory and the facilitation of intrinsic motivation, social development, and well-being. *American psychologist, 55*(1), 68.

Sabo, D., & Veliz, P. (2008). *Go out and play: Youth sports in America.* East Meadow, NY: Women's Sports Foundation.

Sadres, E., Eliakim, A., Constantini, N., Lidor, R., & Falk, B. (2001). The effect of long-term resistance training on anthropometric measures, muscle strength, and self-concept in prepubertal boys. *Pediatric Exercise Science, 13*, 357-372.

Safar, M. (1990). Aging and its effects on the cardiovascular system. *Drugs, 39*(Suppl. 1), 1–18.

Sakurai, S., Chentanez, T., & Elliott, B.C. (1998). International comparison of the development trend of overhand throwing ability. *Medicine & Science in Sports & Exercise, 20*(Suppl.), S151.

Sale, D.G. (1989). Strength training in children. In G.V. Gisolfi & D.R. Lamb (Eds.), *Perspectives in exercise science and sports medicine: Vol. 2. Youth, exercise and sport* (pp. 165–222). Indianapolis: Benchmark Press.

Salkind, N.J. (1981). *Theories of human development.* New York, NY: Van Nostrand.

Saltin, B., & Grimby, G. (1968). Physiological analysis of middle-aged and old former athletes: Comparison with still active athletes of the same ages. *Circulation, 38*, 1104–1115.

Santos, A.D., Marinho, D.A., Costa, A.M., Izquierdo, M., & Marques, M.C. (2012). The effects of concurrent resistance and endurance training following a detraining period in elementary school students. *Journal of Strength & Conditioning Research, 26*, 1708-1716.

Sapp, M., & Haubenstricker, J. (1978, April). *Motivation for joining and reasons for not continuing in youth sport programs in Michigan.* Paper presented at the annual convention of the American Alliance for Health, Physical Education, Recreation and Dance, Kansas City, MO.

Saraiva, L., Rodrigues, L.P, Cordovil, R., & Barreiros, J. (2013). Influence of age, sex and somatic variables on the motor performance of pre-school children. *Annals of Human Biology, 40*,

444–450. doi:10.3109/03014460.2013.802012

Sarsan, A., Ardic, F., Ozgen, M., Topuz, O., & Sermez, Y. (2006). The effects of aerobic and resistance exercises in obese women. *Clinical Rehabilitation, 20,* 773–782.

Scanlon, T.C., Fragala, M.S., Stout, J.R., Emerson, N.S., Beyer, K.S., Oliveira, L.P., & Hoffman, J.R. (2014). Muscle architecture and strength: Adaptations to short-term resistance training in older adults. *Muscle Nerve, 49,* 583-592.

Scanlan, T.K. (1988). Social evaluation and the competition process: A developmental perspective. In F.L. Smoll, R.A. Magill, & M.J. Ash (Eds.), *Children in sport* (3rd ed., pp. 135–148). Champaign, IL: Human Kinetics.

Scanlan, T.K., & Lewthwaite, R. (1986). Social psychological aspects of competition for male youth sport participants: IV. Predictors of enjoyment. *Journal of Sport Psychology, 8,* 25–35.

Scanlan, T.K., Stein, G.L., & Ravizza, K. (1988). An in-depth study of former elite figure skaters: II. Sources of enjoyment. *Journal of Sport and Exercise Psychology, 11,* 65–83.

Schaap, T.S., Gonzales, T.I., Janssen, T.W.J., & Brown, S.H. (2015). Proprioceptively guided reaching movements in 3D space: Effects of age, task complexity and handedness. *Experimental Brain Research, 233,* 631–639. doi:10.1007/s00221-014-4142-3

Schellenberger, B. (1981). The significance of social relations in sport activity. *International Review of Sport Sociology, 16,* 69–77.

Schmidt, R., & Lee, T. (2014). *Motor control and learning: A behavioral emphasis* (5th ed.). Champaign, IL: Human Kinetics.

Schmidt, R., & Wrisberg, C. (2014). *Motor learning and performance (5th ed.).* Champaign, IL: Human Kinetics.

Schmidt, R.A. (1975). A schema theory of discrete motor skill learning. *Psychological Review, 82,* 225–260.

Schutte, N.M., Nederend, I., Hudziak, J.J., de Geus, E.J.C., & Bartels, M. (2016). Differences in adolescent physical fitness: A multivariate approach and meta-analysis. *Behavior Genetics, 46,* 217-227. doi:10.1007/s10519-015-9754-2

Schwanda, N.A. (1978). *A biomechanical study of the walking gait of active and inactive middle-age and elderly men.* Unpublished doctoral dissertation, Springfield College, Springfield, MA.

Schwartz, C., King, N.A., Perreira, B., Blundell, J.E., & Thivel, D. (2017). A systematic review and meta-analysis of energy and macronutrient intake responses to physical activity interventions in children and adolescents with obesity. *Pediatric Obesity, 12,* 179–194. doi:20/2222/ijpo.12124

Schwartz, R.S., Shuman, W.P., Larson, V., Cain, K.C., Fellingham, G.W., Beard, J.C., et al. (1991). The effect of intensive endurance exercise training on body fat distribution in young and older men. *Metabolism, 40,* 545–551.

Seefelt, V. (1980). Developmental motor patterns: Implications for elementary school physical fitness. In C.H. Nadeau, W.R. Halliwell, K.C. Newell, & G.C. Roberts (Eds.), *Psychology of motor behavior and sport* (pp. 314–323). Champaign: Human Kinetics.

Seefeldt, V., Reuschlein, S., & Vogel, P. (1972). *Sequencing motor skills within the physical education curriculum.* Paper presented at the annual convention of the American Association for Health, Physical Education, and Recreation, Houston.

Seils, L.G. (1951). The relationship between measures of physical growth and gross motor performance of primary grade school children. *Research Quarterly, 22,* 244–260.

Sertel, M., Sakizli, E., Bezgin, S., Demirci, C.S., Sahan, T.Y., & Kurtoglu, F. (2017). The effect of single-tasks and dual-tasks on balance in older adults. *Cogent Social Sciences, 3,* 1330913. doi:10.1080/23311886.2017.1330913

Servedio, F.J., Barels, R.L., Hamlin, R.L., Teske, D., Shaffer, T., & Servedio, A. (1985). The effects of weight training using Olympic style lifts on various physiological variables in prepubescent boys [Abstract]. *Medicine and Science in Sports and Exercise, 17,* 288.

Sewall, L., & Micheli, L.J. (1986). Strength training for children. *Journal of Pediatric Orthopedics, 6,* 143–146.

Shaffer, D.M. (1999). Navigating in baseball: A spatial optical tracking strategy and associated naïve physical beliefs. *Dissertation Abstracts International: Section B. The Sciences and Engineering, 59,* 4504.

Shaffer, D.M., & McBeath, M.K. (2002). Baseball outfielders maintain a linear optical trajectory when tracking uncatchable fly balls. *Journal of Experimental Psychology: Human Perception and Performance, 28,* 335–348.

Shakib, S., & Dunbar, M.D. (2004). How high school athletes talk about maternal and paternal sporting experiences. *International Review for the Sociology of Sport, 39*(3), 275–299.

Shapiro, D.C., & Schmidt, R.A. (1982). The schema theory: Recent evidence and developmental implications. In J.A.S. Kelso & J.E. Clark (Eds.), *The development of movement control and co-ordination* (pp. 113–150). New York, NY: Wiley.

Sharma, D.A., Chevidikunnan, M.F., Khan, F.R., & Gaowgzeh, R.A. (2016). Effectiveness of knowledge of result and knowledge of performance in the learning of a skilled motor activity by healthy young adults. *Journal of Physical Therapy Science, 28*(5), 1482–1486. doi:10.1589/jpts.28.1482

Shea, C.H., Park, J., & Braden, H. (2006). Age-related effects in sequential motor learning. *Physical Therapy, 86*(4), 478–488.

Sheldon, J.H. (1963). The effect of age on the control of sway. *Gerontologia Clinica, 5,* 129–138.

Shenouda, R., Wilson, M., & Fletcher, S. (2016). Resistance training in children and young adults: A critical review. *International Journal of Applied Exercise Physiology, 5,* 1–8.

Shephard, R.J. (1978a). *IBP Human Adaptability Project synthesis: Vol. 4. Human physiological work capacity.* New York, NY: Cambridge University Press.

Shephard, R.J. (1978b). *Physical activity and aging.* Chicago: Year Book Medical.

Shephard, R.J. (1982). *Physical activity and growth.* Chicago: Year Book Medical.

Shephard, R.J. (1987). *Physical activity and aging* (2nd ed.). London: Croom Helm.

Shephard, R.J. (1993). Aging, respiratory function, and exercise. *Journal of Aging and Physical Activity, 1,* 59–83.

Shirley, M.M. (1931). *The first two years: A study of twenty five babies.* Minneapolis: University of Minnesota Press.

Shirley, M.M. (1963). The motor sequence. In D. Wayne (Ed.), *Readings in child psychology.* Englewood Cliffs, NJ: Prentice Hall.

Shuleva, K.M., Hunter, G.R., Hester, D.J., & Dunaway, D.L. (1990). Exercise oxygen uptake in 3- through 6-year-old children. *Pediatric Exercise Science, 2,* 130–139.

Shumway-Cook, A., & Woollacott, M. (1985). The growth of stability: Postural control from a developmental perspective. *Journal of Motor Behavior, 17,* 131–147.

Shute, V.J., & Gawlick, L.A. (1995). Practice effects on skill acquisition, learning outcome, retention, and sensitivity to relearning. *Human Factors, 37,* 781–803.

Sibley, B.A., & Etnier, J.L. (2003). The relationship between physical activity and cognition in children: A meta-analysis. *Pediatric Exercise Science, 15,* 243–256.

Siegel, J.A., Camaione, D.N., & Manfredi, T.G. (1989). The effects of upper body resistance training on pre-pubescent children. *Pediatric Exercise Science, 1,* 145–154.

Siegler, R.S., & Jenkins, E.A. (1989). *How children discover new strategies.* Hillsdale, NJ: Erlbaum.

Silva, N.L., Oliveira, R.B., Fleck, S.J., Leon, A.C.M.P., & Farinatti, P. (2014). Influence of strength training variables on strength gains in adults over 55 years-old: A meta-analysis of dose-response relationships. *Journal of Science and Medicine in Sport, 17,* 337-344. doi: 10.1016/j.jsams.2013.05.009.

Silverman, L. (2013, June 20). Nerlens Noel recovering from torn ACL. Silverman Ankle & Foot. Retrieved from www.anklefootmd.com/nerlens-noel-recovering-from-torn-acl

Simoneau, J.A., & Bouchard, C. (1989). Human variation in skeletal muscle proportion and enzyme activities. *American Journal of Physiology, Endocrinology, and Metabolism, 257,* E567–E572.

Simons, J., Beunen, G.P., Renson, R., Claessens, A.L.M., Vanreusel, B., & Lefevre, J.A.V. (1990). *Growth and fitness of Flemish girls: The Leuven growth study.* Champaign, IL: Human Kinetics.

Sinclair, C. (1971). Dominance pattern of young children: A follow-up study. *Perceptual and Motor Skills, 32,* 142.

Sinclair, C.B. (1973). *Movement of the young child: Ages two to six.* Columbus, OH: Merrill.

Singleton, W.T. (1955). *Age and performance timing on simple skills: Old age and the modern world* (Report of the Third Congress of the International Association of Gerontology). London: Livingstone.

Skinner, B.F. (1938). *The behavior of organisms. An experimental analysis.* New York, NY: Appleton-Century.

Slater, A., Mattock, A., & Brown, E. (1990). Size constancy at birth: Newborn infants' responses to retinal and real size. *Journal of Experimental Child Psychology, 49*(2), 314–322.

Smith, A.B. (1985). Teacher modeling and sex-types play preferences. *New Zealand Journal of Educational Studies, 20,* 39–47.

Smith, D.B., Johnson, G.O., Stout, J.R., Housh, T.J., Housh, D.J., & Evetovich, T.K. (1997). Validity of near-infrared interactance for estimating relative body fat in female high school gymnasts. *International Journal of Sports Medicine, 18,* 531–537.

Smith, E.L., Sempos, C.T., & Purvis, R.W. (1981). Bone mass and strength decline with age. In E.L. Smith & R.C. Serfass (Eds.), *Exercise and aging: The scientific basis* (pp. 59–87). Hillside, NJ: Enslow.

Smith, E.L., & Serfass, R.C. (Eds.). (1981). *Exercise and aging: The scientific basis.* Hillside, NJ: Enslow.

Smith, M.D. (1979). Getting involved in sport: Sex differences. *International Review of Sport Sociology, 14,* 93–99.

Smith, N.A., Folland, N.A., Martinez, D.M., & Trainor, L.J. (2017). Multisensory object perception in infancy: 4-month-olds perceive a mistuned harmonic as a separate auditory and visual object. *Cognition, 164,* 1–7. doi:10.1016/j.cognition.2017.01.016

Smith, R.E., & Smoll, F.L. (2012). *Sport psychology for youth coaches: Developing champions in sports and life.* Lanham, MD: Rowman & Littlefield Publishers.

Smith, R.E., Smoll, F.L., & Curtis, B. (1979). Coach effectiveness training: A cognitive-behavioral approach to enhancing relationship skills in youth sport coaches. *Journal of Sport Psychology, 1,* 59–75.

Smoll, F.L., & Smith, R.E. (1989). Leadership behaviors in sport: A theoretical model and research paradigm. *Journal of Applied Social Psychology, 19,* 1522–1551.

Smoll, F.L., & Smith, R.E. (2001). Conducting sport psychology training programs for coaches: Cognitive-behavioral principles and techniques. In J.M. Williams (Ed.), *Applied sport psychology: Personal growth to peak performance* (4th ed., pp. 378–400). Mountain View, CA: Mayfield.

Smyth, M.M., Katamba, J., & Peacock, K.A. (2004). Development of prehension between 5 and 10 years of age: Distance scaling, grip aperture, and sight of the hand. *Journal of Motor Behavior, 36,* 91–103.

Smyth, M.M., Peacock, K.A., & Katamba, J. (2004). Changes in the role of sight of the hand in the development of prehension in childhood. *The Quarterly Journal of Experimental Psychology A: Human Experimental Psychology, 57A,* 269–296.

Snyder, E.E., & Spreitzer, E. (1973). Family influences and involvement in sports. *Research Quarterly, 44,* 249–255.

Snyder, E.E., & Spreitzer, E. (1976). Correlates of sport participation among adolescent girls. *Research Quarterly, 47,* 804–809.

Snyder, E.E., & Spreitzer, E. (1978). Socialization comparisons of adolescent female athletes and musicians. *Research Quarterly, 79,* 342–350.

Sonstroem, R. (1997). Physical activity and self-esteem. In W. Morgan (Ed.), *Physical activity and mental health* (Series in health psychology and behavioral medicine, pp. 127–143). Washington, DC: Taylor & Francis.

Soucie, J.M., Wang, C., Forsyth, A., Funk, S., Denny, M., Roach, K.E., Boone, D. and the Hemophilia Treatment Center Network. (2011). Range of motion measurements: Reference values and a database for comparison studies. *Haemophilia, 17,* 500–507. doi:10.1111/j.1365-2516.2010.02399.x

Sowell, E.R., Thompson, P.M., Welcome, S.E., Henkenius, A.L., Toga, A.W., & Peterson, B.S. (2003). Cortical abnormalities in children and adolescents with attention-deficit hyperactivity disorder. *The Lancet, 362*(9397), 1699–1707.

Spence, J.C., McGannon, K.R., & Poon, P. (2005). The effect of exercise on global self-esteem: A quantitative review. *Journal of Sport and Exercise Psychology, 27*, 311–334.

Spetner, N.B., & Olsho, L.W. (1990). Auditory frequency resolution in human infancy. *Child Development, 61,* 632–652.

Spirduso, W.W. (1975). Reaction and movement time as a function of age and physical activity level. *Journal of Gerontology, 30,* 435–440.

Spirduso, W.W. (1980). Physical fitness and psychomotor speed: A review. *Journal of Gerontology, 35,* 850–865.

Spirduso, W.W. (1995). *Physical dimensions of aging.* Champaign, IL: Human Kinetics.

Spirduso, W.W., Francis, K.W., & MacRae, P.G. (2005). *Physical dimensions of aging* (2nd ed.). Champaign, IL: Human Kinetics.

Spreitzer, E., & Snyder, E. (1983). Correlates of participation in adult recreational sports. *Journal of Leisure Research, 15,* 28–38.

Sprynarova, S., & Reisenauer, R. (1978). Body dimensions and physiological indications of physical fitness during adolescence. In R.J. Shephard & H. Lavallee (Eds.), *Physical fitness assessment* (pp. 32–37). Springfield, IL: Charles C Thomas.

Stadulis, R.I. (1971). *Coincidence-anticipation behavior of children.* Unpublished doctoral dissertation, Columbia University, New York.

Stamford, B.A. (1973). Effects of chronic institutionalization on the physical working capacity and trainability of geriatric men. *Journal of Gerontology, 28,* 441–446.

Stamford, B.A. (1988). Exercise and the elderly. In K.B. Pandolf (Ed.), *Exercise and sport sciences reviews* (Vol. 16, pp. 341–379). New York, NY: Macmillan.

Steben, R.E., & Steben, A.H. (1981). The validity of the strength shortening cycle in selected jumping events. *Journal of Sports Medicine and Physical Fitness, 21,* 1–7.

Stein, B.E., & Meredith, M.A. (1993). *The merging of the senses.* Cambridge, MA: MIT Press.

Stein, B.E., Meredith, M.A., & Wallace, M.T. (1994). Development and neural basis of multisensory integration. In D.J. Lewkowicz & R. Lickliter (Eds.), *The development of intersensory perception: Comparative perspectives* (pp. 81–105). Hillsdale, NJ: Erlbaum.

Steinberger, J., Jacobs, D.R., Jr., Raatz, S., Moran, A., Hong, C.-P., & Sinaiko, A.R. (2005). Comparison of body fatness measurements by BMI and skinfolds vs. dual energy X-ray absorptiometry and their relation to cardiovascular risk factors in adolescents. *International Journal of Obesity, 29,* 1346–1352.

Stenholm, S., Vahtera, J., Kawachi, I., Pentti, J., Halonen, J.I., Westerlund, H., ... & Kivimäki, M. (2015). Patterns of weight gain in middle-aged and older US adults, 1992–2010. *Epidemiology, 26*(2), 165 – 168.

Sterdt, E., Liersch, S., Walter, U. (2014). Correlates of physical activity of children and adolescents: A systematic review of reviews. *Health Education Journal, 73,* 72–89. doi:10.1177/0017896912469578.

Sterritt, G., Martin, V., & Rudnick, M. (1971). Auditory-visual and temporal-spatial integration as determinants of test difficulty. *Psychonomic Science, 23,* 289–291.

Stevenson, B. (2007). Title IX and the evolution of high school sports. *Contemporary Economic Policy, 25,* 486–505.

Stiles, J., & Jernigan, T. L. (2010). The basics of brain development. *Neuropsychology Review, 20*(4), 327–348. doi:10.1007/s11065-010-9148-4

Stine, E.L., Wingfield, A., & Poon, L.W. (1989). Speech comprehension and memory through adulthood: The roles of time and strategy. In L.W. Poon, D.S. Rubin, & B.A. Wilson (Eds.), *Everyday cognition in adulthood and later years* (pp. 195–221). Cambridge, UK: Cambridge University Press.

Stodden, D., Langendorfer, S., & Roberton, M.A. (2009). The association between motor skill competence and physical fitness in young adults. *Research Quarterly for Exercise and Sport, 80,* 223–229.

Stodden, D.F., Fleisig, G.S., Langendorfer, S.J., & Andrews, J.R. (2006). Kinematic constraints associated with the acquisition of overarm throwing. Part I: Step and trunk actions. *Research Quarterly for Exercise and Sport, 77,* 417–427.

Stodden, D.F., & Goodway, J.D. (2007). The dynamic association between motor skill development and physical activity. *Journal of Physical Education, Recreation and Dance, 8,* 33–34, 48–49.

Stodden, D.F., Goodway, J.D., Langendorfer, S.J., Roberton, M.A., Rudisill, M.E., Garcia, C., & Garcia, L.E. (2008). A developmental perspective on the role of motor skill competence in physical activity: An emergent relationship. *Quest, 60,* 290–306.

Stones, M.J., & Kozma, A. (1989). Age, exercise, and coding performance. *Psychology and Aging, 4,* 190–194.

Storli, R., & Sandseter, E.B.H. (2015). Preschool Teachers' Perceptions of Children's Rough-and-Tumble Play (R&T) in Indoor and Outdoor Environments. *Early Child Development and Care 185* (11–12): 1995–2009. doi:10.1080/03004430.2015.1028394.

Storli, R., & Sandseter, E.B.H. (2017). Gender matters: Male and female ECEC practitioners' perceptions and practices regarding children's rough-and-tumble play (R&T). *European Early Childhood Education Research Journal, 25,*(6) 838–853.

Strait, J.B., & Lakatta, E.G. (2012). Aging-associated cardiovascular changes and their relationship to heart failure. *Heart Failure Clinics, 8*(1), 143–164.

Strohmeyer, H.S., Williams, K., & Schaub-George, D. (1991). Developmental sequences for catching a small ball: A prelongitudinal screening. *Research Quarterly for Exercise and Sport, 62,* 257–266.

Susman, E.J., Houts, R.M., Steinberg, L., Belsky, J., Cauffman, E., DeHart, G., et al. (2010). Longitudinal development of secondary sexual characteristics in girls and boys between ages 9½ and 15½ years. *Archives of pediatrics and adolescent medicine, 164*(2), 166–173.

Sutherland, D. (1997). The development of mature gait. *Gait and Posture, 6*(2), 162–170.

Sutherland, D.H., Olshen, R., Cooper, L., & Woo, S. (1980). The development of mature gait. *Journal of Bone and Joint Surgery, 62A,* 336–353.

Sutherland, R., Pipe, M., Schick, K., Murray, J., & Gobbo, C. (2003). Knowing in advance: The impact of prior event information on memory and event knowledge. *Journal of Experimental Child Psychology, 84,* 244–263.

Sutton, R.A., & Miller, C. (2006). Comparison of some secondary body composition algorithms. *College Student Journal, 40,* 791–801.

Swanson, L.R., & Lee, T.D. (1992). Effects of aging and schedules of knowledge of results on motor learning. *Journal of Gerontology, 47,* 406–411.

Swanson, R., & Benton, A.L. (1955). Some aspects of the genetic development of right-left discrimination. *Child Development, 26,* 123–133.

Sweeting, T., & Rink, J.E. (1999). Effects of direct instruction and environmentally designed instruction on the process and product characteristics of a fundamental skill. *Journal of Teaching in Physical Education, 18,* 216–233.

Swingley, D. (2005). 11-month-olds' knowledge of how familiar words sound. *Developmental Science, 8,* 432–443.

Tanaka, Y., Kanakogi, Y., Kawasaki, M., & Myowa, M. (2018). The integration of audio-tactile information is modulated by multimodal social interaction with physical contact in infancy. *Developmental Cognitive Neuroscience, 30,* 31–40. doi:10.1016/j.dcn.2017.12.001

Tanner, J.M. (1975). Growth and endocrinology of the adolescent. In L.I. Gardner (Ed.), *Endocrine and genetic disease of childhood and adolescence* (2nd ed., pp. 14–63). Philadelphia: Saunders.

Teeple, J.B. (1978). Physical growth and maturation. In M.F. Ridenour (Ed.), *Motor development: Issues and applications* (pp. 3–27). Princeton, NJ: Princeton Book.

Telama, R., Yang, X., Hirvensalo, J., & Raitakari, O. (2006). Participation in organized youth sport as a predictor of adult physical activity: A 21-year longitudinal study. *Pediatric Exercise Science, 17,* 76–88.

Telama, R., Yang, X., Laakso, L., & Viikari, J. (1997). Physical activity in childhood and adolescence as predictor of physical activity in young adulthood. *American Journal of Preventive Medicine, 13,* 317–323.

Temple, I.G., Williams, H.G., & Bateman, N.J. (1979). A test battery to assess intrasensory and intersensory development of young children. *Perceptual and Motor Skills, 48,* 643–659.

Thelen, E. (1979). Rhythmical stereotypies in normal human infants. *Animal Behaviour, 27,* 699–715.

Thelen, E. (1981). Kicking, rocking, and waving: Contextual analysis of rhythmical stereotypies in normal human infants. *Animal Behaviour, 29,* 3–11.

Thelen, E. (1983). Learning to walk is still an "old" problem: A reply to Zelazo. *Journal of Motor Behavior, 15,* 139–161.

Thelen, E. (1985). Developmental origins of motor coordination: Leg movements in human infants. *Developmental Psychobiology, 18,* 1–22.

Thelen, E. (1995). Motor development: A new synthesis. *American Psychologist, 50,* 79–95.

Thelen, E. (1998). Bernstein's legacy for motor development: How infants learn to reach. In M. Latash (Ed.), *Progress in motor control* (pp. 267–288). Champaign, IL: Human Kinetics.

Thelen, E., Corbetta, D., Kamm, K., Spencer, J.P., Schneider, K., & Zernicke, R.F. (1993). The transition to reaching: Mapping intention and intrinsic dynamics. *Child Development, 64,* 1058–1098.

Thelen, E., & Fisher, D.M. (1983). The organization of spontaneous leg movements in newborn infants. *Journal of Motor Behavior, 15,* 353–377.

Thelen, E., Kelso, J.A.S., & Fogel, A. (1987). Self-organizing systems and infant motor development. *Developmental Review, 7,* 37–65.

Thelen, E., Ridley-Johnson, R., & Fisher, D.M. (1983). Shifting patterns of bilateral coordination and lateral dominance in the leg movements of young infants. *Developmental Psychobiology, 16,* 29–46.

Thelen, E., & Ulrich, B.D. (1991). Hidden skills: A dynamic systems analysis of treadmill stepping during the first year. *Monographs of the Society for Research in Child Development, 56*(1, Serial no. 233).

Thelen, E., Ulrich, B.D., & Jensen, J.L. (1989). The developmental origins of locomotion. In M.H. Woollacott & A. Shumway-Cook (Eds.), *Development of posture and gait across the life span* (pp. 25–47). Columbia: University of South Carolina Press.

Thomas, J.R. (1984). *Motor development during childhood and adolescence.* Minneapolis: Burgess.

Thomas, J.R., Alderson, J.A., Thomas, K.T., Campbell, A.C., & Elliott, B.C. (2010). Developmental gender differences for overhand throwing in Aboriginal Australian children. *Research Quarterly for Exercise and Sport, 81,* 432–441.

Thomas, J.R., Gallagher, J.D., & Purvis, G.J. (1981). Reaction time and anticipation time: Effects of development. *Research Quarterly for Exercise and Sport, 52,* 359–367.

Thomas, J.R., Thomas, K.T., & Gallagher, J.D. (1981). Children's processing of information in physical activity and sport. *Motor Skills: Theory Into Practice Monograph, 3,* 1–8.

Tibana, R.A., Prestes, J., Nascimento, D.D.A., Martins, O.V., DeSantana, F.S., & Balsamo, S. (2012). Higher muscle performance in adolescents compared with adults after a resistance training session with different rest intervals. *Journal of Strength & Conditioning Research, 26,* 1027-1032.

Tierney, A.L., & Nelson, C.A. (2009). Brain development and the role of experience in the early years. *Zero to Three, 30*(2), 9–13.

Timiras, M.L., & Brownstein, H. (1987). Prevalence of anemia and correlation of hemoglobin with age in a geriatric screening clinic population. *Journal of the American Geriatrics Society, 35,* 639–643.

Timiras, P.S. (1972). *Developmental physiology and aging.* New York, NY: Macmillan.

Toftegaard-Stoeckel, J., Groenfeldt, V., & Andersen, L.B. (2010). Children's self-perceived bodily competencies and associations with motor skills, body mass index, teachers' evaluations, and parents' concerns. *Journal of Sports Sciences, 28,* 1369–1375. doi:10.1080/02640414.2010.510845

Toledo, D.R., Barela, J.A., & Kohn, A.F. (2017). Improved proprioceptive function by application of subsensory electrical noise: Effects of aging and task-demand. *Neuroscience, 358*, 103–114. doi:10.1016/j.neuroscience.2017.06.045

Tomkinson, G.R., Hamlin, M.J., & Olds, T.S. (2006). Secular changes in anaerobic test performance in Australasian children and adolescents. *Pediatric Exercise Science, 18*, 314–328.

Tomkinson, G.R., & Olds, T.S. (2007). Secular changes in pediatric aerobic fitness test performance: The global picture. *Medicine and Sport Science, 50*, 46–66.

Tomkinson, G.R., Olds, T.S., Kang, S.J., & Kim, D.Y. (2007). Secular trends in the aerobic fitness test performance and body mass index of Korean children and adolescents (1968–2000). *International Journal of Sports Medicine, 28*, 314–320.

Tommasini, S.M., Nasser, P., Schaffler, M.B., & Jepsen, K.J. (2005). Relationship between bone morphology and bone quality in male tibias: Implications for stress fracture risk. *Journal of Bone and Mineral Research, 20*, 1372–1380.

Tourva, A., Spanoudis, G., & Demetriou, A. (2016). Cognitive correlates of developing intelligence: The contribution of working memory, processing speed, and attention. *Intelligence, 54*, 136–146.

Trafton, A. (2015, March 6). The rise and fall of cognitive skills: Neuroscientists find that different parts of the brain work best at different ages. *MIT News.* Retrieved from http://news.mit.edu/2015/brain-peaks-at-different-ages-0306

Trappe, S., Hayes, E., Galpin, A., Kaminsky, L., Jemiolo, B., Fink, W., et al. (2013). New records in aerobic power among octogenarian lifelong endurance athletes. *Journal of Applied Physiology, 114*, 3–10.

Trehub, S.E., Bull, D., & Thorpe, L.A. (1984). Infants' perception of melodies: The role of melodic contour. *Child Development, 55*, 821–830.

Trehub, S.E., & Hannon, E.E. (2006). Infant music perception: Domain-general or domain-specific mechanisms? *Cognition, 100*, 73–99.

Trevarthen, C. (1974). The psychobiology of speed development. In E.H. Lenneberg (Ed.), *Language and brain: Developmental aspects. Neurosciences Research Program Bulletin* (Vol, 12, pp. 570–585). Boston, MA: Neurosciences Research Program.

Trevarthen, C. (1984). How control of movement develops. In H.T.A. Whiting (Ed.), *Human motor actions: Bernstein reassessed* (pp. 223–261). Amsterdam: North-Holland.

Troe, E.J.W.M., Raat, H., Jaddoe, V.W.V., Hofman, A., Looman, C.W.N., Moll, H.A., et al. (2007). Explaining differences in birthweight between ethnic populations. The Generation R study. *BJOG, 114*, 1557–1565.

Trudeau, F., Laurencelle, L., Tremblay, J., Rajic, M., & Shephard, R.J. (1998). A long-term follow-up of participants in the Trois-Rivieres semi-longitudinal study of growth and development. *Pediatric Exercise Science, 10*(4), 366–377.

Tun, P.A., & Lachman, M.E. (2008). Age differences in reaction time and attention in a national telephone sample of adults: Education, sex, and task complexity matter. *Developmental Psychology, 44*(5), 1421–1429. doi:10.1037/a0012845

Tun, P.A., & Wingfield, A. (1993). Is speech special? Perception and recall of spoken language in complex environments. In J. Cerella, J. Rybash, W. Hover, & M.L. Commons (Eds.), *Adult information processing: Limits on loss* (pp. 425–457). San Diego: Academic Press.

Turner, J.M., Mead, J., & Wohl, M.E. (1968). Elasticity of human lungs in relation to age. *Journal of Applied Physiology, 35*, 664–671.

Turner, P., & Gervai, J. (1995). A multidimensional study of gender typing in preschool children and their parents: Personality, attitudes, preferences, behavior, and cultural differences. *Developmental Psychology, 31*(5), 759–779.

Turner, P., Gervai, J., & Hinde, R.A. (1993). Gender-typing in young children: Preferences, behaviour and cultural differences. *British Journal of Developmental Psychology, 11*(4), 323–342.

Ulrich, B.D., Thelen, E., & Niles, D. (1990). Perceptual determinants of action: Stair-climbing choices of infants and toddlers. In J.E. Clark & J.H. Humphrey (Eds.), *Advances in motor development research* (Vol. 3, pp. 1–15). New York, NY: AMS Press.

Ulrich, B.D., Ulrich, D.A., & Collier, D.H. (1992). Alternating stepping patterns: hidden abilities of 11 month old infants with down syndrome. *Developmental Medicine & Child Neurology*, 34(3), 233-239.

Ulrich, D.A. (1985). *TGMD, test of gross motor development.* Pro-Ed.

Ulrich, D.A. (2000). *TGMD 2–Test of gross motor development examiner's manual.* Austin TX: PRO-ED, 2.

Ulrich, D.A. (2013). The Test of Gross Motor Development-3 (TGMD-3): Administration, scoring, & international norms. *Hacettepe Journal of Sport Sciences, 24*, 27–33.

Ulrich, D.A. (2017). Introduction to the special section: Evaluation of the psychometric properties of the TGMD-3. *Journal of Motor Learning and Development*, *5*(1), 1-4.

Ulrich, D.A., Ulrich, B.D., Angulo-Kinzler, R.M., & Yun, J. (2001). Treadmill training of infants with Down syndrome: evidence-based developmental outcomes. *Pediatrics*, *108*(5), e84-e84.

Ulrich, D.A., Lloyd, M.C., Tiernan, C.W., Looper, J.E., & Angulo-Barroso, R.M. (2008). Effects of intensity of treadmill training on developmental outcomes and stepping in infants with Down syndrome: a randomized trial. *Physical Therapy*, *88*(1), 114-122.

Unnithan, V.B. (1993). *Factors affecting submaximal running economy in children.* Unpublished doctoral dissertation, University of Glasgow, Glasgow, Scotland.

Unnithan, V.B., Roche, D.M., Garrard, M., Holloway, K., & Marwood, S. (2015). Oxygen uptake kinetics in trained adolescent females. *European Journal of Applied Physiology, 115*, 213–220. doi:10.1007/s00421-014-3005-8

U.S. Department of Health and Human Services, Centers for Disease Control and Prevention, National Center for Chronic Disease Prevention and Health Promotion. (1996). *Physical activity and health: A report of the Surgeon General.* Atlanta: Author.

Utley, A., & Astill, S.L. (2007). Developmental sequences of two-handed catching: How do children with and without developmental coordination disorder differ? *Physiotherapy Theory and Practice, 23*, 65–82. doi:10.1080/09593980701211838

Uusi-Rasi, K., Sievanen, H., Vuori, I., Pasanen, M., Heinonen, A., & Oja, P. (1998). Associations of physical activity and calcium intake with bone mass and size in healthy women of different ages. *Journal of Bone and Mineral Research, 13*, 133–42.

Vahdat, S., Albouy, G., King, B., Lungu, O., & Doyon, J. (2017). Editorial: Online and offline modulators of motor learning. *Frontiers in Human Neuroscience, 11*, 69. doi:10.3389/fnhum.2017.00069

Vaillant-Molina, M., Bahrick, L.E., & Flom, R. (2013). Young infants match facial and vocal emotional expressions of other infants. *Infancy, 18*, E97–E111. doi:10.1111/infa.12017

Valentini, N., Barnett, L., Bandeira, P.F., Nobre, G.C., Zanella, L.W., & Sartori, R.F. (2018),The Pictorial Scale of Perceived Movement Skill Competence: Determining content and construct validity for Brazilian children. *Journal of Motor Learning and Development, 6*, S-189-S207. doi:10.1123/jmld.2016-0043

Valentini, N.C., & Rudisill, M.E. (2004a). An inclusive mastery climate intervention and the motor development of children with and without disabilities. *Adapted Physical Activity Quarterly, 21*, 330–347.

Valentini, N.C., & Rudisill, M.E. (2004b). Effectiveness of an inclusive mastery climate intervention on the motor skill development of children. *Adapted Physical Activity Quarterly, 21,* 285–294.

Valentini, N.C., & Rudisill, M.E. (2004c). Motivational climate, motor-skill development and perceived competence: Two studies of developmentally delayed kindergarten children. *Journal of Teaching in Physical Education, 23*, 216–234.

Valentini, N.C., Zanella, L.W., & Webster, E.K. (2017). Test of Gross Motor Development–Third Edition: Establishing content and construct validity for Brazilian children. *Journal of Motor Learning and Development, 5*, 15-28.

Van Capelle, A., Broderick C.F., van Doorn, N., Ward, R.D., & Parmenter, B.J. (2017). Interventions to improve fundamental motor skill sin pre-school aged children: A systematic review and meta-analysis. *Journal of Science and Medicine in Sport, 20*, 658–666. doi:10.1016/j.samss.2016.11.008

Van den Tillaar, R., & Marques, M.C. (2013). Effect of different training workload on overhead throwing performance with different weighted balls. *Journal of Strength and Conditioning Research, 27*(5),1196–1201.

Van der Fits, I.B.M., & Hadders-Algra, M. (1998). The development of postural response patterns during reaching in healthy infants. *Neuroscience and Biobehavioral Reviews, 22*(4), 521–525.

van der Kamp, J., Savelsbergh, G.J.P., & Davis, W.E. (1998). Body-scaled ratio as a control parameter for prehension in 5- to 9-year-old children. *Developmental Psychology, 33*(4), 351–361.

Van Duijvenvoorde, A.C., Jansen, B.R., Bredman, J.C., & Huizenga, H.M. (2012). Age-related changes in decision making: Comparing informed and noninformed situations. *Developmental Psychology, 48*(1), 192.

Van Duyne, H.J. (1973). Foundations of tactical perception in three to seven year olds. *Journal of the Association for the Study of Perception, 8,* 1–9.

Van Hof, P., van der Kamp, J., & Savelsbergh, G.J.P. (2008). The relation between infants' perception of catchableness and the control of catching. *Developmental Psychology, 44*, 182–194.

van Rooij, J.C.G.M., & Plomp, R. (1992). Auditive and cognitive factors in speech perception by elderly listeners. III: Additional data and final discussion. *Journal of the Acoustical Society of America, 91,* 1028–1033.

Vedul-Kjelsås, V.I., Sigmundsson, H., Stendsdotter, A.-K., & Haga, M. (2011). The relationship between motor competence, physical fitness and self-perception in children. *Child: Care, Health, and Development, 38*, 394–402.

Veldman, S.L.C., Palmer, K.K., Okely, A.D., & Robinson, L.E. (2017). Promoting ball skills in preschool-age girls. *Journal of Science and Medicine in Sport, 20*, 50–54. doi:10.1016/j.jsams.2016.04,009

Venetsanou, F., Kossyva, I., Valentini, N., Afthentopoulou, A.E., & Barnett, L. (2018). Validity and reliability of the Pictorial Scale of Perceived Movement Skill Competence for young Greek children. *Journal of Motor Learning and Development, 6*, S239-S251. doi: 10.1123/jmld.2017-0028 [epub ahead of print].

Vercruyssen, M. (1997). Movement control and speed of behavior. In A.D. Fisk & W.A. Rogers (Eds.), *Handbook of human factors and the older adult* (pp. 55–86). San Diego: Academic Press.

Vereijken, B., & Thelen, E. (1997). Training infant treadmill stepping: The role of individual pattern stability. *Developmental Psychobiology, 30,* 89–102.

Vereijken, B., van Emmerik, R.E.A., Whiting, H.T.A, & Newell, K.M. (1992). Free(z)ing degrees of freedom in skill acquisition. *Journal of Motor Behavior, 24*, 133–42.

Vereijken, B., Whiting, H.T.A. and Beek, P.J. 1992. A dynamical systems approach to skill acquisition. Quarterly Journal of Experimental Psychology, 45A: 323–344.

Verret, L., Trouche, S., Zerwas, M., & Rampon, C. (2007). Hippocampal neurogenesis during normal and pathological aging. *Psychoneuroendocrinology, 32*(Suppl. 1), S26–S30.

Visser, J., & Geuze, R.H. (2000). Kinesaesthetic acuity in adolescent boys: A longitudinal study. *Developmental Medicine & Child Neurology, 42*, 93-96.

von Hofsten, C. (1980). Predictive reaching for moving objects by human infants. *Journal of Experimental Child Psychology, 30*, 369–382.

von Hofsten, C. (1982). Eye-hand coordination in the newborn. *Developmental Psychology, 18,* 450–461.

von Hofsten, C. (1984). Developmental changes in the organization of pre-reaching movements. *Developmental Psychology, 3,* 378–388.

von Hofsten, C. (1990). Early development of grasping an object in space-time. In M.A. Goodale (Ed.), *Vision and action: The control of grasping* (pp. 65–79). Norwood, NJ: Ablex.

von Hofsten, C., Kellman, P., & Putaansuu, J. (1992). Young infants' sensitivity to motion parallax. *Infant Behavior and Development, 15*(2), 245–264.

von Hofsten, C., & Lindhagen, K. (1979). Observations on the development of reaching for moving objects. *Journal of Experimental Child Psychology, 28*, 158–173.

von Hofsten, C., & Spelke, E.S. (1985). Object perception and object-directed reaching in infancy. *Journal of Experimental Psychology: General, 114*(2), 198–212.

Voss, M.W., Nagamatsu, L.S., Liu-Ambrose, T., & Kramer, A.F. (2011). Exercise, brain, and cognition across the life span. *Journal of Applied Physiology, 111*(5), 1505–1513. doi:10.1152/japplphysiol.00210.2011

Vouloumanos, A., & Werker, J.F. (2007). Listening to language at birth: Evidence for a bias for speech in neonates. *Developmental Science, 10*, 159–164.

Wade, M. (1976). Developmental motor learning. In J. Keogh (Ed.), *Exercise and Sport Sciences Reviews, 4*, 375–394.

Wade, M.G. (1980). Coincidence-anticipation of young normal and handicapped children. *Journal of Motor Behavior, 12*, 103–112.

Wadsworth, D.D., Rudisill, M.E., Hastie, P.A., Irwin, J.M., & Rodriguez-Hernandez, M.G. (2017). Preschoolers' physical activity participation across a yearlong mastery-motivational climate intervention. *Research Quarterly for Exercise and Sport, 88*(3), 339–345. doi:10.1080/02701367.2017.1321099

Wagner, M.O., Webster, E.K., & Ulrich, D.A. (2017). Psychometric properties of the Test of Gross Motor Development 3rd edition (German translation): Results of a pilot study. *Journal of Motor Learning and Development, 5*, 29-44. doi: 10.1123/jld.2016-0006.

Walk, R.D. (1969). Two types of depth discrimination by the human infant. *Psychonomic Science, 14*, 253–254.

Walk, R.D., & Gibson, E.J. (1961). A comparative and analytical study of visual depth perception. *Psychological Monographs: General and Applied, 75*(15), 1.

Wallace, C.S., Kilman, V.L., Withers, G.S., & Greenough, W.T. (1992). Increases in dendritic length in occipital cortex after 4 days of differential housing in weanling rats. *Behavioral and Neural Biology, 58*(1), 64–68.

Warburton, D.E., Nicol, C.W., & Bredin, S.S. (2006). Health benefits of physical activity: The evidence. *Canadian Medical Association Journal, 174*(6), 801–809.

Warren, R., & Wertheim, A.H. (1990). *Perception and control of self-motion.* Hillsdale, NJ: Erlbaum.

Warren, W.H. (1984). Perceiving affordances: Visual guidance of stair-climbing. *Journal of Experimental Psychology: Human Perception and Performance, 10*, 683–703.

Wattam-Bell, J. (1996a). Visual motion processing in one-month-old infants: Preferential looking experiments. *Vision Research, 36*(11), 1671–1677.

Wattam-Bell, J. (1996b). Visual motion processing in one-month-old infants: Habituation experiments. *Vision Research, 36*(11), 1679–1685.

Webster, E.K., & Ulrich, D.A. (2017). Evaluation of the psychometric properties of the Test of Gross Motor Development–Third Edition. *Journal of Motor Learning and Development, 5*, 45–58. doi:10.1123/jmld/2016-0003

Weisgram, E.S., Fulcher, M., & Dinella, L.M. (2014). Pink gives girls permission: Exploring the roles of explicit gender labels and gender-typed colors on 334 preschool children's toy preferences. *Journal of Applied Developmental Psychology, 35*, 401–409.

Weisner, T., Garnier, H., & Loucky, J. (1994). Domestic tasks, gender egalitarian values and children's gender typing in conventional and nonconventional families. *Sex Roles, 30*(1/2), 23–54.

Weiss, M.R. (1993). Psychological effects of intensive sport participation on children and youth: Self-esteem and motivation. In B.R. Cahill & A.J. Pearl (Eds.), *Intensive participation in children's sports* (pp. 39–69). Champaign, IL: Human Kinetics.

Weiss, M.R., & Barber, H. (1996). Socialization influences of collegiate male athletes: A tale of two decades. *Sex Role, 33*, 129–140.

Weiss, M.R., & Ebbeck, V. (1996). Self-esteem and perceptions of competence in youth sports: Theory, research and enhancement strategies. In O. Bar-Or (Ed.), *Encyclopedia of sports medicine: Vol. 6. The child and adolescent athlete* (pp. 3364–3382). Oxford, UK: Blackwell Scientific.

Weiss, M.R., & Horn, T.S. (1990). The relation between children's accuracy estimates of their physical competence and achievement-related characteristics. *Research Quarterly for Exercise and Sport, 61*, 250–258.

Weiss, M.R., & Knoppers, A. (1982). The influence of socializing agents on female collegiate volleyball players. *Journal of Sport Psychology, 4*, 267–279.

Weiss, M.R., McAuley, E., Ebbeck, V., & Wiese, D.M. (1990). Self-esteem and causal attributions for children's physical and social competence in sport. *Journal of Sport and Exercise Psychology, 12*, 21–36.

Weltman, A., Janney, C., Rians, C.B., Strand, K., Berg, B., Tippitt, S., et al. (1986). The effects of hydraulic resistance strength training in prepubertal males. *Medicine and Science in Sports and Exercise, 18*, 629–638.

Werchan, D.M., Collins, A.G.E., Frank, M.J., & Amso, D. (2015). 8-month-old infants spontaneously learn and generalize hierarchical rules. *Psychological Science*, 26(6), 805–815. doi:10.1177/0956797615571442

Weuve, J., Kang, J.E., Manson, J.E., Breteler, M.M.B., Ware, J.H., & Grodstein, F. (2004). Physical activity, including walking, and cognitive function in older women. *Journal of the American Medical Association, 292*, 1454–1461.

Whitall, J. (1988). *A developmental study of interlimb coordination in running and galloping.* Unpublished doctoral dissertation, University of Maryland, College Park.

Whitall, J., & Getchell, N. (1995). From walking to running: Using a dynamical systems approach to the development of locomotor skills. *Child Development, 66*, 1541–1553.

White, B.L., Castle, P., & Held, R. (1964). Observations on the development of visually directed reaching. *Child Development, 35*, 349–364.

WHO Multicentre Growth Reference Study Group. (2006). Reliability of motor development data in the WHO Multicentre Growth Reference Study. *Acta Paediatrica* (Suppl. 450), 47–55.

Wick, K., Leeger-Aschmann, C.S., Monn, N.D., Radtke, T., Ott, L.F., Rebholz, C.E., . . . et al. (2017). Interventions to promote fundamental movement skills in childcare and kindergarten: A systematic review and meta-analysis. *Sports Medicine, 47,* 2045–2068. doi:10.1007/s40279-017-0723-1

Wickstrom, R.L. (1983). *Fundamental motor patterns* (3rd ed.). Philadelphia: Lea & Febiger.

Wickstrom, R.L. (1987). Observations on motor pattern development in skipping. In J.E. Clark & J.H. Humphrey (Eds.), *Advances in motor development research* (Vol. 1, pp. 49–60). New York, NY: AMS Press.

Wiegand, R.L., & Ramella, R. (1983). The effect of practice and temporal location of knowledge of results on the motor performance of older adults. *Journal of Gerontology, 38,* 701–706.

Wiese, T.B. (2016, April 13). Women's lacrosse players must adhere to traditional gender roles. *The Beacon.* Retrieved from www.theonlinebeacon.com/womens-lacrosse-players-must-adhere-to-traditional-gender-roles

Wijnhoven, T.M.A., de Onis, M., Onyango, A.W., Wang, T., Bjoerneboe, G.E.A., Bhandari, N., et al. (2006). Assessment of gross motor development in the WHO Multicentre Growth Reference Study. *Food and Nutrition Bulletin, 25,* 37–45.

Wild, M. (1937). *The behavior pattern of throwing and some observations concerning its course of development in children.* Unpublished doctoral dissertation, University of Wisconsin, Madison.

Wild, M. (1938). The behavior pattern of throwing and some observations concerning its course of development in children. *Research Quarterly, 9,* 20–24.

Williams, H. (1968). *Effects of systematic variation of speed and direction of object flight and of age and skill classification on visuo-perceptual judgments of moving objects.* Unpublished doctoral dissertation, University of Wisconsin, Madison.

Williams, H. (1973). Perceptual-motor development in children. In C. Corbin (Ed.), *A textbook of motor development* (pp. 111–148). Dubuque, IA: Brown.

Williams, H. (1983). *Perceptual and motor development.* Englewood Cliffs, NJ: Prentice Hall.

Williams, H. (1986). The development of sensory-motor function in young children. In V. Seefeldt (Ed.), *Physical activity and well-being* (pp. 104–122). Reston, VA: American Alliance for Health, Physical Education, Recreation and Dance.

Williams, J.L., & Corbetta, D. (2016). Assessing the impact of movement consequences on the development of early reaching in infancy. *Frontiers in Psychology, 7,* 587. doi:10.3389/fpsyg.2016.00587

Williams, K., Goodman, M., & Green, R. (1985). Parent-child factors in gender role socialization in girls. *Journal of the American Academy of Child Psychiatry, 24,* 720–731.

Williams, K., Haywood, K., & Painter, M. (1996). Environmental vs. biological influences on gender differences in the overarm throw for force: Dominant and nondominant arm throws. *Women in Sport and Physical Activity Journal, 3,* 29–48.

Williams, K., Haywood, K., & VanSant, A. (1990). Movement characteristics of older adult throwers. In J.E. Clark & J.H. Humphrey (Eds.), *Advances in motor development research* (Vol. 3, pp. 29–44). New York, NY: AMS Press.

Williams, K., Haywood, K., & VanSant, A. (1991). Throwing patterns of older adults: A follow-up investigation. *International Journal of Aging and Human Development, 33,* 279–294.

Williams, K., Haywood, K., & VanSant, A. (1993). Force and accuracy throws by older adult performers. *Journal of Aging and Physical Activity, 1,* 2–12.

Williams, K., Haywood, K., & VanSant, A. (1996). Force and accuracy throws by older adults: II. *Journal of Aging and Physical Activity, 4*(2), 194–202.

Williams, K., Haywood, K., & VanSant, A. (1998). Changes in throwing by older adults: A longitudinal investigation. *Research Quarterly for Exercise and Sport, 69*(1), 1–10.

Wilmore, J.H. (1991). The aging of bones and muscle. In R.K. Kerlan (Ed.), *Sports medicine in the older adult* (pp. 231–244). Philadelphia: Saunders.

Winstein, C.J., & Schmidt, R.A. (1990). Reduced frequency of knowledge of results enhances motor skill learning. *Journal of Experimental Psychology, 16*(4), 677–691.

Winter, D.A. (1983). Biomechanical motor patterns in normal walking. *Journal of Motor Behavior, 15,* 302–330.

Winterhalter, C. (1974). *Age and sex trends in the development of selected balancing skills.* Unpublished master's thesis, University of Toledo, Toledo, OH.

Wishart, L.R., & Lee, T.D. (1997). Effects of aging and reduced relative frequency of knowledge of results on learning a motor skill. *Perceptual and Motor Skills, 84*(Pt. 1), 1107–1022

Witelson, S.F. (1987). Neurobiological aspects of language in children. *Child Development, 58,* 653–688.

Witherington, D.S., Campos, J.J., Anderson, D.I., Lejeune, L., & Seah, E. (2005). Avoidance of heights on the visual cliff in newly walking infants. *Infancy, 7,* 285–298.

Wolf, J. (December 20, 2007). Babies do the driving in Delaware lab. Retrieved from https://www.9news.com/article/news/weird/babies-do-the-driving-in-delaware-lab/73-343111332

Wolff, P.H., Michel, G.F., Ovrut, M., & Drake, C. (1990). Rate and timing precision of motor coordination in developmental dyslexia. *Developmental Psychology, 26,* 349–359.

Wood, J.M., & Abernethy, B. (1997). An assessment of the efficacy of sports vision training programs. *Optometry and Vision Science, 74,* 646–659.

Wood, L.E., Dixon, S., Grant, C., & Armstrong, N. (2006). Elbow flexor strength, muscle size, and moment arms in prepubertal boys and girls. *Pediatric Exercise Science, 18,* 457–469.

Woollacott, M., Shumway-Cook, A.T., & Nashner, L.M. (1982). Postural reflexes and aging. In J.A. Mortimer (Ed.), *The aging motor system* (pp. 98–119). New York, NY: Praeger.

Woollacott, M., Shumway-Cook, A.T., & Nashner, L.M. (1986). Aging and posture control: Changes in sensory organization and muscular coordination. *International Journal of Aging and Human Development, 23,* 97–114.

Woollacott, M.H. (1986). Gait and postural control in the aging adult. In W. Bles & T. Brandt (Eds.), *Disorders of posture and gait* (pp. 326–336). New York, NY: Elsevier.

Woollacott, M.H., Shumway-Cook, A., & Williams, H. (1989). The development of posture and balance control in children. In M.H. Woollacott & A. Shumway-Cook (Eds.), *Development of posture and gait across the life span* (pp. 77–96). Columbia: University of South Carolina Press.

Woollacott, M.H., & Sveistrup, H. (1994). The development of sensorimotor integration underlying posture control in infants during the transition to independent stance. In S.P. Swinnen, J. Massion, & H. Heuer (Eds.), *Interlimb coordination: Neural, dynamical and cognitive constraints* (pp. 371–389). San Diego: Academic Press.

World Health Organization. (2017). Obesity and overweight. Retrieved from www.who.int/mediacentre/factsheets/fs311/en.12

Wright, C.E., & Wormald, R.P. (1992). Stereopsis and aging. *Eye, 6,* 473–476.

Wulf, G. (1991). The effect of type of practice on motor learning in children. *Applied Cognitive Psychology, 5,* 123–134. doi:10.1002/acp.2350050206

Wulf, G., & Schmidt, R.A. (1989). The learning of generalized motor programs: Reducing the relative frequency of knowledge of results enhances memory. *Journal of Experimental Psychology, 15*(4), 748–757.

Yamaguchi, Y. (1984). A comparative study of adolescent socialization into sport: The case of Japan and Canada. *International Review for Sociology of Sport, 19*(1), 63–82.

Yan, J.H., Abernethy, B., & Li, X. (2010). The effects of ageing and cognitive impairment on on-line and off-line motor learning. *Applied Cognitive Psychology, 24,* 200–212.

Yan, J.H., Payne, V.G., & Thomas, J.R. (2000). Developmental kinematics of young girls' overarm throwing. *Research Quarterly for Exercise and Sport, 71,* 92–98.

Yao, C.A., & Rhodes, R.E. (2015). Parental correlates in child and adolescent physical activity: A meta-analysis. *International Journal of Behavioral Nutrition and Physical Activity, 12,* 10. doi:10.1186/s12966-015-0163-y

Yates, L.B., Karasik, D., Beck, T.J., Cupples, L.A., & Kiel, D.P. (2007). Hip structural geometry in old and old-old age: Similarities and differences between men and women. *Bone, 41,* 722–732.

Yeh, T.T., Cluff, T., & Balasubramaniam, R. (2014). Visual reliance for balance control in older adults persists when visual information is disrupted by artificial feedback delays. *PLoS ONE, 9,* e91554. doi:10.1371/journal/pone/0091554

Yekta, A.A., Pickwell, L.D., & Jenkins, T.C.A. (1989). Binocular vision, age and symptoms. *Ophthalmic and Physiological Optics, 9,* 115–120.

Young, A., Stokes, M., & Crowe, M. (1985). The size and strength of the quadriceps muscles of old and young men. *Clinical Physiology, 5,* 145–154.

Zakas, A. (2005). The effect of stretching duration on the lower-extremity flexibility of adolescent soccer players. *Journal of Bodywork and Movement Therapies, 9,* 220–225. doi:10.1016/j.jbmi/2004.07.002

Zelazo, P.R. (1983). The development of walking: New findings and old assumptions. *Journal of Motor Behavior, 15,* 99–137.

Zelazo, P.R., Zelazo, N.A., & Kolb, S. (1972a). "Walking" in the newborn. *Science, 176,* 314–315.

Zelazo, P.R., Zelazo, N.A., & Kolb, S. (1972b). Newborn walking. *Science, 177,* 1058–1059.

Zetou, E., Papadakis, L., Vernadakis, N., Derri, V., Bebetsos, E., & Filippou, F. (2014). The effect of variable and stable practice on performance and learning the header skill of young athletes in soccer. *Procedia: Social and Behavioral Sciences, 152,* 824–829.

Zheng, Y., Manson, J.E., Yuan, C., Liang, M.H., Grodstein, F., Stampfer, M.J., et al. (2017). Associations of weight gain from early to middle adulthood with major health outcomes later in life. Journal of the American Medical Association, *318*(3), 255–269. doi:10.1001/jama.2017.7092

Zimmerman, H.M. (1956). Characteristic likenesses and differences between skilled and non-skilled performance of the standing broad jump. *Research Quarterly, 27,* 352.

Zipp, G.P., & Gentile, A.M. (2010). Practice schedule and the learning of motor skills in children and adults: Teaching implications. *Journal of College Teaching and Learning, 7*(2), 35–42.

Zubiaur, M., Oña, A., & Delgado, J. (1999). Learning volleyball serves: A preliminary study of the effects of knowledge of performance and of results. *Perceptual Motor Skills, 89,* 223–232.

Zwiren, L.D. (1989). Anaerobic and aerobic capacities of children. *Pediatric Exercise Science, 1,* 31–44.

INDEX

Note: The italicized *f* and *t* following page numbers refer to figures and tables, respectively.

A

Abernethy, B. 143
absolute threshold 274
acceleration curves 164, 168*f*
action–perception link 286-295
  contemporary views on 287-290, 288*t*
  historical views on 286-287
  perception of affordances and body scaling 25, 141, 293-295, 294*f*
  postural control and balance 295-298
  self-produced locomotion 290-293, 291*f*, 292*f*
acuity 261
adipose system 179, 181, 186-187, 188*f*, 194
adipose tissue 241
Adolph, Karen 46, 67, 292, 293
adulthood. *See also* aging; older adults
  activity levels in 333-334, 333*f*, 334*f*
  adipose system in 194
  aerobic performance in 210-215, 213*f*, 214*f*, 215*f*
  anaerobic performance in 204-205
  anticipatory sports skills in 141-142, 142*f*, 143
  body composition in 240-241, 241*f*, 247-248
  causal attributions in 327-328
  cognitive processing speed in 195, 350-352, 352*f*
  endocrine system in 194-195
  endurance training effect in 214-216, 215*f*
  flexibility in 232*f*, 235*f*, 236-237
  grasping in 130-131
  intermodal perception in 281-282
  manual performance in 134-135
  memory in 195, 353
  motivation in 333-334, 333*f*, 334*f*, 367
  muscular system in 179-181, 180*f*, 181*f*, 193-194
  nervous system in 195
  obesity in 194, 250-251, 250*f*
  overarm throwing in 110-111
  physical development in 171-174, 172*f*, 173*f*, 174*f*
  reaction time in 349, 350-351
  skeletal system in 173, 185, 185*f*, 192-193
  sport participation in 305, 311
  strength in 226-229, 227*f*, 228*f*, 228*t*, 229*f*
  varied practice in 344-345
aerobic capacity 205
aerobic performance
  in adults 210-215, 213*f*, 214*f*, 215*f*
  assessing 210-211
  in children and adolescents 206-216, 207*f*, 208*f*
  disease and 202, 215
  in older adults 204-205
aerobic power 205
aerobic training. *See also* endurance training
  in adults 214-215, 215*f*
  in children 208-210
  long-term effects of 215-216
affordances 24-25, 141, 293-295, 294*f*, 349
age at takeoff 163
age-related maculopathy 262
aging 5. *See also* older adults
  auditory perception and 274, 275
  balance and 73, 297-298
  body fat and 194
  bone composition and 192-193, 247
  cardiovascular structure and function 211-212
  cognitive processing speed and 195, 350-352, 352*f*
  dynamical systems approach and 24
  fluid intelligence and 338
  gradual imbalance theories of 194-195
  hearing and 194-195, 274
  kinesthetic changes with 273-274
  maturational perspective and 172-173
  maximal oxygen uptake and 213-214, 214*f*, 215*f*
  muscle fibers and 193-194
  physical development in 171-174, 172*f*, 173*f*, 174*f*
  respiratory changes 212, 213*f*
  running and 66
  speed of cognitive functions 195, 350-351
  strength changes 226-229, 227*f*, 228*f*, 228*t*, 229*f*
  vision and 261-262
  vital capacity and 212
air-displacement plethysmography 243
Alberta Infant Motor Scale (AIMS) 57
alcohol, in pregnancy 157, 183
Alexander, G. 58, 60
Allen, M. 58, 60
Almond, Paul 4
alveoli 212, 213*f*
Alzheimer's disease 353
Ames, C. 332
amodal invariants 278
anabolic steroids 220
anaerobic power 203-204
anaerobic training 202-205, 203*f*
androgens 189, 195
angle of gaze 141, 142*f*
angular distance and force 33-34
Aniansson, A. 228, 228*f*
anterior cruciate ligament tears 178
anterior pituitary gland 188, 188*f*
anthropometry 170-171
anticipation 139-143, 142*f*
appositional bone growth 184
Apted, Michael 4
arrested development 10-11
arthritis
  body scaling for 25
  in children 235
  as constraint 7, 73, 128
  grasping and 131
  obesity and 251
  osteoarthritis 73, 236
  overarm throwing and 24, 111
  strength training and 230
Asmussen, E. 223
Assaiante, C. 296
associative stage of motor learning 341-342
Astill, S.L. 138
asymmetric tonic neck reflex 49, 50*t*, 51*f*
atherosclerosis 212
athletes
  older adults as 77, 333
  Paralympic 356
  supplements used by 220

attributions 325-328
atypical development 9, 58, 60. *See also* interacting constraints
auditory development
  auditory-kinesthetic intermodal perception 281
  auditory pattern perception 276-277, 276*f*
  auditory perception 275-277, 275*f*, 276*f*
  auditory sensation 274
  auditory-visual intermodal perception 279
  figure-and-ground perception 277
augmented feedback 347-348
autism spectrum disorder 94, 182
autonomous stage of motor learning 341-342
aversive socialization 315
axons 182*f*, 189, 191
Ay, L. 169, 184, 186
Ayres, A.J. 287

B

Babinski test 52
backswing 101, 103*t*, 110
balance
  assessing 298-299
  in children 295-296
  in creeping 67, 67*f*
  in infants 60-62, 61*f*, 134, 295-296
  motor milestones in 55, 58
  in older adults 73, 297-298
  stability and 38-40, 39*f*
  training for 298
  in walking 39-40, 71
ballistic skills. *See also* overarm throwing
  assessing 124, 124*t*
  interventions 125
  kicking 112-114, 112*f*, 113*f*
  overarm striking 121-123, 121*f*, 122*t*, 125
  overarm throwing 100-112, 101*f*, 102*f*, 103*t*-104*t*, 104*f*, 106*f*, 107*f*
  punting 114-116, 115*f*, 116*t*, 117*f*
  sidearm striking 116-120, 118*f*, 118*t*, 119*f*, 120*f*
Barela, J.A. 62, 273
Barnett, L.M. 24, 253, 254, 324, 325, 328, 329
Barrett, K.R. 70
Barrett, T.M. 134
Barrett, U. 222
Barsch, R.H. 287
basal metabolic rate 242-243, 249
baseball. *See also* catching; overarm throwing
  anticipation in 140
  body scaling and 25
  forces in 33
  gender typing in 305, 307
  perception-action approach 26
  strength and 220
basketball. *See also* catching
  body scaling in 152, 358-360, 358*f*, 359*f*, 360*f*, 362
  developmental changes and 85, 137
  flexibility and 236
  injuries in 177
  task constraints in 8, 362
  vertical jump in 84*f*
Bayley, N. 54-55, 57
Bayley Scales of Infant Development 54-55, 57, 59
BDNF (brain-derived neurotrophic factor) 289
Bennett, S. 143
Bernstein, Nikolai 23, 342-344, 343*f*
Bertenthal, B. 61, 61*f*, 134, 290, 295
bimanual reaching 133-134, 134*f*
biomechanical descriptive period 20, 21*f*
Birch, L.L. 276
Bisi, Maria Cristina 152
Blakemore, J.E.O. 317
Blimkie, C.J.R. 223
blocked practice 344
block rotation 104*f*, 105
blood flow 206, 212
blood pressure 212
BMI (body mass index) 171, 243, 248, 370*f*, 371*f*
body awareness 271-273
body composition 240. *See also* obesity
  assessing 242-243, 369*f*, 370*f*, 371*f*
  exercise in adults and 240-241, 241*f*, 247-248
  exercise in children and 192, 244-247, 244*f*, 246*f*
  exercise in older adults and 247-248
  fat distribution 186-187, 188*f*, 189
  fitness and 251
  importance of 241-243
  maximal oxygen uptake and 213-214, 214*f*
  obesity and 248
  over the life span 194
  Parizkova studies 244-246, 244*f*, 246*f*
  short-term studies on 203-204
body proportions 165-166, 166*f*
body scaling 130
  in affordances 25, 141, 293-295, 294*f*
  for arthritis 25
  in baseball and 25
  in basketball 152, 358-360, 358*f*, 359*f*, 360*f*, 362
  in grasping 120, 130-131
  in learning 362-363
  in sidearm striking 120, 363
  in tennis 294
body sense. *See* kinesthetic development
bones
  epiphyseal plates in 183, 183*f*
  estrogen and 192
  growth of 183-184, 184*f*
  low birth weight and 184
  mineral density of 184, 192
  in older adults 193, 247
  ossification of 183, 185, 185*f*
  osteoporosis of 171, 173*f*, 174, 174*f*, 193, 236, 298
  remodeling of 192
  shoulder 31, 32*f*
Bouchard, C. 163, 188*f*, 203*f*, 206, 207
boundaries, visual perception of 132*f*, 264
boys and men. *See also* sex differences
  body composition of 186-187
  body height in 173*f*
  body mass index chart for 370*f*
  bone loss in 192
  catching by 137, 137*f*
  epiphyseal plates in 183
  gender typing and 307, 311-312, 316, 366-367
  grasping by 130
  growth spurts and motor skills 152, 163, 171
  head circumference chart for 372*f*
  muscle mass in 186, 206
  overall growth patterns 158-166, 159*f*, 161*f*, 165*f*
  overarm throwing in 106*f*, 107*f*, 108-109, 125
  secondary sex characteristics 167, 172
  self-esteem in 326-327
  skinfold measurement charts 188*f*
  stature by age 159*f*
  weight by age 161*f*
  weight-for length percentiles 161*f*, 163, 165
brain
  development of 166, 181, 189-192, 190*f*, 191*f*
  motor and cognitive development and 192, 195, 287-290
  structures 190-192
brain-derived neurotrophic factor (BDNF) 289
brain stem 181, 190*f*
Brodkin, P. 330-331
Bruner, J.S. 132, 134
Burton, A.W. 364
Bushnell, E.W. 293
Butterworth, G. 130

C

calcium, bone density and 192
Campbell, A.J. 298
Canada 203, 203*f*, 208*f*, 312, 328
capability, ability versus 339
cardiac muscle fibers 194, 211, 212
cardiac output 205, 212
cardiorespiratory endurance. *See also* motor development
  aerobic performance assessment

210-211
aerobic performance in adulthood 205-206, 210-215, 213*f*, 214*f*, 215*f*
aerobic performance in childhood 206-210, 207*f*, 208*f*
anaerobic performance assessment 205
anaerobic performance development 202-205, 203*f*
cardiovascular structure and function and 211-212
endurance training effect 214-216, 215*f*
motor skill proficiency and 202
muscle mass changes and 213-214, 214*f*
respiratory structure and function and 212, 213*f*
cardiovascular function 211-212
Carnahan, H. 131
Carr, G. 37, 40
case studies 366-367
cataracts 262, 281-282
catching
anticipation in 140-143, 142*f*
assessing 145
by children 136-138, 136*f*, 137*t*, 138
observation plan for 138, 139*f*
by older adults 143-144
proficient 136-137, 137*f*
in sports 141-143, 142*f*
catch-up growth 169, 172*f*
causal attributions 325-328
cell differentiation 153
cell plasticity 155
center of gravity 38, 39, 73, 297
central nervous system. *See* nervous system
cephalocaudal growth 155
cerebral cortex 189-190, 190*f*
cerebral palsy 9, 58, 362, 367
Cheney, Dorothy "Dodo" 100
children. *See also* infants
adipose system development in 181, 186-187
aerobic performance in 206-216, 207*f*, 208*f*
age grouping 367
anaerobic performance in 203-204, 203*f*
anticipation in 140, 143
attributions in 326-237, 327*f*
auditory pattern perception in 276-277, 276*f*
balance in 295-296
body awareness in 271-273
body composition in 192, 244-247, 244*f*, 246*f*
body scaling for 363
catching by 136, 136*f*, 138
changing constraints in 31-32
cognitive processing speed in 349-350
coincidence-anticipation in 139-140
endocrine system in 188-189, 188*f*
endurance training effect in 208-210, 215-216
flexibility in 231-236, 232*f*, 235*f*
galloping, sliding, and skipping by 90-93, 91*f*, 93*f*, 96-97
grade-level expectations 367
grasping by 130-131
hopping by 85-90, 87*f*, 87*t*, 88*f*, 89*f*, 89*t*, 91*f*-92*f*
intermodal perception in 279-280
jumping by 77-85, 79*t*, 80*t*, 81*f*, 81*t*, 82*f*, 83*t*, 84*f*
kicking by 112-114, 112*f*, 113*f*
kinesthetic perception in 270-271
laterality and lateral dominance in 272-273, 272*t*
maximal oxygen uptake in 205-208, 207*f*, 208*f*, 210-211
memory in 353
modifying constraints for 358-359, 358*f*, 359*f*, 360*f*, 361-363
motivation in 329-333
motor and cognitive development in 60
motor competence perception in 328-329
motor skill interventions 125
muscular system in 186
nervous system in 189-192, 190*f*, 191*f*
obesity in 248-251, 249*t*
overarm striking in 121-122, 121*f*
overarm throwing in 100-109, 101*f*, 102*f*, 103*t*-104*t*, 104*f*, 106*f*, 107*f*
punting by 114-116, 115*f*, 116*t*, 117*f*
running by 75-77, 75*t*, 76*f*
self awareness in 271
self-esteem in 324
sidearm striking by 118, 118*f*, 120
skeletal system in 183-185, 183*f*, 184*f*, 185*f*
social interactions of 57, 301, 310, 323-324, 334
socialization in 306-307, 397*f*
strength in 221-223, 221*f*
strength training 224-227, 224*f*, 227*f*
variable practice in motor learning in 345-347, 346*f*
visual perception in 261, 262, 264-268, 265*f*, 266*f*, 267*f*
walking patterns in 68, 69*f*
Children Who Run on All Fours (Hrdlicka) 67
choice reaction time 349, 350-351
circumference measurements 171
Clark, J.E. 349
Clarke, H.H. 232
"clean house" game 361, 362
Clifton, R.K. 275
coaches 40, 313-315, 324
cocontraction, in infants 48
cognitive development. *See also* action–perception link
aging and 195, 338
brain and 287-290
information processing speed 195, 349-352, 352*f*
memory and 195
mobility and 60
cognitive processing speed 195, 349, 350-352, 352*f*
cognitive stage of motor learning 341-342
cohorts 12-13
coincidence-anticipation tasks 139-140. *See also* anticipation
Colcombe, Stanley 351-352
competence motivation theory 330
computerized dynamic posturography 299
congenital defects 156-158, 158*t*
congestive heart failure 194
constant bearing angle strategy 142, 142*f*
constraints 7. *See also* environmental constraints; individual constraints; interacting constraints; psychosocial constraints; sociocultural constraints; task constraints
atypical development and 9
in case studies 366-367
changing views on role of 8-9
in dynamical systems approach 23, 24*f*
ecological task analyses 364-366, 365*f*, 366*f*
enhancing learning in physical activity 357-361, 357*f*, 358*f*, 359*f*, 360*f*
functional 7, 301, 322
modifying for children 358-359, 358*f*, 359*f*, 360*f*, 361-363
motor milestones and 57-58, 58*f*
Newell's model of 6-8, 6*f*, 196
Paralympic Games and 30
structural 7, 8*f*, 358-359, 358*f*, 359*f*
Title IX and 308-309
types of 6-8, 6*f*, 8*f*
variability in behavior and 14
Contreras-Vidal, J.L. 135
controllers. *See* rate limiters
coordination 9, 11-12, 18, 22-23
Corbetta, D. 133
co-twin control strategy 19, 19*f*
crawling 46, 52, 58*f*, 67-68, 67*f*
creeping 67-68, 67*f*
criterion-referenced scales 59
cross-sectional research studies 11-13
crystallized intelligence 338
cultural constraints. *See* sociocultural constraints
Cumming, R.G. 192
Cureton, K.J. 226

D

degrees of freedom 342-344, 343*f*

Delacato, C.H. 287
DeMar, Clarence 215
dental eruption 172
Denver Developmental Screening Test 59
depth perception 263-264, 290
Der, G. 350
detection thresholds 267
detour tasks 292, 292*f*
development. *See also* auditory development; kinesthetic development; motor development; postnatal development; prenatal development; sensory–perceptual development
adipose system 181, 186-187, 194
arrested 10-11
atypical 9, 58, 60
of the brain 166, 181, 189-192, 190*f*, 191*f*
cognitive 60, 195, 287-290, 338, 349-352, 352*f*
embryonic 153, 154*f*, 154*t*
endocrine system 181
fetal 153-155, 154*t*, 155*f*
maturational perspective 18-20, 19*f*, 23-24
muscular system 179-181, 180*f*, 181*f*, 186, 193-194
nervous system 181-183, 182*f*, 189-192, 190*f*, 191*f*, 195
perceptual-motor 60, 257, 287-290
physical 171-174, 172*f*, 173*f*, 174*f*
skeletal system 179, 179*f*, 183-185, 183*f*, 184*f*, 185*f*, 192-193
in sliding 89, 90-93, 91*f*, 96
of strength 221-223, 221*f*, 226-229, 227*f*, 228*f*, 228*t*, 229*f*
visual perception 262-266, 263*f*, 265*f*, 266-268, 266*f*, 267*f*
developmental change
in catching 137-138, 137*t*
in early and later running 76
in galloping 92, 96
graphing 10-11, 10*f*, 11*f*
in grasping 129-131
in hopping 88-89, 89*t*
in jumping 85
in kicking 114
in overarm striking 122-123, 122*t*
in overarm throwing 102-109, 102*f*, 103*t*-104*t*, 104*f*, 106*f*, 107*f*
in punting 115, 116*t*
recalibrating movement in 71
research design for 11-13
in sidearm striking 118*t*, 119-120, 120*f*
in skipping 90-93, 91*f*, 96-97
universality versus variability in 14
in walking 71-72
developmentally appropriate teaching 363
developmental motor learning
augmented feedback in 347-348
Bernstein's model 342-344, 343*f*
definitions in 338-340, 340*f*
Fitts and Posner's model of 341-342
information processing speed 195, 349-352, 352*f*
learning curves in 339-340, 340*f*
online and offline components of 350-351
practice and 344-347, 346*f*
teaching 367
developmental profile 138
developmental trajectory 10-11, 11*f*
Diamond, A. 289
diaphysis 183, 184*f*
Dienes, Z. 141, 142*f*, 143
diet. *See* nutrition
differential threshold 274
differentiated trunk rotation 105, 120, 120*f*
differentiation of cells 153
directionality 273
disabilities. *See* constraints
disease. *See also specific diseases*
distance curves 164
distances, visual perception of 263, 267*f*
domains 323
double knee-lock 71
Down syndrome
assessing motor development 94
genetics of 156
hypotonia in 60
walking development in 54, 54*f*, 69
driving 144
dual-energy X-ray absorptiometer (DXA) 243
Duda, J.L. 333-334, 334*f*
Duijts, L. 169
dynamical systems approach 22-24, 24*f*, 67
dynamic balance 298
dynamometers 222, 223
dyslexia 182, 289

E

ear structure 268-269, 269*f*
eating disorders 240
Ebrahim, S. 313
ecological perspective 22-26, 24*f*, 289-290, 293, 349
ecological task analyses 363-366, 365*f*, 366*f*
edges, visual perception of 263-264
Ehsani, F. 350
electromyography (EMG) 299
embedded objects, visual perception of 264, 265*f*
embryonic development 153, 154*f*, 154*t*
emotions, self-esteem and 325
endocrine system 179, 181, 188-189, 188*f*, 194-195
endurance training effects. *See also* aerobic performance
in adults 214-215, 215*f*
in children 208-210, 215-216
long-term 215-216
environmental constraints 7. *See also* sociocultural constraints
in grasping 49, 130
in infant locomotion 47
modifying 358-359, 358*f*, 359*f*, 360*f*
in Newell's model 6*f*, 7
physical 7
teacher-centered versus student-centered 332
epilepsy 182
epiphyseal growth plates 183-184, 184*f*, 185*f*, 189
equipment, as constraint 357-361, 357*f*, 358*f*, 359*f*, 360*f*. *See also* body scaling
ergometer tests 203*f*, 210
Espenschade, Anna 20
estrogens 189, 193
ethnicity, socialization and 312, 318-319
Ewart, C.K. 327
exercise. *See* physical activity
exercise capacity 206-207, 207*f*, 208*f*, 212
exploiting degrees of freedom 342-344, 343*f*
extrapyramidal tract 192
extrinsic factors
in abnormal prenatal development 156-158, 158*t*
in nervous system development 181-182
nourishment as 155
in postnatal growth 167, 169, 172*f*
eye anatomy 261*f*
eye-hand coordination 272

F

face perception 265
facial profile/vase image 21*f*, 260
Faigenbaum, A.D. 224, 225
falling, in older adults 73, 194, 274, 297-298
family members 310-312
fast-twitch muscle fibers
in the muscular system 181, 181*f*
in older adults 110, 297
sex differences in 227
fetal alcohol syndrome 157, 183
fetal development 153-155, 154*t*, 155*f*
fibular hemimelia 30
field hockey 304
fielding 136
56 Up (film) 4
figure-and-ground perception
auditory 277
visual 264, 265*f*
fitness
aerobic training and 206-209, 215-216
anaerobic training and 203-205,

203*f*
assessing 205, 210
body composition and 251
cardiorespiratory endurance and 202
flexibility and 231, 233
maximal oxygen uptake in children 205-208, 207*f*, 208*f*, 210-211
motor skill proficiency and 253-254
obesity and 248-252, 249*t*, 251*f*
peak oxygen uptake and 206-207, 207*f*
pulmonary oxygen uptake and 211
quality of life and 199, 202
self-esteem and 327
sociocultural constraints and 313
Fitts, P.M. 341-342
Fitts and Posner's model 341-342
flexibility 231-237
in adults 232*f*, 235*f*, 236-237
assessing 234, 234*f*
in children 231-235, 232*f*, 235*f*
flexibility training 235-237
importance of 231
strength training and 225, 227, 231
fluid intelligence 338
fNIRS (functional near infrared spectroscopy) 191
force, in Newton's laws 33-34, 35
force absorption 37-38
forced vital capacity 212
force platform 298-299
forearm lag 102
freezing degrees of freedom 342, 343*f*
French, K.E. 21
Frostig, M. 287
functional constraints 7, 301, 322. *See also* motivation
functional near infrared spectroscopy (fNIRS) 191

G

Gabell, A. 73
Gagen, L. 25, 32, 33, 34, 35, 38, 294, 358, 361, 362, 363
Gallagher, J.D. 353
galloping 90-93, 91*f*, 93*f*, 96
Galloway, Cole 60, 63
games, socialization in 316
gender, definition of 307
gender differences. *See* sex differences
gender typing
case study in 366-367
coaches and teachers in 313-315
in lacrosse 304
in play environments and games 316
in play with toys 316-318
significant others in 310-313
as sociocultural constraint 307-309
Title IX and 305, 308-309, 311
Generation R Study 169, 184, 186
genetics
in abnormal prenatal development 156-158, 158*t*
body composition and 242
brain development and 190
in dominant and recessive disorders 156
in maturation 18-19
in nervous system development 181
in obesity 248-249, 251
Genome Project 190
Gentile, A.M. 346, 346*f*
Gesell, Arnold 18-19, 19*f*
Gesell Developmental Schedules 59
Getchell, N. 25, 26, 32, 33, 34, 35, 38, 73, 89, 129*f*, 253, 254, 333, 358, 361, 362, 363
Getman, G.N. 287
GH (growth hormone) 188
Gibson, E.J. 292, 293
Gibson, J.J. 24-26
girls and women. *See also* sex differences
body composition of 186-187, 188*f*
body mass index chart for 371*f*
bone loss in 192-193
gender-specific stereotyped behaviors 307-309, 316
gender typing of 304-305, 307, 366-367
head circumference chart for 373*f*
height growth curves 160*f*, 161, 163
jumping by 85
maturation status in 172-173
menarche 167, 168*f*
ossification in 183, 185, 185*f*
overall growth of 158-165, 160*f*, 162*f*, 165*f*
overarm throwing in 108-109, 125
running by 76
self-esteem in 324
skinfold measurement charts 188*f*, 369*f*
skipping by 96
socializing agents for 304-305
stature by age 160*f*
Title IX 305, 308-309, 311
weight by age 162*f*
weight-for-length percentiles 162*f*, 163
Giuliano, T. 309
Glassow, Ruth 20
glia 189
Goggin, N.L. 144
Goh, H. 348
golf 38, 117, 123, 220, 362
gonadal hormones 189, 195
goniometers 234
Goodnow, J.J. 279, 280-281
gradual imbalance theories of aging 194-195
graphs
anaerobic performance 203*f*
body fat and activity 244*f*, 246*f*
body mass index 370*f*, 371*f*
cognitive performance after exercise 352*f*
developmental level in hopping 89*f*
developmental trajectory 11*f*
exercise incentives and age 334*f*
flexibility and age 232*f*, 235*f*
growth in childhood 10*f*
of growth velocity 165*f*, 168*f*
head circumference 372*f*, 373*f*
height in adulthood 159*f*, 160*f*
isometric strength development 221*f*
maximal oxygen uptake and age 214*f*, 215*f*
muscle force and age 228*f*
muscle force and test repetition 227*f*
muscle strength with training 224*f*
obesity and age 251*f*
of puberty and menarche 169*f*
skinfolds 369*f*
stature 159*f*, 160*f*
strength and age 221*f*, 224*f*
weight by age 161*f*, 162*f*
weight in adulthood 174*f*
working capacity and age 208*f*
grasping 128-131, 129*f*, 131*f*
gravity
center of 38, 39, 73, 297
as constraint in movement 31
gravity (postural) reflexes 50*t*, 51-52
Newton's laws and 33-34, 35
Greendorfer, S.L. 312-313
Greenough, W.T. 294-295
grip strength 135, 254
growth. *See* physical growth
Growth: A Study of Johnny and Jimmy (McGraw) 19
growth factors 289
growth hormone (GH) 188

H

habituation, visual 265
Halverson, H.M. 108, 128-130
Halverson, Lolas 20, 21*f*
hand dominance 272-273, 272*t*
hand–mouth movements 133
Hands, B. 254
hand transplant 128
HAPPE (high autonomy physical play environment) 332
haptic memory 271
Harter, Susan 324, 330
Harter's Self-Perception Profile for Children 254, 325
Hartshorne, J.K. 338
Haubenstricker, J.L. 114, 137
Hawkins, Julia "Hurricane" 66, 97
Haywood, K.M. 109, 110-112, 123, 125, 140, 144, 262, 294
head circumference 171, 372*f*, 373*f*
Healthy People 2020 322
hearing 268-269, 269*f*, 275-276, 275*f*, 276*f*. *See also* auditory development

heart
cardiovascular structure and function 211-212
congestive heart failure 194
development of 186
ischemic heart disease 212
maximum heart rate 212
in prolonged exercise 206
height
in aging 171-174, 172*f*, 173*f*, 174*f*
maturation age and 167
measuring 170-171
osteoporosis and 171, 173*f*, 174, 174*f*
peak velocity in 163, 167, 168*f*
sigmoid pattern of growth 158, 159*f*, 160*f*
Heinze, J.E. 309
Held, R. 290, 291*f*
hemoglobin 206, 212
Hesketh, K.D. 250
high autonomy physical play environment (HAPPE) 332
Hogan, P.I. 328
Hohlstein, R.E. 129
Holland, G.J. 236
hopping 77. *See also* jumping
characteristics of early 85-86, 87*f*
developmental changes in 88-89, 89*t*
developmental sequence for 86, 87*t*, 88*f*, 89*f*
integrated approach to 90
observation plan for 90, 91*f*-92*f*
proficient 88, 88*f*
rate controllers in 90
hormone replacement therapies 195
hormones 179. *See also specific hormones* abnormal prenatal
development and 157, 188
in adulthood 192
bone loss and 192-193
early development of 188-189
gonadal 189, 195
hormone replacement therapies 195
pituitary 196
regulation of 181, 188
thyroid 188, 194
trigger hypothesis 209
Horn, T.S. 237, 324, 326
Hughes, S. 135
human genome 190
Huntsman World Senior Games 77
Hupprich, F.L. 232
hydrocephalus 171
hyperplasia 153, 179, 186
hyperthyroidism 194
hypertrophy
in adipose tissue 186
in fetal development 153
in muscle fibers 179, 226
hypokinetic circulation 206
hypothalamus 188, 188*f*
hypothyroidism 194
hypotonia 60

I

IMAX movies 260
immune system, aging and 194
individual constraints
body scaling and 25, 293-295, 294*f*
definition and role of 7
in early walking 68-69
in infant motor development 25, 293-295, 294*f*
in Newell's model 6*f*, 7
Paralympic Games and 30, 356, 360
as rate limiters 23
in walking by older adults 72-73
inertia 37
infants
affordances 25, 293-295, 294*f*
anticipation in 49, 129, 141
atypical development 58, 60
auditory figure-and-ground in 277
auditory perception 275-277, 275*f*, 276*f*
Bayley Scales of Infant Development 54-55, 57, 59
brain structures 190-191
crawling 46, 52, 58*f*, 67-68, 67*f*
Denver Developmental Screening Test 59
Gesell Developmental Schedules 59
grasping 49, 50*t*, 54, 60, 128-130, 129*f*
hand–mouth movements 133
individual constraints in 25, 293-295, 294*f*
intermodal perception 279-280
kinesthetic perception 268-269, 271
lateral dominance 58, 272-273, 272*t*
locomotion and perception 290-293, 291*f*, 292*f*
low-birth-weight 184
motion perception 61-62, 61*f*
motor development 289-290
motor milestones 54-58, 55*f*, 56*t*, 58*f*
muscle fiber types 180-181
nervous system 181-183, 182*f*
norm-referenced versus criterion-referenced scales 59
object perception 264-266, 265*f*, 266*f*
perception–action loops in 289-290
postural control and balance 60-62, 61*f*, 134, 295-296
preferential looking 266-267
reaching 47, 60, 132-134, 132*f*, 133*f*
reflexes 47, 49-54, 50*t*, 51*f*
socializing agents for 310
spatial perception 263-264, 263*f*, 264*f*, 289-293, 292*f*
spontaneous movements 47-49, 48*f*
supine kicking and walking 47-48, 48*f*
tool use 294, 294*f*
visual perception in 261, 263-264, 266-267
voluntary movements 53-54
information processing perspective 21-22
information processing speed 195, 349, 350-352, 352*f*
insulin 189, 195
interacting constraints
basketball modifications for children 358-359, 358*f*, 359*f*, 360*f*
case studies 366-367
designing learning tasks 361-363
ecological task analyses 364-366, 365*f*
Paralympic Games and 356, 360
intermodal perception 278-282
auditory-kinesthetic 281
auditory-visual 279
spatial-temporal 281-282
visual-kinesthetic 280-281
invariants 141, 143
Iowa Bone Development Study 246-247
ischemic heart disease 212
isokinetic strength 222
isometric strength 222-223
isotonic strength 222
Ivry, R.B. 289

J

Janz, K.F. 246
Japan 305, 311, 312
jumping 77
characteristics of early 77-82, 79*t*, 80*t*, 81*f*, 81*t*, 82*f*
developmental changes in 85
observation plan for 86*f*
prelongitudinal screening 82
proficient 83-84, 84*f*
rate limiters in 85
standing long jump sequence 80-82, 80*t*, 81*t*, 82*f*, 83*t*
types of 79*t*

K

Kane, E.W. 311
Katch, V.L. 209
Kauranen, K. 135
Kelso, Scott 23
Kephart, N.C. 287
Kermoian, R. 291
kicking
assessment of 124, 124*t*
characteristics of early 112, 112*f*, 113*f*
developmental changes in 114
ecological task analysis of 364, 365*f*
by infants 47-48, 48*f*
observing 114
proficient 113, 113*f*

Kim, R. 140
kinesthetic development 268-274
auditory-kinesthetic intermodal perception 281
body awareness 271-273
directionality 273
kinesthetic perception 270-273, 270*f*
kinesthetic sensation 268-269, 268*t*, 269*f*
lateral dominance 272-273, 272*t*
in older adults 273-274
proprioceptors 268-269, 268*t*, 297
spatial orientation 265-266, 273
tactile localization 270, 270*f*
visual-kinesthetic intermodal perception 280-281
kittens, motor development in 290, 291*f*
knowledge of performance (KP) 347-348
knowledge of results (KR) 347-348
Kobayashi, K. 209
Kornatz, K.W. 135
KörperkoordinationsTest für Kinder (KTK) 254, 329
KP (knowledge of performance) 347-348
KR (knowledge of results) 347-348
Krahenbuhl, G.S. 211, 232
Kramer, Arthur 351, 352*f*
Kugler, Peter 23
Kuhtz-Buschbeck, J.P. 131
kyphosis 174*f*

L

labyrinthine righting reflex 49, 50*t*, 51*f*, 269
lacrosse 304
Langendorfer, S. 111-112, 122-123
lateral dominance 272-273, 272*t*
laterality 272
laws of motion 33-34, 35
lean body mass
in body composition 171
maximal oxygen uptake and 213-214, 214*f*
measuring 242
physical activity and 204, 207, 242
lean tissue 241
leaping 77. *See also* jumping
learning
body scaling in 362-363
brain structures and 190
designing the learning task 361-363
ecological task analyses 363-366, 365*f*, 366*f*
motor learning 338-340, 340*f*
structuring the environment for 361
learning curves 339-340, 340*f*
Lee, M. 130, 243
leg length 170
Lenoir, M. 142, 142*f*
Lindquist, C. 305, 312
Lockman, J.J. 294
locomotion 66. *See also* running; walking
balancing in 296
creeping and crawling 46, 52, 58*f*, 67-68, 67*f*
Down syndrome and 69, 94
fear of falling in 46, 73
galloping, sliding, and skipping 90-93, 91*f*, 93*f*, 96-97
hopping 85-90, 87*f*, 87*t*, 88*f*, 89*f*, 89*t*, 91*f*-92*f*
interventions 125
jumping 77-85, 79*t*, 80*t*, 81*f*, 81*t*, 82*f*, 83*t*, 84*f*
self-produced 290-293, 291*f*, 292*f*
skills assessment 94-95, 95*t*
vision and 290-292, 291*f*
locomotor reflexes 50*t*
Long, A.B. 273
longitudinal research study 11-13
long jump 82, 82*f*
Looft, W.R. 273

M

Malina, R.M. 251
Mally, K.K. 114
manipulative skills
anticipation in 139-143, 142*f*
bimanual reaching 133-134, 134*f*
catching 136-138, 136*f*, 137*f*, 137*t*, 139*f*
driving 144
grasping 128-131, 129*f*, 131*f*
hand–mouth movements 133
in hand transplants 128
in older adults 131, 135-136
piloting 144
rapid aiming movements 135-136
reaching 132-134, 132*f*, 134*f*
recognizing objects using 271
tool use 294, 294*f*
Margaria step-running test 205
marketing, gender-typing in 317-318
master athletes
anaerobic performance in 205
Cheney, Dorothy "Dodo" 100
DeMar, Clarence 215
Hawkins, Julia "Hurricane" 66, 97
Rogers, Orville 66
Senior Games 77, 333
mastery motivation climate 332-333
maturation 5
assessing physiological 172-173
in children 18-20
exercise capacity and 207, 212
genetics in 18-19
hormones and 189
physiological 167, 168*f*, 169*t*
skeletal 173, 185, 185*f*
stages of 172
maturational perspective 18-20, 19*f*, 23-24, 172-173
maturational threshold 209
maximal oxygen uptake
in adults 210-211, 213, 214*f*
in children 205-208, 207*f*, 208*f*, 210-211
endurance training and 208-210, 214-216, 215*f*
muscle mass loss with aging and 213-214, 214*f*
peak oxygen uptake versus 206
maximal working capacity 210
maximum heart rate 212
Mays, Willie 136
McAuley, E. 323, 326, 330, 352
McBeath, M.K. 142
McCallister, S. 309
McConnell, A. 140
McGraw, Myrtle 19-20, 19*f*
McKenzie, B.E. 292
McLeod, P. 141, 142*f*, 143
McPherson, B.D. 311
mean power 203, 204, 205
Meltzoff, A.N. 280
memory
aging and 195, 352-354
growth factors, BDNF, and 289
speed of cognitive functions and 195, 338
strategies 353
men. *See* boys and men; sex differences
menarche 167, 168*f*
Messick, J.A. 122-123
meta-analyses 13-14
metaphysis 184*f*
MGRS (Multicentre Growth Reference Study) 55-57
mind–body dualism 287
mirror recognition tasks 271
mixed-longitudinal research studies 13
Morris, G.S.D. 140
Morrongiello, B.A. 275, 276, 276*f*, 277, 279
motion. *See also* locomotion
constraints in 31-33, 31*f*, 32*f*
detecting and correcting errors in 40-41
force absorption in 37-38
Newton's laws of 33-34, 35
open kinetic chain 36-37
perception of 266-268, 267*f*
rotating limbs and projected objects 35-36, 36*f*, 37*f*
stability and balance in 38-39, 39*f*
motion parallax 263
motion sickness 260
motivation 329-333
adult activity levels 333-334, 333*f*, 334*f*, 367
in children 329-333
dropping out 331
in older adults 367
persistence 330-331
personal incentives 333-334, 334*f*
teacher-centered versus student-centered approaches 332-333

motor behavior 5. *See also* action-perception link; motor development; motor learning
motor competence
health-related fitness and 254
perceived versus actual 328-329
physical activity and 240-241, 241*f*, 252-254
weight status and 251, 254-255
motor control 5
motor development 5
assessing 94-95, 95*t*
characteristics of 4-5
cognitive development and 50
constraints on 6-9, 6*f*, 8*f*
ecological perspective on 22-26, 24*f*
in infants 289-290
in kittens 290, 291*f*
maturational perspective on 18-20, 19*f*, 23-24
motion perception and 266-267, 267*f*
Newell's model 6-8, 6*f*
psychosocial constraints on 322-335
stability–mobility trade-off in 39-40
in super athletes 220
weight status and 254-255
motor learning 338-340, 340*f*. *See also* developmental motor learning
motor milestones 54-58
atypical development and 58, 60
in balance 55, 58
constraints and 57-58, 58*f*
development of 54-57, 56*t*
in grasping 129
in jumping 79-80, 79*t*
in postural control and balance 60-62, 61*f*, 295-296
motor skill capability 338-339
motor skills
gender typing and 307, 366-367
growth spurts and 152, 163, 171
obesity and 26, 251, 252-255
observing 70
perception of 241
teaching 367
movement-perception link. *See* action-perception link
movigenics theory 287
moving-room technique 61-62, 61*f*
Mullins, Aimee 30
Multicentre Growth Reference Study (MGRS) 55-57
multiple sclerosis 191
Murray, M.P. 72
Muscatine Study 246
muscle atrophy 228, 229*f*
muscle fibers
in adulthood 186, 193
aging and 193-194, 204, 297
cardiac 194, 211, 212
early development of 179-181, 180*f*, 181*f*, 186
fast-twitch 110, 181, 181*f*, 227, 297
sex differences in 227
slow-twitch 181, 181*f*
strength and 221
muscle mass. *See also* strength
developmental changes in 222-223
maximal oxygen uptake and 213-214, 214*f*
in older adults 193, 204-205, 228
strength and 220-223, 228
supplements and 220
muscle spindles 268-269
muscular system
development of 179-181, 180*f*, 181*f*, 186, 193-194
muscle hypertrophy 179, 226
structure of 180-181, 180*f*, 181*f*
music 276-277, 358
mutations 156
myelin 182*f*, 189, 191
myelination 191-192

N

National Children and Youth Fitness Study II 233, 234
National Senior Games 333
near-infrared interactance device 242
Nelson, C.J. 76
nerve tracts 192
nervous system 179
Babinski test 52
brain structures in 190-192, 191*f*
choice reaction time 349, 350
development of 181-183, 182*f*, 189-192, 190*f*, 191*f*, 195
growth hormone and 188
influence of maturation of 189-190
perception-action approach 24-26, 141, 142*f*, 143
prenatal development of 181-183, 182*f*
self-produced locomotion 290-293, 291*f*, 292*f*, 294
signal-to-noise ratio in older adults 350-351
simple reaction time 349
neural network model 195
neural pruning 182-183, 189
neurogenesis 195, 289
neurological organization theory 287
neurons 181-183, 182*f*, 189-190
newborns. *See* infants
Newell, K.M. 6, 129-130
Newell's constraints model 6-8, 6*f*, 358-359, 358*f*
Newton's laws of motion 33-34, 35
nicotine 183
Noel, Nerlens 178
normative descriptive period 20
norm-referenced scales 59
nutrition
body weight and 171
bone density and 192-193
motor milestones and 55
muscle mass and 220
nervous system and 189
obesity and 249
postnatal growth and 169
prenatal 156-157, 156*f*

O

OAC (optical acceleration cancellation) 141, 143
obesity
abdominal 194
adipose tissue development and 186-187, 194
in adults 194, 251-252, 251*f*
body mass index and 248
causes of 248-249, 251-252
in children 248-251, 249*t*
health effects of 251
interventions in 249-250, 252
measuring 171
motor skill competence and 26, 251, 254-255
prevalence of 248, 249*f*, 251, 251*f*
object perception 264-266, 265*f*, 266*f*, 267*f*, 293
object permanence 291
object recognition 271
observation skills
for catching 138, 139*f*
for galloping, sliding, and skipping 96
for hopping 90, 91*f*-92*f*
for jumping 86*f*
for kicking 114
for motor skills 70
for overarm striking 123
for overarm throwing 105, 106*f*-107*f*, 109
for running 77, 78*f*
for sidearm striking 119, 119*f*
older adults. *See also* aging
activity levels by 333-334, 333*f*, 334*f*, 367
adipose system in 194
aerobic performance in 210-214, 213*f*, 214*f*
anaerobic performance in 204-205
as athletes 77, 333
attention in 351
auditory acuity in 274, 275, 276, 277
auditory figure-and-ground in 277
augmented feedback in 348
balance in 73, 297-298
body composition and exercise in 247-248
cardiovascular structure and function in 211-212
catching by 143-144
cognitive processing speed in 195, 350-352, 352*f*
driving by 144
endocrine system in 194-195
endurance training effect in 214-216, 215*f*
falling by 73, 194, 274, 297-298
flexibility in 236-237

grasping by 131
intermodal perception 281-282
kinesthetic changes in 273-274
manipulative skills in 131, 135-136
manual performance by 135
memory in 195, 352-354
muscular system in 193-194, 213-214, 214*f*, 215*f*, 228
nervous system in 195, 228, 350-351
osteoporosis in 171, 173*f*, 174, 174*f*, 193, 236, 298
overarm striking by 123, 125
overarm throwing by 110-111
physical activity motivation 367
piloting by 144
rapid aiming movements 135-136
reaction time in 349, 350-351
respiratory structure and function 212, 213*f*
running by 76-77
self-esteem in 327-328, 334
sidearm striking by 123, 125
skeletal system in 192-193
strength levels in 226-229, 227*f*, 228*f*, 228*t*, 229*f*
strength training by 229-230, 247
visual disturbances in 264
walking patterns in 71-73
open kinetic chain 36-37
opposite-side neck flexion reflex 269
oppositional arm and leg movements 35
optical acceleration cancellation (OAC) 141, 143
optic array 141
optic flow 263
Osgood-Schlatter disease 184
ossification 183, 185, 185*f*
osteoarthritis 73, 236
osteoblasts 184*f*, 192
osteoporosis
height and 171, 173*f*, 174, 174*f*
hormone replacement therapies and 195
in older adults 171, 173*f*, 174, 174*f*, 193, 236, 298
walking and 298
Oudejans, R.R.D. 141
overall growth 158-165, 159*f*-162*f*, 165*f*
overarm striking 121-123, 121*f*, 122*t*, 125
overarm throwing
in adulthood 110-111
assessment of 124, 124*t*
Bernstein's model of learning stages for 342-344, 343*f*
characteristics of early 101, 101*f*
"clean house" game 361, 362
developmental changes in 102-108, 102*f*, 103*t*-104*t*, 104*f*
gender differences in 108-109
making noise in 362
observation plan for 105, 106*f*-107*f*, 109
practice schedules in 344-345, 346-347
proficient 101-102
oxygen uptake. *See* maximal oxygen uptake

P

Paillard, T. 248
palmar grasp reflex 49, 50*t*, 51*f*
Paralympic Games 30, 356, 360
parents 311-312, 317
Parizkova studies 244-246, 244*f*, 246*f*
Payne, V.G. 140, 362
peak oxygen uptake (peak $\dot{V}O_2$) 206-207, 207*f*, 209-211, 214-215, 215*f*. *See also* maximal oxygen uptake
peak velocity (growth) 163, 167, 168*f*
peers 312-313
Pennell, G. 318
percent fat 171
perception 260. *See also* action–perception link
of affordances 25, 141, 293-295, 294*f*, 349
auditory 275-277, 275*f*, 276*f*
image of vase/facial profiles 21*f*, 260
intermodal 278-282
visual 262-266, 263*f*, 265*f*, 266*f*, 267*f*
perception-action approach 24-26, 141, 142*f*, 143
perception-action loop 289-290
perceptual-motor development 60, 257, 287-290. *See also* action-perception link
perceptual-motor programs 287-289, 288*t*
Perrin, P.P. 297
persistence 330-331
Personal Incentives for Exercise Questionnaire 334
Pfeiffer, R. 224, 225
physical activity. *See also* sports
body composition in adults and 240-241, 241*f*, 247-248
body composition in children and 244-247, 244*f*, 246*f*
bone density and 193, 247
cognitive function and 195, 287-290
cognitive processing speed and 351-352, 352*f*
falls by older adults and 194, 298
gender-typing in 304-305, 307-309, 316
memory and 195, 353
muscle mass and 221-223, 226
obesity and 249-250
prolonged 205-215, 207*f*, 208*f*, 213*f*, 214*f*, 215*f*
self-perception and 328-329
short-term exercise 202-205, 203*f*
Physical Best test battery 234
physical growth 5
abnormal 188
adolescent growth spurt 152, 163, 171, 189
age at takeoff 163
anthropometric measures of 170-171
assessing extent and rate of 164, 170
catch-up growth 169, 172*f*
extrinsic influences on 167, 169, 172*f*
overall growth 158-165, 159*f*-162*f*, 165*f*
physiological maturation 167, 168*f*, 169*t*
prenatal 153-158, 154*f*, 154*t*, 155*f*, 158*t*
relative growth 165-166, 166*f*
velocity of 163, 167, 168*f*
physiological maturation 167, 168*f*, 169*t*
physiological optics program 287
Piaget, J. 132, 287
"pickle" game 362
Pictorial Scale of Perceived Competence and Social Acceptance 328
Pictorial Scale of Perceived Movement Skill Competence (PMSC) 324-325, 328
Pigott, R.E. 345-346
piloting 144
pitch 276
pituitary gland 179, 188, 188*f*, 196
plasticity of cells 155
play environments, socialization in 316
PMSC (Pictorial Scale of Perceived Movement Skill Competence) 324-325, 328
Posner, M.I. 341-342
postnatal development 158-171. *See also* children
extrinsic influences on 167, 169, 172*f*
growth spurt 152, 163, 189
measuring 170-171
overall growth 158-165, 159*f*-162*f*, 165*f*
physiological maturation 167, 168*f*, 169*t*
relative growth 165-166, 166*f*
postural control 60-62, 61*f*, 133-134, 295-296
postural reflexes 50*t*, 51-52
power 203-205
power grips 120, 120*f*, 128-129
practice 339, 344-347, 346*f*
precision grips 129-130
preferential looking 266-267
prefrontal cortex, in infants 191
prehension 128. *See also* grasping

prenatal development
abnormal 156-158, 158*t*
of the adipose system 181
embryonic 153, 154*f*
of the endocrine system 181
fetal 153-155, 154*t*, 155*f*
of the muscular system 179-181, 180*f*, 181*f*
of the nervous system 181-183, 182*f*
nourishment in 155-156, 155*f*, 182-183
of the skeletal system 179, 179*f*
prereaching 132
presbycusis 274, 275
presbyopia 262
pressure epiphysis 183, 183*f*
primary ossification centers 179, 184*f*
primitive reflexes 49, 50*t*, 51*f*
proficiency barriers 10-11, 11*f*
Project ACES 322
proprioceptive system. *See* kinesthetic development
proprioceptors 268-269, 268*t*, 297
prosthetic limbs 30, 357*f*
proximodistal growth 155
Pryde, K.M. 131
psychosocial constraints
memory as 352-354
motivation as 329-333
perceived motor competence as 328-329
Project ACES and 322
self-esteem as 323-328, 324*f*, 327*f*
puberty 167, 168*f*
pulmonary oxygen uptake ($p\dot{V}O_2$) 211
punting 114-116, 115*f*, 116*t*, 117*f*
pyramidal tract 192

Q

quality of life, fitness and 199, 202
Quebec 10-second bicycle ergometer test 205

R

Raag, T. 317
race and ethnicity, socialization and 312, 318-319
racket lag 121-122, 121*f*
random practice 344
rapid aiming movements 134-135
Rarick, G. Lawrence 20, 226
Rasmussen, R.L. 223
rate controllers. *See* rate limiters
rate limiters
concept of 23-24
in early running 75
in galloping, sliding, and skipping 96-97
in hopping 90
in jumping 85
Reaburn, P.R.J. 204, 205
reaching
in adulthood 134-135
bimanual reaching and manipulation 133-134, 134*f*
hand-mouth movements 133
in infants 60, 132-134, 132*f*, 133*f*
postural control and 134, 295
rapid aiming movements 134-135
vision in 132-133, 132*f*
reaction time 349, 350-351
reading, spatial orientation and 287
redshirting 286
reflexes. *See also specific reflexes*
appearance and disappearance of 52-53
infantile 49-53, 50*t*, 51*f*, 269
kinesthetic receptors and 269
locomotor 50*t*, 52
postural 50*t*, 51-52
primitive 49, 50*t*, 51*f*
role of 53-54
voluntary movement and 53-54
rehearsal, in memory 353
relative growth 165-166, 166*f*
relatively permanent 339
releasing degrees of freedom 342, 343*f*
research
criterion-referenced scales 59
experimental design 11-13, 13*f*
meta-analyses and reviews 13-14
norm-referenced scales 59
universality versus variability and 14
resistance training. *See* strength training
respiratory structure and function 212, 213*f*
retention test 339, 340*f*, 348
retinal disparity 263, 263*f*
review papers 13
Roberton, Mary Ann 12, 115
Robinson, L.E. 328
Rogers, Orville 66
Roncesvalles, M.N.C. 296
rotational movement 35-36, 36*f*
rotational velocity 35-36
Royce, W.S. 309
rubber hand illusion 271
rubella virus 157
Rudisill, M.E. 332
running 73
aging and 66
by children 73-75, 75*t*, 76*f*
developmental changes in 76
Margaria step-running test 205
observation plan for 77, 78*f*
by older adults 76-77
proficient 75-76, 76*f*

S

Saltin, B. 247
sarcomeres 180, 180*f*
Saunders, Len 322
schema learning 344-345
Schmidt, R.A. 344
Schwartz, R.S. 248
Scott, Matthew 128
secondary ossification centers 183
secondary sex characteristics 167, 168*f*, 172
Seefeldt, V. 137
self awareness 271
self-esteem 323
in adults 327-328, 334
causal attributions and 325-328
in children 324
development of 323, 324*f*
emotions and 325
measuring 324-325
in older adults 327-328, 334
perceived versus actual competence and 328-329
social interactions and 323-324, 324*f*
self-perception, motor competence and 328-329
Self-Perception Profile for Children 254
self-produced locomotion 290-293, 291*f*, 292*f*, 294
Senior Games 77, 333
sensation, definition of 260
sensorimotor coupling 62
sensory pathways 192
sensory-perceptual development. *See also* auditory development
in infants 61-62, 61*f*, 261, 263-264, 266-267
kinesthetic 268-274, 268*t*, 269*f*, 270*f*, 272*t*
visual perception 262-266, 263*f*, 265*f*, 266*f*, 267*f*
visual sensation 261-262, 261*f*, 262*f*
sequential research studies 13, 13*f*
SES (socioeconomic status) 156, 318-319
sex, definition of 307
sex differences
in adipose tissue 186, 187*f*
in anaerobic performance 203-205, 203*f*
in body composition 245-246, 369*f*, 370*f*, 371*f*
in catching 137
in fat distribution 186-187
in flexibility 232-233, 232*f*
in gonadal hormones 189
in growth patterns 158-164, 159*f*-162*f*, 164*f*, 166
in head circumference 372*f*, 373*f*
in maximal oxygen uptake 206-207, 207*f*
in muscle fibers 227
in muscle hypertrophy 226
in muscle mass 186, 220, 223
in ossification 183, 185, 185*f*
in overarm throwing development 108-109
in peak height velocity 163, 165,

167, 168*f*
in peak oxygen uptake 206
in perceived versus actual motor competence 328-329
in personal incentives for physical activity 334, 334*f*
in physical growth 171-174, 173*f*
in secondary sex characteristics 167, 168*f*, 172
in skipping 96
in strength development 221, 221*f*, 224, 226-227, 227*f*
in weight with aging 174, 174*f*
"shake-hands" grip 120, 120*f*
shape constancy 265
Shephard, R.J. 227, 227*f*
Shirley, M.M. 54-55, 57
shoulder bones, as constraints 32, 32*f*
shoulder-to-hip ratio 171
Sibley, B.A. 289
siblings 312
sidearm striking
body scaling in 120, 363
characteristics of early 118, 118*f*
developmental changes in 118*t*, 119-120, 120*f*
grip in 120, 120*f*
observing patterns of 119, 119*f*, 120
by older adults 123, 125
proficient 118
side preference 273
SIDS (sudden infant death syndrome) 57
sigmoid curves 158, 159*f*-162*f*, 180
signal-to-noise ratio 350-351
significant others 310-315
Simoneau, J.A. 186
simple reaction time (SRT) 349, 350-351
sit-and-reach test 233-235, 233*f*, 234*f*
sitting height 170
1,600-meter run test 211
size constancy 265, 267*f*
skeletal age 173, 185, 185*f*
skeletal maturation 173, 185, 185*f*
skeletal system development
in adults 173, 185, 185*f*, 192-193
in children and adolescents 183-185, 183*f*, 184*f*, 185*f*
prenatal 179, 179*f*
skinfold measurements 188*f*, 242, 369*f*
skipping 90-93, 91*f*, 96-97
Slater, A. 265
sliding 89, 90-93, 91*f*, 96
slope perception 292-293
slow-twitch muscle fibers 181, 181*f*
Smith, R.E. 314-315, 324
smoking, in pregnancy 183
Smoll, F.L. 314-315, 324
Snellen scale of visual acuity 261, 262*f*
Snyder, E.E. 311
soccer
anticipation in 142, 142*f*
forces in 33-34, 34*f*
gender typing in 311, 316
heading in 345
stretching in 236
variable practice in 347
social interactions 323-324, 324*f*
socialization process 306-307, 307*f*
socializing agents 310-315
aversive 315
coaches and teachers as 315, 318
parents as 311-312
peers as 312-313
play environments and games as 316
race and ethnicity and 312
siblings as 312
toys as 316-318
sociocultural constraints
as environmental constraints 305-307, 306*f*, 307*f*
gender stereotypes 304-305, 307-309, 316
gender typing 307, 311-312, 316-318, 366-367
play environment as 316
race, ethnicity, and socioeconomic status 318-319
significant others in 310-315
socialization process 306-307, 307*f*
socioeconomic status (SES) 156, 318-319
somatosensory information 61-62, 268
Sonstroem, R. 323, 330
Soucie, J.M. 232-233
sound differences 276. *See also* auditory development
sound localization 275, 275*f*
sound pattern perception 276-277, 276*f*
spatial compatibility, in cognitive processing 349
spatial orientation 265-266, 273, 287
spatial perception 263-264, 263*f*, 291-293, 292*f*
spatial-temporal intermodal perception 281-282
spina bifida 362
spinal cord development 190, 191-192, 191*f*
Spirduso, W.W. 194, 211, 213, 228
spontaneous movements, in infants 47-49, 48*f*
spontaneous self-organization of body systems 23
sports. *See also* motivation; *specific sports*
causal attributions and 325-328
flexibility in 231
gender typing in 304, 307-309, 311-312, 366-367
parents and 311-312, 322
peers and socialization in 312-313
self-esteem and 323, 324, 325
sociocultural constraints in 305-307, 307*f*
Title IX and 305, 308-309, 311
withdrawing from 331
spring-loaded dynamometers 222
SRT (simple reaction time) 349, 350-351
stability 38-41, 39*f*
Stagni, Rita 152
stair climbing 293
standardized tests 20
standing long jump 80-84, 80*t*, 81*t*, 82*f*, 83*t*, 84*f*, 86*f*
static balance 298
stepping reflex 49, 50*t*, 51*f*, 52, 53-54, 54*f*
stereotypes, gender-specific 304, 307-309, 316
stereotype threat 319
stereotypies 49
Sterritt, G. 281
Stodden, D.F. 26, 108, 252, 254, 256, 329
strength 220. *See also* strength training
in adolescence 221-223, 221*f*
assessing 222
importance of 220
in middle and older adulthood 226-229, 227*f*, 228*f*, 228*t*, 229*f*
muscle mass and 220-221
training effects on 224-226, 224*f*
types of 222
strength training
in adolescence 224-226, 224*f*
in middle and older adulthood 229-230, 247
in prepubescence 224-225, 224*f*
supplements in 220
striking. *See* overarm striking; sidearm striking
Strohmeyer, H.S. 138
stroke volume 205, 212
structural constraints 7, 8*f*, 358-359, 358*f*, 359*f*
student-centered environments 332-333
sudden infant death syndrome (SIDS) 57
sumo wrestling 305, 306*f*
supplements, athletic 220
surface perception 292
Sutherland, R. 352
swim reflex 52
synapses 182

T

tactile localization 270, 270*f*
Tanner, J.M. 172
Tappe, M.K. 333-334, 334*f*
task analysis, ecological 364-366, 365*f*, 366*f*
task constraints 8
in anticipation 140
in driving and piloting 145
modifying 357-361, 357*f*, 358*f*, 359*f*, 360*f*
in Newell's model 6*f*

task goal 361-363
teacher-centered environments 332-333
teachers, as socializing agents 318, 324
technology 12, 141-143, 347
Telama, R. 216
Temple, I.G. 273
tennis
  body scaling and 294
  by older adults 100, 123, 125
  overarm striking 121-123, 121*f*, 122*t*, 125
  serving 35-36, 36*f*, 40
  sidearm striking 116-120, 118*f*, 118*t*, 119*f*, 120*f*
tensiometers 222
teratogens 157
Test of Gross Motor Development (TGMD)
  catching 145
  locomotion motor skills 94-95, 95*t*
  self-esteem and 28, 324
testosterone 189
Thelen, E. 47-49, 53-54, 132-133, 299
theoretical perspectives
  biomechanical descriptive period 20, 21*f*
  dynamical systems approach 22-24, 24*f*
  ecological perspective 22-26, 24*f*
  information processing perspective 21-22
  maturational 18-20, 19*f*, 23-24
  normative descriptive period 20
  perception-action approach 24-26
thermogenesis 249
Thomas, J.R. 353
three-on-three soccer 362
threshold discrimination, in tactile localization 270, 270*f*
threshold of detection 267
throwing. *See also* overarm throwing
  "clean house" game 361, 362
  ecological task analysis of 364-366, 365*f*
  Newton's laws and 33-34
  observation plan for 105, 106*f*-107*f*, 109
  practice schedules for 346, 346*f*
  shoulder bones and 31, 32*f*
thyroid gland 188, 188*f*, 194
thyroid hormones 184, 188, 194
Timed Manual Performance Test 135
Title IX 305, 308-309, 311
toddlers. *See also* children; infants
  running by 74-75, 74*t*, 75*f*
  walking by 40, 68-69, 69*f*, 71, 73-74
tool use 294, 294*f*
toys, as socializing agents 316-318
traction epiphyses 184
transfer test 339, 340*f*
Trappe, S. 215-216
trial blocks 345
trials 345
Trick, L. 262
trigger hypothesis 209
trisomy 21 156. *See also* Down syndrome
Trudeau, F. 216
trunk rotation
  block 104*f*, 105
  differentiated 105, 120*f*
  in kicking 113, 113*f*
  in punting 115
  in sidearm striking 120, 120*f*
Turvey, Michael 23
twin studies 19, 19*f*
twitch 181, 181*f*
two-hand underhand throw 100
Type I muscle fibers. *See* slow-twitch muscle fibers
type 2 diabetes 195
Type II muscle fibers. *See* fast-twitch muscle fibers

U

Ulrich, Dale 60, 69, 94-95, 95*t*, 124, 124*t*, 328
underwater weighing 242
United States, socialization in 312
universality of development 14
Up series 4
Utley, A. 138

V

validated developmental sequences 102
Van den Tillaar, R. 346-347
Van Duijvenvoorde, A. 353
Van Hof, P. 141
VanSant, A. 110-112
variable practice 344
vase/facial profile image 260, 261*f*
Vedul-Kjelsås, V.I. 253-254
velocity curves 164, 168*f*
vertical jump 80-85, 81*f*, 82*f*, 84*f*
vestibular apparatus 268, 268*t*
virtual reality headsets 202
vision
  auditory-visual intermodal perception 279
  in balance 297
  directionality and 273
  figure-and-ground perception 264, 265*f*
  in grasping 130-131, 131*f*
  lateral dominance in 272-273
  preferential looking 266-267
  in reaching 132-133, 132*f*
  visual-kinesthetic intermodal perception 280-281
  visual perception 262-266, 263*f*, 265*f*, 266*f*, 267*f*, 293
  visual sensation 261-262, 261*f*, 262*f*
visual cliff experiments 263-264, 290
visual-kinesthetic intermodal perception 280-281
visual perception
  of faces 265
  of motion 266-268, 267*f*
  of objects 264-266, 265*f*, 266*f*, 267*f*, 293
  preferential looking 266-267
vital capacity 212
$\dot{V}O_2$max. *See* maximal oxygen uptake
volleyball 362, 363

W

walking 68
  balance in 39-40, 71
  characteristics of early 68-69, 69*f*, 71
  crawling versus 46, 292-293
  in Down syndrome 69
  on hands and feet 67
  in infants 23
  infant supine kicking and 47-48, 48*f*
  in older adults 71-73
  proficient patterns in 71
  stability–mobility trade-off in 39-40
  stepping reflex 49, 50*t*, 51*f*, 52, 53-54, 54*f*
  by toddlers 40
Warren, W.H. 293
weight. *See also* obesity
  in adulthood and aging 174, 174*f*
  growth patterns in 161*f*, 162*f*, 165, 170
  infant 23, 53-54, 69, 156
  measuring 171
  in motion and stability 39-40
  peak velocity in 164, 165, 169*t*, 186
  prenatal 154*t*, 155, 169, 179
  walking patterns and 71
weight-for-length percentiles 161*f*, 162*f*, 163
West, Robin 178
whole-and-part perception 264-265, 266*f*
Williams, K. 110-112, 123
Witeba Test of Auditory-Tactile Integration 281
women. *See* girls and women; sex differences
Woollacott, M. 298
Wulf, G, 345

Z

Zetou, E. 345
Zipp, G.P. 346, 346*f*

ABOUT THE AUTHORS

Kathleen M. Haywood, PhD, is professor emerita at the University of Missouri at St. Louis, where she has researched life span motor development and taught courses in motor behavior and development, sport psychology, and biomechanics. She earned her PhD in motor behavior from the University of Illinois at Urbana-Champaign in 1976.

Haywood is a fellow of the National Academy of Kinesiology and the Research Consortium of the Society for Health and Physical Education (SHAPE America). She is also a recipient of SHAPE America's Mabel Lee Award. Haywood has served as president of the North American Society for the Psychology of Sport and Physical Activity and as chairperson of the Motor Development Academy of SHAPE America.

Haywood is also the coauthor of four editions of *Archery: Steps to Success* and of *Teaching Archery: Steps to Success,* published by Human Kinetics. She resides in Saint Charles, Missouri, and in her free time enjoys fitness training, tennis, and dog training.

Nancy Getchell, PhD, is a professor at the University of Delaware in Newark. For nearly 30 years, Getchell has investigated developmental motor control and coordination in children with and without disabilities. Her current research focus is on brain/behavior relationships in children with developmental coordination disorder and other conditions. She teaches courses in motor development, motor control and learning, research methods, and women in sport.

Getchell is currently the president of the International Motor Development Research Consortium as well as a professional member of the North American Society for the Psychology of Sport and Physical Activity, and the International Society of Motor Control. She is a research fellow of SHAPE America and has served as the chairperson of the Motor Development and Learning Academy. Currently, Getchell serves as an associate editor for *Research Quarterly for Exercise and Sport* and on the editorial board of *Physical Education and Sport Pedagogy* and *Frontiers in Psychology.*

Getchell obtained her PhD from the University of Wisconsin at Madison in 1996 in kinesiology with a specialization in motor development. In 2001, Getchell was the recipient of the Lolas E. Halverson Young Investigator Award in motor development.

Getchell resides in Wilmington, Delaware, where she enjoys hiking, geocaching, and bicycling.

HUMAN KINETICS

Books

Ebooks

Continuing Education

Journals ...and more!

www.HumanKinetics.com